MIRAGES

SWALLOW PRESS BOOKS BY ANAÏS NIN

FICTION

Children of the Albatross

Cities of the Interior

Collages

The Four-Chambered Heart

House of Incest

Ladders to Fire

Seduction of the Minotaur

A Spy in the House of Love

Under a Glass Bell

Waste of Timelessness and Other Early Stories

Winter of Artifice

NONFICTION

D. H. Lawrence: An Unprofessional Study

The Novel of the Future

A Woman Speaks: The Lectures, Seminars, and Interviews of Anaïs Nin,
edited by Evelyn J. Hinz

SWALLOW PRESS BOOKS ABOUT ANAÏS NIN

*Arrows of Longing: The Correspondence between Anaïs Nin and
Felix Pollak, 1952–1976*, edited by Gregory H. Mason

Recollections of Anaïs Nin by Her Contemporaries,
edited by Benjamin Franklin V

MIRAGES

The Unexpurgated Diary of Anaïs Nin

1939–1947

Edited by Paul Herron
With an introduction by Kim Krizan

SWALLOW PRESS / OHIO UNIVERSITY PRESS
Athens, Ohio

PUBLISHED IN ASSOCIATION WITH SKY BLUE PRESS

Swallow Press
An imprint of Ohio University Press, Athens, Ohio 45701
www.ohioswallow.com

Digital trade edition published by Sky Blue Press, San Antonio, Texas, USA. Inquiries about worldwide electronic sales from all digital trade vendors should be directed to Sky Blue Press (skybluepress.com).

Print edition and institutional digital edition published by Swallow Press/Ohio University Press, Athens, Ohio (www.ohioswallow.com). To obtain permission to quote, reprint, or otherwise reproduce or distribute material from Swallow Press / Ohio University Press publications, please contact our rights and permissions department at (740) 593-1154 or (740) 593-4536 (fax).

1st Edition. Unexpurgated.
All content unless otherwise stated, copyright © 2013 The Anaïs Nin Trust (anaisnintrust.com)
This edition published by arrangement with Sky Blue Press.
Introduction copyright © 2013 Kim Krizan
Preface copyright © 2013 Paul Herron

Excerpts from *The Diary of Anaïs Nin, Volume Three*, 1939–1944 (copyright © 1969 by Anaïs Nin and renewed by Rupert Pole and Gunther Stuhlmann) and *The Diary of Anaïs Nin, Volume Four*, 1944–1947 (copyright © 1971 by Anaïs Nin and renewed by Rupert Pole and Gunther Stuhlmann) reprinted by permission of Houghton Mifflin Harcourt Publishing Company. All rights reserved.

Typesetting and design:	Sara A. Herron, Sky Blue Press
Cover photo:	Courtesy of The Anaïs Nin Trust; Deigh-Nevin
Cover design:	Ohio University Press/Swallow Press

All photographs copyright © The Anaïs Nin Trust, with the following exceptions:

Edward Graeffe:	James Abresch, photographer
Valentina Orlikova:	*Soviet Russia Today* (April 1943)
Anaïs Nin in Provincetown:	José Alemany, photographer
Anaïs Nin in action coat:	Soichi Sunami, photographer

Printed in the United States of America

Swallow Press/Ohio University Press books are printed on acid-free paper ⊗ ™

23 22 21 20 19 18 17 16 15 14 13   5 4 3 2 1

Library of Congress Cataloging-in-Publication Data
Nin, Anaïs, 1903–1977.
  Mirages : the Unexpurgated Diary of Anaïs Nin 1939–1947 / [Anaïs Nin] ; preface by Paul Herron ; introduction by Kim Krizan ; edited by Paul Herron.
    pages cm
  Includes index.
  ISBN 978-0-8040-1146-4 (hc : alk. paper) — ISBN 978-0-8040-4057-0 (electronic)
  1. Nin, Anaïs, 1903–1977. 2. Authors, American—20th century—Biography. I. Herron, Paul, editor. II. Title.
  PS3527.I865Z46 2013
  818'.5209—dc23
  [B]
                      2013026626

To Gunther and Barbara Stuhlmann

ACKNOWLEDGMENTS

The editor gratefully acknowledges The Anaïs Nin Trust, Sara Herron, John Ferrone, and Kim Krizan for their guidance and dedication to this book.

Anaïs Nin at Provincetown

TABLE OF CONTENTS

PREFACE

Mirages is the untold story of Anaïs Nin's personal struggle to keep alive what she valued most in life—the dream—in the face of the harsh, puritanical climate of 1940s New York. It is a record of a journey across what Nin called the "desert before me" and witness to her painful rebirth as a woman and writer. It is the story missing from *The Diary of Anaïs Nin*, particularly volumes 3 and 4, which also cover 1939 through 1947.

This book finally answers what readers have been asking for decades: What led to the demise of Nin's love affair with Henry Miller? Just how troubled was her marriage to Hugh Guiler? What is the story behind Nin's "children," the effeminate young men she seemed to collect at will? How was it that Nin wrote so prolifically during such a tumultuous time? What is the truth about her mysterious relationship with Gore Vidal? And what was it about Rupert Pole that seemed to assuage all the pain Nin had endured?

In 1939, shortly after fleeing wartime Paris for New York, Nin wrote: "Over and over again I sail towards joy, which is never in the room with me, but always near me, across the way, like those rooms full of gayety one sees from the street, or the gayety in the street one sees from a window. Will I ever reach joy?" By 1946, her search had devolved into agony: "The greatest suffering does not come from living in mirages, but from *awakening*. There is no greater pain than awakening from a dream, the deep crying over the dying selves..."

As World War II spread across the world, Nin waged her own war against a reality she found so horrifying that she repeatedly contemplated suicide and sought temporary salvation in numerous doomed love affairs with an assortment of men, ranging from the staid critic Edmund Wilson to seventeen-year-old Bill Pinckard, searching for the "One" who could respond to her, not only sensually, but *completely*. When none of her many lovers could live up to her ideal, she exclaimed to the diary: "Oh, someone, someone love me as I have loved." It was only after abandoning her quixotic quest that Nin met Rupert Pole, the ardent lover who seemed to answer her needs—and who would eventually prompt her to swing back and forth across the continent between him and her husband for the rest of her life.

Nin wrote in 1943, "I feel like rewriting the entire diary in two columns: the actual diary as it is and its completion à la Proust—filling, rounding, objectifying, encircling, encompassing all."

While Nin never actually put her diary into two columns, this aspiration was achieved, to an extent, in her publication history. She published the "objectified" version in the form of *The Diary of Anaïs Nin*, but with one major omission: because her husband and some of her lovers were still alive at the time, she was forced to excise an entire side of her character—the erotic—from the text. While *Mirages* could have been a simple accumulation of what was left out of the *Diaries*, the higher aim was to assemble the most meaningful material from the missing "column" and reconstruct Nin's story, and what a story it is.

Here, the hazy, almost imagined images and the vague angst of the *Diary* snap into eye-searing focus, cast in a strong, sharp, defining light, laid bare for the reader. It is sometimes shocking, sometimes beautiful, sometimes agonizing, with little left to the imagination. The personages of the *Diary* become real people with real flaws and real problems; the transformation Nin undergoes is made brutally clear.

Mirages is a document of heartbreak, despair, desperation, carnage and deep mourning, but it is also one of courage, persistence, evolution and redemption.

PAUL HERRON, EDITOR

San Antonio, Texas
March 2013

INTRODUCTION

Anaïs Nin's diary is a remarkable work of art. Because she believed "the topsoil of our personalities is nothing," her diary chronicles her interior life, the "uncensored dream, the free unconscious," and it unspools like a tickertape. It is a deeply personal document, one that not only reveals the psychological topography of one woman, but one that unveils something of the interior life of all women, all people.

This new uncensored diary is particularly explosive. It will no doubt enflame the usual brigade of outraged moralists who have heaped scorn upon Nin for daring to live by her own moral code, write about her adventures, and then allow that writing to be published for all to read. The vitriol with which she has been attacked proves her diary hits a nerve, but as H. G. Wells said, "Moral indignation is jealousy with a halo."

We know that in the great experiment that was her life, Anaïs Nin did things few of us would admit—or even consider. Most of her secrets involved her sex life, an area women have fought to control on their own terms. Nin had what appears to have been an incredibly full and exciting life, but she believed she suffered from "neurosis" or "sickness," and she fought to understand its cause. In the meantime, and without even a high school education, Nin forged a modern art form that will finally find its place in this century of internet communication, full, as it is, of personal confession. But Nin was decades and light-years ahead, trailblazing the exploration of an area of human life so mysterious, so elemental, so beyond politics and social mores, so personal, and yet so universal. To Nin's detractors one must ask, "If one's lens is too small to fit the mysteries of one complex life, if that life must be condemned, what in the critic's own complex psyche do they condemn and attempt to destroy?"

Nin's story must begin with her father, Joaquín Nin, a respected Spanish composer who abused his children and then abandoned his family, leaving them nearly destitute while he married a wealthy young music student and toured in luxury throughout Europe. Nin, her mother and two brothers were forced to sail for America in 1914, and while on board the ship eleven-year-old Anaïs began writing a letter to lure her father back to the family. This letter was never sent, but was the beginning of her diary—a letter to the world, a sixty-three-year-long cry from the heart.

Mirages opens at the dawn of World War II when Nin fled Paris where she lived for fifteen years with her husband, banker Hugh Guiler. She had married "Hugo" in 1923, and though he loved her and she trusted him, she found the union deeply unsatisfying. In spite of this, the 1930s had been an idyllic period for her and she continued her diary. At a time when it was considered shocking for her to have done so, Nin wrote a book-length analysis of D. H. Lawrence's fiction, including the infamous *Lady Chatterly's Lover*, and had it published. She also wrote a long, surrealistic prose piece entitled *House of Incest*.

In what proved to be a dramatic turning point in her life, Nin met writer Henry Miller and his wife June in 1931. As is detailed in Nin's first unexpurgated diary, *Henry and June*, Nin and Miller championed one another as writers and began an affair. Nin and Guiler also supported Miller financially and paid for the printing of his ground-breaking novel, *Tropic of Cancer*. Then in 1933, after a twenty-year separation, Nin met her father again. Daughter and father were strangers, he a notorious Don Juan and she a thirty-year-old woman. They fell into a brief, incestuous affair, which Nin unflinchingly described in her second unexpurgated diary, *Incest*. Shortly thereafter, Nin sought psychoanalysis from Otto Rank, a close colleague of Sigmund Freud, but he too fell in love with her and this story was revealed in the following unexpurgated diary, *Fire*. In *Nearer the Moon*, Nin told the story of her intense relationship with Left Bank Marxist Gonzalo Moré, with whom she is still deeply involved at the outset of *Mirages*.

Mirages begins in 1939 with Nin's arrival in America and ends in 1947 when she meets the man who would be "the One," the lover who would satisfy her insatiable hunger for connection. In the middle looms a period Nin describes as "hell," during which she experiences a kind of erotic madness, a delirium that fuels her search for love. As a child suffering the loss of her father, little Anaïs wrote, "Close your eyes to the ugly things," and against a horrifying backdrop of war and death, Nin combats the world's darkness with her own search for light.

Mirages is just that: a series of mirages that dance tantalizingly on the road, one after another, promising refuge and water, but then cruelly evaporate like so many hopes and dreams. As with all artists, Nin's fodder was her feelings, and she created from the vantage of shattering pain originating with her father's rejection. In this volume, Nin writes movingly of her "sickness," puts herself through repeated self- and professional analyses, and comes what seems perilously close to annihilation. In the end, this book serves as a 20th century Persephone's journey through the underworld.

The reader who wishes to cross this particular desert with Nin must be willing to trust that an oasis will be found at the end. Finally, after meeting Rupert Pole in early 1947, Nin will enjoy a fulfilling relationship at last, one that will end her frantic search for love, though it will not conclude her story. Instead, she will then embark on a "trapeze" life in which she swings between Rupert Pole and Hugo Guiler for years—a nearly impossible feat and one of the most gripping periods in her story.

Out of abandonment, tremendous pain and "great hunger," Anaïs Nin created a life-long work of art that is unparalleled, one that breaks the false barriers between fiction and non-fiction, diary and novel, conscious and unconscious, societally-sanctioned and the unsanctioned, public and private. It took courage for Nin to write about that which exists beyond words in a period of such censorship that society demanded that fictional characters be seen paying for their "sins." She seemed to foresee what we today take for granted in the 21st century: that consciousness is a streaming tickertape of words and images spooling from us as long as we live, and something to be shared. For those who dare to ride along the precipitous twists and turns of Anaïs Nin's fantastic story: proceed.

KIM KRIZAN

Los Angeles, California
February 2013

AGAIN TOWARDS AMERICA

Will I ever reach joy?

ABOARD THE SEAPLANE CLIPPER, DECEMBER 7, 1939

I carried you above the clouds in a little blue cloth bag—you and the volumes not yet copied. So fast we fly over the distance I no longer feel the pain of separation. So fast we fly, it is a dream and not reality, and in the dream pain is short-lived and soon dissolved. Again towards America, as during the other war. From high above the life in Paris seems so small and dark, and I ask myself why I wept so much.

I am still baffled by the mystery of how man has an independent life from woman, whereas I die when separated from my lover. While all these threads of desire and tenderness stifled me, I climbed into a giant bird and swooped toward space. Up here I do not suffer. Distance is magically covered. It is a dream. It is an inhuman bird that carries me to a new destiny. I rise. At last, like Henry, I know detachment, enter a non-human world. For this voyage I threw out a great deal of weight, to permit myself to rise. Constantly I am throwing out ballast. I never keep bags or old papers or objects I no longer love. It is not masochism. A spiritual nature is aware of its faults and seeks to perfect itself, and can only achieve this by suffering and accepting. I needed to be humanized. I keep nothing that is dead, only what I wear, love, what is my living décor, my living symbols.

About a week ago I awakened with strange fears. Gonzalo had delayed his trip. I said, "I am afraid now it is I who will leave first." Two days later Hugo telephoned from

London: "Get ready to embark on the *Clipper* Tuesday from Lisbon. Be ready to take the train to Lisbon Saturday night."

This was Wednesday at three. When Gonzalo came to see me, I was weeping. Guided by a premonition, I had dressed beautifully for him. Instead of shopping for his winter coat, we went to the United States Lines, to the Portuguese Legation, to the Spanish consulate. All this hurts me less up here in the light, but in Paris, on earth, I suffered to leave Gonzalo behind, Gonzalo with his gift for tangles, his love of difficulties and darkness. I felt too the wrenching from Henry. I had hoped to go to Greece after Gonzalo left for New York and wait there for sailing time, but Hugo fulfilled my wishes with such speed and power. Henry cabled me that he would sail for New York later.

Until I took the plane I felt every cell and cord snapping, the parting from Paris a parting from a form of life, an atmosphere, from rue Cassini, the oriental niche, from a rhythm, a mystical life, from mysterious nights, the menace of war, the sound of anti-aircraft guns, of airplanes passing, of sirens...

The time on the train was so long and sad, with a glimpse of the tragic face of Spain, its hunger, its ruins, walking into a square at Fuenterrabia and feeling that there many had died, and seeing afterwards the bullet holes and stains on the walls of the caserne.

The diaries were not examined at the frontier. Jean Cateret had predicted it. "No one can put heavy hands on you, no one can touch you." No one opened the blue cloth bag where lies hidden the story of four years. In Lisbon, when I felt so uprooted, torn, split, I reread two volumes, and I felt the grandeur and the force of my life, the fire of it. I warmed myself to my own flame because I felt small and sick and powerless at that moment.

Just before taking the *Clipper* I suffered from nervousness, fears, confusion, doubts, intangible insecurity.

New York Savoy Hotel, Room 1410

We landed at the Azores. So true it is that an island is isolation that I felt absolutely severed from all the world. Our giant bird rested on this fragment of the Atlantide, made of black sand and black rocks, and pastel-colored houses which look uninhabited. People on islands are always ready to disappear. They do not suffer because the separation is already made and they are accustomed to isolation. Walking there I felt like a being whose legs and arms were cut off because Gonzalo was in Paris and Henry in Greece. A misty rain fell on us. The sea was rather stormy. The women who passed us wore long dark capes with enormous stiff hoods, large enough to shelter several heads.

The takeoff was difficult. The bird seemed too heavy, its flanks colliding with the waves, but finally it rose with much faltering and trembling. Everyone went to bed early. Hugo's bunk was over mine. At midnight I saw lightning illuminating the wings of the plane and the masses of dark clouds. It was then I felt the full loneliness of space and sea and danger, the loneliness of man, his smallness. All the diaries lying at the foot of my bed, encasing so much suffering and passion, so fragile in the immense night, carried by the wings of man himself, made small by lightning and hail. How the plane trembled. I felt its weight struggling against the wind, the strain of its body piercing the storm clouds. I lay back feeling light and unreal and fragile, without fear, only aware of great darkness, of fatality. No fear of death, just awareness. I looked again and I saw the wings emerge from the black clouds as if tearing through them and capturing enormous stars. I thought the plane had lit its lanterns, the way they fixed themselves on the tips of the wings. Then I lay back and slept because of my faith in the stars.

Over and over again I sail towards joy, which is never in the room with me, but always near me, across the way, like those rooms full of gayety one sees from the street, or the gayety in the street one sees from a window. Will I ever reach joy? It hides behind the turning merry-go-round of the traveling circus. As soon as I approach it, it is no longer joy. Joy is a foam, an illumination. I am poorer and hungrier for the want of it. When I am in the dance, joy is outside in the elusive garden. When I am in the garden, I hear it exploding from the house. When I am traveling, joy settles like an aurora borealis over the land I leave. When I stand on the shore I see it bloom on the flag of a departing ship. What joy? Have I not possessed it? I want the joy of simple colors, street organs, ribbons, flags, not a joy that takes my breath away and throws me into space alone where no one else can breathe with me, not the joy that comes from a lonely drunkenness. There are so many joys, but I have only known the ones that come like a miracle, touching everything with light.

Bermuda should have appeared at dawn, but it only came five hours later because of the storm. The next day the plane took off again and, to elude the stormy area, rose very high above the clouds. We came down gently at Port Washington. Mother was there. My brother Joaquín was in Boston giving a concert. I landed with my diaries but without my soul. I feel like a ghost. I enter a palace of Byzantine luxury. New York. The Bank for the moment takes care of us, so we live in great luxury. The luxury lulls me, but at the same time it makes me more aware of my misery, as a sick person under exceptional care is more aware of his fragility. The more comforts, warmth, luxurious baths, abundance, service, cleanliness, the lonelier I feel, as one can only feel in a palace. Bathe her, scent her, let her feet rest on soft carpets, let her eyes rest on shell pink lamps, let her seashell jewels lie on top of an ivory dresser, let her bells ring for tea, for a regal breakfast, for a letter to be mailed…but she will die. It is a hothouse of magnificence, but my life, my roots, are elsewhere. This is the vase for the marvelous, the rootless. Of course, the Princess is ill. Send for the doctor. I need a medicine man who will demand the return of my soul into my body. He doesn't sense the missing flame, the empty body. He is too used to the brilliant emptiness of America. It is a grippe, he says. Perhaps, I write to Gonzalo, I will begin to live when you come.

DECEMBER 12, 1939

I made a superhuman struggle and plunged into activity. I saw Thurema Sokol all aglow with her love for a Spaniard. I saw Frances Steloff, the gentle Jewess who bought all my D. H. Lawrence books and *House of Incest*. I saw Dorothy Norman, who published my "Birth" story in *Twice a Year*. I met Alfred Stieglitz the photographer, who admires the "Birth" story. I looked at the Babylonian splendors in the shop windows. I unfolded the wings of coquetry and vanity.

I feel nothing. I did not feel the death of Otto Rank, which happened a few weeks ago. It was unreal because I live only in the depths. When I come to the surface for pleasure, I don't live. I live only in passion, pain, depths, darkness. But I try to breathe above of the deep ocean of sensation. New York gives me fever, the great Babylonian city. Byzance. All gold and glitter and sumptuousness.

The Winter of Artifice is selling, the copies which escaped censorship. I work on the Albertine story (the Mouse) which does not belong in the houseboat book, and which I want to print separately. Gonzalo thought it should be printed in Russia because it revealed the suffering of servants and the injustice of abortion laws.

It is snowing.

DECEMBER 20, 1939

The telephone rings while we have breakfast in shining silver and starched linen. Engagements. Receptions for French War Work, vernissages, the French Ambassador, cocktails, dinners, lunches at the Cosmopolitan Club. Flowers arriving constantly, a package of Pall Mall cigarettes offered graciously at every breakfast with compliments. Steaming radiators, soft rugs, an array of enough starched towels to last a month, immaculate waiters. Blanche and James Cooney telephoned me from Woodstock. We're going there Saturday. It is a merry-go-round.

Cable from Henry—the consulate advised him to leave Greece, and he is sailing this week. This is a dying, dying love, I know it now. I am desperate for news of Gonzalo. It is now three weeks that we have been separated.

I shook off my anguish. I look beautiful. Luxury enhances me. My body needs it—the hot baths, the care, the soft water, the perfume, the warmth. I take on the colors of the flowers, the bloom, the delicacy. It becomes me. It is true my astrakhan fur coat is molting with old age, but I can look dashing in it.

The shops are a feast, the Christmas decorations are fantastic. The whole spectacle is regal, but the Americans are not—they are the common, commercial types who created this but who cannot wear it. The women yes, they all look like mannequins, but they do not reign over this luxury. They obey a uniform order and all wear the same things. Each work of art is made to be multiplied to infinity and killed, so a million fur coats walk the streets, all shaped alike, a million tiny hats worn low over the nose.

Think only of today. I cannot be as Henry is, a separate entity, fully alive, without the presence of my love Gonzalo.

JANUARY 1, 1940

Great sadness last night as I heard the New Year celebration from my bed—I have lost a world of deep feeling and found one of mere noise and matter. Ever since I came I have lived as you do when you are visiting a fair. I only felt the gravity and harmony of Dorothy Norman, the holy and humble life of the Cooneys, and a moment of cosmic religious emotion before a film of the people of Ceylon, in which they are walking up the mountain to worship a reclining Buddha. Everything else is terrifyingly empty. I did feel, at Kay de San Faustino's, talking to Yves Tanguy and Caresse Crosby (whom I met with Hugo, who forgot she is the woman I was supposed to have known intimately in Paris and to have stayed with in the country), the poignant regret for the dying France. There was a real sorrow in all of us, Kay wishing she had died there, with them. More of us met at the Gotham Book Shop and admitted how we all had run away from America and now we want to conquer it. But how is it possible to conquer this desert of inanities, this ocean of vulgarity, this abysmal immaturity?

JANUARY 1940

Henry sailed from Greece on the 27th and Gonzalo the 5th from Marseilles—I fear their being on the same boat. I feel such anguish that I cabled the Peruvian consul, begging for the name of the ship on which Gonzalo sailed.

The visit to the Bank was a nightmare. Before the black marble entrance I felt that this is a prison, a tomb of marble, steel, iron, oppressive. In the vaults I was shown a billion dollars in paper bonds. I said I would prefer to see gold, that paper meant nothing to me. The head of the vault must have thought I lacked imagination. Seeing all these heavy, complex iron doors closing upon so much paper gave me the feeling of an illusory, unreal possession, a false, fake, empty activity of man reduced to paper. It all seemed like ideological superstructures, something without humanity or substance, a man's game, leading always to great disaster.

Hugh sailed for Europe on business January 17, and I moved to the George Washington Hotel. His departure affected me. I feel anxiety about the war, the possibility of danger to him. I broke down when he left.

Arrival of Henry. I waited for his telephone call quietly at the hotel—he landed in New Jersey four hours late, and I didn't want to wait there in the cold. When I heard his voice I got nervous, and I rushed down to his hotel, nervous but passionless. Henry received me with a passionate embrace and desire, and possessed me quickly, impatiently. I only felt tenderness, but at the same time, I knew I was beginning to live again, deeply. As I was driving down to meet him, New York seemed transformed—it was as if everything else I had been doing was peripheral, that only now was I beginning to feel again. We fell into our familiar rhythm—deep talks.

In a few days Gonzalo will arrive. All his letters are filled with doubts at each delay of my letters, imagining the worst, reproaching me because he met someone to whom

I had sent a card when on the same day he had received nothing. "I must sail soon, and put an end to this torture, and all the things I imagine you are doing when I get no news of you. I am angry, I am suspicious, I am jealous, I am sorrowful, I am full of love."

Letter from Hugo: "Was broken-hearted to leave you this morning but it was better not to come to the steamer. It was very cold, and the departure was silly and formal. I ran into a rather nice fellow from Paris whom I knew there so I will be with him a good deal. I have one of the deluxe cabins and will be terribly comfortable—only wish you were in the other bed. What a connection there is between us—the most delicate—and yet the strongest of all threads, unbreakable, my darling, and partings like this always prove it to us again. I think of you so delicate and so strong. I love you deeply, deeply. Forgive me for leaving you. It is only to come back again soon, soon, remember that and think of when you will be coming to the pier to meet me. I kiss you tenderly, my love, my only love, my sweet one."

I met Robert Symmes (Duncan) and Virginia Admiral, a painter. He invites me to send writing to the *Ritual* and says: "In your *House of Incest* which I read just this last fall I was inspired by the courage you have for the intense visionary experience, the new ritual…I wrote the uncompleted poem 'Arctics' after I read your *House of Incest*… if there is a chain between your story 'Birth' and your magnificent *House of Incest*, it is that, in the profound sense of ritual in the act and in all experience."

January 29, 1940

The other morning I awakened at six-thirty to meet Gonzalo's boat in the freezing cold, half sick. I waited two hours. He didn't arrive. I was stunned, then anxious, then desperate. I sent cables to Paris, Milan, to Genoa. Then I came back to my room very ill with bronchitis and a fever. Dr. Max Jacobson took care of me. I couldn't sleep. Gonzalo's answer only came two days later, "Leaving Monday." No explanation why he didn't give me news for nearly a month. What pain, and anger too. What happened, I don't know. His last letters were full of jealousy. When I thought I had lost him it was like death.

Hugo arrived safely in London.

I rewrote "Houseboat," the barge story. As I write it, it gets dehumanized and becomes a fairy tale, another *House of Incest*. It is a process of evaporation.

February 4, 1940

Last night I was able to go to White Plains with Thurema. I packed my valise. We went to dinner together. My chest began to ache again and I came back and went to bed. I have no energy, no desire to go anywhere. I stayed alone all day. I inserted pages on my father's downfall in my old diary, a development which belonged there.

I felt physically weak but mystically strong. I faced my eternal problem—I want to publish, to give, to communicate, but I can't publish the diary. I have reached an impasse. I brood over my relationship with Henry. The last two afternoons he took me into his bed, I responded fully, though there is no passion, no tenderness even. Henry is remote, dehumanized. I yearn for Gonzalo's fire, tenderness. Yet I cannot break the mystical relationship with Henry. His attitude about me is fixed, unmovable. He acts as if it is natural I should always be there. He has a faith which baffles me—Henry, the man of change.

February 7, 1940

Again delays and frustrations—I was all ready to meet Gonzalo's ship, and it will be a day late, naturally, for he is always late. I am so keyed up it is painful.

One evening I did enjoy myself with Brigitte and Hugh Chisholm. She is flawless, a delight to look at. A Viking, but full-breasted, with rich hair, a rich voice, a wonderful ease. She was sitting cross-legged on a satin divan, wearing slacks, she the natural beauty, I the artificial one, the created one, the one who needs a certain atmosphere, a certain light, a certain mood. That night, in the warmth of their admiration, I too bloomed.

Everywhere now I see people seeking the deep current in me, that which they seek in themselves. I no longer believe it is that they think me beautiful, or that I can dance, or write, but that it is the deeper current they feel. Brigitte showed me her design for a bathing suit. For this she undressed herself completely, which affected me, enchanted me. Later as we were going out and I was powdering in the salon, she called me vehemently to the bathroom where she was absolutely naked, to dress herself again. Only when she was dressed did I feel courage enough to kiss her. I came away filled with colors, flavors, bathed in luxury and beauty.

February 10, 1940

Waiting for Gonzalo at the docks I experienced the wildest feelings and fears. I suffered the bitterest cold for three hours, because I had seen him on deck—he was there. I would die waiting for him in the cold. He was detained, the last one to come out. I thought for a moment he would not be permitted to land. I had to telephone his consulate. We shouted at each other across the pier, looking at each other for three hours, unable to touch each other. I was desperate; Gonzalo was pacing the deck. And then…Helba, the trunks, taxis, hotels, lunch. And then…Gonzalo came alone to my room and kissed me passionately. We were so keyed up, so tense, that we went out and walked the streets together. Later, lying in bed, I felt him so keenly it was painful, and he was so bound up and panicky, as he always is before a climax, that he could not possess me. But what burning caresses, what wildness of feelings, what a bath of passion. Last night we got into bed naked and caressed each other wildly for hours with such hunger as I have never known, moaning with the pleasure, but he could not take me. His emotionalism was overwhelming. He repeated, "I am knotted, as when I was courting you."

I felt such violent love that I understood the difference between my feelings for Henry and for Gonzalo, the difference between passion and love. We were so exalted, we walked the streets laughing, swimming in space. We needed height. We went to the top of the Empire State Building, looked down on this unique creation and kissed. Gonzalo said, "I have not been happy for months." And then: "American women look ugly to me. Perhaps because I am with you." I felt his love, the fire of it. Fire. Fire. Fire. A human fire. Everything was transfigured. All the feelings one has at the beginning of love, a love of the whole world, ecstasy. I was ill again, with the grippe, feverish, but I didn't care. Now my room is filled with objects from Paris, the Chinese lacquered chest, the Madagascar bedspread, the African leather bottles.

Gonzalo and I together produce fire. My power for ecstasy and his earthy fire produce this white heat all the poets and all the lovers dream of, this raging fire, heaven and hell.

FEBRUARY 14, 1940

We have a quarrel, and then I rage and suffer so…I cannot sleep, and it ravages me. Then I feel my loneliness so acutely, I go nearly mad. I stupefy myself with aspirin because I cannot bear the long night, and I think of Hugo. In the morning I set out in a blizzard, intending to stay out all day, to not see Gonzalo, but then I realize, as I have often before, that it is better to see him, to face the quarrel. I walk back to the hotel just as he is coming to see me. I explain to him about the loneliness, that if he hurts me I fall into an abyss. And Gonzalo is so tender and warm, that soon we are lying in bed and his sex is quivering and leaping at my nearness. It is over. I can work again, sing, sleep. I can even be alone. Why such terrible pain, such desperate suffering at a small incident?

MARCH 25, 1940

During the days after Gonzalo's arrival, I felt the wholeness of our love and began to plan to tell Henry the truth, to break with him. Henry was in Washington, and when he returned to New York, I would face the danger of losing Gonzalo, and this I could not bear. At the same time the anxiety over Henry made me sick. I felt that there was a bond beyond the human, that Henry was alone without me in spite of his admirers and friends. It was while I struggled with the idea of telling Henry that he lost the Indian love ring he had worn since our "marriage" in New York.

The day he returned I found him so frail-looking and sad, I could not say anything. He was anxious about meeting with his parents, whom he had not seen for eleven years. He was going to see them the next day. His father was ill, and he dreaded the reunion. Perhaps they would need his help and he could not give them any. I offered to give him fifty dollars so he would not arrive empty-handed. He said it was not his to give and asked why he should deceive them. I said: "You ought to give them the illusion. Such illusions are life-giving." But Henry would not do it. The day he visited them, he found them as he feared—poor, and his father ill with cancer of the prostate. Henry came home and sobbed all night with pity and guilt. The next day when I came, he sobbed again. He was altogether changed, human, quite broken and soft. He said he now understood everything he had condemned in me, my care of my mother and Joaquín, that one could not really escape one's karma, and that with his evasion all he had done was to accumulate guilt. As it happened that very day, a rich collector had given him fifty dollars for a piece of writing to order, which Henry was now taking to his family. All Henry's intoxication with Greece has vanished. He suddenly began to see his family every week, taking gifts to the three of them, visiting his cousins, aunts, etc. We passed the days sharing his feelings and pity.

One night I pretended to think he had been unfaithful in Greece and teased him. He teased me about Gonzalo, and said that if he put certain facts together about my behavior, it might seem like treachery. I retorted that I could analyze what he wrote and what I heard about his time in Greece. The whole theme was once again pushed aside, and we resumed our life together.

While visiting Caresse Crosby, I had an intuition that her house would be a good place for Henry to live. Coincidence. Sometime later she informed me that there was a room for rent in the same house. I took Henry to see it and it is just what he wants, the kind of room he can write in, large, spacious, peaceful, secluded. Intuitive too because finding this place dissolved his desire to travel, which would have created a conflict in me because I would not follow him. He settled in this room, where I am now, and began to write. I took a tiny studio on the same street where Gonzalo lives, on West 20th, and as Henry's place is on Lexington and 54th, it is a completely different quarter where the lazy Gonzalo never goes.

I sleep with Henry, enjoy him sensually. I leave him in the morning and return to my little studio, small and modern.

I went through a black storm because Gonzalo would not stay all night. I discovered the real reason—his liver trouble and its humiliating consequences. Poor Gonzalo, paying dearly for all his drinking. During the scene, he used the identical words Henry once used: "I'm happiest of all with you. I'm so happy with you I no longer care about my friends." In my anger, I had broken the little blue *veilleuse* he gave me in Paris, the one whose tiny glass lampshade broke the day we moved out of the houseboat *Nanankepichu*, and which he had replaced.

When Henry was jealous of Gonzalo for a day, I realized the terrible pattern of his destiny, how I was acting exactly as June did, which prevented me from revealing what does not seem right to reveal, while our relationship is still alive.

Meanwhile Jacobson has to take care of my stubborn anemia, and I have to accept my physical limitations. I cannot enjoy late nights, parties, strain. After one night in Harlem (a magnificent night of dancing until five o'clock in the morning) I was tired for a week. As soon as I feel well and strong I spend my strength as recklessly as I do my money. I cannot save, conserve, reserve.

I have to learn. I refuse invitations. I copy diaries. I waste feelings of anxiety over Hugh being in Europe. The news of the war getting violent causes me anguish. It drags on like a nightmare—ghostly, neurotic.

Gonzalo reads either the newspapers or the Spanish classics and fails to notice the very world in which I breathe.

The grotesque evenings at Mabel Dodge Luhan's, the self-conscious discussions. All America is still in elementary school, with its catechism, declarations, preparations, definitions, mere prefaces to living.

APRIL 13, 1940

Once a month I get the moonstorm, and it is madness recurring rhythmically, only each time more violently. In a week I get persecution mania, obsession, fears, doubts of all kinds—I feel everything I described in my novel. Each time it is more powerful. It is a reversal of what I usually feel: faith, sense of wonder, illusion. Everyone becomes a monster. I trust only Hugh. Wind in the street appears malicious, people's slightest words a humiliation. I see desertion all around me. I feel hatred, rebellion, resentment, loneliness. I am very near to absolute despair. It is a lie, it is madness. With it come violent erotic longings. I dream of whorehouses, of being possessed by many men, of being possessed to the point of exhaustion, saturation, of touching the depths of sensuality such as one touches only at the beginning of passion. Strangest of all, I write, I create, and stranger still, I am physically stronger than I have ever been. For the first time, I have gained weight, from 107 to 114. A thread of lucidity saves me from insanity. I see it now. I see the insanity in my loves—the obsessions—in my need of the diary as a proof of reality, of the reality of my life.

APRIL 30, 1940

Gloomy days, darkened by Gonzalo's bad health, neurosis, insomnia. Gonzalo cannot conquer his laziness. Add laziness to illness, and there is little charm left—big and fat, lying prone on the couch, always reading newspapers and listening to the news.

Very rarely have we recaptured the beauty of our days in Paris. I think it is all dying from inertia and laziness. When there is no spirit to exalt the body, to dominate disease, to force and create, it becomes stagnation, and soon stagnation will overpower Gonzalo—then I will cease loving him because I hate death.

The life of Gonzalo and Helba is nothing but stagnation. They lie like animals, doing nothing all day, complaining, frightening themselves. Gonzalo does not get his teeth fixed, does not answer his letters, does not see the Communist Party or his friends. Everything rots around them in dirt, neglect, sloppiness.

Meanwhile I struggle to write. I wrote pages on the house of Louise de Vilmorin— the glass house. I finally sent the manuscript to Rae Beamish, the editor. But underneath lies despair.

Kenneth Patchen, whose work Henry admires, moves me because his body has some resemblance to Gonzalo's, but he is too young, too unformed, naïve. *Il n'y a personne.* I seek escape—new passion. My life has lost its flame.

I have asked myself whether there is something wrong with me. Henry says, "In dissolution there is life," but I recoil from dissolution. I struggle *against* the demons—I struggle *for* light—desperately—*against* disease, ugliness, fears, madness, monsters, nightmares.

May 4, 1940

Hugh sailed today from Genoa. I do not feel happy at his coming, only grateful that he is out of danger. I can only think that I will be separated from Gonzalo and Henry because Hugh wants a vacation.

I am working on 1000 pages of the abridged diary to give to Caresse Crosby. Dorothy Norman was overwhelmed by it.

I am in debt again—America is monstrous. I close my eyes and ears and I write. I wrote pages on June's way of talking for the diary.

Gonzalo comes to me to eat with me, to fall asleep in my arms. He found me lacing my jacket, and began unlacing it, gently, tenderly, but the fire has died. It lasted four years, a great deal of time for fire, intensity, fever. In Paris I had a superstitious fear of its transplantation, felt something would happen if we left. Something happened to all of us from the uprooting. Something died in all of us. I can see it in the others. We are only surviving.

May 20, 1940

When Hugh returned he said: "I want peace. No more separations. I have missed you too much." For a week he was extraordinarily possessive, jealous. I got desperate. I was cut off from Gonzalo and Henry and thrown into the bourgeois life again. The luxurious hotel, visitors, dinners, cocktails. I suffocated because I was not wise enough to see it as a phase. Hugh himself revolted, said he could no longer live a life tied to routine, working on Wall Street without trips or escape. But when all this was added to the ugliness of life in New York, I became so desperate I wanted to die. I pulled myself out by writing "The Prison of Fear," the first writing I have done dictated by hatred. I wrote pages on the bus on my way to Henry. Creatively, I have entered the objective writing Durrell and Henry tried to push me into long ago—but emotionally, I have entered the destruction and dissolution from which I struggled to save others. I have struggled too much. I have been sickened by their poison as I sucked it from their wounds to save them from death. I *feel* and understand for the first time the pleasure in dissolution. I felt this only once before, with June.

Suddenly I have lost my courage and desire to struggle. I have lost all enthusiasm and faith. Perhaps the war has done this. I suffer with Europe and participate in its agony. Everything seems dark and futile. I have lost my appetite for everything. I pray only for passion, a new passion. Passion can give me life again, otherwise I shall descend into the inferno, because I have nothing to live for. Henry is sad, Gonzalo is ill, Helba is nothing but a burden, Hugo is grey. It seems like we are all ending like Europe is ending, perhaps out of love and sympathy because of our roots there. I understand what I struggle to heal: despair and hatred. Hatred of Helba has inspired the "Rue Dolent," the "Prison of Fear." May it liberate me from hatred. Dissolution—I fought against it—always. I was the enemy of destruction, but now it is universal horror and despair, as Henry prophesized for years. Perhaps ours is no longer a personal despair, but a deep, universal one.

May 24, 1940

Hugh falls asleep early, around ten. I slip out noiselessly to meet Gonzalo at Park. We wander about or sit in one of those impossible American places where the radio jangles my nerves and the faces of the people are like those of a proletarian nightmare. The news is bad, everywhere there is panic and selfishness. Fear makes people evil. All New York is nothing but a school, a clinic, a factory. In Europe there are machines which deal death and terror. Here there are machines which have already dealt death: Americans are robots—nothing else. I live in a machine with robots. Robots are afraid. Robots commit crimes. Robots write Americans books. Not a human voice anywhere, only voices coming through the radio receiver. The dancing is a parody of the negro's joyous movements. It is all repulsive and monstrous. The machine in Europe is killing people, and here it is canning them. It would have been better for all of us to die in flames, rather than this kind of death. Hugh is cornered in his dying system of capitalism, and the communists utter fanatical, narrow, crystallized statements, as many deformations and falsities as the others, committing the same crimes for their religion as the Catholic inquisitors did for theirs. Everyone is wrong—the pacifists too, for they are weak. The followers of D. H. Lawrence run away to Guatemala or Mexico. I see the twistedness in communists too, the errors and abuses and dogmatism. In the end I return to my mystical concepts. I see only nature, chaos and horror, and I see only one heaven—in the eternal. I know that communism has appealed to the weak, the bitter, and the deformed beings, but they want it as protection, as relief from responsibility. I see so much ugliness, so much horror, so many monstrosities, that I return to god. The communists are those who are born in matter and cannot believe in the eternal, and they are utopians because there cannot be a world without cruelty, envy and jealousy. Europe is being destroyed, but the demons are never conquered.

May 30, 1940

Hugh and I took a furnished apartment at 33 Washington Square West, which gives the illusion of a European quarter, smaller and more intimate than the rest of New York. We are struggling to act as if we were alive.

Gonzalo and I used to have a special caress, like that of cats, howling our needs—his need over mine. Now he says, "Let me lean on your neck." He takes it like a support. He pretends to lean on me, like this, in a caress of utter helplessness. I am afraid I have only augmented his weakness—no strength has come out of Gonzalo, no creation, nothing. I feel my love dying, my passion. And this, happening now with the war, drives me to despair. I see him in his true light, as the clochard he loves to draw: dirty, unkempt, unshaved, sitting all day on a bench, or sleeping, talking with other clochards. Suffering and death everywhere.

JUNE 11, 1940

The Germans are thirty-six miles from Paris, and as if that were not enough, now Italy is invading France. How I feel all my love for her. We are all tense, guilty, angry, cruel to each other—selfish lives, all of ours, saving our own souls only—why? I am absolutely ready to enter the conflict. I would like to have died for France because of my love of it…simply. People everywhere are at war because they do not live by simple human feelings. I feel for the whole world. I have lived a purely individual life, and I am ashamed, but the same laws of pity by which I lived I can easily carry into the drama of war. In loving, I looked for my pleasure and found mostly suffering. So war is a drama no more terrible than the drama of love, and I am willing to serve and die as I have served and died for the love of individuals. My lovers have killed—at least they have killed me— and I return to the feeling I discovered as a girl: personal life is not important.

JUNE 13, 1940

Desperate at the news. Paris is encircled, about to surrender. Ill with pain, sympathy, a desire to die with the past. My cousin Eduardo is saved, but we have only saved our bodies—the darkness of the world is swallowing us.

One still can only cling to immediate human life, the last little bits of love and devotion. That is all there is; everything else is darkness and chaos and horror. Gonzalo upbraids me for not talking like a Marxist. The whole world will soon be at war, all of us engulfed, even the innocent ones—so many innocent ones, so many who never caused war. Henry was saying if people only would behave with love, generosity, unselfishness, as they sometimes do when death is near.

Gonzalo and I are in a little room, where, in the darkness, the dream survives. I tell him I am sad because he wants to be a clochard, and I can't be a clocharde. Would you like me to be one? Would you like me to become one? Gonzalo protests vehemently, saying that being a clochard is all right, but that clochardes are ugly. He likes lovely nails and fine skin and perfumed hair. And I am consoled by this because it seems to me that in his vehemence there was a little condemnation of Helba's unkemptness. I had been thinking how the two of them harmonized—but Gonzalo needs a contrast to himself. I have been feeling the death of our love because of its transformation from passion. His bad health has made this transition bitter and cruel. I am six years younger than Gonzalo. He is paying for his extravagances, his excesses. He has aged. For three weeks I was tormented by sensual desires—not satisfied with Henry's possession, or Gonzalo's, I yearned for violence and fire, dreaming of negroes, dancing at Harlem, to permit this strength to overflow in the drum beat of the music.

JOHN

I believe I have defended myself against suffering

One night Caresse said, "You *must* meet two young poets who have come all the way from Des Moines to meet you and Miller." I had dinner with Henry first. I thought this would be another bore—young, immature hero-worshipping. I felt lifeless and old. We first met Lafayette Young, who looked a little like Rank behind his big glasses, and who was stuttering with nervousness at meeting us. His worship for John Dudley, his friend, was amazing, a complete devotion like a woman's. Then came John, a young man of about thirty, looking like a young English aristocrat, tall, blond, with a beautiful voice. I sensed vitality, a leaping quality, faith, fervor, craziness, and great humility. We looked at his drawings, which were interesting. I was not prepared to meet Dudley as an equal, and his age separated us at first. I was merely touched by his enthusiasm. Caresse had begged us to be nice to them, so I asked them to come see me. Impulsively, I suggested we all go to Harlem because he loves jazz and is a fine drummer. Instead of dancing we talked, John and I. He was full of vision and penetrations—uncannily so. We sat alone by a window and forgot about Harlem. At the end of our talk he said, "I love you" with great warmth and impulsiveness, but it was a love like Durrell's. I felt his warmth and charm. The next day he telephoned while we were visiting with Eduardo. He was depressed by a day full of failures (he was struggling to get help for a magazine called *Generation*)—could he come? I said come. The four of us went out and sat in a café, and came back. By the time he left I felt moved by the force and fire of John.

I could only talk to him, dance with him, but I was getting a little intoxicated. The next evening, when I went with Eduardo to see Henry, John and Lafayette were watching for me on the stoop (they live next door to Caresse and Henry). We again spent the evening together, listening to a beautiful talk between Henry and Eduardo, which lifted our minds beyond the present to its cosmic meaning again.

When we returned from the restaurant, Henry, Lafayette and Eduardo went to get a beer, so John and I went up to the room alone—this I felt like an explosion. I felt his excitement, the suspense. I talked to break the unbearable tension. Across the philosophic airiness of the conversation, our emotions flashed signals at each other. I loved his utter absence of passivity.

The next day, while Hugh was home, John called up and asked, "Can I come up and draw your picture?" I said no because we had to go to Kay de San Faustino's housewarming, but asked if would he come with us. He said no. I felt his disappointment. Then Hugh decided to play tennis, which meant I could have seen John. I felt that he would call again and come to the de San Faustino cocktail with us just to see me. And he did. Then I said, "You can come at five and I can pose for an hour." I knew he was going to come alone. And he did. We were tense. He tried to draw. The night before I had noticed he was wearing a ring too tight for his finger, and I said it constricted him and that I could not bear it. He took it off and, as a symbol of his expansion, never wore it again. We talked, but what we really wanted was to kiss each other. He did not have the courage until we stood by the elevator. By the time we got to de San Faustino's house, after wandering around dazed, we were absolutely exalted. I forgot about age. I heard everyone saying: "We are mourning the past in Paris as the White Russians mourned the old Russia. We are mourning the death of France, of Europe."

John does not feel this death. He is outside of it, as an artist, as a youth. As I write this, it is a half hour before I go to his room. I pray for a new passion, which comes with the sound of his slender fingers drumming on the table at Harlem, full of sensuality and savagery. He said I was a legend in Des Moines, known for my glamour. He was afraid of me.

Yesterday, after the kiss, I met Gonzalo, who talks only of what he reads in the newspapers, who complains of the heat, of fatigue, of pain...a Gonzalo without fire, dull and heavy, like a sad animal.

JUNE 17, 1940

John was looking for me from his window. He was tense, highly strung, overwhelmed. We talked a little, and then he came over and kissed me. He took all my clothes off. He was amazed by my body, the body of a girl, yet more than a girl...ageless. I felt his fear, but to tell the truth, I was afraid too, as if this were my first love affair. I was intimidated because I knew what his imagination had made of me—a mythical figure. I knew he was overwhelmed and that I could not live up to my reputation of an experienced European woman of the world. It felt unreal, and I told him so. I was quiet, timid, passive, feminine—my own humanness put him at ease. He became impulsive, dynamic, violent, and our caresses were entangled in strangeness.

He is truly Henry's son, a young savage, with the same blue eyes, same white skin, a laughing face, but with great strength. He is only twenty-six. I pushed aside the literary aura, the past, so that we could breathe. I said this was something happening in space. I wanted life…and there is life in John, an abundance of it. At first I dreaded my age—thirty-seven—but when we talked I realized I have no age in his eyes. John said he could tell everybody's age, but not mine. He knows, for instance, what his wife will look like ten, twenty years from now, but he cannot tell about me. He feels I will live forever and that I have had many lives, far into the past. He said many poetic things—he is full of faith and ardor. Henry and I have expanded the world for him. I know this is to be a creation, and for that I am sad. I wanted something else, but I am so grateful for John, for his worship and his youth—he is a young giant, a force to come, full of potentialities. He is explosive, alert, violent, active, a strong personality. I enjoy his electric youth. It is better than living in the past, clinging to Gonzalo's heaviness and inertia, to the tragedy of France's death. A few days ago I was dying with France, dying with Gonzalo. Today I went to John's room and forgot all about death. I felt my own youth; there was music again. At least my body is not dead. I told Eduardo I was going to pose for John, and Eduardo said: "It's dangerous. He has his Moon over your Sun."

John says poetic things about my voice, is awake to my hair, my clothes, my skin. Is the current of life set in motion again, by John? He is tender, worshipful, too excited to sleep. Because he is romantic and idealistic, there is the danger of him mistaking this for love.

JUNE 23, 1940

I went to him every afternoon this week. At first it was like a game, an electric game, but we have transcended the phase of unreality. The second time he delighted me with his fervor, his newfound strength, and I responded to him sensually. His awakening, his gratitude, his chivalry, his romanticism, his excitement, are contagious. I came dancing, always with a pounding heart, left after a bath of love. That second afternoon, after I left him, I felt my gayety stronger than death. The dawns in his eyes, the wonder.

I met Gonzalo, who, of course, was amorous again because I was turning away from him. He began to pursue me again, was desirous, asking for a whole night with me, because I had broken away from him after suffering the torture of his lack of passion. One afternoon, after being with John, I went to Henry. We went out together for dinner. I had said many things to John about living on the peaks, how he only needs intensity, that his going away will not matter, that this is a violent dream in space. Then, as I was having dinner with Henry in the Chinese restaurant, they came in, the boys. I felt a pang of pleasure, and then a stab of pain at the thought of losing him. They had no money; no one would sponsor the magazine, and they were in danger of having to return to Des Moines. I cannot help them. Finally, someone gave them a little money, and they will stay a few more days, until Monday.

Strange boy. He is a descendent of the Earl of Dudley, the favorite of Queen Elizabeth, of Thomas Dudley, Duke of Yorkshire. His family owned Kenilworth, of the Walter Scott novels that once enchanted me. And that is how he looks, like a figure out of a novel, a darling of women, a fighter, a tyrant, reckless, courageous, romantic. Fine, tall, white body, hair around his head like a faun's, curled and golden. Half artist, but a good one who makes marvelous drawings with character. Aware, awake, alert, luminous. When near him, after telling myself I do not love him, I feel sensual warmth. Once I came to him in the middle of a violent storm; I came to him on Sunday, a day when I am usually a prisoner. He is extraordinarily aware of me. His drawings of me are accurate and interesting. He has protective impulses and asks if I had been hurt living with Henry, asks what he can do for me. I said: "You rescued me from death. One rescue in a week, is it not enough?" When he feels unequal to me, I say, "Can you say you are less than me only because I've been to exotic places and you have not?" He says: "You accept me. You challenge my strength and make me whole. I feel stronger with you. At the same time I feel weaker than before other women. I was an egoist. I did not consider woman…as an equal." He has a small, childish, dreamy wife, married only for a year. She is even too small sexually for him…too small, not a giant. He will be someone. He will be loved by women, by everybody. He is already. People listen to him. With him, miracles may happen. He is a conqueror, in a way. He is determined; his only hesitancies are those of youth. He has strong hatreds and strong loves. I see him as light and joy.

His worship revives me so much that I return to Gonzalo full of charm, fancies, rid of the tightness and bitterness of absolute dependence, the poisonous, acrid fears. I return nonchalant, imaginative, and he falls in love with me all over again, takes my clothes off and makes love to me all over the body as I like it. I'm like a drunkard, drunk on love, spending most of my life in bed, in an orgy of caresses. Mad, absolutely mad, lying with all of them, creating, laughing, inventing, writing. Liberated, liberated of the fears which made me clutch at Gonzalo. What pain these last months, watching the passion die, but then replenishment at the source of love itself, a tender, young, passionate love, drinking there and gaining strength, sexually, spiritually, emotionally, all in one week. A miracle. And everything around it is nourished by the miracle, a life transfusion of love given to all. I asked John, "Have you the courage to live something inhuman, the poem?" But as I began to leave him and saw the pain on his face, I yielded to a human impulse and said, "You know there is no more passion between Henry and me."

Henry took us all last night to 662 Briggs Avenue in Brooklyn, where he lived nine years of his childhood. We walked through it all, listening to him recollecting. John at my side, silent. Jealous? The night was beautiful. The past, so rich and full to the point of bursting, and the present—John—walking together.

What John and I joined together were two quick, pulsing rhythms, quickening blood, adventure.

I have infinite patience with his youthful stuttering, his youthful errors. I tell him when he retracts or apologizes, "Never retract with me." When he stumbles or hesitates, "Go on." He asks: "Is that clear? Do you understand?" I say: "Don't write. You are a painter." He only wearies me when he tries to make it a great love instead of hunger, electric sparks, everything but love, when he tries to carry me to see if he can *carry me away from all the others.*

Because he has no past and I had no future, we have traded, but I feel airy and strange. Eduardo said: "You have no center of gravity. You live outside of yourself, in your relationships. You are really mad, in a way. Hugh is your only foundation, which may be wonderful for poetry, but you seek only the peaks."

I am so grateful to John that I can feel, laugh, and pulse again. He said to me: "Henry has something of death in him, a greyness, Hugh too. But you are of a different color altogether—you are barbaric red." As an artist, he sees me as beautiful. I see the shadowless translucence of his skin. I like creating him sensually, unleashing him, inflaming him, opening him. I feel his body as if I were making it with my own hands, touching off new cells of responses, new sparks. There are flames again—they leap in my hands.

He is full of delicacies. I have never been served and adored like a princess. He says when I go down the street he wants to push everyone away so I can walk alone, guarded by him alone. When he says romantic things (almost like the ones I said to Henry) I laugh gently, mockingly, a soft laughter. He said after our first afternoon, "This room is now immortalized." Sensually he is learning; he was fumbling at first, but he is gifted for nuances, he is gifted for love. Can I bear his going away? Will I miss his caresses, his exaltation? He does not sleep; instead, he spends his nights making drawings of me.

I did betray Gonzalo—oh, not by sleeping with John, I do not consider such acts betrayals. No, betrayal is when I brought John a piece of Japanese wood Gonzalo stole for me once, to light and produce the most unique incense perfume, a wood Gonzalo and I only burned for ourselves, to make strange hotel rooms smell like us. That is betrayal: stealing what belongs to the other, to the very soul of the relationship, and desecrating it. My sensual gift is only a great expansion of the self, drawing on new worlds, new senses, new experiences, another self totally unrelated to Gonzalo. I dedicated *House of Incest* to both John and his wife (of whom I am not at all jealous), which touched him. He places her under my protection. When I was sixteen, I used to read *Kenilworth* with passion. It had a magic meaning. I shall call John Kenilworth. John I do not like, because of the other John (Erskine), and because it is too simple.

I often can cut through the manifestations of anger and recognize the suffering behind it. Many people react to suffering with anger.

Death and disintegration require passivity like Henry's and Gonzalo's, which I do not have, even in small things. Gonzalo does not know when he is hot or cold and goes out for a week in the same costume; if it is too light and the weather changes he gets a grippe. He suffers. He waits. One day I said: "Gonzalo, you're so hot in that suit. You're suffering. I saw fine-looking slacks in the store with light shirts." We go and look at them. I urge him to get them. It is I who had to help Helba and Gonzalo find an apartment. I urge them into more expensive places because I do not want them thrust into dark rooms again, into a drab past.

Orienta Apartments. Mamaroneck, July 4, 1940

A strange, terrifying thing has happened to me twice now. As soon as I feel the downward curve of love I throw myself into a new one. This time I threw myself into desire for John, a meeting of two fires. After our fourth afternoon together he asked me, "You have never said you loved me." We were separated for two days. During those two days he was like a wild horse suddenly corralled. He rebelled against my power over him. No woman had ever touched off such deep responses, sensually or imaginatively. Until now he had been the loved one, and here I had taken hold of his body and soul without even saying, "I love you!" On one of those nights of rebellion, he saw the film *La Femme du Boulanger*, saw the handsome shepherd whom the woman eats like a beautiful fruit. John asked himself if that was all he was to me. I was away with Hugh during those two days, and John was to wait until Monday to see me again before leaving. He cried out, "It hurts, it hurts." It was a storm of revolt against the wounding pain of passion. He was going to leave before I returned, but Monday morning Henry told him, "Anaïs is coming later." My name struck John like a bombshell. He waited. Then I came, and he told me all he had suffered, but still I would not say I loved him. We plunged into caresses, and his were violent, hungry. I liked the fire in him—I bathed in it.

All the time I knew it was not love. Then came the last day, when we possessed each other like savages. The last evening we all went out together, Hugh, Eduardo, Lafayette, John and I, to Chinatown. As we walked the streets I was drunk with desire. We wanted desperately to touch each other again. The intoxication was too strong; it was torture. I felt myself on the threshold of doing something mad—I could not let him go away. I promised to see him again. And suddenly, it was all unreal; the exaltation disappeared. I did not feel his departure. I felt nothing. I fell into an abyss. Back to the familiar loves, to human life, grey days, sickness, bad moods, fatigue, back to aging and dying, to sorrowing over a lost world. John left me nothing of his goldenness, not a tremor of desire. I cannot remember his words. Nothing he said left an echo. No caress left its imprint on the blood. It was all a mirage.

I do not want to see him again.

Hugh and I came to Mamaroneck for Hugh, so that he can enjoy his boating and fishing. I hate it. I want to run away from it.

Tonight I lie in bed hating my bourgeois life, feeling desperate and destructive while Americans celebrate the Fourth of July, throwing whistling bombs that remind me of those which terrorized us in Europe.

I should learn to accept twilight, deserts, impasses. I am liberated of my obsessive love, but not of the love itself.

JULY 13, 1940

After four days in Mamaroneck with Hugh, I spent a night with Gonzalo and took a plane to Richmond, Virginia, telling Gonzalo I was meeting Hugh in Washington. Gonzalo came to see me off after an intimate and emotional night.

At Richmond Henry was expecting me, with John Payne, Caresse's young lover. We arrived at Hampton Manor, another enchanted house, like the Grand Meaulnes or Louveciennes, with its white columns, its deep frame of old trees, its large harmonious rooms, its extraordinary stillness, the enchanted sleep to the tune of whip o' wills.

Caresse, whose life at the Mill (the *Moulin du Soleil*) was spangled with all the personalities of her time, felt that life might repeat itself with Henry and me at Hampton Manor. When she saw us there, writing, talking, she felt perhaps it was the Mill again, with Harry Crosby like a meteor, with Breton, Éluard, Frank Crane, Ernst, the painters, the aristocrats, the wealthy, the capricious. Now she had invited Henry, Salvador Dalí, and other artists. There are so many currents in Caresse's receptive being that she brings forth more friendships, links and currents created by her life force. She sits stuttering, rubbing her eyes, rubbing smooth the wrinkles on her face, flicking her tongue, her small, sensual pink tongue.

We slept through long, hot afternoons. Henry wrote in the morning, adding many pages to *Sexus*.

We received telegrams from the Earl of Dudley that he might arrive Thursday or Friday with his wife, but I was not stirred. Yet when Thursday evening came and Caresse took us off to the movies I said, "Dudley will arrive tonight." Henry said, "No, at three o'clock in the morning" Caresse said: "Tomorrow." So we went to the movies, but I knew. As we were driving back to the house in the darkness, I said: "They are there. I know it."

And they were.

As soon as I heard John's voice, the sensual turmoil reawakened. His wife is small, dead, insignificant, lifeless. John stole a kiss from me in the dark stairway, and then we all went to bed, Henry and I in one room, John and his wife in another, Caresse alone because Payne is now in the army. I lay awake desiring John, whom I do not love, wishing he had the audacity to rise in the middle of the night, imagining how it would feel to meet in the dark, secretly, feeling each other's bodies, as I read long ago in a novel which stirred me erotically at the age of nine. Darkness and nakedness.

In the morning the current of desire between us was so strong it was unendurable. I was leaving for ten days in the afternoon, and John's wife followed him every minute with a fear of me. But Caresse took destiny in her own hands. She took John's wife in her car to shop an hour away. Henry was trying to get in touch with his friend Emil Schnellock at Fredericksburg, so I suggested lightly that he too go to town and telephone him, and he did.

John had just finished taking a shower. I entered his room, and he began to kiss me hungrily in front of the window while we watched them driving away. The tension was so acute, a storm broke out during our caresses, a violent electrical storm. I stood by the window, John behind me. I pressed against him and felt his desire so hard and strong. He opened my blouse, took my breasts in his two hands and pushed them upward as if to drink from them. The storm over our heads, all the peace gone, fire and lightning bolts coursing through the body. We threw ourselves on the bed, and he took me with violence.

How grateful I was to Caresse for this moment, Caresse with her knowledge of passion. How joyous I was to have discovered this joy divorced from the pangs of love, this purely sensual vibration which alters in no way my deep love for Gonzalo, a vibration which takes place only when John is there, a drunkenness which lasts only while he is there, and of which I am free as soon as I leave him, free of love. Yes, he is the shepherd, and all I want is to bite into him when he is there, his flesh so alive, the summer perspiration fresh as dew, the sensual underlip. He is alive. Electric joys.

Nothing else about him interests me; his atmosphere of Middle West America homeliness, the cult of the ugly, the drinking, his dreams and talk, which I cannot even remember. Absolutely ordinary, youthful, too simple. He is imitating Henry. So when I leave him, the spell is broken, and I am free.

Caresse and I were in the airplane, talking, confiding. Caresse thought Hugh was going to meet me in New York, but I told her Hugh did not know I was arriving, that Gonzalo was going to meet me. Poor Gonzalo was desperately anxious—we were an hour late due to fog. He was waiting for me on the curb, anxiously staring at all the taxis. We spent the night in our little room. The next day we went together to Mamaroneck, to look for a place for him and Helba near Hugh and me. But they are so slow they will move in by the time I am ready to leave.

Here, in Mamaroneck, I have no excitement or fever, so I fall into an abysm. The smallest frustration makes me despondent. If I am thwarted I can easily think of suicide.

This place: a bourgeois apartment house near the bay, everything genteel and well regulated. The husbands all go to the city in the morning. The beaches are dull, the people stodgy and uninterested in each other. It is all plain and homely and tidy and colorless.

Now I think coldly like a demon: John will help me get through the summer, I will get strong, and in the fall I will throw myself into the fullest, most hectic life possible. I must find another love; I must get free of Gonzalo. It is all painful and negative now.

He weighs on me heavily. I am only made for passion; it is the temperature of love that I cannot endure. I am afraid, and I think it is death—everything but passion seems like death to me. Only in fever do I feel life.

JULY 28, 1940
On the train from Fredericksburg to New York

Back in Hampton Manor again, Flo followed John like a shadow every minute. We could not even talk to each other alone. We could not touch each other. Tuesday, Wednesday. He does not know ruse yet. At night when we walked—we swayed in the dark to touch each other's hands. Powerful currents traversed us. At any moment we could have made a wild gesture. The excitement mounted and became pain, the body aching with desire. One afternoon we went to the Potomac River to swim, and when I walked towards John in my bathing suit I saw the desire on his face. We knew we had to act.

Thursday morning Flo was not well, and she let John drive the poor negro, who has a tumor on his finger, to the doctor. We sat in a café and stole kisses, the tension growing so keen that I wanted to scream. We took the negro to the doctor, and then we drove to a pine forest I had observed on the way. We entered into the heart of it, walking on pine needles. We kissed voraciously. He slipped his hands into my shirt. What strength in John's hands, what firmness. I felt his desire hard. We lay on the pine needles, and we almost shouted with the wildness of it, the ecstasy. When we returned to the house, we were gentle and appeased. When Henry and Flo took a siesta, John and I went down to the cellar, to the Mexican room, where he wanted me to see his drawings. I was naked under my cotton dress. He bit my thighs. Again delirium.

The last day we had only one hour together. Unable to unleash our desire for each other, I was forced to notice John's character, and I saw the points at which we touch, the sensuality, the electric tensions, the positive onrushing natures, a likeness of swift, proud, domineering and active temperament, the capacity to burn. But he has a timid, plaintive, shrunken wife, who wants him small, who is afraid of the violence in him, afraid of a mistress who can give him a tremendous sense of expansion, set him on fire, challenge all his forces. The first time John and I returned from the ride in the village, she was weeping—and she said, without knowing anything, but out of pure intuition: "I was thinking how it would be if someday you loved somebody else." The day of their wedding she had already lost him; he was already beyond his marriage. He calls her the waif.

Strange thing: wanting to reassure Henry, I took a siesta with him, knowing he would take me, and I responded fully. And it was after this I went down to the Mexican room and could still vibrate under John's earthy caresses.

Mars of the earth again.

John can do something none of my other loves could do—he can make me feel joyous, sensual, free of pain.

I enjoy my power. I can say John's name in such a way that he says it feels like a knife. I can make him tremble with desire, quaking with it, keep him awake and tortured. He has given me what woman should value highly—a young man's first passion, so total, so romantic and fervent. I feel beautiful, desirable, potent in his hands. The light in his face at times is dazzling. After a walk in the dark when merely brushing each other, we could create ecstasy. Even in the dark his face is resplendent.

John, it is marvelous to arouse desire. Do not be too hurt. So much in the world we should caress and love only with the blood and the flesh because it is beautiful, brilliant, alive—as we love fire. No small role—giving me pure joy—giving me life in this body, a miraculous current without pain. For the first time the Sun. I was never given the Sun.

Poor little Flo—she taps John's knees lightly with a small, helpless hand. I dig my nails into them and he trembles like a racehorse.

MAMARONECK, AUGUST 12, 1940

I believe I have defended myself against loving John, against *suffering*. I believe that just as in the beginning when I still loved Henry and couldn't yield to Gonzalo absolutely, so have I defended myself against yielding to John. Whenever I arrive at Hampton Manor, I am prepared not to feel. And so it was the last time. Because there was Flo, because John is poor and not free, because of his youth, there were obstacles. Anyway, I arrived cold. And for a few hours all was well, but soon the warmth returned. John may have been talking. I saw his eyes on me. I looked at his mouth.

The next day the torment began. I found him depressed. Flo attacked him each time they went to their room. Her instinct is not blind: she told him: "I am not the woman for you. Anaïs is the woman for you." And then, more obscurely, she fights to diminish him, crush him. She tells him he must not be crude (when he is merely impulsive), that he talks too much, or she attacks his work. Poor John.

All the time we were watching for a moment together, and all through the first day it was impossible. The next day Caresse arrived early in the morning. She sent us on errands, which included two huge valises so that no one else could get into the car. John and I went—and we went to the woods. The moment was too short for me to respond fully in spite of my excitement, but I still feel the starved kisses, the violence. That evening, a walk in the dark with sparks burning through us.

Caresse announced her publishing partner was failing her. Somehow or other we all simultaneously began to talk about doing it ourselves. Caresse was very concrete and determined. We sat at lunch, planning to run a press in Hampton Manor to publish the books she had intended to do: *Nadja* by Breton, translated by Jolas, a novel of Kay Boyle's, memoirs by Marianne Gold, Cendrars, Radiquet, etc.

We walked over to the barn, but found it was too open for a press, and we would not be able to get it heated later. Then we walked to the house built for the servants, a lovely little white house all of natural wood inside, with many rooms. We decided to install the press there. As this was shaping into a solution to John's life (penniless, nowhere to go, a good craftsman, he could live on running the press), it became all intermingled with our love. John saw it as *our* work. I could see him working, incited by love, and the excitement took the form of an intense personal joy which we wanted desperately to share together, to share together like a bottle of wine.

While everybody was looking through the rooms, talking, I caught John alone, walking behind me. I turned fully on him and whispered: "I love you!" which completely set him on fire.

That evening we were so full of emotions, we could not talk. John is so different from Gonzalo—so creative and not twisted. Things take form in his hands. He loves to build, to work, invent, discover. The night before—while Henry argued against us—we had talked about the necessity of recreating the universe from the beginning with our own hands. John has that. He likes to dominate matter. This likeness, this capability we both have attracts us to each other. That night the accord between our temperaments was so visible that Flo left the table and went to her room.

Next morning. It is the day of my departure. We find ourselves alone in the library, sitting far away from each other because we are in turmoil and John says he wants to pounce on me. Every time we look at each other we feel we are sent reeling. The whole world is reeling around us. It is unbearable. John comes over to me, takes my face in both his hands and quickly covers it with kisses.

He is despondent. He feels defeated, imprisoned by Flo, frustrated. I am depressed too, from so much supervision and repression.

A little later when I am all packed, I find Henry has fallen asleep. I leave the room. I go to Caresse and ask her if she will call John for me (Flo is ill in bed) so that I may see him a little while. She suggests I go to the little white house and wait there. She'll come with John later. And this she does so deftly that Flo thinks John has been called to help Caresse carry things to the little house where the press is to be.

She leaves us there. My heart is beating. We kiss. John is ecstatic. "Everything you do I love, everything. You are perfect, marvelous! I like your audacity. I like all your impulses. Now I am happy."

In the train I travel with Henry, who has to go to New York. I don't know if it is Henry who has changed or my image of him, but he seems faded, grey somehow. In the train I am anxious because I fear I am going to fall in love with John, but there are reservations in my desire for him which do not exist in my other loves.

The night before I left for Virginia, lying with Gonzalo, after his possession of me, he moved his head in such a way that his long black hair brushed my breasts, and this I felt so deeply, as if every strand of hair were tangled with a strand of my own hair and tied around a cell of my blood. John's gestures do not have this sort of effect on me. The intoxication is there each time, the need to embrace, kiss, to lie with him, but only while he is there, and it never grows roots into my being. Even this time, though I remember the intoxication, I do not feel those blood roots stirring in me, the kind that makes a woman know the man is inside her womb as a child would be, stirring at the center of her being.

AUGUST 22, 1940

Saturday I discovered I was pregnant—three months! Days of anguish over the money and the complications I feared would arise. Jacobson put me in the hands of a good German Jew who works for rich women. He said it would have to be done in two operations, one to insert a bag which dilates the womb (this is done without ether) and then a final one that is done with ether.

I set the date for Wednesday, the 21st. I arrived at nine-thirty and was strapped like an insane person, wrists tied, arms, waist, legs—a strange sensation of utter helplessness. Then the doctor came in. As he began to work, he found the womb dilating so easily that he continued the operation in spite of the terrific pain. And so in six minutes of torture, I had done what is usually done with ether! But it was over. I couldn't believe it. Hugh was so full of anguish, and Gonzalo.

The only wonderful moment in all this was when I was lying on a little cot in the doctor's office and another woman came in. The nurse pulled the curtain so that I could not see her. She was made to undress and lie down, to relax. The nurse left us.

Soon I heard a whisper to me: "How was it?" I reassured her—told her how I had been able to bear it without ether, so it would be nothing with ether.

She said: "How long were you pregnant?"

"Three months."

"I only two—but I'm scared. My husband is away. He doesn't know. He must never know."

I couldn't explain to her that my husband knew, but that my lover had to be deceived and made to believe I had no relations with Hugh. Lying there whispering about the pain, I had never felt such a strong kinship with woman—woman—this one I could not see, or identify, the one who was also lying on a cot, filled with primitive fear and an obscure sense of murder, or guilt, and of an unfair struggle against nature—an unequal struggle with all the man-made laws against us, endangering our lives, exposing us to inexperienced maneuvers, to being economically cheated and morally condemned—woman is truly the victim now, beyond the help of her courage and aliveness. How much there is to be said against the ban on abortion. What a tragedy this incident becomes for the woman. At this moment she is hunted down, really. The doctor is ashamed, deep down, but falsely so. Society condemns him. Everything goes on in an atmosphere of crime and trickery. And the poor woman who was whispering to me, afterwards, I heard her say to the doctor: "Oh, doctor, I'm so grateful to you, so grateful!" That woman moved me so much. I wanted to know her. I wanted to pull the curtain and see her. But I realized she was all women—the humility, the thoughtfulness, the fear and the childlike moment of utter defenselessness. A pregnant woman is already a being in anguish. Each pregnancy is an obscure conflict. The break is not simple. You are tearing away a fragment of flesh and blood. Added to this deeper conflict is the anguish, the quest for the doctor, the fight against exploitation, the atmosphere of underworld bootlegging, a racket. The abortion is made a humiliation and a crime. Why should it be? Motherhood is a vocation like any other. It should be freely chosen, not imposed upon woman.

And today I am home, lying down most of the time.

Gonzalo came to make lunch.

AUGUST 26, 1940

Days of convalescence. Gonzalo's behavior has restored my faith and calmed my doubts. Finally today, as we were resting side by side, I felt his desire stirring, and he placed my hand over it and let me caress him. I was warmed by his desire. I am in love with Gonzalo still. I know it now.

In utter despair at American emptiness and homeliness, we began to dream Paris all over again. Gonzalo told me one story after another, and I urged him to write them down. He recreated the atmosphere for me. Listening to him and remembering, I began to write, starting with the pages on the rue Dolent, a fantastic story about Hans Reichel. With Gonzalo, I could abstract myself from the American scene. It was a collaboration. After working, I often telephone him and say: "Look what you have done! It is your book." His stories are terrifying. I started to write flowingly last week, two days after the abortion. Yesterday I wrote the pages on the café. I am working to weld it all together… the barge story, the rag pickers.

A corrupt man is like a woman. Corruption is a kind of passivity, a pregnable, open, yielding element which attracts one. One feels like plunging into this corrupt, lax, open being, through which all currents flow, raping it, mastering it. During Gonzalo's storytelling I suffer sometimes to see the expression of yieldingness, of abandon, which took him everywhere…the abandon… That must be the way a man feels about woman, the desire to insert the hard erect knife of his will and desire into this soft, open flesh.

Poor John. I think of him now as the brightest son I ever had, but I love the dark one best of all, the one who has shown ugliness, envy, fear, weakness, criminal negligence, corruption. Corruption is revealed by a choice of ambiance, and Gonzalo's choice was of the darkest, most diseased and corrupt of all, monstrous.

AUGUST 27, 1940

Strange days of loneliness, barrenness and inner burning. I live absolutely in my past and partly in Gonzalo's. We meet like conspirators, while Hugh is fishing, and we talk, talk, talk. Then I work. Physically I am at a very low ebb, but spiritually I carry a demon of restlessness, hunger, imaginings. I want a rich, multiple, dazzling life. I want abundance, recklessness, sumptuousness and the heights of passion, up to the hilt.

I want to be burned, to be burned. And now I want to live out everything within the very layers at which I am creating. I have set the climate and I must find it—but where?

SEPTEMBER 1, 1940

I must beware of my imagination. At the moment when love becomes pale, I begin to suffer from doubts. Gonzalo, on the contrary, has nestled in this love and does not expect catastrophe now. He expected it during the passion. I expect it now. Last night I told Hugh I was leaving for Virginia at midnight, and I arranged to have dinner with Gonzalo in New York. I told him I could leave, or not leave, whatever he wanted. He didn't say anything, so I finally began to tell him how, because of his passivity, I had suffered and was detaching myself from him. He was immensely surprised, and he laughed good-naturedly, absolutely innocently. He said all I seemed to be missing was his tyranny, and that he had changed deeply, felt more balanced, less crazy than before, that he now believed in me. I said I loved our rhythm before, when he took the active role, that now I was lost. Gonzalo explained that all men were stupid when it was a question of ruse, and that he had grown to depend on my ruses for our meetings. He showed great tenderness, but I did see the change and felt that this Gonzalo I don't like, that I preferred the crazy one who made scenes. This Gonzalo is old, fat and peaceful. But I have become aware of the demon in me that is the cause of my suffering, the demon of doubt. It may cause me to destroy the very love I want, as I destroyed my life with Henry, because fundamentally, Henry having made his love of June the theme of his work, I never really believed in his love. And Gonzalo, being enslaved by Helba's helplessness, her deafness, I feel equally that in the end, when the passion is over, I may lose him. I have a feeling I should make Gonzalo jealous as I made Henry jealous by running away to New York. But that only reassures me for a little while, and then Henry's egotism destroys my faith again. They clutch and cling and howl when I leave them, but how badly they love.

It is my fault. I love with so much devotion that I make everybody selfish… I know there is something very wrong with me. I need proof of love constantly, and that is wrong and cruel for the others.

All day Sunday I tortured myself needlessly with doubt. Monday morning I didn't telephone Gonzalo. Then he telephoned me to say that because of the weather he thought I should not leave for Virginia. He was afraid for me. Such a small thing can make me happy for a day, but then an equally small act of thoughtlessness can plunge me into despair.

To rise beyond this emotional weakness, I worked well last week. Then Henry came and read what I had done, and his criticism was negative. He had nothing to say about the fragments themselves; all he could see was that they were not woven together. He said it was bad, monotonous and static. This stopped my writing completely. I showed it to Gonzalo, and he responded. But why should I depend on such responses? Why must I depend on others for everything, never on myself? I am back to where I was years ago, before analysis, to a devouring doubt, continuous hyper-sensitivity and fears. What can I do now? Before I was helped by Allendy and then by Rank. Now I have to heal myself alone. At least I realize it is all in my imagination. But the suffering is there, continuous, haunting, like an infection. No relief. A few hours of peace, and then the gnawing begins again.

Anaïs, stop devouring and fearing. You are a tortured being, you have been all your life. Come out of this darkness and live passionately again, forget yourself. Create. You isolate yourself with your love, and you suspect every nuance and every word and every gesture. It is bad. You must be courageous and ruthless and reckless. If you always need a new love because you only believe in the new, you will lose Gonzalo, whom you still love.

September 5, 1940

Hampton Manor has changed because of the petty antagonisms that have grown between Mrs. Salvador Dalí and Henry and John. She used Henry (she doesn't know English), and she has appropriated the library where we used to talk for a salon for Dalí's work. Meals were full of hostility and mockery. The wife wants the entire place run like Dalí's kingdom, and we are to be his subjects. John and Flo feel humiliated by the conversations entirely in French, and John is critical of Dalí's persistent work and gayety (he whistles and sings all day). I would not have felt all this. I am less rebellious at being asked to help, or to being used. John hates to serve. Henry hates Mrs. Dalí's coddling of Dalí. They hated everything and made crazy statements like: "Dalí only eats lamb," as if this were in itself a crime. Henry resorted to his maniacal contradictions. I liked to hear Dalí talk, but it was impossible. John was jealous when I spoke Spanish, and Mrs. Dalí was on guard against me. Dalí liked me, lost his shyness and retiringness when I came, showed me his work.

But Hampton Manor, the enchanted, has vanished. John's money is finished and he has to go home. He growls at everything. The press plan was abandoned because Caresse didn't have the money for it. John would have to have done all the work, but this I didn't want, because I don't want to leave Gonzalo in New York, and at Hampton Manor I couldn't be with John.

But again, when John and I were in the same room, garden, or road, we felt each other's presence like wild magnets. We only had one walk together, the last day, and he told me how he suffered from my absence and the fear that I should die, how he only came to life when I arrived, how he wanted me. What power draws us together and makes me forget Gonzalo. Desire. Desire. Again our eyes fixed on each other each time Henry and Flo are not looking, and again we hypnotize each other completely, falling into the well of the other's being, compelled, blind, drunk. His blue eyes are firm, fixed like a virile possession, and he takes me. At other times he is dissolved with desire, his voice grows husky and warm, and I feel bathed in warmth and passion.

We planned to meet again in New York, to spend nights together.

In the evening, when Flo was in her room and Henry was in the bathroom, I ran downstairs lightly because I heard John locking the doors. He heard me coming. We stood for an instant in the darkness of the porch, crackling and burning like wild torches—he all gold and blue, I all red and black—hearts snapping with the tension, whispering words of love. He then became the lover, feverish with desire, with the voice and laughter of the lover, the man one wants to be locked in a room with.

I am grateful to have a lover I want to be locked with in a room—a lover on fire.

I sit in the train and I still feel him, where one should feel a lover. He says I am his only joy. I say he is my only joy. He says I am the only one who has his rhythm. I say, "You have mine."

On his birthday, we found a pack of cards fallen around the car. I picked up the ones with their faces turned upward. I do not know their meaning, but the negress said it was all lucky.

Sad days, the last of Hampton Manor. We see the long, long roads before us. From afar they look wet, but they are absolutely dry—a mirage. Many tree branches lie wrapped in cocoons of spider webs, dead leaves and dead insects lying tangled in the gown of white fog ribbons, the maternal fluid weaving its cocoon pockets in the forest, silvery envelopes, snowy white wigs of crystallized saliva. The earth is sienna colored. The negro is singing on his horse. There is a pool crowded with headless trees. Dalí is painting a guitar that is loose and slack like a body without nerves and a woman's body taut like a guitar while the hand plays on her sex. Dalí is painting a horse whose insides contain a woman whose child is kissing his horse teeth while the child's enormous horse-like sex hangs limp. Henry is writing about Greece. John is writing about corruption and rebelling: "Why do we take up your death theme? We haven't died." Why indeed, the gold sun youth of America wallowing in our European death chant.

"Well, can you visualize tomorrow?" I asked. "You are tomorrow."

"I can't—it's true."

So they chant death with us.

SEPTEMBER 7, 1940

Tonight I suddenly realized the demon in me, the one shattering my life and endangering my love for Gonzalo, the demon of intensity which pushes me to feverishly seek it wherever it lies. As soon as I left John, I fell again into a more natural world and was sad, as when you want to play the drum because you are taut and full of rhythm, but the drum skins tear.

I am in an absolutely mad state, abnormally sensitive, magnifying everything, emotional, full of anguish and nervousness. If I am eating in a restaurant and the music begins, I become dissolved and lacerated. If I see an accident in the street, I am obsessed all day, jerking with pain for the others. I feel like June—unbalanced, lost.

At the same time I have a ferocious lucidity which makes me act on Hugh's blindness and ghostliness, and I give him a superb talk, such as Rank used to give me on unreality—the blind man's dog I am! At the same time, I am aware that my *gift* is my *curse*—for as I see into others' lives abnormally with such a keen insight, it sometimes gives me an inhuman role to play—the wise man's role, so hateful, so difficult. At times some depend on my guidance, but at other times they hate it and rebel against it, as Henry did. And yet at other times, they ignore it, and then, because my feelings are involved, I suffer more from their blindness than they do. Hugh said the worst is that in anger I utter truths which hurt. He said nobody could hurt more than I, because I am accurate. I hate my own lucidity—I suffer as a god must suffer when he looks down and witnesses a murder committed in a moment of blindness. Sometimes I feel so desperate I cry out that I will kill myself and put an end to this seeing. Oh, the torture of eyes forever open! Close my eyes, oh god, that I may rest from suffering. I can no longer bear my awareness. How clearly I see! I see Hugh walking off like a ghost when I leave him, and this image of gauntness and isolation saddens my trip to Hampton Manor. I dwell on this and discover the significance of his absent-mindedness, his *absence*.

When I returned, as we were driving home, I told him all I know and how I have struggled to reach the point of living fully in the present, with all my faculties in the present moment. I poured out all that I have attained myself with such difficulties—the *presence*, in contrast to the absence of unreality.

Hugh was vitalized, touched. His gloom and greyness passed into me after I talked, because all my strength is used in these transmissions of life. I am weary of burdens— burdens.

I am afraid to ask myself what John will be for me—he will be my joy for how long? John is absolutely poor, but unwilling to submit to the discipline of a job because he wants the life of the artist. He is imprisoned by his wife's complete dependence and clutching love. She has no life of her own, no creativity, no action. She lives vicariously through him, a shadow—his shadow, his echo.

I am cornered. John is not the man. When will *he* come? Will *he* have the savour of Gonzalo, but with strength...or will I have to provide all the strength again, until I die? I await *him*. It was in this exact mood that I awaited Gonzalo a few months before he came along. I knew then he would be a big man, not from France—I almost felt him. I saw his eyes in Fez. And Jean de la Lune (Cateret) had said, "Watch out for 1940." But it cannot be John.

I think I am a little mad with feeling, with awareness, with obstacles. Create, Anaïs. Every word you wrote was always the golden key which opened the doors of your prison. The Lawrence book brought you Henry. The *House of Incest* Gonzalo. The *Winter of Artifice* John. It is your female chant for man, for the lover. Write. It is your ornament, your grace, your seduction, your chant for courting.

Create, Anaïs. He will come.

NANANKEPICHU II

We saved the dream

I spent all afternoon walking the streets of the Village looking for a place for Gonzalo and me, for a dream, a room that would not be just a room, a studio that would not be just a studio, a house that would not be just a house. I was standing at the corner of my hotel, worn out and discouraged, about to go back in, to surrender. At that moment I felt so vividly the kind of place I dreamed of that I continued to walk, as if I were walking towards it. I walked to an agent, and he took me to three places. The third place was the Place—an old red brick house in front of the Provincetown Playhouse. Top floor—a studio which is an echo of *Nanankepichu*—part of it low-ceilinged, uneven, with small square windows, the other half skylight, high and wonderful for drawing and writing. Old but clean, floor painted black, a fireplace—an air of not being in New York. A big bed and a big desk. Beautiful. My heart was pounding. I took it immediately. The next morning, while waiting for Gonzalo, I took over the bed cover from Paris, the same pair of sheets we had in rue Cassini, the seashell lamp. I bought two bottles of Chianti, two big candles, a bottle opener—and there it was!

When Gonzalo came, he was thunderstruck. He said: "It's the barge!" He was enchanted. The only beautiful place in New York, with charm and strangeness and uniqueness! He threw wine on the floor for luck.

Finding the place made me happy. It seems to me we can find again the dream which New York has destroyed. I was dancing with joy. Gonzalo said: "*Me voy muy contento.*"

I feel more peaceful. I thought I was going mad—such gnawing anguish, fears of every kind assailing me, uncertainty, scruples, guilt, chaos, my nerves taut to a painful intensity, a sense of catastrophe, of malignant demons around me. I was impatient with Hugh's absence, impatient with Gonzalo's laziness, angry at everything.

Dorothy Norman is printing my "The Woman in the Myth." Rae Beamish is printing *Winter of Artifice* in December. I signed a real contract.

SEPTEMBER 15, 1940

Suddenly I am whole again like a diamond. I wake up after dreaming all night of a ballet. I make breakfast for Hugh. I go out to meet Robert Duncan. There is the dream place, under the roof. I brought pillows and blankets, I burned the Japanese perfume, I lit the candles. I waited. Of course, Helba had a "crisis," so Gonzalo came late and could not stay, but I am beyond suffering at this—I expect it. Gonzalo's attitude touched me, his delight and love of the place, his lying down at my side, his tremor at my hand passing over his stomach. My hand slid downward when I felt the response. And he let me caress him—I cannot be possessed yet. And today I began to write pages on the shoemaker with a clubfoot from notes made in the diary long ago. I am flowing again—I have lost my fears, my anguishes. I have multiple desires, curiosities, interests. I can be everywhere.

I am carrying you to *Nanankepichu II*. True that it is an echo, true that passion cannot last forever. True. But I have the gift for making it last longer than most, by magic. It can only be done by supernatural means.

SEPTEMBER 16, 1940

Next day, the first act of witchcraft: the place! We found the low bed again, the isolation and the secrecy—Gonzalo loves the secrecy. He asks me: "You haven't told anybody, even Eduardo?" He wants to draw there—the light is beautiful for drawing. Today he rearranged the furniture, my desk and his table. We made coffee there. The dream is impossible in an American roadside cabin or hotel room.

The second act of witchcraft: creation, which renews the love itself. After I wrote the clubfoot story, I took it to the place and Gonzalo read it. When I was leaving, he said, "Leave the manuscript here," and placed it himself in the drawer of the desk.

It is a place where I *can*. It is out of the world.

SEPTEMBER 20, 1940

Beautiful days. A rich autumn, warm, and the sun. Gonzalo brought his drawing board and pencils to the place. He likes to work there. After a moment of frenzied caresses on the low bed, we got up. He sat at his table, his drawing board on his knees, and sketched while I sat at my desk and worked on the Artaud pages. A glowing, fervent night of many caresses, and then this absorption in work, this out of the world dream. I am happy. This dream gives me life. Gonzalo is eager to go there in the afternoon, and then again on the evenings when I am not with Hugh or Henry.

A tender night with Henry. I cannot be taken completely, but he couldn't wait. I am amazed Henry still desires me. I no longer desire him, except when I get into an erotic mood and desire everybody.

My doubts of Gonzalo's love were purely imaginary. I do not accept the pauses made by nature, the ill health, phases of indifference (such as I have myself), or the deadly effect of ugly surroundings and uprootings. Neurosis and fear do destroy and paralyze, but everything is flowing again, everything is illuminated. I began to think about Artaud and was forced to sit down on a Washington Square bench and write. I feel highly inflammable. I missed John when I went to see Henry at Hampton Manor, missed the breathlessness I felt going up his stairs to find him eagerly expecting me. I missed his violence.

Smooth activity. I went to call for the diary at Duell, Sloan and Pearce. Pearce said it was marvelous, but that it should never be published except in a limited edition. I carried the 500 pages to Slocum, Henry's agent, and liked him immediately. I went home and had lunch alone. I look for Artaud material in the diary. At four, I see Gonzalo at the place. We lie in bed smoking, talking, and then we work. He makes the coffee because my left hand is bandaged—I burned myself badly while cooking.

Reconciliation with Helba of whom my jealous imagination makes a monster—in reality she is merely very stupidly helpless, but she has a disarming humility, and she knows how to tease and beg me into mellowness again: "What's the matter, Conejito? You've got pepper on your rabbit tail again. And I, who love you so much, I get mad at you sometimes too, especially because Gonzalo is ashamed of me. He won't take me out. He says I'm too fat. And that's because he's so used to your slenderness and your beauty. But as soon as I see your funny rabbit nose that comes straight down, not at all like other people's noses, I feel such love for you. And I've been very sad. You never come to see me. I ask myself what I have done. And I feel so badly when you go on taking care of me, but without love…" I said: "You know I do love you, or I would not have got the hearing machine for you."

"But maybe you did that for Gonzalo," Helba said cannily. All this reawakens my pity, so I begin acting again. What is lovable in Helba is her lack of resentment and how she dominates her jealousy. She even tells me quite honestly how Gonzalo irritates her by worrying about me. "He was nearly crazy in New Rochelle—he didn't tell me what happened to you, just that you were sick. He didn't sleep all night and didn't eat. How he loves you, Anaïs—I could get mad at you for worrying him so, but I don't. I know Gonzalo's character better than you do because you're not dependent on him. I blame him, not you. I think he does everything to make us hate each other. He makes me out more helpless than I am—it is his excuse for all he does not do. He uses me as a pretext for all his failures."

Their apartment has a new order and cleanliness undreamed of a few years ago. Helba has learned to dress herself, to fix her hair. I remember my first visit to her.

Helba lying in a cot, death on her face. Rags. Poverty. No lights. Cooking on coal in the fireplace. Torn shawls. Unkempt hair, fever and hunger and weakness, Gonzalo half blind from alcohol.

SEPTEMBER 22, 1940

Evening with Yves Tanguy and Kay de San Faustino—planning to bring over Breton, Pierre Mabille, Benjamin Péret, Éluard. I told Hugh to bring his notebook of drawings so they would understand a Hugh they do not know. His drawings were admired. Yves thought they looked exactly like those he had made himself when he had begun to paint.

SEPTEMBER 24, 1940

We have moved to 215 West 13th, the top floor of an old simple house, a big skylight studio shaped like a peaked roof. A small, small kitchen and bath. Not American. I bought two large pine wood tables with two benches, peasant shaped, two beds covered with Mexican serapes, and lamps—that was all. Hugh has his drawings, brushes, etc., on one table and I have my work on the other. The other tenants left us a wall-to-wall carpet in dark brown. Next to my couch is the bookcase and on top of it I have the sea plants, shells and lamps.

Next to my bed is a crazy little Rococo table I bought for $5 in an antique shop in Mamaroneck with painted scenes of Spanish history, a wrought iron top, two lanterns affixed to the sides. When Gonzalo saw it, he said it was a table that used to be carried like a tray (it has a handle in the center) on feast days to the entrances of the church, to sell refreshments. It was covered with a glass holder and little iron plates and two bottles for syrups. A little feast table! It stands in this ascetic, simple place like my eternal note from Byzance, always a jewel in the center of simplicity. In two days I made the place livable, complete, but I am worn out. Gonzalo helped me with the nailing, setting up tables, etc. Hugh complains that even when I say, "It is going to be simple," it still looks beautiful.

Hugh came and found his table all set for work. He was happy. The first night we slept here there was a violent thunderstorm, and in my sleep I felt it was a bad omen. I know the war is coming here. What is happening in the world is so monstrous that I turn away. I made a home again, knowing it will be destroyed. I bought a safe for the remaining diaries. Deep down I feel the tragedy so I keep busy, so busy that I am worn out.

Last night with Gonzalo in our place, where I posed for him. The night before I slept with Henry, who clings to me. He is preparing to leave for a tour of America.

Tonight at home.

OCTOBER 2, 1940

We saved the dream, Gonzalo and I. In that marvelous isolation we have defeated New York, the ugliness. We left the world behind again, and all the threads are rewoven, sensuality bursts out again, there are wild moments of utter abandon. Gonzalo kissing my sex, hurting me with the violent caresses with eager fingers, keeping his fingers inside of me, his mouth to the sex, losing his head, trembling, shaking, moaning and pushing his sex into my mouth while I caress him with my two hands.

Then he makes drawings of me, and we have the talks we've always had, the fantasies. Gonzalo objects to the publicity written for *The Winter of Artifice*, to the descriptions of my life, saying he will write something nearer to the truth: "She was born in Spain, and at six months of age she departed from reality and has remained out of it ever since..."

We laugh.

Such happiness.

The studio home is in order so that I can copy diary 49 in peace all morning. Then Gonzalo telephones. Now I take the bus to 54th Street and have dinner and a night with Henry.

Hugh is happy. He comes home, takes off his banker's clothes and gets into slacks and a sweater. I give him his dinner. Then he goes to sketching classes for two hours. The studio helps him to dream outside of the world's nightmare.

OCTOBER 17, 1940

Young Dr. Jacobson has taken care of me gratuitously because we had sent him a Vice President who arranged his transfer to America. Jacobson cared for me with a special paternal tenderness and patience (for forty-four visits he fought my stubborn anemia). I showed him affection and friendliness. He is young, attractive, vigorous. He would lift me from the scale with strong arms. Slowly a flirtation began for both of us. He told me about his affair with Nina, whom I had seen in the waiting room, a curious girl—tall, slender, with a masculine walk, a fine head, a medieval page, and long, slender hands. An artist, I thought, and I had divined her link with Max. He introduced us once, and I sensed her timidity and evasiveness. He had kept his hand on the back of my neck, familiarly. Perhaps she was jealous. She said: "*Madame est bien jolie.*" He mentioned going to the beach, the three of us. I did not understand at first, so he clarified: would I go over with him and Nina...he loved to have two women together. The usual fear of hurting people's feelings and a certain piquant attraction for an adventure made me accept. Could I enjoy an adventure now?

I was nervous, intimidated. Max said to come at seven. He would treat my burnt hand and then we would call for Nina and have dinner together. I told him I felt shy, not of him, but of Nina. He said she felt shy too. She telephoned twice with delays, and I felt her resistance.

Max gave me a few kisses and caresses, which were pleasant. The three of us went to dinner at a funny little Austrian bistro, where the patron and the clients joined in singing Austrian songs. Nina is a German Jew like Max. I liked her, with her boy-like simplicity, her youth and her shyness, but she didn't like me. She is in love with Max, and I was in a strange situation. Max was forcing everything to please himself. Nina, so slender, long like a boy, straight dark hair, sensitive. On the bed, with Max's sensuality aroused, he lay against my back and was desirous, his warmth passing into me, but Nina was rigid, talking. I touched her gently, and I said, "Would you like me to go? You said you were tired." I didn't want to force her.

Max stretched out his arm and rolled up the sleeve of his shirt. She was caressing the inside of his arm, saying how soft it was. This reminded me of Gonzalo, so I was glad because Nina's resistance gave me the thought that I could escape. But Max was firm and tyrannical. He forced her hand on my breast; he then forced my hand, but I cannot caress someone who hates it. Finally Nina said: "I'll go into the other room. You do what you want." She went to the bathroom and started to take a shower. I wanted to leave, but our resistance inflamed Max. I was half fascinated by the new and strange situation of hurting a woman when I never wanted to, by the tyranny of Max's simple, direct desire. Then he put me to bed, undressed me, and began caressing me. After a moment Nina opened the door, showing no interest. Max asked her to come, but she said, "You seem to be able to do very well without me." Max made her come. She was wearing a nightgown. I was naked. She said: "I'll get into bed and go to sleep," and at this I felt perhaps she did want it with a part of herself, or she would have rebelled. Or did she love him so much that it was all for him, to satisfy his caprice? Or was she as masculine as she appeared? Her caresses to placate him were so young, so asexual. She turned out the light and lay there, legs tightly closed. They placed me between them, but I asked him to lie next to her. I said: "Caress her." At first she continued to be rigid, and then Max caressed me. I tried awkwardly and gently to caress her, and to my great surprise, her legs slowly relaxed and the honey began to flow. She was such a child—a tiny sex, almost no breasts. I never liked kissing a woman's sex, but I felt I had to. Meanwhile Max was taking me from behind. After a while he kissed her sex, and she responded. Then timidly, awkwardly, she began to caress me. Naturally I could not respond completely because I was not stirred. I felt estranged.

In the darkness she said something in German to him, and a quarrel began. He became angry, and his desire died. I asked if I could leave. The light was turned on. I dressed, glad to escape. Max drove me home. I said: "She loves you and responds to you, and you should be glad of that. I'm not the woman for her—I'm not aggressive enough." He said: "The only thing I have is my profession." He is simple and animal, blind to the entire complexity of Nina's feelings.

A few days later he telephoned me: "Nina sends her love. When are we going to have dinner together?" I said: "I'm not made for this triangle, nor is Nina. You can come and see me whenever you want to—alone—but let's not force something that isn't natural." Nina remains a mystery.

Gonzalo spends his afternoons in our place, drawing, or we spend the evening together and I pose for him. Last night I playfully turned myself into a prostitute, combed the hair over the forehead, exaggerated the shape of my mouth with rouge, and posed earthily. At times he will go there alone and draw until midnight.

OCTOBER 28, 1940

The dream of *Nanankepichu* is intact, and after five or six years, there have been great changes in Gonzalo. It was always I who created the place. This time I began the creation of our *Nanankepichu*, and Gonzalo—an amazing sight—took it upon himself to tear down an ugly partition which spoiled a corner of the studio. This he did with his feet and hands, not a hammer or saw. He leaped and pushed his foot through the boards, leaped again and again, like a savage. The fireplace was free and open. He brought ashtrays so as not to burn everything as he usually does. He tacked a red sackcloth over the big desk and table, which were ugly. He took his drawings of me and the photographs of the Seine and framed them. He draws four to six hours a day.

I realize at times how fascinated we are by each other, with what eagerness we abandon our friends, Helba, Hugh, to find a moment of the dream. Gonzalo talks to me as when he first met me, talks about the beauty of my nose like that of an Egyptian cat, or a tiger.

Henry has begun his odyssey tour of America. I felt his departure as a painful loss.

Fatigue is now reducing my life and its expansion. If I stay up with Gonzalo until two o'clock one night and then get up at eight to make Hugh's breakfast, I'm worn out all day.

The Gotham party, William Carlos Williams' vernissage, was crowded and lively. Many people came up to meet me and tell me what they thought of the "Birth" story, and I was fêted and admired by Williams himself. Robert Duncan, the exalted visionary, was monologuing on the *House of Incest*. I was so pleased to be liked, singled out, shining with vanity as a writer and woman. I do confess I love this, but instinctively I shun it because I am aware of how much I love compliments and admiration. By the next day I am once again hidden and finding ways to break the engagements I made in my moments of weakness.

John Slocum's eyes were riveted on me—he is attractive, but I am wary of the physical elation he causes because John is on the way here.

NOVEMBER 16, 1940

John has lost his power—I knew this as I heard his voice over the telephone, and when I saw him standing at the door of the hotel room. No more heart-beating and electric currents. I let him take me without responding. It was impersonal and distant. After taking me, he spread on the bed his new drawings and 200 pages of writing, talked about his rebirth, his faith, his strength. The mother of the artist had given birth again, but would I destroy this creation for my own sake because I could no longer act for impersonal reasons? Perhaps I had given John his life, and perhaps he could now breathe and create alone. I praised his work; we talked.

The next day I asked John to come to my place, and I told him: "I no longer feel the same way." He said, "Don't be afraid to break me—is it absolutely over?" The manner in which he awaited my answer, as if I *were* going to break him, prevented me from making the absolute statement. He was so gentle, so full of faith, that I left it in the shadows. The following day I went to his hotel. When I found the room in semi-darkness and everything set for possession, I again spoke to him, never saying the ultimate breaking word. Why cannot I operate lustily, courageously? I undermined John's faith, but as I did so, the pity I felt for all his hopes, for his imagined life with me in New York, for his new birth, made me offer my mouth and body in attenuation of the truth, and again I left him between awareness and delusion. Another evening, at my place, which provided me a defense, I pled the moonstorm, but I was tender. But yesterday I would not see him at all. So is woman accused of caprice and cruelty! I can no longer be the mother who gives all. I have no longer the strength to act what I do not feel.

I rushed back to *Nanankepichu*, into my whole love for Gonzalo. He made a violent scene of disguised jealousy, attacking all my friends on the ground that they were Trotskyites. I felt again his jealousy and clutching, but the whole scene falls apart at the touch of our bodies, even when his cheek touches mine. Everything vanishes and is forgotten when Gonzalo falls asleep like a child, with his head on my breast and his hand between my legs. I am here again, Gonzalo, most beloved of all. I want to lock myself up with you and my work. I cannot feel or see the rest of the world, whose nightmare would kill me if I were to become aware of it. The other figures are unreal. Why do they move about, so close to me? Eduardo is in a hotel room taking Robert Duncan like a woman. Kenneth Patchen does not sleep, grappling as all Americans grapple, with too much matter and immediacy and impotent to touch the core of meaning, lost and blind. Virginia Admiral sits on a soapbox, drawing and typewriting in the poorest room of all.

NOVEMBER 19, 1940

A few hours before going to see John I entered the subway at rush hour, which I rarely do, and was pushed by the waves of people, jammed against them, and stood there. Suddenly I remembered pages Henry had written about his adventures in the subway, his pressing against women, their submission, how they stood against each other, and how in a state of excitement he followed one of them out and she eluded him after letting herself be touched. As I remembered this I felt a hand barely touching my dress, as if by accident. My coat was open, my dress very light and this hand was brushing lightly just at the place of the sex. I did not move away. The man beside me was so tall that I could not see his face, but I did not want to know who it was. The hand caressed the dress, then very lightly it increased its pressure, feeling for the sex. I made a slight movement to raise the sex towards the fingers. The fingers became firmer, following the shape of the sex, deftly, lightly. I felt great pleasure. A lurch of the subway pushed us together—I pressed against his hand, and he made a bolder gesture. Now I was frenzied. I felt the orgasm approaching; the fingers seemed to know it and continued the caresses. The orgasm shook my whole body. The subway stopped, and the tight river of people pushed out. The man disappeared.

Again in John's room, set against possession, saying the words: "I have changed," but not saying: "I don't love you." I wrap every phrase I use in tenderness. Deep down, I feel nothing except irritation at his childish hatred of the world, his criticalness, his blind and blundering talk, his echoes of Henry, his drinking of whiskey before he makes love. I do not find in him the embracing acceptance which drinks and eats of the world in order to create, but rather a child's petulant affirmation of himself, either out of proportion to his value, or a complete loss of confidence. All that may interest the mother in me, but I am tired of being the mother. Where will I find a man? Break, break, break. My whole being calls for an act of violence, but I still use velvet gloves. My whole being rejects John. I should have rejected him that day when I first responded sexually and then rebelled at his gesture of tenderness because I did not love him. Desire is not enough. Last night when I saw him vulnerable, tender, and I was using all the words one can say in place of "I don't love you," again I experienced warmth, a purely physical warmth, and again I let him take me, untouched, like Lilith in *The Winter of Artifice*. He said, "You cannot be possessed," and I did not say, "Not by you," but I smiled and refused to feel the orgasm which a few hours before I felt at the hands of a stranger. I lay on John's bed and felt nothing. He did not know this; he only thought I was being capricious. How strangely a man must feel after he has taken a woman he does not love and finds that he hates the nape of her neck, her hair, her hands, or worse, any gesture of familiarity on her part. From the beginning I withdrew from every gesture John made that was not of pure desire, but of love. Now I have a feeling of hatred, of rejection, perhaps as a man must have towards a whore sometimes. I want to reject him. I can only hear the foolish words he says, seeking a form to give my hatred.

Mirages. The mother is dying.

What am I now?

If John had come for a week only, I might have acted for the sake of an illusion. One evening Hugo had just given me the five dollars for the next day's food when John came to the studio and asked directly for money. I said, "This is all I have." He took it and went down to buy a quart of whiskey. I was angered by his childishness and irresponsibility. "Anaïs, find us a studio. Anaïs, I need a painting teacher. Anaïs, take us to hear some jazz. Anaïs, find us a backer for our magazine. Anaïs, help me to write, help me to become an artist."

Last night in the street, wanting an absolute break, I told him: "You are forcing me to tell you the truth—I have loved someone for four years, and I still do."

At last it was done. I was shattered by his face grown pale, by his hurt pride making him suddenly rigid, by all the warmth I had thrown away. I felt not like a woman, but like a murderer. In order not to torment him, I had killed him and his newborn confidence as man, as artist, all at once, and for the first time in my life with a clear-cut knife thrust. Never before. Cutting the umbilical cord clean. Then all night I heard the cries of a woman who was ill and felt they were John's cries. My first crime, on young John. But I am being sentimental. John—how deep is his being, how deep are the repercussions of pain? Pain is creative too. Mother, give me sex, give me food, protect, feed, encourage me, give me drink. And the mother, weary, weary, weary, struck out, and threw out, and refused to nourish. John's was the love of a child, not of a man. I have lived this out to its fullest and bitterest, but I am finished with that. The mother has died, was killed, in fact, by cruel, selfish children. No one can revive her.

NOVEMBER 24, 1940

My child Henry returns from his wanderings. We talk about America. I said, "Were you looking for something to love? There is nothing to love here, it is a monster, a huge prosaic monster, buying all the creative wealth of Europe at bargain prices, buying it as they buy paintings, giving jobs to the refugees, yes, but only jobs, only money, no respect or evaluation or devotion, devouring with huge, empty jaws. It is nothing, a void, a colossal robot, a commercial empire, made for caricature, all ugly because it is all materialistic. Every artist born here was killed. You escaped and found yourself, and now you have the strength to grapple with it; it cannot swallow you into its rivers of cement. Look at America for what it is: concrete, iron, cement, lead, bricks, machines, and a mass of blind, anonymous robots. It is a huge monster, but made of papier mâché with marble eyes."

NOVEMBER 26, 1940

The truth is that when I lose Henry, I lose all the joy in my life. I can go to him in my darkest moods and at the very sight of him I find joy. Gonzalo is my dark child, emotional and tragic. Henry is philosophical and healthy, good-humored and joyous. I realize that I miss him, that without him I close up again as I was before I met him. I withdraw and my warmth dies out. With what pleasure I received him, yet I couldn't respond sensually.

Immediately there is expansion, playfulness, stimulation. Without him a whole range of my life and self dies. He is truly the Sun, my sun. Gonzalo is the Moon, my own tormented moon, driven by fears and emotion and madness. Henry is full of passion for me, full of desire and tenderness. Again a wealth of talk, ideas, and collaboration blooms. Gonzalo's world is small and personal, like a woman's, a child's world.

I came home from dinner with Henry to write these words, and in half an hour I go to Gonzalo.

THE COLLECTOR

I suggested we feed him the diary

NEW YORK, NOVEMBER 30, 1940

Again I opened up to Henry—he had to woo me again. We lay in bed in his hotel room, and talked about my idea which is bearing fruit—that while Henry could no longer write erotica for the old millionaire, I could give him copies of the diary in exchange for money for Henry's trip. Virginia copied diary 32, I revised it, changed the names, but while doing it I relived intensely my new love for Henry. Is it the power of the diary? My love seemed intact. I felt awe, as for a magical event.

And here I am with Henry, who is still fragile, lean and ageless, merely a little too tired for big nights, a little harassed by invitations and people's dependence on him. The first volume of his life with June is on his desk. I cannot read it; I have not the courage. It is Pandora's box. I close my eyes and yield to Henry's desire. He makes me lie over him. We again find the sensual frenzy, the same violence, followed by peace and tenderness.

Faced with Henry's dependence again, I suggested we show the diary to Barnette Ruder, the collector of rare books. This is a strange story—he is a Jew who looks like Rank. I have never seen him, only a snapshot of him. When Henry came to New York, Ruder liked him and often invited him to dinner, gave him presents and a little money now and then. At the same time, he talked about himself. His life was a failure, he was alone and could never win a woman for himself. He was always reading and hankering for life, and wanted Henry's guidance. Henry took him out, but Ruder didn't want to pay for his women. One day he told Henry that he had a client who was an elderly man, very rich, who had no sensual life at all, who was interested in Henry's writing, especially the sexual element, and thought it might have a miraculous effect on his own paralyzed life. He was willing to pay Henry one hundred dollars a month to write one hundred pages or so especially for him, mostly on sex. And then, almost like in Dante's *Inferno*, Henry was condemned to write about sex. At first it seemed easy, but it became unnatural and forced, and finally it was hard labor. He did this for a few months. Ruder said that he did not even read the pages, that he immediately sent them to the old millionaire down south. When Henry got the contract from Doubleday for the book on America (*The Air-Conditioned Nightmare*), he dropped the writing for Ruder. I suggested we feed him the diary as I have no money for Henry's traveling expenses. Ruder assented but will make no decision until he reads it. Monday I turn over volume 32, beginning with my love for Henry and June. Not without mischievous intentions, I pasted one of my most becoming Louveciennes photographs on the inside of the cover. Now I wait.

At the moment my love for Henry is strong, but I do not seek to hold him near because my love for Gonzalo is more violent, more emotional, and I live in constant, anguished fear of discovery.

John is going home. I do not feel him, hear him, or see him.

December 1, 1940

Henry for the first time is experiencing being used, being asked to help Patchen, being begged to solve others' problems. He is amazed by the spreading of needs—when you help one, five more appear. For the first time I found Henry depressed because he has awakened suddenly to the needs of others and is overwhelmed. I said, "I have lived with this knowledge since I was a child." "I couldn't bear it," Henry said.

On the very day Hugh gets paid, all he gives me for food, the house, and myself, is given away (half to Henry, half to Gonzalo—the half I give to Gonzalo Hugh knows about, but not the two hundred a month I give to Henry). The second day my pocket is empty, and then begin the antics which wear me out emotionally. I have to cheat, lie, intrigue, borrow, steal the rest of the time. Finally, a few days before the next allowance, I have to confess to Hugh: "I'm broke." Hugh scolds me. Sometimes he notices I pay with checks for things I said I would pay with cash given to me. I never can tell him when I get paid for my writing. Dorothy Norman's check for the Elena story went to Henry. It is as wearing as Henry's old way of living when he had nothing (getting himself invited to dinner, borrowing and stealing). It keeps me on edge. I never buy anything for myself. I have to expect Hugh's revolts and take his scolding as if I were extravagant. When he relents and forgives me, I feel even worse. I feel I am harassing him. That is why I was able to rebel against John.

DECEMBER 13, 1940

Revising diaries from 32 to 38, overwhelmed by the reading. Such consuming pages, such ecstasies, such fever, expansion, dilation, joy, drunkenness. The love for Henry looms immense and deep. At moments I feel that it is the first time that a woman has opened herself up. I had forgotten. Will it warm others as it warms me, consume them as it consumes me? Where am I now? In human life, not so drunk, and not so open. I have locked my door.

Henry's "Essay on Balzac" appears in *Twice a Year* with my story of Elena.

I am sad. The world is heavy without the dream.

DECEMBER 14, 1940

Telegram from Ruder: "Very much impressed (diary 32), have forwarded my client making clear that he is under obligation to pay for this installment. I think he will be interested in others provided the material is similar. What do I do now?"

Got one hundred dollars from Ruder when I was borrowing from Millicent, the maid, with four days until Hugo's payday. I got one hundred dollars when Gonzalo needs money for his teeth, Helba needs a mirror to work with, Hugo needs material for his engraving. There are no promises of more—Ruder does not know what his client will say. The client is interested only in the erotic passages. I was highly excited, happy, dancing around.

The joy I have in giving money away, oh, the joy, the joy. Why can I never have enough of my own money so that I should not feel guilty about giving, why?

DECEMBER 15, 1940

I have amorous dreams about Henry after rereading the old diaries. No sense of pain. Joy only.

Sometimes Gonzalo and I watch our neighbors undress across the way in another house. Gonzalo has seen them make love. I never have, but they like to walk around naked. She combs her hair, brushes her teeth. They pick up the black cat, turn out the light as they enter the bedroom. He puts his hand around her breasts. We talk about a rape we read of in the newspapers. A woman declared that a negro raped her three times, once when she was coming out of the shower, once on her bed, again in her automobile. It was untrue. She may have wanted him to.

JANUARY 4, 1941

Robert Duncan. He stands near and clear in me. At first I did not entirely hear him. He spoke through the poems. He is beautiful. He is at times in a trance, and he talks flowingly then, like a medium. I first loved Robert when we sat and talked alone, after I read his diary. We must never touch physically, but I am under his spell. After he leaves I want to run after him and say: "I love you," but this assertion is annihilated because the possession takes place mystically and more swiftly than words.

Robert as a woman—his great charm, the seduction of his eyelids, nose, ears, hands—I let Eduardo court him for me, make love to him. Others make the motions of love, but we do not. The passage between us is free, open, profound; we are two slender Egyptian bodies in a posture of dance, immobilized by the fulfillment of meeting the double, the TWIN. It is haunting. He talks about consuming hunger, his own "children," his renunciations, his quest for the father, his need of love; when he acts, I am at times frightened.

I think I am talking all this that I have written here, forgetting Hugo and his world, feeling uncensored, free. I am talking. I hear my words.

I feel pain again. I dreamed Hugo died. I have never before had such a clear, absolute feeling of death in dreams. I had killed him with anguish. I had to get into Hugo's bed to be reassured. It was all the guilt I have for sacrificing him to the care of my children. Then I went to see Henry. I was lying over his bed with my coat on. He lay over me like a child, with his head on my breast. I asked him if he would have preferred a human life with me at his side but with all the imprisonments, submissions to poverty and dependence on the world, or the freedom I gave him. He said he preferred the freedom. But how was I? he asked, was I all right? I didn't say. Henry took my waist between his hands, almost spanning it (I have lost weight again).

The old man accepted volume 33. I was again given one hundred dollars, which paid for the doctor for Helba and part of Henry's trip. The old man asked me for expansion of the sexual scenes. I let myself go and wrote descriptions of sexual scenes for volume 34. It was during the moonstorm, and I was powerfully excited by my own writing. I had an orgasm while I wrote, then I went to Henry and was passionate, then to Gonzalo, who was passionate, and I responded to both!

Henry left yesterday. I always feel his leaving; it hurts me. He seems frail, has lost the joy he found in Greece, is not happy. He is forcing himself to travel, to write.

JANUARY 7, 1941

Needing the money urgently for Henry, I set about satisfying the old man by writing four sexual scenes for volume 34. Now I'm inserting some in 40 and 41, the father volume.

Robert is being analyzed, liberated. He too puts all his faith in others. He gives faith, but has none in himself. For this, we depend on our love. He too feels great strength from me. We can talk about all things because we travel equally into the myth or the human. In the legend, women slept with their fathers or brothers. In the legend, one can make love in a mirage, one can be haunted and possessed. It is so strange. Robert in my world has taken away the loneliness.

Tragic love. Why must I suffer so deeply in my earthly loves and find joy only in the mystical ones? The joys with Jean Cateret, the ecstasies! The ecstasies with Robert! Ecstasies of penetration.

JANUARY 8, 1941

Robert fecundated me. I was able to turn to *The Winter of Artifice*, to see its falsities, to separate the fragments and make them individually perfect. I was able to take up the houseboat story, see where I had deviated from the dream and make it more complete. I extracted the Mouse incident and gave it its own legs to stand on. I worked and worked. I wrote sexual passages for the father volume (as his adventures). I cannot give the real volume so I gave *The Winter of Artifice* with expansions.

JANUARY 15, 1941

Gave Ruder volume 35, working on 36.

Eduardo came. I saw Robert change, become the woman, seductive, tantalizing. I saw them caressing, enjoying each other. There was such a current of love that I was taken in and saw, through Eduardo's presence, Robert's feminine body dilating, becoming passionate. I saw Robert in the atmosphere of love and desire. It was like being admitted into the secret chambers of sensual love and then seeing in Robert what would be otherwise concealed from me. It was a strange transition.

Eduardo said, "You two are exactly alike."

"But Robert is more truthful," I said.

"He loves less," said Eduardo. "He is a narcissist."

There was warmth in the air. The taboo between Robert and me which makes us act somnambulistically towards each other was annihilated for a moment. The love flowed through and between the three of us, shared, transmitted, contagious, the threads binding us. I could look with Eduardo's eyes at Robert's finely designed body—the narrow waist, the square shoulders, the stylized body he has, the corrupt, dilated expression. His face expresses dissolution; it reveals the flow, openness, and changefulness. It is so mobile that it seems like an act of exhibitionism. Everything is revealed to the naked eye.

JANUARY 19, 1941

Working on volume 36.

Robert did not give his true self to Eduardo. I saw Robert give one night of pretenses, then withdraw into creation, then detachment, then the "male fury," the rebellion, and finally cruelty. He could not conceal his feelings. I pitied Eduardo, but I knew that it was he who failed. We had scenes, talks, tears, shared torments, confusion, and I had to help and console Eduardo. Eduardo had said: "You love him more, you defend him." So I had to do for Eduardo what Robert could not do: prove to him my love was greater for him, that I judged Robert's acts as those of cruelty. (In the next room where Eduardo could hear, Robert caressed and took Marjorie [Duncan's friend with whom he was staying] without reaching the orgasm himself, and afterwards he excluded Eduardo from all our talks, as if he didn't exist.) I knew this changed nothing in my love for Robert, for Eduardo I love as one loves a sick person, an impotent person (Eduardo is not the artist), but Robert to me is potent and does not need my lies. I knew that I was acting *for* Robert, to do what he did not have the patience or compassion to do. So I was full of love for a broken and weeping Eduardo and helped him out of the confusion. I knew everything Robert felt—I could not truly judge the cruelty because it was an act of honesty. I knew he was acting more nakedly and naturally within his own drama of confusion between myth and human life. Deep down I love him for this too, because it is the sign of the creator. Secretly, while knowing it is inhuman, I admire it. He has more courage. He acts as I would want to, with a clean wound.

The incapacity for cruelty has been my weakness, and in this Robert is a male twin. He often says: "Am I going to live your life?" I am glad he is not going to live my life, but rather what I failed to live in my life. He stopped reading the diaries, not wanting to be engulfed. He teased me about living to make his diary more interesting for me, as interesting as mine. When he was making love to Marjorie, she said to him, "You have done this before." "No," he answered, "I am just very well read."

There is a sexual drama too. Eduardo takes him as a woman, and his knowledge of the danger of this is far more terrible than the woman's abandon—in this abandon woman finds her fulfillment, but the man who yields in this way is condemned to a passivity which destroys the active part of himself. It maims him and produces the caricature of the woman which the passive homosexual represents, because in him it is not a fulfillment of the deepest nature, but a destruction of one side of the hermaphroditic body for the sake of the other, a crippling. So what is left in this feeble half-woman—the defeated woman with only woman's weakness, still flaunting her seductions superficially as the whore does when she is no longer beautiful or potent— is doubt and uncertainty. This is what Robert could not become. He had begun to assert his male aspect with me, in my presence. I feel that what I transmit to him is the masculinity in me, the strength. I feel this current passing from me into him. Robert, I give you the masculine in my own soul, for I am fulfilled as a woman, complete. When Robert is in my presence, erect, firm, stylized, pure, there is a coalescence that takes place, and then he is the perfect hermaphrodite, balanced, effective.

When Eduardo came, Robert's body softened, his hips swayed, his face became that of the *cabotine*, receiving flowers with a coquettish batting of the edges of the eyelids, oblique glances, like an upturned corner of a coverlet, the edge of a petticoat, the stage bird's turn of the head, the little dance of alertness, the petulance of the mouth pursed for small kisses that do not shatter the being, the flutter of the birds, all adornment and change, a mockery of the evanescent and mysterious little darts of invitations and coy exposures, a burlesque of the small gestures of alarm and promises… He becomes the woman without the womb in which child and creation coil and erupt, the woman without the womb in which terrible mysteries take place—but the travesty of the whore's invitation is that it never leads to the magnificent marriage of blood.

While all this happened, I stood in the room staring at Robert, and perhaps through my eyes he saw his disguise, the eyes of my strength calling to him to stand erect and cease these gestures. I am filled with the tears of Eduardo: "I know I risked losing Robert when I took him as a woman..." The tearless, smileless life of Robert flows into his diary because we all talk to each other through diaries. Robert lays the diary open on my knees. He says: "At first with you and me it was the myth. But now I feel it is human."

I felt guilty when I remembered Robert had read in my diaries about my experience with Eduardo in Paris when we tried to make our love actual. I asked myself: did Robert act out this pattern of outgoing and then withdrawing, like the magic dictation I received from June, the June in me pushing me to abandon Henry and then return to him? Patterns, repetitions. "Your only weakness," said Henry to me many years ago, "is your incapacity to destroy."

It only came to me this year—I revolted against being a saint, a martyr. Today Patchen telephoned me: would I send him ten dollars. This request came three days after I had already given him ten dollars. Hugo and I eat for a week on ten dollars. And just a few minutes before I had telegraphed Henry all I had! The injustice riled me. I wrote Patchen a long, stormy letter. I told him we all knew the world has never taken care of the artist, and no one counted on it. He is like an angry beast demanding to be fed, and one knows as soon as one stops feeding him he will be full of hatred again. I do not forgive hatred.

Three people have aroused my hatred: Helba, John, and Patchen. Perhaps it was necessary that I should learn hatred too. I feared it so. I always strove so desperately for harmony. I could not bear hatred, but it is a force. In Patchen I rebel against what Helba and Gonzalo made me suffer, and I refuse to pass through this state again. I have no pity for Patchen, because his hatred is stronger than his love, and his self-love greater than all, and above all, his stupidity, his denseness... I now have the courage for anger, of being hated. Before I had to win all the loves, even the ones I did not feel, but I no longer can pretend.

JANUARY 25, 1941

My letter to Patchen was mad. My madness now is: why do people want to use me, my strength, my courage, my devotion? Why? Is it my weakness they immediately exploit?

The moonstorm makes me insane, but my insanity is nothing but revolt, the revolt I never expressed or lived out. I no longer want to be the victim of the criminals. I want to *be* the criminal, and this has come simultaneously with the birth of the artist. I want to be the artist now. I have begun to create. I am sad, humanly I am sad. The saint in me was killed by excess. I had to know hatred.

JANUARY 27, 1941

I can write about everything. Erotic scenes for the old man, the Conrad Moricand story, Jean's story, the barge, the diary. I am stirred, rich, fertile. I faced Ruder, who is selling the diaries, enchanted him. His rejection of the mystical in the diary pushes me into the human. It is good for me. I possess both powers, but I must strengthen the human. *I was stopped when they clashed.* When I get confused, when they invade each other like my loves, they must be kept separate. As soon as I try to make ONE love, ONE creation, I am broken by the impossible. LET NO ONE EVER DARE TO SAY I DID NOT TRY TO GIVE MYSELF TO ONE LOVE OR TO ONE CREATION—LET NO ONE DARE TO SAY I AM RESPONSIBLE FOR THE PAINFUL DIVISION.

But all of them must live, be heard and written. There lies the strength. I felt it in Paris when I wrote the journal on Fire.

JANUARY 30, 1941

Deliver me from obsessive love. Let me dance. People think I only crave lovers or worship. Nobody knows I am crying out tragically for my very existence. I only exist in the body of my lover, as a body within the body of my lover. My creation exists in its communication and openness. My mystical world, my force, my power, exist only in the twinship voyage. How can I go anywhere alone? I do not exist outside of love. I have never been to a museum alone, to a movie alone, for a walk alone. I have written not to be alone.

FEBRUARY 7, 1941

The Myth story begins to exist because Robert likes it. The Artaud story he sees before it is written so that now I can write it. Robert as a creator has great strength, as a revealer, a prophet. Robert is sitting there writing. For days we locked ourselves in, got drunk on writing.

As the male soul, he says, "Declare your treacheries." My female soul says, "Protect those you love." When I destroyed Patchen, he said, "You cannot judge anyone truly *because you are expecting someone.*" Patchen is not the one, but Robert is. I am content. I seek nothing else.

Mr. Ruder telephones: "More realism! More realism!"

FEBRUARY 9, 1941

In the afternoon, when we met in our corner, Gonzalo said: "There is a change in your voice." He made us get under the covers, took off my panties, took me with fire and delight—a long orgasm which he ends with grateful, tender kisses. I left him all warmed.

This morning I met Henry. His father died yesterday. He arrived two hours too late. Henry was, as I expected him to be, Chinese, mystical, full of tender acceptance. He met me with passion, hunger. I gave myself so wholly, feeling his fragility, his preciousness, the unbroken bond, the well of tenderness, of devotion. We lay in bed talking about New Orleans, his trips, what he saw. We did not talk about his father. There is such tenderness in his leanness. He seems so small, so delicate; I look at his wrists. He has to go back to his family, to watch over the body of his father.

Journals 32, 33, 34: they recreate a state like opium smoking in which one little incident, one caress, one scene, produces enormous diffusion. The writing is all about the feelings produced, removed from reality, the enormous expansion in sensation. Life comes in small pieces, little scenes. I was an opium dreamer—I could not focus on reality.

35 to 45: later the diaries become focused on human drama, movement. The writing grows tighter, concerned with essentials, terse, sparing, strong. 45 to 50: the focusing gains in intensity and accuracy. Greater sincerity, greater clarity. In the last volumes, 50 to 60, there is a fulfilled climax, a fusion of the dream, the mirage, and human life. They flow together.

FEBRUARY 13, 1941

The day before yesterday, a day of orgy.

I met Henry for lunch, and we got into bed afterwards, so eagerly, so completely, grasping the asses with our hands, clutching at them to bring them more violently together. Henry fell asleep. I slipped out of bed.

Dinner with Gonzalo. Our corner. A prolonged enjoyment, prolonged to exasperation, a wallowing into flesh, a hunger of the hands.

Orgiastic day, no writing possible. Hugo called me to scold me: the telephone bill has grown huge, immense, and unpaid when he had given me the money for it. The net of economic difficulties closes in on me. Everybody is irresponsible, unaware that we are going to be shipwrecked.

Yesterday, a Day of Work, thirty pages of writing. Today another Day of Work. I could ask myself, as Patchen does, why does no one pay me for all the work I have done? Ironically, it is not the real diary I am paid for, but the false one.

Story of Ruder, continued. Who is the client? Is it Ruder himself? I said: "Soon I am coming to a volume that brings up the political question. What side is your client on?"

"Bourgeois, of course."

I hesitated eloquently, baffled. "Well, that will be difficult; I myself have swung to the left."

"Oh," said Ruder excitedly, "that will be terribly interesting. I'm very much left. I think you must put all that in. It is all related. Have you tried to reconcile Freud and Marx?"

He was speaking for himself. And his client was bourgeois!

The mystery remains. He repeated his invitation to dinner and the theatre. It is the return of Rank's body without the power and greatness, the same dolorous begging eyes, the intellectual attitude, the incapacity to enter life, all the energies spent on analysis. He is a pepper, this Mr. Ruder, hoping sometime to be able to make an entrance. But because I see his inadequacies and ugliness, I laugh to myself and think: *entrée payante*, Monsieur Ruder.

Laughing with a hundred dollars in my pocket, I went to Henry, who was waiting for me in bed. I said to him, "Mr. Ruder is beginning to contradict himself. He says he likes simple, nonintellectual women but he invites me out to dinner!" We talked until late.

Today I said to him: "When you return, if you still want to marry me, we will get a place and live together. I will leave Hugo."

At this moment I had forgotten Gonzalo. I imagined a whole life of creation and love with the One. Henry said, "I thought you could never separate from Hugo." Separate or break. When the moonstorm comes, I separate, and then it is madness. I write heavily, with the stone of realism weighing on me.

MARCH 4, 1941

One infernal week. Robert brings me all his children to feed. I write for Ruder, who is never satisfied. My period is late, and I am worrying already about the expense of an abortion, about where I can get a cheap one. Coming every morning are angry bill collectors and threats. Feelings of defeat, exhaustion. Henry becomes aware, tender, asking questions he has never asked. I had to beg Ruder for the hundred dollars for Henry's departure. He at first refused, then offered me an advance of forty dollars, but today he rejected the hundred pages as definitely not erotic enough. I took it quietly, but I am beaten.

I went to see Slocum, who advises Henry to stop traveling for a while and write, to catch up. Henry cannot break his contract with Doubleday, so he must go on with his trip. I have spoiled them. It's too late. When I asked Gonzalo only to be careful with the money, he had a crisis of guilt and desperation. The guilt turned into fear, then jealousy. He made a scene again as violent as those in St. Tropez. This one was directed at Robert. He shouted: "I want purity! Purity! You're still going around with the degenerates." He got wild, monstrous. He said, "You are still forming groups around and for Miller. That is what it is, Miller's world. You won't give it up!"

Saturday Henry left. Last night Gonzalo took all his clothes off, I mine. He was caressing, voluptuous, with his whole body. It was like the nights of rue Cassini, sex through the whole body, a whole love. I became baffled. Why, why? I asked myself. How did this wave of passion return, like the waves of its highest peaks, in spite of the day before, in spite of the poison, in spite of Gonzalo's bad health, in spite of my doubts of him and his love? When one stops demanding it, it comes; the passion came, flooded me. I said, "*Estoy contenta.*" "*Yo también,*" said Gonzalo. "It's been a long time since I've been this happy," as if he knew Henry was gone. It was one of those dazzling nights. I felt strong.

MARCH 8, 1941

I am down to my last pair of stockings, and they are torn. I sell my books. Every morning I get angry, threatening letters from somebody or other. My only fear of war is: what will happen to my children? If Hugo loses his job, how will I protect them all? What saintliness Hugo has, accepting to sacrifice for others with me. When he scolds me it is always just. He does not ask for himself. He is concerned for me.

If Hugo is the husband of me at twenty, at least he has not deteriorated—he has grown. He has become the artist. He is more today than he ever was.

All my strength goes into the erotica. The diary was abandoned. I look at it tonight to just to assure myself it is still there. I have nothing to say.

Wrote forty pages of erotica with the possibility of selling it.

MARCH 27, 1941

Robert is gone, ordered to report for induction. I could not eat; I walked the streets. Hugo began to work for his return, his liberation. They do not want homosexuals in the army. When Robert left, for the first time he did not give me a child's kiss, but a lover's kiss.

What I want to tell Gonzalo, but cannot, is that his love for Helba is destroying mine for him. When one brings, as he does, the past into the present, one surrenders the present to the past. His blind, foolish devotion to a person who is willfully and voluntarily enlarging every little pain, magnifying every discomfort and malaise in order to command pity and attention, finally tires out my love for him.

I know this is not true—it is my own sickness that makes me feel this. Perhaps Gonzalo feels the same about Hugo or Henry. Even of Eduardo he is jealous. He was insanely jealous of Robert. Now I am the one insane with this trauma.

How can I surmount the feeling? My life is full, but is there always to be one point of disease in it? Before it was fear of losing Hugo, then Henry, and now Gonzalo? Do I fear losing him? Fear alone causes jealousy, and my fear is invading me—it invades the love and eats into it. The hatred for Helba is growing stronger than my love for Gonzalo. It is a monstrous thing.

I write ten or fifteen pages a day. I see Eduardo, Thurema, Slocum, Ruder. I write to Henry. I paint the benches. When I am with Gonzalo, we paint together when we are not making love. But as soon as I am alone, I fall into this obsession.

I read this tale as if I had never known all this.

I wanted to join Henry, but I do not have the money. Robert is in army prison. I shy away from people. I have isolated myself.

In my own love there is duality, which is why cannot I accept another's duality when it has forced me into mine (or when my duality forces others into theirs). Who is waiting for a whole love, to give whole love? Henry gave me a whole love when he separated from June, but I did not consider this separation absolute, because after June the human being came June the legend, the theme of his work. So I threw myself into a new love only to meet with the same situation, only worse.

APRIL 15, 1941

Still restless, restless, not to be able to meet Henry in Santa Fe, to escape. Then came a day of defeat, the diary finally ending its tour of the publishers, rejected, then the exhaustion of my erotic themes, the debts.

Caresse came. Her lover Canada Lee is a star on Broadway, in *Native Son*. She asked me to accompany her to Harlem, where I met him. I had given her the courage to live out her love. We both worried about our lives growing shabby because love has brought us both poverty and restrictions. I have what all women want, love, but it has enslaved me, not freed me. It is devouring me. I am tired of writing. I am losing everything, the little beauty I have, my gifts for expansion. I am imprisoned by devotion. Look where I am! I am watching *Native Son*, sitting by Mr. Ruder, who is ugly, vulgar and familiar. This is the prostitution I have entered into for Henry and Gonzalo. Look at Anaïs Nin in her dark wine-colored velvet suit (seven dollars at the Lerner shop), in her frilled grey blouse from New Orleans, given to her by Caresse, in the six-year-old wine-colored velvet hat with a feather, the one I wore on the Avenue des Champs-Elysées, with a cape cut out of the dilapidated princess fur coat, with mended stockings, walking with a twaddling, deformed monster who invades the privacy of others! Who wants to enter my life and meet my friends?

However, people still say I look dashing and elegant. I discard my costume *d'époque* to better match Gonzalo's workman's clothes, his corduroy trousers and leather jacket, and down Broadway again we walk to see a jungle film, the only film I would see twice, in which the savagery of the animals trains me for the savagery of man and war.

Henry's adventure trip around America is catastrophic, a wasted sacrifice, for he is creating nothing out of his trip; he is only spitting in America's eye, like a preacher in an endless sermon casting it to hell.

MAY 4, 1941

The madness reached a climax, where I banged my closed fists against my brow, awakened in the morning dreaming I was murdering Helba…and then I fought it, dissolved it. How? There is a way of bringing the monster out of the cave, and in the clarity of the day it shrinks.

What a strange night, when Eduardo asked me: "Come with me to the Tavern" (the night before he had been there and had picked up a homosexual boy). This tavern was next door to my place with Gonzalo, 132 MacDougal Street, a basement room full of monsters, ugly, mediocre types. It was the rhythm of the two negroes playing the piano and cello which Gonzalo and I could hear from our little studio, the music Gonzalo and I lay down to and caressed each other into druggedness and desire. And to this same music, Eduardo and I sat before a little table, watching the door for the marvelous being that might enter, but no one came. Rats and mice and rabbits scurried, snickered, dawdled, munched, hunched, but there was no marvelous being to love. Eduardo watched with anxiety. Another night without love. For Eduardo sensual hunger is also a hunger for love. And if I were sitting there without love?

Tam, tam, tam...the piano and cello while Gonzalo and I lie on the bed, and his black fingers drum on my skin and play the cello between my legs. We are laughing at the music because it is always the same. But what goes on inside of us is never the same. The millions of days, nights, and moods varying in color, smells, form, climate, depths are never repeated. All the millions of nuances of one love, one love turning its million faces towards each other, the millions of gestures altered by the mood of each day, colored by fear, misunderstandings, revelations, creations, books, films, the past, voyages, other loves, dreams. Tam, tam, tam...Gonzalo's body each time is sufficient to awaken erotic feelings—his hair, his neck, his chest, his smooth back, his iron legs, his odor, his color, his laughter, his voice. Gonzalo is unfastening my new panties with the garters attached, and saying: "It looks like a *pulpo* (octopus)—how many *pulpos* do I have to unfasten? Gonzalo, throwing his cigarette butts still lighted in the middle of the room...

Eduardo's eyes are riveted to the door...tam, tam, tam...of emptiness. His blood will flow back to its source unspent and hurtful; his love flows back like poison. I look at the door too. Gonzalo will come in, as he came in the first time into the small room of Roger Klein's apartment in Paris, looking very tall and demonic, his black hair wild, his body bigger than everybody's, but big like a child's, retaining the softness of contours and the awkwardness... Eduardo said sadly, at midnight, "Let's go."

June 1, 1941

Gave Ruder fifty pages.

Dorothy Norman will print fragments of volume 1, the childhood diary. Paul Rosenfeld, the literary critic, kept the diary a month without reading it. Henry is in Hollywood and refused to do script writing at two hundred dollars a week. Ruder said: "Doesn't it make you angry?" "No," I said, "I expect this. He does not want to sacrifice himself." What a relief from tension when he receives one hundred and twenty-five dollars from *Town and Country* (for his article "The Colossus of Maroussi") for the next two weeks.

Gonzalo makes me happy. He has the secret to the kind of love I want, which only the child-man can give, the child-man who has all the time and freedom to love, who gives himself to love like a woman does. What a continuous multitude of kisses and tender gestures. When he meets me, he hides to surprise me. He is always touching me, on the street, in the movies, in the restaurant.

Everyone rages against the child-man: he is irresponsible, he lets his women take care of him, he permits the mother's sacrifices and care, he takes it for granted. It is not selfishness. He accepts his weakness and need of protection. He trusts, believes, and it is all natural. Henry never tells himself that writing scripts for Hollywood would unburden Anaïs. No child ever thinks of unburdening the mother. Henry has not tried to find other protectors…he wants protection with love and understanding from someone who lets him be free. I have never asked him to accept the Hollywood offer, which is merely for money, and Henry has never done anything for money.

What no one understands that this child-man also has a precious gift. His very irresponsibility makes him relaxed, soft, gay. Very often after grim hours of responsibility with Hugo, who worries about the future, who has stomach troubles because he worries *too much* about the future, as I do with him because of the children, I go to Gonzalo and enter his insouciant child-world of such absence of reality and sense of burden that I relax, I forget, I am free. As with Henry, there is purity, almost an innocence regarding the commercial basis of life.

Care often debases one. I have written a hundred pages, which I do not believe in, to take care of my children. I have accepted many humiliating things.

If only people would accept that each one has a role and fulfill it without guilt. Eduardo is not a delightful companion because he is a guilty child. He is not a man, but he is not a child either. He cannot play unknowingly, nor can he be mature and responsible. He never chose between being a bourgeois and an artist—he is always in between.

June 4, 1941

For three days I thought Henry was lost to me because of his enthusiasm for Luise Rainer, born the same day as his mother and June. I was sad, but not desperate as I would be if it were Gonzalo. I was sad like a mother losing a child. I thought of Henry with tenderness, a deep tenderness.

I took a humorous, teasing letter of Henry seriously. He teased me because of his own jealousy aroused by reading 180 pages of erotica, which he is trying to sell for me in Hollywood. "I'm not in love with anyone," writes Henry.

June 10, 1941

I said to Gonzalo how strange it is that the spermatozoa sometimes lingers in the womb before fecundating the egg. He said, "Yes, it's slumming!"

I said, "Janet saw a hermaphrodite, half of her body a man's, half a woman's."

"And the sex," said Gonzalo, "was it a banana split?"

He talked to me for a whole evening about the activity of microbes. Coming home, we saw lovers sitting in Washington Square. Gonzalo said, "I wonder what makes people fall in love." I said, "Don't tell me it's microbes!"

Gave Ruder another fifty pages. Hugo says, "I need money," so I wrote fifty more, then fifty again about Elena, and about a seductive man who is Gonzalo with a will.

Robert is awaiting his release after weeks at the hospital, after he declared himself as a homosexual to the army.

The old man is begging me to write, to write *now*. He wants my erotica like a drug.

Jealousy is a small undercurrent, and all I can do is to recognize it, to be honest about it. It is ugly, and I want to conquer it. Henry says: "You have no confidence in yourself." So gently he answers me, my alarms, my panic. I knew he would laugh at my angry telegram. He writes: "Do you really mean that if you had the money you would join me? You're not stringing me along?"

Hugo, poor Hugo, has regrets now for all he has not done. He has regrets when he reads *Picasso et ses amis*, whereas Gonzalo says, "I thought I was reading my life."

Those who do not enter life—I live in the Village yet I stand outside of it. I walk the streets and I am estranged from all promiscuity. I live only within my deep loves. My last adventure was a fiasco.

Je vis en marge. I have regrets. I have saved one hundred dollars for Henry, which he does not need. I can keep it for joining him—but do I want to?

Stuffed with French books, I write for Ruder.

I only feel I am living when I am meeting my lover, or walking with my lover, or lying down with my lover; I feel that everything else is death, that I should have had many lovers. An evening of soft climate, animated streets, open bars throwing out music and confused voices, gives me no peace, only restlessness. Outside of the orbit of love I do not exist.

Why do I find everything but peace? Great, deep human love should give peace. Every day I abandon a mystical belief, a psychic interpretation. Every day I find new physical roots to the dream.

Jacobson has taken the place of the analyst, and of course I am less happy because only the illusions and delusions create ecstasy. The discovery of the physical and of the earth saddens me. That is why earth people are sad and mystics alone know joy.

When Gonzalo and I sat on the porch this morning and I looked out into space above the houses, he said, "You look as if you were preparing for flight, right out into space." I had asked the airline for the cost of a trip to Hollywood.

I carry armfuls of books back and forth from the library and write…it is like a beehive…pollen and semen indeed.

JUNE 18, 1941

When I think I have conquered the monster, it attacks me again. I awaken in the morning charged with poisons. I see failure of my writing, failure to live for one absolute love, failure to free myself from economic tyranny.

Then Henry's letter this morning quieted me: "If you can't join me I'll be starting back slowly." Is that all I needed? I felt that if I don't join him I will lose him altogether to the Roman life of Hollywood, or to Luise Rainer, who resembles June and me, or to the waitress who talks like Seraphita in an empty restaurant, or to luxury and someone else's protection.

Je cherche mon rêve. Most of the time I am not in New York at all, but in some corner of Paris, reliving the marvelous peaks of my life there.

What I cannot understand is that although I hate Hugo physically, I suffered one night when he was enchanted by a mulatress at the negro ball. I can bear Henry's absence and only feel maternal solicitude, yet when he wrote me that my erotica had affected him powerfully like an aphrodisiac and that he was at that moment going to visit Luise Rainer, I had a black day. In both cases I felt I should abdicate, that it was only right to let Hugo enjoy what I had enjoyed, to let Henry find a new love when mine for him is no longer a passion, but I could not bear it in the end. I believe Hugo's sexual venture might deprive me of his love, which I need. Henry's love is inhuman, lasting, a strange bond.

I did not finish writing, in the red diary book (begun in 1932), the story of the passage through the eighth house of astrology, the book of poisons, the book of rebellion, the book of disillusion. All through it I still clung to the myth, and there was an undercurrent I did not touch—the story of our aging, all of us, aging. I never was aware of age except for one day in Louveciennes, when I looked at myself in the mirror and thought: I am growing old. But that was before I loved Henry, and when I loved I forgot about my age again, completely. I lived in the illusion I gave to people of my youthfulness. In Mallorca the children called me *la niña casada* (the married girl). People were always surprised at my real age...I did not feel it. I did not identify with the subject of Balzac's *La Femme de Trente Ans*, but I do now. I did not notice others' ages then.

I first noticed Henry's aging when he worried about a sexual *défaillance*, his growing interest in mysticism and diminishing interest in women, his first periods of physical fragility, his desire for tranquility. Hugo has a stomach, grey hairs on his temple. Psychically, we left our youth in Europe. Facing America, we showed the lack of suppleness and adaptability of people at forty. I was the youngest...I struggled not to age, not to accept physical handicaps. I took young lovers (a bad sign). Henry submitted quietly to a change of rhythm...he is always submissive. He cannot bear late nights, and his health has weakened. Earthy Gonzalo resents the failing of his body; it depresses him. He has little to spiritually nourish him. Hugo had no such crisis. He is peaceful; he accepts.

And I? In Europe I was about to enjoy the ripeness of maturity, but here, in the country of youth, I became painfully aware of something others do not see. The young men seek me out, they make no distinction. I join them in dancing and equal them. In Harlem I am the maddest dancer of all. For John Dudley I had no age. Physically there are no signs: my body is that of a girl—I weigh 113 pounds and my waist is still pronouncedly indented. My breasts are dainty, the tips are roseate. My skin is translucent. My hands alone have aged, but they always looked old. There are fine wrinkles around my eyes, and I have a few grey hairs. On tired days my chin is less firm, but the experienced girl at Elizabeth Arden said: "Apart from the lines around your eyes, all is well. The muscles are firm." I can deceive anyone, even a doctor. I pass for thirty easily. My walk is easy and free, my steps are light—but the feeling, the agedness given to me by the American life, its immaturity! Everywhere there are unformed beings, awkward ages. That has aged me in my awareness. Fatigue. The passage into human life, detachment from the dream. Once, Luise Rainer and I ran away together when visiting Dorothy Norman, to talk. We slipped out of the house, and she drove us to see the ocean which faces Europe. We stood on the edge of the beach, yearning for Europe together. Laughingly, sadly, I said to myself: for this romantic escapade in an open car, hair flying in the damp night, I will pay dearly. The next days were filled with pains and overwhelming fatigue. I left the weekend defeated, shattered. While walking today, I thought I would write a book on aging, *le déjà vécu*. The tragic motif comes from my not being physically and spiritually in harmony. I await the moment of retreat, and each one seems to be a victory over pain. What pain? The pain that lies in everything. I...once so prodigal... The book of age is the book of caution. I seek tranquility and the absence of pain. The Monster lies all around me, gigantic in the world today. The outer image is too horrible for human awareness. Contemplate the news—the war of Germany and Russia—and you go mad.

I have created the isolation in which I find myself. Life shrinks in proportion to one's courage.

Letter to Henry:

Do you want a divorce, Henry, so you can live out west, quietly? Are you ready to live alone in your Shangri-La? I have felt at times that you were approaching that Tibetan cycle. Should I free you of me? Are you ready for the ascension? Should I be Seraphita now and vanish, is this the moment?

Robert escaped from the army, came back, seeking a place to nestle in. He slept two nights curled up in a parked car, and then went back to Marjorie, who has room for him in her apartment. He is thoroughly dehumanized now.

INTERMEZZO

Please lead me into the world of pleasure

PROVINCETOWN, AUGUST 8, 1941

I fight against the madness day by day, find relief in writing. What silences me is Gonzalo's illness, and so not to hurt him I keep my hatred of Helba a secret. I start out to the beach with Hugo, who is, as ever, gentle, contented. We prepare our lunch, we get on our bicycles, we swim, we lie in the sun. I never know at what moment my obsessive hatred will be aroused, when it will be there to eat into me, devour me, poison me. I begin to hate Gonzalo for submitting me to the woman who represents all that I hate. Then I conquer myself, get a few hours of peace, forgetfulness and contentment. I say, like someone who has been very ill and is now well, what a relief. I am free and well again. I fear the return of the obsession at night. If it comes, I cannot sleep, I suffocate, I suffer. Why can't I be free of Helba? Hugo sees it, says she is a devil. The emptiness of this place, of America, the failure of my writing, has turned my thought only towards what hurts me. When I return to New York I must take up something that will fill my life. What?

AUGUST 10, 1941

Hugo, with his divine goodness, is the only human being who has never hurt me. Yesterday I was saddened by his leaving, and the liberty I was gaining did not seem so wonderful. Gonzalo did not seem so wonderful and could not console me. I did not respond to his passionate lovemaking last night. He took his clothes off and there he was, but I was not moved. I felt Hugo's goodness all around me, like a cloak of tenderness, and for once I looked down upon the passion. I crumbled last night, my body was cold, and passion could not reach me. I have locked myself away from all the pain that accompanies passion, the jealousies, the fears, the cruelties. I awakened this morning to weakness and smallness in me, a hyper-sensitiveness, to a loneliness which neither Gonzalo nor Henry ever filled, a sickness they cannot heal. Hugo alone gives me life, but when he is here I yearn for the violence of passion. I awakened weak, but then took hold of myself. I wrote Hugo a beautiful letter in which I tell him I love my children (as I have told him they are to me, and he believes it) less and him more. Then I answered letters, set order in my life, took the decisive step of buying the press from Robert to do volume 1, the childhood diary, and planned to give Gonzalo and myself an occupation. I dressed myself in my most becoming costume, the *pareo* of St. Tropez, red and white, with shells in my hair and around my throat, and walked down the street to see how many men would turn their heads, and all of them did. Now I sit in the café writing, and again my diary gives me the sense of wholeness, which having so many loves takes away from me. Love in me is a wound. Again and again I repeat this, and the only one who loves me in such a way as to heal this wound is Hugo. I am in truth a very, very sick person, and I need a love like Hugo's to keep me from insanity and death.

August 13, 1941

It is because I see no expansion in my life—it has fallen into a static sameness—that I have to anguish. No hope of a new passion. Last year, when I returned to Gonzalo from the John adventure, I was hoping not to find a new love that would separate me from him. Now I do hope for it. All dreams of the absolute are gone. Passion gives the illusion of an absolute, but then the eyes open, and there is no absolute union. My eyes are painfully open, and I want to escape. But Provincetown—this is no place in which to find new passion!

August 14, 1941

Terrific happiness tonight, all anguish dispelled. I talked to Gonzalo, gently, almost in the words I use here, quietly, movingly. I found that he not only understood everything about Helba, but that he had the lucidity I begged of him. He said he had no guilt towards Helba, that his only crushing guilt was not being able to work, to earn a living, to take care of her, because of the paralysis of his will, his laziness. When I said, "She will separate us," he answered me so seriously and wisely about his independence, his differences from Helba, I felt all my fears dispelled.

A strange night, for when he wanted to leave, I didn't want to stay alone, so I walked out with him. At eleven o'clock the town is quite dead. Gonzalo urged me to play Beano, although I had been losing for weeks. To please him, I played. I played indifferently, sadly. Then came the lottery, and my name was called. I won ninety-five dollars! Gayety! I gave Gonzalo half because he had forced me to play and brought me luck. I planned to send Hugo the rest so that he could come for the Labor Day holiday. We went to the Flagship for the first time at night and drank three whiskeys each. I carried it well, but they closed at one o'clock in the morning, and I had to go to bed. I fell asleep immediately in a euphoric state, but awakened early to send Hugo the telegram and the money. A turn of luck, faith.

AUGUST 16, 1941

The night Gonzalo and I went to get drunk at the Flagship, there stood at the bar a magnificent man. So magnificent, so arrogantly handsome, a blond Nordic Viking, that I made fun of him to Gonzalo. I said: "There is the *gallo*, the cock. Such wonderful Don Juan plumage." But I did feel: here is a MAN. The MALE.

The next morning he arrived at the beach, walked in front of us. He expanded his chest, held himself as if in a state of euphoria. I was still mocking his magnificence. But as he passed, with a free, large, lyrical walk, he smiled at his male companion, so brilliant a smile, so wild, so sensual, that I felt a pang. He was the Sun Man smiling. He stretched himself near us. Beautiful skin, not pale but golden. Curled golden hair. Something so noble, royal, that it shattered all the rest of the people around us. From the first I felt him aware of me as I was aware of him. I wondered at his solitude. I felt: he is foreign to America. He does not mingle with them.

The next morning I awakened so gay, so irrepressibly expansive. I met him on the street. I smiled at him. I broke away from dinner with Virginia and Bob DeNiro and their friends and ate alone at the Flagship in hopes of meeting him there. I ate alone and was exalted by the music and candlelight and thought: if only the people were interesting. There is nobody but him. How well he answers what in me wants music and dance. There is music in him. Yesterday: same place at the beach. When Gonzalo moves away we smile at each other. Walking home: as I reached my place, he reached his a few doors away, moved forward extending his hand, introduced himself. We talked a little while. "I knew you were European," he said. His teeth were dazzling. His smile exactly like my father's, with the milk tooth protruding mischievously. I said, when he asked me what I was doing, I was having dinner alone at the Flagship. He said: "We'll have it together."

Beautifully dressed in my Morocco-blue jacket, in the candlelight, we created a sensation together. All the women were pursuing him. "But American girls," he said, "I can't be with them." A delightful gay dinner. He is Viennese, and a singer of opera. Subtle and full of nuances and beautiful manners. He flirted so delicately. Said I had a beautiful figure. And I discovered he had been observing me all along, everything I did, that Gonzalo read the newspaper at the beach and deduced that we were married. At nine-thirty, having to meet Gonzalo, I left. He was disappointed. "I thought we could go to the White Whale nightclub together." I said I would try to join him at eleven when Gonzalo leaves me. At eleven Gonzalo left, but two things deterred me from going: the fear of discovery (the nightclub is right next to Gonzalo's house, and he prowls about when he can't sleep) and the feeling I should not appear, leaving the taste of brilliance at dinner and then making Edward Graeffe feel my presence. He missed me.

The next morning he was watching for me on his porch. I said I might be free to go to the beach with him (it was Helba's turn to be taken to the beach by Gonzalo). But Gonzalo came. I insisted that he had come with me for four days, that it was Helba's turn, and sent him away. My heart was beating. Edward had waited longer than he had said he would wait. I knew everything as it would be. It was a fantasy I had often indulged in. A beautiful man, the sand dunes, the sun, sensuality and no sorrows. This fantasy I would have liked to fulfill with Gonzalo. But we never did. Since St. Tropez I wanted it.

Edward flung his long legs, singing. His gorgeous torso naked, his golden curls shining, his steely blue eyes gay. Euphoria. A long tramp through the sand dunes. I had grown a little shy. His big hand now and then falling on my shoulder or neck. It was romantic, to an amusing degree. I in my St. Tropez *pareo*, Hawaiian seashells on my hair and neck. In the heart of the sand dunes, he threw himself on the sand. I fell at his side. Lying back, he began with the most delicate caresses of my fingertips and wrist. Such delicacy. And now and then he smiled at me. Slowly I got undressed as his hands searched for buttons and bows. Afterwards, his nakedness as he stood in the wind, laughing. Truly godlike in his physical magnificence. The waist and hips slender, not thick, the torso marvelously ample, shoulders wide. A golden blondness. If only I didn't have the usual stage-struck feeling, it would have been magnificent.

Last night, a secret meeting at the Flagship. He will make his debut in *Siegfried* at the Metropolitan. Taking a bath, preparing for him, I laughed to myself: Siegfried was lacking in my collection. I must have all the mythological figures: the son of the Inca Sun Gods, the Lord of Essex, the Demon of Literature. A sensual, romantic fantasy fulfilled. His free, swinging walk, a conqueror. Man of aristocracy. And power. He was once the leader of the Olympic skiers and nearly married the daughter of an English Peer.

Next morning he waited for me. I was not free. Gonzalo took me to the beach. On returning from the beach, I found Luise Rainer and Dorothy Norman looking for me. With other friends we drove around and stopped at the Flagship for coffee. I went to get Graeffe because he knew Luise. We had a most animated party, with everybody watching Luise and asking for a photograph. Luise and I had one intimate talk while I changed into my dress. She said beautiful things about my writing. Someone in the street said: "They are sisters." Then they drove away.

It is strange to choose someone blindly, intuitively, and then to begin to discover the world he lives in, the details one likes. In this brilliant moment he fitted in so well. "He looks like a god," said a French singer who had come with Luise. Physical royalty. The blue eyes charged with lightning, the teeth incandescent, the golden curls so smoothly brushed. His hands are long and aristocratic, smooth, well-groomed. He dresses beautifully. He carries a Spanish leather hunting bag, with its niche for bullets and a beautiful net pocket which he fills with oranges. A thick wide leather belt for his money and keys.

"My father was a general."

How like a fantasy to have him for a dancing partner, talking by candlelight, listening to music. Now and then he sings a fragment. A rich, colored, free voice. Another Caruso, people have said. He is thirty-two but he looks manly, a man really, with poise, savoir-faire, polish, finesse, humor. He is playful. He remembered a few Spanish words (his mother was from Malaga); when we parted he thundered after me, amplifying his voice: "*El Barón de la Mantequilla saluda la Condesa de la Santa Burro,*" rolling the words as if he were saying: "*La Duchesse de Guermantes…*" We laugh a great deal. He is exuberant, gay, poised, joyous. Luminous, brilliant atmosphere. The nightclubs are transfigured by charm and desire. As we dance I feel against his leg, in his pocket, the hard little French leather case of his watch. He laughs and says: "It is only my watch. I regret to disillusion you." But soon, when he has taken out his watch at my request, he ceases to disillusion me and we have to stop dancing. The misty lights of nightclubs. Mystery. When we move from one to the other, he has to go ahead to see if Gonzalo is not about. People are stunned by us. The homosexuals had all tried to interest him (because when he first came he was with a male friend). He is taller than Hugo or Gonzalo, taller than anyone here, holds himself erect and proud. Talking. Drinking. At one o'clock all the places close (New England). He walked home with me. Before my door in the black night he began to caress me. We entered. I didn't turn on the light. Naked in bed. His caresses, from the lightest to the most violent… I cannot yield entirely yet, but what pleasure I feel, what voluptuous currents of sensations. I say laughingly that I, being Ondine, instead of catching him by my singing, was caught by his singing.

Siegfried is not always romantic. He is often Rabelaisian in his speech, but grandly. All the Americans who tried to interest me look at this couple where all the European charms center, his and mine together. The three of us, Gonzalo ("the motorized Inca," Graeffe calls him, seeing him on his bicycle), Graeffe and I are like personages out of a myth. People think I am an actress or a dancer. Luise's coming heightened everything, and all the stagnant obsessions which haunted me a week ago have vanished. I have escaped, changed climates. The most terrifying, tempting aspect of infidelity is how attractive it makes you to your deepest loves. The afternoon I came back from lying in the sand dunes with Edward, Gonzalo came and took me with the greatest desire he has felt for a week. That has always happened. Love and passion form a current which must be nourished and sustained and renewed and retransmitted. Fixed upon one object it stifles and strangles itself. Desire. Twice I have known desire free of love.

I awakened singing. It was raining, cold, but I was singing. So strange, the passage from sorrowful, shrunken days to luck with money, with desire, with Luise's visit, expansion and flight.

Gonzalo, Gonzalo, I cannot live in the caverns of my obsessions and doubts.

It was strange and terrible, the night Gonzalo talked to me so wisely about Helba. He reassured me of the love, but not of the passion. It was the first time one of our reconciliations did not take a sensual expression. I felt the love and the tiredness, the deep tiredness of the man who is burning out, as Henry was burned out, the loss of vitality, and my passionate youthfulness celebrating a remarriage without a night of passion. This very night, under my joy at spiritual nearness, there ran the sense of loss and separation. And like a floating uncertain, rootless being, I caught at Siegfried, all shining, and was drawn magnetically to the source of desire again.

Brilliance again. Music.

Pouring again. No beach with Siegfried. Alone. Dreaming. Lying in bed, glad of the rest, for my body always takes on more than it has strength for. It always cracks when I begin to soar. So marvelous to reach for your dream when you are outside of the nightclub and you hear the music and you are locked out, not dancing, you are alone in a room watching the candlelight of the Flagship, but knowing tomorrow you will be inside, dancing, with a new lover.

August 21, 1941

In spite of Edward's playfulness and the carefulness with which he preserved himself from this relationship, as I did—the impersonality—a new element entered into it yesterday. The day we planned to go to the beach, it rained, so we did not meet, and I have asked him not to call at my studio. Once I passed by his house and he was out. At a quarter to twelve I passed by the Flagship and he was not there (he came at twelve and did not find me). Meanwhile friends dragged him out all afternoon and evening, took him to the beach at one o'clock, made him drink, etc.

He came home at six in the morning. At twelve we talked. Gonzalo was taking me to the beach. So Edward came, but sat with a friend a few yards away. At three Gonzalo left to teach Helba how to swim. I pretended to leave on my bicycle but I returned, talked to Edward, and we went together to the other end of the beach. And then, because he was tired from the night before, a little less invulnerable, perhaps because I had the intuition of what he needed, I ceased to treat him as a lover. I talked fantastically about Peru, and later at the Flagship I drew him out to talk about his life, and he told me about his first deep love for the daughter of a Peer, whom he could not marry because he was without money.

At this moment the romantic Edward appeared, the one I had sensed through the delicacy of some of his caresses. From this he passed to talking of *Tristan and Iseult*, the sensuality and eroticism of the music. As it happens, the motif of our dancing music at the Flagship is stolen from *Tristan and Iseult*. I felt his disgust of the night before, his desire to dwell again in music and poetry. I made the evening beautiful. How true my instinct. He confessed to me how women pursue and demand the lover in him. And at my door he gave me the most delicate of kisses, mere brushings... We had lifted the experience out of the realm of *une affaire de rêncontre*, a pick-up, a banal incident, into another sphere. The other women saw only a desirable body. It is quite a feat to construct a dream out of an ordinary seaside flirtation and after playing the accessible woman. But I did it. I detected a certain regret when he said: "All this will soon be over. I am leaving the 28th for Nantucket. Will we see each other in New York?"

Je voyage. Je voyage. What I trusted was his smile. There is a Nordic fierceness to his eyes, a power to his neck, but his smile opens like a feminine Iris. In the grandeur there is softness. I could fall in love with his smile. The very image of him makes me breathe more deeply. My pride is reawakened, the desire for beauty and elegance. I feel a curious physical euphoria. Why does the joy of complete yielding elude me? Twice he has taken me, and I do so want to feel him entirely.

AUGUST 22, 1941

We went to the beach together by bus. Went to the farthest end of it, opposite to where Gonzalo was with Helba. We lay on the sand, near people at first. Edward caressed me furtively, when no one was passing, the breasts, between the legs. As I had told him the story of the little animal in Peru who inserts his beak into women's wombs, he was immensely amused and started to call his ever-rising sex "*chinchilito*," and I "*chinchilita*." We went into the sea. Under the water he caressed me. How beautiful this was. I could see his marvelous body under the water and I caressed his *chinchilito* and we laughed so together. So much that when Edward came out of the water he looked for a secret place behind the beach, hidden by the grasses, and there we lay naked for a while, until his desire grew again and we caressed and he took me, too quickly and vigorously for my pleasure, but the sensuous pleasure, the feast for my eyes which he is, the erotic images of his body a feast for the imagination and senses, gave me such joy. I had dreamed once of lovemaking in harmony with the sea and the sand, and here was a laughing god of the sun, teasing, imitating the growling, rather swollen ways of Gonzalo, my alertness and Gonzalo's old, tired lion manners. I was in such a high mood, exalted with pleasure, shedding radiance and full of charm. I know I enveloped him in essences new to him. How much he perceives, feels of me, I cannot tell. I know he is enchanted.

We were invited to a cocktail at Peter Hunt's together. He always says, "I would rather be with the *chinchilita*."

After the cocktail, we gravitated again together for dinner. He grew talkative, more and more expansive, telling me fantastic stories. The sensualist is there, in a phrase now and then. Always women. More and more the project to see me in New York appears in his talk. I never mentioned this. I accepted his being born of the sea and vanishing with the end of the summer. I have doubts. About love I would know, but about pure pleasure and sensual caprice I am ignorant. Every day I think it is ended. The story of his frustrated love is the alibi all men and women give who cannot love ever again. He is impenetrable to me, because this climate without love is new to me. Yet now and then, unexpectedly, he will press his forehead against mine. He is mysterious to me. A new kind, proud (he was short of money today and would not accept the smallest loan), arrogant, independent. Yet I say to myself: why is he so aware of the motorized Inca? Why does he tease me so persistently? Is it a kind of jealousy? In a climate without emotion to guide me, I am rudderless. It is all new. True, I had no feelings for John, but he was sentimental; he was in love.

A whole day without thoughts of Gonzalo. I went so far away from him in a few days, it was difficult to return, to become aware again that he is spiritless, half-ill, lifeless. We met at nine. My ebullience was contagious, and of course he desired me. What encouragement to unfaithfulness. He took me. I was still talking like a drunkard, amusing, high-spirited, impossible to suffocate again, irrepressible. My thoughts were all centered on the charms of Edward, his infinitely alluring smile and his hands, his *coups des belier*, his clowning imitations, his cries of Chinchilita! The humor in him.

Alone. The enchantment of Proust, the web of profundities. Alone. Reweaving each glance of his eyes, each modeling of his lips. Seeing him over and over again on the crest of the dune, wind-blown, or emerging from the water. Neptune. He repeats for me the ice-cold inscrutable eyes of Henry, and the sensual softness of the mouth, in terms of beauty. His deepest love, of which we talked, was dreamlike. The book of age became the book of renewal. For once, I was not prophetic. The beautiful adventure. To find in the physical body, in the physical world of pleasure and sensuality, always the shadow of the dream being fulfilled, always the fantasy, always a body capable of a dream. Never mediocrity. "*Je suis contente*," I said to him, "*d'avoir si bien choisi*." We are not in love. We are playing. It is a fantasy.

AUGUST 23, 1941

Suddenly my wings no longer carried me. I fell. Leaving Siegfried at the beach, I suddenly fell into an abyss. It was too impersonal, too lonely, not tender enough, this brilliant affair. Though we lay four hours on the sand and talked about his family, and he caressed my hands so delicately, still it was not love. I cannot carry it off. I glided on the wings of his humor, and then I fell. I wanted love, love, love. When my exaltation fell, I saw Gonzalo ill and sad. I said: "Come and eat with me at the Flagship." He said, "Restaurant food does me harm." But we went. I took a whiskey. Suddenly I understood people's feverish seeking of pleasure. I drank a whiskey, and Gonzalo can't drink one— he drank two. Then we went out for a while, to buy bicarbonate of soda for Gonzalo. At eleven he took me home and returned to his room to listen to the news. People were going to the costume ball. Edward had not asked me to go to the Flagship. He was engaged with friends. This caused a terrible feeling of desertion and loneliness. I wept. Gonzalo could not understand. I cannot escape into surface living, and I wanted to! I thought I was saved, that I could leave the caverns of desolation and regrets and little deaths, but I cannot do it by desire alone. It must be love.

Siegfried said yesterday, referring to the evening before, when after our dinner together I left him to meet Gonzalo at nine: "Change of guards at Buckingham Palace."

When one says I cannot reach the world of pleasure, one should add: you can only reach it if it is in you. Siegfried, please lead me into the world of pleasure.

AUGUST 24, 1941

Ce chagrin étrange de hier soir. This morning I met him at the coffee place. He said playfully: "Is the Inca's wife not well today so you have to go with him?"

"I don't know yet, but whichever it is, I am free all the same."

"You must not be so revolutionary," he said. "It will hurt him. He may need you."

This angered me, though it was delicate. I said so. I left then, to see Gonzalo. He had planned to go with me. I yielded. I returned to the coffee shop to fill my thermos and to say: "I cannot come. *Chinchilita est fâché*" (annoyed).

He was so soft then, gentle. "Don't be *fâché*. Will I see you later?"

"If you can *défâché* me!"

I left. He told me later, "Last night, at the dance, it was dull. An American girl appropriated me. I cannot be with them more than an hour."

But why didn't he stay with me then? Or take me to the dance? He always says: "I prefer to be with Chinchilita."

I do not understand him.

AUGUST 25, 1941

He went to our place on the beach, alone, and waited. But I…I imagined him arriving with friends. My eyes are not good for distance. I was a little sad. When Gonzalo left me to teach Helba to swim, I stood there and again imagined it was Chinchilito in the water with another woman, probably caressing her as he had caressed me. Jealous. I turned away and rode home. But at six o'clock I could not stay away, and I called on him at his rooming house with some pretext. Then I heard he had waited for me. Even in playing, I spoil it with my lack of confidence. Of course, I am not altogether unjustifiably jealous. The night before he had made love to the American girl. And at the restaurant he pointed her out to me, but saying, "I always return to Chinchilita, and I would give up all the others for Chinchilita." We had dinner together. He talked expansively, about the wealthy people he knows (he is the singing coach for one of the wealthiest American families), talking like a revolutionary, an independent being who is detached from the world, as he is detached from bohemianism, and most all, from American life. At nine o'clock, change of guards. At eleven, the Flagship (for Gonzalo I appeared to be falling asleep so that I could slip out early for Edward).

At the Flagship he was in a tender mood, saying: "Tonight what I would like is for you to come to my room, undress me, and cover me, and put me to sleep!" So his invulnerability breaks down. But in the crowded, noisy, chaotic nightclub, he places my hand where I can see he is not asleep yet. He walks home with me, and as before he has eluded kisses on the mouth except at the moment of possession (which is the proof that we are not in love—men never kiss the whore, and I didn't like to kiss John because I didn't love him), now he kissed me lingeringly on the mouth and pressed me against him so that I could feel his desire. But he did not come into my studio out of delicacy for Gonzalo. So that while I play and follow with Edward the capricious outline of pure desire, at the same time I am looking for the wild frenzy and abandon of passion and forget how this is lacking from the world of desire and pleasure.

In the world of desire and pleasure I am in danger, in danger from my imagination which embellishes, from my tenderness which releases in the man the cruel tensions imposed by other women when faced with the sensual relationship (the old Don Juan talking to Colette: "They did not forgive me for one *raté*, one *défaillance*, they kept such strict accounts and compared notes with other women to see if I was always at the same level"). This tension of the men chosen by women for the role of lover, unrelenting women, as in an Olympic championship game of sexes, a night without lovemaking is his only refuge from women's pursuit. Poor Don Juan. Edward is fated to this role. Women have marked him for the stallion. They disregard the human being, his moods, his needs, his fatigues, his moments of detachment, everything but the erect phallus.

He talks at times delicately: "My father was born in Samoa. He did not leave until he was sixteen years old. When he took the boat home it snowed. He had never seen snow or cold. He thought the snowflakes were butterflies. He tried to catch them and was amazed to see them melt." Then again, he talks like my father, suddenly a *voyou* (guttersnipe) with a Rabelaisian language, cynical, gross, with obscene gestures, but playful. He uses obscene words and then, just as suddenly, becomes tender again, delicate, or once more clownish, like Henry in his writing.

He eluded all the women, came to the beach alone, waited, got impatient, came to where I was with Gonzalo (Gonzalo had just left to see if Helba had arrived), sat near us, waited. When Gonzalo finally left, we went together to the other end of the beach. I told him tenderly what I had already told my diary, and my intuition was right. He was amazed at my understanding of his Don Juan problems, and he talked openly about women. I heard astounding things about women. He dropped his role completely, all the impersonality. He talked about all that he is passionate about, the development of his voice, his studies, his feeling that he is ready as few singers are ready, not only by an arduous, extraordinary discipline, but all of his life, being, experience, feeling, all dedicated to the one end, his singing. He, who said that he always listened, now talked flowingly and confessed how right I was, how he was sick of women who hated him if he didn't always make love. And as I leaned over with a curious wisdom and said, "When you need a friend you do not have to make love to, you can come to Chinchilita," the look in his eyes was almost a look of love, whereas for the other women he shows brutality and cynicism and contempt. I wonder if it is because he realizes that it is their self-love and vanity they reveal in their relentless need to be made love to which is more about their power and charms than a true desire which would consider Edward as a human being. Anyway, he gave me his sincerity. All the other women cannot hold him for more than a moment. I am the only one he spends hours and hours with. He told me how angry they were. One woman whom he refused to accompany to the ball said about me: "But she is not very young…"

Our afternoon was so sincere and mellow that the poor, persecuted Don Juan said at the end in a lugubrious tone: "This evening I have to go to a birthday party." He yields. He will always yield. The woman who will love him deeply will enter an inferno. Like my father, he also accepts his role and needs it. This loveless gift of himself preserves his integrity, his independence, his equilibrium. He has the strength of the isolated, the invulnerable. He will not be in bondage. He will not love. Like all the stories of the whores, the frigid ones, the narcissistic ones, the story of the first frustrated love is said to have locked the doors for good, but it is not so, it only served as an alibi for the nature whose course was not to love. My first frustrated love did not keep me from falling in love anew each time.

Tonight he may yield again. It is always the women who attack him. Not for them the delicate caresses, but the ferocious irony, more ferocious after the yielding, the invincible smile, the abandon. He walks proudly, head high, untouchable. Women can touch his body, but not the core—I touched both. After he has gone, I still see him vividly. It is a kind of enchantment, like love. To discover his qualities, compassion, human evaluations, his absence of vanity, I found more delight in these qualities, and the essence contained by his beauty turns out to be in harmony with it. So that the adventure which, for other women, has turned out elusive, unrepeatable, unseizable, for me has left such a dreamlike taste that I feel content, rich, perfumed. I breathe more deeply when I remember it.

Gonzalo came when I returned from the beach, took me, and I responded fully.

Content. My only wish is that I may feel Edward once, physically, completely. Why do I resist the final abandon? Morning. The flavor remains. I awaken singing the imitated melody of *Tristan*. In this little book, I passed from death to life, beyond age and change, into the eternal in relationship, lived out a dream with an echo instead of a trite adventure *sans lendemain*. How he slipped in and out of other hands, but remained in mine to distill his personality.

So overflowing with gayety that I could not have dinner alone. I thought: let me bring some of this gayety to Virginia and Bob, give it, spill it, spread it, share it. Imitating the booming voice of Edward, I said: "Let's go and have a glamour dinner." They were enchanted. I took them to the Flagship, drank with them. But poor Virginia and Bob, they are caught in a drama of disease: Bob got gonorrhea from Robert.

Where I sit, eating lunch at Taylor's, it is like Coney Island. I live in hope of seeing Edward pass, like a king. Nine o'clock. After missing him all day, a rainy day, I passed by his house and he called me. He was expecting his friends. We sat talking in the little parlor. He was tender, caressing, delicate, mischievous, obscene, with strange gestures, from kissing my fingertips and the hair on my temple to suddenly taking out his *chinchilito*. He said over and over again: "*C'est beau, très beau.*" Then he asked for my address in New York. His friends are driving him away. His expression was beautiful, radiant. The radiance of his smile unnerved me. My god, is this an adventure? When I left his place I heard the wind through the leaves, like the very breath of life of which he speaks, the breath, the feeling I had the first day walking through the dunes, of breathing largely, deeply, freely because of the way he breathes. Why this joy? This joy? I met one of the girls, the one at the party. I had met her in the bus. I see his face: "*C'était beau, c'était beau.*"

It is raining. I am out of the house of death and age. Saved by another dream. I recognize the dream. It carries me. My feet are light. I feel imponderable. All the little contingencies cannot touch me. This morning he was looking for me, pursued me, while I looked for him. But I vanished. He did not dare go to my studio. He is always aware of Gonzalo. He said: "On this rainy afternoon I imagined you would both get into bed and make love all afternoon." Anaïs, beware. *Il faut savoir jouer. Il ne faut pas rêver.*

Midnight. His friends came so we could not meet. I waited at the Flagship. Then I realized that the scene in the afternoon was a good-bye. And what I felt was too deep. I was frightened. In a few days he filled my imagination constantly. I felt him in everything. *Et lui?* Tonight I realize it was all too powerful and dangerous. It will be difficult to forget him. What will he remember? *C'était beau, très beau…* It was very beautiful!

AUGUST 26, 1941

La petite Anaïs ne sait pas jouer.

I was having breakfast when he came in with the friend—the rich woman with the beautiful voice whom he coaches. I did not see them, my back was turned. I walked out to mail a letter. As I passed the restaurant from which one can look into the street he waved at me exuberantly. I smiled. I caught a glimpse of her face. I said to myself: if she is beautiful, I am lost. If she is rich and beautiful, she is his mistress. But the glimpse told me nothing. Merely a distinguished woman, that was all. As I passed them buying fruit on my way to the beach (always at the sight of him I experience a shock, I miss a heartbeat), he stopped me. He came forward and introduced me to the woman (he had already said that he wanted us to meet). She immediately said: "Why, I know your father's music very well. I have often heard his songs, which Ninon Vallin used to sing. And I have heard your brother's concert at Town Hall." She asked news of other people. She was very cordial. I felt very proud for him because he seemed proud of me. It was all very charming. We bowed and smiled. They went off to the beach in her car. I was happy because she was not beautiful! Such nonsense. I was happy. At the beach, the sea, the sand, the sun. Something to dream and remember which has the indolence, the golden colors, the capriciousness, the nature moods of the place. His body the color of sand, with the sun on it, his eyes the color of the sea, and how he lay on the beach, the bigness tapering towards the slender ankles of the aristocrat. My desire detached itself for the first time from the body of Gonzalo and clung to Edward's image. It finished *en beauté* like a very elegant dance, with a strange symbolic scene in which he bowed his head over my fingertips and kept his mouth over them like an homage.

Returning from the beach, preceded by a flurry of autumn leaves, the sound of the sea in my ears, I felt the flow again, the mellowness, a sense of connection with the currents of life. I am in the dream again. Intact, as I was at the beginning of dreaming. It is the dreaming which creates the innocence.

Evening: haunted by mirages. I see him whole, entire (sometimes one does not see people full length, but some part of them, an oblique aspect of them), the very image of physical plenitude. By a sensation: the firmness of his skin against mine, the fineness of it, and his powerful sexual thrusts. By an emotion: the discovery of his tenderness, the penetration of his voice. I keep the brilliance like a precious essence, fearing its vanishing.

I say to myself: I only want one more night. But am I deceiving myself? I wish I were not so vulnerable or impressionable. If he loved me, were moved equally, he would have been with me all the time. But there was the barrier of Gonzalo ever-present in his speech and teasing, like a danger sign, and perhaps I felt his own fear of ever being enslaved, his own desire to safeguard himself against it.

So I will not know until I reach New York whether this is to have a continuation. Yesterday I felt on that dark, rainy day that it was the end. But then I always fear the end. With Henry, every day was the end. With Gonzalo too. Yes, I am in love; it is a feeling that opens one like a flower, fills one with essences that make one mobile and singing like the wind or the sea. Even in passing, I react with a deeper romance.

August 27, 1941

Yesterday another meeting, the lady, Edward and I in the streets. He asked me to join them to go to the ocean, but I had already told Gonzalo I was going to meet him, and it was the day before Hugo's arrival, so I couldn't, but I asked them to meet me at the Flagship for a cocktail. The lady and I found much to talk about because she knows music and musicians, but I suffered from a paralyzing uneasiness again from an attack of discouragement, timidity, doubts. The magnification of small incidents with which I torture myself. As I had invited them I had arranged with the waitress beforehand not to present a check. Characteristically Edward discovered this, and he said playfully: "If I had known this I would not have asked for a sandwich." I replied playfully: "No, you would have asked for a lobster!" A maladroit remark, made out of nervousness, maladroit because of his pride. And I fancied he was hurt. When we parted, finally, it was like the end of an ordeal. I was full of anguish. *Tout est perdu.* Everything went wrong. I was nervous. I wanted so much that she should like me so that he would be proud of me. I walked past his house several times in hopes of a meeting which would reassure me. During the tea he had continually touched my knees with his, and before she had arrived he had run in to excuse a few minutes' delay and had said tenderly: "Chinchilita, I will see you in New York." But last night I thought I had spoiled it all, the dream—I, who never hurt people's feelings!

Gonzalo was having dinner with me. I lured him into the Flagship. I took two whiskeys. Then Edward and the lady came in. We smiled at each other. Gonzalo was jealous. It was a pleasure for me to be able to see him now and then. Strange, she has come alone to see him, she has a room next to his, he drives her car, they are together, yet I feel no jealousy at all, as if she were the mother. She is a woman of my age, ugly, but intelligent and charming, distinguished.

Because of the whiskey I could not sleep all night, not until five in the morning. Then at nine I yielded to an impulse and slipped a note under his door (the door of the house is always open) to come for a minute. I would like to efface last night's error. I cannot tell what he feels at all. His behavior is contradictory. His obsession with Gonzalo is very pronounced. His need of being the center of love is equally clear. I lie waiting for him. Hugo arrives at twelve. I should forget him.

Twelve. He came. He was very caressing, tender. Opened my blouse and kissed my breasts. Teased, played, admired the fishing net overhead, spoke again of New York, no shadow of anything wrong. All I needed to calm my anguish. But what I should not have had to do was to nourish my dreams. Always he repeats: "How beautiful it was in the dunes!" As if it were for him the highest moment too.

They leave today.

Everything so beautifully timed as Gonzalo was beginning to grow alarmed, observing the difference between Edward's formal early bows and the irrepressible cordiality of his last ones. Last night I did not desire Gonzalo, but Edward. I have the clear feeling today that I will see him again, that there is a suspended feeling in him too, a question.

I feel a mysterious, soft happiness.

I see again in him the elegance of my father, the pride and the nobility. Once, when I went into the house where he stays, the doors were all open, there was no one around, and I did not know which one was his room. Three rooms all open on the parlor. I peered in and saw on the dressing table the silver hair brush, comb, clothes brush, and mirror, like my father's, and I knew they were Edward's. His signet ring too, in gold, like my father's, and his beautiful long-fingered hands.

I would like to have beautiful clothes again. All that I surrendered for Gonzalo— the automobile, the servants, the good meals, the house in order, the comforts. I can give, with what I have, the illusion of beautiful dressing.

With Hugo returned the budgets, the accounts, the bills, the calculations, the sense of restrictions, the meals at home, tenderness, absence of fantasy, ennui, gloominess (he always errors in his calculations which makes our situation seem worse), talk of insurance, taxes, indulgence towards my stories, towards the smiles I gather from so many people, the forced lovemaking, the refuge from the sickness.

Becalmed. The sails no longer swollen by great winds.

Then last night I touched the roots of Gonzalo's sadness: no longer supported by alcohol, he is faced with an impasse—the realization of his life, awareness. At the age of forty-four he is faced with a complete paralysis of his will and activity. He cannot even write a letter now, a letter of vital importance. He is completely paralyzed, guilty about his laziness, fully aware of its destructiveness, of all he could have done, of the love and support he got from me.

Eight in the evening. It is all in Proust: "*mon mal*," "*l'amour maladif*," the anguish of love, of doubt. I have never understood Proust so deeply or loved him so much. It hurts me to read him, the craving for the love of the mother, the suffering over a lost kiss, over a phrase carelessly uttered. Every day I live these *angoisses* and want to be free of them. When Edward filled my being I was happy. Now I am prey again, waiting for Gonzalo and thinking he might not come; all the beautiful Portuguese girls here seek him out. Calling for him and hearing him converse with Helba. Being with Hugo on the beach and seeing Gonzalo alone, waiting for Helba, and wanting to run to him and having to hold back. If he does not telephone. Finally my anguish, like Proust's, was only calmed when he began to telephone me every day and I could see him every day. As I know that the disease kills the love, I keep it secret. I get deeply disturbed when I reveal it, when it betrays me, as if I were ugly and monstrous.

Both Hugo and Gonzalo have successfully destroyed my ecstasy. It lies imbedded, deep down. When I am at the beach, I abandon myself to it. But it fades, like the emotions aroused by John Dudley. I think of it in terms of pleasure, an escape, a joy, but not in terms of love. I wish it were.

Gonzalo no longer gives me life. He is like a dead planet.

Since Edward is not my love to come, what then? Or can I have a new, a joyous, a carefree concept of love, devoid of pain perhaps, as I thought Gonzalo's was at the beginning? Proust: "For what we mistake for our love, our jealousy, is not the same uninterrupted and indivisible passion. They are made up of infinite successive loves, of discrete jealousies, all short-lived, but which, through their uninterrupted multitude, give the impression of continuity, the illusion of unity."

I am becalmed for the moment.

Ready to return to New York with the full conviction of my unhappiness and the desire to escape into pleasure or merely to escape.

AUGUST 30, 1941

The day after Edward's friend arrived, my perfume bottle disappeared, was either broken or stolen. What did it signify? A bad or a good omen? I have been trying to discover the name of the record we dance to, the motif of Provincetown. I was told it was called "Intermezzo," and it made me sad. I heard it while taking coffee with Gonzalo. I tried to find out its name again and failed.

So it is that the Montparnasse of most people's knowledge never existed for me, but the dream and essence of it was mine in Henry and Gonzalo, who were both beyond it while they lived its life. So it is that Provincetown, which is vulgar, mediocre, and stupid, was not Provincetown for me, but Siegfried and the dunes, the dunes of Alemany's photographs. So it is that the Village is not for me the home of poseurs and fakes and mildewed poets, but the Village which does not exist for anyone else, the Village of my painted windows and benches, my autumnal life with Gonzalo, the autumn of my face and not of my body, the autumn which has marked only my eyes and a few strands of my hair, but not my soul yet because my soul was always aged. The afternoon I called on Edward in the prim little New England parlor, which looked too small for his magnificent body, when his head touched the ceiling, and the little New England rocking chair protested at his weight, when he bowed his tender-skinned temples against mine, his mouth on my fingers and kissed me inside my ear and teased me, and it was raining and grey, when I walked away with my breasts heaving as if filled with a potent wind, my sails swollen by the long draughts of life-breath he filled my lungs with, I heard the autumn wind rushing through the leaves, the old trees, like the sea sounds at the beach, like the sea sounds of Proust's phrases, rolling infinitely and ebbing, throwing tides and echoes all through the marvelous edifice of lucidity, through the tragedy of this too great and too deep lucidity.

Autumn. Only the tender leaves of the laughing wrinkles have withered in me, only the hope of happiness and peace in love, only the hope of living free of anguish and the deep malady of exaggerated sensibility.

The smile of Edward is gone. Simultaneously, the sky clouded, the beach grew cold, the sea icy, the leaves fell on the old library steps, Gonzalo and Hugo became like dark caverns in which my luminosity died.

The poet knows too well, too acutely what vanishes in others' eyes. When I read Proust I rush to see Gonzalo as if I were not sure of ever seeing him again.

I am so hungry for pleasures, for dinners with music. Last night I lured Hugo to the Flagship. I was fêted by the hostess and waitress there, two girls who are painters. One stole dessert for us and gave me *crème de cacoa*, and refused a tip. I asked the violinist to play "Intermezzo," and it was Edward I dined with.

Return to New York. Telegram from Henry asking for money to return. Telephone to John Slocum to borrow money for a few days. Visit to Miss Steloff of the Gotham Book Mart. Patchen's book is selling well, and Henry's *World of Sex*. My books are in great demand, but they are all out of print now. Visited Henry Volkening, the publisher dissatisfied with Henry's book on America. Saw Eduardo, who has rented a room near me.

Organizing my clothes. Alas, trickeries, rearrangements, *rafistolages*. Organizing my home. Dreaming of Chinchilito. Telephone conversation with Luise. She has serious anemia.

Henry's agent says: "Henry's book on America is unacceptable." Henry owes Doubleday five hundred dollars. His new article for *Town and Country* was rejected. I had to beg for him, and I can't write for Ruder. The music "Intermezzo" haunts me like a dream that I would like to repeat. I would like to fall asleep and dream the same dream. As in a dream, I did not possess him, feel him enough. It has no substance. I prepare my clothes as if for a dream.

SEPTEMBER 16, 1941

Curl my hair, I said to the hairdresser, I am going to a dance. What dance? In spite of war and broken beings and disease and death, I am going to dance and to dream, as I dreamed with Edward. I am not in love with him, yet he remains the symbol of the luminous. I dress for him. When I walk into the Savoy Plaza to see Tia Anaïs, I expect to meet him. I see him in luxury and music. He has not telephoned, but he is in the city and I may meet him, only because he lies for me in air and light, and when I remember him I raise my head, my feet are lighter, and I feel light.

Henry is slowly traveling back, but I wish he were not coming. I feel separated from him.

Last night a night of pleasure and lovemaking with Gonzalo. Like the past, his sensual enjoyment was tremendous, as was mine. A younger and slenderer Gonzalo, made beautiful by the sea. But the desire for fever and pleasure remains insufficiently answered.

Every day a little weight is added to my shoulders until I will be bound again: the lack of money, so acute that I hesitate to write Robert "come back" because of the impossibility of taking care of him (Marjorie has refused to do what I did last winter—feed him and his friends and give him pocket money—so he left for Chicago). Eduardo has a room nearby and lives on a small allowance. Why has the dream of luxury returned after years of drabness and sharing the renunciations and denials of others? With Edward I reach into a dream of luxury, abandoned for so many years. Poverty is monstrous. I see it in the life of Virginia and Bob. Gonzalo is weary of it. I returned to the few years when I knew comfort (Boulevard Suchet and Louveciennes) before I met Henry. I have a need of ascension, not to the same possessions but to a purified luxury, the poetic quality of it. I realize the value of what I surrendered. I asked myself: What is this exaltation? A premonition? An illusion? A mirage again? A preparation for a new love?

NEXT MORNING HE TELEPHONED!

I jumped with joy. I can't sit still or eat. I'm joyous, joyous, joyous. "I missed you in the café," he said. "I arrived last night. When are you free?"

"Chinchilita!" he cried gaily as he arrived in his small car. I led him to the studio. He glowed, beamed, purred with contentment. "It's beautiful here. The painted windows! The benches. You are a real artist. What am I doing here, me with my two vocal cords only?" I gave him the *House of Incest*, saying: "I give you here dreams you already know." I showed him my photos and he took two for his pocketbook, he said. We sat in the porch on the swinging hammock. He caressed me, my breasts, my legs. I saw a new Edward, softer, more tender, feminine. At the beach his physical arrogance, which is purely of the body, predominated. In the city it is attenuated by the clothes. And the softness appears. We spent an enchanted hour. And it occurred to me that we were living in a dream. All I could feel was a slight physical pleasure, a great airiness, brilliancy, an entirely new feeling. I wonder what I give him. He called me as soon as he arrived. He took me driving in his toy car, his hand over my legs, sometimes stealing between them. He talks about next year in Provincetown. I was terribly nervous, yet at one moment I divined his own unsureness. The strange thing is that he is so much like a dream that sensuality is dissolved. I would like an orgy in which to feel him more violently. I was exhausted from nervousness. I wanted to enchant him. And I was not sure. Afraid he would vanish. He said: "Provincetown was marvelous…when I met you."

When I came home, Hugo was not yet there. I stretched myself out as with an opium pipe to remember EDWARD…

In a few days I'm broken by so many marvelous moments: the night with Edward, the arrival of Robert, the night when Luise invited us to see her act in Barrie's *Cinderella*. The life I wanted. And Robert, as always, understands this idea of the myth dimensions, my desire to live only with myth people, and he is ready to discard all that does not answer to this. The bond between Robert and me unshakable and pure. The new emotions roused by Luise's acting, my love for her. I sent her a letter together with one of my glass slippers. A telephone call from Edward. In a few hours I am consumed and burn through all my strength of body.

SEPTEMBER 21, 1941

Robert makes such a true distinction between disguise and transformation. He also said as I say: one person cannot suffice to my great hunger. So again I lie writing in the diary. Hugo is engraving at his table before the window, and Robert is painting the coffre to match the benches.

Last night I was exalted, so vulnerable…every sensation intensified. Music threw me into exalted joy—an intoxicated state, like love. I had dinner with Gonzalo, swept him off his feet. Did he feel my mood for an orgy? He said: "Let's go to Harlem." I was delighted. But in the end he led me to our *rincon* and got me under the covers, naked, and we threw ourselves into pleasure, long, drawn out, a long-lasting orgasm, a bath of caresses, of strong odors, mouth filled with sperm, fingers imbued with honey. A night of joy and plenitude, so like the past that I could not believe in all the little songs of waning love I had been observing.

Conflict in myself: I first took to our *rincon* the Madagascar bed cover, which I had in rue Cassini and which was stained by Gonzalo, but now I keep it in the apartment because it looks beautiful and I see it more often, and others admire it. But I feel this is a betrayal, a lessening of the passion, a throwing of the objects surrounding our love back into the current of my individual life. I do not feel the same betrayal when I take something from my home for my life with Gonzalo—as if all I had should naturally go into the passion, the passion being at the center.

SEPTEMBER 24, 1941

Last night I went downstairs at nine o'clock and there was Chinchilito already there, moving towards me, crossing the street, with his phosphorescent smile and singing voice. We came back to the studio. We read his horoscope together, which is beautiful and confirmed my heightened image of him, the expansion, the largeness, the idealized figure. When we read of sorrow in love he said: "That's Chinchilita." As he recognized my handwriting (Eduardo left me stranded with only a few facts, and I had to complete the horoscope with a book), he was grateful and amazed too. He said, "But what is this, Chinchilita?" Playing upon my horoscope design he said: "There she is, a painter, here a goddess, here an angel, here an astrologer, and down here, a little devil…" and he kissed me on the mouth. Kisses, kisses, kisses, and caresses, but no invitation to make love. We sat at a bar and talked. And then he almost destroyed my mirage by telling me stories as bad as Henry's or Rabelais, but all concerned with excrement and urine, etc., about himself, which I particularly detest, and which left a bad impression on me. I returned home, baffled.

Robert said: "What makes *Winter of Artifice* a failure are the falsities, the interchange of personalities and the disguises."

Eduardo said: "In *Winter of Artifice*, we get the second transformation of a reality already once transformed in the diary. This twice transformed reality being wonderful but not accessible to all." Obviously, my idea that my work consists now in retelling it all with greater completeness is implicated in all the criticism of the diary's incompleteness, but for the moment I prefer to continue and be more complete in the present.

OCTOBER 6, 1941

I am not ready to retire from life and do the masculine creation of the other face of the diary, to labor on what the woman could not complete—the circle from feminine personal to masculine impersonal. My human life means more to me.

Luise does not believe in pretenses, playing roles, because she thinks it leads to disaster. I said I had done this often and without catastrophes. My deceptions! But it is true it requires alertness and tension. To answer in front of Hugo when thoughtless people ask me over the telephone: "How is Henry?" To prevent Hugo from receiving the telephone bill on which are noted telegrams to Chicago (when I haven't the money I am forced to telephone the telegrams to Henry). For my mail: care. When I was in Provincetown I had to send a check for the "corner" on MacDougal. When I signed as Mrs. Moré, I said with infinite care: "Mrs. Moré, care of Mrs. Guiler, 437 Commercial Street," so the receipt could be returned to me. But the postman, knowing everybody in Provincetown, took it upon himself to deliver it to Helba. Fortunately Helba does not read English. When I wrote fifty pages for Ruder in the summer, and Henry needed the money, Ruder asked me not to mail the pages, but to send them with somebody. Hugo was leaving for New York, but if I gave them to him he would know there was fifty dollars coming to him, and Ruder had already telegraphed the money to Henry. I told Hugo they were pages written by Virginia, and I sealed the envelope (when someone else writes for Ruder he does not pay cash but makes them wait three weeks for the answer).

OCTOBER 9, 1941

Feeling very exalted and inspired, I tried to work on the Jean story, but all the time it is Luise I feel and see. My friendship with women are like love affairs, and such a fervor takes me, such vividness, that it inspires me like love and haunts me like love.

Chinchilito telephones me from a life charged with singing, rehearsals, mysterious trips (the Lady? a floating personage, growing vaguer in me). Yet the thought that he is coming Monday afternoon gives me the suspense of a high perilous trapeze leap. The long intervals between our meetings, the absence of sensual connection, makes it like some brilliant trapeze incident, spangled, accompanied by music, in which I can admire his deftness and my accuracy. I sense he too is keeping himself outside the circle of pain, and the little poison of jealousy to which he is so vulnerable has germinated, and my image becomes inseparable from the black shadow of Othello. (Even over the telephone he asks: "What is the motorized Inca doing?") And the tone of his voice, the kind of fatigue and discouragement of the person faced again with his fatal pattern of recurrence (the rival) when he said: "He lives so near to you!" As if he had said: "Too near!" And I, I do not again want the man with a wife (Gonzalo), who belongs to the public (Henry), or the fêted singer-idol (my father, who received applause and the flowers of all women's tribute, the flowers of their sex with the fern garnishing of multi-colored pubic hairs, pistils of desire, the corolla of the orgasm that is given to the interpreter of music, to all the figures on the stage where the illusion we need for love is already prepared). Those who fall in love with performers are like those who fall in love with magicians—they are the ones who cannot create the illusion with love alone. The *mise en scène*, the producer, the music, the role, will surround the personage with that which love needs: the myth. In this love Edward will receive, in the bouquets of women that will rain upon his voice, I would find again the pain my father gave me, and I do not want it. But because we touched the ring around the planet of love, we touched the aura of it, the long beautiful leaps we take together in space, leaps of grace and beauty, across visitless weeks, are marvelous, like demonstrations of the agility our souls are practicing to escape from the prisons of tragedy, the incarcerations of jealousy, the caverns of deep love's tortures…

I lie here awaiting Henry's telephone call and my being is against his return. I no longer feel him. It seems to me that I am struggling to free myself from the burdens, too heavy now, which threaten my existence.

Evening: What defenses against Henry! Luise telling me I should break with him, be free, live for myself, seeing Gonzalo while I awaited Henry's telephone call, all to prepare myself to say: I feel separated from you, it is time to separate. I added in my mind the proofs of his detachment so that I could reveal them to him. He stayed months in Hollywood when it was not necessary for the book, he showed reluctance at returning to New York because he would have to see his mother and face the problem of the rejection of his book on America, and feel again the association of New York to his past (it was then I decided to go to Provincetown and no longer wait for him). And it took him a month to return.

When I arrived Henry himself was timid and nervous. He sought my mouth and I turned it away. I was tense, quiet. I looked at him, feeling: "I am free of him." I looked at what I never liked, the coldness of his little eyes. He was shaky, from the long trip, the tension. I thought: perhaps he is free too. We talked. It was he who softened first, came to my chair and kissed me with passion. I did not desire him, but I did not feel any distaste either, like something sweet and familiar. He made me undress, but once in bed he was impotent. Then I was tender and at the same time I began to talk and to say what I felt, but he was merely humoring me as one might a sick person, humoring my doubts, laughing even, absolutely confident that nothing was broken, unbelieving. All this in a quiet tone. I said: "Since freeing you was my obsession perhaps the time has come to also free you of me. You were happier out west, liberated of restrictions brought about by my marriage."

Henry was soft, tender, and listened to me as a man listens to a woman who is complaining of some little defect, and he loves her, and sees her doubts and knows it is not serious. We lay there. He repeated how nervous he felt. I said: "Let us get very quiet." We put out the light, we talked. After a while he took me. Then he laughed: "You won't believe me, but I have only gone with one woman once in all the six months, and she was a prostitute. I was almost atrophied!" And we went back to our old "scenes," of his merely reassuring me of his love while never for one moment doubting mine or fearing its loss! By this time I was completely disarmed and I could not see the separation, as if the mystical law by which we live created the kind of bond that survives the death of the body, and created a continuity such as we know will happen only to our highest thoughts and feelings. On certain days I know clearly what in me will survive, that highest moment of illumination that comes from effort and courage—so that the highest peaks of my relationship partake of the same immortality.

So it was the same hotel room of six months ago, the same dinner at El Pezzo... In one moment Henry made the most confused statements. I realized anew his weakness and softness. In one moment he asserted that he had no needs and would live on nothing, that he would never live as Eduardo did, on one dollar a day, that he felt so good he could even take a job, that his integrity prevented him from doing scenario writing in Hollywood.

At last I said: "And what of my integrity, doing the writing for Ruder all last winter?"

Henry laughed, admitted the paradox, the contradictions, the injustice, laughed again and dismissed it.

In this entire scene what affected me most was his trembling, his weakness, his childlike confidence. What is lifted, distilled from ordinary life, by the one who has the creator's eyes. My pattern is the dream. I seek to approximate it—when I do not get drowned in the depths of my too-human loves.

OCTOBER 13, 1941

Chinchilito came, lay back on the couch looking at the colored windows, caressing me, and said: "This is the place where I am happiest..." He stands apart, observing the inflated idiocy of singers and severely watching himself, ready to ridicule himself if "I talk like a dramatic tenor." He said my book on my father was tremendous, that he could not believe little Chinchilita had done it. He quoted lines from it.

He murmured: "How beautiful it is here. I would like to come and stay here for a whole day. We have not enough time together. We should have a whole day together." Delicately, closing his eyes as if he were smelling a bouquet, he kissed my fingertips, laid his brow against my temples, against my cheek. There is dissonance in him, from crude phrases to tender ones, constant contradictions, or is it between the Chinchilito I see and the one I hear? It is lovely, this dance we have together in space...

OCTOBER 17, 1941

Henry took me with hunger and I did not want it. But something remains of the old sensuality so that, in contrast to my complete closing against Hugo, after a moment with Henry I can yield even if I began without desire. His desire has outlived mine. Everything externally is the same as before the trip. I take the same 8th Avenue subway to East 53rd Street. I go to a house near the one he used to live in. We eat in the same chop suey restaurant and go to the same movie houses. But I am changed. And Henry does not know it.

Gonzalo gets passionate and wild over world events and reproaches me for not feeling them as violently. So again we quarreled. My blood flows somewhere else. My passion goes to human beings, near, and in need. I hold a whole little world together—I hold Hugo, Gonzalo, Henry, Luise, Eduardo, and Robert together.

In writing for Ruder with indifference and detachment, I attained a smoothness and technical perfection I can never attain in my rarefied writing.

OCTOBER 25, 1941

Henry is reading the abridged diary from which all the love affairs are deleted— nothing left but the outer relationship with Allendy, Rank, Artaud, etc. He is discovering how neurotic I was, which in all the years we were together he had not realized. He discovered my little treacheries, my accusations, and his failings. He praises the diary as a big, absorbing world.

My old anguish returned, and I asked him: "I haven't really hurt you, not seriously."

"No, no," said Henry, laughing, shaking his head, as if to say: there you are at it again, the old obsession with hurting, wounding. It is all so old, the past.

Henry said: "Now I have no need of returning to the past, to the story of June. It is all dead. I may write a book completely detached from the ego, the personal, the autobiographical."

Time. I once lived in the tragic fear of having to read the story of Henry's life with June. Now time has effaced this story, and all he has written are the myth pages already in the *Tropic of Capricorn*, the summation, the poem, not the full exposure and development. Henry said that my fear of hurting others produced more pain in the end.

NOVEMBER 1, 1941 ·

Last night with Henry, a Henry full of desire and tenderness, a Henry growing older, unable to bear great activity or too many visitors, dreaming of a peaceful place, so tired that I left him at eleven.

At midnight I was in bed. Hugo was still working at the New School preparing for his exhibit. Gonzalo telephoned! He had been at the School to get the prints in order to frame them, and he telephones! I knew what a pleasure it must have been for him to find me at home and in bed. I fell asleep enjoying his pleasure, his sense of security. This morning he referred to it. Said he was disconcerted to find me so "sage." I laughed. Gonzalo laughed too, saying: "You laugh because you think how lucky it was that I telephoned last night and not some other night!"

Henry said: "No, I was not wounded by what I read in the diary, but then I ask myself what could be in the missing pages. You're so clever you may have fixed this version just for me!" (That is just what I did do, Henry. And why does this act of protection always make me feel gay, as if I had defeated all the evil forces and the pain in the world by my trickeries!)

Coming up the stairs, home, tired, I felt gay and strong because I had defeated the cruelty of life, the tragedies of time, of love's great expansions and treacheries, by disguises only, only by disguises! Henry discovered after our many years of life together what I always knew: the power one can have over the world by gentleness. He no longer fights his editors; he seduces them and wins them over to his ideas instead of alienating them further. He treats them humanly and wins concessions and privileges instead of breaks and wars. He has lost his vanity and pride which made him unable to recognize his superfluous explosions, his failed bombs (like the moralizing in the American book, which is ineffectual). He said again he had nothing to worry or irritate him—only the money problem. He dreams of cheap, peaceful, isolated islands. Soon he will ask me to escape with him into peace and paradise.

NOVEMBER 4, 1941

This diary opens on a cool morning of a delayed winter, upon Gonzalo making frames for Hugo's engravings; upon Hugo producing his twentieth print for the exhibit; upon a copy of *Twice a Year* with seven pages out of volume 1 translated by me; upon Robert and me dancing last night in Harlem celebrating my meeting with Kay Boyle; upon Eduardo drinking and reading poetry with Harvey Breit and George Barker; upon an aging Henry finishing his American book; upon Luise reading a play on Rachel; upon Veronica Jennings of the *Saturday Review of Literature* saying my diary has no universal quality, that it is too intensely personal; upon Henry saying it is beyond the personal; upon Stieglitz dying and the long ago dead Dorothy Norman receiving Henry and not giving him a copy of *Twice a Year*; upon Edgar Varèse starting a choir and Paul Rosenfeld writing that we must listen to him; upon Moscow's heroic defense and people still unable to recognize Russia's greatness.

Eduardo says perhaps I am, after all, a witch. I gather the poets around me, and persuade them to write erotica, communicating eroticism and spreading this writing that is usually suppressed, giving them both the poison of disintegration and perhaps a way of purification, for all of us have violent explosions of poetry, and we eject the purely sexual as fervently as if we had taken vows of chastity. A purge, and not debauchery, results from the infiltration of erotic confessions. Breit, Barker, Robert. A house of prostitution. I, the Madame, supplying the Old Man with moments of perverse felicity, his drug...so that he has come to beg for it, and I gathering the poets to sell their erotic writings. The homosexuals write as if they were women, satisfy their desire to be a woman. The timid ones write about orgies. The frigid ones about frenzied fulfillment. The poetic indulge in pure bestiality, and the pure ones in perversion. Henry appeared as the mythological Animal. Barker has an English flavor, Robert is metaphysical. None are truly erotic, because eroticism is born of impotence, of extreme decadence. So we enter openly into the secret world of sex, rebelling at the bondage of sex, and exploding into poetry which we have to cut out afterwards. Haunted by the dream which stupid Mr. Ruder forces us to deny...forced to walk when we would rather dance.

Gonzalo's jealousy is alarmed again by my new dressing, my renewed elegance. He has no cause for it. All my desire has withdrawn from Henry. I am more wholly Gonzalo's than ever.

And it is at this moment that Henry is nourished by reading of my passion for him in my old diary, nourished by this past so beautifully captured. He telephones me: "I read the last one hundred pages. It's wonderful. All that about Rank and New York."

His voice was exalted. The last pages of this abridged version are all about the love of Henry as my absolute—the most beautiful pages on our love (after the birth illumination, the return to France, etc.). So I said: "You liked especially the last page?" He laughed. "That sounds like the diary. You would remember what was on the last page! Well, go back to lie and dream on your couch, and write more in your diary!"

Chinchilito telephoned: "I have been in Chicago three weeks—can I come today?" He never vanishes altogether.

NOVEMBER 7, 1941

In bed with Gonzalo. Laughing.

"Gonzalo, your confidence in me has not grown at all."

"We'll have to water it and put it in a hot house."

"You can't say it hasn't been in a hot house!"

Gonzalo laughed, had to recognize the high temperature of our love.

NOVEMBER 9, 1941

Telephone from Michael Fraenkel: "I have to see you alone." (How could have Henry have had a relationship with so repulsive a man? What a commentary on our life in Villa Seurat.)

Telephone from Ruder: "Old Man says none of the manuscripts you sent of Breit and the others came up to the standard you set."

Telephone from Caresse: "Saturday night I want to take you to Peter Powell's."

Telephone from the telephone company: "Your bill is overdue. You will be cut off."

NOVEMBER 12, 1941

Luise is too ill to be a good friend. Every word and emotion in her is now negative. When she is alone with me, she recognizes the greatness of my writing. When she introduces me to an agent, she diminishes me, as parents diminish their children by patronizing me or discussing the imperfections and immaturities of my Henry-June novel, and she thinks it's quite natural when the agent says: "Put away all your European work. It doesn't go here. Read *Collier's*, *Saturday Evening Post*, see how they do it and go ahead." She brings moral and idealistic judgments upon me, for the "crime against love I committed against June." She is so confused, she switches, oscillates, sways between identifying herself with a violent, destructive June and being defeated by me. She orders me to write how she is both June and me. But already I see that she is harmful, destructive, and that her softness and love are not basic, fundamental, but like atonements.

NOVEMBER 14, 1941

Talk with Henry, who is disturbed by the news that his first wife Beatrice believes he has made money under a pseudonym and is inquiring as to his whereabouts to see him for unpaid alimony (amounting now to $20,000) and by the news that his daughter suffers from epilepsy.

When the past haunts him he wants to run away. When he wants to run away he wants me to do it with him. Then he is faced with a recurrent doubt he has of my ultimately breaking with my past to follow him. Now and then he says: "And when we do get a big sum of money, you won't come. What will be your excuse then?"

Then tenderly, half playfully, I deflect the question as I always have, by pointing out how catastrophic it would be if I had not remained exactly where I am to be his guardian angel. I said: "You know, you always talk about faith, about everything coming out well, about your having no anxiety, but you know all the time that why you have faith is because I never let you fall or go hungry. If I dropped dead today you would be completely helpless again." (Last year he made $1000 and of this owes $500 to the publisher.) "I do not reproach you. But I know you are a dreamer, a child, and I know too you have had bad luck with your two publishers." (Jack Kahane was a dishonest and avaricious exploiter and now so is James Laughlin.) "I must continue to be what I am, where I am. I have given you a taste of freedom, traveling. I expect you to want it again, to get restless. I know you hate New York. When you can't bear it anymore you can go away for a few months, but for me it is impossible."

Henry said: "If I ever become aware that each move I make is a sacrifice for you and that my trip was the cause of your slaving for Ruder, I'll go crazy."

It is always the same answer. When they become aware (Gonzalo too, periodically) they become desperate, tear their hair, feel guilty, but that is all. They cannot remedy it. They can only protect themselves from the awareness, seek to be blind to it. In all these lives they have made the mad breaks, run away, traveled without money, but each move, instead of freeing them, has closed upon them like a net. The abandoned wife seeks retribution. The unpaid landlord keeps the trunks and most precious possessions. The starvation creates an endless trend of maladies. The papers not in order lands them in jail. The editor treated anarchically avenges himself. Nature avenges herself. Those from whom they begged, borrowed, stole, exploited, avenge themselves.

Henry took me with fervor after the talk, then said: "I did pretty well for a depressed man!" The illness of his daughter he looks at as a punishment too. Poor Henry.

When I say they are innocent it is because they are unaware. I can see in Henry the inability to grasp the reality of money. It's as if the basic concrete fact they cannot see, as the poets cannot see biology, chemistry, astronomy, physics. And that is why I justify or excuse them. As they become aware they always become sad. It is so much like the process of the child becoming aware of the evil in the world, of duties. I see in their eyes first of all clarity and gayety that goes with irresponsibility, then slowly a sadness which I hate to cause. Only when I was cornered and unable to do more have I dared to say to Henry: "In seeking to fulfill your dream of traveling, I have made you less able to accept the limitations which today are universal. Today we have to be in America. Even if you had a fortune you could not tour the world."

NOVEMBER 19, 1941

A week of disillusion. When my back is turned Robert uses my telephone to call up Massachusetts—one dollar for me to pay. Miss Steloff and Rae Beamish put in their pockets checks received for *The Winter of Artifice* which Beamish did not print, breaking his contract with me. Henry continues to moralize in the American book. Dorothy Norman believes her dreams are works of genius and receives me, marveling at her own work. She returns volumes 51 to 54 unread after asking for them and keeping them for six months. Gonzalo now wants to work, but when I asked Dorothy if she could advance me $200 for a press and that Gonzalo, in exchange for this, would do a piece of print for her worth twice as much, she immediately demurred and shrank. Suddenly I feel an immense fatigue. When I lose faith, when my eyes are opened, then for me it is like death.

Monday morning Virginia came with typed diary pages. I wrote eighty pages for Ruder. To help those who needed money, I spread the writing of erotica recklessly and reached a point of danger to myself. I bear the responsibility of their writing, supplying paper, arranging meetings, interceding for advances, advising, correcting, and the brunt of the rejections and Ruder's complaints. The only moment of pleasure is when I carry in my pocket the money so eagerly, so desperately awaited by the hungry poets.

Seon Givens telephones (she was working at the Gotham Book Shop, met a rich young man, may marry him and become a publisher). "I love *The Winter of Artifice*. I want to do something of yours." She has the fervor and the love that it takes to do things.

NOVEMBER 23, 1941

Dr. Jacobson: "You've lost five pounds in three weeks. There's nothing I can do for you. You're spending yourself so fast no amount of injections can help you recuperate. Your heart is strained. You have to rest, eat at home, get calm."

Trembling, taut, vibrating, exhausted. Stayed home two days, revised *Winter of Artifice* for Seon Givens and Wayne Harris, the delightful and intelligent young couple, my future publishers. Seon was born on the Island of Aaron, masculine, exuberant, Harris is feminine and like Durrell in appearance. Their understanding of my work is exceptional.

NOVEMBER 26, 1941

Successful tea at the New School for Hugo's exhibit. Paul Rosenfeld bought a print. The warm bloom of many friends—the Imbs, Caresse, Kay Boyle, Eduardo, Frances Steloff, Lucia and Francesco Cristofanetti. Hugo expansive, glowing, Jupiterean, with a healthy color, warmth, efflorescence. Grateful to me, telling me: "You created it all."

I can only see my future work as a completion, for each day I see more...even looking back into the past, the figures do not grow less distinct, but infinitely more meaningful... Often I look back, from the Eduardo of today to the youthful one. Today he is thirty-seven but he looks youthful, he looks innocent, and, but for hardly perceptible signs, like a man of twenty-seven. He is graceful, charming, golden. Only now and then I catch the suddenly loose, lax expression of the child, the decadent immaturity. Then it is as if he were deteriorating as a perverse child might and not a man, as if I caught the contortions of the baby's face when it is about to cry, the feeling of lack of control of the muscles, the too easily opened mouth, the disintegrated laughter. Then again he can easily hide this, and I see the suave man who still can deceive women as to his tastes, as he never has effeminate gestures, but merely the actor's smoothness. So women are still drawn to him. Luise said: "He is like the first man I loved. He is quite beautiful." Caresse preferred him to George Barker. Robert was warmed by his glow until he discovered the child where he was looking for a firm, severe father, and an analyst where he desired a poet. To cover up his timidity and paralysis in writing, he puts forward frightening edifices of quotations. He is practically drowned in research work. He thinks the source of his statements will be questioned. He seeks reinforcement and stilts.

I REMEMBERED THIS

My first erotic feeling

NEW YORK, NOVEMBER 26, 1941

Notes on future work: While writing the erotica I remembered this: In Brussels we lived in a two-storied house. I was seven or eight years old then. My father always took us to the attic to be whipped. He did not want my mother to hear us. She would interfere and get angry at him, and the struggle usually ended in a great battle between my father and mother. So the punishments always took place in this low-ceilinged room, cluttered with trunks, rags, broken dolls, old curtains, moth balls, old books and music. As far as I can remember, we all hated this and begged to be forgiven. The walk up the stairs was usually spent trying to persuade our father that we were innocent and did not deserve punishment. I remember I wept violently at the humiliation and hated my father. Now I ask myself if the hand which administered the powerful spankings must have awakened, at the same time as the pain, a region of pleasure. I do not remember feeling the pleasure then, but much later when I remembered the beatings it was as if the warmth of the hand had awakened not only the pain at the blow, but the dormant regions of sensibilities around the backside. It was as if the beating had come too near to the place where pleasure is felt and then entangled and related in the body, both the pain and the pleasure suddenly revealed as close to each other and related. I never became aware of the link between them until I was walking down the boulevards one night and I entered one of those places where they show erotic lantern slides for one penny. I had already seen four or five scenes of embraces, men and women rolling

86

over on the grass, women caught in their bath, whores undressing, and then I saw the following scene: It was in a schoolroom. Many little girls sat on a bench, wearing very short skirts such as I wore as a child. The teacher was growing angry at them. Finally she ordered one of them to walk up to her desk and she scolded her. The little girl answered impudently. The teacher took the little girl, laid her across her knees, lifted her skirt, unbuttoned her pants, and began spanking her sharply. As I watched this scene I felt the most amazing pleasure. I was stirred, I grew wet between the legs, and began to palpitate, almost reaching the orgasm. This was a revelation. I could not remember experiencing this pleasure as a child. It must have come as an aftermath of the pain. The pain created the warmth, and ultimately a feeling of pleasure.

When I discovered this it became a fantasy which I used when I could not feel the orgasm with Gonzalo. I would imagine this scene in the attic from the very beginning. I would close my eyes and imagine the attic, and my father spanking me. In doing this his hand would slip and touch my sex. The warmth of the spanking spread to the sex between my legs. I would say to myself: now my mother is slowly coming up the stairs to stop this, slowly coming up to see what my father is doing. She will catch him spanking me and she will try to stop him. I must enjoy it before she comes up (and how clearly I felt this warm hand on my backside, or was it Gonzalo's warm hand, and Gonzalo's Spanish words). He is spanking me, but it is like a violent caress, and it arouses me sexually. I must open and enjoy it more and more before we are stopped by the mother (before Gonzalo satisfies himself and stops moving inside me). My father is spanking me, my backside is warm, feverish, and all around it, it is spreading, the warmth and fever… And seeing this image I would have the orgasm.

My wedding night: Hugo very exalted and romantic. He read me a poem. He kneeled before me and uttered wonderful words of worship. Then we turned the light off and slipped into bed. I wore a white satin nightgown. He was inexperienced. He had never made love to a woman before. He rubbed his body against mine. I did not know what to do either. All I knew was that it would hurt and that there would be blood. I did not even lift my nightgown. Hugo never got his sex into me at all. He rubbed his body against mine, the penis against my belly until he came all over my nightgown. I was so amazed to feel this enormous penis where before I had felt something soft and small. I was so amazed by the wetness of my nightgown. My nightgown was stiff with sperm when I awakened. I felt sad, vague. Hugo was sad too. I thought that he did not love me. He thought that he was impotent. When I went to the hairdresser at the hotel to get my hair fixed he was jealous and went with me. That night we were to take the train home. I thought then it would happen, that he would take me really. But this time he had no erection. He began to weep, to excuse himself. I had a vague feeling that something was wrong. But all I felt was: he does not love me, he does not desire me. We were both terribly sad. When we got into our first apartment, then what Hugo liked was to get me to lie on the bed with my clothes on, and to raise my legs so that he could look. That was all he wanted, to look up between my legs, without pushing it and rubbed until he came. I would come too rubbing against him. That was all. We wore ourselves out this way, with excitement and frustration. Then one night I determined he would possess me altogether. He was afraid to hurt me. Every time he had tried he had found me too small and tight, and timidity and fear would make me even tighter. He was very big, I discovered later, unusually so, and I was rather small. But it was I who incited him one night to push in, it was I who made him. I did not complain about the pain. I incited him until he finally broke through the virginity, and the blood came, and it was done. But we were never made for each other. He was too big for me. And then he would always come too quickly, almost immediately, and I was slow. In fact, for months I did not know the deeper orgasm. I only felt the superficial orgasm of the clitoris, which he excited with his hands, but nothing deep down. The amazing thing was that it was only a year later in Paris that I felt the deep orgasm. We were living in a two-room apartment separated only by a curtain. My mother came to visit us. She slept in the salon, on the couch. She was tired from a long journey and fell heavily asleep. Hugo and I tried to get into bed without awakening her. Hugo wanted to take me. In the dark I was pleading with him. I was afraid my mother would hear us. My resistance inflamed him. In the darkness, in the secrecy, with the anguish I felt at the possibility of discovery, I suddenly felt this marvelous expanding, ecstatic rush of pleasure all through the body, like a strong liqueur bursting through the veins. I was spellbound. It was nothing like the pleasure of the clitoris orgasm. It was deep down inside of the womb, and such violent enjoyment. It was a revelation. Then I was aroused to the entire world of sex. I began to search through the quays for books on sex. I bought French dime novels which were illuminating. I found in the closet of the old bachelor whose apartment we were subletting, a memoir of a prostitute. When she was a little girl she was touched and tampered with by the tramps who slept under the bridges. But that was just the clitoris orgasm. Then at sixteen she was really possessed and she described what she felt at the full orgasm. This man placed her in a whorehouse. She could receive eight or ten men a day and feel nothing. But when her lover came he could arouse her to a frenzy.

Later my Spanish dancing teacher fell in love with me. He was about fifty but vigorous and agile, a man of the people. Below the dancing studio there were little dressing rooms, stuffy and small and badly lit. After the lesson the teacher would follow me into one of the little dressing rooms, and then, as I stood against the dresses and shawls, he lifted my skirt and kissed my sex until I grew dizzy. But I could never bring myself to go to his hotel room as he begged me to.

It also amazed me, much later, to discover that a man could rarely know when a woman had felt the orgasm. The penis is not sensitive enough to register the palpitation of the orgasm. If the penis is lying quiet inside of the woman it can feel the voluntary muscular contractions which imitate the contractions of the orgasm, but those of the orgasm are more feeble. A man could make certain by the accelerated heartbeat, but even this can come about from the sheer physical exertion.

When you are in love, you love every part of the body; when you are not in love there is always a part of the body you want to push away. When you are in love, after the desire is satisfied, you still love the body of the beloved. When you are not in love you want to push it away.

My first erotic feeling I experienced at the age of eight. I was playing with four or five children of my own age. We had exhausted all the games we knew and it was getting to the end of the afternoon. I remember the growing darkness, and how we passed from the room where we were playing into a glass hothouse. It was very hot and perfumed in there. The only lights came from the street. I don't remember whose idea it was, but someone suggested we take our pants off and show ourselves to the little boys. We did, but out of timidity perhaps, when we took our pants off, instead of facing the boys we turned our backs to them and leaned over as if to receive a spanking. I think we believed this was the interesting part to show. One of the little boys was not content to look. He approached me and placed his hand on my backside caressingly. Just at this moment we heard a noise. We all got dressed quickly. We were nearly caught by the parents.

DECEMBER 2, 1941

Since yesterday, there has been elation and power at the realization that I am completing a work, not about to begin one, but bringing my life task to full effulgence, efflorescence, fruition. Joy. The joy at discovering the diary is not just a sketch book, but a tapestry, a frieze being completed. When Gonzalo referred to its being hidden in a box, I answered, eluding all personal secrecy: "The condition of the work required it being done in darkness, inside of a box. Its condition of life is secrecy. It was born out of timidity. I lacked the audacity of the artist working in daylight (I write my stories in the morning, my diary at night). Secrecy produced this truth, and each day I grow farther away from feminine reflection and nearer to art, to objectivity. I have written the drama of the process, from the blurred reflection of the emotional waters to the terrifying lucidity of the mystic poet. I feel calm and lucid now, patient (before I was turgid, impatient, chaotic, hysterical, occasionally clairvoyant, often blind, careless, living so fast, writing in rhythm with it, negligent, excessive). Now I write more slowly. I even condescend to caress words and phrases. Before, I had contempt for technique, of words in themselves, of my tools, of labor. I have care and patience now. Timidity has marred my creative work outside of the diary (daylight). In the presence of others I assume poses, mannerisms, or the ultimate defense of perfectionism, the perfect diamond phrase no one can attack or wound, the perfection of *House of Incest* and my stories. A shield, shiny and polished. But inside of the box, my soul speaks, truly and simply. Secret.

Memories of my trips to Switzerland alone, which I considered my "healing place."

Every trip aroused in me the same curiosity and hope one feels before the curtain is raised at the theatre, the same stirring anxiety and expectation. With me it became almost painful, because I expected more than a spectacle; I expected my very life itself to begin, at any moment, there on the quays, and as I watched the people it was almost too painful, this expectation of the person who would make my life marvelous, who would transport me out of the impasse in which I had placed myself (the hopeless love for John Erskine, the paralyzing timidity). It was a hunger which did not come from any clear, precise region of my body, but it was gnawing and persistent like hunger. I was unaware of its nature. I was expecting someone. Every time a door opened, every time I went to a party, to any gathering of people, every time I entered a café, a theatre, I was expecting someone. My keen awareness made me quite clearly picture the worlds I imagined to exist, the personages in them. But my timidity locked me out from them. The flights of my childhood repeated themselves over and over again. Because of my father's brilliance, our house was always full of people who wanted to live in the effulgence he spread around him, people who delighted in his articulateness, in his gifts as an actor which made him enact every story he told like a play. I wanted to participate in this, yet my fears were even greater than my desires, and I ended by hiding myself in some corner of the house, in a place where no one could find me. Once there I meditated on the neglect of the world, on people's indifference—I reversed the process which had taken place and felt as if they had abandoned me, those who were laughing and talking (I always feel abandoned by those who are laughing and talking as if they had left me out, whereas it is I who get cut off by my own nature and separateness). I did not know that I had made the move out of the enchanted circle, fallen out of grace through my own timidity. And every day it was the same. I stood alone at the station, yearning to be a part of every intense, every joyous, every tragic moment, longing to be the woman who was weeping, the woman who was being amorously kissed before everyone, the woman who was handed flowers to wear, the woman who was laughing, the woman who was being helped into the train.

My marriage was a part of the hiding away, the refuge. It was a soft, dark, secure hiding place where I was sure of not being hurt, taunted, exposed. My husband was a shadow of myself then, projected all around me, who never separated from me, who echoed my moods, my joys and sorrows, who applauded my efforts, my courage and my weakness equally, who loved every aspect of me... As I boarded the train I was clearly aware of how difficult it was for me to move away, without my shell, without Hugo, without his reassuring presence.

Then I read *Lady Chatterly's Lover*, and I made two discoveries: first that I had never experienced the sensations described by Lawrence, secondly that this was the nature of my quest. But I was equally aware that something had created in me a state of perpetual defense against these very experiences, the same urge for flight which took me away from scenes of pleasure and excitement. I had stood many times on the very edge of it and then ran away. I myself was to blame for what I had lost.

My being was now urged to move forward and into the current of life. The book acted on me like the revelation of a submerged self, the one who wanted to feel love, desire.

The Hugo of that early part of our marriage—he spread his big body over mine and clawed at me, quickly, lightly, like a quick, heavy bird, and was soon satisfied and exhausted. A few short stabs into me and then his pleasure, and it was all over. Very rarely I felt the orgasm, and never again the deep one I had felt the time of my mother's visit. He made no caresses before, did not linger, or seek to create the mood. He walked towards me firmly, briskly, as if his will in this were sufficient to arouse the same desire in me. He never watched my face, my mood, waited for a certain light to appear in my eyes. He did not notice that I had no time to grow moist. He accepted the fact that he had to leave the bed and go and spread Vaseline between my legs to make it possible for him to penetrate me. In everything else he was sensitive, in this completely blind. He thought it was natural this way: the woman's immediate response to a willful act of desire. He was not disturbed when at times I could not pretend to have pleasure. He would say very quietly: "You are not in the mood for it? Then just be my little slave, just let me make love to you." These were the times when I did not have the courage to pretend, when he had already taken me the night before, and I felt unable to pretend. Then I would lie back absolutely inert and passive. I would even turn away my mouth so that he would not kiss me, and his kisses fell on my ears and neck. At such moments I hated him. I could not understand this great abysm between the man I liked to live with because he was so attuned to me, so sensitive, so enveloping, so protective, and this man who appeared at the moment of sex and who was an autocrat. This will which he did not show in our life together, which he yielded up completely during the day (for I was allowed to choose everything, the place where we lived, the movie, the book, the friends, the kind of life…he left everything for me to create as I pleased). But all this was somewhat like an abdication in exchange for the reversal which took place at night. During the day he refused to reign. He gave me a kind of worship, together with an acknowledgment that I was the leader and creator of our life together. But at night it was the will of the man, straight and firm, simple and direct, and to be obeyed. The will of the husband. No attempt at charming, seducing the woman, playing on her moods, awakening her desire. Merely the immediate consent to the sexual urge which came up in him with such firmness, like an order.

He never desisted or turned away, was not discouraged by my passivity. The little game that had grown between us, the habit of saying "be my little slave," then, became the usual story of our sexual life. I would lie down and take off as few clothes as possible if I were dressed. He would watch me undress. I would take off my panties, my garters, and stockings, and then nothing else. He would have to beg me to take off my dress when he wanted to touch my breasts. I exaggerated the difficulties. I would say: "This jacket takes too long to unlace. It's awkward. Let's not wait." I had a feeling against undressing completely. I did not like to feel his body. At times I felt obscurely that I had chosen him as one chooses a brother, a father to live with, some personage of one's family one likes to live with, but that I had not chosen him to lie naked with. I did not like his body. I liked the fervor of his love which was like some perpetually warm climate around me, but actually at the moment of possession I disliked to undress, and I disliked his mouth on mine. His penis was big; it entered into me with difficulty. Once inside of me it did not move nimbly; it was so big that it remained rigid, moving only in and out, quickly. And quickly it was over. Hugo always lamented this: "How quick," he would say, "Too quick!" And I lay like one that had been murdered, feeling the whole scene to be like an act of death rather than an act of life. Very often I felt angry at his forcing the sexual act on me against my unresponsiveness. I compared myself to the wax mannequins he liked so much. It was his only act of unfaithfulness, his love for the window mannequins. I felt sometimes their inanimateness must have reminded him of mine or that he must like this unreal wax inhuman coldness, or he would not walk out of his way to visit a particularly erotic one, and come to me speaking of their charms. He knew just where they lived, how they were dressed. He had his favorites: the one who wore a transparent black nightgown (like mine), the one in London who was naked under furs. He disliked violent, passionate, primitive women. The bestial nature of women frightened him.

All this was not apparent during the first years of my marriage. Our games sufficed then, and I enjoyed them, especially the caresses of his hands. I desired Hugo then, and could feel passion. It was only when my desire turned to John Erskine, and finally to Henry, that I discovered the deeper sensual joys which finally separated me from poor Hugo's inexperience. Was it inexperience which failed to awaken the deeper response, or merely sexual inharmony which became clear to me and not to Hugo? Hugo improved as a lover as I learned from Henry—but it was too late. My love for him had fixed itself on a fraternal pattern—my passion had turned towards Henry. Even today when I have no desire for Henry, I still can give myself without the revolt I feel towards Hugo. Towards Hugo I feel a tremendous obstruction, as if we had never been lovers, as if it were a case of incest, and this is no delusion because the proximity of our birthdays marks us as brother and sister. How is it that Hugo's nature adapts itself so well to incest and not to my nature? Because I have known authentic passion, perhaps.

Every book I wrote has brought me new friends, new realms, opened new houses, new experiences. The imagination brings forth personages which lie in the obscure regions of our being. They come to the surface, take form, appear in the book. And then the answering personage appears. I am sure when Lawrence wrote *Lady Chatterley* that Lady Chatterley appeared. When I wrote about Lawrence, Henry appeared, who was to represent the Sun for me, expansion and fertility. That is my own interest in writing, not to make a name, not to be exposed in libraries, or celebrated after death, but to create life, immediate life around me. I cannot go into new lives without my books. They are my boat and sail, my passport and map, my compass and telescope.

I write too, because creation is my way of reaching the "cosmic consciousness" of the mystics, because this highest point of my being is the point which survives and continues, and I know my highest self is the one who will not die.

If I were a man and I read the passages in my books of expectation, waiting, suspense, I would feel this: "This is my cue. I can enter now. This woman is ready to receive me. The atmosphere is propitious."

When, through lack of audacity, I turn back during my adventures and go home and write the book, the book I then use like dynamite to blast my way out!

DECEMBER 3, 1941

American style in writing—current and general—is commonplace, prosaic, pedestrian, homely, as French never is. Even in *Harper's* and *Vogue*, so-called aristocratic publications, there is a total absence of elegance, subtlety, nuances. Even there the plainness and ugliness is apparent. No wonder I have failed here. I am their antithesis. The poet is the antithesis of America. Just as they don't know "race," clothes, distinction, of any kind, their writing reflects vulgarity and looks shabby, seamy, like faded slippers for tired feet. Mongrels. But real mongrels acquire a personality from their wanderings. The American mongrel is bourgeois and colorless besides.

A speech I invented in the erotica which I wished someone had made to me: "You are the little girl who hid in fire escapes when people came to the house, in corners of balconies, under a shawl. Of course you realize that is a very subtle way of calling attention to yourself. It is another way, a most insidious way, of cutting a separated figure. Think what impression a woman makes if you find her sitting on top of a tree. The most haunting woman is the one we cannot find in the full café when we are looking for her, the one we must go on a quest for and seek through the disguise of her stories."

For Hugo I was perpetually traversing mysterious states he did not even seek to penetrate. He was there merely to console me on every return. He was always there to receive me from every kind of journey, secretly aware of my ordeals, never aware of what caused them. Blindly he showed his own joy at my return, from a night out or a trip to America, from France, or a return from Virginia. Blindly he consoled me for the grief caused me by John Erskine, and then by Henry, and then by Gonzalo. He asked no questions. For him it was a sufficient miracle that I should come home—his entire concern was that I should come home. My transformations he did not try to understand. I returned from the ordeal of John Erskine dead. He did not see the death. He was only aware that what exuded from me vivified him. Since the luminosity still attended me, he did not detect the death. When I returned at dawn with a Spanish cape and candle wax on my shoulder, he did not seek the cause. Now the *déroulement* of his own life supplies beautiful explanations. In Paris he stayed out with Jean in cafés, talking all night, or walking through the city. So Hugo thought: that is how Anaïs spent her nights. Now he gets sad and restless at ordinary cocktails or an evening with bank people or rich clients, and he thinks: that is how Anaïs got restless and sad, and what I saved her from when I gave her liberty.

When I first met Eduardo we were two children, two cousins lost in a huge family of many cousins, aunts and uncles. Eduardo rang the bell of 158 West 75th, when I was about fourteen. He came from college with his two brothers. They stood at the door and asked for my mother. I wore a pale lavender dress and my face was very pale. I was intimidated and flustered so I answered: "My mother is not in—she's out." "Of course she is out if she is not in," laughed the tallest cousin. Eduardo was taken into our games in the rooms that were not rented. I was presenting a play. We had made the costumes, and the scenario was my own invention, but it was not written because I held the theory that once I had told them the story (Thorvald, Joaquín, friends Eleanor and Gertrude) they should supply the words so that it would be spontaneous each time. It was torture for my unimaginative playmates! They stuttered. I was the *souffleur*. When Eduardo came we were having difficulty with the curtain. The programs were already painted, printed in handsome hand flourishes. But the curtain did not work. Eduardo helped. The costumes were made of all kinds of materials, mosquito netting for the princesses, Christmas tree tinsel, old dresses, discarded curtains. I was the Machiavellian, intriguing Black Queen.

Eduardo and I met again at big family dinners, holidays. We read each other's diaries. In Richmond Hill he began to write me letters and send me flowers he picked in the forest lying on moss in a shoe box.

But we were like two transparent myth people who never touched each other. We never even held hands. We got exalted, poetized, soared together at Lake Placid. I was the first one to experience a human emotion. All our life until then took place in the air, in words, on paper, in poems. Then, when I was sixteen, we went to a dance at Forest Hills Inn. There I saw that there was a great difference between the attraction other young men felt for me and my relation to Eduardo. The others wanted to hold me, found dancing an excuse to. They complimented me. And then I noticed that my body felt Eduardo's presence, and I wanted him to flirt with me, to admire me. But his body was dead to mine. It took me years to discover he was already a homosexual, and that of all the women in the world, I was the most tabooed one. I bore the name of his mother and his sister. Three Anaïses drawing around him the circle of incest.

When Hugo courted me Eduardo was passively, mysteriously jealous. But he accepted Hugo. Hugo was, in contrast to Eduardo, extremely present, vital, warm, powerful, assertive. The fantasy with Eduardo paled. Yet during my honeymoon, I wrote to Eduardo!

Gonzalo was sitting on the edge of the bed, had slipped his pants on and was fastening the buckle of his belt. I was not dressed yet. He showed me his belt. It had once been a strong leather belt with a silver buckle, but now it was so completely worn and frayed that it looked about to tear. The tip of it was completely frayed. The place where the buckle fastened on it was almost as thin as a piece of cloth. He held it in his hand and looked pensively down at it. "It is wearing out and it makes me sad because I've had it ten years." As I looked at him I became sharply aware of that moment so often repeated before he unfastened his belt to let his pants down. Each time it came with a little suspense; it was the prelude to a joy. He never unfastened it until some caress, some embrace had aroused his desire so that the confined penis hurt him. I never once unfastened his belt. There was always that moment of suspense before he unfastened it. Then he either takes out his dark sex for me to touch or places my hand within the pants for me to take it out. Sometimes he merely unfastens it and lets me fumble to unbutton the trousers and take his sex out. If I cannot unbutton the underwear quickly enough (I have a shyness about this, a fear to scratch or hurt him) then he does it himself. The little sound made by the buckle always affects me. It is an erotic moment for me. This time what I felt when he spoke of the ten years was a strange, sharp pain. I thought of the five years before he knew me, of the many times he must have unfastened it. I saw him unfastening it in other places, other rooms, at other hours, for other women. I saw him so vividly with his dark hand taking his sex out and some strange woman bending over it, another mouth. How often he had made this gesture for other women! I felt acutely jealous. I wanted to say: "Throw the belt away. Do not carry the same belt that you wore for them. I will give you another." It was as if his feeling of affection for the belt were an affection for the past that he could not rid himself of entirely. I remembered his early spontaneous confessions like mine. Early in our meetings he let fall: "I could always get whatever woman I wanted. I don't know why. It's a kind of magnetism." Later he amended (as I amended): "I had less women than you imagine. Many times I desired a woman and then because I didn't love her I couldn't do anything sexually."

Dr. Franz Horch, my literary agent, praises my work highly. But a new disappointment in my publication history—Wayne Harris and Seon Givens are dreamers. What money they had they already sank into poems by Patchen. I have to wait for this to appear and then sell, and then this money will pay for *Winter of Artifice*. This plan cannot come to any good. Patchen cannot feed my books. All this hurts my pride and adds to the lost time. One year lost when Caresse took the book and failed to print it. Another year lost when Beamish took it and failed to publish it. There is no protection for the writer.

How rich in meaning is The Voice in *Winter of Artifice*. What a *rouleau compresseur* I use, and how carefully it must be read. It's a perfume. Every word is weighty, full of implications. I can reread it, and extract nourishment from it like "compressed tea," a synthetic meal made for the modern age, even for parachute jumpers!

December 7, 1941
JAPAN DECLARES WAR ON UNITED STATES.

We are all asleep. America was caught asleep and schizophrenic. We, Henry, Eduardo, Gonzalo, Hugo and I are caught dreaming, loving, creating.

DECEMBER 12, 1941

Since Robert returned from the army, what crystallized was his external behavior, his attitudes, and he took the form I had persistently refused to see because of the inner Robert I knew from his diary. First what became clearer was his schizophrenic coldness. He always came in without a greeting, entered like a stone figure. Then, like some primitive, but without a sense of ritual, he sought food, directly, ruthlessly. He asked me for two dollars (I wept because since Robert read my diary I could not understand how he could have the insensitivity to ask me, knowing all my struggles). He looks dissolved, vacant. He cannot flow. He has eluded all external discipline (earning a living, etc.), and he has no spiritual discipline to hold him together. Suddenly I saw, and he acknowledged it, that he was eating my writing for his own pleasure, a young cannibal, not out of love. I turned away.

DECEMBER 13, 1941

Preparing for air raids, buying flashlights, tape for the windows so they will not shatter, dark curtains.

Eduardo wants to go to war to have the current, fraternal experience like the others...

"To escape your conflict," I say.

"I can't return home to bourgeois life and capitalism."

"Then give your life to communism, that's heroic. Going to war, for you, is suicide. Don't expect me to be objective," I said. "I am your mother. I can't send you to war."

Henry says, "Let him go." Gonzalo says, "He won't go. He is merely talking."

I copy twenty pages a day of diary 60 to catch up with the others. The diary is a gigantic rumination.

DECEMBER 25, 1941

Robert reading my diary and feeling nothing. Letting me serve him. Asking for money. Finally I see the insanity of this, the shut-out feelings, the disconnection. He took Bob sexually, a whim, causing Virginia pain, not feeling her pain, hating Bob. He found it necessary not only to inform Virginia of all this, but to read her full descriptions of the scenes from his diary.

With Henry I had a tremendous talk. He takes the side of the crazy Hitler, the ego, the criminal genius. I of Stalin, the sane, the powerful, the impersonal, the benefice. Henry likes the man who he thinks obliterates limitations (I said it isn't true, he merely refuses to see them, as madmen do, and overcomes them only by brutality and sadism). Henry takes the side of the inflated ego who justifies his acts by speaking of a divine guidance. These are the symbols of our drama: Stalin, true power by a contact with reality, conquering by real strength, not fanaticism. Hitler the Satan, the dark, the criminal born of humiliations. I said to Henry: "The criminal is the man who revenges himself for the harm done to him by society a MILLION TIMES—that is the criminal, the man who, because you denied him bread once, kills a hundred persons. That's Hitler. Germany was humiliated always for its aggressiveness, its brutality. It has become a monster." Hitler will fall, of course, because he has a false power, the power of the madman who cannot see the human limitation to power (the generals who failed in Russia he punished, not realizing it was natural they should fail, faced with a stronger enemy, not seeing the real profound reason for their failure). War is only the drama we made on a higher scale, out of our weakness, hatred, negativism, neurosis, fear, schizophrenia.

There is a side to Henry that is criminal, identifies itself to the criminal. In *Cancer* there was a total absence of feeling. Today his absence of feeling for France is appalling, inhuman, after ten years of life there. Why? I have sometimes a feeling for even a particular tree in Paris, a sudden tender remembrance of a certain street. Henry nothing.

JANUARY 5, 1942

I had an amorous and beautiful dream of Chinchilito, and the next morning I received a card from him that he was going to telephone. He didn't telephone at the appointed day, but Saturday night I had another dream, and the next morning he telephoned. He came at four—the afternoon before New Year's. As we talked he caressed me, raising my skirt. His long-fingered artist hand, smooth and soft and nervous. More and more caresses. He hid his head on my breast, tenderly. More and more caresses of the hands. Then he took me—lingeringly, with strength, with power, with tenderness, uttering caressing words in German, his youthful vigor and maturity, his wonderful knowingness, strength and fervor, our mouths together, his beautiful face bowed over mine, amorous, luminous. *Point lumineux de ma vie. Point lumineux de rêve*, outside of human life. At the end, small moth kisses on the face, romantic kisses. Silence, and hushed words in caressing tones… Chinchilito, I whispered. And I, of course, timid, unable to enjoy it fully, yet enjoying all but the orgasm. I rose with a desire to dance. Feeling light and joyous, the only joyous moments of the holiday. His wavy gold hair, his luminous teeth, his fantastic tallness. Siegfried—the Nordic God. So beautiful the moment. When I hear music it is this moment I love again. When I dance alone, it is this moment that makes me dance. *Chinchilito!*

THE PRESS

I don't want to think—I want to do some typesetting

NEW YORK, JANUARY 8, 1942

Hugo has given me $100 for the press. Press $75, type $30, miscellaneous $20. We shall begin reprinting *Winter of Artifice* (the "Father" and the "Voice" sections only).

I have been copying volume 62, arranging carbons and pages for Virginia and Janet (when they are finished I will have a double of the whole diary except for the first ten volumes in French), binding the work already done in black folders, clipping the rice paper copies for the boxes to be deposited at Thurema's (in case of air raid). Work has integrated me. I am content. I have no time for obsessions.

I had to console Henry for his one failure: the American book. His worst book. I hope it is the deadly effect of America on him and not the disintegration I have seen take place now in every artist around me who has abandoned himself to his every whim, lack of discipline, fancy, dadaism, instinct, negativism, that falling apart of the self-indulgent, the liberated unconscious, the loss of contact with human reality. I am concerned over Henry. In freeing him, protecting him, I have nurtured both his dream and his weakness. He has a cult of his own naturalness; he has defended his defects. Whatever influence I had on his writing was indirect—it was an effect on his being—but when I judged a fragment directly, Henry never yielded. A very lurid piece of writing which I fought to keep out of *Black Spring* he had printed in the *Wisdom of the Heart*.

When I began to feel this break with the insane, the delirious, with Luise, with Robert, I also broke with my own obsessions, negations, weaknesses and confusion. It was to enter an integrated world of work and synthesis.

But Henry? In the American book the ego appears in its ugliest form: irritable, irrational, contrary, quarrelsome, petty, prosaic. Here he is no prophet, and he exposes only his unrelatedness to the present. His great habit of not living in the present, which may be the mark of the prophet, in the case of the American book simply becomes an expression of the same confusion in the childish youth of America. And here Henry praises the blubberings of Dudley, the abortions of Patchen, the uncreated. It is a dadaist world, but no longer humorous. A cult of off-values.

There is great confusion between the Henry of detachment, the mystical impersonality, the cosmic attitude, and the schizophrenic Henry who is not wholly present in the experience. It is not the sage's removal, but the unrelatedness of the schizophrenic. I am not certain where he stands now. I have left him so free—perhaps too free. I should say rather I have abandoned him and his work. I myself went through a dark age, but today I feel whole again. I am not confused. I may be able to help him. I see everything clearly. Through communism I have faith, a sense of reality. It gives one strength. When Hugo thinks to overwhelm me by saying: "Your work would not be accepted in Russia," I am confused. First I say: "My work was not accepted by the bourgeois world. If I had lived in Russia I would not have written that kind of work—it would have been acceptable to Russia, what I would have written. My present work reflects the decadent world I lived in. In Russia it would have been something else."

Everything is clear. I made my break with the inhumanity of Robert and the absence of creative discipline in all of them (Barker drinking the $68 I helped him to earn after I spent two sleepless nights thinking of his need). I turned away from the weakness I cannot share.

But Henry? Where is Henry? How can I help him? What can I impart to him now? Gonzalo is a transformed being now. He is becoming integrated. Henry? The reviews of the Greek book are not good. People attack his rantings, affirmations, contradictions, the same defects I fought. Several irritating wild shots, egotistical shots, mar the beauty of the work.

JANUARY 16, 1942

The press is put together. I began typesetting, took me an hour to do half a page. Did the first page of *Winter of Artifice*.

Henry gave me $25 and pushed me. Hugo $150 and Eduardo $25. Barker too, spoke for the press.

Monday I finished copying the recent diaries (all but this one) and will go to work regularly at the press, morning and afternoon.

Overwhelmed by tenderness again when Henry suffered from the failure of the American book, but I had to be truthful, I had to say it was not good. I see him fragile, bowed. I see him again in relation to money, unable to cope with the problem, and sad that I was the only one who helped him on his trip. Today even, nobody helps him.

TUESDAY, JANUARY 20, 1942

At six o'clock in the evening, the first proof print. Setting by Eduardo and me, printing by Gonzalo.

JANUARY 21, 1942

We learned the hard way, by experience, without teaching. Discovering alone, inventing, testing, seeking, searching, initiative. Eduardo got books on printing from the library and tips from Cooney. Mostly application and effort. We worked with fervor and intensity.

JANUARY 25, 1942

We reset the whole thing. It was too loose. Worked eight hours a day. Eduardo is patient, Gonzalo uses his strength, and I my deftness. We dreamed, talked and ate the press. So much to learn. All three of us very enthusiastic. Sovietic. Gonzalo is active, dynamic. Getting up early, doing everything at once, organized, transformed. Eduardo for the first time passionate. Halfway through the work Seon began to quarrel with the Gotham Book Shop. So many factors intervened (Wayne's laziness, Seon's drinking and chaos) that I decided to break with them and work independently.

JANUARY 28, 1942

Did the final version of the announcement (the original is wider). I had to cut it up to paste in the diary, and do Hugo's engraving.

Overworked. Took care of Henry for two days (laryngitis). Today I'm home with a cold. The corner has become a workshop. When Hugo comes to the press we draw up the bed against the wall, cover it like discarded old junk. We talk press, invent, plan. I have no money for the paper.

The relation to handicraft is nourishing, beautiful. Related bodily to a solid block of lead letters, to the weight of the composition tray, to the adroitness of spacing, the tempo and temper of the machine—you acquire some of the weight of the lead, the strength and power of the machine, the bodily conquests and triumphs. You live in the hands, in physical deftness, in the development of your faculties pitted against concrete enemies. The victories are complete, concrete, definite and proved. How much greater than abstractions and theories. Eduardo says: "I don't want to think—I want to do some typesetting."

FEBRUARY 5, 1942

Battle with Robert. For once, I did not elude battle, did not let him leave for Berkeley thinking there was a bond. I told him what I thought of his behavior, and an ugly monster suddenly appeared, mean, small, poisonous, using all his knowledge of my intimate life, my vulnerability, to attack. At one moment I was so repulsed, I said: "How ugly you look." Robert's weakness and impotence makes him ugly and evil. He tried to destroy the protective edifice which holds my world together, tried to reveal Henry's presence to Hugo, my deceptions to Gonzalo, out of impotence.

FEBRUARY 16, 1942

After I threw Robert out of my house, with scorn and the desire to beat him, I went to the press, and I was happy in the work. And then at night, happy in the moment of frenzy with Gonzalo, Gonzalo crying out his pleasure. Home to Hugo, delicate and sensitive—then I knew I had a whole, complete, wonderful life on a level which makes others appear as barbarians and failures. I know I have reached one way of fulfillment, not like Henry's, but *fulfillment*, and I was deeply, deeply grateful. I understand the impotent rage of those who approach what I have—which they cannot create or reach—and why they tear at me, try to hurt me and destroy what I have: because they can't have it.

FEBRUARY 24, 1942

The abridged diary was considered by Houghton Mifflin of Boston who writes: "There is no doubt it is a remarkable performance that should someday be published and may well achieve permanence as the ultimate in neurotic self-absorption—a kind of decadent Saint Teresa. Certainly the writing is extraordinary: the cadences, the ability to communicate an intensity of emotion. But I don't think this is the time to bring it out. Today such morbid preoccupation with one's inner life will seem trivial. My guess is that it is a book to see the light about five or ten years after the war is over. When the author does prepare it for publication my advice would be to cut out the redundancy rather than the sex. In fact, I'd trim lightly here and with an eye merely on the law. The erotic element is part of its uniqueness. It underlines the impression of candor and leads even the unwilling reader on."

Suicides all around me, particularly of refugees, uprooted people. When I hear Djuna Barnes is a broken being my heart stops for a moment. I feel I should go to her and print her books. Meanwhile John Dudley had a breakdown, and Flo tried to commit suicide with scissors. Seon is drinking herself into sottishness. Wayne is being coerced by his family into going to war in order to save the "family honor" tainted by the rumors of his homosexuality.

APRIL 22, 1942

Taking the letter out of the box, placing it next to the T, then a comma, then a space, then on and on...Gonzalo running the machine...day after day. We are nearing the end.

Gonzalo no longer lazy, degenerate, self-reproachful, ashamed, stagnant. No change in Eduardo—his pettiness and jealousy are stronger than ever, his shrinking, miserly soul. He is an abstraction with so few human feelings, so small, not the man of tomorrow, not communal, fraternal, or expanded. Reading Algernon Blackwood, I know I am the woman of tomorrow. I know I can expand to the new consciousness. I know too that I have been so subtle in *Winter of Artifice* that my meaning escapes everyone. I have said so much, so much in a mysterious way.

I am the woman of tomorrow, and that has been the greatest cause of my suffering—not just an unstable neurotic mystic, fighting against the insanity which has overtaken the artist and the oversensitive in this period of violence and horror, but a highly developed instrument seeking not to be destroyed by the great violence, not to be rendered deaf by the machine guns, to be able to carry on its vibrations, its extraordinary wave perceptions.

In the evenings I lie in bed addressing envelopes, copying lists, writing letters. There have been days of great sensuality when Henry desired me and Hugo and Gonzalo desire me, and I give myself to the two lovers sensually—with enjoyment. There have been days of disconnection when Henry wrote so much that he was empty, without desire, and when Gonzalo was ill and impotent. There have been days of great jealousy and suffering when I met Gonzalo taking Helba to a communist evening reunion, and I wept. And when Henry, after feverishly writing a rape story June told him about, was nervous, taut, and so cerebral, so transposed he got me into bed and was impotent. I said: "You are living with June now, not me." But he denied this completely and said on the contrary he was truly burying June now, a real burial, a real death, though even that he did not need to do because it was all dead already and he had no compulsion to write. It is true—he is only writing to fill the void of our American life, composed merely of reflections of our life in Paris, sad echoes of a finished experience. As I am printing to fill the void, others are committing suicide. While I finish *Winter of Artifice* in which *La Vida Es Sueño*, The Nightmare grows immense, bigger than my delicate registering faculties can enclose. I may be Spanish in my courage, but I am not the *Passionaria* who can bear the chamber of horrors of an entire tortured world.

JUNE 7, 1942

The book was finished Tuesday, May 5, at eleven-forty-five at night. Gonzalo and I, alone, did the cover. It was delivered by the book binder at my home Friday, May 15, at noon. Then began a series of successes, compliments, letters and continuous sales. A triumphant tea at the Gotham, a crowd of people. The book created a sensation by its beauty. The typography by Gonzalo, the engravings by Hugo, were unique, enough to put the big publishers to shame. Today, three weeks later, I have sold sixty books, Gotham fifty, and they have asked for twenty-five more. I received compliments from Otto Fuhrman, teacher of graphic arts at the New York University, from art galleries, orders from collectors, a letter from Laughlin of New Directions offering me a review of four thousand words, which William Carlos Williams will write.

SEPTEMBER 23, 1942

New York again. In July we worked on Hugh Chisholm's book of poems, against the odds of heat waves, Panamanian humidity, swamp fumes, and all the filthy climates of the world which concentrate in New York. In August we went to Provincetown. Gonzalo was supposed to have landed in Truro, to create a distance and pacify Helba, but he couldn't do it. He came to be near me. But the summer was peaceful. Hugo being there all the time, I did not see much of Gonzalo. Only one night together, as we sat on a dark wall by the Bay and caressed each other. As Gonzalo lifted his face in the exaltation of his pleasure, I saw it against the water and dark sky—a mask of emotional ecstasy.

I knew I would not need the diary. I divined that nothing would happen, no more Chinchilitos. Helba was busy choking on a fish bone and stirring up the neighborhood, Gonzalo was bored, the town was almost empty and dead. We swam to the continuous sounds of depth charges. My only pleasure was to swim under water with my eyes open, and my hair floating. I did not return as strong as I did last year.

Henry is still in Hollywood. Eduardo is called for his physical examination for the draft. Ruder has been drafted and has disappeared altogether.

NO PUEDO MAS

I do not want you back

NEW YORK, SEPTEMBER 23, 1942
Letter from Henry in Hollywood:

I think we're both confused in speaking of WORK. There's nothing wrong, I'm sure in the idea that what we are all seeking is to do the work we like and are fitted for. You shouldn't be angry when I call you a worker. You've always been—it began long before you knew me. What embitters you in regard to me is that you fear your work has borne no fruit, or that it's in danger of being nullified. I admit I owe everything to you... I've said it time and again. What mystifies me is this: that if you, or anybody, make such sacrifices for another, is it because that the other has something more important to offer than the mere performance of his duty? The question, in my own mind as well as yours, seems to have shifted from the accomplishment (due to protection) to the means employed (dependence on others). Perhaps the whole trouble is that I am thinking as an absolutist. That's either my virtue or grand defect. All you're asking for is that I take a relative view of the problem and circumstances. Perhaps I have a great fear, unacknowledged, that if I compromise I will go under completely. I am possibly the only writer in our time who has had the chance to write only as he pleased. Perhaps this was bad. I wonder. Because actually on all sides life imposes compromises. I make compromises in daily life—too many, according to you. And I don't, or won't, with the writing. Logic dictates that to hold that position, I should make greater compromises in life. Perhaps I have never made any real ones. I may have written you foolishly about renunciation versus sacrifice. One might say of me that I have done only what I wanted to do, that I derived pleasure from my so-called renunciations. How can I answer that? Everything depends on the motive behind the question. If I am to be judged, then I am guilty. If it is not a question of judging but of understanding my behavior, then possibly it is not so easy to answer that question.

I know from previous discussions with you, when we are involved emotionally, that the very thing you blame me for when angry, you condone or even approve of when you are calm. One thing is clear—I am not angry with you. I am listening to you like a child. I feel I have done wrong. But you know that is not something I did just yesterday, or the day before. I am not acting differently now than before. I am true to character. At these moments you make me feel that there is something fundamentally wrong with my whole character. I don't say you're wrong. If there is something fundamentally wrong with me I want it to come out. I'm perplexed. I'm tormented. I'm looking for the light. I am not even riled when you use words like hobo and clochard. I know I am not these things, I am essentially a worker—contradictory as all this sounds. Can't you see that my desire to create instead of work is a sound, natural instinct, based on a worthy impulse? Of course you do—or you wouldn't have done everything for me as you did. Maybe it all boils down to this: if the present circumstances will not permit me to create then I should at least work, just as everybody else does. But I wouldn't be writing you these irritating letters if it wasn't that I gravely doubt this, and honestly, not as a dreamer or idler. It's the old Chinese proverb problem, of whether inaction (sometimes) is not better than action. I admit it is difficult to defend this when you commence hurling accusations of inhuman at me. But damn it, you know I am not inhuman. And if you don't, who will? [...]

For a long time now I have honestly never tried or even wished to cause another pain. But to eliminate pain (to others) is almost an impossibility. Especially if it comes about because I am being myself. That is right and just…that's one's destiny. I don't quarrel about that. All my troubles, at the moment, are caused by the mere fact that I am trying more and more to be myself. If this self is a monster, then the sooner it is recognized the better. You have doubts at times, you question the wisdom of all you have done to help me. But if you were just helping me to be more and more myself, how could that be unwise? Or are you implying that I am not myself now? And if I don't know how can you? If I am perplexed now how can you be so clear? I know that you're trying to help me see clearly. But what I also think is that you're worrying about something else…perhaps that I am concealing something from you. You're hammering at me for one thing and meaning another, isn't that it?

Well, listen, don't think that way—you're wrong. You had the same uneasiness when I was in Greece. But I tell you that whenever I am away from you, you only grow in stature. It would be impossible for me to fall in love with someone else. You have no rivals. All other women seem petty, insignificant. I couldn't be faithless if I tried. You've made me immune. What you can't understand is that I can say this and mean it, and yet act apparently indifferently. Talk about wonderful climates, the joys of creation, the pleasure of being alone, etc. There are no contradictions here—only those made by your own fear of losing me. I don't have those fears about you. Not that I don't think it possible for you to fall in love with someone else. Everything is possible. But I don't go after you and chide you for wrong reasons.

As a matter of fact, I haven't anything, and never did have anything, to reproach you with. You have been, and still are, perfection. I admire you more and more and respect you more and more. Where I get baffled is that, the moment I talk about realizing our relationship more fully and deeply still, you say I ruined that possibility, and that my actions are a betrayal of any such desire. True! But only because you have no faith in my desire. Because in some uncanny, feminine way, you succeed in making me say: "I prefer liberty" when, with a little more honest effort, you could just as well succeed in making me say: "I prefer a life with you above everything." This is not recrimination. I know as I write the above that you are just as powerless to act differently as I am.

We have this situation we are in because of what we are essentially. By choosing to live above the ordinary levels we create extraordinary problems for ourselves. You mention Russia and Shangri-La, as though you look to the one and I to the other. I've been all over the Russian experiment in my mind. For me it would not be a solution. Neither would Shangri-La. Both are initial, preparatory steps or modes of existence towards living the life of this world with and for other human beings. The ultimate goal is to make this earth a paradise. But that's how I'm trying to live all the time—as it were. I don't have to conquer any capitalist in myself, nor do I, as in Shangri-La, have to strive towards moderation. I am the ideal citizen for both these states of being. I am ready—but the conditions are absent. It's as though I had to live backwards, from some better condition of the world (which is natural to me and which I was born into) to some stupid and deplorable one. I have already lived the life people are dreaming of not only imaginatively but actually. So have you. The difference is that you adapt yourself better to the backward state. That's what you call being human. You may be right.

Another difference is that with this criterion of human you emphasize the need for struggle. But to me struggle is relatively unimportant. How can I struggle when I have already achieved? [...] This struggle is on a level which I have outgrown. Both the materialistic philosophy of the Russians and the Oriental philosophy aim to lift man above this struggle. I believe in a collective life unqualifiedly. I've often told you I don't mind in the least what would be asked of me—I would willingly dig trenches, ditches. I could even be a slave—it wouldn't disturb me. Notice, too, that wherever there are monks, people are devoted to spiritual ends, they always practice a high form of collectivism. I am not against doing dirty work—I merely see and feel the futility of doing work for no good purpose. [...] It seems absurd for me to fight with you concerning my essential character.

Whatever truth is in me will assert itself, no matter what I do or say. I accept you as you are. I wouldn't want to change you one bit. The more I go along the less I want to change anybody.

And now I want to answer you about Hugo and yourself. You say we would all like to do this and that...the easiest thing. First of all, it isn't the easiest thing—what we are talking about. Doing what one wants to do is the very hardest thing in the world. The easiest thing is to compromise, to do what others want you to do. Hugo did not fail to become an artist because he had to protect you. He much preferred to do what he did—it was easier for him, considering his nature and temperament. I don't think you can accuse me of quibbling here. And as for you, you know very well, you've often admitted it—self-sacrifice has been your curse. We all have different roles. There's some deep, inexplicable reason why we live out both the virtues and defects of our character, not just the one or the other. The virtues are perhaps the flowering of previous inner struggles, in other existences...who knows? [...]

And yet, despite all I say, it devolves upon me to do something. If, thanks to you (and maybe thanks just a little to my own efforts), I have been lifted out of our time... even at the very worst, if I am just dreaming (and how wonderful to dream! Why is it such a sin?)...nothing will put me back except chains. I can do forced labor, like the convict. I tell you, I can forget everything that ever happened, forget all that I ever did, all I dreamed of, and live the life of a dolt...I can do it.

But what will it prove, what good will it do? Will that prove me to be human, like everybody else? I don't say that is what *you* wish. I know very well you don't...I know you are trying to tell me that is what the world wants. You are trying to get between me and the world, act as a buffer, intermediary, *accoucheur*. But why spare me? What happens if you die? And sometimes I ask myself: who is protecting whom? Can one protect another? Isn't there a mutual need, a mutual dependence? Why is there always someone to protect the artist, the non-doer, the non-utilitarian? Is it because some few people realize the preciousness of art? Are they protecting the artist or are they helping to perpetuate something which they vitally need? [...]

You express a fear of having to live with others, by their grace, etc. I respect that. For me it's less difficult. I am always curious to see how far people will go, how big a test one can put them to. Certainly there are humiliations involved, but aren't those humiliations due rather to our own limitations? Isn't it merely our pride which suffers? It's only when we demand that we are hurt.

I, who have been helped so much by others, ought to know something about the duties of the receiver. It's so much easier to be on the giving side. Much of the scrupulousness which people evince is due to a real lack of magnanimity. Giving seems to confer upon them a sense of superiority. To receive is much harder—one has actually to be more delicate, if I may say so. One has to help people to be more generous, more magnanimous. You do them a service—if you are honest about it. And then, finally, no one likes to do either one or the other alone. We all try to give and take, to the best of our powers. It's only because giving is so much associated with material things that receiving looks so bad. Ultimately it's only an accident that one is on one side of the fence and the other on the other. If it were not so there would be no giving…one would eliminate the beggars. But that would be a terrible calamity for the world.

The beggar is just as important in the scheme of things as the giver. If somewhere there should be a true and just form of collective life in which begging is eliminated, it will only be the crude aspect of it. Actually there will always be the beggar—if only the beggar of mercy. God help us if there should be no longer the need to appeal to some other human being, to make him give of his richness. Of what good is abundance then? Must we not become strong in order to help, rich in order to give, and so on? How will these fundamental aspects of life ever change? The trouble now is that people are poor in spirit, low, mean, envious, jealous. The change they envisage is not towards the expression of greater magnanimity, but of protection against humiliation, protection of their petty egos, their petty pride, their petty prejudices.

You use the word "confused." I'm not nearly as confused as you might suppose. You know, I'm always on guard against your clarity. You spool it off with invincible logic always. It seems very clear—on the surface. But I am not so sure of your innate clarity. With you there is a racial clarity. You're diamond pointed. You must see well in order to act. With me it's rather the opposite—I must act in order to see. I'm always making discoveries…perhaps in circles. Sometimes I do succeed in leaping out of the clockwork. Miracles I'm not finished with myself, with my self-experimenting. Sometimes I have to lie still, like the possum, and just watch and wait. You are always ready for action, always armed, always on the alert.

I admire that in you—but I haven't those qualities. The faster you run the more I want to slow up. I look for ambushes. You leap precipices like a *chamoix*. My god, Anaïs, the one great torment I have always and forever is—how can I repay all the kindnesses done me? When I speak of magnanimity of being able to receive as graciously as giving, can't you see that I take that to heart first of all myself? No matter how much I do I shall never become generous enough. I pay not in the coin of the realm but out of my own substance. Sometimes you perceive in that something akin to the whoring spirit. Yes, at its worst it might be that. But at its best, it's an endeavor to pay with a better, cleaner coin, to pay with blood. In the end I will pay with my life, that's what it amounts to. So part of my struggle is to conquer this vicious round, to get free of debt and payment… not to give or take, but to give and take equally at the same time…so that it becomes different, something like radiation. That means transubstantiation. Alchemy of the spirit. How does one achieve that? By fulfilling all his earthly duties? By living up to the letter of the law? No, somehow it must happen like a revolution, a swift inward turn, a different tempo, different rhythm, different orientation. I don't know yet.

Letter to Henry (sent before previous letter from Henry was received):

Henry: Yesterday I wrote you an emotional letter, probably as contradictory as yours. I reread your letter, the last one, and now I see it more clearly. My attitude is a necessary balance to yours and I need not defend it. What has happened is that when I asked you to help me, I pushed you into a conflict. Now listen: we are making it too important. In the first place I always said lately: help me until I get the press going. Also I said: help me partially. Now look: the press is making a success. I feel confident now. I have work until December. What complicates the issue for me, and confuses it, is your sudden insistence on one place rather than another. I can cope with the problem of taking care of you, but I can't cope with the problem of how to do so in Hollywood. Now look, Henry. The place has become important to you because you feel the conflict less when you're away from me. For one thing, you don't see me anxious or tired, and that's a relief to you. For another the climate and lessening of expenses gives you the feeling again that there it is easy and here a strain. I'm ready to do whatever you want. I'm not asking you to take a job. I want you to cease suffering from this conflict, to cease fearing New York merely because it becomes more acute here. On vacation I get lulled too. I could forget even your needs. But not for long. And you want to maintain that vacation insouciance. All right. You know I never want to push you into anything that causes you misery. Stay away as long as you need to. Determine to do what you can, like showing my manuscripts or what you want to. And don't create a monster out of New York, not permanently at least because I can't live in Hollywood. You also torment me needlessly because you enjoy Hollywood and then you get afraid that so many separations will in the end separate us, and then you start to talk about our *partial* life and blaming that, when it isn't true at all, and what threatens to destroy us is your own quest for a paradise which can only be obtained at the cost of my not being in it. *Voilà.*

What I should write to Henry is that I no longer love him except as a child, and that I will continue to take care of him as a mother and thus free him to live where and how he pleases. Can I do this? *That is the truth.* Can I say it?

OCTOBER 7, 1942

The day I asked myself, "Has the time come for me to tell Henry the truth?" I received in the evening a voluminous letter in which he says he cannot fall in love with anyone else, that I am perfection and have immunized him! So again I kept my secret. It would be cruel to abandon him when he needs me, when I am the only one who takes care of him, the only one. Henry has written ten books which everybody reads, and can't have security even for his barest needs. Ben Abramson of the Argus Book Shop printed *The World of Sex*, sells it for $7, and Henry gets nothing.

Fraenkel sells the *Hamlet Letters* and gets $100 checks from the Gotham Book Shop, and Henry gets nothing (he wrote half the book, and it is selling because of his name). His books are reprinted *sub rosa*, and he gets nothing. Poor Henry.

Meanwhile *je me débât* with the money problems, a hopeless tangle. We are heavily taxed, and after Chisholm's poems we have no other orders. Caresse is poor and crazy, has plans but no money. This all makes me work for very little money, the poems of Kay Boyle's daughter, worthless echoes of adolescent readings. Finally I am forced to ask myself: are my stars bad? I have always believed myself responsible for everything. *La fatalité intérieur*, but slowly I see now outer incidents I have not caused: the war, my bad luck with the critics. Paul Rosenfeld, with the best will in the world, writes a review that betrays the secret I threw a veil over and proclaims loudly that the father in the *Winter of Artifice* is Joaquín Nin. Also he creates for everybody a confusion between the diary and the novel. William Carlos Williams, with the best will in the world, the best intentions, presents me as a female ogre, and makes me an enemy of man, by my honesty, and misunderstands me magnificently, regally! These two are the only reviews. Harvey Breit tried to write for me, but the editor of the *New Republic*, who normally accepts his work, is deposed, and the new editor does not like him. Fatality? The others ignore me. Complete silence from the *Times, Tribune, Time,* etc.

My underground success is continuous, from person to person, secretly, and quietly. But no *éclat*. And for that I am ready to *éclater*—I am rebelling against the petty restrictions, anxieties, the destructive, small, constant, harassing needs. It seems to me all the wonder of my life is being devoured. I must jump out of this. I thought the press would do it. A mirage. We were going to make $200 a month, but instead zero! Now what? The stairway. Always I think of the five flights I have to climb to get home. Somehow, in those stairs I climb after leaving Gonzalo or Henry, feeling the fatigue of the whole day and night, always what I meditate on, as I climb, is that Gonzalo needs a new pair of glasses and where will I get the money? As I climb, it seems to me that I am heavily burdened, and I see no way out of it. I cannot make money. I'm a worker, I'm clever, I'm dexterous, I'm talented, yet I cannot make money.

I wept. I am a failure.

In that alone!

OCTOBER 9, 1942

Shook off the wretchedness. Tried to get Sam Goldberg, the lawyer, to give me something to print. He read the diary. He was overwhelmed, he was moved, but does not help. I believe the whole world is jealous of my care and love of others—Henry or Gonzalo—and that is why they refuse to help me. Everybody thinks I am, symbolically, rich enough. Luise didn't want to give me anything. She felt poor, poor in love. I'm rich in love, so the world denies me material riches. I suspect it is malicious jealousy. Goldberg is devoted to me as a writer, yet when I turn to him for help, nothing. I turned to Dorothy (not begging, merely asking to be given something to print) and she failed me…all of them failed to help me. I am never helped, but I suppose it is my self-made destiny, carved out by my character.

Today my courage came back. Jacobson is helping the courage by fighting the anemia. The poor mystic Anaïs is watching the blood count rising, and as it rises, so do the courage and the power. The mystic is troubled. At three million red globules I felt the burdens crushing me, and Henry's attitude cruel. At three million five hundred thousand I felt myself soaring again, confident, ready to take the whole burden on myself again. At four million I feel expansive and all-powerful, although nothing has changed. Hugo meanwhile acts the role of Saturn at the bank: he makes people think of making testaments, advises pension trusts, reminds them of old age, sickness, counsels savings, investments, caution, foresight, and naturally brings some of that undertaker gloom to the house! With the same gravity he discusses the budget, the taxes, his pension.

Though I fully realize our inadequacy and spontaneous nonchalance (Henry's, Gonzalo's and mine) make Hugo's existence necessary and indispensable, I suffer from the cramping, sad realism, and I want to save him too from his burdens, lighten his life and free him.

I'm convinced that if one loves three highly selected men as deeply as I have, one has experienced everything. Every other experience is a reflection or repetition on a minor scale. Dudley was the son of Henry, as Robert was. I have known smaller and lesser Hugos. Many Spaniards would have been to me smaller, less fervent Gonzalos. I have known all the scales of erotic love, of spiritual love, mental and physical contacts, all the contacts. I never read a scene of love that I did not already know, had already lived. I never need to read with envy and hunger. I am conscious now of how we learn to live from certain books, and how I am doing the same for others. My diary will inflame, rouse, expand others equally.

This is Gonzalo's image of the mystical life. He tells me: "It is like a powerful searchlight turned towards the sky. It becomes weaker and weaker as it points towards the infinite. Whereas look how strong it is when it is turned towards the earth." As he says this, his own eyes are ardent, turned towards the earth always, with an earth fire and intensity!

I tried in vain to explain to him the cosmic consciousness which solves all dualities and divisions. People's ideas usually divide and separate. Gonzalo cannot grasp this that is above all ideas.

OCTOBER 13, 1942
The World of Aesthetics
The Imbs. Linked to the world of fashion and fashionable events, in Paris mainly. Irina Aleksander's dresses from the grand couturiers are works of art. Their decadent decor, in white and black and plum color, with Chirico designs on the walls to give

perspective, iron garden furniture which gives ephemeralness (*meuble de saison, de jardin*, transient, and vaporous and rust-inviting). She lacks beauty but is stamped by a distinction never seen in America.

The Cristofanettis. Francesco's decadent painting, artificial and fragile. Lucia's designs for Rodier clothes, her coral jewelry sold at Bonwit Teller, her elegance and originality.

But my books always open the secret doors to the underlying drama, and immediately I can no longer enjoy the decor, the elegance, the games with clothes and jewels. I am taken behind the scene, into the drama. And then the people are like me, amazed when the drama suddenly dissolves all the beauty and reveals instinctive, primitive ferocities. "Oh, the ugliness," cries Lucia, "the ugliness." So Francesco, the mute, dark, jealous Italian aristocrat, foams and hurls the ugliest phrases. Naked they are now. Bestial in hatred, animal pride and savagery. Out of the decadence, sensibilities, elegances, appear the ugliest demons: revenge, hatred, self-love, envy, the wish to murder, destruction, all the crimes of the soul. Jealousy! Again the ugliest of all the demons. Jealousy which makes a murderous animal of the most delicate and sublimated human beings. Now we see Lucia, the exotic Syrian woman, no longer made of satin and velvet and colored stones and feathers, and he no longer somber and trembling and shy, who becomes the women at the market uttering obscenities! The depths of the soul. The first time I saw this spectacle was with June. Do I not possess such a well of horror and monsters? Do I disguise it? In my greatest anger there are phrases June used I could never use or invent. No, I have often wished to kill, in anger and jealousy, but I do not possess virulence, such vitriolic wells of poison. It is this exposure of the Apache insults and sudden descents into ugliness which shocks the idealist Lucia. Au naturel is not very beautiful to people concerned with illusions and delusions and art. I have never seen Henry au naturel except when he chose to write a veritable leprosy. I have seen Gonzalo au naturel, but he thinks it is natural, and forgets it all the next day as if it were a storm. In a storm, he implies, every word is possible, but it is not valid. They attach a permanency to good behavior, and an ephemeral quality to the attacks of bestiality. When I yield to milder forms of these attacks I am humiliated and ashamed. It is possible I am more transmuted in my karma, further from the animal.

OCTOBER 23, 1942

Jacobson discovered a new mixture—the most potent vitamin—which rid me of anemia in three weeks and transformed me physically. This sent me soaring at last with a physical power equal to my desire and imagination. The effect of this on my whole life was prodigious: no more fatigue, no more sense of ruling my body by will and courage, like some old horse driven by a youthful jockey, no more strain. An inrush of power, and physical exaltation. A sense of equilibrium. The obsessions from which I suffer, the incubus, the morbid inner states in regard to Helba and induced by Gonzalo's defense of her, disappeared. I lost my timidity. In the first place I have become beautiful. I glow. In consequence I enjoy dressing and attending big gatherings and shining. At the Guggenheim Gallery vernissage I aroused attention and created a *sillon* of whisperings behind my back: "There goes Anaïs Nin, that's Anaïs Nin." A full expansion. I talk. I am *petillante*. *Je fais même des plaisanteries*. Nothing has changed around me, but I have changed. I am not affected. I feel confident. A desire to shine, to expand—euphoria. I embrace Jacobson with gratitude. Life is a dance again. For the first time I accept a soirée at the Imbs' in place of one with Gonzalo. I never did this before, but I am hungrier for pleasure, and the deeper joys of love are always mixed with pain. Pleasure—it comes all at once. Gonzalo is forced to take me before the soirée, and he makes love to me as if to make certain of his ownership and then lets me go. I dressed up in black lace, taffeta, *frou-froutant*, and lace mantilla, and sparkled for Marcel Duchamp, Denis of the *New Republic*, James Sterne of *Time*. Valeska Imb said sincerely: "You look so beautiful."

Hugo arrived later from his engraving class and was fully shocked, said I took his breath away, was completely seduced, and was eager to take me home and make love to me.

Again I am surrounded by love, by warmth, by magical happenings. I am full of ideas, plans, desires. Gold alone eludes me persistently. On a copy of my book for Marc Slonim, because he talked so much about the *jeux* of detective stories, I wrote: "*À la Récherche des Jeux Perdus*." Let that be the title of my next journal.

This is the heaviest and thickest diary volume I have ever written in. Henry gave it to me. And such a light title (*À la Récherche des Jeux Perdus*) I have given it, in the darkest and heaviest days of all history for a good Marxist, such as I am in my actions, seeking a world removed from pain and horror. However, much shall be forgiven me, because of my being a Marxist in my acts whereas most people, outside of Russia, are the reverse. It is only with their tongues they support the Russian religion, and their acts are acts of bourgeois drug-solutions, bohemian anarchism, or creative egotism and individuation. I am at peace as far as my behavior goes. Now for the direction taken by my flighty mystical soul—that I can't account for.

I have started my new phase with a report made for Dr. Jacobson which is an acknowledgment to the materialistic concepts: his injections have given me renewal, a transformation. I was getting ready to see a psychiatrist, being defeated by my obsessions. I did not need to do so. After three weeks of treatment all my activities are so exalted, so positive and expansive that the obsessions are displaced. They have faded so completely.

Externally, nothing has changed, but the body withstands the wear and strain of daily battle, and I am sure of victory. The worse the state of the world grows, the more intensely I try for inner perfection and power. It is not a challenge. The bestial world and evil can, and do, deal physical death. But that is all.

I fight for a small world of humanity and tenderness just as Jacobson fights the illnesses that are brought to him. He cannot do more.

Last night: while Hugo was bending over his engraving in the quiet of the New School, Gonzalo was bending over me and kissing me with the gratitude he feels after his pleasure. Henry I cannot see or imagine. He is in a place I do not know. This brings us up to date. In the public library around the corner people are reading my *Winter of Artifice*.

NOVEMBER 2, 1942

When Hugo told me again how he loves me I asked: "Why do you love me?"

"Well, for twenty years you have kept me interested."

After twenty years he loves me like a lover: ardent, eager, enthralled. When he saw me healthy last week (I reached a pinnacle of perfect health, never reached before and which intoxicated me—alas! I cannot sustain it) he begged me to retain this. He said he could not bear it, the expression I have sometimes. "You look...you look..." He searched for a strong enough word... "You look crucified."

NOVEMBER 3, 1942

Letter from Henry:

Just got your letter about resuming the role of analyst. Well. That sounds better. Yes, I do think you could do that well. [...]

You know, when it comes down to bedrock, I don't think it's so much a question of "caring for the sick," as you put it, as it is one of our getting results. You can see the results of creation, dealing with your neurotics, and that's pleasurable. It also puts you out of the competitive world, which is so abhorrent. You may remember, I said it to you more than once—that if you feel you must minister to the weak and ailing, then you should do it with all your heart and soul. You can't play at analysis any more than you can at art. Remember this, that you will profit more from it, in the end, than your patients. Because there is something defective in the analyst which drives him to this work—it is like the relation between master and slave—so I firmly believe. Don't fool yourself by thinking that you are doing good, that you are alleviating misery, and so on. No, you will be treating yourself, that's what I think. In this way, and maybe in only this way, you can complete your own analysis—and then see beyond it. This is not to deter you—on the contrary. I think it will be excellent. And don't tie it up, your work, with the idea that it is a solution of my economic ills. Do it for its own sake, purely. Enjoy it!

I want you to put an end to your anguish about my physical comfort. I want you to get like a rock and not worry whether I sink or swim. There's undoubtedly something wrong with me, or I would have solved this primitive question long ago. Better let me face it. You're absolutely right that it is not your place to be humbling yourself before these idiots. Maybe I'd get on to another tack too if I had to take a good dose of that medicine. (Though it seems to me I have. Somehow I get inured to it. I think I am less easily deceived than you, by people. I don't expect too much of them. But that, it seems, only leads to expecting everything of you, and that's wrong.) But I don't want you to think that I would ever get the idea that you failed me. No matter what you did, you couldn't fail me. I hold myself responsible for whatever happens to me. You, having greater wisdom, probably have more fear of what may happen than I in my blindness.

The last three days have been marvelous. Such perfect weather! Almost as good as Greece. I've been in bliss—and feel two hundred percent better. Solitude does that to me. I feel enriched. One doesn't need people, theatres, bars, etc. Just to step outdoors, see the light on the hills, the stars at night—that's enough. People in the East think this is a bizarre place, because it's Hollywood. I have almost nothing to do with Hollywood. I might be a thousand miles away, for all it matters. It drives me nuts, sometimes, to think that one can't live where one wants, especially when the place is not on the moon, not at the Antarctic. Places are important, just as important as food or other things.

I'm going to return, but I tell you, as long as the war is on, I am going to make an effort to convert you to my way of thinking. In some ways, you know, you're a fatalist. Generally you accuse me of being too soft and yielding. Generally you're right, but about this thing, living in the right place, the right climate, nothing on earth can convince me that I'm wrong. I look to New York with loathing. Two days, such as these last two, wipe out years of living in New York. You must realize that I'm not crazy when I say this. And I say it, living an incomplete life. I haven't had a taste of sex since I'm out here. And oddly enough, it doesn't bother me. It's wonderful to live alone like this, but it would be more wonderful not to live alone. But it's like choosing between the concentration camp and going to war. I'd choose the concentration camp.

Anyway, what I'm trying to tell you is this, that the West is utterly different from the East. I wanted you to see this country—you have seen hardly anything of America, you know. I am at the point where, failing to know the people I'd like to associate with, I can get along with anybody. It's enough for me now to exchange a few words with the grocer, or with Honest John, the Greek who runs a hash joint up the canyon. People stop and talk—they always do, you know. But I don't care whether they do or not. I get to the point of complete enjoyment of life, and then bango! The old question— how do you make a living? I'm not a bit sorry that I didn't land a job in the studios, callous though that sounds. I've had a rich, wonderful time of it, these four months. And please don't hold that against me. What gripes me is that I had it at your expense. Margaret and Gilbert Neiman were wonderful to me. And, if I did drain them a bit, I repaid them in other ways. It's something to know that people do recognize more than one way of being repaid.

You know, I meet more people who know Frieda Lawrence than you can shake a stick at. They all tell me what a wonderful life she leads up there in San Cristobal, New Mexico. Somehow Frieda has solved her problems—in a very humble way. She must be a grand person, quite different than we think from reading Lawrence. I begin to suspect that she was the bigger of the two, when it comes to life.

And that's what I'm getting at all the time…to arrange things so that one can live simply and easily, very humbly perhaps.

You seem to get frightened, whenever I mention this. I don't know what it is, whether you need the cultural elements more than I or what. All I can tell you is that I have grown to appreciate the life of the country these last few years. I don't need the cities anymore. You can always have music and books, even in the most remote places. And sometimes it's good not to have even these, but rather to be thrown completely on your own.

Well, I'm going to stop. Maybe you'll be able to give me a job as secretary or something. Better not ask me to do analysis—I might drive the patients away. Somehow sick people infuriate me. And God knows what I'd want to adapt them to.

NOVEMBER 17, 1942

Henry: Your letter this morning made me very angry. You repeat the same thing, just as if we didn't write countless letters about it. You're completely blind about one thing, and always will be. I'm responsible for that blindness. You start all over again to exult in the life you lead—and then you dare to say to me: "When I speak of this life, this humble life, you get frightened—you seem to need the cultural background, etc." as if it were a choice for me, a simple choice. What is this humble life of yours? You admit it's possible because of the Neimans and me. Then it isn't a humble life—it has a basis on dependence. Then you go on converting me to it. What a clever woman Frieda is! Yes of course. What do you expect me to do? I am tired of repeating that I do not choose to print, choose to analyze, choose to stay in N.Y. I do not choose to struggle.

You put me in the place by your attitude. I again bowed my head and accepted this attitude—which means always for me to be and continue to be what I am. The trouble is you're unbalanced and can't see that. You think I can take your attitude. At whose expense? If I can only get my liberation by staying at somebody's house and letting someone struggle for me I don't want it. For a long time I have been fully aware of our separation. My saying it first only happens because I always see first. The last straw was your thoroughly irresponsible remark about sex. "It's fine to have it but I can do without it." It isn't in anger that I say this, but now *I don't want you to return.* You told the (John) Cages you were never returning to N.Y. I should long ago have given you the ultimate liberation. The time has come. I do not want you to return. I don't want to bring you back to any place you loathe. You do not and never have made your life around me, by the climate of my presence. You are now complete, by yourself. I say this without pain or anger. You have prepared me for this. I only regret that you have failed to complete yourself in one simple truth: *two* people can't take your attitude—or they sink into ignominy. *One* can, and the other must struggle. Your passivity has created my struggle. When I met you I stayed in Louveciennes doing nothing—and I like the easy life just as much as you do. I began to struggle because your debacle at the time proved what happened to you whenever someone didn't protect you.

You have always refused to see the necessity of this. You have blamed me as if it were a temperamental defect.

Your passivity increased in proportion to my creative and protective activity. Ironically, you never recognized that my struggle was at the basis of your magnificent renunciations and independences. You mocked the people who struggled. You said: "Look, look how I do it." And it was all utterly crazy and inhuman. I can't bring myself to let you down and show you. You think your way of life is wisdom—but it isn't. It's the way of life permitted to those who are protected by someone else's struggle. That's all. There is no triumph and no conquest in it. It's a crystallization of the ego—that's all. I repeat it, Henry: I do not want you back. There is no need of it. I shall continue to help you. I have always wanted you fulfilled. I have my own plans and it won't be Hollywood. This is not a surprise or a shock. You mustn't be concerned. This separation has been going on since you went to Greece. I have been fully aware of it. Your letters have effectively detached me from you. They are more revealing than you know. Believe me when I say I feel completely detached and you are free—to live as you please. Only I do not want any more letters on this subject. I shall be grateful not to hear any more about the foolishness of my struggles, my love of the city, my refusal to lead an enchanted life at the cost of begging. That I shall be thankful for.

I didn't want a separation to come out of a quarrel—but that is how it happens. One suddenly discovers after ten years that one is fundamentally misunderstood, which means not loved, and there you are. I'm very definite about this however—and it is not anger which makes me do it but complete disillusion—and that can't be altered. Sooner or later you were going to be alone, for your efforts were never towards union but *towards aloneness.* The time has come.

Second letter to Henry:

I'm no longer angry—just very sad at being misunderstood—but I kept my first letter for a day, and read it again. I still feel the same way, but I understand what makes you write me such irritating and unjust things. I understand and feel for you too. You mustn't be hurt by my use of the word "child." You are a man, and more than all other men, as creator, as lover, as everything in fact, but in relation to money you're helpless. This helplessness is so intolerable to you that you can't acknowledge it, and so you also find intolerable the awareness of what I have to do for you—so between guilt and pain you simply refuse to realize the rightness and necessity of what I do. You would feel much happier if I became a child like you, joined you and repeated your life with June, for I repeat to you, I'm as helpless as you in regard to money, and it is Hugo (another unbearable idea) who has guarded us both. What you want me to do is destructive—to join you and become blind with you. As you can't solve this, you ran away. You ran away to Greece. At that time your trip was a break from me and your unsolvable problem. We broke physically and emotionally. You found you could live without me—physically and emotionally. I did too. It became clearer and clearer that the only bond left was a mother and child one: you demanding, capricious, unwilling to make sacrifices, and running away again. Your last demand was the biggest. You really want to stay where you are, you still need my protection, and there you are. You're too honest to pretend anything in order to keep this protection. You have always been honest—your letters are very honest about the fact that you feel fine, alone. You are furthest away from your own guilt. In fact the best deliverance would be utter destruction of the bond, because you would be back at the place before you met me, starving but free of guilt. Alas—it's tragic that we won't escape that, though I struggled to free you. Now if we are both honest, I will say that I will overlook all your foolish, nonsensical statements about your independence and humble life and need of nothing, and I will not let you starve—if only you stop writing me destructive, cruel, thoughtless letters. You, who are so honest, can't face a simple truth like this. It is unnecessary for you to return. We are not bound as man and woman anymore. If we had been, you wouldn't have put so many small things in the way of your return, a city, a climate, your personal gratifications, your well-being. It is unworthy of us to be so deceptive. Now your problem is clearing, isn't it? You have all you want—the impossible always—at any cost. There it is. May you enjoy your peace, your solitude, your choice of life. Do not destroy my peace and the strength I need by constantly being critical of my attitude. I shall respect the kind of bond which makes it impossible for me to leave you without protection, no matter how often you have denied and denigrated the way I achieved it.

November 19, 1942

Henry has definitely chosen his life—escape and delusion. He has surrendered only to himself—to his self-gratification. What he wants of me is destructive, and I will not do it.

November 20, 1942

Before getting my break letter, Henry writes me:

Just got your letter with the postal check—yes, I did get the other, didn't I say so? You will not get the ms. for a few days yet, I fear—it went by ordinary mail…

Each time I open a letter from you I expect another somersault now. You are really veering around like a weather-vane, do you know it? I have no doubt it's all due to the terrible financial anguish you're going through. I'm determined to take a job when I get back: we'll see if that will steady you. I feel excellent—morally, mentally, physically, spiritually.

I have to smile the way you polish off Greece in your enthusiasm for Morocco. How do you know it's so much better? Better than here, by a thousand times, that's certain. What are you doing, working on Hugo now to put him in the consular service?

This morning I was rereading the last volume of my *Rosy Crucifixion*, and do you know, I was delighted with it. Wondered if it was really me who did it. That's the truth—and this leads me to say that I am sure I can both work for a living and do my writing too. So many men and women have done it. And done it well.

Well, Lafe has arrived. I'm going to meet him now at the Satyr Book Shop. Give my regards to Frances and Tom Brown.

...So I write, calling him Mr. Weather-Vane, telling him I had given him what I thought he wanted me to give him: his liberty—and now he was veering again. What will be the effect of my letter? It is the first time I said to Henry what ought never to have been said, the fateful breaking words. He forced me to.

NOVEMBER 24, 1942

There appears what I call the drama of woman's development. Woman—in her new development—has chosen the weak child-man who will not interfere with her evolution, on whom she can use her strength. His weakness in the end destroys her. She no longer wants to be the mother of children, which demands immolation and abdication. She is the sublimated mother of the child-man, the artist, the poet, the primitive. Today the primitive, the poet and the child are the weakest in the new world realism, and woman chose to protect him, recognizing his needs, protecting creation again, and thus giving birth again to the artist.

I count innumerable marriages of this kind: Abe Rattner and his wife, Frances and Tom Brown, Thurema and Jimmy, myself and Henry, Gonzalo and I. But the real child becomes a man and ceases to take the mother's strength and becomes her protector. The artist/child never becomes a man, never ceases to live off her strength, and the woman grows older, tired, exhausted, and finally emptied and weak. If she weakens and needs protection she finds herself alone, even abandoned. The biological drama is distorted, tragedy sets in. The mother's love, diverted of its natural channel, does not find the rhythm of nature which made the child stronger as the mother grew weaker.

This is a phase in the development of woman's strength, in the diverting of the strength away from biological motherhood into sublimated motherhood, into higher forms of creation.

Working with Caresse proved to be an ordeal (she has given me *Misfortunes of the Immortals* by Max Ernst and Paul Éluard to print): she is changeable, fussy, capricious, exigent, wavering, uncreative, egotistical—above all changeable, unsure, which adds to our work, anxieties and expenses. She's made mere laborers of us.

Her catastrophe issued from the lack of depth in her life, her waywardness and lack of fundamental values. Today she is poor and alone and sick. Yet she strains to recapture her "prestige" as a publisher out of vanity. Actually her "designing" and "typography" consisted of stealing my idea of printing on cellophane—immediately she appropriated it—and copying the format and *mise en page* of the original French *Sans Pareil* Edition. So Gonzalo's initiative is killed and we have no interest in the book.

Letter from Henry:

You know, about our mutual veering around. The best thing to do, as pure strategy, when you want someone to do as you wish, is to give in to them—give them the whole hog. (Not in anger, or rebellion, or despair.) Really give in—and you'll always get what you want. I had made up my mind to return quite a while ago...

That I wrote and harped about the beautiful country here, the solitude, etc., was no contradiction. The two are not incompatible. Didn't you yourself teach me to overcome one of my great faults—namely, that of destroying a thing or place or person when you wish to leave it? (I did that with France a bit when writing about Greece—and have repented ever since.) I don't hate what I have to give up or what I can't have. It's hard for me to get angry anymore. (Except about trifling things.) Nor can I be greatly deceived in people anymore. You must not expect very much of people—only the few, and of them one should demand, or expect everything.

I'm sure I'll land something quickly when I get back. There must be thousands of jobs open now. I don't care a hoot what it is. Factory work, if needs be. Have you noticed, incidentally, what a jolly time of it people are now having, working for defense? If only the poor buggers could learn to work this way in peace time—instead of cutting one another's throats.

You always get a retarded anger, which mystifies people. That's from holding it in, of course. You have to get angry on the spot—or not at all. Else you poison yourself.

If I should have to send a telegram about departures, etc., I'll send it to Frances to give you over the phone. Don't worry about money—I'll get there. I'm awake now.

Letter from Henry (after receiving the break letter):

Well, that was a real blast from the Arctic you hurled at me! You certainly don't leave me a leg to stand on. But how can you say that I have never recognized that I owe everything to you? Why, everybody knows that. I've never tried to conceal it or disguise it. Look, aren't you confusing things? Wouldn't it be possible for someone to be wholly dependent on another person—and be miserable at the same time? You must admit that I have achieved some little thing for myself, don't you, won't you? It's true that I might have not experienced the depths and joys of solitude if you hadn't made it possible. But because I tell you of these things (and I'm only saying what others have said before me, those who have tried it), you must not infer that I deny your part in it. You remember Lawrence's words about "the morning star," about being alone but having the woman there with him—which John Middleton Murry found so ridiculous and contradictory? Well, I was expressing the same thing, really.

Damn it all, you do confound what I mean whenever I talk about "aloneness." You consider it the opposite of "union." As a matter of fact, it's the only way of achieving union, because you can only unite with others when you have achieved your own unity. And dependence! I tell you, we're dependent on one another, every one of us. No one can stand alone, no one is self-sufficient. And I mean more than mere physical or financial dependence. But the strength we get from one another is for the purpose of nourishing that portion of our being which demands "aloneness." It sounds contradictory, but it isn't.

You've interpreted my words as some kind of slur on you, which is something I could never possibly bring myself to do. You always get your pride up at the wrong moment. I've been admitting to you all my faults, all my weaknesses. And then, crack, bang! You suddenly come to the conclusion that I am denying you, that everything is wiped out. Certain words and phrases make you see red. I'm truly sorry when that happens, but I never know what will produce this effect. I am not thoughtless and cruel. Whether I am a "crystallized ego," as you put it, I don't know. If I am, then I have accomplished nothing, then I am deluding myself utterly.

No, as I said in my last letters, I'm serious about returning to N.Y. and earning a living. I admitted that I wanted to change the situation. It seems to me now that if I don't earn my own living I have no right to open my mouth. I must do as everybody else does and then see if I can boast of being wise, serene, gay, etc. You're absolutely right. I had come to that conclusion myself. I have been living a lie, and writing it, I guess. I have given a false impression.

Yes, I've run away from so many things—and finally I've had to face them all. And this makes me wonder sometimes—was that all I accomplished by my writing—what every jackass knows? Really if that were it, it would be absurd. I'd be the first one to laugh at myself. You lay such emphasis on the word "choice," I always notice. You give me credit for making choices. I wish I knew, sometimes, what was choice and cowardice. Things are terribly interrelated, more than we dare to believe, I think. My present situation for example. I didn't choose—but there's no doubt I unconsciously brought it about. There's no doubt that I wasn't ready for that job, no matter how much I protested I was. That's being honest, as you say. God, but I'm not flattered anymore about being honest. I've seen the weakness of that too. But I suppose this trait is ingrained, like your pride. It's something we have to wrestle with, and not fall back on as if it were a Maginot Line. In short, it doesn't comfort me merely to say yes to your accusations. I want to do something about it. If I can't prove myself in your eyes, then it's all hopeless. I don't ever again want to write a letter defending myself.

I don't think we misunderstand each other at all. I'm sure I don't misunderstand you. If there's any misunderstanding it's myself that I misunderstand. It does strike me as ironical, though, that at this moment when I imagine myself to be really at my best, that I should produce such a harrowing effect upon you. You make me think of myself as someone performing a successful experiment in a vacuum. And that makes me open my eyes.

It will sound outlandish to say so, but it reminds me of the time when I was a child and my mother dragged me by the ear back to kindergarten to ask the teacher to give me back the presents I had given away to the other children. I had always hated my mother for that. But I guess she realized that I was too sure of the better gifts she would give me, and too pleased with myself over my dubious generosity. Though at that moment, I had no thought of generosity: I was being Sovietique, taking from those who had and giving to those who needed. That was all. If we had been very poor, if I had needed those homely things, I am sure I would have acted differently. But my mother wanted me to be grateful, and I just couldn't be grateful for gifts I didn't want.

But believe me, today I am grateful for everything. I have eaten humble pie since then. Only today it is not so easy for me to distinguish between the giver and the recipient. I would like to see the giving and taking happening indiscriminately. But that's looking at things from the standpoint of perfection, which is wrong, I suppose. There's only one thing I know clearly—we all have different things to give and we also are in need of different things, one from another. And I have no defense to make out for myself. I took what I needed and I gave what I pleased. Now it's time I turned about—give what is needed and take what it pleases to be given me. And even for that turnabout I can't take any credit. It's as though I had been a bandit all my life and then, when given hard labor, I take it cheerfully. So much has to do with the fact that I find the work of the world ugly and stupid. Perhaps this bugaboo will disappear too, now that I am face to face with it. And yet I feel that on my dying bed I will rise up on one elbow and have a last say at the world—"Don't work so hard you poor fools! Give over...do as little as possible!" You see, it isn't the easy-going, happy-go-lucky people who cause sorrow and misery in this world. It's the go-getters, the reformers, the conquerors, the fanatics, the hard-working ones. They think that Paradise is created by sweat and labor, by making everyone think alike. *That*, that sure knowledge that at the bottom of all this toil and effort is simply a miserable, sadistic gloating—that's what kills me. Well, as the monk said in Shangri-La—I'll be moderately industrious. And maybe moderately happy, and moderately independent. Moderation—that's the hardest thing for me to learn.

I understand a little better now, as I write you, what riled you so much. That phrase you quote—that *could* sound like the greatest insult. But would I think like that deliberately? You say my letters are an unconscious revelation. But you always say that when you want to perceive bad things. And you, or anyone, always perceives the bad the moment the ego is in jeopardy. Some crazy kind of fear comes up and then suddenly all is clear, ah yes, terribly clear. But it's not clear! And that's why the over-emphasis on the unconscious, by the analysts, is wrong. If we were to be judged by the unconscious we'd all be guilty of the most heinous crimes. I want to remind you of the story about the Buddha returning home and how he was greeted by his wife whom he had deserted. You spoke of "running away" from problems. In a very true sense, that's what the great Buddha did. He ran away because when his eyes were opened he could not stand the suffering of the world. (A very great difference here, I must admit, between our running away and his. He could not stand seeing *others* suffer. We can't stand our *own* suffering.) Anyway, he went away and his great problem was—how to rid the world of suffering. Apparently, no one has imitated his behavior, at least. (Not that

that destroys the rightness of his viewpoint.) When he returned it was with honor. No one accused him of running away from his wife and child, or from the responsibilities of the court. Nor did his wife complain that he had denigrated the female in her.

I am not comparing myself to Buddha. I have found no solution to world problems. I don't think anything, any element of life, can be eradicated. Don't you think, when I watched Margaret and Gilbert together I had many a pang? And yet I knew I also had something which they didn't have.

I don't believe in these parting quarrels. You know my vice, or weakness, or whatever you want to call it. You stood it for ten years, and you abetted it. I am not the least bit hurt or angry by what you write. I sympathize with you—deeply. It's just as bad as if I had been an alcoholic. And if you really meant it that you didn't want me to come back, or if you ran away, no matter what you did, I would not be angry or hurt. I would only blame myself. But I want to point out something to you. You know what my fears and obsessions are. You know so well, that it makes you overly heroic and self-sacrificing. You want to spare the other person pain. But do you know this—if every day you had come to me and said (instead of pretending that you could manage things): "Henry, things are bad, things are serious—you must do something. I know you don't like to take a job, but you must now, it's imperative. Today I will only leave you half what I promised you, or a third…that's all we have." That would have had a lightning-like effect upon me. I'd have been out on the double-quick. We are all weak in that, when we know the other one is strong, we lean on him or her. It's human, even if deplorable. And, as I said before, that's what strength is meant for—to be used by others. The strong feed on the weak just as much as the weak do on the strong. They're bound, inexorably. Now I know you had too much tact and grace and delicacy to act that way with me. And I was too weak, too passive, too yielding. For a dreamer you have to use thunder and lightning. (Only now and then heat lightning—like now. You certainly turned on the heat, as they say.)

But just as you write me soberly and thoughtfully and considerately in your appendix, so I can write you. I am not going to do as you say. I am coming back and I am going to work. And I am not going to make you miserable because I take a job, you can depend on that. I won't even make my employer miserable. I'll be thankful that I got a bit of sense. All this I had intended to do anyway. You were wrong to interpret my letter psychoanalytically. You've been nursing that unconscious of mine too sedulously. We must give attention to the conscious processes too. That's the part of us that is in the world and doing battle with it. You know the Spanish saying, "No man is a hero to his valet." Well the valet is the conscious mind. It's the mind that knows, because it has to dress the lazy self every day.

I couldn't help but read the parts you had scratched out. I like that line about when your day of pleasure comes it will be at the price of mine. Fine! Now you're talking. I'm going to give you a bit of luxury and idleness. I want to see you take a perpetual vacation. I don't think there's any danger of working! It's a new experience.

And all experiences are good. I'm sure I'll become a foreman or superintendent in no time. Maybe a vice-president. You forget that I was once slated to become the vice-president of the Western Union! I couldn't have been such a slouch then. And now I've got something more than muscle. Yes, I'll want a little sexual intercourse too. I didn't become a guru—quite.

Letter to Henry:

Henry—I didn't make myself clear. I'm not trying to make you say you owe everything to me, or even to feel grateful, or harping on the giving. You know that all this is inaccurate, that deep down between you and me everything was right, an exchange of art, a mutual giving. What makes me see red, as you say, is something I want you to understand once and for all: it is when you are in your euphoric states, talk to me as if what I did do was unnecessary, that all I do can be abandoned, that I can just step out blithely, magically out of the problem, as you do. Don't you see, what angers me is not that I want you to feel the dependence, but only because I serve as a foundation and give you the feeling of liberation, then you turn and say to me: "Why don't you live as I do, do as I do—just ignore it all, enjoy yourself, etc." Then it hurts me because being the realist in this case, the dreamer who has accepted to work, I feel that you are not convinced of the need of what I do. Surely you know I get no pleasure from making you admit I take care of you—none—but I get hurt when you say: "It's too bad you like the big city and not this life I lead here. Why do you struggle so? Why don't you print for yourself, etc." It's like a criticism—as if I could not enjoy dreaming. You ask, is all your writing only going to lead you to find that you have to work like other men, for a living? No—of course, it's absurd. There is no other way. Wonderful men have yielded to that. All the French writers had professions. It didn't kill them. You say then that to make you see this I should have cut you off—to make you see it. But that is not my way. I tried to make it clear to you, but each time I talk about it you make it sound terrible—like a creditor—and that is humiliating—that is not what I mean. It is a blind spot you have. It's Don Quixote saying that it is not a windmill, it's a castle. I'm not opening your eyes to what I do—but to the simple fact that it has to be done, that if you don't do it, I have to do it, that I am deeply, very deeply tired, physically so, and that I want you to share with me, because I can no longer do it all. In America it is too heavy for me, too much for my body. To make you see this, do you think I have to do it cruelly—cut you off, so that you will face it absolutely, really, concretely? Can it not be done otherwise? I have not abetted your desire to do nothing else but writing the last years. Since we came to America I told you: I cannot do it. Hugo still has a European salary which doesn't go far enough. N.Y. is nightmarishly expensive. I can't pay $40 rent and your meals in restaurants. You knew I couldn't. You know I wrote for Ruder, I tried the press, etc. The most I can now make is $100 a month, but the press rent and running expenses take some of that. And the physical wear is tremendous. Wasn't all this clear to you when you left? Isn't that why you left? But as soon as you got to Hollywood you forgot it? And when the press is put on a paying basis, I get sad and lose interest, I am a dreamer. I hate working for other people. You do misunderstand my letters. You think I want you to thank me. God, no, Henry. It's only that when you start dreaming you start asking me why I don't do the same! Then the struggle appears in this light as grotesque. No one can work when the other denies the *need* of it. Can't I make this clear? No—I know it isn't—it can't ever be, to you. That is why you are not convinced. It is utterly hopeless. I repeat the legend, you've been disconnected from all life on earth and no power can reconnect you.

What I don't like is that this forces me to give terrible emphasis to something I don't naturally want in the foreground. Your lack of earth-recognition of the need to earn a living forces me to represent something I'm not. In the end I'm getting deformed in your eyes and in my own. And that depresses me. The dreamer in me is being killed because I'm condemned to be the food supplier—and meanwhile Henry is saying: "It's absurd to have food suppliers. We don't need them!" In short—you are not ready to return. You are not ready to give up whatever drug that protects you from accepting the ugly side of life—your delusions. There is nothing to do but for one to accept the incompleteness of the other and set about to substitute for it. It is too bad that there cannot be a *sharing* of responsibilities so that neither one should get deformed. I'm being deformed because the problem is much too heavy for my body's capacity. You're being deformed because this omission or blindness in you is sooner or later going to catch up with you—in spite of me.

Do you know why you mentioned Frieda Lawrence? I know. It's because it is such a person you need now. You have mistaken the nature of my strength. Hers is a physical, earthy strength. Mine was psychic, spiritual. It was courage with not much of a physical basis—just the desire to protect the feeling. You speak of strength—but you see I'm not an oak—and that's what you need. Trying to be an oak with a body not made for it has broken me. I do not say this ironically or with jealousy—I do think you should visit Frieda—see her life—you must find the life you really want, and the woman who can give it to you. For the first time I realize I am not the woman for you—you need an oak!

Tuesday Night
Letter from Henry:

Anaïs, your last letter was full of sadness and despondency, with genuine despair. There is only one thing I can do, it seems, and that is to relieve you once and for all of this heavy burden. I *am* looking for a job, in earnest. I will know something definite in a very few days. At the worst—or maybe it's the best—I will take a job in a defense plant. Meanwhile I've become quite good friends with a man who has just begun to publish—he's the vice-president of a printing plant. He likes my books—and preferred the "Colossus" to all, which I rather liked. Had dinner with him and his wife the other night. The question is, what can he publish? I am giving him the *Letters to Emil*, which I have been rereading with that in mind, and which are publishable, I think.

Meanwhile, let me say in passing, I won't need any money, probably for quite a while. And if I land a job, I won't need any ever—you'll be free. [...]

FRIDAY
Letter from Henry:

Anaïs, what am I to say to your last letter? You've apparently lost all faith in my ability to solve this question of independence. There's only one thing left for me to do—to prove it. So I'll look for a job here.

I'm truly sorry to hear that you are in such a state of mind. I don't question anything you do, or wish to do. One must act according to one's nature. We can't always understand why a person acts as he does, but we can be tolerant. You must do as you see fit—it's obviously imperative. [...]

Letter to Henry:

Henry: We're still writing at cross purposes. This morning you say sadly that I do not believe in your capacity to take a job—and that you will be *indulgent* towards the step I take—towards my attitude. Henry—for god's sake—when a man has written twenty pages to prove he cannot make concessions, that he cannot compromise, when a man shows the deep resistance you did to your life in N.Y.—how can this man turn around and do the opposite? And for what? For me? How can you expect me to turn around and ask you to do what you have spent twelve years proving to me you can't do? I get my integrity from doing repulsive things *for* a human resource, for you. You can't do these things for another human being. Also I haven't asked you to do anything for me, but for yourself. *I have only given you what you wanted again* as always. What you desperately *tried to get from me.* Again I am letting you be yourself—choose your life, etc. You did everything to prove to me your deep resistance to life here. I can only envisage your return as tragic for me. I have to slowly make you conscious that the rhythm between us is broken because you asked too much—you set about to be true to yourself, to your wishes and dreams. This has been so superhuman a task that I am now drained—weak—and only ask for respite, peace. *I feel broken.* I cry in the streets and I can't climb stairs. I feel absolutely weak. *Je n'en peu plus.* Today I said in the middle of the street to the passersby: "*No puedo mas*"—I wanted to shout it in Spanish—I don't know why: "*¡No puedo mas!* I can do no more!" If you come back I know what awaits me: feeling your misery, your rebellion. I can't bear it. Because I'm a dreamer, I dreamed your dream of freeing you, but I didn't know that the human being breaks—and there you are. The human being broke. You dreamed impossible things and left me the work of fulfilling them. You escaped every constraint, ever discipline, every slavery to love, to human life, every sacrifice. You're at peace with yourself. Well, that's an achievement. Either I have given you the strength to stand without me—or else I gave you only delusions. I believe I merely freed you to dream crazier and crazier things. But don't be *indulgent!* For nothing I am doing comes out of me—women have no life of their own. I have only reacted to your destiny. You destroyed the life in N.Y. You made it worse than it was—you made no effort to make it better. I knew at the time what you were doing, the meaning of it. Each whim, each rebellion was significant for me and a source of pain—but I couldn't stop you. I know you don't understand what has happened to me. I am being destroyed. But I know all my letters mean nothing to you. We now speak a different language. By sheer suffering I have become merely a human being. All I want is tenderness and humanity. You have become something else. If it pleases you to think it's Buddha—let it be Buddha. Whatever it is, it is something that has killed the dreamer in me. My real self was in the fantasy stories, in the *House of Incest* and the fairy tales. I can't write those anymore. My devotion to human beings has killed me. *The mother has finally been murdered by the dreamers.* For me the nonsense and the dreaming and the madness are all alike, they are a way of killing me because I have served them with my life. What I want you can't give me now. Now I want only a corner to sleep in, and recuperate my lost strength, and a human being beside me. I want to hide away. I think you're unbalanced because all these things I talk about don't mean anything to you. You don't know how to answer me. Just give me time. I have my own desert to traverse. It is my turn to go away and find what I must do.

DECEMBER 4, 1942
Letter to Henry:

Henry: There is no blame and no accusation in this that I write you because we have done it together. But you must make the effort with me to understand it and not let it crush us. There is one truth you have persistently evaded and that is the material reality, the need of food and bed. I have equally failed *to have a sense of reality about my body and the limitations of human sacrifice.* You have counted on my heroic attitude, my romantic belief in your creation. Today it has cost me my life, almost, and where will you be when I am dead? As far as that goes, the way I am is worse than death. I am like an invalid. I tried the impossible. I am as weak as when in Paris I collapsed and was given a blood transfusion. Because you have never done for anyone what I have done for you—you cannot understand what it is, *never* to sleep one's fill, to be economizing even on what I eat, to beg, to steal, to work. Do you know the old galleys, where on the deck people took their pleasure while others below rowed until they died? That is what our life has been. And with this a complete awareness in you, a persistent conviction that it would be absurd for you to work. We live out a legend because I believed in your creation, I believed the world should take care of you, and so I set out in a crazy way to serve this until I cracked. There is something wrong there, don't you think? Several times you have been on the brink of realizing the wrongness of it—but it meant a sacrifice on your part, so you ran away. You have practically said: "At the cost of your life I must follow my beliefs"—other times you have said: "If I realized each move I make creates sacrifices for you I would go crazy." Well it is true. And I have paid with my life. My eyes are worn out, my hands are deformed, my body is completely exhausted. I ran the press lately with lumbago. I bent over the typesetting with a painful, stiff back. I can hardly get up in the morning. I come home at six o'clock and go to bed. And you are so far from the reality of this you can't even feel it. You could never feel all the meals I missed, the constant self-denial, the continuous labor, the tension, the anxiety. It is wrong of you to mention Buddha—to make it a religious sacrifice? Haven't I done enough? Buddha didn't burden his wife with the full dependence you did. He didn't talk about meditation and then cause such torment to a human being as you have. Your trip around America was a nightmare to me. You got tired of writing for Ruder in two months. I did it for six months. No Henry—this is deeply wrong—I don't accuse you because a part of me consented to this and I suppose I believe one has to give one's self to death. Well—I have. My real death won't help you—it would be a useless romantic sacrifice. Death as a total loss of strength—that I have reached. I can go no further. I want to give you time to solve this—because it was *our* doing, my mystical exaltation made me a martyr. I gave myself up. The loss of blood—anemia—was deeply symbolical. [...] We have both been equally crazy, and that is why I have no bitterness and no revolt. But I have to make you understand this. I'm trying to do it this way, without violence and without cruelty. If you think that to stop sending you money is the only way to make you aware—then I'll do that too. I still think whatever I do can't be destructive. Your anarchism has been a kind of narcissism. You have dressed up your weakness in wonderful delusions—legends—telling me all kinds of tales to make me believe this was necessary, when only a little communism, a little sharing of the burden, a little humanity might have saved us from catastrophe.

P.S. Your letter today—you are irritated—I'm sorry if in my desperate state I said unjust or cruel things. If I didn't have faith in you I wouldn't be writing you. Neither one of us are to blame. We were both in good faith—we are only to be pitied. [...]

Letter from Henry:
Friday Evening, Hollywood.

Anaïs: Last night I wrote you at some length and now today comes another letter with a check. [...]

Between us there is no antagonism, no war of wills. You are creating a mirage. All that you have asked of me I have readily assented to. Maybe this is what happened— that I fled from the heaven you tried to create for me in order to make one of my own. But heaven is the same everywhere—and it's not a place but a condition, as you know. What does it matter how we come by it, how we arrive? Circumstances now find us three thousand miles apart, but perhaps infinitely nearer than we ever were. You've drawn a line around New York. I'm drawing no lines. Eventually I will encircle you in New York. I feel achieved, at rest, and at one with myself. *Let me help you!* I realize that you are still regarding me as a bit of a fool, but sometimes the fool is nearer to God than the wise ones. How can I make you realize that you have lost nothing? Strength? That will return. You have no more sacrifices to make. That's over with. Incidentally, I am returning this check, because I have enough to last several weeks yet, and I have two or three offers of jobs already. That's demonstration number one. And you don't know how happy it makes me feel. [...]

You say I have killed the dreamer in you. No, only *you* could do that. Imagination is the one thing we possess which is free. Nobody can kill it. It is not "murderable." For the moment, take that on authority. The truth of it will become apparent to you as you come to the end of your suffering. It was you who taught me, in Louveciennes—I remember well that moment—not to blame the world, but to hold oneself responsible for all that happens to one. That was a blessed moment for me, and after that, immediately came the clear vision of my past, of the pattern of my life. I think I made great progress since that day. I know it—don't just *think* it. But I know too that as time unfolds, and vision increases, this same pattern of the past is susceptible of greater and greater interpretation. Nothing is static or fixed, not even the past.

There is a great deal now in your letters about the past. Let us stop thinking of that. Face the future. Don't murder the future with the past. Let the understanding of the past act as a liberating force. I refuse to let you shackle me with my own past. I can't deny it, that's true enough, but I won't be bound by it. And why should you? [...]

I will surely look up the book you mention, and report on it. I hope you won't say anymore that what you write doesn't mean anything to me. It has meant everything, you see. Now you can break your wand, as Prospero did. Don't return any mss. now. Just hold them and let them rest quietly for a while.

Now as I turn over the last page of your letter, I see—"It was all beyond us." Well, you see you were wrong. Nothing is beyond us, if we have the real desire.

Well, enough. I expect to hear another tune in your next letter. And if you still do not believe, still are not convinced, I'll keep answering you on the head. But I hope we're through fighting windmills.

December 10, 1942

I don't know what day I felt: *No puedo mas.* But it came with such violence that I broke down. First came an extreme weakness—so extreme I could not climb the stairs to my home. I had to take them like mountain climbing at the same tempo as my mother who is over seventy. Then came weeping. The uncontrollable weeping. It seemed to me I was broken for good—physically and spiritually. The correspondence with Henry growing more and more confused. Fears, doubts, anguish, confusion. The work at the press monstrously heavy. Strain. Strain. A feeling of unbearable tension— such a painful tension, like lying on a rack. Jacobson unable to give me strength. I can never describe the tension. I had driven myself too far! The daily efforts broke me.

I telephoned Martha Jaeger. Such a beautiful, compassionate face! I yielded to her like a child—weeping, confessing. Immediately she released the tension by her words… "You encompassed too much. You had no sense of reality about the body—the limitations of the body!"

As I talked to her, abandoned myself to her care, I felt less hurt and less confused.

It was as if I had been given absolution and the permission to rest, relax and give up my too-great burden. She was amazed at all I had taken on—"Too much, too much," she said.

The father is absent from this drama. This is the drama of the mother—of woman—I have been drawing closer to all women lately. Woman is only now becoming aware of her individuality, but also aware, as Jaeger said, of how her cosmic relation is different than man's. It is a difficult, deep thing for woman to commune with. She can only do it by a universal motherhood or whore-priestess way.

"The high priestess," said Jaeger when I spoke of my yielding to my father.

It is strange how I turned to the Woman and the Mother for understanding. I have had all my relationships with men—of all kinds. Now my drama is that of woman in relation to herself—her conflict between selflessness and individuality, and how to manifest the cosmic consciousness she feels.

There are depths I have not yet entered—which I struggled to express when I argued against Henry and Durrell and wrote "The Woman's Creation" essay. I reread it tonight and only begin to understand it *now*—because of what Jaeger said about the cosmic life of woman *running underneath.*

It is strange that I have described these feelings and made the somewhat similar statements Jaeger makes but emotionally and unconsciously, and I'm only *fully aware* of them now with her. The diary must be unconscious and emotional, so I can get lost in it and can only regain my vision through the objective eye of another.

Psychoanalysis is our only way of gaining wisdom because we do not have religion.

Confusion in me between love and devotion. All my acts I thought were acts of love: yielding up of the self, the personal. But feeling hurt that they should all be willing to immolate me, and feeling unloved according to my way of loving (sacrifice), I was unloved by Henry and Gonzalo. I felt that the self *must* be shattered in love, love as abnegation, effacement of the self. Henry did not love me this way. Only Hugo. My revolt goes back to all the concessions I made for love (the scene of destruction of my books by Gonzalo because of jealousy).

Coming out of the ether, I said, "You did a wonderful job, doctor."

Why must I fall mortally ill to prove to the world the sacrifice is accomplished? I think I have been completely crucified.

DECEMBER 22, 1942

Hugo feels my "return" and expresses it in the form of a game. He says: "I have been scared of losing you for twenty years. Now I've got you in the trap—at last."

And he plays at laughing villainously (as he does in my dreams of a cruel Hugo) and says: "Now I'm the boss. I won't be so good anymore..."

And pretends to grow into an absolute boss.

We talked about the end of my taking care of my children, that they are grown up and will go away. All this for me is terribly poignant because it is foreseeing events for which I'm not emotionally ready. I'm not detached from Gonzalo, yet my love for him has moments when it resembles a leave-taking. I know the end now. And although I do see that Hugo is the only husband for me—the only one truly married by similarities of character and understanding, the only absolute—I am sad to return. I cannot even say it lacked romantic or passionate value, my marriage. I cannot even say this, because since Hugo gave me the initial shock of first pursuing me and then relinquishing me, he has spent twenty years like a knight of the Middle Ages giving me all the proofs and tests of his love that a man can give, and courting and re-courting and re-wooing me constantly, and waiting like a wife waits for her husband's return!

Jaeger brought out the importance of the abandonment trauma in my marriage—Hugo's departure for Europe before we were engaged. I told Hugo about it, how I had looked for a ring with his last bunch of flowers and did not find it. He had roses delivered to me while he was in the bathroom, with a ring, and this card:

August 15, 1922
Darling, I love you. I cannot live without you. Will you be my wife and marry me when I return from this trip? Hugo

DECEMBER 26, 1942
Letter to Henry:

Henry: Every word you said about the Dreamer corresponds to my feelings. I was puzzled by the same things and I see clearly a great difference between Pellegrina and me. She represents only a part of my nature. This is the very part I tried to live out—*but* she had wealth. And her voice. *Actually* possessed the "horn of plenty." I had the desire to be fully Venusian, and I had the gifts to give, but I didn't have the wealth. And so to live this out and bring magic and creation all around me, I wasn't content to sing (or write) but I had to give *real food*, real nourishment. And as I didn't have it in plenty, I took it out of my mouth, I did it by *denials*. I denied myself even proper eating, thus giving of my very blood, and thus destroying my physical body. That is why you ask me: why should giving have exhausted me? But, Henry, I didn't give what you give, just what you possess—your spiritual gifts, your writing. I gave what I didn't have, whatever the other needed, and to accomplish this I sold myself to prostitute writing, I slaved, I cut on my sleep, rest, comfort. I denied myself all pleasure, all relaxation, all trips, vacations, everything. I even gave up *all peace* because by straining I gave myself constant anguish. I felt responsible—the mother. If I had been merely content with singing—but no, I was the cosmic mother, and like a mother I did all the ugly, menial chores until I died from the ugliness of it all. There is a great difference in the two stories. I had a great deal to give, but that was not enough. I had to give my blood, my strength—and that became a crucifixion. That kind of giving nobody does—giving up even one's self, soul and body. And can't you see that this is exhausting, that this has nothing to do with the mystical giving, that I did it in *reality*—I wasn't satisfied with the symbol of communion. Even Christ was satisfied with a symbolical meal. I gave my body. And that is why I broke and wanted to die. It is this I feel I can't make clear to you because you never experienced it. You gave what was pleasurable, easy and natural, not the impossible. You were really *objective* all the time. You didn't waste yourself away with compassion, wear yourself out with sharing everybody's lives. So you kept your strength. Your question today shows you don't know why I should have fallen and become weak. You don't know that you were in the womb nourishing yourself out of my very flesh—not just a mystical strength. The mystical strength is infinite, but not the body. It is my body I crucified. For it wasn't made for the burden I put on it. And that is where I was the dreamer. Is that an answer to your question?

I am having a pregnancy test made today.

DECEMBER 27, 1942

It is like a detective story, this tracking down of the incidents and misinterpretations which create an image, or distortion rather, or reality. My doubt of love makes me interpret certain phrases and incidents in a certain way.

A re-evaluation, re-interpretation of everything. Objectivity. Could I make a work of art of this—transmute, transform, conquer pain?

Coincidence, or the magical effect of analysis? The day I return from Jaeger, Hugo puts on my lap the first few hundred dollars he has earned outside of the bank, that he has vainly tried to earn for years and couldn't. Is it because deep down he resented how I spent all my money on others and felt it was useless to earn more as I would give it all away? When he felt I was trying to stop giving, he earned it, to give himself the pleasure I have denied him—of giving to me. His greatest pleasure, linked to his erotic passion for me, is to take me out and get me underwear, panties, stockings. Dressing me gives him a sexual pleasure, and I denied him this for years.

The magic consists in my peace being contagious, my relinquishing of struggle and anguish, releasing Hugo and Gonzalo. My lying back, with greater confidence, my ceasing to clutch and fear, affects all those around me.

Neurosis is the real possession by the devil, the real evil force.

DECEMBER 28, 1942
Winter of Artifice—notes

Pure essence of the personality, stripped of racial characteristics—time, place, the better to penetrate the innermost being—the deepest self. Description of states: insomnia, obsessions, coldness. Because I was free and beyond nationalism—

uprooted—mystical. *Rayons X de la vie intérieur.* Describe people as composed of climate elements, race elements, food they eat, animals they resemble, books they read. *Elle était faite de...* Then as layers: living either in feeling, present or past, ideas. Or absent, preconscious, conscious, seeing themselves, or blind or beyond this—into the union of sensation and perception or partly paralyzed, semi-invalids, semi-asleep, atrophied, avaricious, fearful, shrunk. *Day* people, or nocturnal—constant, variable, deflected, focused.

> American Infantilism
> cradle shoes
> little bows in the hair
> gather little girl dresses
> orphan hats
> school girl socks
> eating of candy, sugar, ice cream
> University or school clothes worn by Virginia
> Impotence
> emotional immaturity
> sexual immaturity
> radios instead of musicians
> School
> books on *how* to win friends
> school of *how* to make love
> questions asked of great figures

Gonzalo

I have felt mired in the blindness of their lives. Helba's paranoia, the idea of her great value, the blame of others for all mishaps, the victim complex—Gonzalo believes this.

> Dismantling of a love
> A feeling *décanté*

DECEMBER 31, 1942

The "pregnancy" was psychological. I had all the symptoms: nausea, painful breasts, ovarian pains, etc. Jaeger said I was trying to give birth to something—"What, we don't know yet." After the last attack of poison she helped me again. It is clear that I suffer merely from the knowledge that my love for Gonzalo did not become an absolute, not because of Helba, but because he destroys the mystical me (because he cannot possess it), and I cannot marry him altogether either. There is a part of him I reject, that materialist, *terre à terre*, factual, literal, limited Gonzalo who destroys all that he cannot understand. It is this that causes my sorrow.

I have Hugo. I *see* Hugo as I did not before, and I see the obstacle which turned me away from him erotically. Emotionally, I am suffering, but without despair, rancor, rebellion. I understand. I have to accept this. How sad it is. Gonzalo is blind. Blind. I cannot get any nearer to him. I made all the efforts. I grasped communism for his sake. He never came towards my mysticism. He hates it.

A difficult turning point. I have had too much suffering and so little pleasure.

JANUARY 6, 1943

Jaeger carried me out of the despair, out of the pain. We touched upon a deep well of guilt, great expiation for my only joy—the erotic. My only pleasure was the act of love, but my concept of love was wrong: to give up, to shatter the self in love, to consume the self. And my concept of giving was wrong: to give what hurts to give—myself—I thought was the highest love.

All wrong. And then the suffering from ingratitude, as she said.

The guilt appeared then, in my fear that she should make me renounce my sexual life, the last sacrifice of the last and only pleasure. For days I feared her. I thought she was taking the side of the *others*, not seeing the good I have done (as Helba won't see it). Then we unveiled the guilt, exposed it. So much expiation. Gonzalo too, expiating to Helba for the pleasure he took with me.

The guilt was there and is responsible for the suffering. And today we clarified the relationship with Gonzalo. True, I am not ready to give him up to his next phase of *maturity*, of going to Peru to get his rightful inheritance. True, I fear losing him when he won't need me as a mother anymore.

But it is true he wouldn't go…he waited and postponed and risked letting his mother die without seeing him. He resists facing his home, family, bourgeois background, fears being held there by the threat of the inheritance. He prefers to take from me. And as he said a few days ago, or whenever I doubt him because he sacrifices me to Helba: "The proof that I love you is that I can't go to Peru, as I should."

So it stands, and as Jaeger says, it is static for the moment. She understands so well. She has played the same role, only more terribly. She had no personal life, no husband or child. She could take nothing for herself. She was the giver.

JANUARY 9, 1943

Gradually, led by the lucidity and compassion of Martha Jaeger, the atmosphere cleared. I gained confidence in everything, in Gonzalo's love, in Hugo's, in myself. The tension vanished. And both Hugo and Gonzalo responded psychically. Hugo was relieved and released of his sacrifices, his strain, and we planned our "tour of the world" when he retires, *our* life and *our* pleasures. Then Gonzalo felt free, was happier and even more devoted. He became (because of the change in me) more protective, and expressed his love of domination which I lose sight of.

Resentments and bitterness were lifted. Because I understood everything, I could no longer be bitter. How difficult it is to recapture the talks with Jaeger, so mysterious the process. We don't know when we start, why we are talking about all the women I have loved, and their resemblance to my mother—they have the impetuous, aggressive character of my mother. We don't know why I think that because it was betrayal and abandonment, the suffering my mother endured at my father's hands was worse than any I suffered. We don't know why I expected this for myself. We didn't know how, as a child, I passed into my mother and endured her suffering and her being abandoned... The women—primitive, emotional, uncontrollable, irrational—my mother. This is all that I suppressed, controlled, sublimated. So again I seek "nature" in my lovers, and yet I suffer too, from this naturalness... On and on. And the guilt because of the pleasure I took. I thought Jaeger would condemn me and ask me to relinquish it, which in itself is an expression of guilt. Actually, Jaeger not only does not condemn me, she regrets not having done the same with all the love that has filled her...

Also the masochism, the obedience to the religious phrases.

At what point does the self-injury begin? I fell into a trap because of my compassion. I injured myself, but, says Jaeger, there is a way of giving without injury to the self, a way of being compassionate.

Masochism. What of masochism? The tortures I suffered from Henry's early promiscuity, his stories of going from me to a whore, but that was not deliberate cruelty, and soon he changed. Yes. I suffered, but mostly through my concept of love as sacrifice. My lovers did not betray me. They were childlike, selfish, narcissistic, unconscious, irresponsible, but not sadistic. I suffered mostly from jealousy (without cause) and excessive self-denial. Too great. All that I needed, I gave away, even the essentials.

However, my *weakness* as a mother, my indulgence, was counterbalanced by my mystical wisdom, so that *they* did not become weaker, but stronger, both Henry and Gonzalo. That was positive and creative.

Inner peace now. How strange it is.

I have started again to dream of a new life, of expansion. I dream of going to Peru—all of us—helping Gonzalo to get economically free, enjoying the voyage, the abandonment of America... I dream of voyages, new lives, new relationships...

JANUARY 11, 1943

Dreams of reconciliations:

My father. He is playing a very small piano in a museum in Havana. We are intimate and gentle. He says to me: "You were nicely dressed yesterday but you didn't look beautiful. Today you do." He caresses my hand. He is small, quick, humble.

We traversed the museum before coming to his private apartment. The noticeable fact was that there was nothing to see. It was extraordinarily bare. His own rooms were bare and not beautiful. I felt that he had been given a humble place and that he humbly accepted it.

My brother Thorvald. Also a feeling of intimacy and ease. I said to him: "You know, I used to think you and I were entirely different, but I can see we are growing more alike, and I understand you better." The woman he was married to I liked.

JANUARY 13, 1943

The body still shows the strain, the wear and tear, but it does not rule me. I am in a good mood. I have thrown away my much-mended, much-faded dark red kimono and bought at a second hand shop a sumptuous black velvet *sortie de théâtre* with a satin white lining, worn only a few times by a rich woman, and which I wear as a *robe de chambre*. I have bought oil paints to repaint the now-faded windows. I have bought a muff cushion and made myself a muff out of the little leftover pieces from my astrakhan princess coat, now cut down to a small cape and hood, very Marie Bashkirtseff. I have bought a cookbook and am cooking with care and delectation for Hugo's pleasure (he has waited for twenty years for this new quality to appear in me—I have been indifferent and careless). I have washed my seashells to their pristine whiteness. I have started to dream profusely day and night. The blood is circulating again. I write in my head.

What I feel about Henry now is this: he had ten years of comfort, laziness, self-indulgence, effortlessness, and aside from writing, he gave himself the easiest, softest life, without ever collaborating to make my burden lighter, or at least sharing it in part, or seeking to give me the same share of ease and softness. He never denied himself, drove himself, sacrificed, pinched, or renounced a single whim, pleasure, and therefore I have done well by him, gave him what very few artists have ever been given, ten years of peace and ease, and now he is well known, he is launched, he can easily obtain this from the world. And I do not feel it is wrong for me to put an end to my continuous sacrifices for him. I gave to the limit, of my body and soul. It has to end now. Lately he has not even thought it necessary to compensate these efforts with his presence, has taken without returning even in love or companionship and has made me merely the provider.

Henry gave my birthdate to Pierce Harwell in Hollywood, who never saw me: "First, about Anaïs. Lord God! I haven't come down from the stratosphere yet! Her chart is an experience. While every chart is something of a spiritual event in the astrologer's life, Anaïs's chart is one of those symphonic things that fill the brain and the soul with the music of the spheres. Already I have spent hours in it, like a bird winging through heaven."

JANUARY 1943

I lie in bed and write letters. There is a pause in the press work. I have whole afternoons at home. I am lazy. I enjoy it. I cannot make an effort. When I feel this exaltation filling me again, the surging energy, I lie back. I am not letting it carry me away. That part of me continues to dream great tasks, of going to Russia and working for it, giving my life.

Another part of me dreams of indolence, travels, lovers. Another part of me rewrites the diary to fullness and perfection. As I cannot *invent* people, I don't write.

The house is in order. Beautiful. Papers in order. That is how one organizes for the big dreams which will carry me off. The diaries in the safe, cigarettes in the cigarette boxes, one of leather, one of painted wood. The telephone at my hand, and next to it the little Spanish feast table with its two little red lanterns. On top of it, a glass box with jewels. Marks of Hugo's goodness: the doll house he gave me for Christmas because I gave mine away when I six years old, earrings he engraved for me.

The present. The sensual Gonzalo unleashed last night, thrusting into my mouth…

New stockings bought with pennies saved by Millicent from shopping. She opens the little box on my bed after breakfast, and says: "And now go and spend it on yourself."

Laziness. Laziness.

From my thumb to the index there is a rim of red I cannot wash completely away— the mark of my holding Gonzalo's sex after having marked it with my painted mouth.

Laziness.

FRIDAY, JANUARY 15, 1943
Letter from Henry:

Anaïs, the only reason I keep answering you about these recriminations and accusations is not in self-defense, but to awaken you, because admit it or not, you also have your blind spot. You say I don't seem to understand that it's your body which is exhausted. Implying thereby that there was never anything wrong psychically. And then you send me the Harding book, which I wrote you about last night. And the Harding book contains the answer to your problem. You sent it for me to profit by— but won't you admit that you were equally involved? I am grateful to you, to everyone, when my eyes are opened. But when I try to point out to you wherein you may be weak you think I lack sympathy and you come back to the same theme obsessively—that you are only physically exhausted, because I drained you dry. It is perhaps because you are so physically exhausted now that you refuse to recognize the mutual aspect of the catastrophe. […]

Do you know what this whole thing reminds me of? Of a Cesarean operation. You gave birth to a lusty infant: he's doing well, he has a good appetite, he's gay, even resourceful, young as he is, and the doctors tell you so, but, because it was such a terrible operation, because of the great pain you endured, you just won't believe it. You just can't see how it will get on in the cruel outside world, though the good Otto Rank wrote a book (*The Trauma of Birth*) to prove that's how heroes are made. Here I am, without the ordinary anguish of birth, and you say, "Yes, but look at me!" The important thing was the birth, no? You're alive, you're breathing, you're resting from your labors. Have faith in your creation. When I come of age, you'll marry me. The insignificant one who "protected, incited, inspired, formed, disciplined, nurtured, tormented, perfected and finally created the writer" may perhaps also be able to do as much for the human being who became the writer in order to become something greater still. You cannot and must not give up in mid-stream. The great sorrows, pains and tribulations are reserved for the great. They are fruitful. Let me add this finally. I decided on the beginning from the bottom. I have no illusions of any kind, nor delusions either. I do the utmost I can every day. I'm leading a beautiful, chaste, sober, disciplined life, which keeps me serene. I know that miracles will continue to happen, because I know there is a law of compensation. I atone for any sins or crimes by doing my best towards others. I give myself completely in every direction. I want nothing, and I want for nothing. I consider myself blessed. If this sounds crazy, then have Dr. Jacobson put me in a strait-jacket.

Letter to Henry:

Why can't we stop wounding each other and destroying what was created? You give the weakest and the worst interpretation of my devotion: the neurotic one. That is what hurts me. I never gave the worst interpretation of your dependence: I always gave it the highest one, the justification of your creation. I lived for that highest interpretation. You seek only the *flaw* in mine. That is what fills me with bitterness. Because I wrote it down, you say, proved the wrongness.

You speak of the horoscope but you don't accept its interpretation of my serving. You don't see the tragic drive I had, to consume myself in love. That is not neurosis. Many mystics consumed themselves. That you should treat me as a mere neurotic expressing self-pity is such a poor interpretation of my acts. I asked you not to write me anymore in that tone—I asked for a truce. I will not argue for myself anymore. If you can't write tenderly, humanly, simply don't write me. I don't see why we can't make this change without reproaches to each other. I don't see why we can't be human and simple about it, why I can't just say to you: "Henry I'm tired. You take care of yourself now." And you answer me quietly and simply: "Fine. I will. I feel strong now. You rest awhile." At times you write me like that and I just rest and sleep and feel myself getting strong. But at other times—and believe me in back of all the bitter statements there is always in you and in me a need of self-justification—you write, as you believe, to help me but it sounds like reproaches too. You think I blame you for my collapse but I don't. [...]

You had ten years of what the artist needed to create—and now I'm tired, that's all, just humanly, simply, naturally tired. Is that a crime? When you were tired you slept. You weren't forced to explain or justify your tiredness. After each book you experienced a letdown. You felt drained. Well, I created for ten years without a rest. I'm just plain tired. Do we have to drag in Harding, neuroses, Rank, Lao-tze, etc.? I'm tired like a negro gets tired—like a child. [...]

There is nothing *unnatural* in my being tired. Nothing neurotic. Nothing of a failure. When you slept I guarded you, let you sleep. Can't we be natural, can't I be allowed to be tired, human, simple? That alone would cure me—hasten the return to strength. Your letters have been irritants instead of *berceuses*!

Letter to Henry:

Henry: The way you could have helped me best is by finally regarding me as a human being, with a body. My love for you was far more complete because I regarded you both mystically and as a human being, I treated you as a great creator, writer, mystic, but I took care for your body, and when I met you in Paris it was your body which had broken finally—and I took care then of *all* your needs, regarding them *all* as a whole. But you tend to do to me what everybody else but Hugo has done: to expect the infinite, to disregard my weakness, my illnesses, my fatigues, to have no compassion. This is the reason I obsessively harp on your accepting the reality of the body, for if this had not failed *me* I would still be taking care of you. Don't you see? It is so simple. But you have grown so accustomed to see me only in mystical relation to you. You have lost sight of the other. My insistence on this was because in my mystical desires and devotions there was no end. Will you believe me more when I tell you that this is not my personal interpretation but the very words of a person who can see what neither you nor I can see because we get emotionally involved—the woman with whom I have been talking?

When you had your crisis in France, your change of life, low ebb, you made a transformation from a lessened physical energy to a new expression of it in a more spiritual realm. I didn't call you a neurotic then. I saw you pass from great animal exuberance to a less physical energy and into a more mystical one. Well, I have to do the same which means I can't express my devotion by taking care of people with my body's efforts. I have to do it differently—in another realm, that's all.

Don't you see, Henry? Of course I'll get well, and make the transfer—but it will not be the same pattern. I will have to become a writer, a musician, anything, but no longer the physical mother. That's hard because I am a complete person—the physical and spiritual in me are related. I have not only wanted to give manna, but everything people needed, shelter, warmth, food. I'm *total*. I'm no Ramakrishna. I function on *two* levels, like a combined Stalin-Ramakrishna affair. Can you imagine wanting to be so complete?

January 19, 1943
Music

There is something to be investigated: my relation to music. I think I am a musician *manqué*. It is music I am trying to reach in writing. I am too emotional for writing, too emotional. I ought to be behaving like June to satisfy this violence and excess of feeling. But something controls, checks me. Reason and consciousness. Is it *fear* of the unconscious? When I saw Gonzalo beside himself, crazy, unstable, I felt my own instability and fear of insanity. But music—could this feeling go into music better than writing? How? As a child my reaction to music was emotional, tragic, passive. I hate *solfège*, the technical piano studies, etc. The dream of music, not its reality.

It is the only thing which satisfies me today. I am further than ever from the scientific, intellectual worlds. It is only to save myself from melancholy, depression and insanity that I seek consciousness again. People cannot receive writing directly through the senses as they receive music. Yet it is this way that I write, to communicate directly with the emotions. There is a mystery here.

Why did I reject the study of *solfège* and weep during the lessons? Music has haunted me several times in my life. Why did I give up dancing, which was a joy?

The exaltation which takes hold of me even when I am in a physically low condition is too much for writing. It breaks the mold of words. That is why I have done so much bad writing, diffuse and oceanic.

The kaleidoscope of moods is contained in music, not writing. The second part of *Winter of Artifice* symphonic.

It is always the same story one is telling, but from different ends of the microscope, of the hourglass, of the opera glasses. Through layers and layers of glass one looks, and at times it is an image in the mirror made small by the great distance. It is childhood, a small figure, with its scenery, its climate, its atmosphere. Long distance. Miniature. At another time it is not an image of one figure, but of three large wars that are taking place. For the small diminutive figure of the child, the war between parents and division and separation are as great as the world wars of 1914 and 1940. As great, as devastating. The being is torn asunder, three times. Now it is the giant figures of myth parents, striving and dividing. Now it is the image of nations striving and dividing. The sorrow is transferred, enlarged, but it is the same sorrow: it is the discovery of hatred, of violence, of hostility. It is the dark face of the world which no childhood was ever prepared to receive. Childhood is not prepared for strife. It enters with an expectation of paradise and of play, and to force the tragedy of hatred and destruction upon a child is to force too great a burden on its innocence. The being is sundered, as the tree cracks under lightening, as the earth cracks under the earthquake, as the soul cracks under violence and hatred. Paradise was from the first a place to be swallowed up by the darkness. So it is. The unbaptized children who die are for the devil, but some are baptized by fire—they do not die of it, but are scarred.

There are so many instruments for the eye to gaze through, and to observe. It is possible to see infinitesimal detail, never everything at once, buy only at the moment of the most intense sorrow or pain or death. I have too often looked backwards. Too often, as men return to memories of a battle because the scar hurts them.

Nothing is effaced.

Through the microscope I see the dispersed and sundered being. Every little piece has a separate life. Then occasionally like mercury, they melt together, but they remain unstable and elusive, corroding. The mercury being the matter of our thoughts— the mercurial mind—the indicator of temperature. Blood cannot warm it. The cells of feeling have their own motions, retreats, shrinking. Something always eludes the scientist, the poet, the star-gazer, the informers, discoverers, tabulators. It haunts our sleep. It is what lies in the deformed mirror of the dream.

Fragments.

JANUARY 22, 1943

I feel like Rimbaud, with a desire to turn my back upon all my writing because it is all entangled with pain and to enter a new world. I feel like writing two or three macabre stories I carry in my head.

I feel like rewriting the entire diary in two columns:

the actual diary as it is

and its completion à la Proust—filling, rounding, objectifying, encircling, encompassing all.

JANUARY 23, 1943

I know that the diary should be written in two columns—two versions. I know that the dreams should be *completed*. It is not enough to penetrate into the subterranean chambers. It is not enough to illumine separate cells with a partial light. Some *total* process must take place, some miraculous synthesis, by the suppleness of dialectics. The application of this principle has made the power of Russia. I want to find it in writing. I want to find the true dialectical writing. My problem is that in *action* people repudiate the invisible world which has formed their acts, as people repudiate the influence of the dream. *Je fourmille, je grouille d'idées, des perceptions fuyantes.* I am approaching something new.

JANUARY 24, 1943

How many evenings spent lying down, reading, listening to music, with Hugo. Do I lie content, *savourant* Giraudoux, or ruminating the story I want to write, or improvising in the diary? Evenings at Louveciennes, with the country asleep around the room like a giant foster mother, evenings when people feel at peace and drugged, but Anaïs? Anaïs cannot rest. Warmth, perfume, rugs, soft lights, books. They do not appease me. I am aware of the time passing, of aging, of all that the world contains which I am missing.

Yet when I go out I am disappointed. Every day I am prepared for feasts of love. If only I could enjoy sensual love as men do. If only I were easier to please. If only I were Ninon de L'Enclos…

Frénésie

Frénésie

JANUARY 27, 1943

I have had a fear of public recognition.

All this was subtly suggested by Jaeger. She led me as she does so *invisibly* to the very core of it. I was talking about Helba having had "public recognition—*not that I want that*," I said.

And Jaeger said, "Why not?"

Then I had to confess I did want it and had suffered from the lack of it. I told her the lamentable story of my publications:

The D. H. Lawrence book was published by Titus a few months before his business went bankrupt, and the book was only partially distributed, half lost, not sent to reviewers, and no royalties.

Michael Fraenkel advanced money for *House of Incest*, but lost interest in it when it was out and did not distribute it as he had promised. No reviews, no response. I finally sold about 50 copies to Gotham Book Mart at 50¢ apiece, which she resold at $5, but I was grateful that she took them or they would still be in France.

Durrell supplied money for *The Winter of Artifice*. Obelisk issued it a week before the war—no distribution, no reviews.

I print *Winter of Artifice* myself, and when James Johnson Sweeney receives a deluxe copy from Hugo, he never writes a note of thanks, acknowledgment, or even courtesy. *The New York Times* refused to review it.

I am a slave to love again. I see strongly creative women crushing their men. I have feared this, as I have feared all aggression, all attacks, all destruction.

Henry is trying to make me feel badly, unconsciously. He is merely turning to "begging" letters again, to his dependence on the world. He begged Dorothy Norman, after I broke with her, and groups and organizations. He accepts hospitality, etc. Then he sends me a portrait of Joe Gould, the Bowery Village bum writer.

Then I get a fervent letter from Pierce Harwell, admiring and seduced by my horoscope! And he says this about *Winter of Artifice*, which pleased me deeply:

"Your words are little clay pellets with hieroglyphs on all sides, and on the top and the bottom. Their meanings are not philologistic, but telepathic and cumulative.

"I am going to say something which is peculiar and irrational for me to say to you. You are materially the 'woman of the world,' you have lived hard and violently and roundly. And, quite oppositely, I am eternally pre-adolescent. In a material sense I have been ten years old all my life. So it does seem peculiar and very irrational for me to write to you in this way.

"P.S. I am enclosing a little note for Eduardo. Will you be so kind as to send it to him for me. Henry sent me Eduardo's little book to read, *The Round*, and I am anxious to discuss it with him."

FEBRUARY 2, 1943

Gonzalo's partial impotency, growing more so, leaves me without sensual satisfaction. For weeks he cannot fulfill the sexual act, he merely satisfies himself by my caresses, like an old man. The last time he had a small heart attack. His health is bad. So now, finally, I have nothing, no lover even, just merely the burden, no pleasure, no passion, no understanding. It is a terrible weaning—I have never wanted to *see* that Gonzalo's sexual inadequacy was starving me, together with his spiritual incompatibility. I can't bear the death of this love. I can't bear my being so aware of the crumbling. To separate first from Henry, that was painless, but from Gonzalo it hurts.

Gonzalo, Gonzalo—will you awaken before it's too late? Henry lost me, and now you will too—I am withdrawing. I would give my life to recapture my illusion of Gonzalo.

THURSDAY, FEBRUARY 4, 1943

The talk with Frances today in which we were piecing together a vast puzzle. She described the two kinds of orgasms so clearly: in one she lay back utterly passive, it came out of the darkness, dissolved and invaded her...in another a driving force in her, an anxiety, a tension made her seek it, grasping it as if in fear of it eluding her, and the movements were confused and crazy, cross currents of forces, short circuits, which brought an orgasm which did not bring calm, satiation, but left depression, a lack of satisfaction. The first one brought peace, the second, as if she had *not been possessed*, not fecundated by the male, dissatisfaction and frustration. (D. H. Lawrence has described somewhere the "clutching" of the female will in sex which in turn could be explained by the impotence of the infantile man...)

I have had moods corresponding to both states: I *dread* the second mood.

Is it the strong self in us which is not answered with equality, overwhelmed, conquered?

Is it that in the sexual act of the infantile men (including Chopin, de Musset, etc.), behind the apparent sexual maturity or potency, there is a psychic lack of drive and energy force which the woman feels and is destroyed by?

Is it this, or is it that in us lie two figures: one of the female woman, all passivity and receptivity, and another, a taut, anxious shadow which, to relieve her insecurity, fears, nervousness and panic, always plunges forward as the desperado does and is defeated because this aggressiveness of the psyche cannot meet its *mate* and unite with it? A part of the being does not take place in the marriage, and consequently there is this depression which corresponds to the depression felt by men after a relationship with a whore.

Now I myself have had two fears: of not attaining the orgasm, and of Gonzalo not being strong enough, enduring enough.

The other night I had a reprieve. He took me and I responded. I felt less depressed. But the anxiety has set in, and it is damaging the relationship. Whether the sexual is finally affected by the psychic discordance and multiple psychic assassinations, and whether the cadavers of all the joys Gonzalo killed in me, all the mystical voyages he paralyzed, all the dreams he crippled, have finally affected our sexual life, I don't know. All I know is that I do not have the woman's elation of meeting the strength that will take and possess her.

To really match him I would have to degenerate into a driveling, foaming half-idiot, incapable of opening a door or peeling an orange!

With Hugo I have the same exultancy at mastering, defeating, conquering, meeting the obstacle, at facing truths, at evolving, maturing, advancing, developing, growing. There is no problem of strength. He has his own. It is tested and tried in his work. If only, if only I could fall in love with his body, amorously—I love only his face and hands!

I couldn't save my relationship with Henry, but perhaps there is time yet to save mine with Gonzalo, or is it too late? Have I quieted his aggressiveness, pampered his laziness, increased his inertia in our sexual life?

The lover *inside*

like the child

This struck me because I recognized a feeling which I have had in regard to the lover. The yearning and craving and sense of emptiness come from the evolution in the love which places the helpless child-lover inside the womb, not only as a sexual act, but as a child, *filling* the womb. Now, as the passion decreases according to natural laws, and as he enters less frequently, and as, if the mother is creative, he has been growing *stronger*, there does come a time when she feels him outside of herself, and it is the confusion of the sexual with the material craving which gives woman this terrible misery which she describes as the need of touch, presence and possession. This has been the source of conflict between man and woman. Woman accusing man of not loving all the time, of not being inside of her all the time, of moving away and out. And she is left empty. Woman's tie is the physical. She has a greater need of caresses. And that is why the "weaning" that must come is so painful. When I gave birth to Henry, he lived outside of me. Now I feel Gonzalo outside (for it is a *reality* that he has grown bigger, stronger, more mature).

The suffering is of the womb: a yearning for a thing impossible in love, for a mingling of flesh and blood that happens only between mother and child before the child's birth. Woman's longing has that physical hunger for an impossible tie, the only time she feels secure, tranquil and sure of her possession (as I felt at the early passionate period of the relationship). I believe this is the secret of her "possessiveness." She is a realist and a materialist. Her body is made for this kind of absolute intermingling. Hereafter she will be incomplete without it—no relationship can give the marriage what the woman's body attains with her child. It is fatal to seek it in love, in sex. In other words, while man's tendency is to be born, to emerge, woman's is to take back, to keep, to *contain*. It is this instinct which drives her in love, not desire, not lust, not possessiveness, but that the body is made for this kind of union with the child. And the surrender she must learn, the weaning, the solitude that follows each birth—that, for woman, is her tragedy and her great differentiation from man.

Letter to Henry:

Today I got your gift—am very touched. I didn't want you to send so much—you may need it. I did two things I most wanted: I got my radio out of the repair shop, which brings me music, and I bought paper to print my stories (my pen broke down). When I finish the book for Caresse I'll print my stories and we'll see. When you told me all that Dudley said, I felt sad and ironic. Yes, I was wonderful—wonderful enough to use as the most worthless woman should never be used, wonderful enough to take from, to harass for one's whiskey, to strip and worry, to corrode the wonder and turn it to the use one puts servants and slaves to, wonderful enough not to save, but to burden, to want to feed on, to use for the very menial tasks his philosophy freed him from accomplishing. His rich nature demanded freedom, freedom from work (but not mine!). He has something else to give beyond his subjection to work—(but not I!). He helped to cause the collapse, would have gladly helped to finish me off, but I am "wonderful." I had to run amuck before they stopped, and rebel, and scream.

Well, it's all over. No one can do that to me anymore. I am a deeply injured being. You mustn't be surprised if I cannot agree with your philosophy: it almost caused my death. It demolished our life. I naturally have to find my own. For a while I couldn't read anything you sent me, even the Blake—it seemed to me I had to find a new world or die. Finally I did find a *new* world. I became luminous again, free, joyous. Saturday I'm giving a big party, a celebration of this resurrection. So you mustn't feel badly. But what I do feel is for Dudley's wife, and all the women who will love the sons you will form with your philosophy. I had promised myself to write nothing more about all this because I noticed that my *deepest* letters, where I most struggled to tell you something, were those you couldn't answer. And then suddenly you ask me: are you still against Hollywood? Then it's my turn not to know what you mean!

Letter to Henry:

Henry: What a Chinese correspondence! I never know what you're referring to— or answering—and you say now I mystify you, and all I know is that there is a big eclipse over our communication, for the more I write you the less you understand me. Better to abandon the effort. Surely you can see now the communication is broken. You are trying to understand the big change in me, but since you have removed yourself from all the vital central relations you can't possibly participate. I haven't written because I don't know what to say. We've become unrelated—we read the same books but see different meanings. I'm grateful for the Blake book but at the moment I can't read it. It's unrelated to the big change that absorbs my energy; it doesn't touch the integrity I seek. I prefer not to struggle anymore. The fact that I am the one who helped you get to your stratosphere doesn't console me now when I wish that instead of giving you a stratosphere I had built some kind of... Well...enough. I can't look back. I have to go on. Correspondence is too shabby a substitute. We're trying to make it do, but it's like a weed bridge over an enormous river. It's slight, inadequate. It's better to write as you do: Spring is coming—fine about all the letters, news, offers.

Goldberg doesn't even want to write about the erotica—he's so scared. He saw the man who printed *Tropic of Cancer* out of prison and that frightens him. I have the mss. What shall I do with them? The Cooneys are litigating against a ferocious woman to keep their farm on the eve of ejection—at least insecure and suspected of

145

pacifism, etc. So it is not a good idea mixing with them. Why were you so struck with Joe Gould? What is your interest there? He is a monster, a failure, has created nothing but a grotesque figure of mock liberty, mock creation. It's a caricature. Frances knows him. Was it just comical to you? Something I thought so far from you, unrelated to you…a gory dadaism, a clown of anarchism.

As far as my illness goes, it's over. I have my normal energy again. I'm finishing Caresse's book, but I'm not the same. It's this entirely new Anaïs who doesn't know what to write you. Death and rebirth, but completely changed. Out of the shell shock it is all the ugly and ill I can't bear, the regressions, the negative, the Joe Goulds, the sordid, the weak, the crazy.

I was tempted to tear this up—I tore up two letters. I'll send it just so you won't be without news.

Will I be the musician of literature, will I improvise, will the words emit a sound, will they resound and resound? Will I be the dancer of literature, use the lightest words? Will they dance alone, a ballet even in the most tragic moments? Will I be the actress of literature, wear all the masks, play all the roles myself? Will I be the lawyer pleading for my own exoneration, the jailer making my own prison of scruples?

everything…

the eye of the photographer

the stage setting

the knowledge of lighting

will I use the searchlight of the analyst

the product of my sickness, like the paintings of madmen?

Let me write a book, for I am in prison. Life is too enslaving, too crushing, too stifling. Let me write a book, grow wings, become invisible. Let me forget my sorrows, the lies that were told me, the delusions.

People will say I have changed. I changed. I moved away, only because I could no longer bear the pain.

I must keep to analogies, similarities of processes between body and soul, the analogy between the orgasm and the ecstasies of the soul.

There is a recurrence in the life of my animus, my mystical creative self, in the form of a young man who bears me into the mystic regions: Jean, Robert, and now Pierce Harwell, the astrologer. It is always thus, when I have had a fall from grace, when I am enslaved by earthy loves, by pain…

Henry has passed from the animal to the mystic, skipping the intermediate human emotional state. His mystic state is more that of self-indulgence: it is used to camouflage all painful or disagreeable perceptions. It is used to disguise his inertia and laziness and emotional inadequacy.

FEBRUARY 14, 1943

Last night elated by meeting Pierre de Lanux. As soon as he began to talk it was like a banquet for me—I found again the accents of Giraudoux, of Saint Jean Perse, of Louise de Vilmorin, of Nellie de Vogue, of Cocteau's description of the Comtess de Noailles.

And I, the starved Armenian of the poetical lost words, listened to him with all my attention and forgot my other visitors.

Lanux immediately spoke of the many levels of meaning reached by the French writer not possible to the English—the people, not the language. I am, for the English, committing a sin each time I give a phrase that contains all the meanings: spiritual, concrete, personal and mythological.

"Someday you will wake up and write in French."

But I know my destiny. It is a painful one. I am bringing those nuances into English, as a gift. I am inserting into English writing the subtlety and multi-lateral aspects it lacks. The language obeys me. But it will be difficult to be heard, seen, touched and loved by the English palate and soul. Listen to me, you English readers! I am sacrificing myself for you. I left my own people—those who *understand* my language. I left them to bring you the subtle melodies, the infinite nuances. In doing so, I seek difficulties, I shall be often rejected. You deal in terrible simplicities, in deserts, in primitive in-differentiation. You lack overtones. You lack the oblique, the indirect, the range, the virtuosity and maturity. Listen to me! I am your most intricate and variable musician. I can extend your ears, add hundreds of colors to your eyes, increase your palate's responsiveness, develop your senses. Follow me! I am bringing you a gift. As eyes, you are colorblind. My blood itself, my race brings you color. You lack tonalities. If you would accustom your ears to my scales, to my great variations, wavelengths, how light you would grow, what worlds you would discover! I could make you sensitive all over, thin your skin, sensitize your senses—if you let me! Are you going to punish me for my audacity? The awakener! Proust has not penetrated you. You cannot read Giraudoux. But I speak *your* language—the language of the potential you.

FEBRUARY 17, 1943

Gonzalo and I were talking about the books we are reading. I was telling him of the sorcery of Giraudoux. He said he was reading *Don Quixote* and studying the history of the Party. I said: "What an amazing contrast, exactly like your own nature. In your past life you've been a Don Quixote, seeing beauty where there wasn't."

"What do you mean?" said Gonzalo. I didn't say any more, but he knew I meant Helba. After a while he said: "So I see beauty in the cross-eyed monster—well, several other people have seen what I see." I pretended not to understand, because I realized I had gone too far and could not explain my meaning without running into the same conflict: I attack Helba, he punishes me, then I am hurt because he defends her. How can I expect Gonzalo to see the monster in Helba? We both stopped. The next moment he was tender, as if nothing had happened.

The new Gonzalo lives with me, but the untransformed Gonzalo still shares his weakness with the worthy companion of his incurable anarchism and laziness. What I am is what he aspires to, not *is*—the potential Gonzalo. Helba is what he was. Will he have the deathbed awakening of Don Quixote to his madness? He is trying to awaken. Poor Gonzalo. It is enough.

The rest is the monster in you, Anaïs, your sickness, because you have no confidence, because you fear to be abandoned, you fear Helba's power. That's for you to face and suffer and conquer. In an effort to rise to the surface, to see the surface world, to meet the men of power, the conquerors...*le monde qui brille*...I got myself beautifully dressed, combed, perfumed, and went to a cocktail party at Colette d'Arvilles'...

So I am back again (at the Vilmorins', at innumerable wealthy people's homes), back again into luxury. Everything is warm and brilliant. *Tout cela brille*, like the glasses, the carafes, the ice container, the satin and the damasks, the furniture... *Il ne faut pas regarder en dessous*... Pandora's box. Attention, Anaïs! Can you distill only the pleasure from this? *Les Jeux d'Artifice*.

FEBRUARY 18, 1943

I go out into the world, face new people. I am filling myself with new images, new impressions, new sensations, to renew my poor old love of Gonzalo, to lighten my burdens, and an ocean moves within me with elation and excitement. It is like climbing into the realness of light again. I see too much, I feel too full, too rich, there is the *congestion de lumière*, and out of it I cannot form a book. Any thread I pick, any theme, leads me into an ocean, a cosmos, a labyrinth. I see all the connections and the interrelations, so I am caught in a symphony and cannot play my solo quietly. An onrush. A tremendous circulation, animation...

My night dreams elude me, but it seems to me that I dream continuously. And I cannot seize a structure for *one* book; I can only add to the fresco, to the infinite tapestry to the illimitable.

Je me sens pleine.

That is my most cherished mood—desire, plenitude.

FEBRUARY 22, 1943

Several days of flowing, dancing, inner celebration and inspiration, then last night a dream which has painfully affected me all day: I was working at the press with Gonzalo. I left him to speak to Jaeger. I sat very near her so Gonzalo would not overhear us. But instead of analyzing me, Jaeger went out on the fire escape to show me her gymnastic feats. She did amazing somersaults, with suppleness. But once she slipped down the opening of the fire escape. I was in great anguish. She caught herself by the hand very nonchalantly and continued. Again she slipped, and this time fell down the six flights. I screamed, got completely hysterical, felt a terrible sorrow as if my mother had fallen. Her small son was there—a French boy. He fell asleep innocently on my knees, not knowing his misfortune. I knew his loss and thought: I shall have to adopt him. The house was full of people. I felt the pain of Jaeger's fall in my body. It was unbearable. I didn't dare ask if she were dead. But she wasn't. She was laid on her bed and I felt her pain in my own body, particularly around the breast, the stomach, the body itself, not the arms and legs. She spoke to me quietly as if she would not die. Later Gonzalo and I were looking for each other with desperation. We found each other and clung wildly.

MARCH 3, 1943

Party at Canada Lee's. First I wanted to go alone; an adventure, a new world. *Audace.* Then I felt very close to Hugo and willing to share the experience with him, so we went together. It was beautiful. Half white, half black. The blacks are the best of all, warm, cordial, noble, easy, integrated. They were intellectuals, communists, artists, doctors, sculptors, architects. A new world of human simplicity and deep development. Very moving…but disturbing.

A beautiful night.

MARCH 1943

Then Saturday, March 6, in spite of depression, I gave a marvelous party to give Jaeger the pleasure of seeing me in full bloom of health. A party to health, to pleasure, and it was joyous. And as one party gives birth to another, Saturday I will meet Richard Wright and Carson McCullers, Wednesday I see the James Sternes, while today we all sat around Milton Gendel's table and crayon-painted it as I did my benches. Laughing and talking.

Les jeux rétrouvés! Les jeux. I forgot Gonzalo for two days!

MARCH 12, 1943

The neurotic is the caged mouse, caught in his pain, is fixed upon it and cannot move away. Free of neurosis, even if the problems are still the same, the soul is free. There is the power to move away, to rest from it, to seek new experiences which change the air, change from stagnation to circulation. The problems are there, but I have changed. I can move, dance, forget, rest, renew myself and return with fresh strength.

It is not in the love, but in the friendships that I find gayety…a gayety I needed deeply. So I go out, out, out. And I have lost my shyness. I sparkle. I am so open to the world, so open, so much in contact with it, it is like a huge cosmic love affair!

Then this morning another letter from Henry, and again this feeling that I disagree with every word he says, that he misunderstands me, that the contact is broken.

A DREAM OF HAITI

My desire surges towards him

NEW YORK, APRIL 18, 1943

A visit from Lucas Premice and Albert Mangones, a Haitian evening, a voyage to Haiti. Premice told us a story about an old Frenchman in the Columbian jungle, a political *évadé*, carrying the dead arm of a *copain*, in chains. Premice saved him, taught him Marxism and walked forty days over the mountains to help him escape.

> *On peut toujours s'évader*
> by transcending
> Again my favorite word
> to transcend.

I was happy last night during the journey to Haiti! Upon leaving, they said: "Next time we will bring our drums. Your place has a propitious atmosphere."

I would like to detach myself completely from Henry. I find his letters ugly—how was it I did not see the ugliness? When he gets the small press from Dudley's brother, he writes: "I must find someone to do the dirty work for me." When I refer ironically to Dudley, who like all the others burdened me with himself and his friend he answers: "You are hard on those who use you!"

There is such sterility and dryness in the letters, callousness. The dimension of feeling is missing, as in the criminal and the madman. He is schizophrenic, like my father. I realized Henry's letters only hurt me, anger me, and I asked him to stop writing. I can't bear the ugliness of his letters now without my "delusions" which made me *not see.*

APRIL 23, 1943

On Tuesday, April 20th, we finished *Misfortunes of the Immortals* for Caresse, a big task, a book whose content and design are worthless. On Monday we finished the printing. Gonzalo and I went out and drank whiskey, ate a Spanish dinner, went to our corner, took our clothes off and had an orgy as frenzied as our early passions, with Gonzalo in ecstasy—a peak!

APRIL 26, 1943

I gave a party, for Premice, Mangones, Irina Aleksander, etc. The few parties I have given have been dreams. This party was a beautiful dream of Haiti, with Premice and his voodoo face, his two daughters Adele and Josephine. Josephine is an inspired dancer, savage and violent and powerful (she is only sixteen). Adele is sedate and learned. Immediately they showed affection and used the *toi*, to which I respond with all the warmth of my own being. Albert sat on the drum and sang soft, tangy songs beautifully. Josephine danced. Irina was effervescent, revealing herself as a delirious actress, both comic and tragic, rendering Russian poetry with such eloquence and nuances that it was ensorcelling. She took a scene from the Comédie Française Russe, making us laugh and weep—it was wonderful, fiery, effulgent. Canada Lee was enamored by all the women but crystallized his intention of a love affair on me and, on parting, asked if my green eyes denote passion as the legend assures us. As he looked for something to read to us, Hugo suggested *Winter of Artifice*'s last pages and Canada read them movingly—so I had the unique experience of hearing my work read by someone before me, absorbed before my eyes, a strange violation of the secret lapse which usually separates the writer from his reader. A strange sensation.

APRIL 28, 1943

In his last letter, Henry tells me he met a Greek woman who is *me*, who resembles me in every way, with whom he had a talk like his first with me. *Crazy.* She is the same as me "even to the husband situation." After I sent my letter to Henry I felt slightly guilty of cruelty, for he cannot escape from the truth now, but I wanted to hurt him, to strike against his schizophrenia, his escape from all pain, his great self-protectiveness.

I had the following dream: Henry came to stay at the big hotel where the press was lodged, and I was constantly anxious that Gonzalo should see him. The striking thing about Henry's appearance was his exaggerated, almost grotesque air of health: a very red skin, shiny, thick, healthy hair, while I was mentally and physically sick. He kissed me as if nothing had happened, but I drew away and said, "Help me to tell you the truth."

APRIL 29, 1943

Talk with Jaeger. She believes my collapse came from the finality of the break with Henry. She says the letter I wrote to him was truthful and just, not cruel. She was glad I had made the break. As an analyst she was forbidden to pass judgment on Henry, but today she said she was happy for me because Henry would have merely continued to take my whole strength (the healthy Henry of the dream, and the sick me).

How can I be sick, why should my heart fail me? I have Hugo's complete love, his twinship, I have Gonzalo's passion; I had, as Jaeger said, the most that Henry was capable of giving as love, more than June; I have the whole world before me and marvelous friendships. Let this be the last of the crucifixions.

How Jaeger has tried to save me from sorrow and self-destruction.

MAY 8, 1943
Albert

Albert is twenty-six, and is almost white, golden in fact, like a smaller, younger, whiter Gonzalo. His hair is curly, his face round and soft, but the great difference is in the mouth. Gonzalo's mouth is narrow and compressed, and Albert's is full and sensuous. Albert sings Haitian songs with a beautiful voice, dances, plays the drum, has won a gold medal for architecture at Cornell, and is a painter and sculptor. He is soft, sincere, integrated, a communist. He does not deny his race, though he could easily pass for a Cuban, a South American. He is refined and sensitive. I felt close to him, warm, human. We became friends. At this dinner I turned my attention on him. We danced together, with a lovely warmth. Albert pleases me with the kind of beauty I love in Gonzalo without the darkness. He is made for pleasure. And so my desire wandered—I became all desire and warmth. I got up and danced to the drum…

Then I did a diabolical thing—I let Albert come to the press. He came in and I never saw him look so beautiful, healthy, charming, in contrast to Gonzalo, and I had never noticed the difference and the resemblance. Gonzalo, who has neglected me for ten days, reacted with instant jealousy, instant panic, as if he had been stabbed. And I was glad. I enjoyed hurting him. Gonzalo, you leave me for Helba, and when you leave me, I am unfaithful. I did not try to console him. Yes, I said, Albert was in love with someone else, but Gonzalo did not believe this.

He did not dare explode, but he suffered, and I was glad. Only towards the end of the afternoon did I feel pity for him. I pretended not to know what he was suffering from, and he did not dare to acknowledge it. It is my first experience with sadism. It gave me pleasure. I thought: Well, you like suffering with Helba—I can make you suffer too. When Jaeger called him a masochist I was angered, for I could see I had caused him only pleasure and fulfillment (the only suffering I ever caused Gonzalo was jealousy).

Now, as I write this, my pleasure is gone, and I would like to console him. Has all this come about because Jaeger forced me to face the irrational woman in myself?

Jaeger says I have a rational mind seeking to control my nature, but I have never faced my own irrationality. She thinks I *use* lucidity and rationality only to deceive myself. I have always thought that I face all truth because I do not try to elude suffering, but there is a masochistic suffering masking deeper truths and terrors. Behind all my suffering lies a greater truth I have not yet faced—I am still amazed how a situation can arouse such passion, create such an intense mirage.

I am not sure that Albert is free, and he is not daring enough. I want to wait until someone compels me, courts me, forces me. I want a man. But the very feeling that I could desire others than Gonzalo gave me such pleasure that when I returned to the press, looked out the window and listened to the street musicians, I felt joy, and I said to myself: I am a free woman. I am free to enjoy. I shall know joy. I paid too heavily for my joy, too heavily, until now.

Of course, my causing Gonzalo's pain may have been merely rebellion against the pain he causes me out of his own being, his weakness and blindness.

MAY 11, 1943

Jaeger. She laughs at my "cruelty," its inoffensiveness, laughs that I exaggerate its strength. Then we discover that I have a terror of the irrational, that I have linked irrational behavior to abandon. So I fear it, and as I fear it in myself and repress it, I succumb to its exteriorization in others, and suffer from it.

I have been too good, too saintly, too rational. Now comes rebellion. Gonzalo said during our quarrel (for the next day, of course, we had a big quarrel during which he accused me of being Albert's mistress) that I "was rebelling against life."

I said, "And you don't, and that is why life conquers and crushes you."

Just as I was being reconciled to Gonzalo and realized I didn't want to break but to free myself of neurotic suffering, a new catastrophe places Helba in the center again: her mother died. So immediately came the test! Let us see how I will take it. It is a choice between a break and acceptance. During our quarrel we hurt each other, but the love was apparent. Gonzalo said he had become a "saint" since he knew me, completely faithful to me, that he could not see how I could be hurt. In defiance of the hurt I expect from him, thinking he would say he could not come Monday night, I had invited the Haitians, but then he did ask me, and I had to refuse to see him.

I have had a neurotic fear of being irreparably damaged by my straining and suffering, and of being condemned to semi-invalidism. Jaeger says it is merely guilt for my desire to be happy and to enjoy. There is a violent struggle going on now between the sad, sacrificed Anaïs and the dancing, sensuous Venus Anaïs. It is going on in my struggle with the Haitians in spite of Helba's mother's death with which Helba will involve Gonzalo for several days now!

I am aware of a pain like that of being born, a difficult birth, I assure you. The drama is apparent in my clothes too, and I change from gay feathers and joyous colors to Madonna shawls and black dresses, from luminosity to paleness and thinness, from sleeplessness and heart palpitations to exuberant intoxicating vivacity, which is now released in company.

My heart and nerves have been very bad, but I will triumph. I have saved Gonzalo in great part. What I couldn't save is the compassionate, blind Gonzalo, whose blood Helba is drinking like an incubus; but he has lived, loved, enjoyed, gained health, he is working and creating, while life punishes her cruelly. During the day he was most jealous and angry, he talked all the time about new ideas he had for my book of stories. He is pathetic and sincere. I have been blinded by my pities too...so...

Evening: The scene of jealousy gives me reassurance! So this afternoon at the press, the first afternoon we were without pressing work for months, Gonzalo said, "Let us go to sleep, under the covers." And we took our clothes off and had an orgy—such vibration of desire, such electrical currents that the entire world seemed annihilated—an absolute of pleasure.

Then sleep, peace, contentment. Gonzalo was reassured. He kissed me passionately. Now if only I can keep the poison out of my being, which comes out of fear, and fear out of doubt, and doubt out of self-doubt, and all this comes from illness, just as Gonzalo's jealousy does...

We laughed. We were happy. I was grateful to Martha. I saw her supremely intelligent face laughing at me, "Well, that wasn't such a *very* cruel thing to do, after all."

As we came out of the press, half a block away Albert greeted us—waved. But he had a hat on and was very differently dressed. Either Gonzalo didn't recognize him or was free of anguish, and he kept his good mood, observing that the trees were blooming.

I came home, no longer felt my heart aching, sang, patted my face, and realized that suddenly my "beauty" has *settled*—settled to give others an illusion of beauty.

Ladies and Gentlemen, because I started in the opposite direction of the general run of *grandes amoureuses*, that is, I started with the *amours difficiles* (not *faciles*). It does not mean that after loving three times tragically and deeply I will not be able to entertain you further with more and more enticing stories of seductions and abductions and deductions. I will have many surprises for you, many enchanting adventures yet. All that has happened has made me a "face" and a woman of seduction. After all, my own husband after twenty years still thinks of me suddenly in the middle of his work, with desire. So whoever is reading this diary shall not always be wearied with stories of deaths, hospitals, asylums, but shall get a certain *chronique scandaleuse*, and what else is usually expected of Madame Venus?—who is, as Jaeger says, most positively a symbol of erotic seduction for other women.

MAY 16, 1943

Gonzalo hasn't told Helba about the death of her mother. He is preoccupied and fearful of the moment. I am tender to him, but I run quickly to Albert's studio and find a weak Albert who is very overwhelmed by my visit, timid and uneasy...and as I want to be seduced by a man, I run out again, feather to the wind, full of wild expectations, out in the spring night... Hoping, desiring love. Wishing, dreaming.

MAY 22, 1943

At least my illness is partly conquered. I have moments when I am free of anguish. I had a moment (they are so rare I can note them like important events) when I was laying down at the press, resting. Gonzalo was at the desk finishing a composition. The window was open on a summerlike day. I was watching the clouds passing over the house top. I was content. There was an organ grinder playing. A feeling of peace.

No one has described fully the horror of this illness called *angoisse*, or neurosis. Worse than any physical illness, this illness is of the soul, for it is insidious, so elusive, and so overlooked. You have just left your lover. You have just caressed and been caressed. You are walking home to a perfect, tender, devoted, passionate husband. No great catastrophes threaten you. You are not tragically struck down as others are, by the death of a loved one at war. There is no visible enemy, no real tragedy, no hospital, no cemetery, no mortuary, no criminal court, no crime, no horror—there is nothing. You are traversing a street. The automobile does not strike you down. It is not you inside of the ambulance being delivered to St. Vincent's Hospital. It is not you whose mother died, not you whose brother went to war and got killed. In all the registers of catastrophes your name does not appear. You were not attacked in Harlem, raped, mutilated. You were not kidnapped for white slavery. You were not in the clipper which sank twenty passengers into the sea. You were not in a concentration camp, not on the refugee ship which was not permitted to land anywhere. You were not jailed in Spain, your family was not tortured by France. None of that. But as you cross the street and the wind lifts the dirt and before it touches your face, you feel as if all these horrors had happened to you—you feel the nameless *angoisse*—the shrinking of the heart, the asphyxiation, the suffocation of pain, the horror of the soul being stabbed... Invisible and pitiless drama, the *mute* drama. Only the analyst detects this drama and hears your cries. No one else. Every other illness or pain is understood, pitied, shared with all human beings. Not this one. It is mysterious and solitary; it is as ineffectual and unmoving to others as the attempted crying out of a mute person!

Everybody understands hunger, death, physical illness, poverty, slavery. But no one understands that this moment at which I crossed the street, an alluring personage, a seductive one, every privilege granted me, of love, desire, food, health, house, is more completely annihilated than by a concrete catastrophe. It is the true Tantalus torture: it is given to you, the health of your mother, the loves, the desires, the food, the house, like a mirage. It is given and denied. It is present in your vision and removed from your possession because the *angoisse*, the mysterious disease, the mysterious poison, has corroded your life and being.

This diary has been *le livre des angoisses*. The rarest pages in it are those of peace, contentment. So rare. *Angoisse* is the woman of a nightmare, screaming without a voice.

À la Recherche
des Jeux Perdus

MAY 23, 1943

Wearing the fuchsia bird of paradise, the fuchsia veil, the black velvet suit, the new copper colored nails (I made the mixture myself), sandals, no stockings, I went to the *fête Haïtienne*. I danced with Albert, and I met Jean Brièrre, the young and mythological beautiful black poet, and other Haitians. Josephine performed her voodoo dances.

All of them, the black ones, created this climate of warmth in which I bloom. I was in bloom, susceptible, open, flower-like, and to the first one who courted me, my body acquiesced. Canada Lee came at midnight, and put his arm around me, grasping me so tightly, saying: "When are you coming to see me? I've been wanting you to come and see me from the first time I saw you with Caresse." So I said I would come. His only free evening, because he is in a play now, was Monday, Gonzalo's night, but I said I would come.

It is a blind desire for sensuality, not for Canada Lee, but for all of their warmth and tenderness. It is strange how I have arrived at the flowering of my love of touch, of caresses. My own warmth is so great, but now it manifests itself in touch. I love to touch. I love to touch all of them, to kiss, to put my arm around all my friends— warmth, warmth, a tropical climate.

And now Hugo says, "I am sure I will make money now, in September," and gets masterly. And I say: "Well, if you do, I shall then become completely Mlle. Frou-Frou. I shall do nothing but dress up and be beautiful."

And Hugo answered, equally playful: "Now we are getting down to the truth of it: you *are* Frou-Frou, and I like it, and it makes me desire you."

And it all stood clearly revealed, Hugo's erotic attachment to the exotic Anaïs.

Brièrre, the young African king, noble profile, perfect features. Premice's extraordinary fanaticism of the eyes—a rare noble.

My French ancestors lived in Haiti. When the uprising came they fled to New Orleans. The taboo last night, the separation between black and white, kept reforming itself.

How I wish Albert were more of a man.

Adventures of Frou-Frou

I awakened this morning to the thought of the night with Canada. I awakened hoping to enjoy it, not to be nervous, not to lose my appetite during the day, hoping for the flowering and the joy. As it happened, Gonzalo was dejected, inert, depressed, absent, etc. So I thought: how criminal to expect all life and joy from one human being. When one is born so full as I am, so rich, so overflowing, what a crime it is to be subjected to people less full, less rich, less alive. How wrong it is to take all my moods from Gonzalo, to starve for caresses, to starve for joy at his side, to wait for crumbs when I desire a feast, to rejoice over little fragments of passion when my whole being is that of a *grande amoureuse* with enough passion to flood the world! For the first time, I saw the world as a man sees it! I saw the sentimentality of woman. I laughed at myself clinging to the meager love of Gonzalo and sentimentalizing over him, seeing him unable to master or conquer sorrow, pitying him because I was going to give my body that night. Then, as I came up the stairs of my house, I thought: this has nothing to do with Gonzalo. Why confuse the feelings, the emotions, the pities, with the grandeur of the body's desires, with its climates and tropical orgies? Men know this. Men live by this. That is why they suffer less. Why cannot woman too? Why?

I came home. I enjoyed my bath. I enjoyed perfuming myself. I knew I was born for this, to do it over and over again, the ritual of the dressing, the perfuming for love, for sensuality. I enjoyed everything sensually, thinking of Canada, the body flowering. I brushed my hair with pleasure. I powdered my feet. I put fresh copper on my nails. I was happy, not nervous, free of guilt towards all. Knowing at last what I am, recognizing it, admitting it, confronting it, *une grande amoureuse*, who disguised some of her passions with love—the woman born for love, for man. I denied this. I punished this. Let it flower. It is the life of nature. Do not punish and crucify it, do not sacrifice it, deny it, or kill it.

When I read the life of Ninon de L'Enclos, I envied her, without guilt. How Venus must have smiled upon my *toilette*, and how the tragic gods who cross and thwart my Venus must have enjoyed the trick they played on me!

First, when I arrived, people had dropped in on Canada and were making spaghetti: five or six uncouth, inarticulate Jewish boys. A drunken negro was making political tirades. A young actress, too, was studying her part. Canada and the speaker got into a stupid argument. I tried to talk to the actress, Catherine. I liked her red hair and fiery temperament.

I saw the evening was spoiled, and when Canada went into the bedroom to answer the telephone I followed him there to say I thought I should leave and come another time. He began to kiss me. He was aroused. He closed the door. Then, when he made me lie down and was beginning to take me, the telephone rang! For fear someone would come to the door, he answered. It was for Catherine! So she came to the room and I had barely time to fix my face again. Then he said, "I can't bear to let you go. I'll send the others home." I came out with my coat on as if I were leaving too. Then I saw that Catherine was in turmoil. She was pretending it was because Canada had arranged for the boys to see her home. She was pretending even to herself that this had hurt her pride.

But I knew: I knew it was jealousy. A definite intuition prompted me to say to her: "Catherine, *you* stay, and the three of us will go somewhere together. Stay, Catherine."

But she went away tempestuously. I said to Canada, "She's upset about us." He denied it. But I saw I had hit the mark. He said, "Let's forget all about it. I want you." We went into the bedroom, but by now I was quite out of my pleasure mood. Catherine was on my mind, and he was a little bothered too, but his desire was strong, and he would not give it up. We went to bed. Then came what woman desires in her deepest primitive being, when she craves to be possessed—a mad, violent, absolute carnal act—like nothing ever acted by the white man. A devouring hunger, a complete, violent passion, like a storm.

I could not respond. The curse was on me again.

Canada's pleasure was immense. His cries I can still hear. I bear the mark of his teeth. I loved his possession. It was pure. It was of the flesh, of the flesh alone, and therefore pure and dark and terrible and wonderful, like a source not poisoned by feelings, emotions, sentimentalities, fears, doubts. A strength like the storms, the seas, the jungle, the mountains, the great strength of nature. Oh, Canada, the source of sex is pure in you, and stronger than in us. It is magnificent and of nature. His body was beautiful. A thoroughbred body...

After he had satisfied himself, he awakened to a noise on the terrace. Someone was there. He got up. I noticed he had no fear. Then I understood. I said, "Is it Catherine?" He nodded. He got dressed. I did too. Then the bell rang violently. He said, "It's Catherine." I went to the bathroom to fix my face. When I came out Catherine was still clinging to her story of being angry because Canada had sent her home with the boys. I saw a scene was pending. Canada now looked sheepish, and so I said good-bye to both and left!

It is to nature I want to return, it is my nature I want to accept. Here is an Anaïs whose ancestors lived in Haiti, in Cuba, in New Orleans, who were tropical and sensual. There is an Anaïs whose nature is luxuriant, but the great spiritual torments of love almost destroyed it. With Henry, I was nearer the joyous savage climate of sex than with Gonzalo. Gonzalo is a castrated savage, a timid savage. It was the primitive I loved in Gonzalo, but he was a weakened primitive who took only the pain and suffering from Christianity, its punishments! Poor Gonzalo!

Poor me too! What a crucifixion of the nature, what a starvation of the nature, what a perversion of it! Now that I am fully awakened to its power and magnificence, how criminal I find the constant thwarting of it.

Even Frances was asking me yesterday to transmit this force I felt into creation! No—no more transfusions, transpositions or sublimations! Pure nature and creation will come out of it, but nature will be at the roots, nourishing and plentiful! Nature full blown and wild, and the rest can grow like a superfluous fruit! But no more blood transmissions and transfusions, no more diverting of the courses of the blood into other channels. Let the blood live its own life and throw off its rarified flowers incidentally, but let not the blood be diverted.

I understand our going to the black man, to the source, but I do not understand why they desire us, what makes them prize us. I think it is merely the symbol, merely as a token of conquest by the downtrodden, merely our halo, our taboos, our inaccessibility. But what a poor prize, this weaker, paler, ghostly white race!

JUNE 1, 1943

Albert, his girl Pussy, Irina and her husband, the Premices, we all went to George Davis's house to see Richard Wright. We went like troubadours, carrying the drum. We gave him dancing, singing, drumming, and a taste of Russia, Yugoslavia, Spain, and

France. Richard Wright is a handsome, medium-colored man, quiet, simple, direct. Again a beautiful evening.

I was drawn to Albert, sat by him as he sang, wanted to drink the song from his mouth, his full and beautiful mouth. He responds to my warmth. I feel the current, and he receives it, but in the maze of his shyness, youthfulness, pride and passivity, I cannot tell if he wants me. When we walk towards each other either to dance, or because we are drawn to each other, we walk like two waves surging who do not dare to mingle. In this sea of warmth I am lost. I do not know how bound he is to Pussy, the little Jewish girl. As we left Wright's place, I took his one arm and Pussy the other. I said, "It pains me when you leave." He answered, "*Moi aussi.*" And his hand sought mine and clasped it—I felt him moved. I cannot distinguish between his feelings and mine. When he looks at me I *travaille*. I can't tell if he does too or if the turmoil is in me. Desire. Albert is the image of the joy I seek, the integrity, the beauty, the nature. He is the sea, the island, the warmth, the tropical dream. He is the languor, the softness, the siesta, the hammock, the sun, the dance, the song, the drum. Desire. In waves of phosphorescent foam my desire surges towards him, and I behave like a dancer, moving towards him, then shy, then retreating.

I am blind.

Yesterday, in the sun and warmth of summer, we went with Albert and his statue of a drummer to Jacques Lipchitz's studio for criticism. I heard Albert talk luminously, responding to the cosmic vision of Lipchitz. His intelligence is not like ours, monstrously over-developed like a morbid growth, not reaching the point of dissolution, dissection, separation, but fused, integrated, direct, pure. If only Albert were older, not the shy young son...if only he dared. But now I am faced by a new difficulty: I am the intimidating one.

My impulse is to run to him and kiss him, but Jaeger stands guard, the mythological mother, saying: "Do not run towards pain, do not run into pain, do not destroy yourself again, do not follow the mirages of love! He is the son; he is too young; he is too yielding. Wait for the man..."

Albert's dancing, with the softness and beauty of a woman, his feminine smile.

I live drunk with desire.

I didn't want to see Gonzalo, be with Gonzalo. He was dark and heavy. To come out of the darkness and heaviness, he drank, and when he drinks the savage Gonzalo is released. So he wooed me, with the violence I like, won me, sought a new embrace, sat me like an idol over his body, urged me to move, lay back, and only at the end I made an effort to respond...

June 3, 1943

They all came last night, Brièrre, Albert, Josephine, Adele, Lionel Durant, and Pierre Roumain. We sat on the porch. Albert's hands were on the drum, and I could not resist placing mine on the drum. He only touched the tip of my finger. I felt his feeling following me if I sat by Lionel, his feelings welcoming me when I moved towards him, drawing me to the seat beside him. He said, "I wish I had a gift to make you." I said, "There is something I want—the photo of you drumming in the fields…" He immediately gave it to me, though he had only one. I said I would have one made for him. I took it to the light. He followed me. We were alone in the studio. We leaned over Hugo's pictures, and the emotion caught us together. I had taken his arm, and he pressed mine, our bodies touched. As we could be seen from the window, we walked away, his arm about my waist. Forever and forever I shall feel how he pressed his temple against mine and said, "*Je sais, Anaïs, je sais.*" Delicate brushings, charged with feelings, tensions. A moment later others came. We put on the radio. Albert opened his arms and we danced…he held me tightly…simple acts.

After they left I turned out the light, and I fell back into the summer night, drunk. Over and over again I repeated the scene, the movements, from the very first: the hands on the drum, the dance, the feelings, each time anew, the strong current and the ecstasy, the most marvelous moment in all of life, more marvelous even than possession!

I know, Anaïs, I know…

Evening: Albert and I went to the Blue Angel to present Josephine at an audition. When it was over and Josephine was dressing, Albert and I sat at the bar. He first of all kissed my hand. His face, when he becomes passionate, is beautiful, ardent and joyous. We touched cheeks, temples, and then we could not resist the impulse and kissed. His full, so full, so rich mouth taking mine, the grating of our teeth…

He was not free to stay with me because Pussy had arranged an evening with him. But he came back home with me, carrying the drum upstairs. And for the first time we were alone, facing each other, body to body. A marvelous rhythm took place, some secret harmony which made each gesture exactly alike, a new firmness, like a premeditated graceful dance—I cannot describe it, but it was a dream embrace. We stood up, the bodies fitted so closely. I felt his desire. Strength came out of our similar softness and graceful violence; such intensity, but no brusqueness. How beautiful it must have been to see. First we stood up, and, beside himself, he broke away and went to wash his face. But when he was fresh and clean and prepared to leave, he sat on the drum. I moved towards him, and then, with passion, he laid his head on my breast, and I kissed his bowed head, his hair… Again we separated. "I must leave." But as I stood by the window, leaning against the table, Albert held me again, so powerfully, with his beautiful face resplendent, crushing me so that I lost my breath.

And then he left. And I was full of him, his face, his mouth, his strength. So perfect, so *possessive* were the caresses!

JUNE 4, 1943

Black hair again, lost among mine, black curled hair. Albert's high brow, his slanting upward eyes, his high cheek bones (his father was a white Spaniard from Columbia), his round nose, and his full, finely chiseled mouth, always slightly open, beautiful teeth, his mouth the magnet. His carriage: with all the gentle fullness of his body, its indolent form, the soft outlines, he has an erect carriage of pride, joy, perfection. No perversions or deformities. He reflects dance and music and the sun. His skin is the color of the sun.

J'ai peur de l'aimer trop...

For the night and the day after this, I was in ecstasy, an ecstasy so powerful that I thought it would break me. Everything was illuminated, lightened, the air, the light, the sky... The intensity of the desire carried me out of the world and out of reality! I thought too it would carry Albert out of his entanglements with the continuous presence of Pussy and the "group," for they live a kind of tribal life, always in groups together. But he sweetly, gently, and realistically yielded to the difficulties.

By nighttime, not having heard from him, the ecstasy turned to pain, anguish. I thought everything was lost, that my passionate responsiveness had frightened him. With such anxiety again the next day, I telephoned him, when I didn't want to, only to find him sweet and soft and pliant.

I made him come at six, for five minutes, I said. Found a pretext: I felt I could not go to the Haitian dance that evening without seeing him. He came. I was trembling with anxiety. He came in quietly, passively, accepting the difficulties, but just as passionate. While I talked, he was the one who began to kiss me. We embraced and kissed, and he said: "This will get us nowhere. We cannot be together." His brother had arrived. He was surrounded, encircled.

I was reassured by his embrace, but disappointed. It was what I had feared... softness and the lack of audacity. Lack of intensity too, for he is tranquil and passionate without tension.

At least my suffering and fear ceased, and I felt gay again. We went to the dance. The evening was lovelier than the last, more intimate, no whites but ourselves. I was taken out to dance constantly—and then...

Brièrre, whom I call the *Port de Prince*, Brièrre the Hindu Prince, so black, so intense, nervous, fiery, took me dancing. As soon as he clasped me for the dance, there was a conflagration; such a burning fire came from both of us! He held me closer and closer. He danced almost without moving across the room—we swung our hips. His knee, nervous, wiry, hard, rhythmically moved between my legs with such a sensual simulation of a caress. My knee moved closer between his legs and I felt his desire firm and strong.

A darker, more violent feeling than with Albert.

Brièrre danced with me several times, and each time he aroused me. Once I looked up into his eyes, and his black fiery glance was more like a stab. Those dances were like sexual acts, and I yielded to the drug.

At times I would move my face away…for Jean's temple touched mine…and look for Albert, look at Albert. Albert, in contrast to Jean, looked more and more tender, gentle, idealized, purer. My feelings went out to his gentleness, but the nervous, fiery intensity of Jean compelled me.

What a beautiful evening! How far I was from the dead parties of surrealists and artists, men without beauty or sex. How often I have commented lately on the complete absence of magnetism, of coquetry between the men and women. Last night I felt beautiful, not in an abstract way as I felt before, but beautiful and desirable, as a woman. All the women were beautiful and desirable. We lived in the dancing and singing. My body was joyous and flowering, but what a division again between my nature and my feelings. My feelings go to Albert, and my nature goes to Jean, whom I do not love because he is cynical and vain of his great beauty, because he is affected and literary. I love the great simplicity of Albert.

Dream of Haiti

Varied and beautiful faces. Aristocratic sensuality, emotion, subtlety.

My unhappy Venus wills that both Albert and Jean are returning home to not be drafted.

JUNE 6, 1943

Great fall tonight from the ecstasies, seeing Albert at the Premices' singing, wanting to caress him, seeing him with Pussy at his heels, not being able to be with him, caressing him endlessly within myself and realizing I am going to lose him. In a few weeks he returns home.

Jean Brièrre, too, is leaving in a week. Filled with promises, the drum beating, singing, knowing that here is life, revolted by the whites…but I will lose it all like a dream in a few weeks.

My only pleasure is to arouse a sensation when I come in—the Haitians see me as beautiful. I feel desired. But I cannot reach happiness.

JUNE 7, 1943

I have a feeling Albert was jealous to see me dance with Jean. (I looked so white that night of the dance, ivory white. Our bodies fit together so… And Jean so utterly black…) Was he jealous to see us together today when we called for Pierre? Albert was going to work.

No word from Albert, and I do not have sufficient faith. My ecstasy is shattered. I have lost my audacity, my courage. I cannot give Jean a sign. (In the dance, I yielded to the passion which possessed us—the dark, sensual Jean of the dance, compared to the mannered, timid Jean of daylight.)

Suddenly, because of Jean's darker life (he was in a Haitian prison for fifteen months for revolutionary activity) and Albert's joyous one, I saw them as the two faces of Gonzalo, and I realized I was not free of Gonzalo yet.

This afternoon Gonzalo took me. I was without feeling for him, saying to myself: Well, here is a very handsome man! But he seems to have killed my tenderness. Last night I spoke to him strongly, not tenderly, regardless of consequence—consequence was that he took me!

JUNE 8, 1943

What torment, this mirage of love, soon to vanish altogether. What a cruel torment, this passion for both Jean and Albert.

I am burning continuously, as I have never burned, from head to toe like a torch. I am sensitive and open to all. Even in Eduardo I aroused and released a deep emotion, delivered him of his fear of expressing it, and our parting today was in itself like a romance, a true wave of feeling. It is sad, too, that I have my greatest power of fascination, just at this moment, when I cannot pour the passion into anyone, when I am imprisoned in a mirage. Albert is my soft dream, and Jean is my violent one.

The beauty of Jean is royal. He is slender, a little taller than I am (Albert is the same height but rounder, softer, fuller). His carriage is tense, nervous. Jean is as black as he can be, with a finely chiseled head, the close, short negro hair, but the fine, straight nose, the full, rich, but not exaggerated, mouth. He looks somber, rarely smiles. Albert's mouth is open and smiling, and Jean's is torturous, labyrinthian and perverse.

JUNE 9, 1943

At the most anguished moment of my watch for Albert's telephone call, I lay back and said to myself: I *deserve* happiness. I deserve it!

Days passed. Last Thursday we embraced. No word from him after his visit Saturday. I began to tremble, to doubt, to suffer. Then came Jean, and Jean's poem. And the darkness again. My heart hurt me. My being wanted Albert, not Jean. A moment after I spoke with Jean, Albert called, his voice rich, deep and intimate: "Pussy is not well. I shall go and see her but could be free at ten. But I'm afraid that you, now, will not be free. *Viens chez moi.*"

Je viendrai.

My happiness inundated me, but I was still trembling. I took my anguish to Jaeger, my mythological mother. She quieted my heart, unknotted my nerves, magically. Something wonderful is being born; passion is being born, purified of its masculinity, free of guilt. But in birth there is struggle.

Again I found Albert's mouth, sweeter than Jean's. Again I felt the strength concealed in his softness, a strength that is aroused by my own. I seek his quietness and integrity. I move towards Albert and the light, out of my prison…

JUNE 10, 1943

Again, bathing with the sandalwood soap, the perfume in the hair, copper on the nails, the black lace panties, the turquoise green dress Albert liked, the hair loose. I walked fast, lightly to him, like an arrow, but I did not enter his room directly.

I stood in the street looking up at his two lighted windows, and I thought: a beautiful lover is awaiting me. I walked around the block, to find the lighted windows again, the anticipation…

"Your hair is wild," he said, kissing me. I said, "I walked quickly."

No violence, but quietness and sureness and strength. Aware that it is Albert, it is Anaïs, we called the names… Supple caresses like his dancing. He did not linger enough. His desire impelled him, and soon he had taken his pleasure—all my pleasure was spread throughout the caresses. For each nook and form of the body, there was an answer, cat-like, languorous, voluptuous. The taste of sweetness, of fruit perfection. We lay in the dark. He said, "*Tu es contente?*" I said yes. Later he asked me why I was *amoureuse de lui*, as if he did not believe it. I said: "For many, many reasons—I love everything about you, how you think…I feel your being and your beautiful face… you are luminous." The rolling softness, the warmth we bathed in…after a while I slid down and took his sex in my mouth. All that I knew of caresses I gave him in this—it stirred him; he lay back, sighing. He placed his hand on my hair, and then he moved with my mouth, a soft, continuous undulation, until his pleasure increased and rose to a climax. How I enjoyed giving him this, seeing his body yielding, abandoned, hearing his cry, a greater pleasure than the first. I lay over him now—the silkiness of his skin, the softness, the tranquility, the perfection of the rhythm.

My lasciviousness matched his.

Oh, Albert, how I wanted to know if you felt the miracle. Was it new to you? Were you warmed to the depths of your being, caressed so intimately that the remembrance lingered? I felt near to him, not as in other adventures, but near, near.

I said, "I am heavy."

He answered, "*Non—reste là. Est-ce bon?*"

"*Oui, c'est bon.*"

"*Alors reste.*"

Simple words. Simple, simple. The body and soul can learn happiness, joy. This was joy, fragrant and miraculous. Oh the sweetness, the sweetness! I felt the lightness, I felt washed of pain and darkness, washed, luminous and clear. I could have slept at his side as quietly as he slept after his pleasure. I felt as if he had transmitted his youth to me, his fresh skin and glossy live curls, his laughter and his singing.

What will he remember of this? My body remembers him. My body did not remember Canada or Chinchilito. Balm and fragrance on my soul, a sexual act like a dance. What did I leave on his skin, in his nerves, what flavor, what magnetic waves? He left his fragrance, like his songs. *Douceur, mollesse, chaleur, force souple, force enroulante,* the mysterious currents passing through two bodies, in the night, light of foot.

"Don't you see me through a prism?" he asked.

I didn't notice then.

What does he mean?

Does he think I dream him?

He does not dream.

He is content, he is sleepy, he is hungry, he smokes, he tells me to wear his slippers to the bathroom, he moves quietly, free, beautiful…very beautiful. More beautiful than Gonzalo, because Gonzalo's beauty is marred by the weakness of the mouth; Albert's is rich and full, his face is balanced. Gonzalo's hands and feet are strong and coarse. Albert's are delicate. His body has the savour of his songs…Creole gentleness.

Albert—I took you into my arms, and I take you into my diary, into my devastated life, now blossoming anew because of you. Singing and drumming, but with pale hands and without savagery, you come, soft like your songs, tender like your climate, tranquil like your island, vibrant like your plants, rich like your earth, Albert, I take you into my arms again, into my diary, your innocence and your purity, your luminousness. I take you, take you, take you bending over me, and pray and wish you felt as much as I did… remember, retain, absorb. What I gave you was only the perfume of all my suffering, for there is a suffering that can bear a perfume, a magnificent fragrance of the soul. There is a suffering that is without bitterness, like mine, which can give birth to a deeper knowledge of joy, to a deeper reception of joy, to a deeper love for Albert than those who eluded the pain. In each caress of joy there was the magnetic miracle of love that knows the beauty of what it is caressing, knows it more deeply, for all its deprivations, for all its sacrifices, for all its openness to pain… What my hands and mouth know of your fragrance only pain could have made possible. Exquisite joy created by past suffering. To better know Albert, the childlikeness of his laughter, his fragrance, his fragrance.

Eight o'clock in the evening. *J'attends Jean.*

If only I could live like this, running to Albert in the night, or waiting for Jean.

Gonzalo took me today (his blood mingling with Albert's), and I felt that I had disengaged the erotic feeling from the soul love, separated my soul from him, and that although I could feel without dislike his strong heavy legs on mine, the heavy magnetism which flows from his body, the violent odor and strong hair, still he could not reach me, torture me, possess me as before. The bondage is over.

He does not know yet that he has lost me.

JUNE 11, 1943

Jean came. At first we sat back on the couch and talked quietly. I said to him: "I feel that you are like me, tormented by constant tension, seeking a release from the tension, and at the same time dreaming of an intensity equal to yours…"

"*C'est juste,*" he said.

But he was frightened, frightened by my directness. When he is frightened, he uses literature, talks pompously and falsely. He oscillates between Baudelaire and Verlaine and uses the speech of the Comédie Française.

He recites like a bad actor. Poor Jean. He was so afraid. Poor Anaïs too, tense. Tension is fear, not intensity, and it paralyzed us. He put on the music. Then slowly we danced. And when we danced, we found the flame.

Jean kissed and embraced me with a violence of nerves and sinews, embraced me, as we stood, embraced, embraced, knees interwoven, sexes touching. Slowly we moved towards the couch. He opened my blouse, kissed my breast. He penetrated me violently. Then he withdrew to kiss me. When he had kissed me and lay over me again, he was limp. We lay together. He sought to harden himself with his hand. He said, "*Comme tu es douce, Anaïs*, as you are soft." It was the only murmur from his heart. Everything else was frozen fright and literature. It was late, and I feared Hugo's return home. I had to tell him, though our embrace was not fulfilled. I was sad. He said: "I will call you if I can tomorrow. I will write you." I felt his nervousness like mine, his poses and falsities, his roles and disguises, his forcing of words to say something poetic. Nothing came from his feelings except his wild sensuality, and his, "*Comme tu es douce, Anaïs.*"

I was sad, but not anxious, not shattered. I felt the weight of life, the prison walls, the many abortions… I fell asleep instantly, deeply tired of my efforts.

Today I am quietly sad. Mirages. Mirages.

The ecstasy and the madness still make me unfit for life, for reality. I am projected into space by passion, and I lose my moorings. If I found the equal to this, we would be consumed in one instant. It would annihilate us. Gonzalo had this power for months, and was himself surprised at its duration—three months drugged, he said.

My mother once sang: *mon cœur bat à se rompre*…my heart is beating so hard it will burst…

Be quiet, Anaïs.

So much I had to give Albert for his maturity, so much I had to give Jean to help him smash the formal shell of his work. Too late.

When one sees outside, in the daylight, the image of the desire or dream one carries in one's soul at the moment, when it takes form, incarnates, then one loves.

Albert, the image of joy, the image of my dream of the moment. Albert, the image of my luminous dreams, of my singing and dancing. The hair that has not been tortured, but which curls like leaves, the eyes which have not wept, the mouth that has not known bitterness, the teeth that have not gnashed in anxiety. The flesh unpoisoned by sorrow, the sex pure and strong, the nerves which never tangled, the rhythm which was never broken, the voice that was never wounded, the blood which was never stabbed, the lungs which were never suffocated.

When I went to the press today to meet Gonzalo I felt: I cannot go up those dark stairs; I cannot smell the musty odors; I cannot bear to be shut in with the heaviness of Gonzalo. And I turned away, went to the park and sat on a bench. I have breathed new air, and I cannot return to my prison. I sat on the bench, free, alone, breathing.

When I made myself go to the press, I found Gonzalo without pleasure. He had a toothache. His teeth are all rotting. He wanted sympathy. I had none to give. We lay side by side. I dreamed separately from him. He felt it. I lay at his side thinking: You can go no further. I am going further. It was as if he knew my thoughts. He began to caress me and stopped. He felt the passivity. He asked me: "What is the matter? You seem angry."

I couldn't explain. Each time I have tried to explain he has wounded me. He cannot go further. He is a slave of his own stagnation and weakness.

I don't want his desire.

I am anxious because I feel strong, but I am in transition, between liberation and a void. I have nothing to guide me except this image…Albert. A dream of joy, evanescent, and like the very image of such dreams, ready to vanish, not very substantial… I am merely dreaming this new life. It is not mine yet. It is the gift of the black man to me, because I turned my back on our white *degeneracy*, and because I went to him with love.

JUNE 13, 1943

Evening: Sunday. After four days without seeing Albert, I am devoured with restlessness and fever. I cannot be quiet. I am wildly dreaming of escape, voyages, love, wildly craving love. What can I do? We are in debt. The press rent is four months overdue, and there is no hope of moving. I cannot bear the old, the outworn, the drab. The whole world has become uglier by contrast. The dream I have has only caused me greater torment. It is a vision, but how can I make this vision reality?

There has been a strange increase of my intuitive powers. When Eduardo asked Pierce Harwell, the astrologer, to join him at the Cooneys' Morning Star Farm and said he did not know what he looked like (they fell in love with each other's letters), I immediately had a dream in which I saw him. I said he was as tall as Féri, rather lean, thin, had blond hair, thin features, freckles.

And tonight Eduardo tells me by telephone that I described him exactly, even to the freckles!

I also dreamed Jaeger's face before I saw her.

How, how, how, then, can I find someone to love?

JUNE 14, 1943

Albert came at five.

I say to him, "Will it please you to know you have done a marvelous thing for me, that you have liberated me?"

He says, "I merely came at the right moment."

Slowly the madness comes. Albert closes his eyes.

"Why did you answer my élan towards you?"

"You know I was *attiré* by you from the first."

No, I didn't know.

The madness rises. We touch only the hands, the faces...then, his hand caresses me through the dress, and he returns to the caress he seems to love, gently moving my mouth towards his desire... Then I lie over him and he divines what I want—to feel him inside of me, to bring his desire inside of me. I came nearer to the orgasm—so tantalizing and insinuating he is, so lascivious. He does not thrust, or pierce, but undulates, cat-like, and he is like a woman with a man's virility. Again I felt I brought him only my purity, my own youth.

Albert—how he carries me into luminosity.

"*Tu passe un moment difficile, peut-être...*" (I was thinking of his coming separation from Pussy.)

He said: "Not now. A difficult moment awaits me at home."

His captivating childlikeness, softness of face, yet that mature integrity. Passion and pain have not touched him, fear or jealousy. His deepest love has not yet flowered. He is like some cosmic adolescent...

He gives himself to caresses. He closes his eyes, lies sensual and absorbed, with a *mollesse* so beautiful to see, like that of being born of Venus herself, the very child of Venus.

Moving slowly towards a dream of happiness, without the reality, a mirage of happiness.

JUNE 15, 1943

I am free. The only terror I have is to look into a space without a lover, without Albert. The dream of Albert has been my support, my guidance. A world without a lover! Will I be able to spread this love among friends, in the world in general?

Last night, I heard myself laughing. I lifted this laughter into the summer night like a wine glass. To Albert...to Albert my laughter... Albert's body and Albert's hands in the night, in the air. When I have a lover, it seems as if the summer night itself were in connivance with him, caressing me, the summer a soft duplicity with the lover, the interchange of sun, air, wind, darkness, softness with Albert's golden skin, the softness of his mouth, the voluptuous undulations.

I remember a morning at Lipchitz's studio, when Albert was standing by a statue. He stood with all his weight on one leg, his hip protruding. I was sitting near him, and, roused by his grace, I was overcome with such insensate desire.

When he dances...what a swaying of the hips, without vulgarity. *Enveloppé de bonheur, le fluide de bonheur, la danse de la joie*, desire like tendrils of young plants, the uncorrupted flower-like nature...

Je suis en état de grâce de l'amour.

I can be tender to Gonzalo and once again make him laugh, caress, hope.

I telephoned Chinchilito, intuitively—he has just returned from California and is coming tomorrow night.

I feel Albert's caresses, and in the middle of the street I close my eyes and feel the ecstasy. I lay back on the bed at the press and looked at the sky, letting the light flood and blind me.

JUNE 17, 1943

When I arrived at Martha's yesterday, I kissed her and said: "My life is so wonderful. I'm grateful to you, so grateful. I am in a state of grace."

And then I told her about Albert. She was not concerned over the physical unfulfillment (absence of orgasm). She too felt as I did, that the psychic miracle took place in me first, the mystical communion with my new soul (Albert). So that is why, after being with him, I felt the peace and contentment of communion. A dream has been reached which will slowly take form in the blood too.

I was so filled with this new joy (does anyone know that for the pain-ridden soul even the shivering of the leaves is a sad vibration, even the displacement of a cloud a heart-rending event?), so filled, that even though I could not be with Albert (Pussy, sensing danger, has moved into his place), I was happy to see Chinchilito again. So at nine o'clock it is Siegfried who waits at my door, sun-burnt, with his brilliant Spanish smile and chanting voice.

"Chinchilita," says Siegfried, who now works in a defense plant, whose operatic career has been postponed.

First he took me to an impasse nearby where he wants to take an apartment in September. Then I took him to the press and showed him *Winter of Artifice*. I offered him a choice between sitting on a Washington Square park bench or going to the empty apartment where Thurema is not moving in until Wednesday. "My friend asked me to go and water the plants every day. Do you want to water plants, Chinchilito?"

He chose to water the plants. Playfully, with bottles of beer under our arms, we went to the apartment. He played on Thurema's harp, sang a little, teased, and, as usual, was both serious and clownish. When we lay back on the wide couch talking, he became dreamy and said: "It is very strange, Chinchilita, I have not seen you for six months, a year, it doesn't matter how long, but the thread does not break. I feel something with you I do not feel with the others. I do not forget you. When I saw Luise Rainer in *Cinderella*, and the glass slippers were brought out, I thought: these are La Nin's slippers—I came to see La Nin's slippers, not Luise Rainer's. I feel always relaxed with you, at ease. And you have changed. You are happier and freer. It is strange how familiar you are to me."

He carries my picture in his pocketbook.

He turned out the light. There was moonlight flooding the bed and the head of a tree at the window which might pass for a palm tree. Delicately he woos, as in Provincetown. The courtship begins with the tips of the fingers. Then the rhythm increased slowly and rose to violence.

His teeth shine in the semi-darkness. His teeth sink deeply between my legs. There is a pagan power in him, but he does not reach my feelings, as Albert did. What an infinite, amazing variety of embraces, extraordinary contrasts! Chinchilito brings strength and finesse and knowingness, but it is open like paganism, not mysterious and subtle.

I like his playfulness. He gets up to act for me, to transform himself; he wants to become a gargoyle, the hunchback of Notre Dame, other monsters. He steps out of his beauty into deformity. "I'm tired of acting the hero and the lover when I sing," he said. "I'd like to be Frankenstein!" He frightens me a little. He is naked in the light now—he wants me to be, but I dress.

"It's funny," he mused again. "Wherever you are it becomes wonderful. I thought it was the sand dunes. Then I thought it was your painted apartment. Now we're in an ordinary apartment that does not belong to you, and it is wonderful too."

As we walk homeward, we meet Albert and Pussy on 8th Street.

I am quiet and happy. It seems to me at last I am living my deepest need, the lover. The summer night has fulfilled its purpose, has given birth to caresses, the body has breathed and vibrated. The night is sweet. Chinchilito has his hand on my neck. It is I who sings a little under my breath. The shivering of the leaves is paradisiacal, the flight of a cloud is innocent.

Is there anguish and war in the world, hatred and horror? I have only one weapon against destruction and death: love—to love, to love, to love, to love.

C'est le chant des îles. C'est le chant d'Albert qui a réveillé les ondes de la joie. Un être qui n'a connu que la souffrance est un être malade et incomplet.

I once loved through romanticism (which led to neurosis), and I believe I am now entering a life like Russia's.

Sunday, June 20, 1943

Last night I gave a party, to see Albert, whom I had not seen since Monday.

He came, with Pussy, with his brother Robert and Robert's fiancée, Premice and his daughters, Lionel Durant, Charles Duits, a young poet, Gerald Sykes and his girl, Mrs. Richard Wright and George Davis…

It was a hot night, a sensual atmosphere. We danced to the radio at first, then Albert sang, Josephine danced, they improvised, and we danced again. The porch was dark and cool, the lights low. I wore my fuchsia blouse and danced madly. At the bottom of my heart there was anguish. When I don't see Albert, I think it is over. I have doubts because Pussy has taken him back, with her humble, modest, pathetic sorrow at his leaving, her desire that he should marry her. But I threw myself into the dancing, abandoned myself to the sensuality and gayety. Gerald Sykes became passionate when we danced.

Albert was beautiful last night, illumined with pleasure, knowing his own beauty like a woman does, knowing any woman would succumb to him.

Frances was overwhelmed with his beauty, the beauty in all of them, the beauty of Carl Offord, the Trinidad writer... She felt and understood and loved them as I do. She never saw such a beautiful, sensual party.

Albert, do not hurt me!

I grew lighter and gayer, I danced, danced... One dance with Albert, who pressed me against him, but the ecstasy, too long subdued, I could not release again as before. The anguish was there, the loss of faith.

But I danced, danced. It was late. Suddenly over the radio came Spanish music. I rushed to my closet, got into my Spanish kimono full of ruffles, and danced a few steps of the Alegrias after not having danced for seven years.

After all the people left I was still dancing! I could not stop.

Albert, do not kill this joy you gave me.

The dancing gave me joy, Frances's pleasure, the gayety of the others, Sykes' desire, a hope of life widening into joy...

Today we went to the Premices', where there were more Haitians. Premice was the first drawn to me, the one who chose me, sought me out. They all love my warmth and openness. My own warmth and spontaneity and sensuality are flowing. I am closer to them than I ever was to the Anglo-Saxons—how I suffered from their inexpressiveness, stiffness, lack of grace and warmth! Where is my state of grace? Frances said, "Be happy—enjoy it while you have it." Albert was not gone yet.

The Black world, the magic world of soul and sensuality. "There is purity in them," said Frances. Yes, the sensuality flows into the dancing and singing and gayety... Frances, too, feels revulsion for the whites, shame. It was a dream for her too.

After I wrote this I fell asleep. I was awakened by the telephone. It was Albert. Albert, talking quietly about ordinary things, how good the party was, about the job Hugo is getting for Pussy, about casting his statuette of the drummer of which he wants to give us a mold, etc. No word of meeting, of being together. I fell asleep again, half calmed, but sad. I awakened with anguish. I could not bear the incertitude, the void. I waited for his telephone call. Finally I called him, and he was evasive. I began to suffer. The anguish was immense. I felt unfit for life, for love, for sensuality, for everything. I felt all kinds of fears: the loss of Albert, who is perhaps bound to Pussy, who perhaps did not like meeting me on 8th Street with Chinchilito, who perhaps had heard about my evening with Brièrre... Unable to bear the elusiveness, I said to him over the telephone: "You must come and say good-bye. I am going away to the Bahamas."

Imperturbable. Yes, he would come, sometime. (Frances said: "He is a child, incapable of love; he is also a woman who enjoys being loved. He is not worthy of you.")

The shallowness of feeling, the acquiescence. The love comes from Pussy, surrounds and fetters him. And there he is, receiving it all, responding sensually, a sensual receptivity, effortless, passive.

Why would I put so much feeling into this, so much significance? Yesterday the nervousness and anguish increased, and I was again caught in my suffering: the incertitude, the ephemeralness of happiness, the unfulfillment, the unreality.

I visited Frances, who calms me, who places Albert in his true proportions.

Tom says, "You two lesbians."

We said: "We wish we were. We could be much happier." At this moment I feel strongly tempted to love a woman, rather than the feminine man.

Yes, Frances and I, if we could be lesbians, might have been happy. The same ecstasies and violences propel us, the same need of touch and reality.

My heart hurt me again. I fell asleep like lead. I dreamed I was at a big party. Albert flirted with me, but said, "*I am afraid of the hunter.*" I was persuading him there was nothing to fear. I had the feeling that I bore in myself an arrow, a shaft, a penetrating arm, an instrument, a masculinity of some kind. I said in the dream, "You know I respect and understand your relations to Pussy." Then he was relieved.

This morning I called up casually, said I was leaving tomorrow, would he come at five. Yes, said Albert.

But I know now I must leave him too. He is staying on, I heard, and it caused me no pleasure. I must bring this to an end. It hurts me. I must find a *love*. I cannot live this pagan life so casually.

Will it come to me?

Will he be free?

The moonstorm came in the morning.

Evening: Albert came—caressing and desirous. I told him the truth. I said, "I have to leave because this is causing me pain: I cannot be with you." He was gently surprised. He explained quietly. All along he knew we would not be able to be together. When he leaves his work, Pussy expects him. *He cannot lie.* And because it is their last week together, he does not want to hurt her. Now she keeps him in her apartment where there is plenty of room. Pathetically she clings to him and plays at being his wife. I said, "If you had been so attached to Pussy as to not want to be with me, would you have told me?"

"I would have told you."

And I knew it was true. Again I am the mistress and the passion, the desire, and I am "to respect the wife," as in the dream. None of my men have my audacity to overcome obstacles, know deception, have the capacity to lie, transcend all barriers. None of them were capable of the prodigious feats by which I managed to be with Henry and Gonzalo—all of them children, or women, and I the Lover, the one who leaped the balconies, who risked danger, who managed by ruse and courage to meet the beloved! It's laughable too—poor Anaïs, the very symbol of femininity with the soul and mind of a man! *Le cœur d'un honnête homme dans un beau corps de femme.*

To me the courage, the dynamism, the activity, the action. And Albert, my mistress in the hands of a jealous husband! For the difficulty arises truly from my forgetting myself and betraying my love for Albert, which Pussy quickly divined and which complicates everything, making his visits to me portentous, dangerous, ominous, etc. Anaïs, the Lover of the World. No wonder I cannot find for myself the Lover who will love me as actively as I love others.

JUNE 23, 1943

I shall not describe Pussy, but I will let others. Irina was positively disconcerted: "Is that Albert's girl? That takes away from his value. She is absolutely *quelconque*" (ordinary). She is twenty, small, wears glasses, is indistinguishable, works as a salesgirl, has no particular gifts. She is a mouse, very American.

The child-woman fears me.

I come as the Woman, as the *maîtresse savante*, as the capable, powerful woman, the woman who can make an alluring house, who can be a cook, a head of household, a mother, a sister, a friend, a refuge, a haven, an erotic spell, a witch, a dream…

It is so ironic. When you become gifted, powerful, beautiful, then your rival is the colorless, ungifted, weak, and not beautiful, for such a woman can make a certain kind of man feel powerful, feel his superiority—and I am the challenge, the equal.

Pierce Harwell arrives tonight. It was a marriage *manqué*. Poor Eduardo.

JUNE 26, 1943

The blue water eyes of Pierce, the tender voice, the divinatory phrases. Huckleberry Finn and Rimbaud. The Bright Messenger, as in the book, bringing music and air. The soul of a bird, without the body of a lover, merely a spirit, not a body one can possess. He is a soul's reflection, a dream, a mirror, the fortuneteller…

In the street, I kissed him fraternally and said: "You are all I expected. You're my brother."

Mystically he woos me, courts me, and seduces me. Mystically there is a love affair going on, with charms, enchantments, retreats, coquetries.

To Frances he said, "I believe I went to Eduardo only to reach Anaïs."

I shall no longer court Albert out of his small pale lair, but last night, as I rode upon Gonzalo's body, sitting and galloping, with his sex in me, the movements I made from the hip, the graceful, soft, oriental undulations to circuit the hub of the sex, were those of Albert's hips—I had made love to my own dancing body.

So the dancer is resurrected, through Albert, the hips sway, sway, in the dance of love and desire.

Chinchilito, who admits he hates the telephone, called me twice, and asks me to visit him Monday at his home as he is alone. I say yes.

When Albert telephones, I do not call him back. To possess me, he would have had to be violent, intense and passionate. I passed through the open interstices of his weakness, passivity and *mollesse*, slipping out of his painful spell, rejecting the long watches, waits and *angoisse*…

But the passion in my body torments me—at this moment I want to be Diana more than ever, to violently attack the world and find my Lover.

Always at these violent moments of passion, my bird soul appears to lure me into mystical worlds.

JUNE 28, 1943

Let me celebrate my *freedom*. I am as free as man has been. I am free to enjoy.

Today with Chinchilito, and not Albert, I experienced for the first time an orgasm within adventure. For the first time I did not feel the orgasm linked to emotional fidelity, as an emotional surrender, as necessarily and fatally bound to love. So that love, being slavery to a master who could not fulfill me, became anguish. Chinchilito sent for me. He was alone and wanted me in his apartment. I saw his Neptunian background, his pictures of ships, his tropical fishes, his atmosphere of blue and taste.

Then he took his clothes off, and as he lay on the couch he was already desirous. I abandoned myself to the pleasure of his vigor, his endurance and his knowingness. The pleasure was relaxed, natural, and complete. It was sweet and satisfying. Oh, the joy of the freedom, the freedom. *The freedom man has known.* To discover I could abandon myself, without the deeper love, to enjoy and relinquish. (No fear for the morrow, no need to possess. Chinchilito could disappear, and I would not feel abandoned.) No more linking of response to total giving and total giving to the fear of being hurt. I gave all and relinquished all. I gave it to the moment, to his smile, the beauty of his body.

And I believe woman's great difficulty in achieving sensual liberation and independence has caused her clutchingness and fear.

I returned to Gonzalo soft, more loving, at peace, and when he didn't take me I was not tormented by the inequality in our power. At peace, relinquishing, with a greater sense of the love of man and not of the One. What a torment the absolute is, when the world is full of lovers and love, when out of the smile of Chinchilito and the sexual dance of Albert, out of the intermittent fires of Gonzalo, I can make a total delight. I have a much greater sensual power than Gonzalo, but romanticism prevented me from accepting this. I sacrificed the sensual life, stunted it to his power. Tonight I feel a boundless strength. It seems to me that I have drawn from the very source of desire, as from a life source—a central, universal source. Romanticism to me is now synonymous with neurosis…neurosis is the outcome of our romanticism.

JUNE 29, 1943

The end of *bondage*—of *fear*.

I feel free and strong.

I do not have to court my lover.

He will come.

I can see the trees are beautiful—the vastness of the sky, the immense possibilities of love spreading out. I can see beyond fixation and obsession. How light I feel!

Chinchilito marveled at the swiftness, the lightness of my dressing, like magical smoothness. "Other women make such a fuss, take so much time."

Jaeger is amazed at the evolution. She did not expect such a swift leap. In a week I leaped from the danger of masculinity to perfect femininity, to submission, yielding, passivity and acting from the deepest Eros source.

But free.

Jaeger knew all the time I would not rest until I had found my deepest primitive self. That was my quest.

The theme of humor appeared. I laughed at myself, at my mishaps as a man. I laughed at my mischief, feeling Jaeger would forgive and understand. Her last words to me were: I hope you have a mischievous summer!

Absolution…

Absolution…

JUNE 30, 1943

Illumination

When I returned from Jaeger, I sensed that Albert would have telephoned. He had. He wanted to see me Thursday. I was in the mood to accept, to accept all the joys. The intensity and ecstasy have gone, have shattered themselves against his tranquility, but perhaps he is teaching me happiness.

So I have Albert, Chinchilito, a loving Hugo, an adoring Gonzalo, and I am happy with them all. This morning, lying in bed, I look at the sunlight, and it appears extraordinarily bright.

Yesterday I conquered illness. The heavy Chinese dinner, a shower which drenched me, and at six I felt ill. Then I lay down and I said to myself: Anaïs, this is one of the happiest days of your life. You cannot be ill. Your analysis has come to a magnificent end, you have two beautiful lovers, one deep love, one deep marriage, a mystic brother, you are healthy and beautiful, you are able to fascinate, to enchant, you are FREE. You cannot be ill on a day like this.

When I got up I was well. I went out with Gonzalo, who reflects my mood—we were gay and tender.

I shall never forget the *gout de bonheur* I felt this morning on awakening, like the miraculous new flavors of convalescence. After the deep illness of the soul, the fever, the burn, the pain, the convalescence, the new dazzling appearance of the sun, to new eyes a new vision, the new softness of the bed under a body which has recovered its sensitiveness, aliveness, its sensory receptivity, the new taste of coffee on the feverless tongue. "*Le bonheur c'est l'absence de fièvre.*" Happiness is the absence of fever.

I asked for a second cup of coffee! The beds had been moved to stand side by side near the window because of the heat, so Hugo awakened at my side and found me floating on the cool blankets, bathing in the sun of a new joy which reminded me of the return to life after the child birth, after the illumination, light. I looked at the strip of sunlight by the Venetian blind, marveling how, *because* I possessed it inwardly, I could see it externally. Surely it must have shone other mornings, equally, *but I did not see it or feel it.* I was filled and distorted by my illness. Surely it was the same coffee, but I did not taste it so acutely, I did not ask ever for a second cup!

How I exorcised the illness of the body! Out, I cried, this is a body made for joy. My birth to life again...

JULY 1, 1943

There is no issue for the romantic, except to commit suicide. We were the romantics who were not courageous enough to die (the absolute demands death), but who killed ourselves slowly by degrees (neurosis), had either to die pathologically (Artaud, Helba, etc.), or to transcend the romanticism.

I have now lived through and beyond romanticism, transcended it.

The erotic, open state I am in is openness and fire. I am near and in love with all. There are no more barriers.

I said to Jaeger, "I feel very big things have been accomplished."
"You have a big soul," said Jaeger.

JULY 2, 1943

Yesterday at five I received Albert at Thurema's (96 MacDougal Street).

I felt a new feeling had been roused in him (the deepest layer of his nature has not yet been touched). I felt a new passion. As he came in, I waited for his embrace. It came more brusquely, more impulsively, more aggressively than before. Before, there was a hypnotic quality to it, simultaneousness.

He came as if he had been hungry for me, he came with impatience, a stronger feeling. He was more passionate, more active. And as for me, he entered into my very being and feelings with a terrifying penetration like that of love. It was more than bodies mingling, interweaving. But perhaps for his nature, a youthful singing nature, a *fleur de peau*, this was pure sensuality. In the middle of our caresses he was beside himself, and he said: "*Comme tu es bonne a prendre! Tu es si bonne a prendre!*"

We were naked for the first time in daylight—his body so perfect, so proud and certain of its beauty. Such keen pleasure, delight and anxiety for me. The feelings were roused, the sadness of losing him, the fear, and I did not feel the orgasm. The joy was pain again. It is my very own happiness eluding me. I have been ill for three days now.

I feel something happened yesterday to Albert, like a plant that has lived only a plant life and experiences a human tremor, he, who has eluded disturbance and passion. I may be wrong. It may be pure sensuality which I invest with my own feelings.

JULY 4, 1943

The return of the illness (it is said this happens when the analyst leaves one, and Jaeger has left for two months).

With this comes jealousy again, the feeling Helba is responsible for my estrangement from Gonzalo, the resentment, the regrets, monologues to make Gonzalo aware of this.

As if seeking the magic cure, I invite the Premices, and I visit them today, Sunday, instead of seeing Gonzalo. In their humble and simple life I seek an antidote.

Pierce gives them astrology in such fabulous terms that I hesitate to translate to Lucienne Azar what he says. Like Jean, he talks in symbols. He says, "She swallowed a mirror!"

Adele tells me of the passions Jean Brièrre aroused without himself being caught, of how she almost fell in love with Albert, of how Albert distresses Pussy by his indifference and, above all, by not marrying her.

Then, speaking of Josephine's aggression, she said, "While you, you just sit back and look wistful, and everybody falls at your feet!"

I know the Haitians love me. *D'abord pour eux je suis jolie.*

JULY 7, 1943

Pierce and I last night, walking along the East River, through the ghetto. How light we are together, arm in arm, hand in hand, warm and light. He is bodiless and warm with feeling. The contrast always between the mystic brother and Gonzalo is that the first is all light and air and wateriness, and Gonzalo lacks light and airiness and is all earth and instinct. Only the mystic *understands.*

One afternoon I went up to be with Canada, who was passionately aroused and made violent love to me, but I could not respond, and I felt again: it cannot be without love. I cannot yield to sensuality.

With this came a great sadness at the bondage to love. If I could yield to pure sensuality then I would have yielded to the most marvelous sensuality of all, Canada's violence and Albert's lasciviousness.

Canada's words: "Feel my big black dick in your small white pussy...you've got lovely red hair on your pussy...come all over my big black dick..." At the end, he cried out: "That just one woman should be so good, so good, so wonderful... Oh, your wonderful skin. You throw me, you throw me!"

His ravenous *morsures* leaving their mark on my body.

Unpossessed.

I wore my beautiful white silk suit given to me by Thurema. I looked radiant. I looked equally radiant Saturday night at the Premices' for the farewell party for Albert.

But I was not present; I had removed myself. The dream of Haiti was over. There was Albert singing the same songs and the women acting as if he were taking them all, there was Pussy clutching, clinging, no men to dance with to distract me from hearing the silly chatter, the childish pranks, the emptiness. Suddenly I was no longer there. At midnight I looked at Hugo, saw that he was lost, disconnected, and we quietly abandoned the party.

Seeing Albert in relation to Pussy's insignificance revealed the Albert I didn't want to see. I am always deceived by the heightened selves others give to me, and I only see them smaller in relation to others, such as Henry's relations to the repulsive Fraenkel and Fred. Hugo was revolted by Pussy, and suddenly I was revolted by Pussy's Albert, as I am revolted by Helba's Gonzalo.

The dream of Haiti was punctured.

I wish Albert were gone now, now that I see him clearly, that I may forget his lasciviousness, which answers mine. The dream of pure sensual connection is over.

The anguish about the love that is ending and the new one not here yet, the intermediate state—alas, how I suffer from this.

July 12, 1943

Mon petit journal, I feel as when I was a little girl, and I came to tell you about an unexpected fairytale end to a tale of great suffering...

I doubted again, as always. I suffered to have been Albert's mistress for a few hours. I doubted when he didn't see me for the week before leaving. I thought I had been a passion, a whim, a drug for him, that I had only imagined the *depths*.

This morning he came. I was withdrawn from him. He came to choose one of Hugo's prints. When we stood near, I felt him aroused. But as he reached for me, I stood back and said, "*Je ne comprends pas ta façon d'aimer.*"

"Anaïs," he said simply, looking at me with his entire soul naked, "I love you too much to be content with those small moments. It is my nature to want everything or nothing. I wanted to be with you altogether, and I couldn't bear just being your lover of the moment, so I withdrew..."

"Albert, then you felt as I did, then I didn't just imagine that you felt as I did, something deeper..."

"I felt as you did."

"What I gave you was strong and true," I said.

"I too. That is why I couldn't bear the stolen moments, I can't bear half measures—I wanted a whole measure, or nothing."

"If you feel as I do, then if you tell me to, ask me to, I shall come and be with you in Mexico."

"If I can get work there and can stay, I'll write you. But If I don't get work I will only stay a week."

We embraced. Without touching lips, we let the passion well up through our bodies like a powerful current...it took our breath away.

A tragic moment too, a dangerous moment—I remembered suddenly that just as I had imagined myself going to Peru with Gonzalo, I had sat by Albert's side on the porch once and felt it quite possible to be sitting next to him, married in Haiti. It seemed as natural, as fatal...!

But my imagination plays tricks on me. I never went to Peru with Gonzalo. I went into an inferno.

Is this a spell? This deceptive imagination in which I lose myself is not always blind! I felt the deeper layer of the sensual accord! I felt rightly—I failed to understand Albert's suffering at this partial, incomplete relation. Saturday night I was jealous. Now I remember that while Pussy pursued him, clung to him, barred his way to me, sat between us, he was looking at me dancing, and to explain his looking at me I heard him say to Pussy, "Look what a beautiful dress Anaïs is wearing!"

Albert is imprisoned by Pussy, as I was last night with Gonzalo, tortured by Gonzalo, Gonzalo tortured by his guilt, hating himself, full of anger at himself, humiliated, but doing nothing to conquer it. He said, "I am in hell. You don't know what hell it is to be taking money..." A hell he drags me into. And I wept. To be out of hell, I have to abandon Gonzalo, as I abandoned Henry (Henry now writes Pierce he is in the agony of regret over my loss and realizes now what a drag he was on me). Gonzalo didn't know what I was weeping over. I was shattered, but for a reason he doesn't know. I was shattered before I saw him, for the loss of Albert. To know that Albert felt as I felt, and that I didn't love into a void, which saved me from a fall and saved the dream. But it is worse that this forbidden, restrained, arrested love was about to bloom into passion...

What I felt for Albert was more than desire, it was something that penetrates deeper into the being. I can't let myself think of the sensual harmonies, for it is painful.

Albert...

Albert saw this greater love that was possible and which did not fit into the stolen hours of mere desire.

The mystery remains, then, of the sensual that is not separate from the feelings, as it appears...

Albert. I write his name to bathe in it.

July 14, 1943

After this scene with Albert, I needed love so badly, consolation, someone's nearness, that I turned to Gonzalo, and took his tenderness, drew close to him, seeking to survive the shock I received. *Un amour impossible.*

If I closed my eyes, I felt the wild desire for Albert, and the abysm, and the pain. *Un amour impossible*, Anaïs, you must surrender it. He is between two women, and one is his fiancée awaiting him at home. I must surrender him. It cannot be because he is twenty-six and I am forty.

I returned so nervous I was not even tired, but keyed up. Dinner with Hugo and Gerald Sykes at Jai-Alai. I threw myself into the refuge of sleep. I awoke trembling.

Now I am so nervous and confused I cannot bear it. I asked Albert to see me today. I await him. What I must tell him is that just as he decided last week it was better to forget me, he must now tell me when he gets to Mexico if he decides it is better we forget each other.

I see now he wants to elude the pain, the danger. I run into them so recklessly. For a few moments of ecstasy I am always willing to endure the pain.

How mad it would be to meet in Mexico, knowing we will love deeply, and knowing he can only stay in Mexico six months. Pain again, everywhere I turn, pain and tragedy.

I had said to Albert that I must speak with him for five minutes. Not wanting him to feel I was seeking one of the short meetings his nature drew away from, I offered to meet him in the street. I felt in his voice that he wanted to see me again, was succumbing to the temptation. He came for a "moment."

Then I asked him to please tell me, whatever decision he made in Mexico, to spare me the pain. Then he said: "Anaïs, you are as I used to be, you are dreaming a dream, and you break yourself in this. I have suffered from this, so deeply that now I have given up the personal dreams. I have a sense of reality. We were not permitted the time. It doesn't matter how long, but if it is a week, it has to be a free week. We have not the freedom. If I can stay in Mexico, I'll tell you. I don't know what awaits me there. I am afraid you are dreaming me. Perhaps I do not have the qualities you believe."

"I do not dream you, Albert, I feel you, I feel what you are, and what you are is close to me."

It was strange. He was talking to me like my wide awake self, as if to save me and himself from pain. He gave me the feeling that he had abdicated the individual quest, the search, fulfillment, as if he had become "collective." I could not quite understand if this came out of a shock, as he spoke of having suffered for his dreaming—yes, I believe it is this. Then he found communism and relinquished the self. I am afraid I awakened or reawakened his deeper, more violent desires again, disturbed the peace he had gained. It was strange, this mixture of my dreaming at the same time of this "reality" of Albert's—this Albert who said: "I want to stay on the ground, to keep my feet on the earth," as if it had cost him much to achieve this and he wanted to keep it. So the "romantic" Albert is in me now. "I was like you," he said. I said, "I would rather be like you at this moment," because the suffering comes from the inacceptance of reality. I said, "I believe all obstacles can be overcome." It is strange. His equilibrium attracts me, because I see him always tranquil, and I enjoy it when slowly, slowly desire and passion disturb it. We were talking quietly, so quietly. He was caressing the center of my arm, the softest part. I said, "We have so much to give each other." The understanding passed between us, subtle and equal to the physical. He spoke of the *grande richesse* in our being together. He spoke also as if "personal happiness" didn't matter. He will not cling to the impossible. We walked out on the porch. We stood quietly together, his arm around my waist. His goal is not personal. It is the work he can do in his country for the peasants, his political work. That was why I did feel his "impersonality." He lived in the "group." The personal clutching of Pussy, or the personal intense anguish I felt to be with him, he transcends as "individualism." There it was, his practical, terrestrial, natural acceptance. And I received his peace and acceptance while we stood there, mastering the passion. The wind caressed us. He had a pose I loved (everywhere he is natural, simple, without timidity or self-consciousness). I looked up at him. Then we went back into the studio, and I showed him what I wrote in the *Winter of Artifice* for Jacques Romain, "This scene of what I look back upon as a white decadence which led me to the beliefs we have in common now."

Then we stood and embraced. Bodies pressed together, mouths together. His body began to shiver and tremble. The feelings were violent, electrical...we couldn't break the embrace. The intensity held us together like a fire, painful, surcharged, unbearable. Albert then lost his head and led me to the couch. We undressed. What a passionate, intense possession, then, long-lasting, powerful and filled with love, with a love which strove to plant a seed, a memory, an imprint, a caress full of meaning, like a marriage, deep-reaching and emotional!

Alas. That was certainly a moment to pay highly for, a moment to haunt us, a hopeless, impossible love born in a moment of separation.

Albert may recover his tranquility, as nature does after a storm. Yes, he has the power to do this, to accept the inevitability of the war forcing him home, of his work pointing him home, of the fiancée who awaits him, of his father's power, but I?

I have no resignation, no acceptance! The obstacles drive me onward to master them, to fight! But it is this I must not do. It is the man's role. And it is also against greater forces.

My greatest inner weakness which kills my courage is the knowledge of the difference of age. But how Albert looks at me, takes me with his eyes, and what a strange intuition runs between us, a strange relationship like a twinship. He reminds me of myself at sixteen before the storms uncovered fears and infernos, that calm I had, harmonious, poised, serene.

But deeper in him, there is the passion—how tangled we are! I light the flame in him, and he diffuses the radiance so it will not burn us, hurt us.

His face as he takes me, the desire, the love, the identification. Only this moment to see each other, to express the complete embrace. Oh, god, will I forget this? Can I now forget it?

"If you decide we must forget each other..."

"I cannot forget this, Anaïs, and I do not want to forget."

But I fear what will happen. I would like to haunt him forever, until he returns, but he knows what pain there is in this, and he will circumnavigate it.

JULY 16, 1943

I fell into an inferno. The night before he left, the pain in the body kept me awake. If I slept awhile it was to have a nightmare: Albert's bus was in an accident. He died. I slept awhile but awakened at dawn, at five o'clock, the hour of his departure. The pain was terrible. I felt everything, the intoxication, the separation, the emptiness. My present life seemed unbearable. Nothing could help me. I didn't want Gonzalo, or Hugo, or any of my friends.

Oh, the suffering, the suffering. How could I learn to relinquish this, accept the loss? I thought of so many things: to throw myself into communism, to relinquish personal happiness, the quest for love, as when women used to go into a convent at such moments. Worst of all, when I was all tangled with Albert, while he so vividly lived inside my body, Pierce chose this moment—the worst of all—to make love to me. And what a violent effort I had to make not to murder him! Pierce, with his bodily ugliness! Pierce, playing the role of a woman seeking to tempt a man. Pierce in his kimono, languorous and inviting, showing a little shoulder, a leg!

For the sake of the mystical sensitiveness he showed, I refrained. I let him kiss me, as if to prove to him he was not a man, not a body, but a woman! And I left, revolted and incensed.

That he should dare desire me, he, the impotent, the weakling, the degenerate. This desire of a eunuch, of a castrated being, of a woman! Suddenly the fraternal affection I had turned to repugnance. After Albert's beauty and power, the long, thin, ugly body, freckled, red-skinned, and above all, the degenerate face!

I wanted to hurt him, send him away. He has been using his mediumship evilly, reading only catastrophes, striking terror in Thurema and Frances—he did not dare towards me.

He drinks, he creeps into places and stays, and again I was blind, because Pierce was one person with me and only betrayed the diabolical self on the outside. I had to sum up all the images together to obtain a complete one. But the image of "courtship" (and his fears afterwards, his discussing with Thurema his fear of not carrying through physically!) was enough to revolt me. Degeneracy, madness.

JULY 18, 1943

The suffering became unbearable, and it attacked the body. I got ill. In spite of the illness, I could not be at rest, so I took another trip with Gonzalo, and went on a weekend with Hugo, searching for a vacation place…

Last night in the hotel room, filled with torment and devastation, I took a sleeping pill. Then, as I felt the torpor of sleep, I mistook it for death. I felt: now my hand is asleep, now my shoulder. I am dying. My heart feels strange. I am dying.

It was sleep.

Can I master this alone? Can I relinquish Albert? I have no faith I will see him again. He will bow to "reality." My only reality is passion and its need of fulfillment. He is like all those I love, passive before destiny, events, outer obstacles, lost in them. He hasn't the strength. I must relinquish him.

I am caught again in the wound net of the dream.

Caught.

Will I die?

I could go to Jaeger, but I would like to transcend this alone.

JULY 21, 1943

The illness burnt me. I had to go to Jacobson. I had an inflammation, an intoxication of the kidneys which may be caused by sexual excesses! The pain, the loss of the body, pleasure and life, meeting with a weak Gonzalo again after the magnificence of Albert, Canada and Edward!

Jacobson gave me drugs. Nothing for the pain of the heart. Frances said: "You must give up Albert, because he is the son. He can only make you suffer. You must give up what causes you pain."

Yes, I have given him up, because he is the son, and the mistress. I will have to jump over the obstacles on my Diana horse and court him, and I will have to sweep him off his feet. My whole being craves the man, and no longer the immolation of the mother to the son.

But he still lives in my being, and when I remember him it is with passion.

I sent Gonzalo and Helba to Quogue, to the beach. I am free.

It is only mother and child now. The passion is over. Chinchilito telephones me, wants to see me.

Pierce—we should all have known that his impotence would inevitably make him a criminal. Everywhere he finds the husband, the lover, the man, and he, like Robert, tries to get inside the marriages, to separate the father and mother, the mother from her lover. He tried to wreck the bond between Thurema and Jimmy, "It will not last, because of the difference of age." To Frances: "Tom has two mistresses. He will leave for Hollywood and not send for you, or return." To me: "There is no relation between your chart and Albert's. He is dangerous. He is a vampire. I see no love there!"

Laughable when I see it now. His sadism and then his masochism, seeking to be punished and loving it, knowing I would reject him, knowing I had abandoned Henry and Dudley…seeking the pain.

At four o'clock in the morning, when I am asleep, he telephones me: "I have *The Bright Messenger* here. May I bring it over?"

Hugo was furious, and rightly. I refused to see him, not only that night, but the next day. I told him: "You've destroyed everything. I don't want to see you." Without hesitation I cut him off. He cannot crawl into my life with his weakness and destructiveness. I reject his illness, degeneracy and impotence, his insanity.

As he warned me, out of jealousy, against Mexico, I told him I was leaving for Mexico. He uses astrology unscrupulously for himself, for his personal ends. Since he cannot be loved, or possess, he will destroy.

What does a certain mysticism do to the body? The lack of care, the illness, the neglect, as in the Russian hysterics, saints, maniacs, a punishment of the body which inevitably mutilates it. Pierce was tall, but his face was sickly. His skin was particularly ugly: red, very white, freckled and subject to red patches, rashes, or at times it turned to blue. He had watery, irritated eyes, as if he never slept well, a small turned-up nose like a clown, and teeth with spaces between them which always seemed weak.

I was not surprised that the spirits who understood me looked like this (Rank, Jean). I accept it as a prank of destiny, a cruel prank. I thought again of the fanatics, the insane Artaud, and as a defense against this, the great physical beauty of Albert, of Edward Graeffe.

Lucas Premice: He is about fifty. He has the true African mask face, his hair straight and stiff, standing on his head as if carved out of wood, fanatical eyes, a nose which wrinkles up when he laughs, big mouth and big teeth, emotional and independent character. He had wanderlust and worked on ships so that he could travel all over the world. When he was very young, he was exiled from Haiti for political activities. At thirty he landed in America, was gravely ill in a hospital, met his loyal, devoted wife, married, and had Adele and Josephine. He worked then as a fur cutter, organized the workmen, and lost his job as a consequence. He talks bad French and bad English, almost unintelligible, wanders when he talks. He has natural refinement of manners, sensibility, dignity, practices a noble hospitality. He is deeply homesick for Haiti.

Adele: about twenty, wears glasses which magnify her eyes, so she is not beautiful. She has no confidence in herself, is afraid of her father, is effaced, but kind. Has a beautiful voice and plays the piano.

Josephine is seventeen. Her zest and aliveness are dominant. She is not beautiful, but is very bright, flaming, has a well-proportioned body and intensely brilliant eyes. Her dancing is marvelous, her singing husky. She is full of humor and improvisations. She is naturally coquettish, magnetic and romantic. A stony brook.

I pack my valise to visit Irina for a few days.

WOMAN OF ACTION

I feel ready for this

At Irina Aleksander's, July 23, 1943

I didn't run to Jaeger with my pain, like a child to its mother. I wanted to take the shock, survive it, mature, learn to suffer without dying. And I have triumphed. I am strong again. I haven't died. I took my body to the beach, to the sun, recuperated. I had bad moments, but I haven't died. My senses are alive, and I am no longer ill. I have eaten heartily. Monday I will make love with Chinchilito. Tuesday I will go to Southampton. I will have more lovers, many of them. I will play, be alive, dance, sing, swim—*not die*—not be caught in tragedy, paralyzed or enslaved. I will defeat tragedy.

The image which has supported, inspired me, upheld me, put me to shame, is strangely that of the Soviet Captain Valentina Orlikova, with whom Irina had a friendship. Her photograph gave me the same shock I felt when I first saw it on a magazine cover and heard about her life. A shock of admiration, of love, of identification. She was born February 22.

Life lashes out. I must turn my face, receive the blow, and continue. Every day Valentina faces death, separation from her husband and child, the great tragedy of war, greater catastrophes, universal tragedies. *Il y a une* self-indulgence *dans la souffrance.*

July 26, 1943

I felt I couldn't write about the days spent with Irina under her roof, but now I am back in New York with the captive image of her Rubens coloring, her flaming hair and delicate roses, her soft curves, her deep voice, her irrepressible laughter, her nervous tension which is causing her illness.

For the first time in my life, I felt natural and relaxed while staying with people. I didn't strain. I had confidence. I was passive (I arrived still ill).

Irina said when I left: "There are no visitors coming until August 15. There will be a hole after you leave." *Amitié passioné*—always going as far as a friendship can go without sensuality. I take her bare arm. It is soft, and the skin is so fine, so fine. I left too soon.

I have been captain of the invisible ship, the invisible captain of Hugo's life, of Henry's, Gonzalo's, or Thurema, Frances, so many of them, yes. But am I doomed to invisibility and mystery!

Valentina has a real ship, a real uniform, a real medal, a real direct love from all.

And I? I am weary of the ghostliness of the soul and wish to appear on the surface!

As I write, I am bruised and exhausted from a long orgy with Chinchilito. The independent Chinchilito is now more personal in his lovemaking. Not only does he take me with greater passion, but holds me afterwards with tenderness, a personal tenderness. We talked together delightfully, whimsically. And then, when I thought he had enough, he took me for the second time, something Gonzalo has never done. The sort of feast I like, which satisfies me, quiets me. He feels my detachment from Gonzalo and grows nearer.

In this new physical world I feel strange at times. Certitude. Like the sunlight, I see the new hand of Chinchilito upon my hips, a blond, fair artist hand. As he talks I look at his mouth, his lovely and dazzling teeth. There is friendship, gestures like those of love at moments, paroxysms of desire mounting.

The only element missing is the emotion, the deep inner burning consuming the feelings, but there is the freedom from pain. His wife doesn't exist for me. I powder myself at her dressing table, I see the Arden face tonic, the Arden face powder, dark hairpins.

Of course, I am deceiving myself. To possess the physical world, I am surrendering my emotional depths, the feelings that were a reality of another kind. I lived by them. I also died for them, the feelings indissolubly bound to torment.

How many, many layers the being has, how many folds and fissures the flesh has. A body like mine is shaken in the act of possession, and because of its capacity to vibrate, the feelings too get shaken somewhat (as if the dice alone could not be shaken without affecting the box). Yes, as he kneels, he shakes my whole body with his power; he is a powerful instrumentalist. But the deep emotions are dormant. How easily Albert reached down to them.

Of course I am aware of the *simulacra*.

Because I have often experienced orgasms of the soul, my lonely body, when deprived of its emotions, is not deeply possessed yet. It is only pretending. Yet life does come from these *simulacra*—yes—in the playing and pretending there is a growth too.

JULY 27, 1943, SOUTHAMPTON

Caresse got me an apartment in the plumber's house across the street from the Old Post House, which she manages. I have plenty of rooms, two bedrooms, a sitting room, a big kitchen and bathroom for the incredible sum of $50, but the atmosphere of the place is ugly, chichi and snobbish. I don't like it. I try to think of the beach only, health and recuperation.

I am getting hardened to the blows. My body is more resilient. I feel nothing when Gonzalo telephones me that he is coming tomorrow. I feel drained. All I want is the physical warmth of sensuality. That is why I sought out Caresse, whose sensual life is full and excessive and happy. She has an "official" lover, whom we call the husband, because he is protective, elderly, and whom she doesn't desire. She has a young son lover, *amants de passage, amants d'une nuit,* etc.

When I think of Albert, it is with an acute agony, but it passes like a heart attack.

What can I make of this moment, the present? A day at the beach, at the exclusive beach club where at least everything is pleasant to the eyes and people have an assurance, an ease I have not seen among the poor and bohemians.

Sleep. Rest.

The solitude I hate, yet I can't bring myself to invite Frances or Thurema.

I want lovers.

So.

MONDAY, AUGUST 9, 1943

Thurema and Jimmy came for two days and cheered me. Hugo comes on weekends. August passes, and my love for Gonzalo turns to tenderness...

Sadness.

I had the courage to surmount death, to continue to live, but I find nothing to live for. I cannot live without passion.

SEPTEMBER 3, 1943

I tried to pass through the ordeal of the loss of Albert alone, tried to survive it, tried to take it with strength, health, but in the end I have lost the battle. I have fallen again into my anxieties, my obsessions. I have no desire to live. I think of my work and feel blocked by the stupidity of the response it gets, by its inadequacy, by the fact that I am writing for people who don't understand me. There has been complete silence surrounding *Winter of Artifice,* never any public mention of it. A few individual responses, that is all. How can I print another book? Where will I find the courage?

My body is starved.

My only possession, as always, is Hugo's love, Hugo's devotion, Hugo's passion and desire, Hugo's worship, Hugo's protection, Hugo's total abandon to me, Hugo surrounding me. That is all I have, and ever have had. The rest was illusion and delusion.

Dream: A ship is sailing towards Europe at top speed. I can see it through the enormous lens of a movie camera. But suddenly I am aware that I am in another ship on which is perched the movie camera, sailing towards Europe even faster than the other ship. I see that I am inappropriately dressed in a white lace dress. Then I feel very insecure because the highly elevated ship (to hold the camera) makes it top heavy, and as it is racing against the other ship I feel its height makes it dangerous, apt to overturn. Now we are facing the narrow canal I always see in my dreams. I say to Joaquín, "There it is, I recognize it." It is always apparent that the passageway is too narrow for the large ship. Now we enter it. It is bordered with trees and lined all along with prison bars. Behind these bars are all the prisoners of the war. I see them as we see them in pictures, crowded, idle, ghostly...

I told Hugo I am tired of being a ghost, that I want a real ship, a real medal, action. I always succeed spiritually but fail in action. I failed to become a dancer, a psychoanalyst, and now a writer. Yes, I know my value, but my value always condemns me to the *coulisses*, the mystical, the invisible, the mysterious. I am tired of being a mystery. I want to take form, to *appear*, and one only gains visibility by action. As it is, I only appear in people's dreams, haunt their souls, and they refuse me power in reality, refuse to pay me, refuse to review or recognize me as a writer, condemn me to obscurity. No, I want power and daylight. I am coming out in the open now. I am no longer going to be the transfer of blood that I have been for others. I am going to BE, be myself directly, openly. Every act of mine has been subterranean, mystical, incomprehensible, reprehensible, and suffocated. Just as I cast off my romanticism and magic, I cast off my old form of action. Like Russia, I am going to transmute from hysteria to health, from emotion to action, from weakness to *strength on earth*.

But how? How? How?

Men fear woman's new development. Imagine kissing a woman corporal, a sniper, a captain, a welder. Imagine how they will dominate! It will be impossible to regard them as women or to dominate them! Men's fear. Gonzalo's, even Hugo's fear! Their power is threatened, and their masculinity is endangered.

I know how to answer this.

Women are much more dangerous to men as thwarted wills, perverted power-seekers who dominate man indirectly because they cannot use their own power directly. Their will is frustrated because they are always forced to fulfill themselves through *another*, in the husband, the child, and if she is husbandless and childless, then she is a failure, an incubus, a sick, incomplete cripple.

SEPTEMBER 4, 1943

I dreamed that I was going to die in one week. Then someone was reading a story, a serial about a character with whom I identified myself. I asked this person: what happens to the woman this week? It's a story of her death, and I am sure this is an indication of my own. I was not sad, I was only worried about the diaries. I wanted to burn them.

I cannot fight my way out of death. It has descended on me, engulfed me. Everything seems like death to me: New York, the press, printing the stories, life with Gonzalo. I dread the people I am going to see again, none of them give me life. I give it to them. Irina, Thurema, Frances. The Premices will remind me of Albert, and I will see Pussy at their home. Pain and emptiness—naturally my health is bad.

SEPTEMBER 9, 1943, NEW YORK

After returning to New York, the activity calmed my anxiety.

Ideologically, what has crystallized is the relationship between romanticism and neurosis. I have seen their connection. The result of romanticism is death. I have repudiated it, but I had not seen that it was synonymous with neurosis. Frances pointed the way to Denis de Rougemont's *Passion and Society*, which analyzes the myth of Tristan and Iseult. This theme has appeared in all my relations except with Hugo, though my attitude towards Hugo was romantic and a rejection of happiness for the sake of intensity and passion.

The whole theme of my Southampton lamentations was, "I cannot live without passion!"

Passion and suffering, obstruction, frustration, and death—I see the relationship better now because of the myth images and de Rougemont's cruel exposure of it.

This is no petty experience I have lived through. It is directly related to *war*, the *cause* of war. The relationship was exposed in the heroic defense of Stalingrad: the passion, heroism, death, but the gift of the self—selflessness—reaches the infinite.

I have waited to make this gift. I wanted to give up the personal war of touching the infinite and to die for Russia, to share in the intensification which its drama brings. That is clear.

Now, I don't know what I'm going to do with the great erotic tumult in me. I cannot disown the erotic seeking a personal outlet.

"Write!" says Frances. "What marvelous writing you will do."

I saw Jaeger, and for the first time derived no comfort from the analysis. There is an impasse.

I have no desire to write or to print my stories. I move automatically but soullessly. I see Eduardo. I plan for the printing. I fix the apartment. I attend to my clothes.

SEPTEMBER 10, 1943

Talked to Eduardo about my big, objective work to come, the one I wanted to start at fifty. I said to him I may take myself out of it completely and have everyone in it but myself!

He was enthusiastic. I said I would break all the taboos, expose all the myths, and end by being not the poet, but the supremely lucid revolutionary analyst preparing *new* myths of Valentina, the woman captain. Eduardo was excited.

But I ended by saying: "But first of all I want a *lover*. I won't work until I get a *lover*. I will not sacrifice my body nor the life of my body."

Five-thirty in the evening. I have returned from Dr. Lopez. There is a cyst on the ovary which is infecting me. No lovemaking for two weeks. Treatments, perhaps an operation. I took the news well. I am calmer since I saw Jaeger. No anxiety.

I do not intend to sacrifice my erotic life at all. I will overcome this.

SEPTEMBER 13, 1943

My weekend with Irina
my mother—Wassermann's Ganna
Ganna
hysteria, will, tyranny—

Certainty that I am the myth maker
I have to turn everything into a myth, symbol, legend
Plus grand de nature
therefore I shall never deal with actuality as it is
nor do journalistic writing like Irina's—
Satisfied with my lot. Irina maliciously situates me with the dreamers.
That's a way of
embalming me
disposing of me.
But I don't know that I shall always remain in the rarefied spheres of the dream.
the *dream* of pyschoanalysis
the *dream* of Henry
the *dream* of Gonzalo
the *dream* of communism

"Come down from your stratosphere," says Irina, at the same time feeling a great uneasiness at my adventures, fearing and respecting me, not daring to reject my work merely as perverse, pornographic, or experimental.

I have a vague hunch, a feeling something is going to come of my honest struggles, sincerity, courage, and of my sacrifices.

SEPTEMBER 14, 1943

I cannot begin a work casually. I have a concept of something big. I cannot begin, select, eliminate. I feel whatever I do will have to be all-encompassing.

What happens if I leave myself out? Then everyone will be restored to his natural value, not mythical, not romantic, not enlarged, not symbolic.

With me absent and only the other characters present, it shall be in a human world, purely of feeling. Possibly if I eliminated myself as representing the legend, the vision, the far-reaching and the cosmic, I might get into direct contact with the natural aspect of human beings. It is only in relation to me that they become "poeticized" or translated into a dream. *It will be a diminished world.* A *natural* world, not an intensified one. With me absent, passion and intensity will be removed, as will the mirror reflecting people's potential selves. It might be a way into the human. *If I am there it will be mystical and mythical.*

It might be good to begin writing about characters as unrelated to me.

For example, I see a bigger Ganna to be portrayed, the impossible woman, my mother, the extension of her. In a state of destructive revolution, the black anima.

If I disappeared as a character and became merely the *vision*, if I disappeared as an ego and used myself as the chemical which brought certain elements to light, I might accomplish the objective work of human dimensions which could relate me to the present.

SEPTEMBER 16, 1943

Jaeger was pleased with the development in the creation, but not with my illnesses, which she attributes to the suffering at sexual privation (the pain in my ovary), nor at my dreams which still show traces of masochism. In life I am blocked, but not in anguish. When I returned to New York, I had to face the torment of Albert's presence: here on this couch he took me, on this porch we talked holding each other, before this table we first felt the frenzy and fever, here we parted, here we kissed with a joy so intense it was painful, and then hearing about him from Josephine and Adele, "He is still in Mexico, trying to get a job."

Yes, it is the moment of maturity when "one has to rectify the errors by the imagination." It is the moment of philosophy, but for me it is like trying to tame a tigress: the capacity for madness, frenzy and fever are still there, surging powerfully at a piece of music, a scene in the movies, unused, misplaced. Out of place with Gonzalo, certainly.

My Major Work occupies my mind. I *didn't* want to give myself to it, to be possessed by it. But life and love are fatally denied me—I wanted *to do it later*. Now is the time for pleasure and sensuality, but I cannot reach them. I admit to an external obstruction (as I know the inner obstruction was removed): the fatality of Albert in danger of being drafted and forced to leave, the war keeping me in America, the desert.

SEPTEMBER 17, 1943

Forward again, accepting Gonzalo as he is, taking care of him, repainting the furniture and windows, restoring my clothes, recapturing my elegance, having a suit made out of Hugo's dress suit, very smart. I am planning to print the stories with Gonzalo, to go to fiestas, dances, Harlem, to see Carl Offord, Richard Wright, the Premices. I am ruminating my Major Work because the mind is best occupied with this artistic construction than with the past. Refreshing, re-lacquering, remodeling the old.

So here I am, wearing a sienna-colored corduroy suit given to me by Thurema, Mexican sandals. My hair has been newly curled. Lopez says I'm much better. The economic pressure is lifting. Hugo is making a little extra money. The anxiety and strain are gone.

Voilà. Courage!

SEPTEMBER 21, 1943

Last night, when I did not expect it (for I have given up Gonzalo as a lover), he took me completely and with vigor. But I could not respond. Too much anxiety and repression and control have made me cold. What a tragic see-saw!

After seeing Martha:
Don Quixote
Idealization of myself
   Henry
   Gonzalo
Now I see my Shadow Self in the women I have liked:
   June
   Thurema
   Irina
Here is the dark part of Anaïs.

I have never faced *darkness* except in those I love, and then only for combat. *The enemy is within.*

Let us find the dark Anaïs now.

Jaeger points out the inevitable suffering caused by idealization, dreaming, mirages, illusions. *There is no happiness possible while I am dreaming.*

The firefish falls into the dark unconscious where it must seek to live. The *orgueil* peacock falls too. Jaeger said: "I thought the other day when you came with the fuchsia bird in your hair how good a symbol it was of you. How it represented you. The colored plumage…"

Jaeger can only see my love for Henry and Gonzalo as not *loves*, but mirages, drugs and poisons. That was why life with Henry in New York destroyed my dream. That was why I sustained this dream by isolating him.

This return to true vision modified by experience draws me closer to Hugo, who alone withstands reality, whose character has become what I truly love.

Jaeger has been concerned with my elusiveness. Everything I have placed outside of myself, in others, but it all issues from me. My "shadow" self, my dark self, is in the women (except Frances) and in Henry and Gonzalo. Jaeger says *I must find the shadow in myself, not its projection in others.* It is like a detective story. I am so fearful of my capacity for transformation and illusion that I begged Jaeger not to let me escape again. I have had courage to suffer masochistically, but not to face the reason for this suffering. *I have never accepted the shadow*, but I have fought it in myself. I fought sickness, dark experiences, *yet submitted to them at the hands of others*.

Tonight I feel like Don Quixote, struggling for sanity. Symbolically, I fell in love with a coat, a coat that represents the great change in me. It is not the coat of the firefish or peacock... It is a very beautiful material, masculine tailoring, fitted, with a velvet collar and cuffs. It is expensive, aristocratic, simple, very pure, for action, and far from mirages of Byzance or the dream! I shall wear it a long time. It is enduring, of good quality. I chose it boldly, in an expensive shop, but I hesitated because of the high price. Hugo then insisted I should make him feel like a man of power who is able to get such a coat for his wife, and when I saw it was a symbol for him too, I yielded. It is a coat for a new life, and it will go with the very smart suit made out of Hugo's fine English tuxedo. So I am fully blown *Harper's Bazaar* elegance and out of the masochism of clothes.

I cannot write a book now. I am just barely awakening from a dream, and I am not wholly awake yet. When I am awake, I write the Birth story. *I always feared awakening and what I should find.*

I beg Jaeger to hold on, that I don't know how to seize the dark Anaïs once and for all. She eludes detection. She is clever and artful at deceit and enchantments. Already I begin to feel that I have had enough analysis and that I can abandon it now and live and write, but I say this when I am on the threshold of the ultimate discovery of the dark Anaïs.

Idealization is the rejection of darkness.

SEPTEMBER 22, 1943

Last night when Hugo, according to ritual, sat next to the bathtub while I took my bath, dried me off with the towel, and then asked me to "put something nice on," I wore the black lace nightgown. Then, because I had been concentrating my roving, far-fetched, capricious fantasies on Hugo, on my love for him, I was not only able to control the straining of my imagination towards the romantic lover, but by saying to myself: here I have happiness, a love that is happy and complete, and *I transported myself into the present in order to enjoy it.* I found myself relaxed, not full of resistance, and natural, as if Hugo were simply one of the lovers, and I would have responded if he were not so swift. But progress has been made, consciously and voluntarily, towards reshaping a perverse desire, an imagination and a body wanting always what it cannot have, rejecting happiness, always seeking the impossible.

It was while showing Hugo my coat last night that I realized it was Captain Valentina's coat—it is the uniform, the rectitude, the sobriety, the disciplined!

SEPTEMBER 24, 1943

Ever since I started to track down my shadow it eludes me.

I note the characteristics of the women I was attracted to:

June: hysteria, unrestrained, unconscious aggression, sensation, sensuality, possessiveness, jealousy, fear, *energy*.

Thurema: violence, hysteria, unconscious behavior, emotionalism, extremes, action, energy in reality.

Irina: violence, hysteria, unconscious behavior, action, energy, actuality, reality.

But that applies equally to Henry and Gonzalo: Gonzalo was exactly like June and Henry like Thurema.

I know all this, but it does not reveal my shadow. All I have felt is relief and pleasure at their *reality*, their sensational and violent adventures, but I have not *liked* their behavior, could always see its destructiveness and fought it, never yielded to it.

It was the *unconscious*, loose and uncontrolled, that attracted me, the action, the drama and reality of their acts.

I felt enclosed and bound to my idealistic behavior, not free to act as they did, but compelled to be noble and selfless.

I like their naturalness. As Rank used to say, "Women like the bad man because he is *natural*, closer to nature."

Closer to nature.

I began so far from nature, so *ideally*, that I wanted it, but found it to be mostly black.

My nature has been idealized and *denatured*. My fight with nature was also an expression of love, a desire to instill my spirituality in it—for I *influenced* them all, and I fought them—*I did not yield to them*.

The first time nature appeared to me as beneficial and innocent, it was in Albert. It was nature, naturalism, that I liked in Henry, his enjoyment. It was the savage in him I liked, in Gonzalo too. They are all violent like nature, unpredictable, capricious, stormy, wayward, emotional. But they are also sick, all of them, except Albert. That is as far as I can go.

Evening

This morning I went to Martha, and instead of talking I showed her what I had written since our last talk. I watched her face, with its wonderful expressions of compassion, indulgence, humor, forgiveness, understanding.

She said, "Your expression of all this is marvelous, crystal clear." Her face was full of admiration. I felt it and was elated. Her praise, more than anyone else's, has such significance for me! "You will have much to contribute to the development of woman. I feel that it was a privilege for me to analyze you, read you, that you gave me rich material, that this was a collaboration towards woman's problems. Because you live so deeply and suffered so much, these experiences will mean a great deal to other women." More than her words, her tone moved me. I felt like a starved person receiving manna. The tears came to my eyes. This obscure labor, so overlooked by the world, so little recognition or understanding of what I am doing, the silence around my writing. "Because," said Martha, "you write straight from the unconscious."

Her response was invaluable to me as artist, as woman. I was suddenly glad of all the suffering which opened such deep worlds to me. I was glad it was Martha who saved me when the suffering crucified me. I am glad it was she who gave me back my strength, because her vision reaches very far and is the kind I believe in.

The miracle now is one of synthesis. Martha made me fuse, integrate, synthesize. There is no doubt that all this flowering and renewal came from her. Without her this summer, I was dead. Now I am full of strength.

She smiled about the coat. Yes, it is for simple, direct action. It wasn't hatred, jealousy, or temper I was concerned with in the primitives, but the energy, dynamism, the *passion* being used for life, for actuality, for the present. Passions make us act in the present. That was what I wanted. Mysticism gives us a larger vision, but the human dynamism must be there. Passion pushes the sails and creates the currents of drama and life and action. I feel ready for this.

I told Martha that because I had meditated on my shadow, only now do I see, because it was linked with my illness, the *under*ground activity, my indirect *buried creation*: the diary.

Now I must come out of it at last!

I didn't see the direct relationship between the pursuit of the shadow and the immediate answering dream: the diary! The diary *is* my shadow. I knew even as a child I was putting into it the rages, hatreds, outbursts, venom and complaints I didn't want to use on other people! Enclose the devil in its box, but there it is, immense and dark!

September 25, 1943

I wish I could write the END of the diary and turn to the outside story.

The theme I am interested in is the development of woman. I would like to take June, Thurema, Irina, Lucia Cristofanetti, Frances, their childhoods, their backgrounds, their *indirect* actions, their *underground* lives, their lack of fulfillment. What has kept me focused on myself was first that I was good for *all* the experiences, as laboratory experiments, that I was a supple general subject! Secondly; I *was* all these women in myself, and therefore my story was the most complete one. I was a symbol, the figure that can contain many figures. But instead of creating a character, I can easily tell the same story in many women, divide myself:

Irina: the masculine me writing novels, *chic femme du monde*.

Thurema: the maternal me spending herself on all, the courageous me.

Frances: the dreaming me, the analytic me.

June: the sensational, the unconscious, dramatic me.

Lucia: the oriental harem, timid, childish me—what Henry used to call the Japanese wife of Lafcadio Hearn's descriptions.

Jaeger: the healing, most highly protective, intuitive, guiding me.

And there you are…if I write about these women, it will be more human, more accessible. Now, can I efface myself, like the cathedral builders of old, to focus my vision on these women?

In these women there was, to begin with, *strength*, a strength which impelled June out of her orbit, Thurema out of her ordinary life, Frances out of her poor, arid background, Irina out of her home into international sophistication, Lucia out of her enclosed Syrian harem. A strength which made them choose instinctively not the man who would again master and withhold them from the use of this strength, but the weak, childish man upon whom they could use this strength as mother, husband, muse, and at the same time whom they could become what they themselves did not dare to be: June making Henry the writer because she felt creatively inadequate but wanted to be the character of his creation; Thurema living through her children and wanting to live out her musicianship through Joaquín; Lucia first wanting to be a painter and then turning this into making her husband Francesco the painter; Frances feeding Tom's writing and developing him, rather than facing a man equal to her who would possess her. All these women eluded *being possessed*, being passive. They played the active role, thus suffering in love because by being the aggressor, they forfeited being courted and loved as other women are. They suffer in their femininity, suffer from the man who cannot fulfill their dream (as I suffered from Gonzalo not becoming the *active* heroic revolutionary).

The effect of this active role upon sexual life is the accentuation of the passivity of the man, his limitless taking, (June's giving to Henry was continuous and selfless too). The disastrous effect of the strength—when misused, it results in possessiveness, in great sacrifices, all indirect routes to fulfillment.

These weak men represented not the masculinity of these women, but the weak, newborn consciousness of an active role in life which women obscurely feel but upon which they do not know how to act.

These women could not connect with the totally masculine man as we know him because such a man would endanger this obscure, barely born, active role they felt urged to seek, the role of the new woman. Such a man would insist on passivity which by now has grown irksome and impossible. The weak child-man, on the contrary, was the right one to develop this new strength with, but he left the woman, on the other hand, alone, without a real mate or guide, without the support or the protection of the real man. The real man is capable of playing the father role when necessary, and certainly the husband role, and the child-man has failed even in his role of lover. So woman was left with a child who did not grow up, who did not gain strength from her efforts as the real child does, but became weaker and weaker. What a penalty to pay for this new strength she felt, and what a misuse of it!

Confusion. This strength was meant to be used directly, to have its own fulfillment in activity, not to be used as a lever by weak men—but in women it became confused with the maternal instinct, so woman's first act of strength was always *to protect*.

Confusion, too, when her activity became corrupted into rivalry with man who considered this activity of women as a challenge, danger, a competition. They often punished women by either overlooking or denying the existence of their femininity. Rivalry takes away the love.

There is confusion in woman who feels that she is *only* imitating man and often losing the man in this process, like an exchange which demands the surrender of femininity. Not at all! No femininity lost! Women's *passivity* in life is not necessarily feminine or linked with sexual obedience. Man fears her development as an usurper and arrests her expansion, misinterpreting it as rivalry, not seeing that this arrested, enforced passivity negatively corners her perverted strength into nagging, the domination of the husband and children, imposing her will over them because it is an unfulfilled, thwarted will which cannot spend itself creatively, usefully and positively in concrete action. The concentration on the home, which receives the discharge of these "turned milk" breasts, the sourness and discontent accumulated from the slavish tasks, the lack of more expansive living and remuneration (woman does the same labor at home, but she does not earn money or feel free, and instead is dependent on the man and receives no recognition of her work).

Man says: How can I make love to a sniper?

But didn't women receive love from killers without confusing the issue?

Men fear the activity as a sexual danger. How can one kiss a corporal into submission? But woman is not seeking power but rather the expression of the dynamism of the emotional life. Man's expression of power as negation of the primitive and the emotions is not satisfying to her. (Note: I wouldn't do as a character in the book anyway because I have Hugo—no tragic choice of man, a happy ending as it were!)

Now, this analogy between primitive woman seeking to become articulate, seeking to be given a right to act resembles the problem of the negro. Women have gone to the negro for sexual power because of the degeneration of the white man, but there was more than that which impelled her: the negro's primitivism was the same as hers; the language of the emotions, lost to man (having become the capitalist, the analyst, the man of science), was the same.

Caresse, dedicated to love, turned to Canada for the "best lover of all." Frances is sexually starved by her dry twig of a husband. Thurema is not satisfied with her husband's "financial success."

The problem of primitive races is in great closeness to the revolution of women.

SEPTEMBER 26, 1943

Dream: I get dressed for lovemaking with Charles Duits.

And of course he telephoned today, and we went together to the Premices. Lucas told marvelous stories, Josephine *pétille* like a spangle, Mother Premice gave me a head scarf. The atmosphere was warm and human, with stories of voodoo, magic, etc. Albert has a job in Mexico but has not written me. He has wisely submitted to reality and not sought the painful ecstasies which could destroy him. What would I do now if he wrote me? Today I would not rush so fast to impossible ecstasies for which one pays with one's life, yet physically my body is being sacrificed and denied, and in my dreams I am full of erotic fever.

Today I saw Duits pale and mystically blue-eyed as the eternal poet who haunts me. I resisted him during the summer, but now he charms me, and I see how he charms the Haitians who look at him like a figure from a cathedral window...*illuminé.*

Yes, the light, Josephine, which leads one away from the present into the infinite, killing the body in its journey through space after the divine and impossible absolute. Because passion is a *fire,* one believes the being will be dissolved and *welded* to another, and by dissolution the union of elements will happen. But fire cannot make this marriage. It is not fire which makes it. Josephine's fiery black eyes look at the five-pointed star eyes of Duits, at his pale face and curly hair. She does not see the body without power, the over-developed mind, the orgasms of the soul cheating the body of its orgasms, the marriages of intuition and spirit making marriage on earth impossible. The disembodied Duits, *poète maudit,* who all summer refused the sun and the sea and liked only the night, the dream... Josephine, beware, beware, Josephine and her sensual, lively curves, provocative, animated, full of electricity and fire and wit.

If Albert called me I would go, for that is life. This game of the imagination, the book, is only a poor substitute. I would live and be willing to die afterwards, cries the romantic! Perhaps fortunately for me Albert is natural and passive, not romantic.

SEPTEMBER 27, 1943

Half-awake, I murmured: It is a question of forgetting Albert. I felt the writing would help me to forget Albert.

At the same time I am conscious of a resistance to the writing as if it meant *being possessed by the book* and not wanting my passion to go into that, but into life. As if it were a choice. I see clearly the energy withdrawing from the sex into the imagination, and I refuse this substitution.

I also know I must do it because I am the only one who can, as a soldier knows he must fight, a priest knows he must serve. I am conscious of a role which was often behind my choices and acts, that of initiator and clarifier for others.

Consciously there is no such choice to be made. There is no life demand made on me which can contain this passion. This passion devours me, poisons me. It is right that it should go into creation.

It was being at the Premices' and seeing Pussy which reawakened my suffering at the loss of Albert.

To work, Anaïs. Now the twelve windows are painted, the style is modern and spacious. The colors are ultramarine blue, magenta, turquoise, dark green, and violet. The furniture is repainted in violet. I have thrown away all the old, faded, worn, useless.

Great distinction between the talk of theories, concepts, analysis, and the primitives telling a story. Gonzalo tells me stories, which is one of his greatest charms, and yesterday Premice told us stories (it was by the telling of a story that he won me). I am finding the primitive Anaïs who made a god of her father, who wanted a husband who would tell her stories, who told herself stories, and who is about to tell herself a new one!

Stories, stories, the only enchantment possible, for when we begin to see our suffering as a story, we are saved. It was the balm of the primitives, the way of bringing enchantment to the life of terror.

My "procrastination" consists of having to have everything in order before I begin—the house, clothes, papers—to be free.

I see women, women, women, tragedy in women. I am touched by their plight. I think of their inarticulateness. May each one find herself in all these women and be helped. I have so much to say, but I want to do it with my craft, without intensity, without anxiety, without acceleration and rarefaction.

I am not writing for the elite, but for the confused ones. I would like to have the *Encyclopædia Britannica*. I need it now. I want facts and concrete images, earth, science, body. Everything *made flesh, everything a story*, everything animated and dramatized.

THEME

DRAMA

IS

THE MISUSE OF STRENGTH

It is the misuse of the dream—the dream is the image of what one is to be, to become, to do. The dream is to be used as a guide, as a prophecy, as a creative source.

Women are dreaming the dream of strength and mistaking it for *man's* dream. Man has been woman's only image of strength, her only ideal of strength. It is time for *her creation*.

SEPTEMBER 28, 1943

I put on my tuxedo suit, my black veil, and went to Jacobson. He, expressing fully his knowledge of my evolution, stopped dead and exclaimed in his vague, inarticulate, crude way, "Ah! *Une dame!*" Maturity. As an experiment I have asked him to give me again the same "strength" cure he gave me a year ago in October, at the beginning of this diary, a strength I misused psychically on the struggle with Henry and Gonzalo and collapsed in spite of it. I felt that now I could take this physical strength and turn it into creative action.

From there I met Caresse a block away from our meeting place. She watched me cross the street without recognizing me, spellbound by my elegance and then exclaimed: "You are…you are a *grande dame*, Anaïs. What a change. I saw you walking so firmly, carrying your head high…"

But I sail boldly and luminously until I meet Gonzalo, a sick Gonzalo who is defeated by his weaknesses...

Anaïs, there are no miracles. Your passion and your dream deceived you, drugged you, but in the end you chose to dream with impotent men.

Why do I suddenly lose all my joy?

What a potent awakener the diary is. As I get ready to leave it, I pay it a slight tribute. This should be the last volume. At forty, I enter a new maturity, stripped of my mirages, dreams and miracles, of my delusions, my illusions, and my heavy romantic sorrows. What awaits me is the expression of this strength in action. I am about to lay down my magician's wand, my healer's paraphernalia, and to confront the *act*, in writing as well as in living. Without the diary, the tortoise shell, houseboat, and escargot cover. No red velvet panoply over my head, no red carpet under my feet, no Japanese umbrellas growing on the hair, no stage settings, tricks, enchantments...

Hadn't woman lived for centuries in a state of annihilation before man, dependent and incomplete? The few who had escaped this had suffered equally from deprivation, for man condemned them to sterility, solitude—the state of harem women—a passive infantilism, stunted growth, almost degeneration, for the flesh alone flowered on sweets and pillows.

That woman's strength should have found no impersonal object, no labor to fasten to, was tragic for man, for it became as dangerous to him as the primitive's strength.

Such women are not consumed by the man who could master them, the man so powerful that he can do his painting and music alone, but by the uncertain, vacillating child-man who arouses a devouring maternity with his weakness.

The giant mothers.

You cannot quench a woman's strength with laws, curse it with solitude or abandon. It must be dealt with. It is the woman's revolution, the flower of revolt and injustice. The men who lost their power as primitives are the prey of this woman. It is a kind of vengeance. There is something in it of the cutting of Samson's hair. The nature of woman has not suffered the damages that man has in his struggle to suppress nature. She has not been as exposed to the social poisons. She has been relatively sheltered. Her power is unspent, new.

OCTOBER 1943

Because of objectivity, my *vision* has become like a pure diamond. I see into others' beings so clearly that they seem transparent. Last night Josephine, Adele and I practiced our dancing. Duits was there, Duits the child teasing Josephine the child, and Duits the poet with the pale face fascinated by Anaïs, begging me to wear the glass slippers so he could look at my beautiful feet so extraordinarily naked. Josephine courted him with all the perfect sensuality of her strong body and her dancing. I did not court him, yet he dreams of me. Once again warmth invades me, an enfolding warmth, a yearning to open his delicacy and youth. I was astonished at how I could read all his feelings and his dreams, all of Josephine's perplexed, puzzled emotions at this new species of animal who does not accept the contagion of his fire. At the same time I felt a strange taboo, not out of fear of suffering again, but like a religious mystic order of divination: I believed always that I *saw* more because I loved more, now I feel I see more because I see them all outside of my love. Of course, it is always with some kind of love that one sees, but what I feel now is a love not of Duits, but of all he represents in the long lineage of the poets I have known, in the hierarchy and dynasty of the poets. He the last pale flame of them all.

I see through his body into the bloodlessness. I destroy his legend because I see he is anemic, that he dreams of vampires and sucking blood because of his great need of it. I held his almost transparent hand in mine, light and fragile, and Josephine cried out, "My god, you have no flesh at all!"

A game takes place between reality and the dream. Josephine stretches out her strong black legs, and then prances like a well-bred horse, and Duits watches.

Then we sit in the semi-darkness, telling strange stories to each other. Duits' imagination is nourished by the fairytales of the past, and he does not yet know that it must feed on life.

Thurema and Jimmy understand the diary because it is human—*Winter of Artifice* does not move them. If only I could find my human form, naturalness; if only the human Anaïs could speak now the same human language she speaks in the diary.

I still speak the language of the *voyant*, of analysis. I am learning from Josephine and the Haitians how to tell stories. I used to tell stories as a child, adventure stories. The great adventures of new unconscious revelations can be told with excitement. Jimmy says, "Why read fiction when you can read Anaïs?"

J'approche la fin du journal…la fin, la fin, la fin, la fin…

OCTOBER 3, 1943

Having gathered together the fevers, the conquests, the crusades, having pulled in the sails of my restless wandering ships, having garnered, *ramassé*, called back from the Tibetan deserts my roaming, fervent, mystical soul, having rescued my spirit from the web of the past, having cured myself of the drugs, poisons and perversions of romanticism, having surrendered the impossible dreams, having mastered the madness of my erotic desires, having called back into the hearth the weeping dreamer, the disconsolate idealist, the exhausted Don Quixote, the lamenting, exalted peak-seeker, the divagating nerves, the dissolved, the lost, the frenzied, the twisted, the tortured, having escaped the chambers of torture, the self-punishments, the holocausts, the pyres, having meditated on the present, focused on the present, *I integrated*. I gave Hugo today a whole woman who responded quietly but completely to his desire, who vibrated in the first orgasm of happiness…

A pale flame, after the consuming ardor of passion, but a pale flame that resembles the heaven I perceived now and then as possible through the darkness of my ordeals, prisons and infernos. I can truly say passion is an inferno, and this is felicity, and the body and soul rest in their moorings, the painful tensions are relieved, the anguish, the anxiety, the terrors, the repeated agonies… For the first time I am not ripped apart by restlessness; my imagination does not wander alone in the night, wailing and questing. For the first time body and soul are together inside the window, with the door truly closed over them, and I rest. The music I can bear; it is not an invitation, a provocation to a mad search of the world, a pursuit of ghosts, a desire for mirages, an embracing of a void, and this is no mere interlude to an unceasing pain and hunger, but a possession of the present in the person of Hugo who has, for twenty years, been the haven I did not want, the fulfillment I perversely negated, the patient image of love itself, unceasing and indefatigable, and eternal, and *not* passion, and passion is *not* the marriage but the illusion of union that never takes place. Hugo's every word answers my word, his faith my faith, his constancy my dream of constancy, his concept of love my desire! For the first time I can close the window and say everything is here, everything is here where I wish to put it, in the present, on earth…let dreams and ecstasies no longer torment me. I was weakened and tormented by the magnitude of my desires. I could not fit myself to human proportions. The enlargement and magnifications were made at the cost of tearing the body and soul asunder, at the cost of insatiable fevers and the habit of drugs which caused indescribable pain after the first ecstasies.

It is only as I grow mature and whole that I finally recapture my childhood, and it is only when I grow mature sensually that I recapture my sensuality, which in both elements resembles the sensuality and the childlikeness of the Haitians.

Last night as we danced together and told stories together by the light of the red candles, I felt I had recaptured my true nature, like theirs, sensual and innocent, and my childhood's power of telling, receiving and inventing stories. How strange that it is only when you mature and rid yourself of the *false* childishness, the *false* youth, and the *false* nature, that you recapture the true games of faith and desire…the wholeness.

Childhood: the *bananier* that moved in the night like a woman waving her arms, the mapou trees of evil walking about at night that terrified the Haitian children, the leaves one rubbed on one's arm which caused swelling and saved one from school, the medicine a negro took too frequently, a poison which made him white like an albino, the reading in a glass of water, the eating of the glass, the voodoo magician who could place a lighted candle in the water without drowning its light…the childhood, my childhood, finding its stories and legends in my own rich life, eager to tell them and cause surprise, fear and joy in others.

My nature finds its climate among them because they touch each other so warmly, they kiss frequently, caress each other, make gifts to each other. There is warmth of life and sensuality.

Albert's gift to me, Albert, so young, who gave me his wisdom—do not dream, Anaïs, you are dreaming me—who gave me his youth and his climate, his people to help me find my heaven, who guided me into paradise. Albert, the image in the flesh of Jaeger's teachings—*Jaeger my marvelous Guru, guiding me out of the inferno*, Albert helping me to dance into a new earth.

So I have found the mobile mapou tree of the legends at the same time as my detoxification from fatal drugs, at the same time as the possibility of the happiness I sought, the human warmth and simplicity of reality.

I learn Josephine's dances because they are Albert's dances. I listen to stories because they are Albert's stories. He, the dream of joy, giving me the island in which my human warmth has flowered.

So I can dream, dance, write, enjoy Hugo and the present. *Tu n'es plus malade, Anaïs.* A great shock split you asunder, but now you have welded the fragments together, and from this will issue your strength. And where are the *jeux*?

I found the only mature *jeux* possible—humor.

OCTOBER 6, 1943

I wrote my first four humorous pages about Thurema (on her cooking and on her clothes). I laughed while I wrote them, *enjoyed* writing for the first time.

OCTOBER 18, 1943

For many days I lived without my drug, my secret vice, my diary. And then I found this: that I could not bear the *loneliness*. That in writing the book about other women, there were still so many things I could not give to them, and above all, not one of these women could contain my obsession with the perfecting of my life, its completion. The last visit to Jaeger on this road of mystical development brought an extraordinary crystallization of all the experiences: I achieved integration; I gave myself to my fundamental love for Hugo—as a mistress; I gave myself to my home—I spent hours cleaning, painting, re-animating, renewing; I gave myself to an objective work. But I realized I did not want to write a book, I did not want to give anything. I wanted to *be*, merely to be, to enjoy the integration. So. In my new black suit I felt a new solidity. Suddenly the wanderlust ceased, the straining of an ever-departing ship. This part is comparable to opera glasses at first maladjusted, and then *focused*. I *focused* on Hugo, who changes and becomes always what I want, on my home, on what I have. Thus my vision, arranged for distance, saw the near. The near has become the marvelous. What I strained to abandon, to transcend, became wonderfully animated by my enjoyment. Fifth Avenue: the hustle, the luxury, the movement. Going to an exhibit where I touch people superficially enough so they cannot disturb me. (I never knew how to distinguish between what must be kept at a distance, the valueless, and what can be felt—I felt everything and suffered from nausea. This can no longer touch me.) Returning in the subway in the first car, and looking at the tunnel swallowing me, which I used to fear, caused me pleasure like a *montagne Russe* of darkness, red, green and blue lights. Everything reflects the inner change. The quietness.

Gonzalo does not know what has died. It is too subtle for him. We have moments of dreaming together, but they are nourished by a resplendent past, not by the present or by the future. They are reflections of a violent passion which was finally suffocated in his earthiness, in his weakness.

Hugo is free and strong, and wants what I want. With the relinquishing of the tension and the mad desires, came joy, the joy I craved for forty years from behind the prison bars of my tragic soul, always thinking it was not unattainable, that it was denied me. And it lay dormant, latent in me. Not necessarily in the South of France, or in Haiti, or with Albert, but in *me*, a deeply buried precious stone, like the diamond born of utter coal blackness!

So I tapped the source, and it flowed so easily.

One night at George Davis's house, when we danced madly and humorously to Haitian records, I imitated Josephine's trance dance and became entranced and frenzied to the drums...

With Hugo there is gayety.

With Hugo I never feel the loneliness I did with Henry and Gonzalo. There is a sense of nearness which no passion can create. The loneliness is lessened now that I have fewer secrets from Hugo, and he feels my return. It gives him a sense of power. He has been divinely patient because he dreams my dreams with me, forgets himself in his love, and now he is compensated. He won.

Talking to the diary was part of that loneliness, the necessary unburdening of so many secrets. Now I have fewer secrets, fewer burdens. *But I still feel this is a wonderful story*, and it would be a pity not to tell it.

It isn't that I have forgotten Albert. Strangely, he is as vivid and alive in my feelings as when he was here. Only I do not suffer, I do not rebel, I do not hunger and crave uselessly. He is there. He is everywhere, bright, beautiful, desirable. I melt at the remembrance. I am filled with love. The love and desire are intact. They did not need to be killed for me to survive.

When pain cannot kill me, I am healthy. I can take the pain and transform it, take the pain the whole world is suffering and, without being closed to others' suffering, experience pity and not die. I am not stopped and not murdered. The neurotic transforms pain into an attack of paralysis and cannot continue living. He is arrested, fixed upon one experience, as I was fixed upon Helba's destructiveness. Psychoanalysis and Jaeger have given me something I never knew: happiness. It is like the difference between a body that has known only fever and when suddenly the fever ceases. The entire world has changed. It is *health*. People in the street look *normal*. I cease to feel anxiety and certain diabolical distortions. Before, 14th Street represented the New York I hated and rejected. Now it is merely 14th Street. It has nothing to do with me. I am stronger than my hatred, and it cannot possess me. 14th Street is where I walk, on a very beautiful autumn afternoon to buy gouache specter violet to finish painting my bookcase. It is the street where I buy veils with spangles for 39¢, which I use charmingly and seductively as other women use expensive $15 hats. It is a neutral street, it is not monstrous. Surely it symbolizes the ugliness of New York, but this ugliness cannot penetrate me. I am filled with other things. I must remember to cut four slices of the bread Gonzalo likes to eat with coffee at the press. I must write a letter to Eduardo, who is reliving *The Good Earth* in miniature. I mailed Henry's paintings. I copied volume 64. I wrote Mother in Havana. I cleaned a lamp for Gonzalo. I stayed home alone one evening without feeling abandoned or lonely.

It is meaningful and important that there should be nothing in the house that is useless, cluttering, meaningless. *Épurement*, purification, simplification. Discard, throw away, give, rigorously. No *déchets*, no careless accumulations, no odds and ends, no unworn objects, only the essentials, the living, the basic.

Carnet de route: light baggage.

NOVEMBER 4, 1943

The euphoria of the analysis has worn away. I am no longer anxious, I am content, but I dream intensely (in place of writing in the diary?), and I am tired.

But we did the first page *Under a Glass Bell* today.

NOVEMBER 11, 1943

New development due to analysis: I fight for my rights instead of being passive and hurt. I have a good relationship with Thorvald. Greater firmness. *Action*.

Very ill at night with ovarian pains.

NOVEMBER 16, 1943

Important decision. I wanted to *do* something for the world, for communism, for the negro. Should I join the Party? Gonzalo says no because: 1. I show no aptitude for the science, detail and labor of political work, no professional interest in its routine. That is true. 2. I am not properly educated in the theories of communism, have never studied it thoroughly, and I show no sign of real knowledge. *That* is also true, but it is true about everything I do—I have never studied or labored or worked on the details of writing. I have marvelous ideas about costume, but I cannot sew anything. I have fine ideas for the house, but I'm slap-dash in their execution. I hate technique, applied science. Without Gonzalo I am not a good printer because I can't understand measurements. Am I to forever accept this as a defect of temperament? Am I always going to rely on my talent, inspiration, intuition, improvisation and inventiveness? Am I never going to discipline myself? I thought the Party would discipline me, but Gonzalo says no, that is a *false* effort. But then where can I begin? I want to *act*. Gonzalo says:

"In communism there is no action without theory. Study first of all. Go to the Worker's School. Then you'll be able to act."

So at last I face my lack of action as due to my lack of technical, practical application.

Fine. I have made a good start on the science of writing. Printing made me more careful, tighter, more concrete. Now for politics, the applied arts, crafts, and sciences. I will learn to sew. All this *bores* me, has always bored me. Let us see.

I never knew anything about psychoanalysis, nothing about painting. Everything in me comes from a kind of genius, but I feel this cannot go on. It's like a mystic existence without body. I am always conscious of trying to grasp the meaning, the mystic meaning, but not the body, not the body in action.

This is the book of Action.

NOVEMBER 19, 1943

During the night of ovarian pain, before falling asleep, I was in a very bad mental state. First of all I thought the pain came from a tumor, or cancer, and then I saw myself in the hospital and getting pity. I was glad to worry Gonzalo, but I remembered Helba had her ovaries taken out and thought this would happen to me. I remembered the child had a tumor and felt it was caused by the abortion manipulations.

Strangely, the next day Lopez, who is very thorough, explained that I suffered from a painful ovulation which happens between periods, the egg maturing and ready for pregnancy and being ejected and bursting from its shell, sometimes causing pain.

I have made an unnatural effort to stand on my own feet, not to see Jaeger again. I liked the ideal of a clean finish, no threads hanging, like a perfect story.

NOVEMBER 24, 1943

My happiness with Hugo, based on harmony, is increasing. My health is mediocre and a source of continuous small torments, but I feel strong, and I want action, action!

In public I enjoy the audible cult of my appearance, enjoy creating a stir, even though I dress very simply. Incurable Anaïs, who feels reassured by others' praise!

The whole duality lies between what is dreamed and what is actualized. The dreaming produces anxiety because it is ghostly, evanescent, unstable, fluid, but above all because it is lonely. No dream is shared.

Reality is shared and similar (people's dreams can be similar, but they cannot create a human relationship), and the similarities of human experience—war, birth, death, suffering—draw people together. As I come closer to reality, I feel greater strength and greater companionship.

Anaïs Nin, 1940s

Henry Miller at Hampton Manor

John Dudley at Hampton Manor

Anaïs Nin at Provincetown

Edward Graeffe

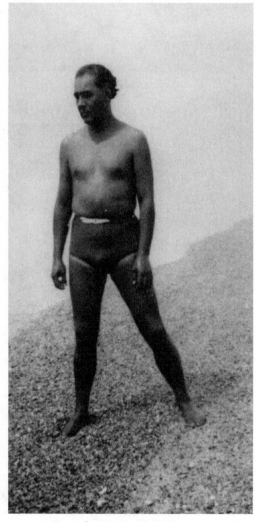

Gonzalo Moré at Provincetown

Anaïs Nin at her press

Albert Mangones

Publicity photo for *Under a Glass Bell*

Hugh Guiler (Hugo)

Valentina Orlikova

Anaïs Nin in her "action" coat

Publicity photo for *This Hunger*

Anaïs Nin with some of her "children"

Gore Vidal

Anaïs Nin and Gore Vidal

Rupert Pole

UNDER A GLASS BELL

My own soul has reached into other souls

NEW YORK, DECEMBER 20, 1943

Today we reached page 35 of *Under a Glass Bell*. I've received 56 subscriptions, but am hurt when people do not respond, people who have the means. People expect everything from me as from a priest. They think it natural that I spend 6 hours of back-breaking labor on each page of the book, work 70 times 6 hours or more and *give* them my work, not only the writing but the complete book!

People to whom I gave *Winter* do not subscribe to *Under a Glass Bell*. Ben Abramson, the Chicago book shop man, did not pay me what he owed me for more than a year and a half and still owes me $18. Peggy Guggenheim obliged me to an exchange of books and gave me her gallery catalogue in exchange for *Winter*! Charles Henri Ford asked for a copy of *Winter* for review, never reviewed it, and has plenty of money. This list of defections, of selfish grasping without response, is much larger in my mind than my loyal supporters are, and this affects me deeply.

The struggle is full of humiliations. In order to print my work for the few who consider it a breath of life, I have to beg for support that I do not get.

In return, I get the total, sincere allegiance of a few. But the reality is there. Of 500 *Winters*, I gave away 100, sold 250, and 150 are left. I'm only printing 300 of *Under a Glass Bell*. Most of the subscriptions were obtained by my writing pressing letters, telephoning, etc. The end result is injury, disillusionment and pain.

The support has been infinitely small, not sufficient enough to sustain me either spiritually or materially. I am going to surrender.

DECEMBER 25, 1943

About a week ago the dreaded depression possessed me again. The happiness with Hugo seemed unreal, and I fell into an abysm of obsessions, brooding and resentment. I had a violent quarrel with Gonzalo like a chess game in which nothing is gained or lost. He accepts Helba's interpretation, "Anaïs rejects me because I am poor and sick!"

Well, the grotesqueness of this should make me laugh, but instead I quarrel, I defend myself, I *see* his stupidity.

When I prove to myself that his being influenced by Helba is proof of his lack of love, he defeats me by saying: "If I didn't love you I would be in Peru and not poor. Because I love you, I'm here, dependent on you and humiliated, mocked by my friends."

Then he brings out his grief: since his friends can't come up to the press to see his business, they suspect the worst, and gossip about me is in the air. They all live in the Village. People connect the press with me. No matter what the reality is, he is humiliated and full of guilt, and because the opinion of others matters to him—his pride!—he suffers. I offered to get a true business place, to retire from the press altogether, and to let him show his "business" to the world. I had not foreseen this consequence of our romantic venture. It is the negative aspect of a positive effort to make him work, create.

So that is the end of the press as far as I am concerned, and, besides, the lack of adequate response to my writing and printing is forcing me to withdraw. Another failure, another unrequited passion. The world doesn't respond or support my efforts. Everywhere except in my life with Hugo lies failure and pain.

I accept the failure of my romantic life, the error of everything into which I put my feelings, my wasted love for Gonzalo. But I don't know where to turn or what to do…

DECEMBER 26, 1943

It was like a crisis of insanity. I *felt* the exaggeration and distortion of which I am guilty, I felt the obsession: I want to force love to be unlimited, infinite, from the world, and from Gonzalo, *because mine is infinite.*

Today the crisis passed, and everything resumed its normal aspect. Gonzalo was tender and close. We spent the afternoon in bed, in the dark, half asleep. He was abandoned, trusting. Hugo is always there, infinite, unshatterable. A bath of love, and I am healed.

To help myself believe in the world's response, I pasted the letters I received the last week on the wall, all of it a pathetic proof in order to cure a woman condemned to death, a woman without an inner core of faith, without strength or independence, her life depending on outer proof, shipwrecked at the smallest doubt, devoured by a self-destructive demon. *I meditated for two days how to kill Helba to save Gonzalo, to free him, describing it to myself as a mercy killing.* This is insanity.

JANUARY 1, 1944

The depression lifted. I went to Harlem with Hugo and Lucia, warmed myself to the gayety, felt the caressing hands, captured the vitality and humanity. And now all my mysterious efforts on behalf of Gonzalo have begun to materialize. I talked about printing, writing of political value, about the negroes. I welded the idea of the press with economic independence and service to communism.

Now I end the period of my slavery to be printed, of the sacrifices to my writing, of my personal creation.

The group I condemn and want to break from: Mr. and Mrs. Bernard Reis, patrons of arts; the *VVV*, the surrealist review; Irina Aleksander because she is a bourgeois; 57th Street Galleries for their snobbism and commerciality; Max Ernst, Breton, Jolas, Zadkine, Léger, Kay Boyle, as dead; Peggy Guggenheim for completing the corruption of the surrealists; Charles Henri Ford for publishing disintegrated and clownish views; Kurt Seligman as false, mimetic, and decadent; Tanguy for stagnant self-repetition.

The group as such is corrupt, malicious, perverse, decadent and stagnant, but still they are a force because of their coalition, certainly the only true art group.

I wanted to break with them, but my work tied me to them: they were my public, and Hugo's public. None of us could break with them until we found a new group. And I see this new group as the uncorrupted negroes.

To close with the old, I must also turn my back upon my own work. That is what I will do. Make a new start. I will bring my taste and my knowledge of art to bear on political writing.

I am pinning my faith on the negro, because he is not corrupted by our old art development, because he is vital and revolutionary and pure like the workman, because of his *character*, which has suffered humiliations but without becoming twisted and ugly. The character of the negro is admirable, his sensitivity, feeling, intuition, sincerity, simplicity. I want to give my life to this, to the negro.

The poetic press, the personal press, is to become the political press.

Hugo says, "How creative you are!" It seems like a miracle, but it is the product of much labor, pain, churning and sincere struggle. The opposition between art and communism, between action and my capacities, is resolved.

Next week I start going to the Worker's School with Frances.

JANUARY 12, 1944

Hugo went through the same breakdown as I did, the same total loss of strength. Jaeger helped him, relieved him of the tension. Our rhythm is changing. As I become more of a realist, I burden him less and less. He had reached the point at which he could go no further. My effort now is to unburden him, to make Gonzalo stand alone, to take some of the strain away from Hugo. My love for him grows.

JANUARY 13, 1944

Dissolution of the Communist Party in America.

For three days Gonzalo was full of poison. He was dependent on the Party, its mature development, its long-range wisdom which he cannot grasp for himself. For three days I hated him.

No matter what I do, there is one demon I cannot conquer, and that is depression. It has haunted me all my life. I can understand why people commit suicide. At such moments it seems very natural to me.

I am killing myself to print this book of stories, and my efforts are unrewarded. There are times when I cease seeing my destiny within myself, and I begin, like Gonzalo, to believe in some external fatality. I have a frightful feeling of having been cheated, deluded, exploited, used. I've been nothing but a fountain, and everybody has come only to drink my life. Hugo knows and sees this.

I turn now on people who come to seek my blood.

JANUARY 21, 1944

Working at double speed and time because I am reaching the end—page 64. Tension. Exhaustion.

There is a mystical joy at achievement, at the certainty of the stories' value as mystical and poetic, and even the severe test of typesetting failed to dissolve them. The words are just as pure, unalloyed and meaningful, after all the scrutiny and the lead concretion.

JANUARY 24, 1944

One week of obsessions, horror and suicidal impulses, then the period of calm, sanity and a definite knowledge of the cyclical nature of my instability. I did not turn to Jaeger because it is a repetitive crisis, and I can come out of it alone because I take an objective medical attitude towards this *mal*. Astounding.

If I cannot break with Gonzalo, at least I can break with everybody who behaves as he does: the primitive Lucia, Josephine, crazy Mrs. Lipchitz, Lucas Premice, my mother, etc.

Primitive passion causes suffering, but then mystical and romantic élans cause sacrifice, martyrdom and self-destruction. Compassion, art, all these we pay for with our lives.

What alone can give peace, contentment, harmony, felicity?

Realism means to treat each person according to their reality. You can't treat a primitive with "evolved" ways, or a brute with gentleness, a combatant with passivity.

Duits said, "My god, Anaïs, you give up the diary, you give up the press—what are you going to do?"

Yes, analysis is a cruel process of truth, a truth most people cannot bear. I have ceased to consider passion as the absolute. I see that I confused ecstasy, frenzy and violence with the absolute and suffered because every moment in between showed the relativity of the tie with Gonzalo.

I am aware now of the oriental in my religion (belief in karma, continuity, Buddhism), of the northern fantasy from my Danish origins (fairytales, magic, affinity with Isak Dinesen), from Spain sensuality and fervor, and from France the need of clarity, construction, analysis.

The diary is obviously the diary of neurosis, the labyrinth, and I am in it again, drawn inward.

There is a severity in me, a rigorousness and discipline. It has to do with the will to organize, lead, and create.

Hugo says, "You must know your material, as the artist does."

I write only invisibly now. As I live, phrases form themselves, and then it all dissolves like a dream, and I have no desire to make efforts.

Effort was the key word. Effort must cease.

JANUARY 27, 1944

I have not seen Jaeger since the beginning of the winter. Alone I surrendered the romantic press, alone I faced the reality of economic problems and the misery they create, alone I faced my recurring obsessions, alone I built up my relationship with Hugo, liberated him, supported him when he was broken. Jaeger guided all this, gave me the principles to adapt to new experiences, to surrender what destroys one, first Gonzalo, then the press.

Now...

"Now," said Jaeger, "you will do your most important work."

I complain that we, the evolved ones, had to go back and find our lost primitive natures, and that when we find this nature it revolts against the sacrifice of the self caused by evolution.

I spoke of my revolt against writing.

Martha said: "We return to find the primitive, but to continue and find a higher synthesis. There is an evolved life which combines the pleasure with creation and is not martyrdom. At this point it is difficult to distinguish, but later it becomes clearer. You and Hugo are now ready for the best part of your life...free."

Suddenly, when Martha spoke of her feelings as she heard of my discouragement in December, *she* opened her heart to me and confessed it had not been fatigue which strained her, but that Hy, her husband, had tried to commit suicide. And she wept. I held her hand and asked her: "Why didn't you come to me? I could have helped you."

"I wanted to. I felt you were burdened."

She feels Hugo and I are mature. It is strange that no matter how neurotic I was I could always understand the other person and forget myself. It was to give Martha pleasure, not myself, that I invited her to my parties, divining her need.

Transposition of my sexual tragedy with Hugo. He said today (after a complete response from me), "I'm much happier, much happier."

"Just because I make a bit of noise, that's all. I was merely a silent cat before. Now I miaw like the cats on the roof, and you like it!"

"Yes," said Hugo, "I like it."

Now the crisis is purely material, stripped of all its disguises. Hugo and I are shipwrecked, $1000 in debt, just when we need $1000 to start the new press. Hugo has given his maximum effort. Now it is up to me and Gonzalo, and to whether Sam Goldberg will lend me the money.

During Hugo's physical collapse he said, "I can no longer cope with the economic problem. It is for you to solve now." Then, because of his goodness, he felt guilty about his fragility.

My assuming the responsibility means I have to start a new press to give Gonzalo a means of livelihood, and for this I depend on Goldberg, who is elusive and neurotic and resents being depended on.

When I ask Thurema for help, she shifts the talk to a *scène de jalousie*, that I don't see her enough, that I see other people, etc. I must be the *woman who has inspired the most selfish passions in the world*.

FEBRUARY 3, 1944

Jaeger asked, "You remembered the loneliness of neurosis—do you fear the aloneness of individuation?"

"Yes."

What will happen when I free myself of the incubus? I am full of terror and anxiety. Gonzalo's dependence gave me a certain security. Now I have none, none.

Giving up the press as it is—the place—seems like the end of my life with Gonzalo. Breaks, breaks, surrenders, losses, because I was dying.

The *Action*. There it is: acting, deciding, advancing. I rejected Thurema's financial help because it would mean submitting to her possessiveness. I will have to do it alone. Hugo will get a loan from a bank which I will have to return, which will be *my responsibility*.

FEBRUARY 9, 1944

I have discovered why people refuse to help: because I am not asking for myself, but for others, for Henry and for Gonzalo. Thurema resents Gonzalo, as does Goldberg. They are jealous and envious.

Today I finally broke down with bronchitis, the day before the end of the book. The last straw came yesterday. I went to the press at ten o'clock in the morning, already sick, and worked steadily till five. At five o'clock came Miss Decker of Graphic Arts and a man named Stricker to discuss the cover. He was insolent, patronizing, and said: "In the first place you shouldn't be doing this. You should get published by a big publisher.

No one is interested in an unknown writer. Your book isn't worth 50¢. Why don't you offset instead of printing from the plate? It's easier and cheaper, if you know anything about printing," he said to Gonzalo. Never looked at the work, flaunted his ignorance, gave destructive "advice."

But in contrast to the past when I would have controlled my anger, I jumped at him: "You're insensitive, patronizing, insulting. Why have you come here? I won't take your bad manners." And I cowed him.

And earlier, Gonzalo had said, "We're going to lose the press if we don't give a deposit tomorrow."

I didn't have the money, and here was this man saying, "To do this cover go out and buy yourself a $50 proof press." I came home, the bronchitis like a fire in my chest, and I sobbed. I have such an exaggerated reaction to people's brutality, insensitivity, gross ignorance, selfishness, cruelty.

How people hound me. A sample of my days:

Irina: "I must see you. Can you help me?"

Jimmy grabs me one morning on the way to the press, to pour out his sufferings with Thurema.

Thurema comes to the press to tell me about her destructiveness and quarrels.

Gonzalo's pain at his brother's death in an auto accident becomes violence, irascibility, disproportionate scenes.

After I visit Jaeger, she leaves me with her husband, who tried to commit suicide, because I am good for him. I get him a job on a barge, like Jimmy's.

Frances comes to relieve herself of her sister's cruelties and attacks.

Helen Burlin, having met me only once, wants me to read her poems and give her my opinion.

To talk about the reverse, what I have been refused, hurts me. I have never found anyone who paid for the publication of my books, have never found anyone who made me large gifts, or loans. It has been hard even to get subscriptions. Though the book costs $5, I mark $3 for subscribers, and it is the rich people who take advantage of the reduction.

If I didn't have Hugo, nobody else today would support me.

It is because I built a legend of strength. We indulge the weakling, but we do not forgive the strong one who has moments of weakness. Why is this? Is it the revenge of those who were under the power of this strength, under its domination, or is it the hatred people have for any change of pattern?

Hugo has also been helped by Jaeger to throw off his burdens…his over-abundant goodness, responsibility and compassion. In some obscure way he does not condemn anything that I have done, first because he perceives that in *part* his lack of aliveness was the cause for my seeking life elsewhere, and second because when I broke the shell, I liberated him and transmitted life to him, saved him, enriched him. He takes his share of the responsibility as I take mine. So few people have this courage, this honesty, this generosity of not blaming the other.

But now he is free too, has made gains and has earned his freedom. He won it, and he won me.

Gonzalo made the first payment on the new press. It has to be moved by March 1. Jaeger offers to help if we cannot meet the payments on time. This on the terrestrial level!

On the writing level, I'm developing a form of association, such as the one made in psychoanalysis, to form the new psychological structure of the next book. Not James Joyce's "wanderings," but a detective game of revelation, a chain which leads to the uncovering of the mystery. The plot of psychoanalysis is always so full of surprises, dramas, changes, paradoxes.

FEBRUARY 15, 1944

Letter from Henry:

Dear Anaïs: I just mailed you back the pictures you lent me for the Hollywood exhibition. Hope they reach you in good shape. Your birthday is about at hand, and I want to send you a sincere message of congratulation. It has been hard to write you, knowing that you preferred silence.

Well, I am about to leave here now, for an extended vacation. I may never return to this place. I have no definite plans—only an urge to get out and relax. The experiences lived through here were of enormous value to me. By a strange irony of fate I was put in a situation which enabled me to realize, as I never could have before, just how I must have appeared in your eyes. It makes your stature even grander. I learned the lesson. Everything (I think) that you wished me to do I have done. I went through a veritable ordeal, for which I am most thankful.

I hope your own struggles have proved as fruitful. I would like to know, if you care to tell me. All my strength came from the example you set me. There is no one on earth I venerate more than you.

My address for the next few weeks will be c/o Jean Varda, 320 Hawthorne Street, New Monterey, California.

I would like to make you a gift of the handsome book which some friends have made for me—"The Angel is My Water Mark." Would you accept it? You wouldn't get it immediately—each book is composed individually—but in the course of the next few weeks. Yes? I hope I hear from you. And more than anything I wish you could believe that my only desire is to be of help to you.

I have been waiting most impatiently to see the new book. All the important book stores here have ordered copies and are eagerly awaiting it.

I once—more than once—told you that if ever I had the money I would give it to you to publish the diary. I still mean that. Seventeen books are coming out this year, here and abroad. Should the windfall come you will hear from me. I have repaid my most pressing debts with the unexpected returns from the sale of water colors. I wanted to clear all this off in order to leave a big blank space for *you*. I hope you won't deny me this great privilege when the time comes. Bless you, dear Anaïs.

Helba
the poisons expressed physically
vesicule biliaire
pocket of poison
psychic pocket of poison
struggle against toxic anger and hatred
physical illness for every psychic illness
appendicitis
cancer—worry
syphilis—guilt infection
fever—unleashedness
arthritis—unnaturalness
Gonzalo
the poisons absorbed from the outside

Anaïs: when anxiety sets in like ague, cold and hot waves, chills, *frissons*, as you might feel on the edge of an abysm
be calm
know it is anxiety

Do not explain it away by the last painful incident. Do not attach it to any particular moment, place, person, as then it becomes magnified, and what it fastens on gets devoured as by cancer.

When depression suffocates you like a London fog and enters your lungs, think that the cause is probably not as great as you believe. A small defeat, a small frustration, discord, seem to obliterate the sky for you and to become the absolute. You can never see the transitoriness of the mood, its ephemera. You exaggerate until the obstacle stifles your entire life. Anaïs, beware of enlargement, exaggeration and dramatization. Beware of associating the bad weather, a tactless work, a rebuttal letter, a rejection, with a *total* picture for despair.

You have courage, but this courage is severely strained by your enlargement of the obstacles and the way you hurl yourself against them as if your life depended on it.

The first copy of *Under a Glass Bell* is in my hands, a beautiful and exquisite piece of workmanship. Last night I was enjoying its birth. I sent Gonzalo with it to the engraving class and the New School so he would cull the praise of Stanley Hayter (Hugo's engraving instructor), Lipchitz, etc. He did. He was highly praised. Whether he feels guilt or succeeds, or whether he must destroy every pleasure he gets, I don't know, but instead of being content, he said: "I don't get any satisfaction from this, as I got none from writing or drawing. My heart isn't in it. It is detached from me. It isn't *hard* enough. It isn't my line, my passion."

"But what was your passion, Gonzalo?"

"I wanted to be a pianist. That I failed to be through circumstances beyond my control."

I feel utterly sad. Only the other day Hayter was speaking admiringly of Gonzalo's work, amazed by his gift. Is it merely guilt? Can he not bear to excel in any way? I confess that all my understanding is useless in the face of Gonzalo's reactions, perhaps because they are all negative and I cannot conceive the negative aspect of all things. My imagination cannot conceive of the *NÉANT*!

My pleasure was destroyed. I could not respond to him sexually, and he had difficulty reaching the orgasm. His entire attitude is mirrored in our sexual life.

When I came home and saw that Hugo worries when he gets his due as an artist, wanting me to get all he gets, I said to him, "I want you to know that there is no man in the world as generous, as sensitive, as full of beauty as you are, that your work is born of your character, that you deserve everything you get more than anyone I know, that your work and mine are one and the same to me, so that what is given you I feel is the same as if it were given to me. You had an equal part in the birth of my writing because you supported me, sustained me, nourished and protected me on all planes. You gave me *all* I needed, you played all the roles and tried to balance all the suffering I endured." (I didn't say "at the hands of others.") "So enjoy your success." (He is being photographed for *Vogue*, and he is concerned because *Vogue* never gave me any attention.)

SUNDAY, MARCH 5, 1944

At Wakefield Gallery with Hugo, Lucia, Thorvald, Betty Parsons—hung prints, worked hard, early to bed.

Thurema: "The stories are *darling*."
Irina: "The stories, the preface, the engravings are *adorable*."
Lucia: "Such imagination and poetry! It seems terrible that people can pay their way into such a magical world."

MARCH 7, 1944

Great success at the exhibit. Excitement, fatigue, pleasure. I am receiving my due! Affection, response, *feelings to answer my feelings, sincere success*. No falseness. No hypocrisy. A wonderful harmony with Hugo's work, his prints and plates, and our book. Telephone calls, letters, praise. I am happy and Martha was there—I shared everything with her. We had dinner together after the exhibit. Spontaneous reactions on all sides. The stories are preferred to *Winter*... People love "The Mouse."

I feel immensely stimulated. And strangely, before the response came to the surface, I was walking along a few days before the show and thinking with the utmost certitudes. I know now what I must do: I must be true to this *deep* psychological investigation, to this bottom layer of consciousness. Dolly Chareau said a very accurate thing: all the stories end in B minor, almost monotonously so. An expression of a secret revolt, despair perhaps. It is my only criticism. (So there is a downward and negative curve in my spirit after all, which is betrayed by the writing, the sudden failure to attain the orgasm as it were, the unsatisfied act. So it is to be thought out.) Success itself makes me sad because it is the story of having to *prove* your value, to convince, to assert. Just as I wanted to be protected without defending myself, to be loved without doubt of this love, to be treated as I treat others, and to have others see the potential me as I see *their* potential selves, none of this happened. I had to fight for everything, as if people in general were blind, deaf and dumb. My gratitude goes only to those who believed at first, without proof.

MARCH 9, 1944

Excitement, the exaltation of activity, of greater assurance. I was so charged with electricity that Paul Rosenfeld jumped up and kissed me passionately! Telephone calls. Miss Decker of Graphic Arts: marvelous! From everybody: I love the "Mouse" and "Birth." I'm a little drunk, exhilarated. To be related to the world at last! To burst the bonds of personal relationships, to overflow. Many voices, moved. The telephone is our modern life, carries all the tonalities of feeling. Gonzalo and I look for the new press place. Fell in love with a little two-story house. The little box with three little drawers in which I put away the money I receive for emergencies: the new machine, rent, moving, the mechanic. Hugo's exhibit is drawing people. No rest, no repose, no relaxation. The feeling I have is that I am bursting from the shell, the mask of my own persona and *becoming visible and audible*. When the journalist exclaims: she is moving in the clouds, it is no longer true. *J'ai fait enfin mon apparition terrestre*—I have finally made my ghostly self earthly.

I cannot fathom the miracle. Is it merely a piercing of the hard crust of indifference, of doubt? Is it the culmination of long, multiple efforts? Contagion, accumulation. Is it Martha's work on me, this increase in my confidence? I thought people would find the stories esoteric and remote!

MARCH 14, 1944

This time, with *Under a Glass Bell*, people are stirred and feel with me. The atmosphere is full of feeling and response. My own soul has at last reached into other souls—at last, at last. *I do not feel the loneliness.*

APRIL 15, 1944

It was a breaking through a shell, a second birth, becoming visible and tangible. The sense of being a mysterious influence ceased. I was brought into daylight. First of all, Rosenfeld mentioned me to Edmund Wilson, who went to the Gotham Book Shop where Frances Steloff talked about me. He went home with a copy of *Under a Glass Bell* and wrote a review which appeared in April in the *New Yorker*. The morning the *New Yorker* appeared I was being photographed by *Town and Country*. They had telephoned me; I did not seek them out. It started when Jon Stroup wrote a review of *Under a Glass Bell*. I arrived in my best plumage, a lace blouse borrowed from Barbara Reis, my tuxedo suit, and the Coat, the tailored coat of the woman captain of action. *The New Yorker* was lying there, the pinnacle of authority, with a review by Edmund Wilson. Then *Town and Country* appeared with a review (the photo is for the June issue). Then telephone calls and letters. Then the mystical, magic present of a marvelous collage by Jean Varda, with a letter of dreams. Then Washington D.C., 150 visitors at Caresse's Gallery, praise, autograph signing, etc. When I returned, the edition was sold out (in three weeks) and I was asked to reprint it (orders are pouring in, said Miss Steloff). Then Steloff encouraged me to print one thousand. Sam Goldberg loaned me the money. I begin today a trade edition at three dollars, linotype, not hand set.

When I returned from Washington, something had altered in Gonzalo. He was softer, he was more on my side, he was nearer. His passion burns free. I expect and demand nothing, so we work in harmony. He is healthier, more active, he takes responsibility. It is now his press. He opened a bank account. I give him the money he gets from my book, which is in great part due him for his printing work, and I made him feel it is his, that it is well earned. Hugo is happy. He has my complete love. We feel it is the end of struggle and pain. Gone is my sense of unrequitedness, my feeling that I am condemned to obscurity, to love more than I am loved. My success itself was due to friends, loves, devotion. It was born of warmth. There is a sincerity about it and in my friends' rejoicing. I have few enemies, only out of jealousy and envy. Most people feel I deserve all I receive. And I have been happy, have known days of serenity, days without anxiety. Gonzalo can again share his troubles with me and talk naturally, and he is full of passion, could not wait when I returned from Washington to take me.

Spring. Work. Serenity. Sense of effectual action.

April 19, 1944

Today the machines were moved to 17 East 13th Street. It is to be called the Gemor Press.

Gonzalo is active, excited, transformed. His pleasure gives me pleasure. He has discovered of his own power and will. He exclaims, "How well I have done things this time." How well they have worked out because he was up early, he kept his appointments, he was coherent and organized. My creation is over now. I can begin to rest.

There has been a scandal. For Gonzalo's sake it is necessary that I disappear from the press, surrender it. What is Gonzalo doing? Pretending to be working in a room with a bed. The Spaniards mock him, "The Anaïs Press." Such a sad scene. Hope, the woman in Paris who wanted Gonzalo and could not have him, always jealous and malicious, showed the *Town and Country* to all the Spaniards, saying, "Which one is faking, who did the book?" I regret the lie told for the sake of publicity, its boomerang against Gonzalo, who has been saying it is his book. The need is growing to deny the partnership because no one believes it's a partnership of work. I wept at this negative aspect of my frantic efforts to free him. Gonzalo is very active, devoted, tender, jealous. For myself, I no longer want effort, but peace, the leisure to write.

Tremendous labor, the installation of the press, the work with electricians, window cleaners, movers, packers, packing and unpacking, transferring twelve trays of type into type cases. We are counting paper, beginning to work on engravings (the edition will only have nine engravings instead of seventeen), unpacking twelve boxes of paper, books, plates, tools, etc., buying a scrap basket, bulbs, blotters, files, pasting Gonzalo's work in a scrapbook to show clients. It was all done in one week. Gonzalo has assumed leadership. He is proud of his place, his machines, his independence. I feel very tired but content, and I am proud of my human creation.

May 9, 1944

La Vie en Dehors. My faculty for reliving in the diary, the mirroring inner eye, all this has gone. I see it now. The withdrawal in order to commune, relive, ruminate, conserve, has gone. It is like being constantly out of doors, in the light, in the daylight.

I gave Hugo Henry's $1000, thinking of the time he gave me the money to publish *Tropic of Cancer.* Hugo is now rebelling against his own goodness, sense of responsibility and patience. He is going through what I felt before I went to Martha's, utter exhaustion and rebellion. I help him to rebel, to free himself. Goodness is bondage.

May 18, 1944

Printed 1200 pages. Gonzalo has started running the new machine successfully, is very proud of himself. Six o'clock, dinner with Mother. Nine o'clock. Gonzalo, the MacDougal Street place is kept to meet him. It has become again the secret, silent place of secret meetings, the peace after the workshop atmosphere, the reinstated dream.

May 19, 1944

Ten in the morning to six at night at the press. Printed 1700 pages. Broke four nails and had to buy false ones. At ten in the evening, the Haitian flag dance, but no longer the dream of Haiti. That ended with Albert.

Returned home with Hugo to find a sneak thief had broken open one of the locked tins in which I kept carbons of the diaries. If Hugo had come before me he would have seen it all, and it would have meant a disaster worse than death.

June 16, 1944

Writing preparations: sent all diaries in a trunk to storage, the overflow, kept only the originals and the Japanese paper carbons in a safe to work with.

June 22, 1944

Harry Herskovitz, Henry's friend, has the rich voice of Henry, is the son of Henry, the adventurer, the seaman, the dark, lean, ardent Jew. The first night he talked about June, Mona, Alraune. He was writing about Henry, about June as the illusion of love. I rejected him because he was plunging me into the past. I told him so over the telephone. I didn't want to see him again. He pleaded, wrote me a love letter. After two weeks I let him come again. Now he was filled with me, and Mona-June-Alraune disappeared. Harry loved me, I was the most beautiful woman he had ever seen, the very image of his soul, his counterpart. I sat silent, moved. Then I let him come again, and now he was free of his identification with Henry's life. I made him write his own story (we take our identifications for love: they are self-love, self-seeking), to start his own book. He telephones every day, and today I had an impulse towards him. I could have gone to him. I invited him with people. (I must fear him a little, as he feared me. He brought a ballet dancer to his first visit.) His eyes move me; they are aware, fiery. He is violent and primitive. And confused. And perverse. Because of this I did not go to him. But I had the desire.

JUNE 28, 1944

I left for a weekend with Martha and Hy, but I was in such a state of erotic openness, of creative outflow, of exaltation, that the quietness and earthiness of the mountains were torture. I had a choking feeling. I awakened choking. Too much food, too much earth, Martha's anxiety which is blind, and Hy's confessions: "I am sexually desperate, hungry. Martha does not live with her body. She cannot go further. I want a response to my sensuality. And she is too sensitive and too complex for me to deceive her." And Martha's strange relinquishing: "What you represent for Hy is the symbol of feeling. I want you to have a relationship. You can help him." In her distress, she places him in my hands.

When Harry came, he was merely writing about the symbol of Mona. A few days later he began his own book, his own story. "Once, in some dingy city, I lay on a couch and read Henry's article on your diary, and I felt: I must know this woman. My fear was that you were perhaps trapped in Europe. Anaïs, when I first saw you as I came up the stairs of your house, it was fortunate I did not come alone, or I would have become violent. You are the woman the soul seeks and the body desires. I was seized with madness when I saw you." I let the desire mount like a wave, surge, and then fall, foam, disperse. The new mastery, desire that is not a wound, a defeat, or a bondage, but an exquisite game to be played, an instrument of enjoyment, the new mastery, ruled by pleasure. I want the night lifted and dilated, the summer night, I want the fire to warm all it touches, but not to consume. Impatience and immediacy had come out of fear and anxiety.

JUNE 29, 1944

Harry. He awaits me at the corner of the street with the eagerness of a young lover. He is there before me, young, his hunger immense. Because I am animating his writing, when we reach his room he lays his manuscript on my knees. The pages are of violence, horror, terror, crime and punishment. It is the world of instinct, of the animal. But as with Henry, this animal world has suddenly found its soul in me, and so while he is writing lust and crime and madness, he is before me gentle and soulful. My warmth, my warmth floods us, and I can never resist it. Oh, Anaïs. So now the faces are very close (after he confessed he was looking for the flaws, he had tested this love of his cruelly and found me flawless). He and his writing, like Henry, are full of flaws, falsities. But his soul must be perfect. I too had been seeking ways to defeat the spell. I looked at him to find the ugliness that would kill my warmth. But actually, before me, there is only a man seeking his soul, and a man shaken with desire, a young man who was denied everything. His sincerity is there, and there is a force in him. So the faces are very close, and desire retreats. There are obstacles. My hand on his arm was so light in the street that he could not feel it. There is a point of desire, but without body. It is a trap, I know. How can I walk into it again, knowing? But I do. There is a difference. I am the master for the first time. I am the one who gives, takes, leaves, commands. This is new. It is the sign of the new power. I am not in bondage. I say, "Wait. I am going away four days. I will see you Tuesday." It is not I who will suffer, or count the days, or fear Tuesday. I will not come. This is new, this power over desire. It is perhaps not love. Finally the mouths touched, and there was frenzy, but not ecstasy. It is a dream, like the encounter with Jean.

JUNE 30, 1944

I am having a second karma, a second relationship to the nature of Henry with Harry (the similarity is amazing. He utters the same phrases: I will destroy Hugo. I must know the woman's soul. When I know that, I will know all.), but one in which I dominate. I will inflict upon the innocent Harry my new firmness and power. His worship adds to this new power. Here I am the conqueror, not the sufferer. It is not a story of love, it is a story of power. Poor Harry. I should deliver him of myself, for he has a dream of love. I have made all other women distasteful to him, and he is entirely at my mercy. Every gesture I make affects his body and soul. It is an unequal encounter. Yet he feels he is being given heaven itself, the answer to all his hungers. The hunger of the poor Jewish boy born in ugliness and deprivation.

JULY 7, 1944

I stayed away four days at Lucia's, at Amangansett. In a state not of grace, but of love. Such a state of love that I desire all of them, the day after a full orgy with Gonzalo. As unreality recedes, reality assumes a new strength which produces a different but more powerful ecstasy. It is comparable to the differences between caresses and the orgasm. Reality is the orgasm.

I have never enjoyed more violently the orgasm. The whole body participates, a free body filled with a passion so strong that it is instantly renewed. I have never grasped so strongly the body of Gonzalo. Reality. I have never looked at his brown nakedness, hips, sex, with such voluptuous awareness. I see more. I feel more. Before, it was filtered by the dream, the outlines and the physical flavors were distilled. How clearly I see his body (since I feed myself of the romantic dream of union) and the violence of our physical union, an orgasm divinely timed, a rhythm of equal intensity. My god, how the state of passion continues, embracing Hugo who bathes in it at night, embracing Harry *en passant*, embracing, embracing.

I am now like pure fire without the vacillations of doubt.

Four days at the beach, of calm, warmth, desire, peace, and the image of Harry lost its haunting aspect. I knew I would not be compelled into a false role, of giving more than I wanted to give. His deep warm voice drew me to meet him, but I told him: "Do not be deceived by my warmth. I have too much feeling for you to obey a passing desire and to hurt you. I am not free. I love someone." Harry trembled from the shock. I knew this pain was better than the pain of being my lover for a short time and then abandoned.

There is a moment when the person disappears to give way before a cosmic ocean, an emotional and nameless ocean. This is the reversal of my drama with Henry and also its outcome, its finish. The spiritual adventure of meeting with the primitive, the negative, the destructive, and *not* being submerged, victimized, or led into a long, arduous, cruel combat. It is completed by a test. I am above Harry's confusion, his crazy statements, his inaccuracies. If I had had this strength when I met Henry, I would not have suffered.

July 18, 1944

Depressed, deeply so by my night with Harry. I knew that I had done the wrong thing, that I would be trapped and that I must free myself. The phrase that ran through my head was: "Can you live a lifetime in a moment? That was the moment and there is not to be another." I wanted to write this and not see him again, but I didn't. I faced him tonight, so tenderly and firmly, but there is always the same struggle to say anything instead of, "I do not love you." There is always the weaving a web so as not to injure or wound, to not give him a sense of defeat, of obstacle, of inadequacy, but merely all the other reasons that cannot injure him.

He is too young. I have already lived this. He is an echo of my life with Henry. (Dear diary, haven't we heard all this before—you don't really want me to repeat myself with lesser Henrys.)

July 22, 1944

Last night I met Gonzalo. When we return together and he enters a shop to buy fruit, I meet Harry—dark, ardent, tormented. I move towards him so tenderly. What did he feel afterwards when he saw Gonzalo join me? At that moment I would have preferred his frenzy to Gonzalo's sensual well-being. I do not telephone him, call him back, or relent. I do not obey my feelings this time, but my wisdom.

September 14, 1944

LIBERATION OF FRANCE

Tremendous month of joy, hope, hope of the war ending, hope of returning to France.

I gave myself to the sea and returned with strength. I saw Gonzalo there twice, caressed on the beach, with sweetness and tenderness. But the night before I left for Amagansett, I yielded to Harry's passion, and we had what for him was a night of love, for me merely a night of sensuality. It took me a lifetime to be able to enjoy a man without love. I also spent an afternoon with Chinchilito, who doesn't forget me. At last, at last, pleasure, without pain.

I even take a little pleasure in tormenting Harry. I let him dream all month, and then again I exile him because he is disintegrated, chaotic, unbalanced, because he is sick, because he says to me: "I want to read all the diary. I want to know the secret of woman, to incorporate the knowledge in my writing. I feel I must know it. No other woman can give me the truth." My nature rejects the predatory invader. He complains: "Everything is locked to me. You, and now the diary." The nakedness of his appetite and greed revolt me. His audacity and demands. He is aware of the shocking rape of the *House of Incest* Henry committed in his *Scenario*. The excuse is that what you want to possess is something you love, need, but in them there is ruthlessness, a taking for the self, and there is no tribute, giving, loving. I am to Harry a jewel, and he wants to possess this jewel without ever asking himself: has he ever created a jewel, or been a jewel himself? No, it is greed. Harry wants his dream. I have a feeling of revolt almost when he begins to rant: "You and I will be together someday. We will have a child." His invasion makes me recoil. He never sensed frontiers, respected my withdrawals. I won't let my sensuality carry me into the morass of stolen goods. Nothing comes out of his own being. It is all borrowed from others.

The diary as a project. The diary covers the period between 1914 to the present, and the setting moves between Europe and America. It is immensely rich in activities, voyages, relationships, and it encompasses all classes of people and nationalities. It was not written for publication and therefore the quality of complete truth is developed strongly, revealing more than the usual novel does about character and events. It is the diary I wish to convert into a long novel. From it I have already transposed one novel, *Winter of Artifice*, and short stories, *Under a Glass Bell*. Many themes are contained in the diary: the theme of emigration of a European child to America, her reactions, drama of adaptation, conflict with language, habits and education; the theme of the father and daughter relationship (partly treated in *Winter of Artifice*); the theme of the return to Europe, voyages, the artistic life in France, the aesthetic world, international worlds; the development of the world of dance, music, writing; the theme of development of an American writer in Paris; a life of the aristocracy. One volume will deal with drama of psychoanalysis, a full description of it in process, its effect upon the artist, its relation to the present, its significance. Woman will discover her own significance. There is the theme of political conflict in France; the theme of love relationships, developed in multiple directions, encompassing a study of love from a feminine point of view.

There is the conflict of woman with her maternal love, with her creative self, conflict of the romantic and the realist, of expansion versus sacrifice, conflict of woman in present-day society, the theme of development of woman on her own terms, not as an imitation of man. This becomes, in the end, the predominant theme of the novel: the development of woman finding her own psychology and her own significance in contradiction to the man-made psychology and interpretation; woman finding her own language and articulating her feeling, discovering her own perceptions; woman's role in the reconstruction of the world. The women who will appear in the novel: the masculine objective woman novelist; the chic woman of the world; the maternal woman spending herself on active, devoted love; the dreaming, passive, analytical woman; the sensation-seeker; the unconscious dramatist; the oriental, childish woman; the cold, egotistical, inhuman woman; the healing, intuitive, guiding woman. From subjectivity and neurosis come objectivity, expansion, fulfillment and evolution.

OCTOBER 1944

We have to reprint Berthie Zilka's book because it was full of errors. Gonzalo had told me he had taken the proofs to be corrected by a French person, and I trusted him, but whoever corrected them did not know French. I struggle to keep press afloat. While I am working the electric company comes to shut off the power. I work from ten to six, and Gonzalo from two to six. He works three times more slowly. One day he is sick, the next day Helba is sick, the third day he has to appear in court for the money he owes Dr. Lopez, on the fourth he has to see a lawyer. Result is that I bear almost the whole burden of the work. To do a whole book over again is demoralizing. When I come home the telephone begins to ring: Thurema, Jimmy, Frances, Elsa de Brun, Berthie, Lee ver Duft, Harry, Duits, Martha, Josephine, Jon Stroup, Henrietta Wegel.

My greatest joy has been Hugo's blossoming. He has finally come alive. He has a body, and it is alive. He is more alert, more intuitive, more talkative, more emotional, more vehement, more jealous, more relaxed, more irresponsible, lazier, happier. Last night he took me with frenzy and cried: "Oh, I have come into joy at last. I'm happy." He was a dead man.

And now he says: "With your beauty and your intelligence, how did you bear me before? You would have been justified in leaving me." So he unknowingly gives me absolution for all my abandonments. My betrayals of the dead Hugo, my quest for life and passion, saved him, ultimately, and returned to him in the form of life.

OCTOBER 11, 1944

I received a letter from England that the English publisher will print *Winter of Artifice* and *Under a Glass Bell*, a letter from *Print* magazine that they cannot review *Winter of Artifice* because it is improper, a letter from Henry that he is coming to New York because his mother is ill.

With Martha, as with Rank, I entered into a false relationship. She has the marvelous personality of the analyst and the tragic element of her personal life (poor, deprived, loveless, lonely) that led me impulsively to bring her into the life she helped me to create. I wanted her to have a share in the joy. Soon it became apparent that there were two Marthas, absolutely distinct. As the analyst, I felt connected to her compassion, understanding, subtlety, intuition. But the personal Martha is different: she is passive, cold, analytical, critical, detached, willful. By this time Martha, like Rank, wanted to live, to enjoy, and was drawn to us, to our group. We made her more aesthetic, healthier, handsomer. To draw closer to Hy, or to charm him, she entered into our way of life. Lucia invited her to Amangansett, where she was hopelessly out of place. She was the mother, the nurse, the doctor, but for her it was beneficial. She became more alert, more connected. I feel constrained with her because of her unnaturalness. Poor Martha, she is courageously pretending and simulating, is absolutely mechanical, consciously making efforts. It is all terribly conscious, analyzed, a curse, and I am back again at the same point I found myself with Rank. Analysis should be used like a medicine for a crisis and then left alone. Martha cannot leave it alone. I am finished with it, free of it, and now I am living. I do not enjoy the relationship. Analysis should lead to mature naturalness and then fall away like a vehicle. As I once told her, "I am now going back into my submarine." But Martha cannot do this, to learn, step by step, how to live. She is conscious of every error, every gain. What a curse. Mine is different. I can plunge into unconsciousness, follow it, yield to it, as I yield to the dreams or the impulses. Hy complains, "She verbalizes everything." I am swimming, I am walking, I am hungry. There is in her the cancer of idealism, the consequence of which is neurosis.

Martha is not content with our becoming "natural." No, we must behave "evolvedly," one of her self-deceptions. She suffers anguish each time Hy talks to a woman, no longer listens to Hugo when Hy talks to me, yet she asks me to help him, that I am for him the animal image, that he dreams of me, etc. She does not understand when to avoid catastrophe and pain—Hy will fall in love with me, and I am not interested in him. When I try to explain that I no longer desire the negative, sick person, she is hurt and protests that Hy is making more efforts than all the others, the very opposite of her advice to me during analysis, to keep away from the sick, the negative.

I wage a battle against psychoanalytical language, which I never used—the medical, banal clichés, deadening, powerless. Instead, I tried new words, made deep efforts to be articulate so that the patient could become articulate. A cliché phrase is standardization, neutralization of the experience.

I am at work on a new book. I took the character of Luise Rainer, and gave her my father, my lovers, and my friendship with Thurema.

I am bewildered, lost in the maze of the diary. I cannot disguise myself as Luise, as any other woman. I cannot find the thread of development. I work unconsciously on fragments. I perceive and follow associations such as walled, blind, wall, whorehouse for the blind and blind love.

OCTOBER 26, 1944

When I smother under the weight of the press and Gonzalo's perverse destructiveness, I can only recover my life by breathing in the climate of love.

Sunday evening I worked on my new book, and while seeking material, I reread the incident on the dunes with Edward Graeffe, the *chinchilito*. The same evening, he began to think of me and wanted to call me, but didn't because he thought Hugo might be home. And he called Monday morning. Tuesday evening I let him come. With the Bright Messenger, the myth personage, enters physical beauty, harmony, power. He has been studying astronomy, but as he enters with his powerful voice filling the studio like the sea of sound, he lays in my hand the bouquet of his desire! First desire, and then astronomy. And my fatigue lifts as we stand in Union Square studying the Pleiades. "With Chinchilita," he says, "I can always talk as I feel. No need of disguise."

Elation fills me when Pablo comes. Pablo is nineteen, is from Panama, has a Cuban grandmother, a mixed background, and is all openness and naturalness. Last night in a dream I had a love affair with him. My nature responds to his warmth and naturalness, and I have turned against the closed, negative beings: Eduardo, Jimmy, Hy. I want pleasure, openness, naturalness, warmth. I wrote to Albert.

NOVEMBER 1, 1944

How Pablo reminds me of Albert, reawakens my desire for Albert. How I see the full mouth and desire it, and how I recognize the very slender, very feminine hands of the feminine man. Pablo is probably homosexual, but the reaction of the sensitive me has changed: if I answer impulsively in my dream, or in my nature, at least I do not act and let the danger pass.

The way Pablo came was this: One day he telephoned. "You don't know me, but I have been reading your books and I love them. I love *Under a Glass Bell*. I am in the navy. I am only in New York for a day. Won't you let me call on you for just a moment? I have been sitting in a café in the Village, alone, reading the stories, and I got drunk on them, and this gave me the courage to call you."

The voice was warm, cheerful, elated and young, and sincere. But not knowing him, I said: "You can come for a moment. We are on our way to dinner."

As he walked up the stairs and I held the door open I saw first of all his irresistible smile, a lithe figure, reddish brown hair, freckles, laughing eyes. As soon as he came in we liked him. He stayed for the whole evening, and we became friends.

NOVEMBER 6, 1944

The reason why I sometimes feel capable of suddenly committing suicide is because when I reach a moment during which I feel awake, I feel everything is delusion and deceit. I have been cheated—that is, I can live when I have faith, but there are moments when I feel my faith is illusion. Today I feel this terrifying sense of reality which makes me doubt everything. I feel I did not make Henry strong—it was I who was strong, because of his strength. I wrote his books. Today, without me, he is again flabby, wasteful, in error, egocentric, lazy, and not creating. When I left him, the Henry I dreamed ceased to be—I never accepted the reality of Henry. Now, I work at the press with Gonzalo merely to give him the illusion of being self-sustaining. In reality, I do most of the work. I give him this illusion that he is capable. He doesn't really care how much I put into the press, because (like Henry) he thinks I have the strength. Hugo and I have not only denied ourselves comfort and peace, but in addition we have worked for two human beings, of which one is utterly without value.

L'HOMME FATAL

My difficulty with the feminine man

DECEMBER 7, 1944

I touched the bottom again and then liberated myself. I decided to eliminate the cause of friction, to not care about the press. I never go there unless Gonzalo calls me. I battled for my health by going to Jacobson. Then Jaeger reminded me we are never in a trap unless we want to be. I had to choose between breaking with Gonzalo and accepting him, and I accepted. I began to write, first out of the intolerance, out of despair—I saw art so clearly as a drug, the only drug left to me now that all illusion is removed.

Then Lanny Baldwin, the southern poet whose book we are printing, came to the press "to breathe." I like his humor and softness. He took us to lunch. One afternoon he was looking over his pages and I saw his blond, sensitive hands and felt their nudity and sensuality. He was at first merely a handsome man, well groomed, who had been on the stage, not comfortable in business, who has a home in Mount Kisco and two children. Then he became the southern gentleman poet who was gallant and shy with me, became the man whose rich, soft voice stirred me over the telephone. The *homme fatal* for me, the soft, feminine, rather weak man. As I grew healthier, lighter, freer, I began to desire him, to dream of kissing him.

We went out together last night—a French restaurant, red wine, a long talk. He wanted me to read his last poems at the hotel. At first I said I'd wait in the taxi, but he urged me upstairs. I read the poems. It was late. When I stood to leave he kissed me, so delicately and so strongly, so sensually. I left. In the taxi I threw my head back, drugged.

Lanny. Lanny cannot hurt me. He can only give me pleasure. He is born in September, under my father's sign, but he is my flirtatious, tender father. I can take only pleasure now.

DECEMBER 13, 1944

Writing important pages richly, intensely, with strength—I know—for women's history, on anxiety, on a bicycle ride, on Lucia (Hejda), Thurema (Lillian), and Luise (Stella), but I feel I never surpass the diary. I cannot invent character. Hugo is paying me the subtle tribute of weeping, weeping over the difficulty of my destiny. He thinks I am being sacrificed to the writing of the future, that I will not live to receive my due.

I wrote Sunday out of the drunkenness caused by Lanny's kiss. Then yesterday he came to my place. I expected pleasure, but I found a man afraid. He had been dreaming of me, obsessively, but he could not bear the deception, the secret, the partial relationship. He was afraid I would hurt him. We kissed. He held me so close on the couch that I felt his desire against my body. He fought his desire. It was all so sensual, so soft, so tormented. I felt his sincerity, his naïveté, his fears, his absolutism. He was saying good-bye, and he was kissing me and crying out: "Oh, God, to feel this way again. I never thought I could feel this way again." (He is just barely recovering from a cruel break with an actress.) But he cannot lie. He dreads the estrangement from his wife and home that he felt after he left me. There is so much feeling between us that I do not believe he will be able to stay away. But fear can be stronger than desire in him. So I don't know. I felt sad at his loss, empty to be deprived of the drunkenness. Two bad, empty days without joy or drunkenness. Why do I choose so unwisely? I feel he will return and we will have pleasure. I will hurt him and perhaps liberate him too.

DECEMBER 14, 1944

For two days I felt the pain all through my body, of my loss and his loss too. He is too good, too simple, to be free. I had desired Hugo's goodness, Hugo's inarticulateness, Hugo's adolescence in Lanny, and something of Eduardo's physical attributes. It is strange, this excursion into the ecstasy of loving qualities I already possess around me, loving them anew. I never understood, as a Doña Juana, the deeper causes of Don Juanism. The mystical impersonal expansion of love, loving only the dream and not reality, which means to love the beginning over and over again, the ecstasy of a new dream before the morning, the awakening, to love again a young Hugo, a young Eduardo, our young idealism, our young sentimentalism and fears. It is strange, the overflow of love, for I have never loved Hugo better or more completely. I have never loved Gonzalo better, with a purer maternal passion. But the mistress goes on forever, desiring, desiring, pouring out. Creation does not reduce my love output! The strength goes out to the new book. The softness goes to men, women, and life.

I wrote this book yielding absolutely to unconscious images and following associations, and then the symbolism became clear, the awakened thinking of trivial facts. I was haunted for days by the image of mirrors in a garden. I wrote it and found the thread of connection later, one of the essential symbols of the book, that of art and reality. At times I depict nature as nature, and at times I must use the mirror. I call on poetry, on symbols, even on a bicycle to tell a very simple truth. We will respect the taboos created by people's fear of truth. The mirrors will remain in the garden, the mirrors of art and poetry. The sexual scenes must take place in the mirror of the naked garden in Paris. People cannot bear the truth; they have placed mirrors where they can see the bodies possessing each other, but where they cannot see when the bodies fail.

Lanny came back, doubting, protesting, but was carried away by the intoxication. He cannot bear lies, he cannot bear the uncertainty, but when he dreams of me or sees me, he is swept away. We were in the restaurant. His ex-mistress had come to his house, very drunk, and he no longer loves her. We leaned over the little table as if we were going to fall into each other. I was drunk too, and again my intuition did not lead me astray. At moments his fantasy answers mine…above all, our feelings go together. At the same moment we both withdrew from the noise of the restaurant and went somewhere…we imagined a room…we imagined… Oh, the drunkenness of love and desire. The day is illuminated—the press, the winter, the house, the music, the books, writing—Lanny. He couldn't kill the desire I knew. I was physically in pain for a week when I tried to. Today, joy again. Joy. Joy. Joy.

DECEMBER 22, 1944

Alone with Lanny in my apartment, and again the doubts: do I love him or merely desire him? He is afraid. He wants an absolute love, in the open. He doubts everything, himself, and me. And he fears pain. When it was a question of unimportant women he could play and feel no conflict, but now he feels churned and pulled. The contrast is too violent between his life at Mount Kisco and me. He talks like a woman who is afraid to be possessed. Sitting back, tender, vulnerable, he arouses me painfully. And then suddenly the brakes give way, and he holds me with such a fervor that it is like a possession. He says: "Let me sleep. I'm broken. I want peace." So we lie side by side, and as he falls asleep, his caresses grow wilder, all but the ultimate. His passion and emotionalism now arouse me more, and I suffer now. My feelings are captured by his conflict. I know. I know. Let him sleep in my tenderness. From this he cannot be saved. If I withdraw, it does not matter. Lanny cannot kill the passion that is in him, the poetry and the ecstasy. They are in him. They will torment him. I wish I could turn back, but it is too late. I didn't want to feel so much.

The other day I thought suddenly: I can never be happy in love. If Lanny comes to me we will be happy together for a short time and…I suddenly imagined him in uniform. The next day he talked about the re-classification, saying he might be drafted (he was not drafted because he broke an ankle skiing). His exterior is so cool, so contained… he always enters so cool and polite, and then he breaks into flames. Now that I have felt this fire in him, I find myself caught in more than desire, and I suffer from his conflict—the passion, the passion in his free body, and then the fear paralyzing him.

Lanny. It is so strange. There is his external self: the American, neat and dapper, clear and sleek. Everything separates us: his Americanism, his masculine wife, his children, his home, his business life, his bourgeois frame, his bad taste in painting and in music. Only his writing is different. And then suddenly all this breaks down, and body to body we burn together. What a mystery. What a marvelous, incredible, beautiful thing it is, this welding fire. Then again his thinking, his conscious self. We can't meet. But this breaks down at the touch. In the touch there is all: cognition, similitude, rhythm, expressiveness. He is to me all tenderness and warmth, all hidden and sacrificed by his goodness and responsibilities. He is full of innocence and immaturity. He is idealistic. In him I like it, because at the same time he is an *homme à femme*. In this he is knowing and worldly. He has the lover's polish. It's comical too, how the lovers recognize each other and distrust each other. Those made for love know that lovers pursue love and are therefore unfaithful. (Chinchilito—how he distrusted me, feared to love me.)

I know Lanny is the lover, but I have more confidence than he has. I know I can hold the lover, satisfy him, enchant him. I do not fear him. I see Lanny elusive and playful, smiling with charm, soft and debonair too, handsome and distrustful. At the same time, I see now, I am the lover. Oh, god, I am the lover. This moment of frenzy when we lay together, he trying to sleep—the violent embrace is everything to me. Everything else pales. This is the fever and the madness, the flame. I want this over and over and over again. Lanny, Lanny, his softness. I, alas, am courting again, I am courting a woman…the sensitivity of the face, mouth, the warm softness of the features.

DECEMBER 24, 1944

I am so lovesick I can't write. A whole day before me, and what I want is to make love to Lanny. It seems to me that I cannot create unless I possess his femininity, his softness. I have a craving to have him in me, and then I shall feel complete to do my creative work. I need strength, and I have put all my softness on him. I melt towards him, and this weakens me for writing. I have lost my strength. It has gone courting him on Christmas Eve, seeking the yielding of his body. Give me my lover, oh, god, give me my lover so that I may do this arid and strong work, for I have to make clear this chaos of sex, and it drowns me. Today I drowned in my unconscious!

A whole afternoon alone together at Jon Stroup's apartment, Lanny and I. The same scene, the same passionate embracing and the same blocking. He is caught in his fear of life, of pain, of desire. And yet all we say and do together has a kind of harmony. He can do all but take me. He takes my mouth, he uncovers my arm, he slips his hand under my sweater, takes my back, takes the dimples at the beginning of the back, and takes the feelings and the turmoil. No two love affairs are ever the same. In ours there are ballet gestures. He takes me by the waist as if he were going to lift me up in the air, and there is a region of his body I feel under his shirt, his back and ribs, wavering and shivering under my fingers, all the peripheries and dances of a ballet that prevent fusion. We touch a point of fire. He brings me many things: an America I never knew, an aristocratic America, a gallant America, an ideal America. We can laugh together. He can dance loosely. As he dances a little I see the woman in him, the woman who peered out of my father lying down when he fainted after his concert, pale and disheveled, the woman in the golden transparency of Eduardo, with his green eyes, their ardent caress. But this is more than a love affair *manqué*. There are subtle transmissions, as when I received Albert without the orgasm. There is a penetration. Will the obstacle be removed? As we come out in the street, I miss the elation that follows lovemaking, yet I feel the intoxication of half-possession. We talked. I sat away from him. "Don't touch me," he said. "If you touch me, I lose my lucidity." He confessed, and I helped him, perhaps. He was recently annihilated by a woman. (How woman can demolish a man. I wonder if I ever left a man as destroyed. I wonder if I left Dudley demolished—yes, I did, and Rank, and Harry, and others, those I did not want. The wounds of the war of love. The cripples.)

JANUARY 5, 1945

Between the afternoon I spent with Lanny and last night when he took me out, I decided to withdraw. Immediately he felt it. We sit in a dim bar, and I refuse to be drawn into his softness. He questions me, and I tell him, "It was a mirage." "No," he says, and then with great feeling and anxiety, he adds, "But now that you feel it was a mirage will you abandon me?" His face is so near to mine, and my being is again drawn to him. "No, Lanny, no." "What I feel," he says, "is that at any time, any moment, I will get violent…" (And take you?) But oh, his doubts of women, of himself, of this situation. He gives great weight to the fact that I left Henry as Lanny's mistress left him, that I am someday leaving for Europe. His love for the other woman, who was married, was great until he told his wife that he wanted to surrender her and the home and marry the mistress. But the mistress would not leave her husband, would not go all the way, so this situation is the worst for him, and he cannot accept it. It paralyzes him. His instinct is right. This is only a love affair, and it will take him again to an impasse: the failure to have the woman all to himself. He knows. For his own sake I should free him. But we are caught together, for he has the power to melt me. Why? I came last night to resist being melted, but then it is his voice, his full and sensual mouth, his emotional green eyes, his rich dark hair, his slender blond hands, his emotionalism melting me, and I'm drunk again. After we talk, quietly it seems, we stand up to leave, but we are unsteady and swaying from desire.

Why can't he play the role of love and not demand the absolute?

In all mature love, there is the love of and response to certain qualities which run from one human being to another like the theme of a symphony. There is my love for humorous fantasy and playfulness, which come from my father's whimsy, storytelling, imitations, take-offs, etc., which reappear in Henry, in Gonzalo, in Chinchilito, in Lanny. Love does not end but continues like a tapestry, simply passing from one human being to another. One first perceives the continuity and eternality of love in its current.

This flow does not die—what dies is the individual's love for another. If, in the same restaurant, my blood was stirred by the voice of Henry ten years ago and now by the voice of Lanny, Lanny is struck with the tragedy of the passing of love and I with the wonder of its continuity.

JANUARY 12, 1945

Another afternoon with Lanny here in my apartment. We try to talk as friends. He becomes passionate; he cannot go all the way. This hurts me physically and emotionally, and is followed by a great depression. I feel he is bad for me. I should break with him, yet I can't because he is suffering and needs me. He falls asleep, and then when he awakens he suddenly attacks communism. I refuse to quarrel or argue. He is a mixture of Mars and Venus. Because our Venus cannot form a conjunction, must our Mars flare up? So there we are. The next day he telephones and I am out. The day after he telephones again. Can we have lunch? I didn't want to go—I was depressed and ill. But I went, and again it becomes mellow and soft...I feel caught and angry to be caught.

To break Lanny's spell I telephone Chinchilito at his home, and meanwhile he is telephoning me from outside. We always do this simultaneously after months of not seeing each other. I invite him to choose between Monday and Tuesday (Hugo is going to Cincinnati). He chooses Monday. Tuesday it is Lanny. I love the idea of Chinchilito's power to heal the insecurity with Lanny, yet the truth is that I have a more tender, warmer feeling for Lanny—Chinchilito has never aroused my tenderness. What fatality there is in my loves. It seems cruel and selfish to abandon Lanny, yet for me it would be best.

In one week: Hy said to me, "I must not stay near you, I want you too much. From the first I knew I would be attracted, too attracted..." Then Elsa de Brun, whom I have known for twenty years: "I knew nothing about the love between women when I was a girl, but oh, Anaïs, the dreams I had about you, always about your nakedness, your beauty. And with Jaeger we talked about you; I was always obsessed with you. I understand it now." Then Jimmy reports to Martha about having dreamed of me naked, then Thurema's own desires for me are made clear by Jaeger, then letters from Henry. And meanwhile, where am I? Because I see Lanny as Hugo was—imprisoned, human, lost—I am lying down by his side, a shell-shocked Lanny, suffering from paralysis.

Evening with Chinchilito. He arrives again in a state of erection and places his firm desire in my hand at the door. We lie naked on my own bed, and I abandon myself completely, voluptuously, to a marvelously strong, powerful interplay. He is confident, firm, relaxed and potent. My strength answers his in a long-lasting, deep, complete fusion.

He takes the whole body between his hands; I take his, and within the golden-haired pagan tabernacle, a mélange of fluids, wines and palpitations of a golden mass, a mass of pagan silky sounds, rhythms of joyous blood transfusions. There, there, in the billowing flesh, at the core, a soft and thirsty and vibrating wall of flesh, I took him in, enveloped him, and he lay there, waiting, moving, waiting for the sudden spurt of ecstasy, mutual, confounded, perfectly rhythmic. Oh, the sweetness, the repose, the languor, the laughter. No pain in the world of the body and of the sun. I fell asleep afterwards, with a feeling of richness. Love is not necessary. The body has its own sun life which stems from itself, from beauty, from a life that is apart from the darker mysteries of personalities. Chinchilito returns to other women, no doubt, living naturally, free of identity, free. And I too.

The key word is certitudes.

JANUARY 18, 1945

Lanny comes with a speck of dust in his eyes and a guilty nervousness because he has to leave his wife to have dinner alone in town in order to be with me. So I have to bathe his eyes and lull his guilt…then we sit on the couch, and he tells me: "I want to go and live in Mexico, take a house there by the sea. Leave my job, and write. Will you come? I will go only if you come with me, to stay with me."

"I can't. We haven't the means to go."

"But I will take care of you and Hugo. We'll work at farming, all in cooperation. I have the means. Both Hugo and you are creating worthwhile things, you ought to be freed. You have genius. I want to watch your development. I feel I have to live this life with my family. I cannot live two separate lives. I'm not…sophisticated enough. But all of us together, in Mexico…"

So I pursue the elusive, potential Lanny against reality. Always against reality. At home, again he relaxes. He almost falls asleep and asks me to wear my oriental trousers. "You dreamed them. I don't have them." Yes, he is dreaming. Then again he feels desire and makes me lie alongside him, and he caresses me. And again he stops. I return always to the imprisoned ones. Is it merely my desire which catches me helping those bound ones, those of less ecstasy, less freedom? Do I feel the latent passion in Lanny as I did in Hugo, who was so quiet and attenuated and bound when I first knew him? There is more than desire here. I look at his full and sensitive mouth with such mixed feelings. He moves me beyond desire. His laughter moves me.

SATURDAY EVENING, JANUARY 20, 1945

The diary has been my *canto* to love. When I love I cannot write, I can only be with my love. Lanny is in the music I hear. He is in Mount Kisco, behind my green iron gate at Louveciennes, with his wife as I am with Hugo. Lanny tries to reconcile the irreconcilable, to deceive himself and hold back his passion. There is a feminine quality in men (Hugo has it) which arouses me. A timidity.

JANUARY 25, 1945

Yesterday was a day I felt I should break with Lanny because he is not free, and I cannot bear this ambivalence. A day when I rebelled against Gonzalo for not reading my new manuscript (in contrast to Lanny's interest) so that I actually feel pain at his not being the companion of my work. A day when I felt nervous before the ordeal of posing for *Town and Country* again, as different women in different costumes (impersonating Hedja, Stella and Lillian). I didn't sleep, imagining this scene with Lanny. Then in the icy, cold studio, I did pose, successfully in spite of the problem of clothes—shoes given to me by Frances not fitting me, a shirt from Valeska not fitting me, etc.

Lanny telephoned me during the posing, and then later he called for me. We went off together to sit in the Plaza room, which is like a huge baronial room, an awful place. Oh, Lanny. He likes the splendor and the vastness. And there we were in big leather chairs; I was so tired, so tired by the posing, and languid. We drank together, talked. His eyes blurred, dissolved. He drank, and I hardly, but the dissolution always takes place at the same moment. There is a blood rhythm. He touches me, always when I feel he must, when I crave it. He took my hand. I leaned over. When I leaned back, relaxing, he said, "I don't know if it is because you are tired, but you're lovelier than I have ever seen you." Amazing how two people in the Plaza bar room can express such a multitude of moods and gestures.

When the talk got too deep I refused to go further. I said that I knew his demon, that it was like mine, but I would not say at four in the afternoon, at the Plaza, that it was a sensual demon. "No," I said, "If they would put out the chandelier, and then the white mural bulbs, and then the red lamps, I might tell you." So he called the waiter and tells him what I'd said!

How he plays, how light he has become, such gayety. He wanted to go dancing, but he had to catch a train—because of the cold his family may need heat. We walked to the studio. He took me to the elevator. He left me. He came back to kiss me fervently over the eyelids.

JANUARY 28, 1945

Days of feverish inspiration, such a flood of spontaneous and disordered writing that at one moment I took my head in my hands and believed I was going insane. An onrush of associations, of disconnected episodes, utter freedom. What happens is that I reach such a deep level where I touch the cosmic consciousness of woman, and I lose my character as a separate, identifiable personage. They all flow into one another, boundaries are lost, and in the end I am swallowed by the infinite ocean of my own unconscious. So I lose my grip on reality, my construction.

But today I emerge with thirty-eight pages on the snow woman, a beautifully told myth of the virgin woman.

FEBRUARY 3, 1945

Lanny again. We met at Gotham and then had lunch at the restaurant, at the table where we first met. I said: "I am proud of your poems. I want you to bloom. You reveal in them a rich unconscious."

I wrote him a fan letter, unsigned. He will see Martha. Will she unite us, or dissolve our illusion because of the pain involved? I don't know. I have more than desire. I feel a terrible, devastating tenderness, which is worse than passion, when he shows me a missing button on his shirt or a torn glove. His slenderness moves me, his quietness too, the sensibility of his mouth. I write to be nearer to him, to re-taste my happiness with him. My new humor seems somehow to have been born with him. I feel an irrepressible youth with him, my own youth, so free, as it never was.

The beauty of this moment is in my freedom. My abundance of love is able to live itself out, to keep Hugo in a state of romance (the secret of the duration of his romantic love), to keep Gonzalo in a state of romance, to make each hour, each evening, each moment, each love yield to this inexhaustible wealth I feel—to disperse and dispense tenderness, attentiveness, coquetry, desire, feeling.

FEBRUARY 7, 1945

Talk with Martha. She tells me there is no masochism in my relation to Lanny, first because he is different, not egocentric or narcissist as Henry and Gonzalo are, second because I have been able to keep my sexual freedom (Edward Graeffe), and third because of the way I handle it, with airiness, no obsession, no fixation, etc., no neurotic reaction. I am not hurt, only aware of his pain and difficulties. So this morning I let myself express my feelings for him in a note: "You are in the music I hear, you are all around and within me. You give me the fever that is life, and the quietness that is creation. I feel I worked with your quietness, for you have a surer rhythm, against my great disorder and recklessness. Yet I have the freedom, a full, full freedom. And you will have it too. What there is between us is so deep and too strong to be broken by an obstacle..."

After being separated since Friday because he was ill, he rushed down this morning at eleven o'clock and laid a poem on my knees, and I read it while he read my note. His poem was a poem of death.

He was deeply moved by the note. He said: "It makes me happy. It's wonderful. But I give you this death in me while you give me life and the sun." Then he read the new pages in my book describing Henry's insouciance, and he was elated. "I love the freedom of this man." He likes my waking writing better than my dream writing. He responds to my directness. His duality—he passes from warmth to coldness. He is at times remote. Today he did not caress me. I don't know if my body can bear this, especially when I am constantly tempted.

The mystery of freedom. To face the same experience again with a different attitude. In Lanny, it is Hugo who comes again to court me and then to be afraid, to be impulsive and impotent, to be full of desire and full of fear. In Lanny, Eduardo has come again in all his states of death and paralysis. In Lanny comes John Erskine asking me to undress, throwing himself upon me and then not able to take me. In Lanny comes the month of ecstasy with Gonzalo when he could not take me either. In Lanny comes my difficulty with the feminine man who defends himself with all the feminine man's virginity and fear. But I am not the same. With Hugo I wept and thought that he did not love me. With John I wept and became obsessed with the failure. With Eduardo I was frustrated, with Gonzalo too. With Lanny, I suffer physically to have to withdraw my desire, but I am not defeated or hurt or obsessed. I am free of tragedy. I am free. That means my desire can go elsewhere, anywhere. I am not enslaved. I am free. Lanny's poem touched me: "Alone among idolatries, World without compassion, World without passion, I must move alone, in saintly seriousness."

It is the death I felt after John Erskine. But I will not die with him. I will give him life without hurting myself.

To be free means to go on living, not to die under a tragic impasse or a blow. To be free means to go on living, making love, loving even when faced by an obstacle, or pain, or a collision, or a tragic loss. When I first faced pain I was shattered. When I first met failure, defeat, denial, loss, death, I died. Not today. I believe in my power, in my magic, and I do not die. I survive, I love, live, continue. Lanny is in me, but his death does not kill me. He cannot kill my body or my feelings by denial. They are stronger. To be free means to be stronger than your jail. It means to live in the present.

After ten years I see my father altogether differently. At first I saw his Don Juanism as his crime against me, and I the victim of it, and I hated it. But today it is clear that what I thought I hated I actually loved and wanted to be. Ten years later I see his dancing faithless figure in the quest of love not as the enemy, but as myself. I have become him. There is a youthful man in me who has desperately courted the feminine in men. My soul was an effeminate young man. My virility has donned my father's suit (it fits me well, there is no doubt about it, like the suits of Eduardo's young men which fit me perfectly in Paris), and now I am him. It is possible that instead of courting the feminine in men I might be happier courting the women who yield to me, the women in love with me. What has appeared in my last book is a woman who loves all women. I was convinced that Don Juan was desire, not love. And I am love.

Gonzalo's only comment on my book was a criticism of its erotic element and obsession with sex. He gave me the title for it from one of the phrases in it, "This Hunger...this hunger became love."

Such a shock last night. Going with Gonzalo to MacDougal Street and finding it rented to another person, being painted, empty and dirty, because I could not pay the rent for three months. Another *rincon* lost, after three years of love, desire and work. A shock. The fear of change.

Lanny, when I say I will go away, it means I have lost my courage. Today I lost my courage. You have aroused in me a dream of complete love, and I cannot bear to kill it. You do not suffer this because you are in mourning. You are in a state of death. This that I suffer you do not suffer. I suffer from being fully alive, aware and awake. You have lost your faith in love. I have more to kill, more to kill. You can renounce more easily at this moment. You have withdrawn. I am not withdrawn, and I cannot renounce because I don't know how. I feel you have been able to kill your feelings for me, because the other love experience killed you. Oh, Lanny, I cannot bear it. There is too much to kill. Do you want me to do this, to die with you because you cannot live with me? I have been living with you. You are not living with me. You are where your poems told me you are. What an exchange that was, your poem on death and my note to you! That to me was like the final stab. Final. It is final, final, final. My courage was because I did not believe it final. Say the word that it is not final.

Lanny, you killed me with a poem, with your most beautiful poem, one I love so much I wanted to set it by hand, print it by hand. I wasn't thinking of myself then, but of you, and then I didn't want to feel what it meant for me. I will not see you tomorrow. I cannot see you, Lanny. I answered you cruelly at the restaurant when you spoke of *Tristan and Iseult*, because that was a love that ended in death.

FEBRUARY 17, 1945

I touched the bottom of suffering, and then I rebelled, violently, and definitely. I will not submit to this. So when Lanny came yesterday with his negative evasiveness, his hesitations, ambivalence, postponements, fear of conflict, I brought it all out in the open. I said, "I cannot see you anymore." I let him read what I wrote in the diary because I was so hurt and so bewildered that I could not speak. In his attitude I read the final image of his ambivalence and guilt, and I responded with determination. He wants this game with his secret desires; he wants a friendship without sex, but I don't. I felt the masochism of it. In place of sexuality he thrusts out jealousy, the jealousy of impotence, and destruction. He destroyed my spring mood; he destroyed so much in a feminine and indirect way. He criticizes Jean Varda because Henry's article on him appeared next to my story of Jean Cateret in *Circle Magazine*. Something cold and destructive emanates from him, the reflection of his death. And I rebelled. I let my nature rebel. It came so swiftly, like nature's storms. I made the break, tore him out of my being. The pain was deep and terrible. I sent him away. When he left, bewildered, inadequate, I was shaking and trembling. With an act, I had freed myself of pain by tearing out the injured flesh. But oh, the pain, the violent pain.

When I called Frances, I had such a moment of despair it was like dying. She came and tried to help me. When she left and I tried to sleep, I sobbed again. Such a full, open pain. Slept fitfully. Awakened dead. Heart dead. Weak. Rushed out. Could not bear my house. Wept in the street.

Talked with Edmund Wilson at lunch. I felt his distress and received his confession. My suffering has created an understanding which even a stranger like Wilson senses and turns to. He is lonely and lost. I accompanied him to buy his uniform (he is going to France as a war correspondent), his sleeping bag. We walked, talked about his suffering with his wife Mary McCarthy. Suffering opens all the doors to the depths. As

I came home I was consoled by this that I have given. I am walking and weeping but able to give. I rebelled against pain. Will I suffer from this as much as from the loss of Albert? I want to be delivered from these men! What irony. The women are the ones whose temperaments I love and make me happy.

And women suffer from the passivity, the taking, the lack of power of men. Yet the women…we love each other, but we know it is not sexual.

Midnight. Gonzalo came, studied the preface I wrote Sunday, admired it. We were close, tender. He consoled me, unknowingly. He took me, kissed me passionately, fell asleep. I lay quiet, and I began to weep. I called out to Gonzalo. He took my wet face against his and murmured, "What is it?" I said, "I feel oppressed by my work, all I have to do. I cannot do it alone. A woman cannot do all this alone." The feeling was mixed with the pain of losing Lanny, as if my need of him outside of love had to do with the writing. I lost a companion in writing. I need the writer at my side. I need love. I need love so abnormally that it all seems natural to me, being close to Hugo the night before he left, then to Chinchilito, then to Frances, then to Lanny, then to Gonzalo, all the one and same love.

FEBRUARY 18, 1945

There is virility in suffering. Today I went with Hugo down to the sea. I saw the sea sparkling, rolling, white-foamed in the winter, walked for an hour. Hugo talked about Mexico in July. The astrology magazine promises me romance then. I thought of Chinchilito, I thought of how free I am and that I can enjoy other men. I felt the pain, yes, but I felt strength against it too. There are terrible moments, but I haven't wept today. Lanny clung to me Friday saying, "We won't lose this understanding that is between us?" He stood so near. But I do not want his friendship. I want no pain. In his moments of freedom how he came to me, but his fear was greater, his guilt, his masochism. I saw a wild light of jealousy, a lightning of frenzied, denied jealousy when he saw my photographs taken in Provincetown, where I lay at the edge of the sea. "Like a Hollywood star, the half-nakedness, a gayety." He asked, "You won't go away? You won't go back to a devastated Europe?" And then the protective, chivalrous, terrible goodness which moves me so deeply: a concern over my pain. "You won't be alone tonight? You won't stay alone? When is Hugo coming back?"

He haunts me. His sensitiveness and unconscious cruelty, his acting and his ambivalence, like a dance by a cripple, dancing awhile and then falling. But I feel erect in my suffering. I feel strength. I won't die or break.

Yesterday I reached the depths. Lanny told Gonzalo he would come to the press, and I could not face this—at the smallest reference to him I begin to weep. I had to call him and ask him not to come. I had to hear his voice, and melt, and hear him say: "I must see you. We must have an understanding. I wrote you an answer to your letter, but I won't send it. Let's get together today."

"No, no," I said.

"But why?"

I could not say because I am too hurt. I cannot bear it. I hated his Anglo-Saxon control, his Anglo-Saxon self-deceptions, his Puritanism and sexual rigidity. Yet I had not used the word "final."

I have never cut away or rebelled against pain so sharply or clearly. As I heard him react with impatience, "But we must talk this over. I want to know the reason," I was glad. I thought: let him suffer. He has not felt the loss yet. He has so much protection. The whole structure of American life protects him from such absolute feelings of the pain I experienced, his false courage, his objectivity, his home, wife, children, the drinking, his friends, the skiing.

I feel my old demon came to tempt me in its most seductive form: will you suffer again, Anaïs, at the hands of a wife, at the hands of a mistress, at the hands of man's passivity, fears, guilt, indecision? Will you suffer again because the man is in the hands of a stronger woman, a wife and her rights, an inhuman mistress, and will you be the savior at the cost of your life, every step of his freedom paid with your blood, will you be the battlefield, the confessional, the absolver, the priestess, the friend, the muse, the mother, the guide? No, not again. He is not the man for me. I know I am capable of these strong illusions. I create them, and my body incarnates them, and then it sweeps me into tragedy. No. No. If I can overcome this temptation I will be stronger. If I succumb I will be the eternal martyr. No. Anaïs is free. I will be free of pain, of regression. Yet today in the taxi, I saw him as vividly as I saw him the first time, in bondage, slender and neat in his business suit, with his briefcase, on a trip, lonely, his sensitiveness encased in this conventional uniform, and I felt the stoop in his shoulders and back. I felt it so violently in my own body that it was a physical pain, a shock, a terrible identification with him, a bond—how can I ever disentangle myself from him?

I have no defenses. He has been part of my work too. I cannot write. This illusion sustained me. I can't bear the bleakness. The strength of my rebellion and the overpowering tenderness, the compassion I feel. All my emotions are rushing out to him, and all my strength is saying: he is not good for you; he is bad for you; he will kill you. The weaker ones kill the stronger ones. What makes me love so violently when others love so weakly and shallowly? Yesterday I wept desperately when I came home. Today less. May this be my last ordeal as I cannot bear any more.

FEBRUARY 21, 1945

This morning I awakened and tried to write. I wrote the barbaric, primitive raping of the snow woman. I am being possessed by a cannibal, of the *Winter* Paris edition, but strengthened and amplified. I put my strength into the writing. Then I got violently angry at the window I couldn't open and started to bang on it with my fists to break it open, such violence I have never expressed, banging until Hugo stopped me, and I threw the flowers on the floor, those Pablo sent me for my birthday. Suddenly I felt: I have overcome the weakness in myself. I have overcome Lanny and my own weakness.

I felt a new power, born of the violent rejection of pain. I feel my strength at last. I do not need Henry or any man to write my book. Yesterday I wanted Lanny to lead me by the hand towards realism. I have a strength made out of deep suffering. I feel my violence which I never lived except through Henry and Gonzalo, my own pure violence and indestructibility. Lanny was the last image of my bondage and submission. I feel I am the woman who is being unveiled, who is being liberated. I gave myself to Hugo with a sensual frenzy and no devouring regrets or yearning, for my own pleasure. My violence was my strength which I denied, oppressed, submerged. I was the woman in bondage to man's weakness, submitting to pain. And life gives you what you submit to, accept. I am unashamed of my strength.

MARCH 2, 1945

Something persisted and survived the break with Lanny. Had I succeeded in overcoming what had to be overcome, but, as usual, without killing totally, saving the good? Yesterday I obeyed the impulse to write him a note, "I will be your friend." Then I telephoned him: "You can come and talk, anytime. Tomorrow."

"No, today," he said, "I'll come at three."

His first day back, he left his work. I said: "I am not sure that this can be done. It is a lesser thing in place of a bigger one."

"This is the bigger one," said Lanny. "I am not free. I know it. It makes me sad."

"I have never lived in a temperate, neutral zone. I dread the coldness after the warmth."

"But it is just the opposite with me. It is with you I express warmth and with the sexual comes a conflict which leaves me cold. You spoke of weeping for both of us. Do you know—after the break with you, I wept, I wept for the first time, completely."

"Then my weeping was good, if you wept too. It was worth it."

Now that he no longer feared me, the warmth came back, the immense tenderness. I let myself feel this tenderness, confining it just before it overflowed into desire. If this time I can relinquish desire for the Son I am saved. Already I have less desire than before because he is too soft, too yielding. Already I feel the woman in him, but how he arouses my tenderness. He has a tremendous innocence. I realize that because of his innocence, I felt the innocence of my youth towards him too, and therefore I aroused his romanticism, his worship and his fear of his instincts. I couldn't abandon him altogether.

The sun came into the studio. He dreams of a woman to have peace with. I dream of fever.

One learns not to die. One learns to suffer without dying. I suffered deeply, body and soul, but I did not die. Two weeks later I am dancing, singing, writing and loving. A full life is like a powerful current that can take the suffering but continues to flow. I was amazed to be able to see the sun on the sea, to feel the spring, to renew my love affair with the world.

THE TRANSPARENT CHILD

He is my son, my lover

NEW YORK, MARCH 8, 1945

William Pinckard, who wrote me from Yale after reading *Under a Glass Bell*, is seventeen. He was born in Manila to American parents, spent four years there, four years in China, then came to America and its loneliness. He is incredibly slender, with white hands more feminine than mine. There is extraordinary beauty and magnetism in his eyes, in their length. There are curiously pure blue shadows over them when he looks down, a celestial blue. He destroyed his diary, and his adolescence with it, when he came home from college. He brought me a story he wrote, his watercolors, and left them with me (to be blessed?), as Pablo leaves his work, as Lanny left his poems. I am rich indeed with young men's dreams and worship. If they were not Anglo-Saxon, but French, they would be my lovers and I could be initiating them to life as well as to art, but they are the *jeunes filles en fleurs* of America's future, the sexless future artists. Poor America. I am the celestial Madame, and this world will castrate me unless I find a MAN for myself soon. But the marvelous mood I'm in, the pleasure, confidence, faith. I am dancing, practicing the castanets.

MARCH 10, 1945

Last night: Pablo, Eduardo, Bill, Hugo. Bill knows hypnotism, and Pablo wanted to be hypnotized. For half an hour, Bill talked Pablo into a sleep. Pablo obeyed all Bill's orders; he could not hear our voices, only Bill's. He could not see latecomers because Bill told him he would only see those who were in the room when he fell asleep. He was told that he was two years old, and he said in Spanish, "Agua." At three years old he said, "Nanny." At four he sang a little song in an unknown language. At five he broke a vase and stood in the corner for punishment. Bill gave him a cigarette, which he smoked awkwardly, and at the taste of it he made a wry face and coughed and choked. Later, asked about his home, Panama, he said, "I want to lie on the sand."

"Do you want to paint or write?"

"No. I want to lie in the sand."

"Now you are in New York," said Bill. "What do you want to do?"

"Write and paint."

We were all half-anxious, half-afraid, half-laughing. Bill, smiling and dominant, flaunted his power. The beauty of his face was deeply moving, the dark blue, intense, shadowed eyes, the paleness of the face, the fine, lean line of the cheekbone, elongated, then indented at the chin, the full-balanced, sensual mouth, the boy's tousled hair. I said to Eduardo: "He is my mystical son. More than Pablo or Lanny." And Eduardo told me, "He is ruled by Neptune."

Oh god, confessor, analyst, help me not to desire my sons, not to want to be the mistress of my sons. Help me to keep my desire away from the sons of my soul. But how whole I am. Where my soul goes, my body goes. Bill has helped me to free myself of Lanny, because he is mystically and romantically freer, nearer. The spell is broken.

MARCH 17, 1945

Bill and I sat in Washington Square, talking over his wanting to break with his family, sweetly, warmly. We went to the press, where Bill wants to help me.

Blessed am I at this moment with loves that never turn into pain. This mood, this peace, relaxation, freedom and joy, I have never known but intermittently. There is joy at giving life to Bill, at opening up my home, at the youth which surrounds me. I look younger than I did at thirty. I dance. I sing. I enjoy Pablo, his activities and motions. Bill. I love Bill. He looked tired after the hypnosis, as if he had made love.

"Can you make someone fall in love with you?" I asked him.

"That would be a poor kind of love," he answered.

If only I do not fall into desire. He moves me so.

Pablo is my Spanish child, natural, physical, and alive. Bill is my mythical one. Everything is marvelous, a summer day, the beat of a factory nearby, the sun on the meager courtyard and the anemic trees, the sparrows, the Debussy records. Last night as Bill left, I held his hand in my two. He responded.

MARCH 19, 1945

Bill said, "If I had a place to go to, I would leave home." I said, "Do nothing if you don't feel emotionally ready." (He only has two months before he goes into the navy, and he wants to live freely.) But what formed and crystallized his maturity was not only reading my books, seeing me, but sharing our life, the spontaneity and aliveness of Pablo, the vitality of Josephine, the atmosphere of my house, my friends.

Saturday evening I had a party, a warm, lively, joyous evening with Josephine singing and drumming, making us all sing and drum and dance. At the end Bill hypnotized Pablo and Marshall (another beautiful boy), and it turned into great humor and high fantasy, mixed with a little terror (Bill ordered Pablo not to see Hugo after he awakened, so he could not see Hugo for the rest of the evening, but he could see his shadow on the door as he left). During the hypnosis I left the studio and went into the kitchen. I have to be alone at times for one moment when I am in a crowd. My sense of solitude overtakes me at moments, in the warmest, fullest moments. Bill sent for me: I had to be there. Doing hypnosis gives him a sense of power. Such purity and innocence he has.

How difficult it is to be in the presence of Bill's great beauty, his intense blue eyes, his fair skin, his full and languid mouth. When he leaves, I always take his delicate, soft-skinned, feminine hands in mine, and he yields them up with a vibration, as if he placed his being in the shelter of my warmth.

Yesterday, Sunday, was the critical day for him. His father was going to make him work in his business downtown Monday morning. Bill said he was first going to Yale to collect his belongings and to leave home, not intending to return. I told him, "Your life is beginning."

He appeared at my place with the valise, and our dream began. Bill eats with us, shares our evenings, books and music. Frances and Tom gave him a little room. I gave a party with Josephine Premice and her rhythms, Luise and her fantasies, an atmosphere of gayety and invention and freedom. I think of my nearness to Bill, the mystical and mysterious understanding, his great beauty, his fear of death, his understanding of my work, his drawings of me, in which he really sees me.

When the studio is full of people, Bill and I look at each other across the room with understanding. In his face I see the mysteries of the orient, the glow of the moon, the power of insight. At seventeen he has intuition about people. Nothing of his "class," his sheltered life, clings to him. He is the adventurer in spirit in spite of his sensitiveness. He has spiritual courage. He reads everything, he absorbs, he evaluates, he shares. His shyness is physical—his body alone is slightly bound.

MARCH 26, 1945

Another party. When I am near Bill I am happy and feel the tremendous glow of the dream. I also feel a great fear of pain and collision. I love his youthful, delicate, flawless skin and his magician's eyes—what are these shadows on his luminous face, those blue-violet shadows? I love his hair falling over his forehead like a boy's. I love his bird profile and his noble, full face, long, narrow and oval, with a full, generous mouth, the perfect and strong teeth. There is strength in him, in the deepest layers of his being. He is deep right through his youth, beyond his experience.

What does he feel? When I sat near him at the party, I felt as if we were gravitating towards each other, melting into each other. After the party, I felt great sadness—I wish he were older. "By magic, make yourself twenty-seven years old for a while," I said. (That I may know you as a lover.) I fell asleep to the tragedy of time, of my ever-haunting dream of uniting with what my soul loves. Last night we went to dinner, arm in arm. Friday we went to a cocktail at Elsa de Brun's, where Lanny went too. I introduced Pablo and Bill to Lanny, who was constantly uttering disillusioned phrases, making me happy that I was free of him. Bill smiles. How easily he took me away altogether from Lanny—but who will take me away from Bill, away from the love for which my body would be sacrificed, for there is no place for it? When he finds the woman who is his age, I will have to leave him. Bill has great strength, but not enough to be my lover.

I dreamed that Josephine, with her sexual aggressiveness, took both Pablo and Bill away from me. About Pablo I didn't mind, but Bill... Monday night when I left at nine o'clock to meet Gonzalo, Bill was uneasy. "Where are you going?" I returned at eleven. Because of Bill, I began to suffer from Josephine's caressing of all of them, but he did not respond to her endearments. Yesterday Josephine telephoned to take them out when I had to go to the press. It was such an effort to yield up Bill. I wept because I must surrender him...he cannot be mine. Surrender. I went to the press, returned at five-thirty, and Bill was there. He had not gone with Josephine and Pablo. He had called the press. He was looking at my photographs, and he said, "I wanted you here." Such an élan towards each other. I made tea, and we sat on the couch. We lay back on the cushions, so near to each other, talking. He asked me, his face close to mine, "What did you say last night about me...who was nearest to you?"

"You were."

We touched hands. I touched his hair and he caressed mine. It was like a trance in which we kissed violently, violently, and his kiss was a man's. Bill. Hugo was on his way home, and I had to break away. I did not dare be happy because I have such a fear of pain. I was afraid of Bill's reaction, which was one of sadness, not ecstasy. Was it guilt? I could not tell. This morning he was sad, not knowing why. Is it all lost? Too great a burden for his youth? I wait, all day. What does he feel? I cannot tell.

That afternoon, when I returned home from the press, I found Pablo asleep on one couch and Bill awake on the other. I sat on Bill's side and said, "I will put you to sleep," and stroked his hair. He lay so quiet I thought he was asleep, but then he opened his eyes.

"You didn't fall asleep, Bill."

"I can't with you so near," he said. I kissed his hair, then his temples, and it was he who took my mouth in his beautiful, wide, generous lips, so full and red. We kissed deeply. He kissed me as in possession, fully, strongly. When Pablo awakened, we separated. It was the day before this that Pablo was taking a sun bath on the roof, and Bill again kissed me. We stood for a moment together, kissing wildly, and I pressed my whole body against his, swayed against him. I felt his sex rigid against me and felt such joy at his desire and maleness. But how afraid I was of his fears, of his retractions. How I held my intensity in check, amazed that from such frailness and youth desire could emerge, his body slenderer than mine, with his woman's skin, his hands more delicate than mine.

Then yesterday, Easter Sunday, Pablo and Hugo were away. I wore my white kimono. Bill came. Would he be afraid?—no, he lay on the couch. We played at my putting him to sleep, and when I kissed him tenderly, he answered sensually. His whole face was luminous and mystical, but his mouth is so sensual. I lay at his side. He kissed me profoundly. And again I felt his innocence, the passive pause before the unknown.

I whispered, "Am I your first love, Bill?"

"*Oui*," he answered softly. "Take your clothes off."

I opened my kimono and took off my panties. He lay over me, his desire erect. He penetrated me. Then he lay still. I moved slightly, rhythmically. He lay inside of me, and after a while his strength withered. But he continued to lie over me, and I knew it was only the beginning, that he would be strong. When we lay quiet and I had closed my kimono, I said, "I will go and dress." He said: "No, don't dress. Stay this way." And he unbuttoned my kimono, and with his soft, beautiful, golden hands, he caressed my breasts, my hips, my belly, and then my sex. His desire rose and he entered me again. How sweet and tender, how warm it was. Making man, creating man, giving birth to man. The child becoming man in the mother's womb. His childlike abandon, his newborn strength.

After our first kiss, he dreamt that his father and mother came to take him back and that he rebelled and refused to return with them, insulted his mother.

I wanted so much to be his first love. I act like a very young mother, not overwhelming. I hold my ecstasy, my desire, within the boundaries of his youth. Such a mysterious act has taken place, a love between Bill's unconscious, not yet born—the future Bill—and me. The present Bill is still a child, still blind ("How frightened I was the first time I came to see you"), but the deeper Bill obeys his mystical maturity. It is the unconscious Bill who shows us his extraordinarily beautiful face, the mystical knowingness. I saw the sensual Bill in his drawings and in his mouth. Danger. I took the risk of losing him. I wanted to be the initiator. He is my son, my lover, and his life will begin with wonder instead of poverty. It is as it should be, the initiation into creation and life together. May the love be sweet and painless. I am the giver of life. How I loved his delicate body, the gold down of his hair, his long, dark eyelashes, his hand over my breast.

Last night I had to go to see the Gendels. Hugo said he preferred to go to the movies. Bill and Pablo said they would go with me, but at the last moment Bill said he would stay and write. Hugo and Pablo left. Bill made me lie alongside of him. He put the radio on. We fell into caresses and an orgy of kisses, for a long, long time. Shyly, his hands caressed me, shyly but knowingly. He loves to caress my sex. I cannot abandon myself to the pleasure because I feel he is not ready for the storm of the climax. Silently, entranced, we kissed and caressed. The sweetness is overwhelming. The child and the man. A child who enters your being by softness, and a newborn man who asserts himself when he says, "I want you!" We took our clothes off at the end, and lay body to body, his sex erect, and he spilled his seed too soon, against me, not inside of me, so that I felt the warm rain over me. But the sweetness, the sweetness. What strange joys, joys of birth, joys of erotic motherhood, his *angoisse* when I go out. When I went to the Gendels at eleven so that Hugo would know I had been there, Bill went to Frances's and tried to telephone me so that I would leave. I had mentioned the Gendels having invited a man who wanted to meet me. Bill asked me over the telephone when I got home, "What did the man do?" His insecurity, his mind, and Hugo's suffering because, "Bill will grow up, return in a uniform, a man, and you will love him."

I have no time for Lanny, who is courting me again, who wants to reawaken my love. I have put my love in Bill's hands with trust in his hidden, unborn unconscious self whom he does not yet know. His love for me is unconscious, blind. In consciousness, he is a child, confused, inarticulate, reserved, separated. I go to Gonzalo and fulfill the unfinished sensual act, carrying in my body the warm caresses of Bill. I have the child inside me: Anaïs, the undying adolescent who persists in living out this relationship with another child. Bill looks at times like a young Rimbaud.

Hugo is suffering, and together we have discovered that all through the past his "deadness" was a secret, mute jealousy. I found the words to console him, but I cannot stem the flow of love. I drift, float, cannot work or write. I live like a flower now. I cannot hold back, direct, guide, or stop this flow of life. Hugo loves me for it and suffers from it. I love his concentration on me, but it is a burden. I carry this love with Bill like a precious seed of youth and creation. It is a sweet, sweet lover lying upon my breast.

Yesterday I had to meet Lanny for a cocktail at six and the others at seven for dinner and a play. I felt Bill's uneasiness. When we all met for dinner, he was depressed. We came back to my place because the Lorca play was so badly acted we could not stay. Lanny danced with me. Pablo danced with me. Bill had taken a cardboard sign that reads "Reserved" from the theater and placed it on my couch-bed (he always waits in my corner) and was silent. Lanny left early. Pablo began to talk to me about his passionate love affair at fifteen with a woman of thirty. Suddenly Bill got up and, barely saying good-bye, left. I rushed to him. At the door he was trembling. I begged him to tell me why he was leaving. He kissed my hand and left.

A while later, I went to Frances's and knocked on Bill's door. We sat on his bed. He did not know the cause of his sadness, or at least if he did, he would not admit it. I feared guilt and withdrawal, but I realized it was jealousy after he became happy when I showed my love and lay at his side, lulling him. He kissed me deliriously. He embraced my whole body. He was desirous and passionate, but it was midnight and

Hugo was waiting for me. He knew I had left to talk to Bill, and I could not stay. But Bill held me, kissed me, clung to me, would not let me leave. For the first time I allowed myself to feel the joy and passion his love gives me, and for the first time I felt sure of his love, and I felt the ecstasy. We clung and kissed. When I finally got up to powder and comb my hair, he stood behind me. I turned. We stood kissing with complete abandon, desire against desire, his sex against mine, until we were dizzy.

Frances walked back with me. She told me how Bill spent hours looking at my photograph, how restless he is when away from me, how lost he is in his dreams, how clearly in love he is. How beautiful this love is. I am living my life over again, the life that was battered at every turn. This is my second life. I begin again, but not as before, in tragedy and fear. I am Bill's age, before Hugo came to hurt and shock me with his fear and his flight from me. I am seventeen again as I was when I could not touch Eduardo. And now I have a lover who has the face of a mystic and a fiery body. I am blessed in this second life with the joys I did not have, the power I did not have, the deeper freedom I did not have. By my suffering, I have earned this second life. In this life, at this moment, there is no Eduardo and no Hugo—only Bill.

At Bill's first withdrawal I felt deep anguish, fearing his guilt. One Sunday morning I went to his room to awaken him. We lay naked together and he spilled his seed over my body, too soon, before entering me. His silence, his heart beating, and his hands cold, his childish, delicate, knowing hands. The next day he was moody. He teased me, contradicted me, was perverse and difficult. When Josephine brought me closed tulips and I opened them gently to make them seem like esoteric flowers, he reacted strongly against me. I felt all is lost. He feels he is the flower that was opened too soon, too swiftly. We talked, and I was truthful. He said, "I am full of resentments," but he did not know why. And I, fearing his guilt, misinterpreted it all—Frances had said the opening of the flowers was his opening *me*, his guilt for opening *me*, that the young believe the sexual act is an act of cruelty. In the maze of his childish unknowing and confusion I tread so delicately.

"Is it that you cannot bear the burden of becoming a man?"

"I don't know."

"Do you want to give me up?"

"No, I want you."

"I'll wait now, until you come to me."

He let me leave, kissed me chastely. I went out and wept in the street because I fear my destiny and its fatalities. I thought him lost. I felt the loss of his sensual mouth, the mouth I have loved most of all, the loss of his paleness, his delicate hands, his voice, his brilliant smile, his beauty, his boy's body. I came home to be consoled by Pablo's warmth. I went to Frances, who talked about my "loving the man to be," never living in the present, and suffering from what the present is until the dream is fulfilled.

With pleasure, I hurt Lanny, retaliated against his weakness and discarded him. "I love Bill and I cannot love you." Then Bill sat by my side and we talked. I began to sense a deep, deep jealousy which was the basis for the moods, the flight, the resentments. For him it was "only a cloud." He retained his mystery. He is the closed flower, giving but a petal at a time, his mouth above all. We kissed, kissed, kissed, and the delirium returned. We kissed, body against body, his sex erect against mine, his mouth voracious, and the joy returned, life returned.

Josephine came. We danced. Bill, who can dance, now danced with me. Pablo got tired of Josephine's silliness. So our little feasts of magic continue. Bill cut a silver bird out of foil and hung it on a thread from the ceiling. It turns at every breath of air, and he painted it with phosphorescent paint, as well as the tapestry, the lighthouse, the benches, so when we turn out the lights the place glows. Magic. Duits comes. He and Bill invent a duel of fluid forms with a tiny tape measure, which looks as if they were dueling with lightning. The atmosphere is elusive, gay and free, impossible to describe except as magical. When people come, Bill pastes a little piece of mirror between my eyes. He pastes silver paper over my toenails. He paints my legs with gold. He bites my fingers. He cuts copper and tin foil to make earrings. Pablo makes a clay figure, writes twenty pages of his experiences. The music pours out. We dance. My love for Gonzalo is dying.

There is no love on earth for me without anguish, no love without fears and doubts. Bill is naturally passive like a child, and I need an active love. I suffer because my ecstasy is restrained by the measure of what he can answer and bear. It is not the love for me. I know it. But it gives me mystical and selfless joys—to create him, to free him, to see him bursting from his shell, to see him laugh and be natural. I cannot understand how my new life could lead me to this, to a greater, more selfless love, to the child. Yet I feel a lightness too, a youthfulness, a beginning, without knowing the meaning. Frances says I love the future Bill, the older Bill with that mystical, sensual light in his face. He will travel. He will be a great lover. He will pursue mirages, as I did. This vision illumines my love, and this love takes place in the future. That is why no one understands it, not even Bill himself. It is a lonely love, one he will know later.

April 15, 1945

The new life is different: what I fear does not come to pass. The birth of man in my arms gives me such joy. Bill has become a passionate lover. We begin to talk, but he wants caresses, kisses, bites. We lie naked in his little bed. He takes me. I whisper: "Love is like a dance. Move inside of me." Like a shy new dance, the beginning of love, the rhythms of love, move, move, the dance of lovemaking, the marvelous young dance of love. When I think he is exhausted and asleep, he continues to kiss me, to lie over me, and we fall into a trance, half asleep, and again he becomes warm and full of desire, and he takes me again, rhythmically, and his warm blood flows into me.

His awakening power fills me with ecstasy, such ecstasy. And afterwards, no sadness, but lightness and strength. He recites French poetry. He runs up the five flights to my apartment, and makes me run. Joy. I am more romantic than my lover. He has a certain sardonic humor, like Henry's, a sense of caricature, a criticalness in general, which is alien to me. But sensually and mystically we are alike. He brings me back to the depths with his seriousness. He loves Bach and Modigliani's painting. My happiness this afternoon was that of giving birth to the man, and to my own second adolescence, my own early faith before the great pains shattered me. I am whole again.

April 17, 1945

I can hardly believe in my happiness with Bill, whose passion mounts day by day, who expresses it, who is impulsive, who, when we are about to go out, begins to kiss me and does so for an hour until we have to lock the doors and windows and get under the covers naked, who becomes more active, firm and potent, not only once but a second time, bathing in desire, in endless kissing and caresses, and soon he will be strong enough for me to have pleasure. And his gayety afterwards, his teasing, or standing on his head, his gayety as we go down the stairs arm in arm, or when I run up the five flights I could barely climb before.

To see Bill's strength being born! Such a joy! Love is my heaven and my hell, my all, my climate, my life.

April 20, 1945

Just after our hour of passion the other day, Edward Graeffe telephoned. Bill was lying by my side. He encircled me with his arms, and his hand teasingly pushed against my stomach to stop my voice from answering. He placed his small, delicate ear against mine near the phone: he listened. And after a while he said, "Who was that?" The memory of his hand on me has not left me since. I feel the imprint of it. It was the sign of his possession of me, the sign of his appropriation, of the magic stamp, for I felt his hand on me like that of a child, abandoned, trusting, helpless, and yet also like that of the lover, holding and encircling. At that moment I became his prisoner, and I had no desire to see Edward, as I have no desire to see Lanny. Bill, who, with his wild blond hair, his drugged face, his white silk scarf, his aristocratic carriage, his constant oscillations between childhood and manhood, learning engraving in one lesson from Hugo, quick and dexterous with his hands, wanting the experience of drunkenness after the exultancy of his virility, getting drunk at Frances's, then coming to me the next morning sick, to be taken care of. Oh, the yearning over his growth, his feebleness, his anxieties, and the nurturing of his strength. I feel full and complete as he lies in me as only the child can lie. What I wanted of the lover was this child lying in me, becoming man while he lies in the womb. Such sweetness, such twinship, in the shape of his hands, in his slenderness, in his druggedness and trances, his losing himself in sensation. My animus, my poetic male soul. He begged to see what I had written in the diary. I read him the first few pages, enough to satisfy his need to know how I saw him, but he himself stopped me, understanding what I said, that the diary would be destroyed if I opened it to others, for its mystery must be maintained so that I may go on telling the truth. Opening it kills it. He feels this, but he also feels embarrassment at seeing himself. Yet he says if he hypnotizes me he will make me open the safe and he will read them all. There is in his face the mysterious light of Neptune.

I see now the role of personal responsibility in destiny, but I also see the part of destiny which is beyond my power. I had the power to enchant Bill away from his home, his parents, his security, to win his love, to give him life and creation, but not to keep him from war. And so on May 8 he has to leave, and I will lose him.

A terrible revolt shook me today, a revolt against pain and my tragic destiny. All the time I had Pablo and Bill, I could not enjoy them because of Hugo's "crisis" of jealousy, this after he had said to me: "I cannot expand. I can only contract. You have to do the expanding for me. I accept this. It is good for us to have Pablo and Bill." The moment of carefree pleasure is in the past, and now we come upon another obstacle: the money debacle, the payment for all the dreaming. Once again reality destroys all life, all dreaming. An end to parties, hospitality, expansiveness.

Bill's mother sought an interview with him. He went, and I spent the evening suffering with anxiety.

Bill, my love, I write this for you tonight while I wait for you to return from your parents, for you to read when you feel alone. I feel the deepest sadness at your leaving, and I want you to know it. The day you came to my house, you walked deeply into my being, and a dream began which we must protect against the world. We must fight against separation. Remember that in your moments of conflict you tend to destroy, to condemn, to move away from what you dream, want and possess in your own self. Remember that in you, love is not continuous or harmonious, but full of breaks. Half of you is at war with the other half. Remember that I represent the deepest layer, the one that will have the greatest difficulty in asserting itself. In your withdrawal from your unconscious—your moon—you will also withdraw from me, because I am your moon. I understand this. Your greatest need is for integrity and unity. Trust in me, and my love will help you in this, for it is without breaks or oscillations. My love is the great separator and isolator. Feeling is the only unity we have…it makes for wholeness…

Bill saw his mother, passed the test and holds on to his freedom. Then today his father called him "to discuss his future." They want to do the best for him, to save him from being drafted into the army, to forestall it, but in so doing relieve their anxiety over the decadent group he has fallen into. I gave Bill a dream, and the world says I have corrupted him. I gave him strength and love, and now I must surrender him.

APRIL 22, 1945

Last night I seriously contemplated suicide, because what I most want in the world, the only thing that counts, my deepest need, my obsession, is the dream of love, and that I cannot possess but intermittently. I want it all, a continual, frenzied, full orgy, even if I must pay for it with my death. I feel I should leave Hugo, who represents protection against death, but also restriction and oppression. I feel I should surrender everything to my dream and be willing to die for it (because I cannot stand on my own feet without protection). Without Hugo, I would have lived like the romantic poets and been consumed. He has rescued me and restrained me, has been my counterbalance, but he is also the dead weight, the oppressor. If I could only have given myself completely to each dream, or lived alone in order to have been totally Bill's while he was here, if I could have only given way to the intensity and the Neptunian urge that is my life…and my death. If I cannot fulfill this because of my weakness ("your anemia," Hugo always reminds me), I instinctively feel dangerously unsettled and trapped. I cannot bear the restrictions, Hugo's temperamental opposition to the marvelous atmosphere of the house this month. He is hopelessly heavy. His attempts to dance are heavily grotesque. He is grotesque. His weight is always present. The magic is destroyed even though he protects it. He has admitted his cruelties towards me, which I have felt but never admitted, not even to myself. He gives me liberty by word of mouth, but in a subtle, oriental way, he retracts what he gives. He loaded me with guilt with his brooding severity and gloomy inertia. He never did accept me totally, yet he did not surrender me. He wanted me to be what I was, yet he constantly restricted what I needed to be. "*I can't breathe*," I cried out when he threatened to eliminate Pablo and Bill and the beautiful activity of the house. "I would rather die than live as you do." Yet without him, without Saturn, what am I? I fulfill men's dream of love today as no woman can. I want to give myself to this. I want more of it. I want to live altogether for it. Oh, god, give me freedom. Give me freedom. Freedom!

Hugo sits before me. The father. Again I recoil from his desire. I am like a dancer who has to constantly force herself to merely walk. Reality. I came close to it last year, and I hated it. I recoiled from it. My dreams are greater, deeper. And if to fulfill them I must die, I would rather die, but not slowly with only intermittent loves and passions— no, by a vast fire! To die for the dream which reality destroys is right for me. Reality and the dream are hopelessly opposed, irreconcilable. I choose the dream. Bill saw me in his dream as a little nymph running naked in the forest. I see already in the past the luminous afternoon when Pablo and Bill painted the tapestry, when Pablo wrote the colorful history of his life, decorated a bottle, made collages and drawings, when Bill wrote and engraved, cut a firebird out of metal that hangs from a thread from the middle of the studio and turns in the air. I had come back, running, from the press at four to make tea and honeybutter. In the past already is the time when Pablo became *de trop* because Bill and I wanted to kiss each other, and then the restlessness, the stolen kisses in the kitchen, in the bathroom.

APRIL 25, 1945

As the love grew in beauty and strength, the obstacles threatening it grew too. Bill began to sense the tragedy of our separation. He became more intense, more demonstrative. He gave himself wholly. He uttered words of love (he, the silent one). One evening at seven we were alone and were going to the ballet together. I was dressed. We were smoking our last cigarette when suddenly Bill put his hand on my breast and said: "I don't want to go to the ballet. I would rather stay here with you." We became passionate, but Hugo came home for dinner and we had to go out. We saw the ballet. It was beautiful, sad, symbolic, *Pillar of Fire*.

But on our way out we, with our hands interlaced, arm under arm, ran into Gonzalo walking with two Spanish friends. I knew this would provoke a crisis of jealousy. Worse still, the next afternoon Bill came eager and impatient to caress me, possess me, and I had to telephone Gonzalo to give him an excuse for not going to the press. At six Gonzalo telephoned me and said that he wanted to break our relationship. I went downstairs and found him beside himself with jealousy. "The way you walked with that young man was like two people in ecstasy. I know." I denied everything, quietly, quietly, quietly weeping for the sadness of it all, over the sadnesses, the deaths of love, the pain it causes. Today he was gentle again, and had accepted all my explanations. But oh, the turmoil yesterday in the magic studio, with the silver bird turning in mute circle flights, the phosphorescent planets glowing, in opposition to the subterranean jealousy of Hugo, to Gonzalo storming downstairs in the rain, to Bill's father invading Frances's home to see where his son was staying and threatening to harm the woman who had incited his son away from home. "If you get into trouble," said Bill's father to Bill, "I will get all these people into trouble." Power against spirit. His power is frustrated with his deepest wish, for he has lost his son. There is the danger of scandal for all of us, the danger of Hugo losing his job, of my being sent out of the United States. Already Bill's father has harmed his teacher at Yale, Wallace Fowlie, by accusing him of corrupting the morals of the young, including Bill, by giving them books by Miller and myself to read. I wanted to face the tyrant and risk destruction. I didn't want to bow down, or Bill to bow down. I felt the time has come to pay with my life for my beliefs and what I represent. I am ready. I am ready to be burnt at the stake. I said to Frances, "One instant of romantic life is worth all of life itself. I am willing to pay." Frances tried to dissuade me, and Tom went to see the father and talked calmly and gained his confidence. His hatred of me is there, but the lightning was averted in time. Frances said that in reality I have never come so close to catastrophe. The cost of living out a dream is so great, so great.

This morning I felt overwhelmed, but after we heard the father had recanted the harm done to Fowlie, Bill and I were ecstatic and again plunging into passion. Yesterday, before the threats, I had felt my first orgasm in his arms, quietly, deeply, passively, in rhythm with his. We had consumed ourselves in caresses for an hour in the afternoon, and then, in fantasy, we walked through the studio under an umbrella "to Mexico," playing games, teasing, with little scenes of jealousy, with sadness when Fowlie's letter came. But the sweetness, the delicacies, the songs, the caresses, the games (he buttons and unbuttons my kimono with chop sticks). His clothes lie about the room, his drawings, his writings. The obsession and madness of love, its ecstasies, its laughter. He crushed me so hard with caresses, I said, "I'm going to come out thin as a wafer." He answered, "The better to commune with, my dear." Bill treats me playfully like some young animal, tries jiu-jitsu on me, hurts my arm, picks me up and carries me, is altogether disrespectful and calls me, laughing, "The weird Miss Pin" (as my name was misspelled on a card). Every time I get a letter, he opens the envelope and reads it. Every time I get a flattering letter he starts calling me Miss Pin, and thus he and Pablo place me in their youthful world and are amused, treating me like a child. Bill gets rough and tumble, and when we end up on the floor, he cries, "Look at the lady of the legend, look at her, so pleased with my fall into naturalness." I embrace him and say, "This is better than a legend." A human and natural atmosphere of play, full of ecstasy and *angoisse*, because it is so precarious.

Jealousies. When Bill's father visited Frances and we expected him to descend on us, I quickly took down the colored bird. When Pablo takes a photograph of me, Bill demands it back. He won't allow Pablo to possess a photo. Hugo made me copper earrings to outshine the ones made by Bill. A million jealousies keep me tense, for I am aware of all their feelings. All my men are so difficult to obtain, and so difficult to lose. I cannot lose Gonzalo. He clutches at me. So does Lanny Baldwin, who, because he is jealous of Bill, indebts me to him by helping me to do my book. The world of love, the drug, the spell. Frances and Tom watch over us, for Bill and I are entranced and out of reality, except in our caresses. With all his teasing, each time the moment for caresses arrives, Bill's heart beats wildly in his slender body, and I am so deeply moved. I lie so quiet, waiting, waiting for his delicate and dexterous hands to open my kimono, for his mouth on my throat. His is the most beautiful of all mouths I have known, his slender face so rich and sensual. The trance of the mouth, mingled with his incredibly tender skin, silkier than mine. The pauses afterwards, when he does not leave my body and lies over me, still kissing my shoulder. Our hypnotism, he calls it. Who hypnotized whom?

He was such a solitary boy, a rich man's son always at school, without warmth and affection. How he imbibes my sensual, maternal warmth, bathes in it, needs it. How will he live without it? He opened like a flower. How will I live without his caresses and the presence of his complex, mysterious moods so like my own, without the joy of his flowering? His hands, so sensitive and so strong. His frailty, like mine, concealing a strength and power. I love the child in him. The new, vehement young man devours me with kisses. How are we going to live without each other?

APRIL 29, 1945

Testament. What I most value, most want, I cannot have, which is a love without tragedy. I am haunted by sorrow and depression. I cannot bear any more sorrows. I have given enough, creatively, and in love I have given more than I have been given. I love more than I am loved. It is not enough. Nothing is enough, except death.

During Joaquín's quintet at the Museum of Modern Art, the sadness became unbearable. I cannot continue. I cannot rise out of this as I rose out of the Lanny failure, because I have to cut off something that is flowering. The loneliness. I cannot bear the loneliness. I am lonely with Bill, since because of his youth he cannot feel in proportion to what I feel. I am lonely because the mental life in him is stronger than the emotional. It is his mind he uses, his instinct, but not his feelings. I always love the one whose feelings are not as strong as mine. It is my own emotional nature which will kill me, for it rules me, blinds me, sways me, torments me. I feel weak and powerless. It all becomes unreal, and it all dies. Bill looks like the moon, pale and dead, because he is staying with his family for two days.

APRIL 30, 1945

Will I break this time? Hugo takes me back, tenderly. Lanny stands by, gently paternal, admitting his imprisonment, speaking of the emotions that "choke" him, push the tears into his eyes, strangle him.

"It comes like a wave of ecstasy."

"The difference between you and me," I said, "is that I ride on this wave when it comes."

Lanny helps me, reminds me of my work, of my obligations. I have loaded Hugo with debts. I must repay him. I must bring the book out.

"We will help each other."

All my loves stand around me, for I am a suffering symbol of love in a world that is destroying itself with hatred.

Saturday Bill went home for the last days of his stay after his mother begged him, but he is plotting our Tuesday and Wednesday nights together (Hugo is going on a trip) like a mature man. Monday his father asked him to stay at home but allowed him to go out with a college friend to the galleries. I came home at five to talk with Frances, and Bill had arranged to get away. When Frances left, we fell into passion. Bill was expected home at six-thirty. At six, after arriving sad, dead, eclipsed, he began to kiss me and become alive...soft light kisses, brushings, at first, and then hunger. He opened his mouth and bit mine, made me lie down and opened my red robe. In this embrace we expressed all the love and passion and hunger. How can people set themselves against this completion of the dream, this transfusion of sweetness, this marriage act of skin and hair and blood and honey?

Martha is against it, and Frances.

Bill emerged gay and alive—a reprieve from death. I died while he was away, and he died in his home. He could not sleep. He sat dejected and dead. We danced down the stairs, his skin now roseate, his mouth red, his hair wild, his hands warm (they were cold before touching me). And I felt ecstasy, and yet an acceptance of the sorrow.

Frances is proud of herself for not having desired Bill.

I am proud to have given him all and to have received all.

Frances has protected our love, but she does not believe in passion. She believes in its denial, as Martha does, and their rationalization is that it causes pain.

Greater pain is caused by negation and denial of passion.

MAY 1, 1945

A day of happiness. I await my young, ardent lover. He came a while ago, gay and demonstrative, laid his head on my breasts and said: "Do you know what I don't like about Frances? She is too matter of fact, too heavy-handed. She lets nothing rest. Why isn't she as you are…more flighty…more moody." I laughed at the word "flighty," but knew what he meant.

He brought me a photograph of himself.

It is raining. He will come soon for the whole night. We will sleep all night together. A day of happiness. A night of happiness. Remember, Anaïs, when you want to die, this is enough and is worth the death in between.

MAY 2, 1945

I lie in bed with my drug (my love), and my diary (the reflections of my love, my life, to remember, to hold, to relive each hour of fulfillment).

Last night: stretched at Bill's bed, reading, and Bill's little game of flirting with the big moments of passion, his *jeune fille* evasions and retractions, holding me off, reading, making me read, and listening to music. Not abandoning himself instantly to the moment, to the fire, but I, having learned to play this game, lie still, wait until the lights are out and we find our slender nakedness in the dark.

He asks me afterwards: "Were you happy? I never know whether I'm a good lover…"

"I told you that you were naturally gifted," I said.

But then I knew the time had come to teach him more, so I said, "You must learn to prolong the pleasure, to hold back so it will last longer." And when he awakened this morning, he drew me to him, took me again, lingering, waiting, and I had with him a perfect rhythm of fusion and pleasure. Such joy and peace afterwards. I believe in passion. It makes one pure and chaste afterwards. It is a fire which purifies. I am at peace tonight, full of love and without anxiety. I await him.

I can even think of my work and its meaning. I feel I approach the same truths discovered by scientists with art and writing—for instance, Reich and his *Function of the Orgasm*. My function is to present these truths I hit upon long ago in the form of art—for example, the idea of describing and discovering character by observing gestures, behavior, occupation and its sexual meaning (as I described Lillian by her anxieties and achieved a picture of unfulfillment). My task is to give an art form to the new scientific discoveries in psychology. Reich's entirely new theory concerns the relationship of masochism and the pleasure principle, and I discovered for myself that pleasure comes from the realization and the pain of tension. I have been for the greater part of my life in a state of tension and, therefore, pain. Only recently have I achieved a more continuous state of relaxation and, therefore, pleasure (and the orgasm). This relaxation I first encountered in Henry, and for this reason he was able to give me the best of my pagan life…he relaxed me. Anxiety destroys this.

For a moment I thought that the pain of losing Bill would kill me. Now I have accepted it, perhaps because I believe in it and believe it will continue. (Or is it that love will continue? Or that I must surrender Bill soon anyway so he can find a girl his age?) Last night, falling asleep, he talked about his novel about a youth who finds a world he rejects (the world of Yale, of his family, of his former friends).

"Would I like Miss Nin?" asked his mother. "You are poles apart," answered Bill.

MAY 5, 1945

A few days ago, Frances's mood changed from softness and sympathy to sharpness and irony. Bill felt the change. I intuitively felt this: When Frances said, like Martha, I should not sexualize everything, and that she had a beautiful relationship with Bill, intellectual and pure, which could last forever, I felt that this was untrue, that she was jealous of the passion. I answered: "Well, we each got what we wanted. I wanted passion." The afternoon I said this, Bill had come to my place. Tom and Frances were there. I wore my red Chinese robe, long, flowing, with gold buttons and full sleeves. Bill had come from his home, depressed. Tom and Frances left at six. At six-thirty he was due home, but he stayed and made love to me, and when we separated, we were elated. Yesterday I saw Frances in her home. She wore a pale blue flowered robe. I said, "How nice you look in your blue robe." She answered ironically: "In frigid blue, in my frigid blue robe. I should wear a red robe." The red robe of passion?

On Bill's pale face, there is the sign of passion. What binds us is an oriental, voluptuous quality, trance-like lovemaking, charged with dreaming and silence and rich transmissions. He, the remote one, so rarely near human beings, is caught in a trance of warmth and nearness. How can anyone dare to reject the experience of physical union, which is the completion of everything? They all suffer from the denial of this. I know now it is right. I regret no physical gesture ever made. My only regrets are for those I did not make fully, completely, because my anxieties destroyed my enjoyment and the full taste of sensuality. I regret no gesture made to connect with human beings through the great beauty of the body.

The idea that lovemaking is like a dance animates Bill's young, passive, timid body—he moves with the dance, takes, holds, feels, touches, plunges, discovers.

Yesterday afternoon at Frances's, while she was out, Bill took me to his little room and possessed me twice, fully, drawing from me a flower-like orgasm of the purest pleasure. The softness of our skin will soften the words between us. The coldness of his hands, of his rhythmic withdrawals, will find warmth in my body. I no longer suffer from his rhythm of abandon and withdrawal. I understand it. I also understand the limits of his physical power and how he instinctively refuses to face its limit, holding himself from a consummation he cannot withstand. And I have tuned myself to his energy, to his youth, to his power, to his rhythm. "How alike we are," he says. His emotional nature is clouded at times, but it shines through in possession. In this he dissolves and burns. Then he emerges cool and detached. His mind assumes control again, and it is all clear and no longer hurtful to me. I feel peace. I feel confidence. I feel rich.

And I fall asleep dreaming of his orientation, dreaming of how I am living with the future Bill no one yet knows, with his royal aristocratic traits, his aristocratic ways, the young man who, discussing with Hugo the men who ruled the small kingdoms of India, or Hugo's friend who ruled Tunisia "temporarily," to which Bill said arrogantly, "But I will rule permanently." He dreams of the Orient, he dreams of a power that is both mystical and of the world. All this I see and live with in actuality, whereas for others it is in the future. As a woman I like to give him a feeling of leadership. I like to yield to him because it helps the man to be born, and he likes to be tyrannical and possessive. I let him bite my fingers, hurt me, because it pains him and then he kisses these same fingers with tenderness. He has tested his power, and he can now show his love. The true woman knows when to let the man feel his power so that he will grow strong. Bill will be one of my most wonderful creations. My Neptunian child, visionary and instinctive. Suddenly he performs mature, assertive acts, surprising ones of pure instinct. It is while lying naked over me he telephones his father, holding me in his power, as if confronting his father with the victory of his manhood. His father's voice asks severely, "Where are you?" And Bill is satisfied with this as I was satisfied, like an oriental, by my unexploded, silent, secretive revenge and rebellion against those who hurt me. Now he refuses to be with Hugo. His jealousy of Hugo is open. While meeting Chinchilito for lunch today, I wore Bill's white scarf as a shield against temptation.

MAY 6, 1945

Last night suffering at Bill's leaving. He went to his parents' with his valise and I don't know if we can meet again before he leaves.

Put away the toys, the scattered records, the box with the phosphorescent paints, the copper, the scissors, the watercolors, the half-finished earrings, the colored glass. Put away the copper plates, the prints, the poems, the scrap papers, notes, sketches. Bill's poem: "This day / this hour / a dancer / circles in the room. / This flesh / this sound / our life / this round / a secret still simoun / our sigh / our sighs / draw close / and bind us / ask why / I know / it's here / the answer."

MAY 7, 1945

This afternoon Bill telephoned me from Frances's to say he would not be over to see me until four o'clock. I felt such pain at not having him all afternoon, so I called him back and said that his last afternoon belonged to me, and that rather than seeing him so late, I'd rather not see him at all. His answer is always to call me "Stella" (from the novel in which I describe Luise Rainer's doubts). But he came. The misunderstanding was cleared. He has the same reactions, the same doubts as I.

I said to him, "So you must understand mine."

His answer was, "Mine are childish—and so are yours."

Then, because he had a cold and is weakened physically for a day or two after our last passionate afternoon, we sat quietly and had our first clear, deep talk on writing, on the writing of the future. I inspired Bill with the possibilities. Then I spoke of Neptune, the subtle, intangible rapport between us, for which we have used so few words. I realize my love for Bill is greater than his for me, so I would not dare to follow Bill anywhere, for fear of not being loved enough. (Perhaps it is because I cannot believe in anyone's love but Hugo's, whose way of loving is like mine.) I have made no progress in confidence. My feelings, love and faith in others are strong, but not my faith in their love. I have suffered at Bill's first sadness after our first kiss, at his moods of detachment and remoteness, at his brusque manners and cautious statements, his measured words, his rhythmic expansion followed by contraction, his passion followed by coldness. He is not continually human or warm. I realized suddenly that during possession he can be passionate and physically warm, but not in between. What a strange, painful destiny mine would be. I now see that the only person who matched my sensual self was Henry, in extravagance, in love of the orgy, and in potency. The only one who matched my emotional nature in intensity and violence was Gonzalo, in his outbursts and explosions. The only one who matched my protective form of love is Hugo. The only one who matched me mystically was Jean.

With Bill it is both the mystical and physical, but there is no emotional tie. He subdues me emotionally with his reserve and inexpressiveness.

Tonight I feel a sadness deeper than death. I return slowly to Hugo, whom I hated for a month, to ask his forgiveness. I return to Gonzalo. They are both aging, as I am not aging. But I am so weary of pain.

MAY 9, 1945

Bill came this afternoon. Twice now, we have had an exchange of ideas. I gave him my essay on Rank to read and my "Women in Creation" from the *American Quarterly*.

When it is time to separate, we fall into passion. How I love the feminine abandon of his face, its softness, its meltingness. He closes his eyes. He yields. We fall into a trance of mouth hunger, then it is the cool tenderness of his skin, his pale, drugged face, and his hands, so deft, delicate, like a musician's, timid, faltering, but gifted for caresses, opening the skirt, and then nakedness, his new knowledge of timing, postponement, lingering, profusely enriched with kisses. We are under the knitted blanket, heads and all. The little holes of the knitting are like mosque grills. Under this we lie, his body over mine, slender, delicate, long, fitting so close together, our two identical waists, our lean hips, our long legs, our silky skins. No violence. Voluptuousness. He sinks into caresses. He falls asleep. Then he takes me again. I am prepared now for his detachment and cloudiness when he arises, for the break that takes place, his contractions after abandon.

Frances is right that the anxiety I feel is caused by guilt, because he is a child and I am a woman, the active one, and that is destructive. He is feminine and passive, and wants me to assume all responsibility to free himself of guilt, and I feel the anxiety. I want a love without anxiety, without uncertainty.

To each illusion I give a kind of absolute love, intense, too intense, when my feelings are involved. Why can't I be lighter, enjoy Graeffe, not become attached, remain free? I have not been free. I gave my all to Bill. I abandoned Hugo and Gonzalo, my work, Graeffe, Lanny, all my friends. Bill. His pale, pale face, his hair falling over his eyes, his voice grown rich (the first time I heard his voice it was dead).

Dream: A ballet is taking place, and everybody is wearing highly colored costumes. There is a choice to be made between red and yellow chiffon. Yards and yards of both colors lie draped for me to choose from. I choose red unfalteringly.

MAY 12, 1945

Hugo is almost always in a continuous depressed state, grey, dim. He has a silent, subconscious way of making me feel guilty for my expansions. His weapon is guilt over the money spent. Now, when it is jealousy and fear of losing me, I understand and sympathize with him, but this does not apply only to Bill (or whomever he is jealous of), but to all my friends. He does not evince interest in anyone, in nothing, not even his fellow engravers. In fact, he has no friends but me. He wants to come home, eat quietly, read his paper and go to sleep, sometimes right after dinner. After a week of this, I get ill, desperate and restless. I love people. How can I reconcile this radical difference in our temperaments? Eliminating Bill is not the solution. It doesn't solve my wanting to talk to Frances, to laugh with Thurema and Jimmy, to see Russian movies with Gonzalo, to dance with Pablo, to write with other writers, to walk down a sunny Fifth Avenue with Lanny. What compels me to expand is stronger than any oppression, but I have been choking for three days and nights from the lack of air with Hugo, his tightness. When it is jealousy, I feel compassion and I am ready to surrender. But when he says I should not publish my D. H. Lawrence book because he will be disgraced at the bank, or that he is driven to live a bourgeois life, then I lose my compassion and begin to suffocate. When he has a "fling," he gets an apartment at Mamaroneck such as his family would get, or he buys a car or a motorboat. I have been dependent on his kindness but emotionally submissive and in bondage to his tyranny. Each step of my liberation was a painful one. Expansion and contraction is a normal rhythm, like depression and elation, but Hugo is all contraction, all depression. I'm willing to have flings and then contract, work, pay debts, etc., but the expansion I will not surrender. I have given Hugo the largest portion of my life, the most basic one. He gave me all, but he demanded a sort of annihilation.

This morning we wept, quarreled, got hysterical. Hugo feels guilty for having constantly put the brakes on me, and, simultaneously, for wanting what I get by expansion. I feel guilty for having spent his money on my life (because he separated himself from all I did—Jean was the only one we shared). My only freedom came when he traveled. Since we live in New York, he not only does not travel, but he never leaves the house in the evening. I can't always meet my friends on the outside. If I go out, I must be home by twelve, apparently not to disturb the sleep which he needs, but actually, when he has fallen asleep and I have accidentally arrived late at one, he awakens to look at his watch and say, "You are late." Because I left him in the evening to go out with Gonzalo twice a week, he plays a game intended to make me feel that I abandon him. His fear of losing me was never open and clear. We lived for twenty years on the assumption that I was the fearful, unstable one, and Hugo was the confident one, not the neurotic.

Lately I have rebelled, in many ways. I have ceased to feel guilty even for the money I spend or give, for I could be spending it on clothes, playing cards, or as Hugo's mother and sisters spend theirs, on chichi, comforts, luxuries, etc. Twenty years ago Gonzalo chose his way of life, and nothing could stop it, no love, no human being. Henry made his choice, ruthlessly. I have tried to be human. I have admitted interdependence and interrelation. Hugo and I needed each other. Neither Hugo, nor Martha, nor anyone can imprison me. No one. When Bill hurts me now I feel detached. I move away. What lingers in me is Hugo's pain.

Bill and I get into all kinds of dissonance. When he is uneasy, does not feel well, or does not feel equal to the situation, he suggests we call Frances. I get hurt because he has just arrived, perhaps, and I want to see him alone. So I say: "You go to Frances. I have something else to do." Then he feels I don't want him, and he becomes sullen. If he reads, on the other hand, he won't talk. He is full of small cruelties. He burns my hair with his cigarette. His power is expressed with cruelty, autocracy, arrogance and demands. He has hardly any compassion, very little sympathy for others, a great deal of detachment. I need detachment, and I have gained in this. I became free and far from him in between times. I achieved this by not exacting and not idealizing, but slowly my power to exalt will be killed, and I shall hate those who helped kill it.

May 14, 1945

The tension grew so high between Hugo and me that he went to a hotel to get away from it. I spent the day with Bill and maintained my rebellion against Hugo's oppression. The next day I hardly saw Bill because he had to see his parents, and in the evening we all went to a dance recital. Hugo left for his hotel, and Bill would not come upstairs with me! The pain of this was unbearable. When I am not free, he wants me. When I am free, he perversely shrinks back. He kissed me goodnight, multiple kisses, like those of a child, and left me. He associates me with his passionate expansions and also with his withdrawals, instead of sharing peace and tenderness. I was completely shaken. And for this I was making Hugo unhappy. I thought I could live alone, without Hugo, and at a childish act I crumbled. I could not bear to face the empty night. I called the hotel before leaving the apartment at one-thirty. The sordid setting Hugo chose overwhelmed me. It was practically a hobo hotel, for men only. What masochism. I was not even allowed inside, but my inquiry over the telephone had brought Hugo down. I spied him, turned the revolving door fast and shouted into the lobby, "Hugo, come home!" He smiled with happiness. With Hugo back, I could sleep. Battered and defeated, I asked his forgiveness. He asked mine for oppressing me so.

This morning I went to awaken Bill. He was unaware of what he had done, was puzzled. But I had a desire to hurt him. I made him jealous, so easily, when I showed him a thirteen page letter I had received from a young writer in Richmond, who was on his way to New York just to see me. Bill became anxious. Then I went out with Gonzalo, and Bill thought I had gone out with the young man from Richmond. He asked me: "How was he? When is Hugo coming home?" I've lost interest. He is perverse and difficult, possessing a world of cruelties and perversities, of loneliness and terror. So today I feel cold and tired. I am ill (the same illness I had when Albert left). Any illusion of happiness with Bill is gone. *La passion est dure comme l'enfer.* In passion one must be hard, not deep. I will learn. Today I felt strong, but it was only because Hugo was there. I have no illusions about my strength. None.

MAY 17, 1945

Bill stayed long enough to break the illusion of nearness and understanding. His behavior, his whims, his changefulness, his fears, his selfishness, his insincerity, give me anguish. There was a mutual and inhuman fascination there, another mirage. When he paints a picture he tacks it over one of Frances's paintings, or one of Hugo's.

I can see what I dreaded: that the future of America is schizophrenic; the youth has been born dead at the roots of feeling. They can think, they can desire, take, absorb, but they cannot feel or give. They are automatons, born of Puritanism, of loneliness, of hardness and callousness of American life. Their souls are atrophied.

Miller was the first symbol of this I had encountered. Should I say America? My father was a schizophrenic. But it is America. Then what am I? An exaggerated, feeling nature, captured always by the non-human, by my compassion, for the isolated, the lonely, the cripples, the lost, and paying heavily for it. I can never answer this—it is the mystery of my life. Does my constant dissatisfaction with the love given to me proceed from my lack of confidence, or is it in reality less than what I give? Why do I feel Hugo is the only one who loves as I do and that even he loves me as he perceives me and not as I am? Why did I feel Henry's and all the others' love less than mine, and yet anyone who looks into my life will say I was greatly loved? I can see in my early diaries the disparity between the facts I note down faithfully and my reaction to them. I can see that. Then what is it I don't see today?

Is it neurotic of me to suffer because Bill has not been passionate for many days, or because he did not stay the other night when Hugo was away? Will I continue to suffer from anguish and uncertainty, because last night he said it was crazy for Thurema and Jimmy to marry due to the difference in age, that she would become old and withered? His egoism is like Henry's. He takes, he feeds, he absorbs, and he gives nothing. Yes, he is enchanted, as Henry was, but for his own pleasure and delectation, for his vanity, his pride, his future, and his creation. How can I ever enjoy my loves with this anguish corroding them all? I don't want to believe that this anxiety comes from the deep knowledge of illusion and mirages, for it seems to me that my mirages have often created miracles. What I pursue, which others do not believe in, has often materialized. If I surrender my power of illusion, I surrender my power of vision into what others do not see.

Now I come to the critical break with America. If I am convinced that the youth is schizophrenic and therefore dead at the roots and incurable, then I should not sacrifice myself to America. I want to leave it.

MAY 18, 1945

As inexplicable as nature's moods, Bill's suddenly melted into a flowing, illuminated sensuality. Yesterday afternoon while I wrote to detach myself, he was delayed when he had a quarrel with his mother, who reproaches him for his coldness, indifference, and his bored air at home. As he didn't call, I went to Frances. I also arranged to meet Gonzalo at Henrietta's place. (Now that we have no place to go, our meetings have been rare, and I wanted to reassure him, but I also need his great volcanic warmth again.) At Frances's, at four-thirty, Bill telephoned imperiously that he was waiting for me at my apartment. I returned. He was painting a watercolor. We talked. Because he had gone through the storm with his mother, I was gentle, tender and relaxed, concealing my hands which were trembling with the anguish of doubt of the love. I was thinking again of his need, not mine. He was tender, playful. He left regretfully at six. At seven he telephoned me: "My parents are going out for dinner. May I come down?" He came, embraced me, followed me into the kitchen. From his remoteness and silence, he becomes the golden boy, melting in gold light and softness, his hands so delicate on my skin, on my hair. I served him dinner. We lay down together. He read the papers and I the *Manifeste des Surréalistes*, which asserts all I assert: the right of the imagination.

It was eight-thirty, and Gonzalo was calling for me at nine. Bill left his paper, stretched, yawned and relaxed, slid down on the couch, laid his head against my stomach. He looked up at me. I know this look, this pose. It is a woman with a man's sex lying down, inviting caresses with the eyes, the eyelashes, the open flower face, the opened flower mouth. He lies there, inviting, timidly caressing my hair, his body nearer, melting, opening until I melted, burned, and fell into voluptuous kissing. I tried to extricate myself, reminding him the bell would ring, but his passion was aroused. And from passivity he suddenly emerged virile, lying over me, his sex hard against me, becoming willful. Why at the wrong moment, when I am not free? Remembering this capriciousness, I did not yield. When the time came, I left.

Gonzalo surprised me with a wild attack, with voraciousness and power like that of our first year together. He, who rarely shows sensuality of the mouth, now took my mouth for a long time. I answered, and the passage from one passion to another was made almost imperceptible, without shock or conflict, as if it were the same ocean. The distinctions efface themselves. Passion burns in all directions, in the past and the present. The silky, gold hair of Bill and Gonzalo's heavy, black, coarse hair; the silk feminine skin of Bill and Gonzalo's violent sandalwood skin; Bill's lightness, Gonzalo's heaviness.

I came home and fell asleep, dreaming that I met Henry's wife and liked her, free of all jealousy. Why can't I conquer my doubt of love, the source of all my anguish? Bill's behavior would not hurt me if I did not see it in terms of my doubts of love. He himself says, "You imagine things." Why? Why? Is that the brand, the scar of guilt? Is it guilt? Passion is my only certitude, and passion is nothing but the intensification of the love, the love forced by the obstacles, circumstances, outer pressure, to concentrate its force into one moment, therefore exploding and causing violent physical embraces.

In a few moments I have loved Bill as much as I have loved Hugo, or Gonzalo, or Henry. That is passion.

Friday afternoon we were together, and Saturday he left. He called me on the telephone and said, "I'm at the recruiting station and taking the train for Fort Dix at six." I wept. Then an hour later he appeared. He was free for a few hours. Half of the time we spent at Frances's, half here. I had to make him some supper. He was tender, playful, but afraid of our feelings. He lay over me and, like a true Anglo-Saxon, he said: "Now I want you to smile. I don't want you to get upset." And I obeyed. So we kissed, but not on the mouth, knowing the danger of this. And he left.

Seeing his laundry today, his small shirts, his small underwear, I experienced the abysmal yearning of the mother, tenderness and concern over his fragility in the army, over his being cold, over his food. A terrible, painful concern for his boy's body, so tall and underweight, his little boy's neck and ears. And yesterday, an hour after he left, I sobbed uncontrollably. I awakened to the memory of his mouth, and then I yearned for his caresses, his touch. Oh, the pain. I wanted to sleep, to become unconscious. Such a human, simple, deep pain. I hated the sunlight, a day I could not enjoy with him. He became small, frail, distant, and I empty and lost.

I went to the press and worked to tire myself. I slept. I could not climb the stairs. Oh, Bill, *mon enfant précieux*, my beautiful, voluptuous child.

If you are not neurotic, you are not fixed, caught, trapped in suffering. It does not become geological, pressing and oppressing the flesh into frozen layers, crystals of defenses, petrifying, arresting life. If you are not neurotic, the pain washes through you, absolute and terrible, from head to toes, dissolves you, and flows out again. You either die instantly, wholly, or you return to life. I have learned to suffer without dying. The being becomes accustomed, yields to the grief, cries, sinks, and then lives. What helped me was Bill's letter, like Henry's letter, without expression of feeling or loss. His child's letter quieted me and revealed the disproportion—oh, not in age, for at seventeen I was capable of pain, grief, loss, abandon to feeling. So I wrote him with a tender lightness, not fully charged with my love, but with gentle emanations, allegories, symbols. And then I returned to the surface, to the sun, to the summer. I opened the coffre with summer clothes and gave away old dresses associated with old pains, such as the green dress in which Albert possessed me for the last time. I began to live in the future, to surrender the depths where all suffering lies, the depths of attachments, the intensity. I have learned to suffer and to flow and live.

MAY 22, 1945

Il y a des souffrances vraies. True sufferings purify, like the excesses of passion, like the orgies of creation. I have my moods. When I receive his child's letters, their coolness subdues me, detaches me. When I went out onto East 13th Street, I was suddenly stabbed by the vivid image of his luminosity. The day he walked with me to get cigarettes on 3rd Avenue, he wore his white silk scarf negligently. It was a grey, cool day. He walked with me to the press. I saw him cross to the other side and walk away, the very symbol of poetry. He was marked as if by a drug, by an orientalism, a voluptuous mysticism, a blue light from not sleeping, those who dream at night and do not sleep deeply. He was marked for trances of unreality and for trances of the flesh. He was illumined by mysticism and a small, burning arc of desire. Was it symbolic that we spent our last minutes together comparing the twinship of our hands, their length almost the same, the slenderness of the fingers the same, the width of the wrist, the color golden, but mine more creamy, his of Anglo-Saxon milk whiteness, mine of ivory and ermine? Yet I must see not always into the future, not always into the deepest layers of people's beings…I must see the little child…

My *jeune fille en fleur*, my precious Bill, fainted when they gave him a needle thrust to test his blood. He is now trembling at the idea of more injections. And this is the child America sends to war. My love, *mon enfant précieux*, I am listening to music and thinking about how, in order to become a writer, you must learn to express your feelings, that this is linked with creation. Miller wrote because he was not repressed in any expression…he expressed all. I the same. The flow in the diary was the flow of response. Let your letters become the diary of your other self that is just being born, instead of a carapace, a disguise, an oblique evasion of your feelings and thoughts. You may say what you felt when you were *mon enfant précieux*. But you must seek to know, for it is in this tapping of the source that lies abundance. The secret of writing lies in your moods, your feelings, not in the exterior self. To stay near this inner self, either write your diary again, or write to me, since you know I love the Bill who slept in the little cot, the Bill who had a thousand moods in one second. Trust and confide, for that is writing. You intend to be a novelist, so open, expand, speak, name, describe, paint, caricature, say everything. Speak for your moods, make your muteness and silences eloquent.

Frances is studying my Rorschach test. The mind is fine and clear but has no power over emotional impulses. The emotional nature, the neurotic drives, sweep me away. I have floating anxieties, not schizophrenia, but hysteria. I must either act or use writing to prevent the explosions. Sexuality causes my anxiety and tension, but also relieves it. There are sadomasochistic tendencies, idealization of pains inflicted on me, and I give mystical explanations of my roles and destiny, mystical reasons for my sacrifices. I hold a romantic image of myself as from another world. It is this self I fear to open to the world, because when I do give it, open it to all, it gets shattered. I have no defenses against pain, no hostilities. It is in this alone I am passive. Wanting life and contact, I found no other way than that of pain—my ecstasies are rooted in pain. So I get shattered, and then my intellect comes to the rescue, or my capacity to yield to the direction of others (as I yielded to my analyst, recently to Frances when Bill's father threatened me, because I felt lost in a dream, a myth), or my creativity in which I manifest great active strength. But there is a strong, modern woman in me—if only she could act directly in the world, instead of obliquely. I did not face the world squarely, but created obscure, legendary writing. My protection is mystery and feminine elusiveness. There was a moment after analysis when I almost became the woman captain, integrated and strong, when I began to put my strength in writing, but then I met Lanny and Bill, and again my strength was dissipated in anxiety and in this painful love of the feminine man.

Will Bill be my last romantic love? When Bill left, I fought my pain with activity, but I also accepted the pain, wholly, emotionally, when it came. But now I face reality, problems, debts, the press, etc. The longest hours were his hours: at four, when I expected him for tea; at ten-thirty, when he would come from his parents' home. I miss him deeply, deeply. I hated Hugo violently last night when he took me. Somehow or other, there has been a break with Hugo. I feel far from him. I began to feel peace, to enjoy the peace, the freedom from anguish. I thought vividly of Bill's mouth, its richness, its loveliness of texture, the tender palpitations of his skin when he awaited the kiss, but I remembered the anguish of his failure to contain my full passion, my full strength. I remembered all the delicacies, the controls, the subduing, the way I had to hold back.

As in the Rorschach test, I get submerged by my emotions.

MAY 25, 1945

The day Bill left, Pablo and Duits telephoned. Pablo telephones every day. They all circle around me again now that Bill's jealousy does not close the door on them. I miss Bill deeply, abysmally. I wrote him a long, humorous letter yesterday. I think of him on awakening, during the day, and before going to sleep. I passed by his parents' home and was chilled at the gloomy, severe uniformity of Park Avenue, as if my luminous child escaped a prison but is now in another.

Shock yesterday with Martha. In her usual elephantine heaviness, she cornered me and said, "I had expected to have an intense, emotional relationship with you!" I said I had given all my love to Bill and that my women friends were resigned to my "disappearances" during times like that. But I did not save her feelings by disguising the truth to as I might have done before, because I felt she was committing a violation. She knows from analysis I have fervent friendships with women. I admitted to my acceptance of great differences of temperament. "But you don't know what a capacity for intensity I have!" This from an analyst. Supreme masochism, offering love where it is not wanted, not seeing, not feeling it is not wanted, forcing me to turn my eyes away with *pudeur* before her mental, psychological blunder. "This I no longer feel for women," I lied, "but only for men. Your life is different. I have begun a new way of life, not in reality or ordinary living. I'm more obsessed than ever with the marvelous. It may be my last attempt to live it out, but I must do it."

My dear Martha, I had to reject you for your lack of taste, discrimination, evaluations, your artistic and creative values. You are tone deaf, you belong to the prosaic, and I have been overburdened with this.

Oh, Martha, so inadequate in life and relationships, reaching for me so clumsily, forcing me to say: I do not love you. Outside of analysis, again, as with Rank, is an incomplete and pathetically ridiculous being, large and formless, reaching out so heavily, her big body edging up towards me, her embrace. How can one analyze a friendship into what it is not?

MAY 28, 1945

Depression. Loss of courage. Scenes repeat themselves, but without the illuminations of desire. I feel dead. My friendship with Frances has deepened, strengthened by our sharing of Bill, the child. His letters, like Henry's, are frozen and impersonal, after I wrote him such a beautiful letter, tender, light, glowing, humorous, nourishing.

MAY 29, 1945

Self-discipline. Bill's letters helped to kill the terrible meltingness and softness I feel for him. With Pablo, it is a climate of my nature, seeking expansion, movement, life, motion, dance, music, color, impetuous living, drama, love, relationships. It is pleasurable because we are not in love. It is free and easy and natural. When he smiles, I feel I smile as I can't smile with Bill or with Hugo. I feel like an open flower.

This flower feeling has come with the acceptance of my nature. I find it difficult to make great efforts. I prefer ease and relaxation. For a while I enjoyed the peace of a world without a lover, but now I feel restless again. Anaïs, work, work at the press from one to five, and have patience.

The lover has come, has always appeared, and will come again.

JUNE 7, 1945

Bill writes me: "In the little time that I lie awake after I go to bed, Anaïta, I think of you and wish I could be lying beside you again. Love to my wafer."

I was delirious with joy on a cold, gloomy day. I went forth and bought a much-coveted Mary Stewart hat of black, edged with pearls, something to wear for Bill. With one little word he binds me to him fast and passionately. He has the power to make me dream, to illumine my darkest day.

What a bottomless infinity there is in one personality. Certain elements get buried, dispersed, lost, forgotten. They lie there. Suddenly a mood brings them to the surface. I awakened desiring change and adventure, awakened with a violent attack of wanderlust, and said to Hugo, "I'm going to hitchhike to Mexico." Hugo said, "What about your health; what about money?"

"I'll be healthy if I do what I want. I'll wash dishes for my meals."

JUNE 10, 1945

My week of strength did not last. I feel that everybody threatens the poet in me, the very symbol of the soul, and seeks to destroy me. They do not accept me totally, or understand me totally. They should encourage me into purer and purer fantasy, but they do not. Even Frances wants me to destroy the legend I have created, mocks my idealizations and embellishments, how it seems unreal that I should sit in her place and eat, that I am never seen blowing my nose, never visibly and messily sick, etc. Hugo explains: "You are a living reproach to everyone. Everyone feels that they should immediately give up all their earthly occupations and fly with you. And it frightens them."

JUNE 16, 1945

I find reality to be the enemy of experience, the enemy of intuition. Frances knows the end of it all and cheats herself of experience, dropping the stones of wisdom with emphasis upon the obstacle, the obstacles between Bill and me, for example, rather than on what is being created in the present. They destroy the dream with their realism. Of course Bill will ultimately go to a young girl, and I to my mature man, but it is the present that counts, the boy who needs me as I am today. I needed, in the center of my being, the flower of his skin and his new, uncertain soul, the delicate suggestions of a newly born portrait not yet crystallized. "Your fantasy life," they say, as if it were not the reality of my soul's life. In mystical worlds, Bill's age and mine have no importance—we touched and saw each other in space, and that is enough. I have an intuition about him (true, he shows very little of my intuition about him to others, so they love him as an intelligent, charming and handsome boy). I rebelled against Frances's extreme use of analysis to destroy my illusions, which are fecund. I recoiled from her, Hugo, Martha, and they all capitulated.

But I feel alone, alone, alone. The great beauty of my life was that I lived out what others only talk about, or dream about, or analyze. I want to go on, living out the uncensored dream, the free unconscious. I have made my concessions to reality—I work at the press eight hours. Then I come home and write to Bill, as if he were my diary, but more lightly, more fancifully. Will he become what I have seen in him, and then will he see me totally? This destructive lucidity, analyzing everything under a microscope, is death to experience. "Bill is too young. It is all unwise. It is not good for you. He is too young to give himself, too young to love." Do such words dispel the taste of his mouth, the richness of his kisses, the silkiness of his body resting over mine, the delicacy of his hands, the quality of his voice, this childlike grace, shyness, the voluptuous trances we fell in together? Eduardo says: "Perhaps you will be the one to reveal the positive meaning of Neptune, not as illusion, but as intuition."

When Hugo takes me, Bill's luminous face haunts me, paralyzes me, closes me. It is so near, so vivid, the son against the father.

Hugo always says, "Poor little pussy," and loves me weak, helpless, small. When I grow strong he admits he does not like it. When I say, "I am no longer the poor little pussy," he dislikes it. I was strong for a week and they all battered me. Hugo doesn't want me harder, he wants me soft. The best of human beings are cruel to each other. Hugo wants me soft and tender, yet he does not want me to do soft and tender things for others. When I want to get harder to meet responsibilities, he protests. I have sworn to pay back our debts and to support Gonzalo, and myself, so as to be free of reproaches and to unburden Hugo. I feel lost and bewildered. I have no one to turn to who feels exactly as I do, who lives as I do, who accepts me as I am, and understands me completely. All of them, even Martha, have been possessive and selfish in their love. Frances feels that until I accept her reality, her atmosphere, background, friends, daily behavior, I do not accept her totally. I have always eluded this (poker games, writers from the New Yorker, cigar-smoking lawyers), as I elude Martha's heavy atmosphere, because it stifles me. I feel pursued and loved, but not understood.

JUNE 26, 1945

Work. Work. Work. Seeing people with portfolios, writing the preface forty times. We turned out a beautiful work which sold quickly, so we paid for the linotype and will be able to buy paper. Work, the press, Hugo and Gonzalo, Gonzalo and Hugo, a light dinner, oppressive heat, milk. Every afternoon when I came from the press hot and dirty, I took a bath and wrote Bill beautiful, flowing letters. For a week I communed with him with my best, freest, most tender self.

And he stopped writing. No letter for two weeks, but he still wrote Frances and Tom. All my pleasure, courage and élan fell. I do not want this dependence on love, this anguish. My greatest enemy, depression, clutched me again. All work, no pleasure, no love, no peaks, no sparks, no illumination. The source of my illumination is the lover, whoever he is, and without it I die.

I made my peace with Hugo and ceased living with a caricature of him. After living twenty years with an idealized Hugo, I suddenly saw him at his worst, and then I accepted him again. But he remains the father, old and grey. I'm full of rebellion. To reassert the dream, I bought a cotton dress for seventeen dollars, shaped à la Recamier and of that peach salmon rose which suits me, and came out in my new costume looking, as Tom said, all of fourteen years of age. And now shall I wither? I am writing prodigiously in my head, feeling discouraged with the new book, discouraged by people's lack of understanding.

Martha, in daily life, destroys what she created in analysis: she is full of envy, jealousy, ambivalence towards me. In analysis she accepted me, and in life she doesn't understand. She says she would have had my kind of life and experience if she had had my ego and my narcissism.

Pablo and I, starved for love, not lucky, suffering from depreciation in a world full of paltry natures, not abundant like ours, not being in love, we do a dance together, an improvised dance to *On the Town* music. Beautiful. He rules me, sways me, turns me… it is a dance in place of lovemaking. I feel the intensity of his body, the fullness of it, but I do not succumb. He is not deep enough, only his physical nature is fully alive, but afterwards, when he talks, it is all dispersion and froth, exterior, and too light. I was untrue to my diary, giving Bill all that came to me and flowed. I closed the diary and wrote to Bill. And there you are. But Bill was too small, too small to take it. I hope I can detach myself from him, soon, soon, be free of him, free of the physical memories.

JUNE 28, 1945

Six-thirty. I finished writing, and then I telephoned to find out how expensive a call would be to Michigan, where Bill is. I had a crazy impulse to call, but I controlled it. I lay on the couch dreaming of talking to him. *And he phones.* He had misaddressed several letters, and when they were returned with the mark "not at this address," he got frightened. He called because he was afraid I had left. Telepathy? Connection? My mood changed. I always expect the worst, always think it is the end.

I took the chop sticks, the white scarf, the "Reserved" card, the tin foil bird, the poems, the drawings, and wove a story for Bill. Each letter is a part of the tapestry. One day I wore the white scarf of faithfulness, the one he wore that dark day I watched him walk down the grey street like radium. I wore the "Reserved" card on my breast when I went to a party. New people come, but none are adept at unbuttoning my robe with chop sticks. I take the red robe and the revolving bird, and I reweave the past into the present. Gaily too, I call him William the Conqueror of the Wafer, and I sign myself the "frayed streamer" from a review of my writing we all laughed at. I court him delicately, surround and envelop him with sweet securities. *Je me glisse a côté de toi et je t'embrasse.*

When he is lost to me, I die, but as soon as he called today I was revived. Yet all the time I know the truth about my Anglo-Saxons: they are frigid; they are not passionate as I am, as the Latins, as Gonzalo. They are all afraid and ashamed of touch. They are colder, more calculating, more awake, not roused to the depths and not in the present as I am. They cannot give themselves. Hugo did in time, but how afraid he was. Frances and Eduardo have doubts of love, so they subtly instill their doubts in others, in everything. They cannot give faith. Frances did not say, "Have faith in Bill's love," but instead, "His is sadistic, perverse." And perhaps it is true, but I may still win, as I won with Henry. Something has been created, and truly the purpose of love is to create, if not the child, then something else, like Henry's writing.

JULY 8, 1945

Today there was a moment of absolute serenity and detachment. I awakened free of Bill. All the intensity and depth are gone, dissipated by his letters, which are prosaic, ordinary, lacking in feeling, pretentious, parsimonious, self-conscious.

JULY 15, 1945

I am yet far from sadism. Out of compassion for Lanny, I spent an evening with him, listening to his poems and was patient with his confessions, confusions, fears, contradictions and chaos. I showed tenderness.

Then at Pablo's birthday I wore my new low-cut peach cotton dress. I felt beautiful and young. The place was filled with five women and fifteen young men. I felt light. I was courted, flattered, surrounded. I danced with Lanny but found him dislocated, grotesque in his exaggerated caricature of "freedom." Already my tenderness has frightened him. He was drunk, jealous, glittering with malice and destructiveness.

"There are too many men around you." Later he took me outside to kill my gayety. He said, "Bill is coming back next week."

"I know."

"You forget too quickly," he said, severely.

"I'm not forgetting Bill," I said, looking at Lanny's petulant mouth and remembering Bill's so much more beautiful and strong. "And if I could, it would be better for him," I added angrily. I hated his moralizing, his disguised, hypocritical desire and jealousy. I had Bill's letter inside of my dress, against my breast.

The atmosphere was easy, lax and natural. Pablo had brought his blue rat in a cage, his beautiful fiancée, Tieko, and Claudia, with her statuesque gravity. All night long I heard: "You are a legend. I wanted to meet you for months. You are a legend. I had a dream about you before I saw you. You are a legend. I can't believe I am talking to Anaïs Nin at last."

Then they went to a bar and discussed me. I have reached the peak of my magic, but not of love!

JULY 17, 1945

In the courtyard this morning I heard a Spanish woman singing desultorily as they do at work. Her voice sang joyously. I felt the weight of my mood like that of a cloud. Why does she feel like singing and I do not?

"Allo ooo oooooooo," sings Chinchilito over the telephone. "What are you doing today? I am free all day, Chinchilita."

"I am free, too."

We went to Pablo's place, which is a small room with two windows open upon a rich elm tree, making it seem like a tree house, like the African huts built up on the trees in the jungle. The tree filled the room with its greenness, with its silk frou-frous, its whisperings. Chinchilito and I lie on the small bed. He is like the sea, the sand, the sun, the forest, lying at my side. When I lie under him I am like the earth being ploughed and churned. A rhythm begins which is like a dance increasing in tempo. The shivering of the leaves is like the silk shivers of the skin and the hair. The green light of the tree and the blue light of his eyes and the glow of his teeth…the swaying of the branches and the swaying of the bodies, the rhythmic undulations of legs and arms. I can encircle him, wind around him, press against him. His strength is there. I can pierce him with my breasts, I can contain his piercing, draw pleasure at will, receive his vigorous thrusts. It is all firm and rooted to the core of his strength, of his power. He is the trunk and I the leaves. He is the hard core of desire. He takes his pleasure at his own time. He is straight and free, and tender when the passion is over, tender and smiling, and pleasure comes from fullness and ripeness.

Later he rose and filled the room with his singing, with euphoria. Later, when alone, I broke into singing, every cell singing out of fullness and ecstasy. When I came home the Spanish voice was singing in the courtyard. I knew why.

It is strange that before I experienced this absolute ecstasy with Chinchilito, I described him in *This Hunger* as Philip, the magician of joy, and with him I have achieved it. Fullness, ripeness, expansion, power, the great splendor of maturity and strength. It was a physical encounter of great splendor, of relaxed, sure, deep pleasure. Such pleasure. This morning I was still in ecstasy, walking in the rain, singing, singing, until I met Lanny, and then Gonzalo, and all their twistedness and poisons of weakness, their pain and impurities. I felt them and lost my joy. But I was content to have attained it.

I am the one who has traveled between subjectivity and objectivity, between romanticism and modernism, christianity and paganism, tragedy and joy. To arrive by *deep routes* to nature and joy, what a feat! To arrive at the ecstasy of joy and nature when having known only ecstasies of the spirit.

THE PROBLEM OF THE DIARY

My own voice is here

NEW YORK, JULY 21, 1945

Another day of joy because my little child Bill writes me: "How happy I was to get the volume (I sent him a diary) you sent me. It helps a lot, for its music takes the place of instrumentals, and I can lose myself in it perfectly. It's my one source of inspiration in the barren world which surrounds me. It makes me long even more to see you again and cleanse and revivify myself in your personal cosmos. I am beginning to understand why I do not write. Every dream of mine cast into a story, put on paper, and made public is one dream lost for myself, and of them I have few enough."

This surrender and simplicity I feel now about my feelings. I want to write out of it and I can't, only in the diary. I want to write as I feel in volume 11, and I can't.

Why can't I find my true key in writing? My own voice is here, in the diary. Why not in the writing for the world?

I was wondering why I could never show Henry my weaknesses. It was because he had appointed me the protector, the strong one. When I showed a part of my weakness, he either did not help me, or he betrayed it. The lover and the child take advantage of the weaknesses. I always felt that the only one who loved me for my weakness was Hugo, but neither Henry nor Gonzalo would have, because both were weak and needed my strength. The same is true with Bill. Yet Bill, and Henry too, were touched by the childhood diary.

JULY 26, 1945

My deepest writing these months has gone into my letters to Bill. Now he is coming tomorrow or perhaps the day after. I tell Hugo I am in need of seclusion, isolation, to write, so he will go away for a week's rest, which he needs, and I will be free. I printed Bill's poem, had his engraving printed, and made portfolios for him as a surprise.

I feel that Frances, as did Rank, has opened Pandora's box and may die because of it, for only the artist can open Pandora's box because he can replenish it with new material. There must be something to motivate a man to make him whole, but analysis disintegrates, dismembers. After you dissect all the separate parts, then what? I cannot be put together like a watch. I can withstand moments of mortal separation because I'm so rich. I can immediately produce another love, another dream, as fast as life dissolves them, as fast as analysis dissects them.

I see my early writing as an early presentiment of the imprisonment to which human beings are subjected. It was my means of evasion, of burrowing my way out to freedom.

JULY 27, 1945

I waited for Bill all day yesterday, and all evening. I had promised myself to be calm, detached, natural, free, but actually I was nervous. My legs gave way when the radio played one of his most loved Beethoven songs. I felt: now he will come in. I tried to write.

I swallowed hundreds of pages of the diary, amazed at its vastness, feeling I can never surpass this, that no writing can ever surpass the hot lava flowing freely out of the volcano of experience. And I am blocked because I cannot handle any of the major themes—Henry, Allendy, June, Rank, my father—without crucifying Hugo. And I cannot falsify either. It revolts me. Something revolts me in both *Winter* and *This Hunger*: the falsifications. In the last one, it was the intermingling of Luise Rainer and me in Stella, the intermingling of Frances and me. It is false. I want to be truthful. The truth is greater. One feels it is the truth. I don't want to write if I can't write the truth. What am I to do? Every word in the diary is perfect, true, and necessary. Complete. I don't want to touch it, mutilate it.

So there is only one outlet: to write about minor themes, as all women do. As Virginia Woolf did, Katherine Mansfield. I am nauseated by *This Hunger*. It is a falsification. I hate this. Everybody lives in a false world, everybody. It is not right to add to the falsities. You define and limit so as to have control and a kind of security. You say this is Tom, this is Bill, this is Anaïs, with a landowner's metrical system, and all the rest (the ring around Saturn, the nebulae, the dreams, etc.) is illusion. And now you have your reality, and your limit, and a smaller world. Lesser beings who cannot go beyond themselves and transcend their New England, their Quakerism, their Park Avenue, their age.

I went to sleep in a kind of pain. I dreamt strangely:

I was walking about naked, but full of confidence, assured of being beautiful. I reached a place which was an art school. A woman said: "Come in. Pose for us. Wouldn't you like to pose for us?" I accepted, playfully, remembering that I once did it for a living (but then I was shy, and I would not pose naked for anyone). But in this dream, I entered the large class, full of men, calmly. There was a gasp of admiration and then an "Oh!" from all. What was implied was that it was not only the physical beauty they admired, but the distinction. I walked nobly, erect, sure, poised. I felt this was only a game, an amusing return to the past, but unlike in the past, I was no longer dependent on this and did not have to pose. When it was all ended, I looked at the men. One was a young ballet dancer dressed in yellow satin, who began an erotic dance. I said later, still naked, to the headmaster, the old painting teacher, "I am not coming back. I am now a well-known writer. I don't need to pose. It was only a lark." He was rather irritated. Then I looked for the toilet and began to walk about. The whole painting school was a series of wooden rooms and stairs, suspended over the earth, very high. On returning from the toilet I got lost. I found that to return to the main room and the way out of the place, I had to climb a stairway in space, and I looked down and saw the earth below and was frightened. I hung on to the stairs. But I let go of a man who was burdening me. He was dead and pale. He looked like a white-faced Gonzalo. He suddenly fell away and I felt I should have held him, but his weight was too heavy for me. He fell down below over a fire. I was horrified even though he was dead and it didn't matter. I felt like a criminal. I felt people would not know that he was dead already and would think I had thrust him out, let him fall, murdered him. Somehow I got back into the main room. Everybody was leaving. Then followed some wild erotic experience I cannot remember.

And this does not help me in my conflict with the writing. I cannot understand the dream. A part of me is free, evidently (my body, my nature, my nakedness, my assurance, my guiltlessness), but a part of me carries a dead man for whom I feel responsible.

I heard the crepitation of the fire in the dream.

I wrote last night about my belief in fire.

I fear I have lost my way again.

Bill arrived Sunday at two. I heard him climbing the stairs two at a time. Eager, impetuous, hungry for caresses, joyous, less timid, it was a real lover who returned, without timidity or retractions. We embraced like brother and sister, like mother and son, then like lovers, lay on the couch, sank into kisses, and he said: "Let's wait till tonight. I'll come for a whole night."

At five he returned to his family. At nine-thirty he returned to me. But he could not wait. He lay in bed and made me lie beside him. We turned off the lights. We undressed. He sighed as if this were his home, his all, his voyage's end. He sank into caresses, hid in them, took me passionately, and fell asleep like a little child, lying upon me. I couldn't sleep. I was too tense. I watched over him, covered him, went to the other bed, tossed, finally slept. Awakened early. Read. Looked at him asleep. A Bill less pale, less remote, less poetic, healthier from a life in the army, more present, less mysterious, charming, innocent, erotic, with his pure brow, pure eyes and sensual mouth. At last he awakened. I made breakfast which we had in bed together. But I lay outside of the sheets in my white kimono. And we talked and read together until he took my book away and nestled against me, slipped his hand inside of my kimono, caressed me, undressed me. Oh, this moment when the naked bodies first touch. We melt into each other. This embrace I have never known, this loss, this vanishing, this melting of similar substances, of softness, slenderness. How passionate he was. And I never get hurt now from the boy's errors, tactlessness, confusions. I laugh. His conscious self is unformed, stumbling and awkward, but his other self is mine and gives me joy. At noon he left. He will return tonight. I see no one. Hugo is in Westport. I work at the press in the afternoon. That is all.

Bill said: "In seventeen months when my training is over and I am sent to Japan, then you can go to Europe, and I'll invite you to Japan..." He stopped, frightened. We have no future, only the present. Only the present.

I do not hold on now. I live openly, ready for the pain, the separations and losses. I am not holding on. Open and free, sad at moments, but knowing the deep joys are worth all that follows. Deep joys. One must be willing to suffer, to surrender.

I feel rich, sweet, living deeply. Bill.

August 2, 1945

Hugo's words—"I am jealous of all you write about. Is Jay Miller? You loved Miller, didn't you?"—so paralyzed me last week with terror that he should discover my Volume Two, that I had loved Miller, that I fell into the deepest despair and discouragement.

I am hopelessly frustrated. When I had only my work and Bill, I was happy. I got ill from the nervousness of waiting for Bill two days, ill too because of the conflict. I mused, meditated for hours in my enforced solitude (I could not leave the house in case Bill got free of his family). Finally it was very much like an airplane which has to soar higher to escape the storms. I rose into vaster mysticism, where personalities were not so important.

And I found this:

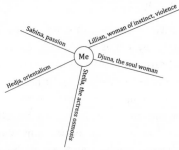

These women were all aspects of me which I developed to their utmost. I could split myself, and above all, for Hugo's sake, the important thing was that I should not have loved Miller (Jay), so Jay is married to Lillian, in which Hugo does not see a part of me, and related to Djuna the anima (Hugo will see Djuna as he sees me: the mystic). So the mystic guides Jay but is not in love with him. There is no physical relation between them. Now the strange truth: what I hit on here, instead of a deformity, is that the mystical self in me was the one who did not love Henry, the one who condemned his pleasure-seeking, loveless ego, his cruelties and callousness, his lack of soul. So far all is well. Jay has lost nothing by not sleeping with his anima (it is as if I had known Henry while he was married to June before I met him). My only problem is that for Djuna's development she had to have a physical life and find her body. So we will see. But this way I can write.

This protection of Hugo will perhaps become creative and force me to become an artist, to create (not falsify). Frances said with amazement the other day, as if she only now had become conscious of this: "In the end you are always really writing the truth. People think it is fantasy, but it's psychologically real." Of course! That's what people don't see. They think because I've discarded realism I'm not in reality. The character of Hedja is absolutely true of Hedja psychologically. It is less invented than Henry's characters.

AUGUST 3, 1945

One more night of passion and he is gone. A summer night. Windows and doors open. The noise of the city. The fog horns. The birds revolving up in the ceiling, the tapestry flowering. All the lights out. Bill in his soldier's uniform. I in my light chiffon dress, sheer and clinging. We lie on the striped Madagascar bedspread. We kiss teasingly, then frenziedly. I move my head away so that he has to pursue me with his mouth. Oh, his mouth. He bites me then, my whole mouth, my shoulders. He kisses my breast. In the dim lights from outside, the whiteness of the bodies are illumined. He kissed more of my body than ever before. He kissed the indent of the waist. Oh my darling, oh my darling. He took me and then fell asleep. After a moment he awakened, "Are you there?" He kissed me, took my hand and put it on his body and fell asleep again. And this is all I have, for he cannot write warmly, he can never utter warm words, he can never make gifts or acts of love. His little, cold soul, brought up in the devastating atmosphere of schools, colleges, and the cold atmosphere of his home (his mother's cold voice and "my father does not believe in emotion"), his little, atrophied feelings. Do they lie there concealed, suppressed, or does he truly not feel? This love expressed only in passion is difficult to believe in, but this time I believed. I did not get hurt. When I said to him this morning, "Nothing about you worries me except that you have grown up in an atmosphere in which feeling couldn't grow, and it concerns me whether it can exist always in hostile surroundings," he said, "You have nothing to worry about." Meaning what? That for me he feels, yes, but for how many others?

In his moments of youthful helplessness his only assertion of power is to criticize, to pick out flaws. He is not moved or carried away by anything—he analyzes, he applies his mind. He does not know yet what he feels, what he is, or what he thinks. When he argues with Tom and Frances he uses my ideas. When he argues with me he upholds Frances and Tom. I ask him, "But you, you, what do you think?" "I don't know yet," he answers truthfully.

All these days struggling with my work, writing. Writing in between. This morning awakening before him, I corrected proofs of *This Hunger* in bed, wrote two pages, and watched him sleeping, his hair over his forehead, his heavy eyebrows slanting, his blue-shadowed eyes closed, so pure, his mouth so sensual. In his slender, lean face, so childlike and delicate, his mouth is incredible—all his maturity is in his mouth. When he left, my heart hurt me for an hour. It contracted painfully. Then I felt dead. My legs gave way. I dragged myself to the press, worked. I saw Hugo and arranged to go to Westport tomorrow, to work tonight. This is not right. My destiny is hard; this passion cannot be lived out and must be denied for three months again.

And now to live on, to take revenge upon my destiny, which starves me in passion, to take all the passion I can find.

AUGUST 6, 1945

The way we have power over our destiny is that we can alter our attitudes, our subjective reactions, and therefore we can free ourselves of what at other times may enslave us. I no longer love what I cannot be happy with. I no longer cling to what is impossible. I no longer want what hurts me.

I had a strange impression from Bill's last visit, of physical passion but disharmony in everything else, a lack of closeness, of understanding. When he left, I suffered, deeply. I lay in bed calling his name, but my awareness of the obstacle became stronger, this obstacle which would have incited me before. I cannot cling now, and I can no longer be hurt. That dissonance now detaches me. I love less. I realize it is passion, not love. I was sad, depressed. I had not been filled, fulfilled, or answered in any way but physically. I had no joy, no ecstasy, no freedom, nothing but a boy bursting into desire when we lay down, and that was all.

Loneliness.

And now I am free for another love. Perhaps what I should do is leave for Europe where I can more easily forget him.

AUGUST 9, 1945

Atomic bomb
atomic force
used first for destruction, but with fabulous, incalculable possibilities.
A new world has been born.

There is an effect of this scientific discovery. I believe it has a bearing upon our psychic life, that there is an analogy: the bombardment of the personality by analysis, the dismemberment and separation of the elements of the psyche, may release new energies, perhaps a kind of triumph over death. I believe the scientific principles can all be applied to the life of the psyche and in fact have a direct connection with it, a direct interrelation. I feel it in another realm.

I must embark upon the study of scientific principles in order to make clearer the workings of the psyche. The time has come. I feel something new in the world. I felt it before. I was born with the airplane. I felt a new rhythm which I possess in my being, the radio, radio waves. I always understood the transmissions, as I now understand atomic force.

I feel I am on the edge of my own private discoveries in the principles and life of the psyche. There is an analogy of what takes place within us and what takes place without. I feel an immense new world in my head corresponding to the scientific worlds, the spiritual echo of the scientific discoveries.

The dream of Bill is over. Because I am no longer enslaved, my being has learned to turn away when there is no joy, only pain and difficulties. It is like a current. I keep it from flowing to him, remembering his harshness and his not savoring the passion, how he limits and tightens me, binds me to smaller measures.

Je suis libre, libre, et ivre de ma liberté. No dream can now bind me to any pain.

AUGUST 10, 1945

I have found the secret of joy (I remember being haunted by *La Joie de Bernanos*, more by its title than the description of the ecstatic states of the girl). I remember a long quest for joy, for all its outer aspects, places, faces, people, for its appearance in Henry. I remember listening for it, yearning for it, through others' memories.

Joy.

It appeared this morning in the form of a leaf fluttering in the sun outside of the window. It appeared in the taste of the coffee. It appeared as I walked through the press, as I worked, singing. Joy, the secret of joy is in the mastery of pain. It is in the life of the senses. It is in the enjoyment of all and the giving of all, in being.

Chinchilito gives the *coups de bélier*, the powerful thrusts of man. Rhythm. There is a rhythm in caresses, like the rhythms of dancing which some cannot learn. It is instinctive. It is like a crescendo in the blood, a circle, a cycle, an intensification like Ravel's *Bolero*.

Chinchilito's room is interesting. One wall is hung with a black cloth. On this cloth he has a wooden colored peasant eagle symbolically holding balls and crosses, then old historic lead soldiers in a row. On another are old sheets of music, the piano, photographs of singers and other musicians (so much like my father's photographs). He has aquariums and watches newborn fish with delight. He grows plants in his porch. He has astronomic maps on the walls. I suggested he paint them with phosphorescent paint so that they would shine at night. He is also busy photographing my erotic postcards (which I kept in the diary) to make a little erotic movies. He is instinctive, intuitive, not intellectual (although he was a brilliant lawyer in Austria).

AUGUST 16, 1945

PEACE!

AUGUST 19, 1945

Bronchitis, bad general health, but great inspiration. I wrote pages on the attributes of a lover, Sabina and the fire ladder, Eduardo, me, and Robert. "From the very first Jay hated her." I began writing about Djuna and her city (the pawn shop, the whorehouse of the blind).

AUGUST 29, 1945

Began printing *This Hunger*.

AUGUST 30, 1945

140th page. What I used to feel only in the ecstasy of a deep, absorbing and single obsessive love, I now feel continuously in a state of freedom from love.

Today, after printing heavily and hard, I felt the machine giving me back strength. I felt the lead, so heavy to carry, giving me back strength and weight. I left the work elated. I met Edmund Wilson, back from Europe, who turns to me to read his stories because he is separated from Mary McCarthy, a lonely, soft man who has suffered because he likes clever women, but clever women are so impossibly neurotic. As I sat waiting for him at the most banal of all restaurants, Longchamps, I felt that the orange walls were as beautiful as fruit, and the noises and the lights of the summer gay and wonderful. No one can hurt me. I can even be alone. Hugo is away and yet I am content. When I want lovemaking, Gonzalo is there drawing from me such a long-lasting orgasm, or Chinchilito is there with his violent virility like a negro's, or anyone else.

All the tragedy lay in trying to fit a boundless and insatiable love into human proportions, into one love. I found first of all that one was not enough, then that two were not enough. I added Henry to Hugo, and Gonzalo to both, and then it was not enough and I finally became the *grande amoureuse* of the world. Now I love Gonzalo, but I don't think of Helba or of possessing his whole love, and he gives me his unchanged passion. Tonight, I am alone, full of music, full of physical delights, conversing with the warm summer night, full of inspiration, writing.

Now we enter into the night, we enter chaos, and the mystery of woman. We enter where all women melt into one, into the layer that is common to all. We melt Stella, Lillian, Djuna, into one. One and the night.

SEPTEMBER 2, 1945

Yesterday I reached the 184th page of the deluxe edition. Then I rested, bathed, dressed up for Marshall Barer, descendent of a famous Rabbi Barer, handsome, with heavily lashed, dark, olive and blue-green eyes. He designs layout at *Esquire* and writes, paints, dances, etc. He is impulsive, generous and outgoing. One day he brought in a makeshift box a fierce-looking black bird he had found near the Metropolitan, with a broken leg. Marshall looks very much like Albert, which is why I like him physically. He is intelligent, fanciful, quick. He first of all pursued Josephine violently, with desire. He loves both men and women. He invited me to a dance with his friend Estelle (he seems afraid to be alone with me, so I invited Chinchilito).

SEPTEMBER 9, 1945

All this is nothing but courage, multiple acts of courage not to sink, not to despair.

I let Marshall take me out dancing. I felt elated, but he knows I love Bill.

I let Chinchilito come with his violent masterful caresses.

I let Hugo return from his vacation sunburnt, lean, handsome and full of love.

And then suddenly I fall. When I received a letter from Bill, my world turned black: he has chosen of his own free will to go to Japan.

I wrote an answer but did not mail it. He is a little child. He does not know what he is doing. Like all romantics, he must destroy fulfillment.

Then I wrote a light, objective letter which I can't send either.

Marshall planned an evening for us. Dinner, then dancing together at a little place on 8th Street, and then back home. During the dancing he desired me, and I responded. But at the table he said, "You are so unreal to me, yet very real things keep happening." When we returned to my place we sat on the porch in the hammock. It was warm. He lay down with his head on my knees. He said: "I'm frightened. God knows it is not what one should feel before you." From then on he began to create a web in which to conceal his fright. He sang little songs in a childish voice, a little off key, songs from musical comedies, about not knowing which sex he belonged to, about not wanting to lose his heart and suffer. It began to drizzle. But he wanted to continue to lie there, with his head heavy on my Venus mount. In a trance, he said, "I have never been happier," while holding my bare arm and caressing it.

His phrase, "I'm frightened," subdued me completely, killed my desire.

Monday we went out again. He met me at the bottom of the stairs, looking up at me, moved and worshipful (like Lanny?), and he kissed me. I returned his kiss. (Oh, I want to love, I want to love whoever is not Bill, not Bill who hurt me, whose love I doubt.) We danced together. We listened to subtle jazz at the Three Deuces. He was tender, expressive, humorous. He said, "You always have the right reactions." (He was born on February 19.) He brought me home, kept the taxi, kissed me, and said, "Don't smile, don't smile," and left. Poetry, dreams, mysteries, to veil, "I am afraid."

"*C'est fini*," I answered passively. I lay back. I did not seek, court, wish, struggle, regret. I lay back and let Marshall vanish. A sweet, tender, warm child, lavish and hungry.

I plunged into work as if it were a drug. Then Gonzalo unconsciously began to sabotage the end of the book because he hates hard work and intensity. But I was possessed, an almost self-destructive possession, not caring, not caring. At other times, I seek consolation in imagining what new world this book might create, what new person, what new love.

On my good days I think of my new book, the 100 pages of "Bread and the Wafer." I invent, plan, create great things.

On my bad days I feel despair because I cannot find happiness in love. On my bad days I think my writing is nothing but a substitute, an effort to find new worlds, an instrument for enlarging the world and peopling it—but where is the man for me?

September 18, 1945

How the pattern weaves and re-weaves itself. Jean writes me. I wrote in my story that he was a "prisoner," using the word symbolically because of all that bound and fettered him. In reality, he was in prison in France, for taking part in the resistance. His psychological research now is along the same line as mine. Then I hear that Louise de Vilmorin, a heroine of *Under a Glass Bell*, has the best literary salon in France. Everything pulls me toward France, the rich literary activity, the feeling that I am now ready for its maturity which before frightened me.

Tonight I am drunk with fatigue, nearing the end of the book. Worked from nine-thirty to seven without stopping, except for lunch. My heart is weak. Where do I get the psychic energy? What carries me when others with my kind of body would collapse? It is the dream. The dream sustains me. I see reality corrupting the dream, corroding it, destroying it, and then I lose all faith and strength.

I dream of a man who will know a great deal about science, who will help me concretize and strengthen my psychic knowledge, who will help me incarnate, as Henry helped me to incarnate. Oh god, I pray he may be strong, a match to me so I shall cease feeling guilty for my power, one who can hold his own with me, live with me. I feel I can't do my work alone. I feel so feminine and dependent, yet at the same time so unyielding. It is a mystery. I did not yield to Henry's way of life. I did not yield to Gonzalo's way of life. I make my own atmosphere and bring others into it. I do not assimilate America; I have withstood participation in politics, in bourgeois life. People struggle to make me a realist, and three psychoanalyses, from all of which I derived my own course. I am spiritually strong, sure, full of faith and certitudes, but I am emotionally weak and dependent on others, on love, on affection and devotion.

Il y a des chagrins de l'idéalisation, la comparaison constante entre la réalité et le rêve, the collision between reality and the dream. The strength of the ideal concept determines the extent of the suffering. A tragic sense of life means an ideal sense of life, not a primitive, natural one. Where did my path turn towards such ideal concepts which determined my tragic reaction to Henry rather than a joyous participation in his destructiveness and irresponsibility, my tragic struggle against Gonzalo's inertia, his fatalism and destructiveness instead of a willing submission to it? As a child I must have been aware of my physical weakness and substituted exaltation, intensity, enthusiasm, fervor, for actual, real strength. They became my strength.

Poor Hugo, he was to court me with his goodness, woo me with it, win me with it, to extract from me the gift of my body which I can offer prodigally to others. It is his goodness which finally overcomes my physical indifference to him. His goodness is so amazing, continuous, human, his love so great, so loyal, so total, that I finally am warmed by his love itself and can bring myself to love him as he wishes to be loved—physically. He has been working at the press and is convinced that Gonzalo is insane. He is also convinced of Gonzalo's selfishness, perversity, self-destructiveness. He says, "Such behavior must kill your feelings."

THIS GREAT HUNGER

Now you must find reality

NEW YORK, SEPTEMBER 20, 1945

We finished printing *This Hunger*. I fell into a suicidal depression, had to resist the impulse to throw myself before a truck, knowing that all this effort did not bring me what I wanted, that my "faith" is not faith at all, but courage. This terrible, terrible feeling of giving more than I received, this doubt of attaining happiness in love, this void in place of passion which is the core of my life, this silence from Bill, this feeling of obstacles, of Gonzalo's destructiveness, of the fact that Hugo is my wife and has been swallowed by me, that he is mine absolutely as the child is the mother's, this feeling that I have reached beauty and power, but not love, not what I crave and need.

And now I face the opposition to my new book. Edmund says: "I must be severe with you...no form...no movement...not concrete enough, artistically less than *Bell*, but amazing, marvelous insight. I marked many passages which describe Mary."

Worse than all of this is Wilson's courtship, dinner and wine and his shattered home (Mary McCarthy stripped it of half of its contents). Before the evening was over, he was under my spell, wanted to make love to me, was amazed by my gentleness.

"You are a friend of man's, aren't you? You don't demolish him?"

"I never forget that when you demolish a man, you lose a lover," I said.

I'm weary of everything, the lack of understanding. I give them jewels, and they ask me for earth. I give them precious stones, and they ask me for paste and papier mâché.

The strange thing is that I have arrived at an unshakable faith in my writing. No one can influence me or turn me away from what I am doing.

If only I could reach the same unshakable faith in love.

It looks to me as if I will be fulfilled only as an artist, never as a woman. I cannot find the man who fills my whole being, my match, my equal, my all. Will my writing bring him to me? My only joy is writing, a sad joy, a lament disguised, an Arethusa fountain in place of tears. Oh, someone, someone love me as I have loved. One loves in proportion to one's vision. I see more, so I love more. Will someone see me entire, complete, past and present, encompass all of me, see me as I see others? I promise to have faith, to have no fears. But let someone love me for what I am. Let someone come who can contain me, assent and accept me entirely, who can receive all that I have to give and return it.

SEPTEMBER 26, 1945

Bill did not write for three weeks. I telephoned him. He said, "I wrote you last night." Then, after having written that he wanted to go to Japan, he suddenly referred to my dream of France and said: "You said you knew someone who could transfer me to France? I won't finish this course here."

"We'll talk about this when you come at the end of October."

"Will you be there?"

"Of course," I said, not understanding the question. And the next day I received his letter, which shattered me and our relationship. He chose paper such as I use to write such cruelties. My heart beat and I suffered deeply. I tried several answers. And then the hopelessness of it struck me and I decided not to answer, but this morning I mailed him the white silk scarf and the chop sticks broken in two.

Bill's letter:

I can hardly think of a better wife for anyone than Tom and Frances from Tom's point of view. Of course his prosaicness that you mentioned isn't any good for Frances, but she understands him as hardly anyone else does or could. Frances, it is true, does not take pains with her personal beauty, and she is older than Tom, and more passionate. *Dommage*. However, I think they could be happier than even you and I could, if we were married. As I mentioned before I couldn't last long in a marriage with one such as you. Your passion is more far-reaching, inclusive and perhaps deeper than mine is. You require a passion that would reciprocate your own. Except in moments, you couldn't find that in me, at least not at present. Moreover you require someone to give as much as you give; you have already remarked how little I am willing to give of myself. Your heart seduces your soul. Try and figure that out. I want to seduce someone who would love me but who would never claim me... *Et c'est ça*. As a wafer, you can be eaten and still be there to eat again.

Last night I broke down, not as for Lanny, not a flowing pain, but a deeper one strangling me, the torment of having to surrender him because he is bad for me, and to remember only the good moments. But it is done. At the same time I know it was the end of my dreaming. This last dream, betrayed by Bill, was my last dream. I must abandon the dream because it has caused me too much pain. I wept. I saw Frances, who was tender and helpful. She suggested analysis again, because I must dissolve this illusion which destroys me. I must find reality. The morning I mailed the scarf and the chop sticks, I felt so weak, so broken, that I called up Dr. Clement Staff, a Marxist analyst, different from all of them, earthy, rough, plain-spoken, who immediately said, "This great hunger" (the title of the new book!) "which you have disguised and idealized into giving, you were ashamed to take to gratify your needs. You created a work of art and a life out of starvation, and the child and the woman have not been fulfilled. You were ashamed to take, crave, need. You were ashamed to take so you gave. But now you must find reality."

I said: "Reality says a boy and a woman cannot love each other, but don't you see, Doctor, I was in love with Caspar Hauser. I loved Caspar Hauser in Bill. And Bill acts only according to his fears and his egotism. I transformed my physical needs, my sexual needs, into a golden goblet (Rorschach test), idealized my hunger, and therefore created something that deluded my hunger but didn't fill it."

"What is it you fear about reality? What makes you hold on to the dreams, the art? Your writing holds you together, but it is part of the delusion."

So illusion is delusion, and I have been Don Quixote, and nothing that I loved or dreamed existed. I am empty-handed now, a woman with an aching body. Lost. Weeping. Weeping. Saying yes to the analyst like a child.

SEPTEMBER 30, 1945

The pain over Bill has been the worst of all because it means relinquishing the dream itself, all romantic love, my need of the child, my need of beauty. I never came nearer to death. I had to resist suicide as never before. I stood for one hour on the porch fighting a terrible impulse to throw myself down those five flights. To die, to die, rather than surrender the dream, this impossible dream. This knowledge of another Bill who does not know himself, this knowledge of the bond he does not know, this feeling of the bond.

By violence only did I cut the cord.

Two talks with Staff, and his emphasis is on the void, the self-cheating, on all that I did not have. I disguised the woman. I regressed. I made myself small again, a child with Bill, so that I could re-enter the little house of innocence and escape the woman. But Bill is not deluded. He is not lying beside a child like himself. He is lying beside a woman who gives him a love he cannot answer, letters he cannot answer, who overwhelms him. The air is too rich, too powerful. He does not see the child in the woman who experiences his fears and his helplessness.

He does not see that it is because at times I feel the same timidity and fear that he does, that I rush with my strength to give him power.

With this failure I have to face all my failures, my creation of an unreal world, a beautiful world where I am humanly starved. After talking with Staff I did not dream, but the next morning I awakened to a grim, cold, grey day. I shivered and said: that is reality.

That afternoon Chinchilito came, with his violence, his animal violence, and I answered fully. His German realism is what has always prevented me from romanticizing him. I gave myself fully, physically, but I did not have ecstasy, because deep inside of me I am mourning Bill, Bill lying gently over my body, Bill's dreamlike, shy presence.

That evening I went out with Edmund Wilson, and suddenly I succumbed to his worship, his desire, his ardor, his madness. "The first time I saw you years ago at the Gotham, you were wearing a little cape and hood. I thought you were the most exquisite woman I had ever seen. I was so enthusiastic that I went and told Mary. As I took my marriage very seriously and it was the first time I had praised another woman so much, Mary was very angry. When we began to become estranged and to quarrel, among other things, she accused me of being in love with you. I had tried to see you again. I found out that Paul Rosenfeld knew you. He arranged a cocktail. But we didn't talk very much. I gave up hope of seeing you because, as I said, Mary demanded all my attention. Then Steloff put your *Under a Glass Bell* in my hands. I hadn't liked your work before, but this book I did. Then when I met you I thought you were beautiful, but inhuman."

All through dinner he courted me. I lost my timidity. I enjoyed receiving worship. He took me to his house, and in the taxi he kissed me. I liked his eagerness, his hunger (oh, Bill, Bill, my little Bill, this is the moment when you retracted, moved away, sat in a taxi, remote, removed, unattainable, inhuman).

Another's fire, and I took it. I took the worship, and I gave myself. I felt relief at a man pouring out words of love, words of worship: "Oh, you are beautiful, you are flawless! I have never seen such a waist, such feet and hands." He kissed my feet, he lay at them. He was ardent, sensual, potent. I forgot his ugliness. In one day two men, two hungry, desirous men, palpable, strong, and positive, but neither one of them able to enter my heart, my breast, my inner being, as Bill had done.

God save me, save me from the love of Bill; it lacerates me, tantalizes me, torments me with its lack of plenitude. What is it, what is it? Is it the cheated mother trying to unite with her child? Is it the dream?

I took.

My body was quiet after the orgy. I felt power; I felt I was taking revenge. I was inflicting pain, being unfaithful, desecrating all the delicacies in Bill and in myself. Wilson, who has big needs, needed me, wanted all I could give, wanted me for a wife, a collaborator, a mistress, one to enjoy power with, his two houses, his position of power, his last ten years of achievement, but I starve him, elude him. He telephones. I inflict the suffering on him that was inflicted on me by another, but only because I do not love. So it must mean that those who behaved as I do now do not love.

In the dream there is no human life. I am the only one who gave her human self to the dream. I loved my dreams humanly.

I saw the filmmaker Maya Deren, and from her I got the inspiration to defend and explain my own work. She accomplishes this. She fights. She asserts herself. She writes about her movies. She is stronger than I. I was hurt when Frances said: "Your women are two-dimensional. They have no body," or when the analyst said, "There is no sweat in your work."

The pain of Bill and the pain of being creatively unanswered intermingle. Something is dying in me, but I am in danger of dying with it. I could bury myself when I bury the romantic in me, the visionary, the mystic, the magician, the poet, Bill, and face the unknown.

Dream: Throat obstruction, pulling it out, as in my first book, *House of Incest*.

I can only make notes. With Staff, it is my idealization of myself and others. Behind my masochism lies sadism. Behind my indirectness does not lie femininity, but a crippled, fearful self who does not dare. Behind my idealizations lie a primitive woman, indirect uses of power, subtle forms of destructiveness, this hunger.

Rock bottom. Bitter truths. My face changes. Others' faces change in my eyes. I face my fear of ugliness, of strength, of power. A mass of subterfuges and transformation.

The face of Bill changes. He is no Caspar Hauser, but a rough, objective, cruel, little brat, who uses whatever he can in place of strength.

I lose my great softness towards him. I shall return his bites, his hostilities. (You make the child feel small and he hates you. Need is not love.)

Where is your hostility?

One discovers one is not a saint.

Then there is the affair with Wilson, accepting his frenzy, his adoration, his passion, hearing my own words in his mouth (those of praise and worship, such as I gave Bill). His feelings are like mine about Bill: desire, passion, fire, lust, hunger. It is he who says all I wish Bill would say: "You are beautiful, flawless, different than all the other women." Wilson suffers pain after our first encounter: "I felt such pain at not seeing you, such a desire for you, did you miss me as I missed you, I couldn't get interested in anything else, just wanting to see you." Frenzy. Tenderness. Worship. His words and acts fill the void left by Bill: "I wish you could stay all night... If we lived together, if we were married, I would make love to you all the time."

OCTOBER 5, 1945

Dr. Staff's outline: Masochism produces nymphomania. To escape pain, to relieve pain, I seek pleasure (as with Chinchilito). It balances the pain, saves me from utter catastrophe, but it is not happiness. I have repressed all my natural functions, accepting only the outlet of sex (I have an unnatural stylization of life, I do nothing distasteful in public, I don't over-indulge in eating, etc., only in sexuality, like my father, who was austere in everything else). I use masochism as a devious way of seeking love (Christ, look at my wounds). I use writing as a discharge of unbearable tensions too, to express neurosis. With all but Hugo, I act a role, an unnatural role. I have an unnatural role in writing. *Show the world only a perfect face.*

In bed, the breakfast tray at my feet, Hugo shaving, winter coiled outside, bright and cruel. The new book is on the table, not wholly accepted by anyone, not wholly loved and very much opposed. I nearly sank into death.

OCTOBER 9, 1945

Real play-acting for Maya's movie in Central Park West, where I once played as a child, or rather didn't play because I had to take care of my brothers. Nine o'clock. Sunshine. Marshall loving, Pablo loving, Maya loving, Anaïs dancing, smiling, acting. Freedom, loveliness, fun, creation. Play.

I am detached from the deep desire for Bill. He is not the child who gives me joy. He is the sick child who gives me pain. Now I desire Marshall, who is soft and caressing, but I will no longer desire what I cannot have. I feel soft and iridescent.

Staff: "Your face, a mask…"

The doctor: "You have a tumor in the left ovary."

Staff: "You were in grave danger of breaking."

Dr. Jacobson: "You have anemia."

Wilson: "A great wistfulness in your face."

I thought my great illness was over.

I'm peddling my new book without joy because I don't get full understanding, only partial, and yet I know what I am doing is right.

Faith.

Do I have to resort to the passion of Wilson to see myself again as desirable, beautiful and wise, because a little child treats me harshly?

Wilson: "You are the only beautiful thing in my life now. You don't set off my neurosis, my hostility. I'm a very quarrelsome man."

He buys me a lovely, luxurious kimono, a black lace nightgown, dainty slippers, lays them on the bed as a Christmas gift, but I feel I am borrowing them, that they do not belong to me because I do not belong to him. He is trying to make me a wife. "Stay all night. Come to my house on the Cape."

There is a deep split of the roles I play. I have suddenly rebelled at the role of ideal mother and muse towards Henry and Gonzalo. I played a lesser role with Hugo, that of the sick child, the suffering woman (when he didn't know the suffering was at my

Don Juan life). And there is my role of showing the world a legendary figure, a perfect jewel, an idealized woman, to which the world responded. The dream others have of me stimulates them to create.

Sunday, October 14, 1945

The child, who was not allowed to be a child, who was overburdened with responsibilities, became a problem child, a sick child. Staff will let the child live, but not the problem child. I bring him an image of happiness. The next day it is "reality," selling a book, difficulties, humiliations, money problems. Staff says all this comes out of my hostility to reality, to the adult world.

I have split:

the world of the child; the world of realism

the world of the artist; money

play; power

purity; hell on earth: war and politics

creation; self-interest

imagination; corruption

freedom; the dullness and restrictions of bourgeois world

My hostility towards authority, money, organization of the world, the father and mother world.

I love the child because I wanted secretly to *be* the child. I played the role of ideal parent to the child, in opposition to my violent, childish, severe parents.

At Staff's I weep, feeling the helplessness and why I love the child so much. "The child is the dearest part of you." Such an effect these words have. I kept them in mind while facing Maya's camera for a close-up, and it came out beautifully.

I have a strange relationship with Wilson. I never want to see him, but when I do, his fervor burns me like a fire. I let him love me, but I barely answer. I hate the dismal house because of the father in him, his solidity, good manners, his choice of Hogarth prints, the bourgeois bedroom. But I like his ardor, his physical vehemence, his articulate world, his passion, his worship. I enjoy his possession because of its vigor, its energy. I enjoy his mind, his humility, tenderness and possessiveness, his enjoyment of me. "You are the best woman in bed I have ever known. Marvelous. You are without flaw. You are a darling, a sweet, marvelous woman. I long so much for you in between your visits I can't work. I want you all the time. I want to have you here. I want to show you a bigger world."

"You won't," I say, "You'll keep me all to yourself."

"If Hugo is worried, tell him you're going out with me so I will write you a good review."

"Oh, I can't say that, he wouldn't believe that, it is not consistent with my character."

At times he reminds me of Henry in his florid, frank sensuality, at times of Rank. He takes me to the same German restaurant, Jaeger's on 86th Street, where Rank took me. I wonder at what moment I will cease to enjoy his passion for me and turn away.

Meanwhile, I like his power and palpability. He gives me such a balm to my insecurity, such a vigorous climate after the evasion, mysteries and impalpability of Bill. Bill does not write me, so I take my revenge with others.

I give my love to Pablo. We establish a cajoling, caressing relationship, all but possession, and the same with Marshall. A little dance of attraction and fear, fascination, a dance, nothing more. As soon as I come near Marshall, his mouth trembles. He is afraid.

"The intensity of what I feel for you, Anaïs, terrifies me."

"Stay near me, at least," I say, "and feel the bond, as a constellation, spreading my intensity."

Meanwhile, the terribly human, vulnerable, womanly Anaïs suffers, wants love, caresses, a human love such as I get from Hugo, but she is not understood and feels the continuous presence of the illusion starving the human being. The worlds of the child and artist are, for me, the same world. I have drawn the children around me—and again they cannot love.

How can you escape from illusion and its tentacles, its webs, its torments?

Reality: a man who utters words, who dwells on your body, who hears what you say.

Did I have a secret wish that Wilson would encompass me? No, he cannot, because he is not of the future. He is the classical critic. He is crystallized, inflexible. There is a hardening of the arteries. He has set ideas. He looks like one of the Dutch bourgeois in the Dutch school of painting, with his florid skin, the satiated flesh, the small eyes, the solidity of the earth and its heaviness. He has no sense of beauty, no lightness. He grunts like an animal. He wears unbelievably ugly brown army underwear. He is didactic, makes definitive statements, has conventional ideas about style and form. He has learning. He is all in brown, earth brown, and fire red, but oh, to feel a man's strength, a man who knows what he is and what he wants, the certitude.

OCTOBER 20, 1945

There has always been at the very bottom of my being a little girl who was afraid of life, afraid of death, and afraid of man.

On the doctor's couch she does not dare breathe too deeply.

Dr. Staff says, "Breathe."

I breathe deeply, and it makes me sob. It is too painful.

As a poet, I wrote this: This little girl loved Bill, but then this half-woman let Man worship her, a man who said: "I long for you. I have dreams of possessing you. You are divine. You are more wonderful than your writing."

Let the classical critic bow to the flawless feet, the one I thought was my enemy: the father, the man, the critic, a man of culture, the enemy of the child, the woman, the primitive artist (he hates Henry Miller).

How alight his eyes are, how lusty his possession, to which the woman responds. How fiery his coloring is, animal and terrestrial.

And then I say, because I have been truthful, "I am not in love with you." As he leaves me at midnight he is strangely moved and says, "Don't ever forget me!" as if it were a farewell, and this I hear with my feelings. It is the first time something he says enters my feelings, is audible to my heart.

"Must I order a new girlfriend?" he teases, to draw from me some word of love I cannot utter. But now I am tangled with his emotion, his vigor and his certitude. I am "a woman who does not destroy man."

No, it is true, but I destroy myself and consequently the relationship. I commit suicide and thus harm the man.

I listen to his criticism, at peace with the father for the first time.

I was opened. Staff saw my fears. I said, "If I go on breathing deeply (into the present) I will get hysterical, go crazy."

But yesterday, breathing deeply was not an ordeal. It became pleasure, warmth, sensuality.

I faced my fears, my helplessness, my substitutions and roles to disguise weakness. At the moment I acknowledged my weakness, I felt weak, but I also felt real love entering into me, though it may be neither Bill nor Edmund Wilson (both born May 8). I feel I have been a little mad, like Don Quixote, and am in convalescence. Withdrawing my passion from Bill has produced a constellation of lesser loves, but painless and rich. I desire Marshall for his softness and whimsicality, his ivory skin and black, curled hair, his full mouth and his emotional intensity. I desire Pablo when he is near me, so fiery and ecstatic and flowing, so full of movement and impetuousness. I desire Duits' attitude, his delicate hands, his timidity and unusual intelligence. He brings me Gerard de Nerval to read. Marshall brings me a humorous collage. Pablo brings a "dream boat" made of tulle and paint and spangles.

The conflict in my writing is the conflict in my life: the opposition by an ugly reality to a marvelous dream; the forbidding the human to destroy the illusion; the opposition of the artist (child) world to the adult world of authority, limitation and power.

Staff says I have written like a medium. I fear criticism because I think it will destroy my spontaneity. I fear all delimitation, and that is why I cannot construct (or find what I want: I would have to define what I want, to make a choice). When Staff asks me what I want, I flounder. I live by impulse and improvisation. I have no plans.

I set up Wilson as a symbol of the man's world. I chose a man I do not love, do not desire, so as to tear him down and say: "You see how a man behaves? Impossible man."

He wants to shape my writing. Beneath his interest lies tyranny. When I went Saturday afternoon under his pretense of talking about my writing, I went determined not to be possessed, and he would not accept my excuses (no time, etc.) but forced me, imposed his lust, afterwards asking my forgiveness. This way I can tell my analyst (and myself): see what would happen to me in the hands of a man of power?

Yet I liked his sexual strength and his power in the literary world. At first I felt elation at his passion, but now I feel it as tyranny, a burden. Already he sees that being married to me would not be so marvelous because I am "such an important personality that people would fill the house (as they do) with their cult of you."

"So you see, dear Doctor, I can't advance. I can't move towards the mature man who would dominate and crush me, and I can't move towards the child who feels afraid and overwhelmed."

"So you act to maintain the split."

And I feel helpless. Lost.

Coming home from Wilson, I wept in the taxi for Bill, who abandoned me to my fate by his inhumanities. I pray to be reunited with him. I think of his coming.

I shiver to think he may feel towards me as I do towards Wilson.

But if Wilson had been handsome and desirable, I wouldn't feel this way. I have to close my eyes when he descends upon me. As with Rank, I feel I am living out *Beauty and the Beast*. It is not Wilson, but my image of reality which I chose according to my concept of it—force and authority—that I rebel against, hate, justifiably reject. The concept of ugliness: his house is ugly, his writing is ugly, his taste is ugly, his body is ugly.

Still, there is a force, like Henry's force, a force of certitudes, convictions, acknowledged wants and attitudes, and I felt this would give me strength at the time I felt the weakest.

Staff points out the receptivity, passivity, reflection in experience, while I reflect on it with great sensitivity. How am I going to use this? Where is my direction, construction, purpose? I must limit, define, construct. It's funny. Wilson used the same words, almost: "You reflect. There is no movement."

I have expanded into the infinite. I must contract of my own volition. My search for freedom led me to chaos, and I feel overwhelmed.

The street of trucks. My first sensation of returning to a diminutive state came while I walked down 16th Street towards the river, which is a street lined with truck garages. I found myself with huge trucks all around me, coming from the left, right, front and back. They were enormous, painted red, with vast prows and sterns, the wheels alone being taller than I am, and I felt small, helpless, cornered. I lost all sense of power and maturity. In one instant I became a child in a hostile and threatening world. That was the first day. The second time it happened was in the evening, when I had to get somewhere. I stood at the corner of 14th Street deliberating. People were pressing into the subway. I visualized the rush and the violent efforts one had to make to enter, and even more to come out of it. I felt discouraged. There was also a crowd waiting for the bus, and two busses passed too full to stop. I tried to hail a taxi. Two or three people got one just before I could. I suddenly felt small again, lost, left out, disconnected, helpless. I wanted to give up, sit on the curbstone and weep. I felt like the beggars, the bums, the tramps. I felt like making no more efforts and letting myself fall.

Staff stripped me of my pretenses, my false courage, false powers, false masteries, false maturity. So I stand again at the beginning, to find not the crippled child, but the one who is mature but free and without chaos, hysteria or madness.

I am so tired.

As I was made small again, I felt nearer to Bill, and I wanted him. If only he were the tender child and not the callous one, if only his weakness and fears did not make him hostile and rigid, if only he would give me his softness and trust me. *Enfant méchant, enfant malade, enfant terrible.*

The end of another diary, one of confusion, of terrible pain, of being torn asunder. I broke again, and this time it was a little child who helped to break me.

So it is to be Bach, the quartets, organization and form.

Life changes according to revelations which dispel the blindness of our acts. I have discovered what I want: human feeling, human emotion, human response. On the way to see Wilson, I mailed a letter to Wallace Fowlie, who is the opposite of Wilson.

NOVEMBER 2, 1945

I could not close the diary without enclosing in it Bill's voice over the telephone saying, "I am here." Our meeting downstairs by the door, and our impulse towards each other, our lying later on the couch and kisses, and his uncontrollable orgasm happening before he took me.

Then he escaped to Yale to see Fowlie, was swallowed once more by his mother, and returned one afternoon and lay beside me, fearful again, timid, heart beating. My own heart began to beat like his. We took our clothes off and flowed into each other. He said, "Make it slow." His mouth was so hungry, his hands and skin so delicate. The intensity, the joy, the consuming flame of this. It is no wonder he takes flight again from this abandon of ourselves. To a little child this must seem like an earthquake. Yet this perfect moment of softness and utter possession reaches me more deeply than any other. I can accept his flight and his guilt when I see the way he comes out of the prison of the army, of his family, and of his own fears to mingle with me. I feel sympathy for his brusque anxieties, his shame, his resentments, his split self. My adored Bill, who says: "You take what I say too seriously. You know I'm confused." He is so fearful of these sudden losses of himself in passion, and yet those rare, intense moments are everything for me. He is too small to contain me. My little prisoner only can escape for a moment of passion, only one, after a week of hope, of waiting, of frustration.

I also was a prisoner. I did not dare to reach for what I wanted except indirectly, subtly, by pain, concessions, sacrifice. I felt nearer to his timidity, but he cannot see mine, and when he lies with his head on my breast, he says suddenly that I have to put my head on his alarmed, small heart. Meanwhile I not only discovered my own timidity and a child in me fearful of rejection, but I have also discovered a powerful, rich woman in need of a great passion. I have split up my loves, taken away some from Bill, because he could not bear its weight, and divided it among Pablo, Marshall and Charles, between Hugo and Gonzalo.

But I could not bear to close this book without enclosing in it again the fragrance of the child Bill, half-child and half-man, as I am half-child and half-woman. His delicacy, his fears, his unreality, his ghostly life, his solitude, his transparency, his purity, his erotic desires, his small, fearful evasions of his prisons, my pale and fragile prisoner, and my love for him and our passion, and his flights, and my new belief in his inarticulate half-love, his child's love. He is here, light and airy like this paper, silky and transparent. He lies here, and it is a marriage of children touching each other's fragility, two sick, imprisoned children, one that I was and am no longer, but then am I not always tied to my suffering twin, the one who is not free…

We walk hand in hand.

NOVEMBER 1945

After reaching the depths of weakness, helplessness, of childlike terror and anguish with Dr. Staff, I asked him why I feared appearing in public.

"As a child you are rejected for being yourself, loved only if you are good (according to your parents' concept). You fear to face the world with your real self. You fear not to be loved. So you are afraid. Your art is an act of defiance. It is your act of self-assertion."

So I faced my fear of lecturing. I accepted to appear November 3 at the Young Men's Hebrew Association Poetry Readings. I awakened in the morning thinking, this is my new birthday. I was calm all day. I made myself beautiful, quietly. I wore my black tailored suit with a fuchsia blouse. Hugo, Frances and Eduardo came with me. At moments my heart beat wildly. I did not sit at the table as Parker Tyler did. Then I stood up. The lights were strong. At first I was a little afraid. I read my lecture, and then a passage from *This Hunger*. They clapped. I could not tell what people felt, but this is what I discovered later: they were deeply moved by my voice, my appearance. I was simple and emotional. My voice became deeper. I felt what I was reading, and I made them feel it. The applause at the end was warm, spontaneous. I won them. I signed books. I felt free, elated to have mastered my fear, to have communicated with the public, to have come out of my shell.

"The soulfulness of your eyes," said Hugo. "I almost broke down." I feel the love of the world flowing back to me. A letter from Edmund Wilson: love. A letter from Wallace Fowlie: love.

The same evening my love Bill was leaving, but I felt no pain. He does not let me. He wants me "not serious."

He puts too many obstacles in the way of my love, so I must love him more lightly, in proportion to his age, and so the love flows out to others, all around.

I dreamed of a transparent child. I am the transparent child. I flow clear and free.

Hugo said, "Do not feel guilt."

"I burdened you financially, overburdened you."

"But you carried the spiritual burden. You pioneered for me, you suffer for me."

"Yes, I suppose I did carry your soul, and at times it was a pretty heavy one."

Dream of the transparent child. Luminous. I saw transparent shoes and wanted them. I love crystals. I love transparency.

Staff says: "Unashamed. Willing to be transparent. All of yourself."

"But," he says to Hugo, "I am not finished with her yet. Anaïs is very *elusive*, very evanescent, very clever. She has many ways of escape. Her way of escaping analysis is to make a success of it quickly. I'm on my guard with her."

He has made me suspect of my own idealized states, my elation. I always come to tell him what a good analysis it is, but he looks for the negative aspects. I dedicated my lecture to Bill. I allied myself to the child as an act of defiance against the adult world. The adult world still appears as a caricature in the mind of Anaïs. I try to tell the analyst, "Look at Edmund Wilson, he let his writing slide downward. He has become conventional. He is full of mechanical statements, uninspired." And Staff says, "In this case you are right."

That I am right is proved by Wilson himself, who is attracted to my "exquisitely spiritual" appearance, and, feeling that his writing has become peripheral and extraneous, he says he is going to tackle more essential themes. He is inspired by me now, rather than I by him, inspired by my purity in art.

"What are you trying to tell me," Staff asks, when I bring him "experiences," "that reality means lust, power, self-interest, money, etc., and that the world of the artist and the child is purity, disinterestedness?"

I say: "When I say something in the form of fantasy I expect people to do the unraveling of its meaning, as when I bring you a dream to interpret. People want me to do the revealing."

Wilson, seeking to use his subtlety to reach me says: "What you are is Ondine. You have not suffered. You have never loved, never wept."

I tell him: "I have not fallen in love with you. You must find yourself a wife. I cannot go on like this—it must be love."

Yet I answer the core of his sexual act because it is so virile, so strong. I answer the power...but I don't want him. Yet I like my peace with him, *the reconciliation with the father*, my invulnerability to his criticism, my clear insight into his limitations. He failed to understand the last chapter of *This Hunger*, that the neurotic can only see the mirror in the garden, and not the garden. Reflections only.

I inhabit the unconscious. I will always write from there, flow from there, more deeply until I reach the collective unconscious of woman.

Staff said to Hugo, "She is a rare perfume."

In his office the hatred of reality takes place (the grey mornings, the exploitative booksellers, the money problems, the critical father, the aggressive mother), but Staff shows me that I choose them for the purpose of caricaturing them. I make up my own little story so cleverly. Man the father is ugly, he drinks, he is heavy, gross, lustful. The boy is beautiful, delicate, subtle. I always invent my little game of drama to suit my point. I choose my personages to prove my point. But Staff is not deceived when I say, "I am free now." He says: "But if you were entirely free you would not be so conscious that it was your 'birthday,' that you wanted a new dress for it. You are a little too conscious of your freedom."

I can tell now about the breathing exercises, which at first caused anxiety, sobbing and pain, but which brought release, warmth and sensuality afterwards. There is confusion between femininity and masochism, a real split. The only release I had was sensual, and since it was the only release, I over-emphasized it and became a nymphomaniac. I feel myself exploding under the great tension of the split between fantasy and reality, the split in the loves, which became more difficult to integrate because I escaped from one relationship to another, to relieve the pain of an old one by engaging in a new one. A dreamed life. I gave myself entirely only to the diary.

I married the diary.

The boy: Bill. His imprisonment touches me (like mine), his solitude, his detachment, his guilt.

November 10, 1945

When I left Staff today, I had a distinct impression of the dreamed life—that I am awakening from a nightmare, discovering again that the monsters are in my imagination, and when I succumb to their victimization I succumb to my own needs and desires.

Dialogues with Charles Duits take the place of my intellectual talks with Bill. Exaltation, ecstasy and dancing with Marshall and Pablo take the place of passion with Bill. The night after my lecture, I had a real dance of sensuality with Pablo which was almost like possession. And last night the very sight of Marshall exalted me; we walked ahead of the others at a great speed, the speed of elation. We sat in a café, his hand so light on my bare arm (light, like Bill's airy fingers between my legs), my hand on his shoulders. When he, Claude and I come to my place (he is living with Claude), he orders me to say goodnight to Claude, leaves Claude at the front door, carries me up the stairs for three flights, then kisses me softly. I went to bed and fell asleep on his kiss (softer than Bill's, not as masterful, but then he is more masterful than Bill in other ways). He treats me like another child at moments and forgets his fears. Such a deep love I have for all of them, with Bill at the center, unattainable, like a dream, who has become a dream, and then the others nearer to me, whom I can talk to, dance with, touch and kiss, each one beautiful, each one bright, each one gifted, each one sensitive and near to me. Duits is the most intelligent and is cohesive, cultured and developed as the European child is developed, with structure, order and form. Bill is intelligent by fits and starts, confused, immature, with sudden illuminations. Marshall is more evenly perceptive than Bill, more developed in living, more emotional and free. Pablo, without intellect, is all impulse, emotion, physical expansiveness, violence. Bill is still a nebula, clouded, misty, dim, sleepwalking. It is this in him that makes me dream him. Marshall is more human, more accessible to human feelings. All of them are elusive and subtle, but they are so near to me, so much a part of me. All of them are fearful of the banal, the trite. The time I spend with them is rich (Frances thinks it is wasted), richer than the time I spent with Wilson. I feel inspired, moved. They understand me better. The exigent idealism of the young.

Dream: I was at a party. The hostess had written a letter to my father. I asked if I could add a post scriptum. She passed me the paper. But when I began to write I found I was trying to write on my rose panties. I made an ink stain. I was in a factory, given a machine to run. I felt a bunch of threads in my throat, choking me, and I pulled them out. I was not good at understanding the machine.

Association: My dislike of mechanics, of all machinery. Analogy between Child and Artist: they both live in a world of their own making, in conflict with the adult world. They both create an inner world according to their own fantasy. They do not understand money values or the pursuit of power. They create without knowing mechanics or disciplines. They invent their own forms and manners and styles. They make no distinction between themselves and art. They are personages in the fantasy world.

In the adult or realistic world there is tragedy for the child and artist. They are rebels against existing conditions. Sometimes they feel loved for their sallies, their whims, sudden honesty, but sometimes too they are punished for them. They both have direct access to people's feelings and cannot be deceived. The world of the child, the world of the artist, will always appear more wonderful than the adults' or realists' world, which is ruled by conscious compromises, self-betrayals, selling out.

Staff: A handsome, dark-eyed, olive-skinned man of about thirty-five, a little bald, looks like a Spaniard. Active, alert, sound, solid, with a very warm and human voice. Dynamic. I was determined not to charm him and made no effort. He gave me my first compliment today, when he noticed my new dress and my new way of wearing my hair. His only slip away from analysis was when he became interested in the idea of my lecture, because it was in accord with something said by his own analyst, "The psychoanalyst must be a novelist, able to construct a character from one fragment."

Staff understands my mechanism, my roles, pretenses, tricks and true aims. He has brought out my hatred of the father, of authority, my need to expose and destroy him, while I am able to love the child, the son, the younger brother, the boys who cannot harm me. He brought out my fear of the big world, my hatred of the bank, publishers, institutions and traditions, my trust of the art world and the artist and the tension between these worlds, my pleasure in stolen joys, the intensity of sexual pleasure with Bill due to its delinquent quality (stolen over the heads of his parents and of Hugo). Today my first transference: my desire for Staff when he asked me what I felt about him, which is clearly sexualized.

"In real love," he said, "the child is brought out and then amalgamated to the man and woman, integrated with man and woman. You brought it out to mother it, because the child in you had not received enough mothering or fathering, so you caused a fixation upon the child element in the man. You were not yourself entirely woman enough to bring out only the man, to relate to the man alone; you didn't want the whole man like Wilson, who would invade you, dominate you..." (Wilson had said, "I can understand a woman like you must be free. I would bully you, force you, want you absorbed in me, and you couldn't develop.")

(I must write about the relationship with Wilson. I have repressed doing so, because it was incestuous.)

Staff: "The slaying of the dragon again, the big dean of the critics. The conventional, traditional critic. You had to seduce him, make him respect you (and you succeeded). You had to see that he had no real power, that he cannot seize you, that he is obtuse, heavy-handed. To lose your fear, you exposed him, as you exposed Rank."

I have been as destructive as other women, only more subtly, more dangerously. I have used my sexual attributes *to destroy the father*. Man was my enemy. Incredible. How I deluded others and myself.

Wilson had said: "You are one woman who does not destroy. I can see the men who loved you will love you forever. Miller has no anger against you, no hatred."

Another layer uncovered, one layer after another exposed. The topsoil of our personalities is nothing. How to do this in a novel, to include all the layers. Character is bottomless. I only now have discovered my own destructiveness, which is hard on my idealism (my idea that I was creative, constructive, positive). Wilson said: "Your men never hate you. I hate Mary now. You give them something. You bring out the best in me. There is something pure in you."

I am disturbed by the discovery of this dark side in myself. I could see it in other women. I could see it in man's fear of woman, and now I see it in my fear of man.

"You haven't loved yet, Anaïs," said Wilson.

How hard it becomes to write when the truth changes every day.

Edmund Wilson's house is narrow, unbeautiful, on a peaceful little impasse. The first time he took me there, after our dinner, he wanted to show me the devastation caused by Mary McCarthy, who took away everything on the first floor except two chairs left in the parlor. I was chilled by the barrenness, the homeliness, his story of the devastation caused by Mary's neurosis. Mary is very much Lillian in *Ladders to Fire*. We talked. I knew then he wanted me, but I didn't want him. I left early. I was playing with my fear and my desire to conquer, to enter the world of tradition (history of Greek art, culture, perfectionism, classicism, convention). Something in Edmund won me too: contrary to the critic in him (the censor), he is enthusiastic, fervent, irrational, lustful, passionate and violent. We discussed my book. He had more to say about the flaws than he did about what I had achieved, yet he recognized the "newness." But the father and daughter story in *This Hunger*, he admitted, guided him in his relationship with his daughter. He wanted me to reconstruct his house, to help him choose a divan and curtains, but I didn't want this, so I subtly substituted his daughter to give him what he needed. He still needed me to talk to, finding me wise and stimulating.

The second time at his house, his passion burned like a fire, temporarily annihilating his physical ugliness. The power, vigor, decisiveness, and the wild torrent of generous praise!

As with Rank, I was without passion, deep in myself.

Wilson grunts like a bear, snorts, is too fleshy, twitches from drinking too much. There is an absence of beauty and fantasy which will make me leap again towards the luminous body of Bill. Oh, god, in the taxi I yearned for Bill, as if the inadequacy of Bill had left me to be victimized by the father. Oh, Bill of the silences, who dared not claim, the delinquent child who stole into me, is back home again, burdened with the guilt that has overshadowed our love. Bill, whose careless letters broke my happiness and who is nearly on his way while Anaïs is overwhelmed by the power of the father.

I lay at Bill's feet the world he cannot possess because he has no real access to it, no perception of it. I do this because unconsciously I feel Bill closer to this world, yet nothing in Bill's exterior proves this, nothing but the revealing beauty of his spiritual body.

Each time I said to Wilson: "It cannot go on. You are the father to me. I must withdraw." But he overruled me. He had a book for me. He had the review of *This Hunger*. He had more worship, more desire, which, like a torrent, engulfed me.

Then Bill came, and to be with him that one passionate afternoon, I abandoned Staff and Wilson. I returned to Wilson as atonement. Staff said, "You love Bill because he is a prisoner, and you both steal your joys from a terrible world."

I love him, but the obstacles are too great. I relinquish him. I feel no pain at his leaving. He stifles and strangles my love in his own imprisonment.

GORE

If I could have loved a woman, it would be you

NEW YORK, NOVEMBER 19, 1945

Kimon Friar asked me to go to his lecture on love at the Y.M.H.A. I was in a sad mood, so I dressed as Mary Stuart, who had her head cut off by a jealous Queen Elizabeth, in a tight black dress with long sleeves half covering the hand, a heart-shaped black hat edged with pearls, and a white veil. Kimon lectured at the head of a long table. At the foot of the table one chair was empty, and I took it (Hugo had to sit behind me). Next to me sat a handsome lieutenant, who, after I had leaned across him to speak to Maya Deren, spoke to me. "Are you French? I am a descendent of troubadour Vidal." His voice is like Bill's. He is luminous and manly. He is nearer to the earth, not nebulous, but clear and bright. He talks, is active, is alert and poised. But he has the same tall and slender body, the same clear skin, and the same full, sensual mouth. He is twenty years old. He is one of the editors at Dutton, and his own novel is appearing in the spring. He knows *Under a Glass Bell* and had guessed who I was. He asked when he might visit me. I said I would be home that evening or on Tuesday evening. He said he would come on Tuesday as he was not free that evening. But after a moment, he said "I'd like to come this evening if you don't mind."

So four hours after meeting him, he walked into my studio. It was his likeness to Bill which attracted me. His voice is rich and warm; he is intuitive. There is too much to tell.

I eluded an evening with Wilson.

I tear up Bill's letter because it is uninteresting, noting, however, that on January 5 he will come for eighteen days. I write him lovely letters.

I feel more insincere than ever. I must break with Wilson.

To separate truth from creation now, what a task. I write about Miller without love in the new book and marry him to Thurema in order to make a new story that is true without telling the truth. If only I could tell the truth, how easy it would be.

My attraction to Gore Vidal is based on his resemblance to Bill, but I like his aristocracy, his French ancestry, his intelligence, his manliness, his poise, his greater worldliness. He is wealthy and free. But at the moment I feel love like a river, not in individuals. I can spend a marvelous hour with Gonzalo in Bill's room at Frances's, and then be with Marshall, and feel both equally. For now I am dulled and numbed to pain, and can only respond to pleasure. Therefore, I love no one.

When Gore Vidal says he will be the President of the United States, I believe him. He walks in easily, not dream-fogged, not unreal, not bemused as Bill did. His eyes are not blue, not shadowed in blue, but clear, open, hazel. They are French eyes. His face is square, not long and narrow. I begin to see *him*, now, and I like him for himself. He came Sunday afternoon. Then this evening we sat at the Number One bar and talked. His father is a millionaire. His grandfather was Senator Gore. His mother left them when he was ten to marry someone else. "She is Latin-looking, vivacious, handsome, her hair and eyes like yours," he said, "beloved of many."

The boy-man is lonely. He rejects homosexual advances. He says, "In the army, I live like a monk." He is writing his novel. He is clear-minded, but emotionally confused and vulnerable. He is less afraid than Bill. (Oh, Anaïs, Anaïs, I know that my love for the disconnected, aloof, lonely child is my own lack of real contact with others. Their imprisonment is mine.)

Will his French troubadour lineage stir in his memory some recognition of Anaïs, whose name comes from a little Greek town in the south of France? I feel yes, unconsciously. He has the courage to say, "May I come?" He telephones, he can command a taxi. Will he dare? I feel the bond, less than with Bill, but one that suits my present self better, for I am returning to my aristocracy and my pleasures, and leaving my bohemianism behind.

Gore talks about his childhood: "When my mother left me I became objective...I live detached from my present life...at home our relationships are casual...my father married a young model...I like casual relationships...when you are involved you get hurt...I do not want to be involved ever..."

Mutely, as with Bill, Gore's sudden softness envelops me.

I am advancing into the adult world of power, leaving behind me the crippled and the weak self. The voice of the analyst is the voice of sincerity. I said to Staff: "I have become terribly aware of my insincerity. I dread the world of power—the world of my father, the salon—because there is a greater insincerity there than among the bohemian artists."

Staff: "We live in an insincere world, full of falsities. All you can do is to find your own integrity, act by your own values."

I am getting nearer to the lost Anaïs.

Roles: the proof they exist is in the loneliness *in between*. My character: where am I? I am here, in the diary, confessing my roles.

My first act of sincerity: I broke with Wilson. He was sad, shocked, tender, sincere. I said I could not go on, that it was not worthy of us, not big enough, not deep enough, not satisfying. I had been afraid of his anger.

"Afraid," said Staff, "because deep down you recognize your false pretenses. You knew you had never wanted Wilson. It was a compulsion to seduce the father-critic you feared, enslave him and diminish his power. Notice that all your relationships are partial, which is a way of eluding control and contact. You have never given yourself, only a part of yourself. A part to one, a part to another. You have never loved. What excites you sexually in these boys is that you do not fear them. They do not demand as man demands. They are little men, not dangerous. Their anxiety in the world of men, which they can only calm by seducing the men, is like your anxiety in the world of men, which you can only calm by seducing them too. You choose those who you know cannot give themselves, because that gives you the courage to let go. You know they will let you down and that you will inevitably suffer from being thwarted. But you prefer this pain to the other, the pain of giving and being betrayed, as you were as a child. You choose unconsciously those who will not assert themselves or claim you. Or if you find one who does assert himself, does claim all of you (Rank, Wilson), then you do not love them, you reject them."

Staff: Departmentalization. Close one, open another. Multiple relationships, not out of richness, but to maintain the split necessary to my life. The split is safety from contact.

"But if I put all my intensity upon one person, it would shatter him!"

"Not if it is well answered," said Staff. "It's only shattering when the other is split too, and feels threatened." (How frightened Bill was when I centered all my passion upon him!)

December 5, 1945

Gore is a lieutenant at Mitchell Field. He comes in on weekends, and Sunday he came to see me. We had a fine talk, lightly serious, gracefully sad. He read me from *Richard II*. "Why was he killed?" I asked. "Because he was weak. I am not weak," said Gore.

No, he is not weak, but he might need Joan of Arc to place him on his throne. I told him his arthritic hand was due to a psychic cramp for writing about an ordinary hero when he himself is no ordinary young man. I teased him, touched upon his depression. His handwriting is chaotic and unstable. He took me to dinner.

Today he called me up, "This is troubadour Vidal." His voice is lovely, musical. He is not homosexual, he says, but he doth protest too much.

Bill is coming December 22.

Two days in bed with bronchitis.

I have to escape from this children's world where the woman Anaïs has outgrown her childhood fantasies. Can I? Am I still in love with Caspar Hauser? In both Bill and Gore the idea of death is strong.

When Bill won me, Pablo declared his love. He showed me his suffering and jealousy, his flight from me, his homosexual ambivalence, his desire to be psychoanalyzed. At the door, he kissed me for the first time as a lover, ardently. I became evasive and elusive, but I feel more for them all than I do for man.

Chinchilito calls up to tell me that he has spent three days making me a Christmas present.

God, god, god, I need love, I need it, I need it. That is what Bill feels, poor Bill. His need is endless. He cannot even answer, only drink, drink, drink of it. The love-starved children. Staff called them the love-starved monsters.

DECEMBER 10, 1945

Gore came, and we slid easily into a sincere, warm talk. He dropped his armor, his defenses, his roles. He confessed that he has had homosexual experiences—casual ones—without love. He has taken women but recoils from them. He may feel attracted to the men, but he cannot love them. He is caught in a zone of non-love, non-desire. He dreams of love but does not know it. "You are the only one I have told this to. I am amazed. I don't like women. Either they are silly, like the girls of my set I'm expected to marry, or they are harsh, strident, masculine intellectuals. You are so different..."

He takes me to dinner at the Lafayette. All the society mothers look for him, for their cocktails and dances. The debutantes write him letters, "Why are you so detached?" As we walk, I take his arm. This gesture has infinite repercussions upon the long distance range of his being. When I relinquish it, a moment later he extends it back and says, "*Mon bras?*"

The part of me that was living out my relationship with Bill is still tied to Gore's voice and full mouth by the thread of resemblance, but Gore's own definiteness and maturity have now taken their rightful place: he is more adequate, answers all I say, and holds his ground. When we return home (he came at four and left at midnight), he makes me laugh with the most amazingly well-acted pastiches of Roosevelt, Churchill, a southern senator, a petitioner at the House of Commons, etc. He is so proud that his well-constructed roles and personae masked his homosexuality from me, that there is no confusion possible between him and Pablo and Marshall. His façade is entirely manly and upright. But now, I abandon my writing, my need of the doctor, to write about him because I enjoy his presence. I enjoy being allowed into his secret self.

His very far apart, clear hazel eyes open into mine, "I give you the true Vidal, a supreme gift." Leaving, he says: "I'll come on Wednesday. Don't let anyone else come. Send Hugo away."

DECEMBER 13, 1945

Wednesday I met him at the restaurant, wearing my fur hood and cape. He had news for me. Dutton had a conference, offered $1,000 and a contract for all the new books! We celebrated.

When he tells me I must finish my new book in two months, I say: "I don't know how I will do it! I'll have to stop seeing people, with a few exceptions, or I'll have to go away."

"Wait till I'm out of the army" (I had told him Hugo was going to South America in February, and he dreams of going south or to Mexico with me).

When he gets up to pay, I watch his body with desire. In the taxi he says, "I am jealous of your young men." I know this is bad for me. He will not be able to take me, or if he does, he will have anxiety. Strange—just before going out, I had received a beautiful letter from Bill, a symbolic love letter, but the fear of suffering is still there. I hold Gore as a talisman against pain. I have Gore. Secretly there is a hope, a hope that Gore may become strong because Bill is leaving for Japan, and I cannot lose all of what Bill is to me yet. Gore's warm voice is that of a male, so different from the homosexual voices. It was Gore who called my attention to the homosexual voices.

Anyway, the charm is there.

And the conflict.

Staff took the diary, and while I was uneasy, I didn't expect the remark he made. I expected a condemnation, a judgment, but not what he said: "You live in fantasy. You see things that are not there. You are inventing a world, not because of a conflict between fantasy and reality, but because of the fear of being rejected in the real world (of the father), of being inadequate."

No. Here I resisted. If what I write here is fantasy then my life itself is in danger. I am alarmed. I stayed away from analysis under the pretense of making love with Chinchilito and to receive his beautiful, imaginative Christmas present, but deep down, it was out of conflict. My fantasy world: Gore, the warmth I feel…unreal? The desire? The elation? Is it all unreal? (Yet today I cannot understand having felt the way I did for Lanny Baldwin.) I believe now that the non-feeling I experienced after Bill came from the trauma. I said to Staff: "I feel I'm getting elusive again. I feel the floating, the absence of an anchor, the absence of solidity, integration. I feel diffuse. Lost. Perhaps Gore is an escape."

DECEMBER 16, 1945

Gore's visits on Sundays are now a habit, but I knew he would telephone me yesterday, not wait until Sunday. He had dreams to tell me about. He had his early novel to show me (written at seventeen), his poems. How easily we talk—it flows and shines. He is so responsive, quick, personal, confessional, natural. He is warmer, nearer, stronger than Bill. Sharp. Sometimes I feel a kind of twinship in his quick responses. He does not elude, but meets and answers. Why, why, why, why can't I enjoy this without desire? Why am I so affected? What makes me so vulnerable to his mouth and voice, so moved by his rootless childhood, his old man ways, his intelligent awareness? Latin and Celt, mystic and realist, he says about himself. I can talk to him. He does not frustrate me, or cut me off, or arrest me, or elude, or waver as Bill does. He speaks of the luminosity of my writing, is so gallant, attentive, observant.

Saturday I made the house beautiful. I bought new couch covers, sewed pillow slips, banished the sea shells, the Japanese umbrellas, the jewels, the romantic trappings.

Monday Gore came. He dreamt that he and I stood at the top of a mountain and had a titanic battle. He believes it was a battle about his ambivalence, his duality in sex. He is not interested in the group around me, only in being with me.

"Oh, god," I said to Staff, "this cannot go on. I can't put my passion into it, yet it is Gore who arouses this passion."

Staff: "Because you do not fear them. Bill, Pablo, Gore. They do not threaten you. You feel adequate. But you know they are not. The castrates can't dominate or engulf you, claim you, possess you."

"Small fry," he says contemptuously of the boys, to whom go all my desires and feelings.

Eduardo does Gore's horoscope and says, "There are similarities to Bill." And now Bill is coming.

Gore is jealous of Bill. I told him that Bill was leaving for Japan and that I must forget him. Why? I thought it would encourage him to know that Bill could take me. I have a deeper love for Bill, but there is desire for Gore because I feel that Bill is a part of him.

Staff, "These are all escapes from the man who could answer your passion, and really take you."

I came back to Staff ready for any truth that will deliver me from these fascinations without fulfillment. I really believe I suffered so much from the disproportion between my feelings and Bill's that it split my love and it began to flow to Gore.

While I ponder this strange fascination which brings me so close to Gore that I feel we resemble each other physically, he notices that our eyes are the same color. We get ill at the same time, we get well at the same time. How to free myself, how, how, how?

"At best," says Staff, "there is nothing there for you. What if you do make him a man, have his desire, do everything for him, so he can marry a woman his age and have a child...and you?"

Why, why, why the feeling?

I sent Hugo away...subtly...on a skiing vacation for ten days, ten of the fifteen days of Bill's vacation. And now I'm in love with Gore.

Gore has won his place. His voice, so warm and rich, issuing from a sensuous, lush mouth, delights me. When he telephones it sings, "Anaïs!" He does not know he feels inadequate, that he is overshadowed by the parents, whom he glorifies and belittles himself in the process. He doesn't see that his homosexuality is a part of his childhood. He thinks he is mature because he carries himself with poise in the world, because he is intelligent, wise and mature in his knowledge, because he likes sherry and waltzes, because he is going to be a "severe" husband. But he doubts his strength. He is afraid of failure.

Gore has a feeling of a power to accomplish whatever he wishes, has brilliance of mind, clarity, decisiveness. On the conscious level, he is manly, capable of leadership, active, dynamic, magnanimous, proud, direct, generous, with an expansive attitude. On the emotional level there is another Gore: hypersensitive, insecure, subtle, but passionate. His imagination and intuition are highly developed but not entirely trusted. He is afraid of this and disguises it with convention. He allows the mystical, sensitive, musical poet little freedom, because he associates this aspect of himself with his nature's soft and feminine side. A true Venus and Mars. He will never be passive, therefore he will not be a complete homosexual.

DECEMBER 22, 1945

In a quiet, harmonious studio alone, I wear a new fuchsia dress just as the couches are wearing new covers, with stronger lamps, with order, cleanliness, renewal, clarity and simplicity, and I wait for Bill.

But last night the one I at first mistook for Bill's substitute is winning as himself, winning his own place in me, by our harmonious, vital connection, our understanding of each other. Gore said, "You are the first for whom I ever wrote a poem" and gave me his poem entitled "The Mountain."

All day I had been painting, dressing, curling, beautifying myself for him as well as for Bill.

When Gore comes, I want to kiss him, but I don't because I know it will precipitate a conflict. He has said he is slow to make decisions, to act, and I want it to be his act, his decision, or else it will not be good.

Can he not feel this pull, this longing of the mouth to touch, this full voluptuousness of his? He took his sensuality elsewhere to a homosexual and felt depressed, hostile, repulsed afterwards. No fulfillment. And I felt the pain of this, the jealousy, even though I knew his deeper being was not touched. Three evenings, three aspects of his life. One with the homosexual author of *Dark of the Moon*, drinking, blind sensuality, and depression. One as the dancing partner of a lovely debutante at the high society Victory Ball, where he felt stifled and bored, where the loveliness of the girl did not touch him, where he was critical of her falsities and her prattle (even though she writes poetry), where he left her early to be escorted home by another young man. The third evening was with me, when he gave me the poet and his poem, two pages of his childhood recollections, the fourth chapter of his novel, his sickness from the war, arthritis and stomach cramps, talk, all that lies in him, his mother, his father, his childhood, his homosexuality. He complains of a feeling of *dédoublement*, of unreality. He talks of death, reveals the mystic. He is obsessed, as Bill was, by the circle of young men around me. This open nearness I have with Gore I could not achieve with Bill, because our nearness was only sexual, while the subterranean and the inarticulate were unknown to him. Bill now seems like the younger brother of Gore.

I should be writing, yet all I do is to dream about Bill and Gore in a strange, interwoven way. It is a symphonic obsession, Gore's absence of cruelty an exorcism of the pain Bill deals me. But would Gore become cruel and anxious if he tried to take me? Would all our pleasure together become pain if we attempted to possess each other physically? Gore might then hurt me too, out of his conflict. He was the friend of a girl for six years before he took her and then recoiled—but he did not love her.

Midnight Sunday. Gore is sitting at the foot of the couch writing his play on the werewolf (a legend attributed to his ancestors). He said, "We met at just the right moment."

"It is so good to be one's self without poses," he said. He loses his overly serious society boy's *tenue*. He becomes soft and warm. Only when he talks about homosexuality does a frown come to his face.

Cornelia Vanderbilt is in love with him, and she is very beautiful, but not "too earthy." But he is happier here. "You inspire me," Gore says. I suffer only when I look at his mouth and want it.

Our love takes place in space, in his poem, and in the werewolf play, for I told him the story of the woman who let the werewolf suck her blood to save him from being caught, and this touched his fancy. I meant it as: let the animal free in you no matter if it bites, hurts, kills, so at least he lives out a love of woman in his play. And I lie here in my red robe. (All day I had expected Bill but I have less suffering with Gore. He is tender, attentive, not cruel to me.) Like Bill, he opens my letters saying: it is probably someone telling you how much they love you, etc. It is strange. If I could only learn to love these young men mystically and find a man for myself.

CHRISTMAS DAY, 1945

Yesterday a flowing evening with Gore writing his play. When he got up to leave he was stiff with arthritis. His face was pale, his eyes glowing warm, and an impulse so strong willed me to embrace him, to warm him, and I could not resist it. I embraced him, body to body, my head on his shoulder, cheek against his cheek, not a lover's embrace, but a passionate fraternity (not daring the other, not daring to look at his mouth), and he responded. He did not stiffen, or grow distant or afraid. He returned the pressure equally, firmly, but sought no more. He answered me as he answers my talk, he meets me. He did not elude or fear me, at least. It was whole, bright and warm. I couldn't bear the evening to end without touching him.

But afterwards I felt anxiety. Have I spoiled it? Will he grow afraid of me? I felt he had not. I felt he took the embrace as it was intended, not as a sexual aggression but as a need of simple nearness. But still I could not conquer the anxiety, the regret of my impulsiveness, even though I felt his love.

I refrained from telephoning him. Gore, did I spoil it, this élan of warmth?

I went to Staff instead. "Why, if I'm clearer about this," I said, "am I in it deeper than before?"

"It's like the exacerbation of an illness running its course."

But the sweet delights attending it, the fever, the loveliness of the sun and the snow illumined.

"I fear the loss of magic."

"No loss of magic," said Staff. "Nothing need be lost, only strengthened."

I'm obsessed with the desire to live like this, alone, to have no need of Hugo, to feel light and free, to lie in bed in the evening dreaming.

The first to call me today was Gore: "Merry Christmas, Anaïs. I finished the play. I'll come Friday evening, may I?"

And I was happy.

Is it possible I am reliving my adolescence with Eduardo, but with an understanding of it, with deeper knowledge? The karma of my sixteenth year with the young man a girl of sixteen would love, only then it was blind, and now it is deep.

"Why," I asked Staff, "why do I have a real desire for them?"

"Because you are sexually normal, not homosexual."

Writing all day with the ecstasy and warmth of Gore's early morning telephone call is all I need. And he uttered the right words about my work, "You have expanded in depth, now it should be in width." Others may have said this, but he says it enwrapped with his love and understanding of what I have done—or is it that he has the magic power of saying what I need to hear?

I feel I own this love.

Yesterday Bill called in his little boy's voice, a prisoner of his family because it was Christmas Eve, and today perhaps he could run away. But with the pain he causes, he has broken the spell. There have been too many futile watches, disappointments, absences, elusiveness. He is not warm and near.

I am writing with a more active, dramatic power. Static analysis was my danger in writing.

Seven o'clock. Oh, my diary. Bill came, brought me presents, two little Japanese birds to wear, a bottle of champagne. We sat on the couch and talked. Then I saw on his face that expression of love, and simultaneously we moved towards each other with such a deep impulse. I couldn't believe in my happiness, couldn't believe in it. His passionate kisses. His words: "I have thought of ways to be free. I'll come Thursday night and stay all night. We will begin all over again. I want to stay all night. I always want to sleep here." "We hypnotize each other," I say.

Such kisses, such devouring, as if he would eat me alive. And then such phrases as, "It will be fun to go to Japan," a complete contradiction except that as a little child he feels going to Japan is inevitable…but he has yielded to it. Yet he loves me. I know this when we lie together. He has only a moment, no time to make love, just kissing. Such torment. He came in a pouring rain. I'm left melted, drunk and pained that he had to leave, but so happy at his behavior. He always comes a little older, a little more determined, a little more impulsive. I see again that blue shadow over and under his eyes, the paleness, the mystic language. And I am pierced again, possessed again, and I see the pretense of all my attempts to escape the pain of losing him. He is too young to know what he is losing when he loses me, thinking perhaps he will not lose me.

This does not change in any way my feeling for Gore. Mystically I feel Gore to be an older Bill, come to woo me without fears, to be with me without retractions and flights. He has come to relieve me of the unbearable intensity of my passion for Bill, to divide and soften it, so that my love can match their needs and youth. *Le vrai partage mystique.*

DECEMBER 29, 1945

Thursday evening. Bill came. We went into a long, endless tunnel of caresses, fell asleep together, awakened to more caresses, talked only a little. Our only contact is physical now, because he cannot sustain a relationship. Then he disappeared again into his family prison.

Last night Gore came. As he arrived he handed me his play like a bouquet of flowers. "Here is what you inspired."

I read it. It was intense, dramatic, emotional, strong. He read me the last act. I was stirred. He made me feel I was the cause of it. "I've never written this way, impulsively, directly, without plan. Never with such intensity. I collapsed afterwards."

I let him read my pages on Eduardo. I have never known the way we talk with anyone else. His answers are so close to my thoughts that we have the impression of hearing ourselves talk in the other.

He wanted to know when I would make his portrait. "I made it in the diary when you gave me permission."

"I gave you permission because I knew you would do it anyway! Read me the portrait."

I hesitated. "You can skip anything you want to skip."

I brought out the diary. I was still hesitant.

"I *know* all that is in the diary."

I looked at his face and saw that he knew. I felt uncovered, happy, but hurt. Happy that he does know me, and terribly hurt that the one who comes so near to my thoughts and feelings should be one I am not allowed to touch.

Our faces were a confession of love. He said, "You are Maria" (the woman who gave the werewolf her blood and is willing to die).

"I am not used to being discovered, known by others," I said. I tried to laugh away the pain, the desire to clasp Gore. I said, "Now we're two magicians using magicians' tricks on each other."

"I didn't mind being uncovered by you," said Gore.

I could not say: "It's different. My secret was my love. Yours was your non-love."

To not show my desire—I was hurt because earlier in the evening he had said, "The situation is the same."

"You've had more homosexual experiences?"

"No, because I've been ill. And I felt all the trouble of getting the hotel room, etc., not worthwhile" (whenever he talks about this, it is as a man talks of whoring, deprecatingly, cynically). And with me, he is melted and warm.

"I must retreat from you," I said, my exposure causing me pain because it was the exposure of love. "I won't read you the diary until I feel I can read you every word I wrote, Gore."

Later he said, "It is something we can't face yet."

Such tension and excitement. Doesn't he feel it? His body, can it be so dead when his eyes are full of love, his face, his words, when he knows it is a play of love he has written, when he is saying in so many ways that I am his love? When I said, "You will hurt me," he was so moved. When I lean over at times, talking, to plead, to tell him something with vehemence, I feel him being moved, answering.

Oh Gore, our thoughts and feelings touch, how can it be that our bodies won't? It can't be!

And for the first time I felt sadness, and the desire to run away from him, because he moves me so deeply.

Will Staff deliver me from this fatal love? I know all the reasons, and yet I am caught again, longing, yearning, dreaming, hardly able to work, to write clearly, my whole body aching.

DECEMBER 30, 1945, EVENING

I explained to Gore, "I didn't withdraw because of your coming near to what I think or feel, but because I became aware at that moment that you are the one I am forbidden to love."

"I feel the same thing, yes, all the sadness of it."

In every gesture and glance there is love. When he first comes in, he wears a formal mask, has a certain coldness. But at a certain moment, when we enter our personal realm, he becomes deeply sincere.

"If I were normal I would take you away from Hugo." And again, "I am jealous of Bill."

He wants to destroy the bird Bill made.

His feeling about writing has changed. He now wants color and magic. He realizes, without my ever having had to say it, the conventional mask of his first novel.

He does not believe he is handsome. He has fears and doubts. His only security is external, material, his family position, of which he is proud.

"My play is the first time I have written about love." As he sits near me I am consumed with desire and sadness. When I leave I cannot control myself, and again I hold him to me. Again he holds me. No more. And again I must surrender the mirage of love. Oh, Anaïs.

He always refers to his mother's warmth, her consuming passion for him. So there it is. I can never describe the excitement, the perverse exaltation that takes place. May I find the man who will answer and accept that for which I am ready.

JANUARY 2, 1946

A consuming life. The desperate intensity with Gore was relieved by New Year's Eve with Marshall. At two o'clock we were dancing together at my place. Poor Luke, who is in love with Marshall, saw the exaltation in the air, in the dancing, and left us. I said: "Let's forget this. It wasn't meant to be. Let's just go to sleep together."

In the dark, naked, Marshall began to speak of my unreality, the mask of my smile. Then he spoke of how he did not feel my desire, how his other woman lover was so open about hers. I realized he was telling me what Staff tells me: my fear of rejection makes me elusive and makes my physical warmth invisible so that the man too is lost in this non-presence. I almost wept when Marshall said this, but he didn't know it was fear which caused it—he thought it was merely a lack of substantiality.

At this I began to caress him, arousing his desire with caresses of the mouth until he took me with cries of ecstasy. (I didn't have time to respond. Oh, Anaïs.) With his hands on my body, as I still lay over him, he said: "You are the earth too, but the finest part of it. Not all earth is just black dirt, but there are the veins of precious metals. You are one of the finest veins of the earth."

He got up. He put on music, and we took milk and crackers and cheese. It was five o'clock in the morning when we fell asleep. In the morning he was exultant. "I feel strong and clean. I've always wanted to wash afterwards, but not this time." He began to build up the relationship, too high, dreamed of taking me to his parents in West Palm Beach so they would know he had conquered homosexuality. He said, "With you I can create." He was tender and whimsical, wanted to stay and write his story. But he had to leave because I expected Bill.

Bill came at five. We always begin to talk, becoming mute and overwhelmed with desire. Then everything is total fusion, our bodies understand each other, we sink into voluptuousness. I feel the ecstasy! Such ecstasy! He no longer gets sad afterwards. He whistles while he dresses.

And he left. One hour together in five days. He is completely mastered by his parents again, has become a child again.

When he left, I dressed to meet Gore at the Charles Restaurant, a sad Gore, pale and sardonic. We sat at the St. Regis bar. He mocks his world and yet draws strength from being on the social register. As we walked we met three of his homosexual friends.

I'm saddened by Gore's vanities, his display of position. I saw a discordant Gore, half detached and half dependent on worldly attributes, terribly in need of glorification. I saw his personae in the world: arrogance, coldness, masking his sensitive self.

He said he wanted to take me to the Stork Club. Sitting at the St. Regis in my astrakhan cape and hat and fuchsia dress, I felt sad and estranged from Gore. If I could only detach myself from his mouth.

JANUARY 1946

Marshall came, completely exhausted from the tensions, ecstasy, emotion, surrounding the "miracle," as he calls it. He came pale, eager, gusty, worn. He said he must not take me because he was consumed and needed strength for his work, but actually he is playing with the fire of his new life. I was in the same state and glad, for I was thinking of ways to avoid intensity. I lay down to answer the telephone. While I talked he lay beside me, caressing my legs and stomach. We kissed: "Oh, Anaïs, I can't believe it. I have lost all my fears. I was lying here and I just got roused by your legs, your stomach. It is a miracle."

Desire overwhelmed him. We moved apart. He had come to see if it could be true, if it would last. All evening we played with our desire, and the perverse denial of it, like moths. Embracing, separating, talking, a game I have learned to enjoy. He said, "I have lost weight."

I said, "That was the little piece of ear I bit off."

He laughed and said, "It's like a door opening! I saw a scene in the movies: when the man and the woman kissed, they showed a door opening, and then another, and then another, and the last one opened into space, the sky! That is how I feel. I have never known this, Anaïs!"

If this could be my gift to Gore. If this could happen with Gore. Gore.

I made him leave early.

I slept ten hours from exhaustion. Then Bill came at one, Bill, who quoted Eliot, "A shadow falls between my feelings and fulfillment," to describe himself. We went together to visit Isamu Noguchi, to see his work. Met a Hindu girl there. Went to the Museum of Modern Art. We were happy together, light, arm in arm, hand in hand. A light afternoon of freedom and an exploration of art for my beloved prisoner, and with my new understanding of this moth dance around the fire of desire.

I think of my own understanding of the great fire within me, the desire to unite body and spirit. Knowing fully now my own fears of the great fire, I allow only my young moth men to touch me with air and light between the interstices of their fears. At last I have found my rhythm with them, the play of fire and light, of magic, of distance, of loss, of shadows. I understand them. It is like a perfect dance now, on the rim of my own dreams. I am ready, perhaps, for my own mature woman's fire, at the center, and they will be able to play on the rim of my soul and body with their light fingers and newborn strength. Oh, my love for them, my love for them, can I ever love a *man* as well! Every shade of fear, of vacillations, of delicacy, of sensitiveness in them touches off something in me so deep, so protective. Oh god, this warmth is flooding me. How can I give it, where? It cannot be given to them; the burden is too large for my loves, my tender, whimsical dream lovers. Three of them could make up the man I will love. Bill is the most childlike of all.

I can't write or work. I am drugged, weak, exalted.

While Bill was here, Gore telephoned. "I'm on my way down to take you to lunch."

"But I'm not free."

"Who is taking you out?" he said in the same tone as Bill had used, severe, jealous and fearful.

Oh, Gore.

The doors have opened for me too, the doors away from frustration. This wild eroticism is centered on the unattainable, for the knowledge that it is unattainable dissolves the fear, but now that it has become attainable, I feel free of frustration. I feel this miracle, that the shadow is being removed. Gore is my only closed door, my last wish. And then I shall be free of fear.

Gore is tall and slender, but more like a Latin, not elongated with a long face or long-legged, but more stocky. He has blond hair which he combs down too severely, parted on the side to make him look older, and eyes that are brilliant and aware with very heavy eyebrows. His skin is pale and smooth, his nose long and fine. His mouth is full, rich, emotional. His smile is his greatest charm, showing two small, white milk teeth protruding slightly (wolf teeth), which reveals the tender and gentle child in him, beneath the austere mask, the frown, the anxiety, the criticalness. His hands are delicate, but strong. When we tried our hardest handshakes (I have a very strong handshake for a woman), he can crush my hand hurtfully.

I write because then I can see him physically. How I desire him, desire him.

I wish I could stop this diary and create. I love my life better than my work. This period, with Hugo away, has been so rich and marvelous. I want to live alone. I want freedom. Such an obsession with love.

The secret of the diary is my illness.

If I could find a man like Bill—Gore, please, please, please—a man who is sensitive and not afraid, sensitive and subtle, who will actively take me, possess me.

I am lost, but happy…happy and sad. *Bouleversé*. A little crazy with love.

Friday. I felt this that I wrote on the next page and let Gore read it, teasing him because he always knows what I think, "You probably already know what you are going to read."

He read: "Gore, forgive me. I wanted to give you strength, but the warmth I couldn't hold back added to your sadness and created a conflict. Women will love you and make you feel their demands. I demand nothing. You can rest in me, and I will be your friend. We will invent a new love. Only take the tenderness, for that I can't hold back, take it without fear.

"If you only knew how well I understand. For me this that torments you is only a part of your true age. You aged so quickly in so many ways, you are so mature, but only in this you are simply the adolescent, and I believe completely in your ultimate strength. This homosexuality is only a part of adolescence. It is not right to force maturity. Let it be. It will come with your strength, your naturally born strength, and not the forced one, hastened and forced by the too early loss of your mother. We will give each other strength, but only admitting truth, your true age, your true softness and sensitiveness, with the maturity. You will not lose me, the bond is too deep. So do not be sad. Let there be tenderness in which this, the loveliest part of your being, will bloom. Let there be trust and no sadness. I have nothing to hide from you now."

He read—with sadness.

I said, "I don't want you to be sad."

"This only makes me sadder," he answered. "You see, if I could have loved a woman, it would be you. Now I know my homosexuality is incurable."

He is worn, pale, sick. Such compassion I felt when he said this. I would make any sacrifice to help him, to give him peace. I would be the mother then, anything he needed. So sincere and true he was at this moment, so well we understand each other. I feel every tension in him, every strain, every "crispation."

So he is to be my son. I embraced him tenderly when he left, "*Bonsoir, chéri.*"

Hugo is coming back. I have lived out two complete loves, and one mirage. I fell in love with my life alone. I wish I could live alone, with this stream of lovers, washed in love.

I can't understand Gore's knowledge of me, a boy of twenty for whom my thoughts and feelings are transparent. He is the same to me, I can see every true feeling, every false role, every pain, heaviness. I know his thoughts. In my presence he is true, and all his vanities fall away. With me, he is so far from his royal life, from Cornelia. He says, "I could walk out of it and not miss it."

"But you draw strength from it."

"No, I draw strength here; that is why I wrote the play here, with you."

His arrogance with others, his sweetness with me. He gives Cornelia my books to read, shows her my photograph. He has a real love for my work. It is the only time he has taken an interest in another writer, pushed one. He admits his egoism in this. He wants first to make a place for himself, but he wants my work known. He wants to bring his friends to my house. If I can draw away from my desire we could have a fine relationship. But what will happen if I fall in love with a man; what will happen to Gore? The mother abandons you for a husband and lover. I'm in love with his aristocracy, his erect bearing, his intelligence, his sensitivity, his *tenue*, his sadness, his loneliness, his fears, with the dimple in his cheek when he smiles, his hands, his body, his voice. I see in him racial images again, his French ancestry, his Spanish ancestry, his link with the Austrian Baroness like mine with Denmark, a tone of North within the South. He suffers from Anglo-Saxon rigidity and frigidity. For the role of Maria in his play he chooses a Latin actress. Accents of love, the true accents of love I have heard in his voice, and I can't say as I should: it is hopeless.

Not a million analyses seem to free me from romantic and tragic loves.

SUNDAY, JANUARY 6, 1946

Bill and I had our most beautiful talk of all on Caspar Hauser. He loves the legend now, sees all I see in it of its application to him. He wants to write the play. I told him the story fully, movingly. Then, passion. In passion he says all, is firm, willful, voluptuous and strong, and then afterwards he becomes again the child, casual, ironic, hating, cutting, stifling warmth.

But the physical ecstasy! The current between us. And the break of this afterwards, as if he is fighting the engulfing passion and trying to keep it in check.

When he was about to leave, Hugo arrived unexpectedly. Bill had to hide in the outside stairs while Hugo came in.

All this made me so anxious, for Bill's reaction to Hugo's arrival, for Hugo's reaction to my reception—how I hated to see him after Bill—for my exploded dream of love with Gore.

Exhaustion. The desire to run away, the need for peace.

Consumed.

Mad Anaïs—Gore, a boy of twenty, who is so old, so *old*! I'm younger than he is. What irony. He loves the Latin world, he loves feeling, articulateness, expression, color. With him I expand, whereas Bill hurts me with his Anglo-Saxon dryness, his coolness and his detachment. Not Gore. We glow, expand, warm each other. I don't play a role with him. He has power where I don't in the world. Authority. Ease.

Hugo threw away Gore's horoscope because of the terrific relation between Gore's and mine, every kind of sympathy, every kind of attraction, every kind of bond, conscious and unconscious, physical, spiritual, understanding. Our Mars is in the same place. His Sun is over my Ascendant. His Jupiter is over my Moon. Emotional ties, mystical ties.

"Good God," said Hugo, "this is too much!"

Mad hopes. And lucidity.

Strange thing, this planet Neptune, a planet of magic first pulling Bill and me together and then Gore and me.

I feel if Gore saw Bill, he would love him. They are so much alike, with the same voice, and similar mouths, but Bill is more feminine-looking than Gore. There is the same arrogance and pride combined with sudden softness, the same cautious writing, the same detachment, only Gore is mature and Latin, and Bill is childish and Anglo-Saxon.

Bill told me about Fowlie courting him, about how often he had been courted, how he could not understand homosexuality. "It's aesthetically impossible. I can't understand it."

Such irony. If only Gore had Bill's eroticism. But then it would be a catastrophe, for he would be the One, and we cannot marry.

Gore, believing I am thirty, asked me to look up in my diary what I felt and did the day he was born.

He doesn't want me to write in the diary. I said, "If I can talk to you, I won't." Over the telephone he asked, "Have you had any more thoughts for the diary?"

"You know what they are. I won't tell you."

"But I like to hear you say them."

JANUARY 8, 1946

Staff seeks to sober me. He says no matter how powerful Gore seems, he is a frightened child. He could not contain the passion in me. It is the children's world. I am putting all my passion in it, and if it could be fulfilled, said Staff, I would be dissatisfied very soon with my role in it. For in the love of the child there is no solidity; it is all uncertain, ephemeral. I would have no feeling of strength, no place to lay my head. This, with Gore, was the greatest mirage of all because of the spiritual and emotional nearness. I seek to put a woman's full, deep passion into the children's world. There is disproportion and therefore pain.

Staff spoke of the child's faithlessness (such as Henry's), the unfixed attractions. He seemed to be describing Bill, the Bill not knowing, being unsure of what I mean, not prizing it, overwhelmed rather than roused to a man's definite selection and possessiveness.

So, Caspar Hauser, you have come again to haunt me.

Staff smiles. He sees me being too sad and too deeply involved with a small world.

"But I don't find men like Bill and Gore."

"Bill and Gore will grow up, won't they? A Gore of forty might be someone for you."

As I went to Staff, I walked along the park. At two o'clock it became dark, a storming dark. I feel again that it is the end of the world. I heard bells on a horse's back. I lost my sense of time and place, didn't know if I were in France, Spain, a child or a woman.

JANUARY 9, 1946

Yesterday—the dark day—Gore telephoned me. I sensed he is lost to me. Symbolically, he telephoned me from outside and we were cut off. I called him, but he didn't call me back until this afternoon. I asked him to come. He did. He took me by the waist and kissed me fraternally, warmly.

I said, "I feel we lost each other."

"I did too."

"Why? Was it what I said last time?"

"No, it was Hugo coming back."

"Was my intuition right? I felt you had gone to an orgy."

"No. I worked. And I went out a great deal."

"Help me get an airplane seat to go south with Caresse," I said.

"That I won't do."

"Why?"

"It isn't safe. I think of airplanes as death voyages. So many of my friends were killed in airplanes." (His father owns Eastern Airlines, and Gore was its youngest air passenger.)

He called up Cornelia from my place. Why? He tries to make Cornelia jealous, and perhaps me. Said he would bring her down Thursday. I said no, she wouldn't understand. He said, "She would envy you."

"My freedom?"

"Yes."

Because there can't be deception between us, I told him the truth about Hugo's position, how we spend our money, everything. I explained my prison break, how I made it, and why. That story surprised him. "It gives me courage to do the same thing," he said. "A break is forthcoming. I can't be an artist and a senator, or a president. I must choose."

"What a story," he repeated.

"This time I surprised you!"

"Yes."

"Where are you happiest, Gore?"

"Here with you. And you?"

"Here with you."

I teased him, "Are you going to help me find a man like you?"

"With all my traits but one."

"Yes, but how did you know I liked your traits? Do you like all of mine?"

"Yes."

He says he is cynical, suspicious, and does not like people. A shadow fell between us when we discussed whether or not we should go to the Ruban Bleu. I said I was free, that I had given Hugo a good excuse and could stay on a little. "I'm good at that," I said playfully. But Gore stiffened: "I don't like this. It makes me think you have done it before." And he became severe. We would not go to the Ruban Bleu. He would take me home. "Are you angry?" I asked. In an effort at reconciliation I took his hand, but he did not respond. We talked of other things. When I explained my remarks that I like freedom, but not destruction, he said, "Oh, no, I like to break things."

"What are you going to break, Gore?"

"The diary and the group around you."

A deep depression. An impossible situation. Jealousy and no fulfillment. He had said, "When are you going to leave Hugo?"

"Not until I find the One."

Later I reminded him that he had promised to be analyzed a year after our meeting. "Then I would become normal and take you away from Hugo."

He is always sad and sincere about this, but I must free myself from it.

He always asks whom I see. I gave him the impression that he dispersed the group, which is partly true.

To divert him I reminded him that I made a wish which he must guess, and I invented a ritual which he must guess too. He is sure he knows the wish (that we might be lovers), but the ritual comes from his werewolf play—I want him to bite me with his milk tooth.

Bonsoir.

JANUARY 11, 1946

When Gore said he wanted to bring his theatre friends down, I went into a state of fear. I imagined them sleek, hard, cynical, scornful, successful. I imagined myself failing somehow. I found it too difficult to accede to Gore's desire to show me off. I lost my confidence.

A talk with Staff restored it. The old nightmare: a half of Gore represents my father's standards—he admires the best dressed, the most beautiful, the highest achievements. This half frightens me. But Staff brought out the truth: actually Gore looks up to me, is proud of me, thinks of me as a beautiful woman of achievement. He brings his friends to admire me. They asked to meet me. The overwhelming mountain disappeared. Staff said: "Be yourself. You are the one these people are seeking out, even Cornelia. They are attracted by your richness."

I wept violently at the realization of my crippling illness. Incredible. The descriptive harshness I have towards myself, measuring myself by wrong standards.

I became free and casual again.

I dressed in my peach Greek Recamier Empire dress, with a long black taffeta skirt which I slip over it, making the bust and shoulders very lovely, graceful. The crossed ribbons laced around the waist just below the breast. Hugo brought vodka, cheese and crackers. The people came, and they were not as I had seen them. The *diseuse* was not a ravishing beauty; the producer and designer were no faultless Greek god homosexuals. The producer was an intuitive man who gave me a ring and read my handwriting: "By great lovingness, you transform everything. At the moment there is a deep depression, which may affect your writing. You seek to tell the truth but are enveloped in magic." He would not say more because everyone was listening.

They were expected to go somewhere else at ten-thirty, but they left at midnight and Gore stayed on with us.

Oh, the bond with Gore, the feeling that even from across the room we make no movement that is not felt by the other, have no thought unknown to the other. Our glances meet at the same moment. Only my body moves around his like an ocean, receding, returning, espousing. My body receives his movements. I feel suddenly melted in his mouth, or I feel the neatness of his hips, his legs against or within my own. If only he felt this. Last night he felt it more. I felt his eyes clinging to my face. How can I escape this physical spell? If only this could become mystical. But as a weapon against passion, I have this understanding of Gore: his gift to me is his knowledge of me and his capacity to love.

He stayed last night. Surely he must feel all these strings pulling mouth towards mouth, paleness towards paleness, slenderness towards slenderness.

I said, "Are these the friends you told me about who are going to take a house on 85th Street together and rent apartments to other friends?"

"Yes, they are." Already he had read my thoughts. "Why, would you like to live there? I had thought of living there too."

We play with the desire, the fear to be somewhere together.

The bond is undeniable, inescapable.

I have faced the extent, the terrifying extent of my neurosis. I conceal it from the world, even from Hugo. I have only now realized how anxiety has devoured my life, thinned my blood, destroyed my pleasures. Everything was contaminated. The rarity was the moments of peace, of enjoyment.

I only confessed to Hugo and to myself recently how after an evening, for instance, I relived every moment in terms of destructive self-criticism. Last night, after overcoming the fear of people, the fear of disappointing Gore, after seeing that all went beautifully, that Gore was relaxed and sweet and himself, that we laughed, I savagely condemned myself for not being comical and humorous.

Because Gore postpones his visit tonight, I feel he loves me less. I could never postpone seeing him.

Staff attacks the anxiety, feeling it is caused by false motivations (the need of approval is really the need to triumph over people I seduce as symbols and not for themselves, which creates guilt).

Oh, god, there is such a labyrinth of suffering from which I'm making superhuman efforts to escape. There is such sadness and fatigue at the struggle to gain freedom, reality and space, but what wonderful art is created out of it. I want to depict the neurosis of our time. But I'm so sick of it. Staff thinks the anxiety caused anemia.

To cure myself of Gore I think of his defects. His lack of security makes him vain, in need of approval, susceptible to flattery. He is perverse, as all homosexuals are. He is intensely jealous and possessive. He is conventional and superficial at times. He is tyrannical, but all of this is external…his defects are neurotic. I love what he truly is; I understand him. He is marvelously gifted, intuitive, tender, interesting, colorful, unusual, sensitive, poetic. I love him.

JANUARY 14, 1946

Gore. There should be no shadow between us now because Thursday night killed the physical spell. Today you came and you were for the first time humorous and objective, and I was at the most painful moment of awareness of what we had lost. It could have been a tremendous love, Gore, changing our lives, helping you to bloom. It could have been a big relationship. The pain of giving it up is unbearable.

Too soon, another blighted, unlived love. All day I've been in the blackest state. This time I won't have the courage to go on. I want to die this time.

Oh, Gore, what I didn't say today, what you didn't let me say. I can kill the desire, but I can't kill the tenderness, the need to touch you when your eyes are dark, when you are pale.

Well, it's done. Yesterday everything died in me, every hope. If after Thursday night he didn't feel as I did, then I can no longer desire or hope.

It is done.

If this be my illness, my feeling too deeply, then I am gravely ill indeed, ill enough to die.

This was the first time we had a false meeting, when I didn't say what I felt because I felt he didn't want the sadness, when his irony and teasing almost stifled me.

So Hugo plays his role again, comes home and finds me ill with bronchitis (ill with forcing the rich love back into the breast, back into the womb, ill with an aborted love). He is tender, anxious, paternal, maternal, takes care of me. I hide in him, relax, want to weep, then try to react for his sake.

I awakened stronger. The fight for health is superhuman. This morning, to fight the bronchitis, I went to three doctors. The third was Staff.

On the one hand, I went to Elizabeth Arden and bought a valise there for my new life. For my new life and new self I want the best. So I have a valise with toilet preparations, black and smart. Today I bought the best vanity case of red leather at Jansen's. I have the best dressmaker (a negro Frenchwoman) making me a smart black dress copied from an expensive one given to Frances. I have the good fuchsia dress I bought for Christmas and one pair of new shoes from Miller. I have thrown away all my old clothes, clothes that have been fixed. I have never been a real bohemian about my own person, never became unkempt, careless. I never ceased to have beautiful nails, clean hair, never ceased loving finery. So that, at least, is sincere. I begin a new life.

I begin A, B, C, with the clothes. I like good clothes, and they suit me. About my home—I don't know yet what I want.

JANUARY 15, 1946

An evening with Marshall. He has made a painting, wants to write a play. When lovemaking, we began fiercely and then he couldn't carry through.

"I'm afraid again, Anaïs."

I was relaxed, humorous. "Oh, don't be sad."

"Too many years of homosexuality. I can't let this happen to me."

"Oh, it's nothing. Maybe I'm not the woman for you."

"Don't say that. I love you, Anaïs."

"I'm not slutty enough."

"You're slutty enough," he said gaily, and we laughed.

"Love me but don't take me too seriously. Take me like a whim. I can stand your whims, now yes, now no."

"But I want you."

"Well, you'll have me. Tonight was just caresses. They were good, weren't they? It wasn't so tragic."

"Be patient with me, Anaïs."

I left lightly, because I don't love him, and I was even glad, for I wanted to slip out of this relationship, which for me was a whim, and which my deeper feelings for Gore and Bill made difficult to maintain.

So I must think that even if Gore had been my lover and all had gone well, the relationship could not be good for me. I would still be the mother, helping him, and never sure of his love, never secure, never free of anxiety.

But I made an important discovery. My hostility was not directed against others, but against myself. It was savage self-criticism, savage self-destruction.

I have never described, even in the diary, the act of self-murder which takes place after my being with people. A sense of shame for the most trivial defect, lack, slip, error, for every statement made, or for my silence, for being too gay or too serious, for not being earthy enough, or for being too passionate, for not being free, or being too impulsive, for not being myself or being too much so.

JANUARY 16, 1946

That was the darkest hole I fell into. I wept. I wept before Staff at the surrender of the dream of Gore. I wept with anger at my choice of weak men. Staff cleared up everything. He revealed my masochism as guilt for stolen pleasures. My hostility has turned inward for fear of it destroying others. A great weight was lifted. Then he praised the deep insight and wisdom in my work, how with imagination I deepened the relationship between Lillian and Djuna, when in others' hands it would have been merely ordinary. I feel light and free and strong.

Then Gore called me up just to know if I were well.

Then Wilson came.

He said, "You're neurotic about not seeing me. You're always sick when I want you to come to my house."

"I'm not neurotic, but you always try to force me. What you want I can't give you."

When he came, he forced a kiss on me, which I recoiled from violently. The rest of the scene is blurred, by his anger, incoherence, irrationality. He realized I was determined never to be his mistress again. He sat down, angry and seeking a way to avenge himself.

He lit upon my writing. "In *Winter of Artifice*, I sympathize with the father."

"That's just what estranges us. You already said that in the restaurant. Then you wonder why I won't see you."

"I will give you lessons in writing for nothing."

"No one can teach me to write. I have my own way."

"I've given up hope of absorbing you—you're too strong a personality. But I could tell you what's wrong."

I stopped him. "What you say now about my writing is not objective. You're angry because I won't sleep with you. I made up my mind long ago, quietly, that you didn't understand me. People who don't understand each other can't help each other, only destroy each other. You can't destroy my confidence in what I am doing."

What I didn't say was: "You're an inferior writer to me. You're not creative. You're dull." No. I've only learned to defend myself, not to attack yet. I wouldn't let him spill his rancor and give him the pleasure of a battle as a substitute for sex. I was cold, silent, superior, and that unsettled him.

"You're unjust and angry. Don't make it seem literary when it isn't," I said.

I had stuck home, because he believes in his objectivity. He doesn't believe his role of critic masks his impotent rage at being a mediocre writer and an ugly man.

He was so ugly.

I hated him, hated his way of saying my name, his brutality, violence, ugliness, and cheapness. I was glad not to have trusted him with the diary.

In the face of Bill's and Gore's beauty and delicacies, what a caricature Wilson was.

"I'd better go," he said.

"You'd better."

He tried a humble reconciliation, "Well, good luck, and do include the Henry part in the *Winter of Artifice*." (He identified with the father and the analyst and felt rejected.)

Tant pis. He is full of meanness.

Gore, my love, I see you so clearly now. I see you insecure and leaning for support on external values, because you don't yet know your inner personal values. I love you deeply for this true inner self revealed to me in your sincerity. This that you do not yet see or know clearly is the most valuable part of you. You need external proof of love, of your value, but they will count as nothing if you do not acquire faith in the core. There alone lies strength. Your faith in the hidden core, the best, where feeling and creation and deep values issue, that is what we must seek together. You found simply that you could love no further, but I had to destroy an already rich, full passion, to kill something already born, already living. It was a little easier for you to remain where you were, at a distance, free of desire for woman, but I had to destroy the dream of a complete love while knowing the tremendous rarity and power of it.

The "values" of your parents, such as Clark Gable handsomeness, top notch celebrities, etc., are superficial, and at the same time they overwhelm you, for you are made of a finer, more sensitive, more intelligent, more gifted, more subtle quality. And if you pit yourself against this you are pitting yourself against a glorified emptiness which will destroy you, for your value lies elsewhere. All the values of your parents are external, for appearances, not deep. Yours are much more than this. You have to separate yourself from this because it causes you uneasiness, dissatisfaction. You could triumph in any realm, but if it wasn't the one which has value for you, you would never be content. The deeper Gore would feel ashamed to be a best seller, or to be a Clark Gable. If I didn't think you were better, that you were more than all this, I wouldn't say this. *Tu es plus que tout çela, mieux que tout çela.* Our life here is more real. My love for you is more real than anyone else's, because it is for the inner you, your imagination, your feelings, your dreams, your doubts, your fears, your soft and your strong self, for your days of weakness as well as power, for your creativity as well as for your lost self, for your gifts and brilliance as well as for your insecurities, for the you that you are becoming. What I love is the courage, the efforts, and the truthfulness. Strength is a rhythm, not an absolute.

JANUARY 18, 1946

A day of happiness. Gore took me to dinner. In the middle of the dinner he said, "I wonder if there could be a marriage without sex."

"Yes," I said, "like Gide and his cousin Madeleine. Why? Is that what you proposed to Cornelia?"

"No, that is what I propose to you."

I was taken aback. I don't remember what I said. I saw his distress.

He asked, "Or do you feel you need Hugo?"

"No, it isn't that. We'll talk later."

At home I explained. "Wait a little while."

He said, "A year." He explained that our relationship was so wonderful, that I was the only one he would marry, that I would accept his homosexuality.

"And would you accept my having a lover?"

"I would be jealous, of course, but as long as you were truthful, and as long as it were only physical, I would accept it."

I had begun the evening in great gaiety and lightness, free of my desire, of tragedy. I came out shining. He said, "You look so dramatic! So electrical!"

And this wish of his gave me so much security in his love that I was in ecstasy. He talked about his constancy. His fear was rather that people should ask what could I see in him, or that he should disillusion me.

If only Bill had made such a wish. Only this from Gore gave me such a feeling of security, of trust, so that now I can give out freely the love I feel. Freely. I don't feel that I gave more than I was given. He had his dream.

For the first time we talked to each other at close range, sitting on the couch near each other, relaxed. Never so near, so relaxed, so tender.

I let him read the last pages I wrote. He was amazed. Understood the difficult, painful transposition I had to make. "How could you?"

"Well, Gore, it was either lose you, run away from you, or kill the desire. It was hard, like death, really, like Maria being willing to die for the love of Stephan in your play. It was a death. But what I feared actually was that the love should be harmed, whereas it is still alive.

And now I fear for Gore, not for myself, for I shall find a complete love and he may not. And at this point he needs me more than I need him. But I feel happy.

At the door I said, "Guess the ritual."

He couldn't.

"I want you to bite me with your milk tooth."

He tried, not very hard. He said, "My milk tooth doesn't touch the lower one so I can't bite with it."

We laughed. I had said I wanted a ritual like no one else's because of the fraternal kiss I give to several, Pablo, Eduardo, etc.

We embraced fraternally.

But what I enjoyed was the disappearance of his fear, his melting, his trust. If I can be light with him, as with Marshall, we will be happy.

We're overcoming his fear. We were playful. I told him how I wanted to smooth out his frown.

He said, "That's what my mother always wanted to do."

I then sat far away and said, "I won't mother you."

"That will fix you," he said, laughing.

I give him his small manly victories. I always answer his direct questions. They are like a masculine thrust, spontaneous and impudent. I evade very few of them.

JANUARY 19, 1946

Analysis gives power. The way I felt last night when I went out to dinner with Gore was like a real Spanish woman: integrated, vivid, electrical, strong, gay. Not grieving, pale, wan, nebulous, but vivid. Today sickness again, weakness, but happiness.

Sunday: Gore came. He lay back, became so gentle and sweet, so lyrical and tender, so pure and simple. He is anxious about Bill. He thinks that since he and I are not lovers, I will want Bill again and he will lose me.

I have told him with Bill it was passion and not this emotional nearness. He said, "A passion could take you away from me. Whereas nothing will take me away from you. I could never love a man. I know that."

"Nothing will take me away from you, Gore."

He was depressed. "Whenever I get depressed, I will ask you about Bill."

The truth is a difficult thing to tell, even when one wants to. What is the truth?

It is true I can imagine myself living with Gore and not with Bill, because Bill is aloof, detached, except in sensuality. Yet with Gore I would suffer from the absence of the physical tie. With Gore I have harmony.

I wanted to, and did, love Bill wholly, but this wholeness was shattered by his passivity, his attitude towards me. Bill...he left without a word of love. Gore is filled with love.

Gore is in Washington for a week. I miss him. I can't separate from him. If I dance an improvised dance, I'm dancing for him. If I hear music, I hear it with him. I like to talk about him, to say his name.

A fantasy: Gore and I are in Zagreb, Yugoslavia, and leading a life like a dance from one brilliant point to another in a current of writing. We call on Rebecca West, who would say, "What a witty young man," on the French, who would like his Latin air and quick mind; on the Greek poet in Athens, who would fall in love with him; on Durrell, who would like his writing; everyone would be charmed and eager to invite us; and Gore and I would seek our solitude by the Mediterranean in the sun, weaving our stories out of our own *Thousand and One Nights*. We would never run out of stories, for we have the body and face to create new ones, to awaken confidences, to receive secrets. People would be open to both of us, love us, and we would illumine each other, say the astrologers. And if I can be cool enough and can divorce myself from his mouth and take my desire elsewhere, if we have this understanding together, we could be happy and free together and find the marvelous everywhere. We could travel, see the Riviera, the Italian lakes, Bali, and also be quiet together and work together in our subterranean life. So at last I would have found Caspar Hauser and live out my love. For the first time I feel this love as a new beginning, as if I were his age.

I never fantasized a life with Bill.

Friday: I wrote in one breath the first ten pages of the party in my new book, in a new way, being able to execute concept of neurotic world vision as we experience life. It is an interior party, a fusing of symbols and externals.

Saturday I wrote five more pages. Yesterday five more, on Djuna's absence from the party.

Thanks to Staff I pay no attention to criticism. I listen only to myself.

JANUARY 29, 1946

Monday towards five o'clock Gore telephoned, five minutes after returning to New York. I had an engagement but I broke it. He said, tyrannically, "Meet me at Charles." It was to celebrate his coming out of the army. We arrived at the same time. He called me from his taxi, leaped towards me, kissed me. He was in his civilian clothes, looking more slender, more youthful, more vulnerable. Gore. He noticed my lace blouse. He has sensual reactions, then retractions, then pleasure. He says: "I feel as if I were coming home. In Washington, I felt lost. You have ensorcelled me. What I used to accept now I don't like. I found my grandfather, the senator, boring…"

We went to Ruban Bleu (where Albert gave me his first kiss). We drank together. We sat close, arm against arm, sometimes holding hands. There was great warmth. He told me about his mother beating him until the blood came. She said to him, "No one will ever love you as I do."

He wanted his mother to die, and he imagined how her jewels would look on me. "This is the most fabulous love in the world today."

I'm so moved that the boy who lived in the most external of all worlds should be most capable of a dream, and of giving himself to a dream, the dream of our marriage. Why do I live in it knowing the obstacles in reality, our difference of age, yet dreaming it, wishing it (long before he said it, I had imagined that he would). We have a world together. It is now real. He wants to live in the Village. I dream of a house in the Mews, a little house where he would live on one floor, and I on another. Why? Why? Are we truly so close, so similar? Is this another spell? It's strange that I like his earthiness. When he is a little drunk, he is very sexual, a realist in his talk. He oscillates between two worlds. His hands are square, not long and fragile. We were both obviously happy. People could swear we were in love. I say, as I only said to Bill, "*Bonsoir, chéri!*" And he asks me, "How is Guillaume?" without knowing that Bill signs himself Guillaume.

I was able to drink five whiskies without bad results. Was cheerful and humorous all of the next day, clowning for Hugo in the morning with a heat pad over my head, pretending to have a heavy hangover. "The logical conclusion to a life of spirituality. Now I'm a night club frequenter and a drunkard."

Lightness and pleasure. I write well. I wrote pages on Djuna's flight from the party. Real wonder lies in the depths; as soon as you look deeply you find the extraordinary. The truth, which only the child and the artist tell, is the real wonder. Magic and power lie in the truth, the truth.

Cornelia is attacking me, has begun waging a big battle against me (she says my work is decadent). She admits she is jealous and feels Gore's devotion to me.

He comes to me depressed, ill, and slowly begins to glow, to come alive.

"Until this moment I felt terrible." His mood lifts. He lives in a world of terrors. He goes through battles with threatening forces. Poor Gore, and his fear of criticism, his resentments. Someone has insulted him. I can help him. I feel serenity. I feel confidence. I feel confidence in his love. I do not fear Cornelia. He says *"cherie"* as he leaves me. (I bring the fraternal kiss a little closer to the mouth.) Oh, Gore. The high sense of romance is there.

He said: "I often feel, when I look into the mirror, I am looking for a skipped, missed fragment of my life, my childhood. I'm constantly aware how they run into each other, how the feelings I have are the same ones I had as a child."

A child shall lead me into the external worlds, a child shall cover me with his mother's jewels, a child shall take me into the world I rejected, and I shall take him into mine.

He is so easily wounded, hurt, destroyed. Cornelia told him she liked his first novel better than his second. Why? She had no reasons that made sense, but her statement disturbs his faith, as all negative statements find an echo in that part of ourselves which doubts, and which is dependent on confirmation. Why does it count so much?

"I must know what everybody thinks," he said.

Most of all you must find out why they say and think as they do. When it doesn't make sense it's because there is another reason. When Wilson can't have me for a mistress, he attacks my writing. Perhaps Cornelia is quarreling for other reasons. "Be sure you can see why a criticism is made so it will not harm you." So now she will take the side of his doubts and I the side of his dreams.

Gonzalo and I are still walking the streets together (in his new suit bought with Dutton's money). We still sit at cafés together, we still lament having no shelter to make love, and have to content ourselves with furtive caresses stolen with the anxiety that Hugo might come, but we are not walking the streets of the present, but of the past, an echo of an early passion, its human echo, a once-shared passion, a flame with enduring reverberations. We are not sitting at today's cafés, but at an extension of the Paris cafés. It is the old passion, the old love which guides our steps, which orders the drinks, guides our talk; it is the old passion which makes pale gestures with familiar warmth. The spark is not there, only a human, lingering echo of the past. The streets of a nine-year-old love are still richly peopled. He is still telling me wonderful, lusty stories, even if I do not hear them as vividly. He is still full of Indian humor, malice, roguishness, rich with experience. He dreams of making a big fortune with a business deal, buying a bigger press, and he is now playing at mature constructions of a life, cheerfully and playfully. But it is all tributaries from a lost central flame, running with mellowness, out of the past, echoes and reverberations.

I always go where life and the flame are, to share what is immediate, my present self with the match to my present self, Gore. Under the warmth of my strength, he is allowed to be what he is, the child cheated of his childhood.

"I told Cornelia about writing my play in your presence. She fights you now."

His first novel is dedicated to his mother Nina, his play to me. His second novel?

"Be careful," said Staff, "to not enter this new world with any need to seduce, charm, conquer what you don't really want for the sake of approval. The frozen moment before the people who belong to Gore's mother's world was due to your fear that they might not approve of you, your desire that they should."

I feel my center now. I feel my integrity and confidence. I want to take from this external world what I want and what is a part of me, not to be corrupted (as my father was corrupted). To add to myself the beauty it gives me. To reach mature playing and enjoyment with my oldest son.

Gore, my love, I lie here listening to music and so filled with you that I marvel that an incomplete love should seem so complete. I ask myself whether you feel this, the intensity of a full love, the sense of completeness, of fulfillment.

(Gore read this and wrote in his own hand, "Yes.")

Hostility

For the first time hostility appeared clearly in my relations to Hugo, yesterday, when the time came for Hugo to take me…I never desire him. I feel I must obey his will because he is good to me, because he has a right to me, because I want to give him what he needs as he gives me what I need. Also, I would like to find satisfaction at home. The asexual relation to Gore, which keeps me so erotically aroused, and the fact I do not desire anyone else, is hard to bear. I am filled with sensuality. So I will yield to Hugo. But my body bristles against him. I can't bear his eroticism, his preliminary caresses. I hasten his taking me because his caresses have the opposite effect they are intended to have. They make me bristle, and I want to cry out, "I don't want you!" That would break his life. I can't do it. So I will submit, close my eyes. Once he is inside of me it is easier to close my eyes and imagine it is Bill or Gore lying over me. I'm angry that Hugo breathes heavily as Bill does not, so that it interferes with my fantasy. I'm angry at all the expressions of pleasure he shows because they break into my fantasy. I close my eyes and I feel not Bill's sex, or Gore's sex, but their mouth. Their mouth! (I won't let Hugo kiss me on the mouth.) And with this I can reach the orgasm. But when Hugo has reached his pleasure, immediately I hate him again, violently. I can't be tender. I would like to destroy him. I find a pretext to get up, to go to the bathroom. I hate lying beside him afterwards.

How can I hate Hugo when in reality there is nothing to hate? The abysm between reality and my feelings is tremendous.

"You do not hate Hugo," said Staff. "Your hostility is towards the one who is the aggressor, the taker, who is doing what a part of you wants him to do but which a part of you has denied in yourself (you rejected self-assertion, violence, taking, as you saw them in your father and mother). These are the elements of which you were the victim, and they are therefore to be hated. But these are also positive elements of life which you need: activity, self-assertion, anger, power. So you place them on others, and when others act them out you hate it in them. Hugo fulfills his natural husband-lover needs and assertions. And you feel hostility towards this which you have repressed in yourself, which you only allow to come through in a perverse form towards those who, with the same perversity towards their own aggression, hate it and fear it: Bill, Gore, and the other children. When your love wants to come through then you have the problem of hatred, which comes through simultaneously with love because of your relation to your parents. To suppress the hatred, you controlled the love and dealt it out in compartments. The hatred still came out, only indirectly: your hostility towards Hugo in faithlessness, in sharing the young lovers' son-like hostility towards Hugo, your hostility towards Miller. Wilson is right to say you are destructive, but it was in so subtle and indirect a form that it was practically undetectable, and greatly suppressed too, almost imperceptible. You let others do it…Miller, for example, who was so aggressive in his writing. And you played at being thoroughly gentle, a victim of the aggressions, which made you guiltless. Bill feels the same way. You express his wants of which he is ashamed, so he will punish his sensuality in you. We project this unbearable self onto others so that we can hate it in them and destroy it. Now, these condemned elements are necessary to life; when you kill them, you kill life."

Last night Gore came—a long, lovely, playful evening, so full of unconscious richness, talk, listening to Wagner, reading his synthesis of his play. He read my party pages. "The best you have done. All I can say is, I wish I had done it."

"That comes out of us," I said. "You inspired me. I will dedicate this book to you." That pleased him.

I enjoy the perversities. I'm not masochistically subjugated or a victim to them. I enjoy his perversities: his love of his father, his hostility towards Hugo, his love-hatred of his mother, his jealousy when I speak of other loves, the lover I would take later (I described Graeffe). "I only ask you never to let me see him," he said severely.

He had said, "I don't want you to live like a nun."

I said, "So you won't be concerned…I'll take a lover later."

I enjoyed his suffering, as he makes me suffer when he describes his affairs. "You know, I need them less. I used to have frenzies of promiscuity, one every night. Now I need less. And it doesn't satisfy me."

What is this? A step towards me? No. I am the mother. When he dreams of his new place (where I will have an apartment in the same house) he dreams that I will feed him late at night when he returns.

But when he left, I asked him to kiss me "for the two weeks you will be away." He was shy and gentle, and a little lost. He had already kissed me warmly on my cheek and neck. This time I put up my mouth fully and we kissed. Again, as with the first embrace, he answers, but does not seek more. We pressed our mouths together and separated. But I felt the sweetness and the fulfillment of a wish, a dream I have had so often.

I haven't conquered my desire.

February 6, 1946

Strange that whomever I love takes on a quality of light. The illumination has withdrawn from Bill because it was not lived out; the life that was being thwarted by his absence has been transferred to Gore.

He is now illuminated for me. I am less unhappy with him (emotionally I feel answered, only physically am I thwarted). But I question this light.

FEBRUARY 10, 1946

My world is so large I get lost in it. My vision is hard to sustain. Last night I had a real fear: am I insane or a genius? I am alone in what I am writing. It's a big burden for a woman.

From Florida, Gore writes me the word YES, all alone, in a letter.

Yes to what I feel, write, think. Yes to all. Such a subtle, aware, accurate way to reach me, to bring us close. For these things I love him.

"There is more equality here," admitted Staff.

When I opened his letter, a flush of pleasure warmed me. Actually, my blood so stirred, it rushed to my face. The word was so penetrating, so warm, so intimate, so direct. Yes, Gore, you have a gift for relationship.

FEBRUARY 17, 1946

Gore rushed back before his two weeks were up, three days early, and telephoned me as soon as he awakened today to meet him at Charles.

"I thought I shouldn't leave you too long. I must watch over you, not leave you long out of my sight. What about the Viennese?"

"I was faithful," I answered.

And it all begins again. I said my feelings were calmer, but when he telephoned my heart began to skip beats and lose its rhythm of peace. Elation. I had been concerned with his saying he found homosexuality boring. (When I mentioned Gore saying he felt unfulfilled, Staff had said, "There is hope for him.") But when he added he would like to meet Christopher Isherwood because their writing was similar and he would like to have written *Prater Violet*, I said, "And if you find him, he may be more than an ordinary sexual experience since he is your intellectual equal."

"Not the same as this, this is the best," he said, so simply, so clearly, so sincerely.

Oh, god, the temptation is great, to live with him, to marry him, to make a new life. In the bus I take his arm, "I'm so glad you're back."

"Why, it's always a beautiful day when I come back to you...look." We looked at the grey, soggy day made beautiful. Gore. What a man he will be someday, when he is made whole. He is not a homosexual, but a split being, split by his mother's violence, and who saw his father harmed by her too.

Such sincerity with me, and, he said rightly, "our insincerity with other people." His wisdom is what characterizes him. He can express violence, too. His violence is not crippled. And his body is not dead like Eduardo's. He reacts to my clothes, charms, notices and responds. He feels.

FEBRUARY 18, 1946

Today I finished writing Part II of *Ladders to Fire* and was so disciplined that I reduced 200 pages to 80. The party is a wonderful section, like one of Martha Graham's ballets, full of rhythm, rich, full of color, and strangeness. It's like a mobile, a modern painting. It satisfies me. I'm exhausted, nervous. My love for Gore and his for me is the drug I need to create. In the sun yesterday his eyes were green and gold, the color of his tanned skin is golden. There is intensity in him, moments of open sweetness, moments of serious manliness and courage. He faces pain, doesn't shrink from it. If only he were but ten years older. He is ripe for passion, capable of passion.

Tuesday. Oh, Anaïs, you're dreaming again. My feelings go out to Gore with wholeness, and the next day, when I wanted to bring him this wave of wholeness and faithfulness, he had already broken the dream, our élan, the closeness, by a night out with a sailor. His need of telling me was an unnecessary pain he inflicted. He needs to put this between us as a way of saying: we cannot be closer; I am not wholly yours.

And so, hurt, I took my desire elsewhere, mocking my own seeking of an unbroken, whole dream. At a party at Maya's, Paul André danced with me and became violently passionate, so passionate we had to stop dancing or he would have lost control. Then a young, slim Austrian said, in a fever, "This is not a dance, it's a spell." And we danced like one person, drugged. Today Chinchilito telephoned me, and I said yes, I would come tomorrow at ten. That ends the dream of wholeness.

FEBRUARY 20, 1946

Today I could relate to Chinchilito better than before. Things are said, revealed, acted, expressed, withheld out of fear, and these make up the tapestry. Chinchilito. We began to invent a room together, a kaleidoscopic, mobile room.

I write to Bill every day because he is in hell, his hair shaved, his skin spoiled by the hardest training among the coarsest men, living in barracks. Bill among those men, my god, is like a young girl among them, a child. So for this I write him every day, not because he finds any words to answer me.

Midnight. I thought my visit to Chinchilito would kill my desire for Gore. As he had insisted on knowing the truth, I said: "Gore, I don't want to lie to you, but I must tell you, I have taken a lover. I must ask you not to make me talk more about it." I wanted to test him (he can't bear deceit). He was deeply disturbed. From then on I don't know what happened. It was if a barrier had broken down. I kept telling him: "If it hurts you, I can't do it. It's my obsession, not to hurt you…oh, Gore."

"How is it, how is it for a woman? It's different. I'm not possessed. It is I who take." (He was struggling with this feeling: Anaïs is possessed.)

I hid my head on his shoulders and confessed, "I thought of you all the time, every moment." Oh, god, it was true, it was Gore I kissed with my eyes closed, not Graeffe.

Then, when I came home, I wept. It is the same as for the man, when it is done without love—it leaves no memory, it doesn't stay in the body. That's why I don't like it. "But tell me, Gore, if it estranges us, I don't want it."

He could feel, of course, that there was no change. I suddenly embraced him and said, "I belong to you, you know that."

"I know that," he said with the same vehemence. His emotionalism, his responsiveness—we never came so close. We sat close, as we never have before. In my desire to reassure him, I expressed all my love. He received it. He answered. He kissed me back, near, near the mouth, not on the mouth. He told me after he took the boys he always thought of me, sad that it wasn't me. We were close, so truthful. He said the homosexual act was like a meal, no more. It was not a break in his love for me. He was afraid mine would be. I said, "When you came here, you sensed no change, did you?"

I had received him with the same élan. My sadness when I left Chinchilito was that this will remove me from Gore, make me cold. I found out that Gore doesn't mind my desire, that he didn't want to be unfair and demand a chastity which he would not practice, that he only feels it cannot be as casual for a woman. Some barrier was broken, a physical barrier. There was so much feeling in his embrace. So many things he said. He didn't want to take and not give. He didn't want to hurt me, ever. It was the nearest we shall ever come to a real love scene. I could not hold back my quick, spontaneous kissing. I was terribly moved. Although, just before he came, I had listened to L'Ile Joyeuese, and I was in ecstasy. If only Gore knew such big waves of love which carry one over the highest obstacles. He only knows the small waves.

Four o'clock in the morning. Awakened by a storm. Inexplicably happy, as if I had had a sensual night with Gore, so much did the emotions make us flow together. It is a magical power to touch a finger one loves. I touched each one of his fingers as we talked, his ears, his cheek, kissed him obliquely, touched his arm. His slenderness is strangely lusty, as his character at twenty is strangely firm. He faces me. His body never shrinks. He has will and courage, and all the possibilities of manhood.

He is proud of my work.

FEBRUARY 21, 1946

Went with Gore to Noguchi's studio. At the moment that I wanted to leave, I looked at him and saw he wanted to leave too. So we went together to eat at the Jumble Shop. He is tormented that there is somewhere a man who has possessed me, who feels he has possessed me.

"I won't see him again," I said.

"I know how you feel."

Well, there is something gained, but actually he cannot accept this without pain, as I can't accept the homosexuality without pain, so there it is: the pain, and the conflict.

FEBRUARY 22, 1946

An hour before meeting Gore at the restaurant, I decided he must have security. He has given me all that he can give, including his feelings. I want to protect him. He needs to grow, and to grow he needs trust. I can do without it because I'm older. For his great tenderness and sincerity of feeling, I will accept my role. I will protect him with a lie. I said, "Gore, I've made a decision. For a year I will belong to you exclusively. This is worth it."

"I can't make the same promise."

"I don't expect it."

I treat him not like my child, but like a passionately loved brother. So after dinner he took me out to share in his perversions. We went to a homosexual nightclub, saw an astounding man-woman who was fascinating, corrupt, stirring in me all my masculinity. I wanted to rape him, attack him. I wanted to be a man. Gore unrestrainedly showed his attraction for a boyish young man, but the young man was violently making love to a woman. I saw in Gore such an expression of avidity, childish lust. The fact that he desired a boyish, humorously innocent boy, not the corrupt fairies, touched me and convinced me of the childish narcissism of his homosexuality (quest for the lost childhood). I felt tender, dissolved. He bought me a flower. He held my hand. He confessed his fears: he either worries about his writing or his health. "There's something wrong with my insides. I have vomiting spells. And I have to be operated on for a fistula which may cause cancer." Anxiety, fear of death. In the street and in the taxi, it is he who now takes my hand. And upon leaving me, he kissed me on the mouth. Very well, I shall love my sons with passion and find myself a husband, but let Gore have his dream, which he needs now to strengthen him. At twenty he is so full of courage, and he has trusted me. I will not hurt him. He has given me the emotional tenderness, warmth, understanding that Bill never gave me.

Yet how it hurt me today that Frances threw away the little bed where Bill slept, where we made love several times.

What Gore most fears is Bill's return, and he is right to fear it, for I have the same kind of love for Bill, and he can give me physical fulfillment. There is a possibility of his giving me greater emotional fulfillment as he grows older, though I believe he will always remain the child of a "father and mother who didn't believe in showing feeling."

In the middle of an evening, at the most unexpected moments, Gore remembers the bird in the middle of the studio. Gore, *mon enfant malade*, has at times the cramped, stiff appearance of anxiety. He then seems to move with difficulty (the mere act of living becomes difficult). His face loses its softness and is set in a forced, false mask, jerky and brusque, which is painful for me to see, for then I know he is bound and pretending, moved by neurotic compulsions. I love him in his natural moments. I know too, he touches the depths of depression, but never fully. Pleasure and elation are rare in him. I've tried for the first time not to treat him as a child, but to relate simultaneously to him both as a child and an old man, for there is in him a side that is not only mature, but even promiscuous and cynical, a side of him that sees people coldly, in the light of their defects. I feel more relaxed to discover his standards are not as severe as my father's—he doesn't care about clothes and luxury. I thought he demanded "perfection." No, he wants freedom, richness, experience.

FEBRUARY 25, 1946

Last night Gore came. After writing under the stimulus of benzedrine, he was depressed. I talked about analysis, had to confess I had been to Staff because "I wanted to die." Although Staff said if Gore were analyzed I would lose him, I want him free and strong. We aren't lovers anyway, and what he wants is impossible to me, to live with me, to be close to me, possessively, emotionally, but to sleep with boys. When he takes me out he does not conceal his interest in boys. He wants me to share this. I get hurt, though I try to act cynically. He discusses them with me, undresses them, tells me how it will be: "This one will be too white, and he will want all sorts of things I don't want. He will be complicated and make a scene. They do terrible things which I don't do. My approach is entirely non-phallic."

I tried then to know more. What does he mean? "I do the least of all, and I am glad when it is over."

In the taxi he takes my hand and talks about our life together. Upon leaving me, he kisses my mouth. He moves me emotionally and erotically. Yet it can't be, this life, but on the other hand, because he has power over my feelings, I can't envisage not living near him at all. Curious. Mentally, he is full of aggression, thrust, directness, essentially active, not passive.

When I hear Gore's voice over the telephone, I am so moved, and I want so much to be with him. I get lifted by yearning, as if I were going to melt into him again, then I awaken to reality and seek to quiet my feelings. I was afraid of this: frustrated in my élan towards Gore, my desire and feelings for Bill have reawakened.

Terrible depression.

Party.

The studio decorated with Hugo's two new immense copper plates. The mattresses are taken off the beds, making four low oriental divans. I installed more lights, hired a flamenco guitarist. Guests brought their musical instruments and sang with great animation. Steve Heidrick is a handsome, suave, elegant young man who dances beautifully, who loves to dance with me. He dances clingingly, caressingly, with his brow against mine, cheeks touching. Gore saw us dancing often together, and although he doesn't like to dance and does not dance well, he "cut in" and said, "I wanted to take you away—no more dancing with him."

"Release me from my promise."

"I will not. You are mine. You said you'd be mine for a year."

Immediately his reaction is to seduce his rival. Steve is homosexual and wears the sign ring on his little finger. I love his active self, acting on impulse. Here, not out in the world, he becomes soft and gentle.

Though I have suffered tension while preparing for the party, once it was on I abandoned myself to the magic of it, and it became beautiful.

After I made Gore jealous, I melted with pity. He is young. I do not enjoy causing him anxiety.

The enormous labor, only four hours' sleep, and cleaning the house this morning exhausted me. I spent the day in bed. Gore calls me. He has written a poem, which I help him sell to *Harper's Bazaar*. He talks about my work to everyone. My responsive man. I say to him, "We teased each other last night, and I always get uneasy."

"You shouldn't." (He has confidence in my love, the rascal.)

"But you can always read something in the diary to reassure you."

"And you always get a poem, and that is even better."

He asked me what I put on my nail polish to give all the colors a warm gleam. "Gold."

"Like your writing," he said.

MARCH 11, 1946

I did a lecture and reading at Amherst, and it was a success. I was fêted, worshipped, and I signed twenty books. There was both tension and elation. I read like a dramatic actress, made friends with James Merrill, a twenty-year-old poet, answered the mathematicians who questioned me on the "fluctuating point of view" before sixty persons. I was surrounded by soldiers. I went to sleep in Jimmy's room, yearning for Gore, loving Gore, filled with desire, feeling him to be the one nearest to my heart and body.

I telephoned him constantly from Grand Central while he was telephoning me from the outside, until we talked together. I saw him the next day, a highly emotional meeting. He said: "I felt terrible at your leaving, even though it was only for two days. I felt it deeply."

But at the same time he told me that he had met the boy nearest to his physical ideal, like the first man he had had sexual relations with when he was thirteen, like his half-brother to whom he has been attracted for years without daring to act. "Now I'll tell you something that will make you happy. This is the best physical relation I have had yet, and with the most beautiful boy, and no ordinary boy either…he is an inventor, a student of mathematics. And still this relationship with you is bigger and means more to me, and I want it more than anything, and if I had to choose, I would choose you."

Still, the attraction for the boy was there, and he could not help talking about it, even telling me when they were going to be together.

We went out. He said conflicting things, "The wall between me and woman is so thin, so thin." He was tender, touching me, was near, but he also talked about the boys.

To make him jealous, I said I would take a lover. The need of the lover was so real, my fantasy of a young lover from Amherst grew. I told Gore I would see him the next evening, while he was with his boy. As we walked home, Gore talked about our place, how we would live together, entertain, how it would be a Mecca for all the artists.

We separated regretfully. I went to sleep in pain. The next day he telephoned. He was not jealous. "As long as you don't love him."

The next day I was completely unnerved. I could not see Staff, and I felt lost. I felt all the pain at once.

That night Hugo took me. I was completely cold. I went to the bathroom and wept. I fell asleep weeping. The next day I couldn't stop sobbing. When I heard Gore's voice, it broke me. I began to whisper, to tell him I must go away. He was so tender over the telephone, wanted to see me, but I couldn't let him. I went to Staff, who again pointed to the identification with the child, why the intensity of the feeling was so strong. But I already knew: I must not sexualize. I would be caught in a painful relationship anyway. He is young, and he must live out his life. Even if we were lovers, he must live out his youth, his whims. At best, I knew it is not for me. Staff said, "That is progress." But I couldn't stop weeping.

Gore came that evening, ill with sadness. He felt my sorrow. He was like an older man. I said: "In killing my desire for you I feel I'm killing a dream of love. I can't bear it. And I can't do what you want me to do. I can't bear sex without love." We kissed more tenderly.

He said, "I will give him up."

I said, "I wouldn't ask you that."

Then he told me the boy wanted to travel with him. He is a student at Dartmouth, but he has an apartment in New York. I suddenly bowed my head, fought against the tears and whispered, "That is the end of our life together, that is just what I feared." At this Gore was pained. "Oh, don't say that, don't say that." The irony is that it is my love warming him that has strengthened his relations to others and made them less casual. He knows this.

Upon leaving he said, "The windows you painted look like you, not Hugo."

"Maybe because I have to stay here a little longer," I said sorrowfully.

The next day he was ill, very ill, and so was I.

His attitude and sincerity, however, had moved me. He does not elude my pain, but shares it. He has great tenderness. I went into death and out again. I faced the truth: he is my child, loves me romantically and passionately as a child.

When he got ill, I said, "What can I say to make you well?"

"Take back what you said about our life together being at an end."

"I do take it back."

When he got well, we went out together, to an exhibit, to a party. He said, "I have faith in our star."

Such nearness. Our romance begins again, the exaltation of love, but I have faced the truth. He is not the one. But he is the nearest now, and he deserves my love. He has given me all he could.

Gore said: "I understand what is happening. I know how you must feel. Mine is a feeling of being split in half, of being divided. I know this, because it has happened to me. I should like to help you fight this thing, to help you feel that it is not necessary to choose, but I think you know that. It is a very important thing to me that you be happy and that I can give you as much as you have given me, so let me say that these attractions I understand and, because of our incompleteness on a certain plane, must exist. What you must find is what I have found, that it is possible to have both without being in any way unfaithful to the other—and so you will fight this thing and conquer it and be happy which is of great importance to me. Don't be sad.

"The feeling of death and sorrow came from the fear that the split might make the love less strong, less big, but you made me feel it is not so. I feel the power and strength of it."

MARCH 13, 1946

Last night Gore made me go to the Pen Club dinner, and, in an effort to "face the world," I instead found mediocrity, cheapness, degradation. I tried to sustain my dream with Gore, and I have finally awakened. His writing and a part of himself belongs to the ordinary world, the world I reject: Hollywood, society, office life, army life—those are his themes. There is a split between the ordinary world and my world.

After the dinner, which he didn't like, we left, ran away. He confessed he had asked me to come because he wanted to see me at eight-thirty and would have had to wait until ten-thirty. So this way, he again wins my heart, again he touches me with his humor. When we sat at the Blue Angel he began to look all around, interested in a young movie actor, then remembered I had said, "When I'm out with you I'm not interested in other people," and playfully, he turned his back on the actor and stared at me intently.

I said, "Why are you staring at me?"

"When I'm out with you, I'm only interested in you!"

I laughed, and then he added in the tone of someone repeating a French lesson, "*Je suis toujours content quand je suis avec toi.*" This was so childlike that I laughed. The truth is that if I am his deepest love, his interest is also scattered, diffused and expanded like Miller's, the child's interest in conquest, in vanity, in "meeting everybody." This is good, for a child. Now I am awake, and my body alone aches, because I am without a lover. I don't want Hugo or Gonzalo. All this richness, and spring, and no lover! The mirage is over. I am free. I have wild longings to clasp him, but they will disappear when I have a lover.

The soft spring forced me out into the street. I bought an aquamarine dress, a gold chain bracelet chained to the ring. I saw Staff. "The child cannot answer your needs."

The ache, the ache, the hunger, the terrible hunger is not acknowledged. Can I really break this pattern? All my love affairs have been that of mother and child, even with Hugo. You could not bear your own helplessness, you had to achieve mastery, and you feel your own drive to helplessness, fighting the desire for mastery. *Je suis bien fatiguée.* Very often I feel the struggle to live is too great and death would be easier.

This diary will end when I find the lover.

MARCH 14, 1946

Gore came and kissed me ardently, as passionately as one can without sexuality. He was responsive to my new turquoise dress, looked so melted, admiring, so near…it is so near to complete love that it is pitiful. I pitied him, his hunger. He was so moved, he was almost trembling, was so vulnerable. For the first time I saw the child's fear in him. I saw, as I embraced him, how drawn, moved and frightened he was. His hand over me had the gentle awkwardness of a child, as he had about our first kiss. I was light and happy, seeking to make him happy, made him feel I would never again get sad or emotional about his sexuality. He was not well, with a headache and neuralgia. At such times it is hard to separate. My feelings want to envelop him, protect him. He is divided, and he suffers. Knowing now what a relationship can be, he can no longer have casual sexuality, so he dreams of W. H. Auden and Isherwood, of writing with Isherwood. He yearns for the complete relationship, and I can see what will happen: no marriage, and no protectiveness. Isherwood is probably egocentric and will not give Gore the tenderness he needs. Poor Gore, he is caught, and Staff won't help him because he is fighting for my life and is afraid of what will happen if we ever became lovers. This way, I at least have a chance to escape my fatality. Gore himself helps me. There are moments when I do feel that I would be lost if we became lovers. *Enfant adoré, enfant mille fois chéri, enfant* who gives himself, gives me more than Bill.

MARCH 18, 1946

The reality of Gore's world, which is based on prejudices and bourgeois standards, is ugly. He is hostile towards Jews and negroes. When it came time to work on Maya's film I told him simply: "This is the way it is. The star is Maya and a negro girl." He answered, "If I can act a part with you, that is all I want," and he joined us. I tried to make him break through his "pose" by acting not as an actor, but as we are together. I incited him, "Let's drop the acting and talk as we do when we are together." In spite of the fact that I suffered with fear of showing my age in the violent lights, I believe we acted well. Gore never left me for one moment, and that is what makes me feel so close to him. He always makes the intimate contact, *"Tu es contente? Tu es fatiguée?"* His personality towards others is what I don't like: he is cold and ruthless, almost the opposite of what he is with me, almost like Miller, full of cruelty and caricature, and without feeling. It is from his narcissism that his passion for me, his mother, and all that belongs to him comes. I like that he telephones several times a day. I like his closeness. But I am now free of the tragic desire to be possessed by him, because I see the outcome: pain. When he gets analyzed he will discover I am the mother, and our romance will be over. Meanwhile, he is mine.

Sometimes I feel the anxiety and suffering are too great, the ordeal of analysis, to be made whole, to break life-long patterns and habits. I got ill. There is pain everywhere, and I feel cornered. I must go on.

Staff, "You are afraid to give up being a mother or a child and to be a woman, for then you will have to face *man*, genitally, and give yourself up."

Yet I can see that in the relation to Gore there can be only pain. I am condemned to be the mother again. No, no, no. There is a pause. I wait for a man to come. Staff shames me by saying that it is something that must happen within me. Confusion. I am lost, utterly lost.

I am in the new apartment, all white, with the beautiful modern stained glass windows, everything clear and fresh. The light of reality is clear and bare.

AWAKENING

Oh, the drug of my marvelous dreams

NEW YORK, MARCH 22, 1946

The greatest suffering does not come from living in mirages, but from *awakening. There is no greater pain than awakening from a dream,* the deep crying over the dying selves. Giving up the children seems like giving up my life, my own youthfulness. Pain, terrible pain. A desert before me. I have no husband, no lover, and no child. At last I must relinquish all.

Gore and I acted in Maya's movie, and I felt my desire for him weakening. I am battling it with Staff, trying to relinquish what cannot satisfy me. With Staff, I go to the end of my dream and face the fact that even if Bill had yielded to me, I could not have been satisfied, because we were both trying to reach the unattainable.

Oh, the tremendous experience of the acknowledged weakness, the acknowledged helplessness.

There is sadness for the dying selves that must be killed for the sake of the new ones.

Accepting my mother role towards Gore, I left him at his house last night, felt no pain in the taxi, and I told him I had lost my wish that he should be my lover. Then, I dreamed of his lover's kiss with his tongue breaking the shell between us, of great joy and ecstasy. The emotional tie is so strong. This morning I am broken again. This is worse than the mirages which crucified my sensual body and killed all my joy. This is barren, like death. This awakening is death.

Staff calls it resistance. "You find new caves to hide in. You say giving up the child is giving up your youth, but it isn't so, because you played the mother. The children didn't free the child in you. They demanded that you protect them."

Then a new resistance emerges: if I give in to my sexual nature, I will live like a whore and want nothing but sensuality. I refuse to create, to write, because it seems like a poor substitute for passion. I suffer physically from want of passion.

I write letters to Bill which I tear up, in which I try to obtain the emotional warmth Gore gives me, while I try to obtain from Gore the physical responsiveness Bill gave me. Impasse. I must turn away, react, activate. I rush out into the spring softness and buy a nightgown, a bag, objects I need to be ready for love. I feel weak, lost, on the verge of hysteria. I called Staff. He can't see me.

MARCH 23, 1946

Yesterday was the worst day of all, worse than the end of the mirages. It was the day when I was like a drug addict deprived of his drug. I opened my mouth to shout, to scream, to call for help. Anxiety choked me. I called Staff. I forced myself to be calm. I went into the street. My writing tastes of ashes. I have lost my dreams. My relation to Hugo is tender but passionless; to Gore and Bill, finished; to Gonzalo tender and dead. I keep pretenses, talking like a wife, cook, nurse, mistress, friend, but I am dead. I talk to Gonzalo, who makes a big scene of jealousy, trying vehemently to reassure him while knowing my love is dead. Gore has gone to visit his boy. I have no loves. Gonzalo took me but I couldn't respond. Hugo takes me and I can't respond. The dream has been killed by the body. Only the body gets cheated in the dream. One does not eat, make love, live with the body, in the dream. The awakening is to a desert.

Monday I reached the highest peak of suffering, when I envisaged the possibility of a relationship between Gore and Pablo, and then I awakened completely. Suffering comes from the dream that does not coincide with reality. In the children's world, I cannot find a lover. I had not been able to surrender my dream of Gore as my lover, but yesterday I did. I said: "To hell with this children's world! It is a dream that cannot be." Tragedy comes from dreaming against reality, and the reality is that Gore is sensually a child, a child afraid. Pablo is a child afraid.

Oh, the drug of my marvelous dreams, the pain of awakening. The most terrible pain came when I dreamed of Gore possessing me, and then I awoke unpossessed. The unreality of it, the emptiness. The dream is a drug which kills the body, kills fulfillment. Don Quixote came to a sorry end, and I too. Awake, Anaïs, Gore is a little child, a very sweet and lovable child. C'est tout. Pas plus. And I am alone.

During all this, Hugo tries so earnestly to be all to me. He reads his old diary and is shocked by the image of himself. He does not like his own image. I had to console him, while I was collapsing from exhaustion and sadness.

We worked all day for Maya. Acting is like freedom. Pablo returned from Panama fiery and gay, as before, his body full of warmth. We danced a new Panamanian dance, we laughed, we embraced. All of the pretense of relationship for the film was a shadow dance, for there was no deep carnal relationship between anyone yesterday. All the men are homosexual, and all of the women are unsatisfied. Rita Christiani, the half-negro girl, is a lesbian. Maya is unsatisfied with Sasha, her partner. The women are drawn to each other. The men are drawn to each other. What is this, a world without vital passionate relationships? "There is a relationship going on!" shouts Maya, directing, "a contact made at the party, talk as if you were related!" They couldn't. We couldn't.

Out of fatigue, after being under the strong lights from twelve noon until twelve midnight, we became hysterical and gesticulated wildly to break down the walls between us. When I tried to relate to the others, it was not from the depths of passion, but from its periphery.

Tuesday: Gore came, and I tried to act detached and light-hearted. I pretended Bill had been here for twenty-four hours (a wish, and a counterbalance to Gore visiting Bill Miller at Dartmouth). Gore tells me: "I know now how everything is. My Bill is my little brother, and we have sex together. But you are *mon âme*. This is more important. Bigger."

And he handed me a poem called "Return."

I tell him I am happy to not spoil his sense of balance, his happiness at having what he needs, but he is too intuitive, too instinctive. He reads my eyes, face, and voice, and says, "You are not happy." He is so soft, so melting, so gentle, so warm, so near, so much present in his feelings that the warm flow begins again. I told him I could be happy and complete if my Bill were here for the passion. He offered to get Bill out of the army. "Though it would hurt me and I will be jealous, I want you happy." His love for me is real. "With my Bill," he said, "I am not myself. I am awkward, and not myself. Why is that? We are not very compatible in bed. He likes women in bed, really likes them but doesn't love them or feel related to them." And there it is. In my presence he is completely himself, and I too because I cannot act before him. He knows all I feel. Sweetly we eat together, walk together. I tell him about my fears of Pablo. "Oh, I don't want Pablo. There are a million Pablos. And he is in the group, and I don't want my secret out."

"What shall I tell him?"

"That we are lovers?"

"But it isn't true."

"This is a love affair. Otherwise we wouldn't feel so alive. We are the two most alive people in the world today. Will you marry me?" he asked me again.

"Not yet."

"Age doesn't matter when one loves," he said later, after he had told me that people of thirty-five or forty are "old."

He knows how to make me feel his love. What he wanted to see on my face as soon as he returned was, "I am still yours." And he can see it. I feel like a woman in love. My eyes tremble before his. He wants to act a love scene in the movies.

It is hard to believe in an analysis in which I choose to starve myself of my hungers and passions out of the fear of the consequences of abandoning myself to them. But why did I choose a man who denies me what I so violently desire?

Staff: "Your instinct tells you: 'This one bears the obstacle that will act as a check upon my complete possession by another. I do not have to check myself; he will do it, first by being incapable of making love to a woman, and second by the difference of age.'"

"But the hunger! The desire! How can I believe that I sought to starve myself, to deny myself?"

"Well, when you were faced with the possibility of escape from these traps, you were filled with fear: either you would become uncontrollably erotic, a whore, or you would fall victim to a man who would impose his will over yours. When you contemplate a world of maturity, you also fear rejection. Your father rejected you. The children cannot reject you. They need you, idealize you. You are in power."

Self-imposed suffering and starvation. Such deformations. I deformed my inner vision of Hugo. I painted him within myself as the father without youthfulness. It is true he is almost continuously depressed, but so was Bill, and I forgave him, and so was Gore before I met him. It is inner fate, *destinée intérieure*. The human being we relate to best is the one who reflects our present psychic state. In me, there was this hungry child in need of another child (while playing at being the mother), the fear of the violent lust of man (such as Wilson's), and the fear of having to live in a state of violence (the same fear Gore had after being beaten by his mother).

Angoisse makes you dash to the end so as to be delivered of suspense (a short circuit): quick sexual acts, quick satisfaction, for I can't bear the incertitude.

Staff discussed altruism as a cover for the hunger, for needs of which one is ashamed. I was terribly ashamed to take, so I gave, and as I gave, I wanted to cry, "This is what I would like you to do for me."

Hugo went to see an analyst. Poor Hugo.

Wednesday. One day softened by Gore's emotional nearness, then the next a letter from Bill, a passionate letter full of physical longing: "Last night I lay a long time in bed thinking of you. You become so real in my mind that I felt your body beside mine; I felt your fingers stroking me, and I felt your lips and tasted your tongue. I was with you with all my senses and desires. I wish it could have been reality; it's been so long and it will be longer after I leave for Japan. I found you in the description of Lillian: the white young body, the vitality... The blue light seeping through the high window, flowing down into darkness, enfolding gently the flower body... Pale straight stem cool in its white repose... Studded with blossoms, black and red and pink...

Crowned with a heavy flower, blooming, whitely among black silk petals... A pale stalk, from waiting sleep awakened. Motionless and in quiet symmetry singing of the burning consummation. The white blossom turns slowly towards the shadow pale stem diving... I am by the two stalks lured into enchantment... Black tendrils winding through my fingers... as the real blossom opens. Your fingers are enfolding my layered selves... Your breath has entered my soul. In the blue light we dance."

And ecstasy! It is spring. The bells are chiming on Fifth Avenue, the shops are full of flowers, the crowds are gay, and suddenly I am in ecstasy.

Joy. Joy. Joy. I saw Gore for lunch and had to leave at two to pose for some publicity pictures with Maya. He left with me. In the dazzling sun, I was almost dancing. In the taxi I talked about Bill's letter, but I was moved almost to tears by Gore. He took my hand and melted completely in my presence. I have starved myself, cheated myself of joy. It is incredible.

Unwisely I write Bill, "I can free you if you wish," thinking that I can tell Staff: "I won't give them so much importance. I won't give them my whole self."

Gore says: "Will you come to my property in the tropics? We will live there together eleven months out of the year and one month only with our Bills."

I have a longing for a free kind of home, a houseboat, a gypsy cart.

April 1, 1946

Staff says, "You help others obtain what they want." I warm Gore, and he attains pleasure and health. His mother had said he could not act because he was self-conscious, but he got over his fear and acted. His mother said he couldn't dance. I said he could, and so he begins. He carries my castanets in his pocket, goes bicycling in the park, calls me when he finishes his chapter. He says for the first time he can give. He is happier, writes more spontaneously. He writes to music as I do.

Then I lie on my bed, convulsed with hunger. I am the one who wants freedom, money, success, power, to act, to dance, to find passion, strength, confidence, but it was Gore I helped because I could not take for myself. But I, what have I? I want love, passion, confidence. Instead I have this hunger.

"It's a breakthrough," said Staff, "a breakthrough with the want, the need."

I came home less depressed, full of tenderness for Gore because of the way he behaves. If my voice isn't alive in the morning when he calls (even if I tease, "I'm practicing how to be an Anglo-Saxon for the next time I see you") he knows I'm sad, and he calls me again in the evening.

"I want the *williwaw* (storms). I don't want coldness."

The tragic element lies in the absurd dream I invented, to see Gore as my husband and lover, putting everything in his hands, as I put everything in Bill's hands. This is the end of the Transparent Child...or the beginning of my own lost, killed, buried child...

L'ENFANT TRANSPARENT C'EST MOI!

One night I was very comical for Hugo, dancing, impersonating, singing, mocking, inventing a song about Hugo's "glooming in the gloaming." I laughed until I wept, but suddenly I felt the despair of knowing, of never really forgetting, of seeing myself, to be so split.

Staff, "The first person you gave yourself to betrayed you." So I split. Ultimate giving terrifies me. I split, split, split, and seek split beings.

Dream: A painter comes with a woman. He has painted the woman in a very obscene fashion on the canvas, with a hole through it. He talks loudly. I have a feeling he has been using the painting sexually. He scoffs at the woman and says to me: "Yes, she looks sensual, but she's got a padlock inside her sex. Can't get her to make love. Can't get any woman to make love." As he goes off, he says, "I suppose you're not willing either, that you haven't even got a towel with you." Such a crude invitation I can't answer, although I wanted to sleep with him.

Tuesday: I told Staff I was free of the dream of Gore, that now he could analyze Gore without fear of me. I felt wide awake. Then I met Gore, but he is still dreaming his dream. He says: "You don't need the diary anymore. This is the last relationship—there will not be any more." And: "I don't need analysis. I have your faith." And: "Do you know why my father is enthusiastic about you? Because he sees you are destroying my mother's image, and he always said my mother had been bad for me."

Then I tell him, "Someday you'll know I did the hardest thing of all when I sent you to the analyst."

"Why?"

"Oh, you may marry Cornelia and have nine children."

I know, as Staff told me, he will lose his "illusion" that we are lovers and see the truth. And I hate to lose his illusion even though it harms me. I hear the words of a "lover." I won't hear them anymore. And it seems like a second surrender, a terrible thing to be asked to give up. Illusion. I never saw it so clearly. "Something would break in him if he knew your age," said Staff. "The illusion will disappear. You will be good friends."

Gore calls me three times a day. My photograph is on his desk. His words are those of love. I must surrender, surrender illusion for the sake of truth.

Gore says: "We are *not* pretending. We *are* lovers."

I said: "We have talked about your complexes. Now let's talk about mine, so that I can convince you I don't want you for a lover. You are Don Juan. You live now for the conquest. You like to add them up on a little blackboard."

And this is what this boy of twenty answers me: "This is only true because I haven't slept with anyone I loved. If I had a relationship with you it would no longer be so. So there, I can knock down your complex right there."

His illusion—and his faith in it—touches me. I observe that as I sit there, the painful hunger, the tension of desire, the excitement, all of it is gone. I am free, as long as I don't look too long at his mouth. Free but sad. I am awake, but he is still dreaming. I have such faith in him, but he is the one who has faith in our life together. He writes me a dedication on the cover of his new novel, "You placed the king on his throne."

Is this illusion necessary to his life and creation, or will the truth give him greater strength?

This was the hardest of all surrenders: to give up being his analyst, the needed one, for the sake of the strength he will get. I want him strong. I want him to suffer less than I have. This is his reward for his own courage, his own capacity to love, his responsiveness, his constant truthfulness. He is so truthful, so direct, so worthy of being given all. I want to give him all the strength, all the power that comes from self-knowledge. This analysis will be invaluable to his writing. The love is real, sincere, and it will endure. When the mother gives up her son, that is the greatest love of all.

April 4, 1946

Yesterday I met Gore at the museum for lunch. He plays at greeting me like an Anglo-Saxon (to get ahead of my doing it), so twice now we don't kiss upon meeting, and it hurts me. The waves of love choke me. I walk the streets with this love that is too big for Gore. I hold it in, and then I go dead, dead. When Gore telephoned this morning and I did not have that electric feeling, I thought I was free. I am dead.

Truth and Illusion. Truth and Illusion. Illusion has been creative. What will the truth be? That is why I always lie. I can't have a truthful relationship. Gore's idealization of me sets my pattern. I begin truthfully, but then I withhold what hurts him, what would destroy his illusion. I hide my psychoanalysis, my real age, my sexual needs, my past lovers and experience, my negro lover, and I give him his dream, his ideal woman. But where am I in the end? He is a boy who loves the truth.

Weeping, I bring Staff my fear of what truth conceals compared to the beauty created by illusion. Staff proves to me that it is not an illusion about me which animates and fecundates Gore, but rather the real Anaïs, whom Gore knows unconsciously, who is rich and inspiring, who created a world he can live in, whose warmth makes him feel alive, and who awakened the depth of his feelings. So what do I fear? At the movies a young woman danced a most gliding dance on the screen, and he said, "C'est toi." When I talked of difference of age, he said, "At forty I will be a cripple, and you will still be vital and shining."

Staff: "But that is not the best part of the relationship. The best part is the real part: his need of you, his real contact with you, your understanding of each other, your helping each other. The 'illusion' that you are lovers is spurious. You aren't. And it will be years before Gore is ready for a woman." He admits part of my illusion was based on reality and that he is only dealing with the false parts, as when I began to lie to Gore when I saw he wanted the mystical, romantic me.

When I mentioned Staff, Gore looked pained and said: "Oh, you aren't going to him now when you have me, are you? I'm not harmful to you. You should not need him."

So, to sustain his great desire to possess all of me, to be the only one I need, I said I had been seeing Staff before knowing him. That was the first lie. Then there was another, then another, until finally my role is shaped by his needs, and I am overwhelmed, lost, unhappy. I am always anxious because I am aware of the falsity, and in this way I lose true contact with him. But illusion was the drug (I confused the illusions I created with my real intuition about people's potentialities), and when I lose its stimulating, enhancing effect, I die.

Reality seems like death. If Gore and I can't believe we are lovers, or may be lovers, what is there? A love which was not intended to be sensual, because sensually he is thirteen years old and I am his mother.

After talking with Staff I felt strong, clear and quiet, felt like writing.

Dream: There is a gathering to listen to poetry. I walk through naked. I feel embarrassed and yet defiant too. I don't sit down, however, I stand. There is to be a party afterwards. I am looking for someone to cover me. Martha is there. Three of us are lying on a bed. Martha wants to make love and slips her hand under my dress. I am ashamed people will think we are lesbians. She begins the caresses and I think how childish this is, how incomplete. People are passing by, and then a train cuts right through the gathering under a tunnel. I look to see if the tunnel is already made, or if the train has to lift the earth and pierce its way through each time. I gave Martha pleasure with the hands, but I felt none.

Association: Sexual relations with Gonzalo last night. I wondered how I could ever have been satisfied with him, with his weakness, his inability to finish the act, his interruptions, the rings, my having to give him pleasure with the hands, and not always reaching the orgasm myself because I feel the vacillations. How could I have desired this lack of power? It would be the same with Gore. I am cured of the desire for Gore. There is only tenderness left. With Staff, I moved away from him. I see him sexually as a child, and I want power. I feel the power in myself, and I want an answer to it.

May this diary bring me freedom from desire for my sons, and a lover and husband.

Letter from Bill: "You must know you put me in a difficult position. For how am I to answer your offering of a way out when you show by every comma and syllable what you wish I would do? The problem is not simple. In Japan I will learn whether or not I am fertile or barren. If I am the first I shall be happy and shall return in the manner of Ulysses who has had his search inside himself; if not I shall return and struggle along with external support. For these reasons I have decided to go to Japan. Until we meet on my furlough (soon) I embrace you in thought, *tendrement, ton Guillaume.*"

With analysis, I may perhaps attain freedom from the diary itself, by watching myself live, by having to create stories to make it more marvelous. I may attain freedom from my idealized self, the idealization of others. I got frightened because I have gained four pounds, so I look less spiritual and look more like what I am: a sensual woman who lives a great part of her life through her senses. As I broke off with the bourgeois world, I also broke with the intellectual world.

APRIL 5, 1946

Gore. I tell him all, how I talked with Staff, how it will be a long time before he is ready for a woman, how I have conquered my desire of him, why I want him to have analysis. I tell him this is my most sincere relationship. "We have much to give each other." I am quiet, strong, and yet full of feeling, full of the desire to be what he needs, to be the woman nearest to him. The pain is gone. I will have little stabs of regret, yes, but now the truth is strong and deep. I want to accept reality and to make it rich and deep. The pain lies in the impossible wish. "Our only enemy is time, now," said Gore.

APRIL 7, 1946

After our talk, Gore came to a party that I had decided to enjoy in a carefree way, by giving up sexual obsession and the obsession to conquer something for myself. When Gore arrived, he kissed me on the mouth so warmly. Hugo was not there, so Gore played the husband. He hooked up my new dress. When Pablo came (and I knew they were attracted to each other), it did not change the steady current between us. I told Pablo Gore and I were happy together. He was jealous and yet happy too, as if I had said, "Your brother and I are lovers." They will sleep together, I know, but it doesn't matter. Pablo made me dance wildly, and Gore came timidly to try. I made him close his eyes and listen to the music and obey through delicate vibrations the movements of the dance, and in this way he found rhythm. The first time he danced, it was true, he had none, but now he held me close and followed the rhythms. Sometimes he fell back into a lifeless, monotonous motion, and sometimes he obeyed the music. To see each part of his body, once stiff, becoming alive was a joy. He watched Pablo, he imitated him, we laughed, we played. "With you, I can dance." With you, you, you. There is no frustration because there is a life current.

Pablo brought five ugly, vulgar homosexuals, who danced among themselves, kissing and talking obscenely. Gore had the same aesthetic reaction I had. "You see, that's the world I don't want to fall into." "You won't, I won't let you," I said. I have no pain. I am free. We danced.

When Pablo left at two for another party with his revolting retinue, Gore didn't go with them. He stayed, waited until everyone had left to take me in his arms and kiss me amorously several times, lingering like an adolescent lover not yet fully awake, a little nebulous, which is what he is. The sweetness pierced me. Our tongues don't touch, just the mouths melting (the sexual thrust is lacking, it is like a communion). It is enough to establish physical contact, so that it is not abstract such as it was with Eduardo. I was very happy. Pleasure is always there, always possible, when one is not obsessed with a quest to conquer the unattainable, to force one's will upon the unwilling, to change the unchangeable, to conquer what is not conquerable, to want what cannot be taken.

I was simply happy to have what I could have, which is all that Gore can give.

Awakened peaceful, eager to write...tired, but relaxed and wise.

APRIL 10, 1946, EVENING

Gore's interview with Staff was a failure. "It didn't sound as if he were talking about us. I didn't recognize you or myself in his statements. He said I should be your playmate and your friend. He tried to say it was good for you to have a relationship without sexuality, that you tended to over-sexualize. He was tactless and crude. I have no respect for him. He tried to separate us, I could see that," said Gore.

He aroused my anger against Staff for the first time, anger that he should speak of me thus to Gore, and that he didn't know how to overcome Gore's resistance, or pride, and win his confidence. He intimated that Gore was not ready for analysis, not desperate enough.

All that I obtain with tact and gentleness, Staff could not obtain by his direct tactics, which caused Gore to rear back. I have to help him alone, with love. My love alone touches and moves him. His Bill slipped away, then came to New York to visit his older friend without seeing Gore, and he saw them at a bar.

"Little boys can't love," I said.

"Is that it?"

"You are deeper," I said. "You can't put deeper feeling into small receptacles." (I should know. I have learned my lesson.)

APRIL 13, 1946

I now believe Gore went to destroy Staff so I would not continue to lean on him. He went with jealousy and hostility. Staff said, "He is nothing. Your idealization again. You would die married to him."

I worked well this morning, wrote pages on the adolescence of Stella, the relationship of Michael and Donald, and then the story of the opening of the tulips, inspired by my incident with Bill.

Monday: I am inspired and flowing, writing pages on Sabina, the fire bug, the café life.

What a man and woman can achieve together is rhythm. When Gore feels fragile, I feel strong. When he feels strong, I enjoy being led and being fragile.

By kissing, we keep the physical current alive.

Bill is coming soon, my passion, but I want more now, and I see this is not enough.

APRIL 16, 1946

I have such a sense of relief because of the freedom from Gore and the thwarted wishes, a sense of great inner richness pouring out in the writing, as well as a flow of emotion, a sense of youth and strength.

All of this I owe to Staff.

The bond with Gore is broken because it is merely a child and mother disguised as a woman submitting to a man who is secure and powerful on the surface, while he depends, leans, and gives his delicate, tender self. There is great tenderness, yes, but now I turn away from his childishness, his little boys, his miniature sexuality, and I am at peace. I wait patiently, tranquil, smooth-faced, feminine, quiet, plant-like, gaining weight.

Strange, the great honesty about my sensuality brings from Gonzalo a new wave of lustiness. He tells me that after nine years I am a marvelous mistress. "How wonderfully you make love!" He is more openly sensual. I enjoy it. I enjoy whatever I have. I dream of Bill. I write about Louveciennes. Dr. Effron, who analyzed Staff, reads *This Hunger* and says simply, "She has genius."

I telephoned Bill. He said: "I'm as well as can be expected. Send me the *Tibetan Book of the Dead*. Are you telephoning from the old homestead?"

"I miss you."

"I miss you too. I won't be coming before two or three weeks."

Hugo is on his way to Cuba, so I have ten days of freedom and no lover.

When Henry couldn't have something he wanted, he didn't care—he took something else. So I have Gore, a party, cocktails, an evening at home, people I want to see, adventures I can try.

Gore wrote a perfect love scene for his novel in which he possessed me.

Damn everything that hurts. I am free of all that hurts. The only true freedom is not to want anything, not to care so desperately, to not depend on love as though it were a matter of life or death. All dependence is wrong. I am sad, free, free of Gore and of his boy, just an ordinary little boy, "not too bright, of a lower class, and who dreams of another life," which is what he finds in me.

APRIL 21, 1946, EASTER SUNDAY

A year ago Bill and I were lovers for the first time. Last night, Gore came early to the party, depressed—he realized last night that the boy bored him, and he longed for me. "I want a boy like you, in every way like you." I smiled. We embraced, kissed, and he lay half over me, with his face buried in my neck. The telephone broke the spell. People arrived. Irina said, "He is adorable." Gore always hovers, plays the husband. His pride and arrogance all gone, he even talks cordially to Bill Attaway, the negro writer, breaking through his prejudice. After the party he gathered the glasses for me. We kissed passionately, and he left. *Le petit fait de progrès*, I thought, when alone, remembering his kiss, its vehemence. Then, suddenly, I lost my gayety and irony and felt pain all through my body not to have him at my side after this emotional flow we had. The passion is aroused again. There was desire on his face.

I feel thoroughly, completely alive.

APRIL 22, 1946

Gonzalo and I.

Gonzalo: "It's unbelievable, we've been together nine years, and I still feel an illusion. I never had this with any woman."

Anaïs: "Nine years!"

Gonzalo: "I'd like to know how often you have been unfaithful."

Anaïs: "I don't want to know how many times you have been."

Gonzalo: "Oh, with me, only a few. When you left Paris that time, and I got drunk. At Provincetown, too, that girl who was so friendly with you at the beach."

Anaïs: "I didn't ask you. I don't want to know."

Gonzalo: "But I do. I know you went off with that singer. Why did you? A singer. I wouldn't make love to a woman singer for anything. Mine were unimportant. You know you're the only one I love."

Anaïs: "But if I had gone off with him, you'd think it was important."

Gonzalo (disturbed): "It's different for a woman. When did you? And why?"

Silence.

Gonzalo: "You won't say anything."

Anaïs: "I don't believe we should talk about this. I don't want to know about you. (Crying) I never wanted to think about it, and now you are making me."

Gonzalo: "You're crying? But it was nothing. I forget about them immediately. And in nine years only a few times, whereas with you, oh, I'm sure it was at least fifty."

Anaïs: "I didn't ask you. Why did you have to tell me?"

Gonzalo: "I'm just more sincere, and you aren't."

Anaïs: "It isn't sincerity, it's revenge. You told me to hurt me."

Gonzalo: "I told you because I thought it would make you tell, drive you to tell me."

Silence.

Gonzalo: "Now you're shut like a clam."

Anaïs: (I no longer love Gonzalo, but he doesn't know it, and I can't tell him, because I know that if I did, I could plunge him into hell. And Gonzalo thinks I am crying over his infidelities.)

Gonzalo: "I would like to know how you learned all you know about love. Where did you learn to move as you do, so rhythmically, tantalizingly? Who taught you that inner spasmodic clutching which is so exciting? Very few women know this."

Anaïs: "Miller's wife told me about it." (I won't say Miller taught me. I can't say one man taught me this, another that, Henry taught me to clutch, this one taught me other things. I can't say either that a great deal more was a natural gift, I learned very quickly and much instinctively. No one taught me responsiveness and quick sensitivity, or the easily flowing honey, or the lascivious turning I later discovered in Albert, native island tropical languorousness, the voluptuous inheritance of tropical islands.)

Gonzalo: "It enrages me to see how much you know. I often wonder where you have learned."

Anaïs: "In every relationship it's different. We have our own ways. We have invented our own lovemaking together out of our own temperament."

Gonzalo: "Yes, I remember, I liked taking you from behind, that excited me. But now I have changed. What a good mistress you are! Other women don't move rightly. You're so soft down here (touching me). It used to make me feel it's so soft I can't bear to hurt you, I used to fear hurting you, I still feel as if I were stabbing you in there, how can it be pleasurable. I see this big dark penis inside of this soft, small, white and rosy part…"

Anaïs: "It is pleasurable."

Gonzalo: "Sometimes I made you weep with joy, didn't I? I reached deep into you, didn't I?"

Anaïs: "Yes, but how is it you talk about this now? You used to be so secretive."

Gonzalo: "Yes, that's true. Now I'm aware of all this. I wasn't before. It was always difficult for me, I found adaptation difficult. Couldn't be satisfied easily. There weren't many women, even when I was young. And you feel nothing here, outside, do you? When I kiss you there you never respond."

Anaïs: "No, I was hurt there once, horseback riding, in that particular place. I was about sixteen and I went horseback riding in Central Park, and it was the first time. I was wearing garter panties, and the garters got between me and the tight riding trousers, and I would not complain. I went on riding for an hour."

Gonzalo: "You're the one who feels more inside, anyway."

Anaïs: "Yes, except when you caress me, that I feel too. But much more inside."

Gonzalo: "Why did you go off with that singer? Why did you do that to me?"

Anaïs: "There was no singer. I just liked to dance with him."

(When I cried, Gonzalo tried to take me. He was aroused, but I wouldn't let him. I was still resentful of his unfaithfulness. When finally he took me I wouldn't respond. It made him angry, but I was still terribly subdued by all the betrayals, the inevitable ones, crying over love itself, its fluctuations, and its ends.)

He couldn't extract a confession. I defeated him in this, knowing how he would torture himself with one fact, let alone all the truth.

Hugo is gone, and I have no engagements. I am free to go adventuring, but I feel anxiety. Suppose I find no one I know, or that I have to eat alone. Suppose I am approached by an utter stranger slipping into the Village underworld, unknown. Oh, so Miss Nin, what an adventurer! You set controls over and around yourself. You say because of Hugo you can't do this, because of Gore, because of Bill, and it is because of you!

Your cage is open, and what? You're shy. You're ready to call someone you know. And what do you do with your freedom? You obey another's need. You call on Nancy Banks, married to a negro guitarist, because she is lost and confused. You meet her and her husband at a Calypso restaurant. You sit at George's and listen to jazz.

Then Nancy tells you her life history. You think about it, and then at ten o'clock you are home for Gonzalo.

The first night of freedom.

The second night you are in bed, tired from the quarrel with Gonzalo, the sentimental yearning for Gore combined with the anger at him for the half-passion by which he holds you, you are not well after the dentist, the cocaine, and a late night.

And tomorrow I try again. But I call Josephine and Pablo. I am led by the hand because I am afraid of the underworld of violence and illness and darkness. Afraid. That is why I went into it only to pull Henry and Gonzalo out.

The cage is open, but I don't know how to fly.

At one moment when Gonzalo was trying to take me while I wept, he managed to slide his foot between my legs, a little game we often played, his big dark foot between my white legs, and I would say very politely, "Oh, your foot has come to pay me a visit," and suddenly I remembered the time I had such a frenzied desire for John Dudley, the wildest of all, and that after we had satisfied it and were lying back talking, he was trying to woo me again, and playfully he placed his foot between my legs and said, "My foot likes you." Because this reminded me of my little game with Gonzalo, Gonzalo's image came before me and all my real love for him, and I brusquely felt violated by John's foot, the falseness and strangeness of our lying there naked, so I got up and dressed. What if I told this to Gonzalo? He could never rid himself of the image of me yielding to another man. It would poison his life. Already the slightest gossip poisons him for days.

APRIL 25, 1946

I gave up the frenzied desire for a new lover after falling into the familiar trap of pain, when Gore's kiss the night of the party bound me to him erotically again. To escape, I threw myself into sensuality with Gonzalo. When Gore told me about a night with the boy, I retaliated and implied I had an affair too. I felt resentful. I broke a luncheon engagement, and his reaction was real illness. He suffers from jealousy. When we had dinner together, he was loving, hurt and jealous. He took my hand, touched my neck, and said, "One more bottle of wine and I could take you."

"What are we going to do?"

"Cut out sex," he said, violently.

We went out drunk, soldered together as one by our similarity of feeling. With a passionate kiss we separated, he to his boy, and I to Gonzalo. It is hell on earth, and then we break, soften, and the tenderness heals us both. I had imagined him and Pablo together, and the image was so unbearable I felt that I must leave for France right now. I must break this.

Staff was scathing when I said sorry, sorry, sorry, doctor, but I still feel as one with Gore, not with Hugo, not with Gonzalo. I feel all he feels.

Taking the subway and recalling his pale face and his hand on his heart, I felt cut in two by tenderness, absolutely weak right through the center of the body. Hunger, a yearning hunger, at times not sexual, so deep it is within the womb. I analyze it myself now: one feels one possesses the child, but not the man. There is a bond which gives security. It is real and physical. I can also identify with the child's needs, his hunger. We are two children ashamed, rejected and deserted, he by his mother and I by my father. Both of us are hungry and insecure, he to find his mother, and I to possess something inside of me, something near.

Yes, I know, the child needs. Mature people relate to each other without the need to merge. D. H. Lawrence wrote enough against merging. There he is, he is tall, he is slender, his skin is golden and new, vulnerable, with the tenderness of newness, youth. He is an old child. Like me, he covered the weakness by acting paternally, as I acted maternally. He dominates, he takes responsibilities, he patronizes his little boys. He doesn't feel overwhelmed or threatened by me, so he loves me, and I yield. When I want to affect him, I do so gently and subtly. I don't run headlong against his prejudices, I don't argue about negroes or Jews. I present him an interesting negro writer and Gore sees. I show him Maya at work and Gore learns. I don't attack his writing as it was. I help him expand. I say, "Write as you are, out of yourself, that is where your richness lies." I worry about his writing. It is conventional, but I at twenty was sentimental, romantic. My first novel was unprintable. Not his.

He made love to me on paper. The day after being apart (I was having my "affair" and not lunching with him) he hands me as a gift his handwritten version of the love scene, not seeing the irony, believing he is "spoiling" me with this chapter seven, our love affair on paper.

Will I ever be free of him, of his neck, his soft, brilliant fawn eyes, his vulnerable, emotional, full mouth? He has the same aspects of Miller—aggression, taking from the world, using people—because he needs to shine, to achieve, to attain fame. As Miller did, he says: "Ask Leo Lerman to review my book. Invite the Book of the Month Club man." He pushes forward, primitive, hard, self-interested, but towards me he turns a soft, truthful, humble, lost self.

As I know what drives him, I cannot judge him. My love will make this less necessary. I don't know.

April 26, 1946

I spent last night alone, fell asleep early, suffering from loneliness, the unreality of my soft, deep yearning for Gore. Hugo is far away. Gonzalo is far away. I feel a mellow tenderness for them, but that's all. I have so many relationships, but none are near enough to the core of my being. Gore says, "You are my deep life," but I wonder how deeply he would go with me.

My art is not artifice. There is no separation between my life and art. The form of my art is the form of my life, not the artificial pattern of narrative, and my life is an unfinished story.

While neurosis rules, all life becomes a symbolical play. It is this story I am trying to tell, the ghastliness of our life today.

Who has not followed for years the spell of a particular tone of voice, from voice to voice, as the fetishist follows beautiful feet, scarcely seeing the woman herself? A voice, a mouth, an eye, all stemming from the original fountain of our first desire, directing it, enslaving us until we choose to unravel the fatalism and free ourselves. The story of freedom does not appear in the new book—you are still in the labyrinth and must be willing to get lost before you are saved. The unreality we suffer from is what I am making clear. The hero of this book is the mysterious malady which makes our lives a drama of compulsion.

Saturday. I was writing yesterday when the bell rang. I expected the drug store, and Bill stood at the door! I nearly fainted. A Bill who has lost his dewiness, opalescence, transparency, from life in the army, with rougher hands, now a lieutenant. A Bill who is tender and less shy. We talked at first, because he wanted to wait until Monday night when he could stay all night, but the hunger was too great, and we kissed, kissed. The ecstasy of his determined kisses, the softness of his hands, the sliding, tender way he enters all my being. Oh, Bill, of velvet and silk, oh Bill of the rich voice, moth-like ears, tender skin and sharp, strong teeth. "I want to undress you. I can't wait till Monday." He kissed my breasts, grown heavier. He undressed. The soft waves, the rolling of our bodies without violence. I melted, melted by the lightest hand of all, dissolved in ecstasy. "I have dreamed of this so often, you look now as I saw you in my poem. The windows are blue and you, so white. I have dreamed of you so often." Bill talks, utters words, lifts my legs to better penetrate me. Bill is mute through the orgasm, but his heart beats faster with ecstasy. One hour of joy. When he leaves, I take a warm bath to music, to preserve this ecstasy. Ecstasy, vaporous, light, mystical, sensual. What a contrast to what follows.

At nine o'clock it was Chinchilito. I was still full of desire, having been barely aroused by Bill. I kept thinking of Gonzalo's stories about the lambs in Peru, the beautiful lambs. At mating season, so as not to wear out the male, they gather all the females and they first send out all the young lambs to tease and caress the females, arouse them, prepare them, and then, when they are warm, alive and melted, comes the male, who is not one for voluptuous expansion, but who takes them quickly and directly.

The young, soft lamb Bill, and Chinchilito, the giant pagan, six feet tall, enormous, heavy now, so violent. I hurt my body against his strength, and in a frenzy of excitement and desire, we meet each other's violence. He is like a beast, aroused, grunting, and violent. I tantalize him, rubbing my breast against his penis, give him violent gestures, and the violent strengths are matched, firm, hard body against body, not yielding, not taken but taking with him, answering with contortions and convulsions, the wide, big, stormy, elemental explosion of what began as a soft, honeyed, secret flower pistil caresses with Bill.

Power.

Violence.

I fell asleep appeased, but today again I'm in a frenzy of desire. This is delirium. This is what I feared after I sought to thwart myself with Hugo.

Evening: Gore has been ill in bed for two days. He comes out to have dinner with me. He is pale. I beg him not to ask questions, not to make me talk about my other life. He wants the truth. How long will Bill be here? Where does he live?

He sees what I feel. I feel our nearness, our bond, our pain.

"Should we surrender each other?"

We can't. He shows me the poetry he wrote at sixteen, emotional and deep. "In school they made fun of emotions." Thus the shell that surrounds him.

I am full of love. Can I heal him?

"My little boy bores me. He is not enough."

"My little boy and I are strangers," I say, for that is true.

Coming out of Lafayette, I lean towards Gore, put my head on his shoulder. "Gore, if you only knew what I feel."

"I know," he says, "neither one of us is happy."

I ride on the bus with him to his home way uptown on 92nd Street to have more time together.

Then I have to console a jealous Gonzalo, who is suffering with suspicion. Three exhausting scenes of jealousy—he had seen me on the street with Gore.

I am tired, and sad.

Duits talks about Bill: "Bill is a deeper person; be patient with him. He is just perverse, very perverse, and frightened. He is more than Gore."

April 29, 1946

While I had dinner with Gore, Bill came and waited on my doorstep for an hour. He was only free from eight to ten, and then had to return home.

At ten Gonzalo came, took me, commenting again on our nine years together and the incredibility of this, and analyzing why I didn't have a hairy and thick-lipped vulva like most women, but that of a young girl, and that, he said, was why he loved me. He took me, then passed to jealousy and fury, working himself up into a rage like a volcano, naming all the men I slept with (wrongly) and took a painting by one of the children down from the wall and smashed his foot through it.

Such violence. I was equally furious, denying everything, saying, "You're stupid and blind."

Standing there, naked, while he destroyed the painting of "one of your lovers," he shouted, "I should break your face!"

Angry, as if I were innocent, so intent was I on protecting him from the truth (a truth far worse than he imagines), like a black demon.

Five minutes later, he called me up: "I'm crazy, I guess I'm crazy. Forgive me." I, feeling deep pity for his suffering and yet knowing it was he who destroyed my love by his own destructiveness, I called him back. He was humble and wounded, and I healed him. We had lunch together, feeling very tired. "As tired as if you had beaten me," I said. He laughed, but I'd rather be killed than confess, because I believe the truth destroys more than it creates. The truth about one's betrayals is not good. I keep begging Gore to let me at least be silent and for him not to tell me about his sexual life. But he insists on the truth.

Ten-thirty at night. I am waiting for Bill and am disturbed by Gore's jealousy. I do not tell him about tonight, but he knows. Yet, he let me look for an apartment for him where he can receive his boys. It is an impossible situation. I would like to go to France, but I can't desert him, at least not until he has someone, a relationship. I find myself surrounded by men who cling to me and cannot surrender me: Hugo, Gonzalo (Henry, too, was not ready to stand alone).

In analysis, the contest is now between the violent and unsubtle men, and the gentle, tender homosexuals.

Chinchilito was too brutal the other night. So was Gonzalo. Bill and Gore are too gentle, too passive, too feminine. Chinchilito so Germanic, Gonzalo so Spanish, with Moorish, Indian violence. I have associated sexuality with violence (my father and mother at war), as the homosexuals do. Going into mature sexuality seems like going into dark violence, nightclubs, villages where men attack and harm you.

Gore: I wait for a lover, yet I am thinking of you. I am filled with you. When we stood waiting for the bus and I felt your leaving me, for you do leave me at such times, I wanted to say to you: I love you more than ever. It is hard to believe. But the reason Bill is my favorite lover is merely because I have more of a feeling of having been with someone like you, and therefore feel nearer to you, and I can't bear men who are altogether different from you. I died once, before you did, for three days when you were with your Bill. I went through a kind of hell. Believe me, I do not exaggerate. It's just that I know better than others the marvelous things which get killed by pain. What I fear, my love, is that you and I will harden, close ourselves up, in order to numb the hurt. Tonight already you were changed towards me. I'm only now aware of this, and I don't know how we can find a way to keep this love alive. The first time I was deeply hurt when you were with your Bill, and that, you remember, ended our dream of a life together. Why I sometimes seem to take things sadly is simply because I am more aware of what happens to feelings. Gore, it is true that the lover doesn't take me away, that I continue to flow towards you in all my feelings. If I read, I read with you, if I hear music, I think of you, when I write, I write with you, for you, and it doesn't, as I had hoped, kill my desire for you. But it is also true that when we hurt each other and feel jealousy, the one who is hurt leaves and wants to break. I found it very hard today to look for an apartment, having so vividly in mind that it is for you and your boys. You have faith. You think we will grow used to it, but you forget at what cost: the cost of hardening towards each other, closing the doors which had been opened. And instead of being happy tonight, I think of this and fear for this strange love of ours. Jealousy is the worst of all pains, and it is worse when love has no completion, no security, no moment of saying we possess each other. I don't lack faith or love, but you know, my love, you have a little of that masculine sense of injustice. You say, "We are even," in such a reproachful way. You forget that you struck the first blow (involuntarily, I know). You feel my unfaithfulness more, as if mine were a greater betrayal, yet all the time I have belonged to you in a way you haven't to me, for I went all the way towards you, remember?

MY NIGHT WITH BILL

My diary, keep for me this most precious of nights, keep, keep in your pages this night with Bill.

There are those who enter your being and truly take you. Every one of Bill's caresses has entered my being. Every one has left its mark. My hair remembers his fingers. My neck remembers his mouth, his teeth. My hips still feel taken in his hands. My skin still raises its down at the remembrance of his light touch...his hands. Why is lovemaking so different, so different, how can a body be touched so differently? He sat on the bed, his legs hanging down, so as to make love to me with his mouth, his head, his shoulders. I buried my face in his thin shoulders, felt the delicate bones, kissed his tender, silky, lean body, his belly, his hips, took his penis in my mouth, his penis hard and leaping, breast against breast, tongue against tongue, mouth within mouth, and flights away from the burning sweetness into the cooler regions of the neck, ears, hair, to rest from the fire of his penis and the warm, flowing honey in which he dipped his fingers. In their light agility he weaves, interlaces, kneads, binds—it isn't just a touch, a weight of flesh, it is a making of lace, a tying of threads, an encirclement, an envelopment. Sliding, smooth, subtle. How some can find the entrances to the being, and others cannot. His hands enter into me, open every pore and tendril, melt me, when the penis comes the body is already so open, so given, so dissolved, the orgasm comes out of the depths, effortless as with no one else, like a flower orgasm, all the regions without violence (only his teeth are violent). He enters, he takes. Never, never have I known this sweetness. My body feels like a flower, turned to velvet and petals. His voluptuous movements, all made out of softness, never a discord, or dissonance, or jerking, everything is of flesh enfolding, unfurling, the movements of merging, of flowing. No impact or hardness, but a complete, total melting, flowering, flowing like a dream with a strong flavor, a lasting, enduring flesh taste as of having been in the ocean. Bill and I swam together in a sea of flesh, so it was, caresses I will never forget, our bodies have the same veins, flow, rhythm, it is languid, voluptuous, rhythmic, but not like a drum, but like a rolling of flames, curling, in satin whirls.

He lies over me as he was when he took me. I let my legs slide down parallel to his. He lies over my whole body, his face buried in my neck, in a trance of oneness. Keep this, keep this here, my diary. It is rare. It will be lost. Keep this, my diary, the flavor of his flesh, the taste of his sex, our legs twined as he sleeps over me, in a dream of abandon, crushing me, so fitted together our bodies, knitted together, his mouth so hungry. Only when he is inside he has not yet learned to control the movements. They are not rhythmic. He moves too softly, though firm and erect within me, and his orgasm comes quickly, like a soft, gentle fruit of his skin, his delicacies. The violence is missing, he flows into me, he doesn't stab, but it is all so harmonious with his age, his newness, his shyness, so natural to his beginnings as a lover.

In the early morning Bill awakened, smiled at me, drew close, slept in my arms, laid his penis against my leg. I could feel it throbbing and pulsating. Then he took me and we fell asleep again, but before I fell asleep I watched his beautiful face, his long eyelashes, his pure skin, the blue shadows under the eyes. I watched too, the little part of his face which is like Gore—the corner of his mouth, the upper lip, the nose—and felt as if Gore were lying there, and the two loves mingled without shock. And I fell asleep trusting, given...

A day of ecstasy, ecstasy and contentment.

MAY 3, 1946

A night with Bill was illumined by his passionate face drinking mine with drunkenness, his long eyelashes lost into mine, his eyes closed the better to drink my mouth, the endless draughts he took, his whole face in the kiss. The touch of his skin, this silk, this purity of silk, the firm softness of his mouth, all over my body, kissing my stomach, my hips, his hands everywhere like so many leaves, his mouth, how he sat and pulled me up so our breasts would feel the impact, how he pulled me against him, how we found each time the gesture of the most utter nestling, fitting, no gestures lost or wasted, each one aimed at the being, each one clear: I take this, I take this, I take this. Every gesture answered, if my head falls between his legs, he pulls my hair up and devours my neck, he devours my breasts until they hurt, he kisses me until it hurts, a trance, a trance of flesh, a trance of throbbing, pale voluptuousness with a core of fire. For such a long time he kisses, caresses, such a long time until my body is utterly dissolved and only then, as if he knows, he enters, only then, with a divination allowed only to the greatest lovers, the divination, every moment he has this, he has this, how can bodies emerge separate after this, I feel we will emerge as one body, deeply, deeply, he takes me, and I know he will remember this forever.

When I reach such fulfillment it stays in the body as if he had made a child within me. It stays in my body and over my skin. Then, as I have caught his rhythm now, and I know he wants this to end like a big wave to roll gently out of the depths into lightness, we emerge together into playfulness. I take him to visit everyone and every place I knew and at every place he enters the game. I say: The house was like this, the person like that, he says this, and says that of you, and even though you don't say very much, I know this person will ask me about you months later. We visit thus, he sketches me. We drink rye together, smoke, talk. Content. And he takes me again before leaving.

And I dressed, washed, and went to a Calypso dance, to not feel, to not break, to not die. Lost and blind at the dance, lost with Nancy Banks. "What am I doing here?" Anaïs, who has lost her identity, is dancing, but at least she does not feel Bill's departure. I feel too much, but my feelings have passed into other lives. I said: "I won't feel. I won't feel." But this feeling passed into Nancy's life, and I saw it. The next morning I got up and wrote the story of Nancy ("The Child Born Out of the Fog"), feeling for Nancy and her negro husband and child. I don't feel for myself. I have had fulfillment. There are others who have never had it. I have. I am rich. I am fortunate. I have no right to die. I wrote the story of Nancy, I went out, I laughed.

But this morning anguish got me by the throat. I wouldn't cry. I opened the window. *Angoisse*. Death passing. Swooping. Anger at Gore. Such anger. I went out, walked, ate, my eyes filled with tears, strangers looking at me. My life I have lost. My life is the peaks, the climax. Life is magic nights with Bill, light and fire. And now? Gore and his foolish boys.

No. I must leave.

Sunday, May 5, 1946

Gore came, having gone through hell, angry, jealous, frustrated, wanting to go far away, to take a woman, to overcome his fear, to come back and take me. This week he knew he did not have me, and that the boys were nothing. At first we were uneasy and tense. I pretended to be well, I assumed a role, I took a drink. The expression of his face touched me. He was sad, sincere, and he could see I was pretending. Then we broke down, embraced fraternally, tenderly, admitted all, admitted the pain, my desire to go away, his desire for flight, his rage last night, his terrible storming. He went into a debauch, an orgy. He called me (after saying he could not see me, he got free, and when he called I had gone out), went to the Astor bar, went off with a group invited to an orgy in which he could not participate. We sat on the couch, caught together again in a sincere, soft bond. After a little while we got lighter. He is more capable of detachment than I am. So I not only have the problem of my desire for him, which was not cured by Bill because he has the same kind of appeal, mouth and voice, and a strong emotional harmony, but there is also the problem of jealousy.

At peace again until the next storm. In the bus he says, "Your hands are like my mother's."

"What else?"

"The color of your hair."

"What else?"

"Your moods."

"But I'm not tyrannical."

"Oh, you are, but very subtly."

He doesn't want me detached. When I propose to leave until I can feel about him as I do about Eduardo, Pablo, etc., he won't have it. He is fully aware of what we lose by detachment. When I pretended to be happy, he was not happy.

MAY 6, 1946

The pain, the physical pain of losing contact with Bill was terrible. It caught me unaware, like death. I opened the window, I went out, walked. After seeing Gore, I fought for life. I kept busy, saw Staff. Gore and I ate at the Caviar Restaurant. He was at peace. I had let him read the part about himself in the diary.

I talked with Staff about my feeling of merging with the child, which makes my sensuality with Bill so acute, so ecstatic. How can I progress from this when it gave me fulfillment? Staff only says: "It was fulfillment because you only took the best from it, but let it be tested by marriage, by permanency. You would run away from both. It's the romantic peaks you took. You try and live on them alone." I know.

It is a beautiful day. Under the effect of gas at the dentist, my heart beat fast and I beat my chest with my hand to communicate to the dentist that I thought it would break. I thought: this is like death.

I must keep active, active.

Gore was sad that "Bill got into your diary." Yes, hurt. Oh, end this diary, end the children's world, if only, if only I could detach myself, be detached. Please, please, I beg no god in particular, help me be detached.

Gore, there is one thing you do which you must stop if we are to have peace together. As soon as I say to you, "Bill freed me of my desire for you," instead of accepting this and letting me be, you set about talking as you did the other night, talking about going away, making love to some unknown woman, to come back to me, etc., all of it sounding more like medicine than pleasure. Now will you please understand, I don't want this kind of willed desire. If it hasn't come out of love, I don't want it. I don't want planned lovemaking! I only wish you would let me alone with my physical fulfillment with Bill. You only make me feel humiliated, for you and for myself. The wish doesn't come out of real desire for me, but merely to take me away from Bill. I need, at the very least, my dream of Bill, and you try to pull me away. Then as soon as I am at peace, you say something to make it clear that we are to stand apart, but only after you think you have won me back with illusions about the future. Then you say, like yesterday, "Oh, we could make an arrangement," or like today, "Oh, no, I've tried that already," which sounds as if you thought my peace came out of this illusion you extend to me, whereas when I listen to you, the way you talk about coming back to take me, I compare this with real desire, and I am at the moment more convinced than ever that you are not the one for me physically. It would be better for both of us if we surrendered this. It isn't worthy of us. It wasn't this prospect of your forcing yourself to take me which gave me peace at last. It was feeling that my physical fulfillment with Bill didn't break our relationship. So please let me be, Gore, don't stir false wishes and let me see you tear them down the next day as if you feared my having believed you, or else we'll never be happy. I was only sad the other day because when Bill is not here I have no protection against the physical loneliness. I have ceased making wishes for us. What does not happen out of love cannot be good. Also I don't like it when you talk about making Bill a homosexual. Why do you want to take him away from me? Why can't you help me not to desire you, to be free? Do you think this way of talking coldly about taking me tempts me? I am utterly convinced and free of this wish, but it makes me angry that you keep it alive in me.

In Gore's handwriting, "You begin to write the way I do."

Gore, with the last pages you read I tried to break the mirage which makes me suffer. Forgive me if I misunderstood you, but I thought that if I could just face the truth and accept it, I would no longer feel this in you which exalts me, pulls me towards you and then suddenly dissolves, and we could be at peace. This is your diary, Gore, because you are at the center of my life. Be a little patient with me because it is a little harder for me to surrender this, and when I get angry I'm really angry at myself for not being able to achieve what you achieve, and because I am suffering in a way that you are not.

This diary comes to an end as you wished it would: no more relationships. I belong to you. I would not marry anyone but you. But I can't marry you because I could not bear the pain. But we can be happy, Gore, we can work together, and I will always be there in between the boys, whenever you want me.

May I be free of desire for Gore when this diary ends. Free of my passion for him. Free of all wishes for the impossible, free of pain and of frustration. I am so tired of pain, so tired of it. I want fulfillment and richness and peace, to write, to love wholly. What makes life tragic for me is thinking of each break as an end, as death. Each quarrel, each separation, each voyage for me is death, the end. I cannot be separated from Gore until I separate from the child in me, who is married to him.

Angoisse, worse than ever. I have feelings of choking, as when one is drowning. I feel I am either drowning or being born to a trauma. I was born asphyxiated. It took a long time to bring me back to normal. My life is definitely tragic. This diary ends as Gore's novel ends: "'Of course, you must go,' she said, gently dying."

We make love to each other only with words, with telephone calls, and on paper. Our love is a dialogue of warm words, taking each other only by understanding, imagination. Nature is shut out. The forest, the sea, the marvels of sun and flesh are silenced. Pleasure is shut out, trances, reveries, softness, touch. How arid this is, a love without fusion, without ecstasies, full of half gestures. He can live without even touching me, without intimacy. Not even tenderness is necessary to him. He can be content with walking crowded streets, sitting at restaurants. His love doesn't need a room, doesn't need a touch. Ah, Anaïs, why don't you have the courage to break this? For the first time I question my dreams, my faith. How I give myself to my dreams. Is this another dream that cannot be? I feel lost. Gore has not forgiven me the truth in place of illusion. He is hurt.

A child's world, a day at Yonkers for Maya's moving picture, a Greek park open to the public, with statues, pools, grass, Greek temples, Helba, Maya, Sasha, Nancy, Sheri, Rita and I.

They won't let me carry anything, saying, "You're too fragile."

Sheri says: "You are a legendary character. I keep thinking in the future I will look back and say, here I was with the legendary character Anaïs."

Nancy: "I'm glad you said you wanted me to sit by you in the train. I wasn't sure you liked me. You're so much more experienced. I must seem adolescent."

Helba was shocked to see me carry a can and eat a frankfurter.

My legend and my gifts created this distance. I fell into a deep despondency, felt locked out, locked out of everything. To surrender Bill and Gore, to surrender my own childhood, to seek equality in passion, I decided to close the diary, for it is an end, and I can't bear ends.

MAY 19, 1946

For three days I struggled to rise to the surface, threw myself into activity, had angry sessions with Staff: "The anger is there now, for giving much and receiving little, not receiving what you need. Good. With anger comes revolt and strength, and you will find other worlds. There are other worlds."

I met Gore at Charles and talked about our work, about getting him a display at the Gotham Book Mart. He dislikes my detachment, and it is he who drags me to the bottom again. "I want you to be yourself."

I don't want to disturb his serenity (he always says: I feel well, I am serene), and when he asks me how I am, I say: "Don't ask me. I want to forget about myself." I gave him a taste for the depths, where reality lies, so it is he who plunges into it: "I want a boy like you, with all you have, and I know I won't find that. I am not serene. I'm full of rage. My boy wants to break with me because he feels I have not given myself. I hold him back merely because I am tired of changing. And yet I'm bored, bored, I'm losing interest in them, even physically." (The battle is on, my poor Gore, the battle between your split selves.)

"I'm looking, and you are waiting for Bill. There will always have to be another person between us. I know Bill will grow up."

"But he won't grow into a person like you."

"I know. You won't find another boy with my understanding of you, nor I a boy like you. We have spoiled each other for relationships."

"If I went away now, you would be content with your homosexual world."

"Never, now that I know you and what a big relationship can be. But I know you want to go away, that you are poised for flight. I know also that you will think of me if you ever leave me, as I will think of you, and that there is no running away. I'm full of anger. I feel now that even if I turned to a woman it might be with the hard side of myself, my angry, revengeful side, eager to destroy them because I hate my mother. So it would never be you, because I won't hurt you."

"But you're revenging yourself on me just the same by withholding a part of you, out of mistrust."

He fears I would be sadistic. He was troubled, pale, angry. I was about to break down, to weep, but I controlled myself. We walked out in the rain holding hands.

"Why won't you allow me to come to the surface?" I said.

"Because I like you as you are, really."

"This time you made the scene. I'm glad. I thought you were getting impatient with my scenes."

As soon as he sees me stirred, unhappy, he feels the bond is strong, that he has taken me, that I am real with him, that he possesses me. Then he is happy. We sat at a little bar, his hand over mine. After the emotional disturbance (as after lovemaking) he said, "One can be happy in the depths."

What made him happy? In the turmoil he extracts his nourishment. I admit we have a special understanding of each other. His love for me is human and personal. He knows my moods, cares about how I feel, and I admit I do not have this with Bill. I admit that I thought of him lying at Bill's side. I admit regret that we are not living together. I admit sorrow and longing. In the taxi we kiss fervently, on the rim of passion. And that is our love scene, a love scene of the impotent, of the castrates, the inadequate, the immature.

Gore, what I cannot accept is that with the surrender of the physical tie, we surrender all that surrounds it, the intimacies, the living together, the sharing of life, talks in the dark, all the multiple exchanges, the mutual creations. It is not just the act of taking each other, but all that it means. We live as visitors now. We do not share a life, the constellations, the changes, all that constitutes being together. When Hugo left the conflict, your fear of my becoming passionate destroyed the intimacy. So each day I rebel anew. I feel the loss. I have so much imagination that I felt I had already married you. I have too much imagination, so in my body I felt your relation to others. Your nights with the boys don't happen far away. I see them and feel them in my body. They happen to me. Such nearness is intolerable. That is what I want to run away from.

Not from you, but the intolerable living so close with you in the imagination and so abstractly in reality. And hoping...

Dream: I go into a whorehouse. The men who are going to make love to me are babies, one of whom is crippled. I ask him to keep his clothes on so I will not see his deformity (he is tight, drawn, pulled together). There are visitors. I want to make love immediately, and people remind me of the visitors. I say, "But if it is a whorehouse, why pretend to be here for some other social reason when everyone is obviously here for sex?" And I want to go into the room with the little boys.

I started with the idea that to be loved you had to become wonderful. So I eliminated selfishness, demands for love, aggression, exploitation. Then I associated with people who practiced this openly—*they did it for me.*

I project many of my sensibilities onto others—I imagine great vulnerability in others. So I summon that part of themselves, gentleness, softness, weakness, and as Hugo says, "You make me feel things I don't feel," meaning they are in the unconscious and that they could be left there. Something else could be summoned out. I remember I used to feel that Henry summoned my strength, challenged it. Hugo makes me feel soft and weak. And so this side of me turns to him. Do I invent feelings as well?

Hardening and strengthening was a terrible process. Strength appears to me like hardness. I have reactions after I hold out. There is a possibility of happiness, then, in the non-caring. I have had a magnified caring, an over-developed sensibility. Sure, it gave me insight into others' feelings, but it also tormented me.

There is a way of living which makes for greater airiness, space, ease. It is like the airplane's rise above the storms. It is a way of looking at the obstacle as something to overcome: if we look at what defeats us as a monster created within ourselves by our fears, it is dissolvable and transformable.

TUESDAY, AUGUST 14, 1946

Letter from Hugo:

Six-thirty in the morning.

Have found the early morning is the time when I feel most deeply about everything. The unconscious is most active in me in this quiet time, and now I yield to it instead of feeling as if I were a sea being tossed against rocks.

The part in *Ladders to Fire* about the powdery gold, the atomizer, the green dress, the green that was never seen before, the mist of perfume, the trembling light behind you, the sounds that become music—"the air of that summer day, when the wind itself had suspended its breathing, hung between the window and the garden, the air itself could displace a leaf, could displace a word. The essence, the human essence always evaporating where the dream installed itself and presided"—all that gave me a pang and a feeling of overwhelming tenderness for this picture of you.

The preciousness of your evanescence and the knowledge of the pain it gives you to be evanescent made me hope that I have protected this one with tenderness and quenched the other with my manhood.

I know I have not always done both at the same time. The parts I have acted, as in your book, have been acted as if by separate people, or by the same person at different times. There were times when, as in the book, the husband merely visited you sensually, as a man, and when the whole lover did not possess you. And that was when you turned to others for what I did not give you. Only once did I lose you both ways. Now I am bringing together both lover and husband, poet and protector—you need both and I know I can give you both, because when I read your book I respond equally to the sensual and the tender evanescence in you, and I think you are going to have a hard job finding those two responses to your satisfaction in anyone else because those two needs of yours are two sides of myself which are now fusing.

As ever, your Hugo

SEPTEMBER 8, 1946
Letter from Bill:

Cherie,

I have been thinking about you continually since I left.

Letters are a poor substitute for what we had when we were together, but I guess they are better than nothing.

As you can see, I am now in Korea, in a little town on the southern seacoast, a place called Pusan.

My address is on the envelope.

I wrote a poem while in Tokyo, or rather a very short verse. I'm working on a longer one, but haven't got the privacy to complete it.

In secret chambers of the city she,
In oriental panoply,
Sits; she weaves a web
With fingers fair
That draws my quickening
Memories there.

All my love, Guillaume

ENDINGS

The hell grew larger as the illusions broke

New York, Sunday November 10, 1946

Letters—work on lectures
Cocktails
Movies, Hugo, Eduardo
The lesbians seek me out

November 11, 1946

Letters
Gonzalo
Exhibition—Crosby
Early to bed
Depression began
Helba answering telephone instead of Gonzalo, screaming instantly: "I will kill you all. Go to hell!"

I made heroic efforts with Staff to conquer the illness. I detached myself from Gonzalo, from Hugo, from Gore, from Bill, from all to stand in a kind of desert as the saints did in their search for god, and so I, in my search for love, have reached nothing but a desert. At first I wept, mourned over the dead selves.

There was a fear: *before*—I had illusions, and then hell, and the hell grew larger as the illusions broke. But now I have nothing, for I no longer have my illusions of Hugo. He was a man who had repressed the natural part of himself and therefore had died. But as he began to come to life under Dr. Bogner's care, everything erupted in great violence. He emerged an angry man—Jehovah, as I called him, still deifying him, the angry father-god, angry and rebellious, rebelling against supporting Gonzalo. Each time he became angry, I felt guilty, crushed, unloved. I wanted to run away from home as I did when I was five years old, but I took his side and struggled desperately to wean Gonzalo off Hugo's money. The press collapsed under a mountain of debts, corroded by Gonzalo's irresponsibility. Even when it was time to move out, it was I who did all the packing, sorting, cleaning. Gonzalo took the small press home. I went away alone, broken in health and seeking strength elsewhere. Hugo demanded to be master of the situation—he would wean Gonzalo, but he couldn't. The only thing Gonzalo did was sell his books, pawn his clothes and his typewriter. Hugo gave him money only for food (because Hugo himself was in debt). When I returned to Gonzalo to give him food, everything was lost, the passion, the faith, nothing left but human fraternity, ashes. Gonzalo thinks I broke with him because of his jealousy of Gore, but it was the attempt to end his parasitism.

In the summer, at East Hampton, I fell in love with John Paanacker, a beautiful boy of twenty-three, driven insane by the war, and his behavior (just like Bill's, tenderness and sadism) nearly drove *me* insane. I saw John as the continuation, the expansion of Bill, even born on the same day! I returned shattered, having walked through the inhuman East Hampton at night, sleepless, weeping hysterically. Staff knew this was only the violent culmination of the illness. Then, upon resuming analysis and my activities, I had days of faith, days of peace, days when my improved relation to the world promised an improved intimate relationship. But to live this unromantic life without passion and ecstasy, merely because I could no longer bear the infernos which always followed, is worse than death.

Curious contradiction: while my personal life sank like a pierced ship, there was a great ascension in my work. When *Ladders to Fire* appeared October 21, three hundred people came to the Gotham Book Mart and fêted me as one dreams they would, each one carrying several copies of the book for me to sign for themselves, for friends. Thrusting, admiring faces, deep glances of worship, words of faith.

Those three days were symbolic and proved to me that the world for which I am writing is topographically much larger than I thought, rounder and vaster, and that the young writers of the future will waste less of their strength as mere surveyors of it.

Three more parties at book shops. People did not offer ordinary compliments, but their souls, a silent votive offering of their deepest feelings, and that reduced the sting of a vulgar Sunday *Times* book review, of Diana Trilling's implacable anger, of Leo Lerman's betrayal: "You should lie low and hide after all this scandal about lesbianism.

You attend too many parties…" etc. Jealousies sprouting like venomous mushrooms. But letters and manuscripts come from new friends every day.

Staff called me up with a voice of lucidity during the din of Gotham to say, "Have faith." Oh, I have faith, but my vulnerability, which is my instrument of creation, the sensibility which is the very vibration of my writing, rejects the ugliness, anger, distortion, and wants to retreat from this exposure.

The stupidity of Wilson and all the reviewers only accentuates the lack of understanding. But other people respond: the young. So I know I'm right.

I don't miss Gore—he is like the others now, just one of my sons. My heart is closed against Bill. I do not feel him. But I can't bear this life without a great passion, for which I am made. To have reached recognition, fame even, at such a moment. I flowed emotionally to Bill Burford because his writing is the twin of mine, but he was frightened because he is homosexual.

NOVEMBER 15, 1946

People are reading in *The New Yorker* that Wilson thinks I have "made progress in the new part of the book, and although the story is a little amorphous, there are charming things in it," etc.! People are talking about me, people are thinking about me, but at five o'clock—a fatal hour when the buses are so full that you cannot climb into them, when the taxis will not stop, when the subway is impossible to enter, when everyone is running somewhere, when the lovers have chosen each other, when I am stranded at a corner of a street, unable to reach home, unable to reach anyone—I feel this wave of choking anguish: loneliness, loneliness, loneliness.

There is no change in the diary. I wanted it *not* neurotic, but I see something is still wrong, for I felt pain while writing it and a desire to evade the pain. I only wrote it out of loneliness…

To love out of loneliness, to write out of loneliness is not good.

I cannot be alone.

Waves of anguish choke me.

It is too late for analysis to cure me totally.

I have terrible moments.

What has happened is that instead of writing in the diary, I now want to talk to someone or write to someone, to be related, to give of myself, to exchange. But I am forced back here. What can I say to Bill Pinckard? He has paralyzed me by not answering my letters. He and Gore killed my spontaneity. They are too small to contain me. Gore gives me the feeling that I disturb his peace and isolation like a raging storm. Such meager letters he writes, such a small life. Flight.

Pauvres enfants! I am too rich for them. I remember when I first began to receive the flood of Henry's letters. Torrents of words. How rich I felt! How overwhelmed, so overwhelmed I couldn't answer. I felt submerged, but I enjoyed it. Perhaps it is feminine to *like* to be overwhelmed, to be swept off one's feet.

Alors, mon cher journal. Me voici du nouveau. Twenty years of illusory loves and passions, and here I am, back to where I once was:

To solitude

To monologues

Soliloquies

Communion with myself

Because everywhere I turned was pain, incompleteness, sacrifice, self-destruction.

NOVEMBER 18, 1946

For days I was copying the diary in which Albert appeared, longing for him desperately. One day, in desperation and frustration against the emptiness of my life, I lied to Gore that Albert had come on a diplomatic mission, that he was here. (I wanted to punish Gore for his inadequacy, or perhaps it was to sustain my own need of life.) I survived two weeks with the myth of Albert, and then, unable to sustain it, I explained my depression to Gore by having Albert return to Haiti.

And today Albert telephoned!

Awaiting him, I admonished my heart: be careful, be quiet, do not hope, do not let joy flood you... It may be a dream...another dream.

But when he stood at the door, my heart lost its caution and opened my arms! We kissed feverishly. We tried to talk...but couldn't. I was overwhelmed with happiness.

Anaïs, je te veux...

I couldn't believe the simplicity of it. After three years! "Anaïs, I want you..." And the richness of his mouth, the vigor, the voluptuousness of his body... Three years without this richness, this utter abandon and enjoyment, the caresses... *Aï, Aï, Aï,* he moans. How he takes me, how he ploughs into me, how he enters, fills me, strong and voluptuous.

"Anaïs!" he cried, "I thought you'd forgotten about me."

"You are not easy to forget."

He said, "Three years...they have been cut short...now they don't seem so long..."

He fell asleep.

But there is sadness in this meeting, a passion which was mutilated at its peak— can it survive? There is *angoisse* at the bottom... He hurt me before, accepted the obstacles between us, yielded to conventions, had the courage to leave me, and did. Yet this is what I want. He is the match to my physical self, the only match to my nature, my island nature, my tropical nature, and nature was sacrificed.

He is sad. He is no longer the golden boy. He is thirty years old, an active communist, not romantic, but a Marxist, sincere, simple. He is married to his childhood friend, to the fiancée who waited eight years for him. He has a child.

Let me enjoy this...enjoy this...

Garden of Eden

    Albert:

We sink into caresses, with tenderness, with strength, with drunkenness, with
    richness, softness, fire, honey, flesh.

Oh the paradise of *nature*

Of sweet flesh

Of unashamed desire

Albert, my island, my song...

So sweet and so present.

He stands erect with the pride of his beauty.

He is hungry, he is caressing, he is free.

I can write now.

Not a diary, but a song.

Sweet flesh,

Sweet...

He came this morning.

Always desire, a brushing of lips becomes a trembling of pleasure and
    his manhood is aroused...

He wants. He takes. He takes time. He plunges. He enjoys.

He tastes.

He is perfect, like a leaf, like rain, like dew, like a tree, like a storm.

He has sad thoughts, a sad face. Why? Because he has negro blood, because
    he stands between two worlds, rejected by the communist party in Haiti for
    his light skin.

He looks like the son of Gonzalo, paler. He works at the U.N.

Saturday:

    At the center lie fire and the earth

    I am at peace

    Where there was emptiness there is now fullness

    I can work

    I am not cheated by life

    His warmth is in me

    His blood

    His cries

    His enjoyment

    I am rich

Oh, his flesh, so full and firm. He is all roundness and firmness, so beautifully
    made, so rich to taste, his strong odor, male and bitter, and rich...

Garden of Eden—*Now* I have the sea, the sun, and I can write, work, sleep.

Albert, I am grateful to you. I am far from perversions, decadence, complication,

paralysis. So far from Gore, the paralytic, the sick.
Sweet Albert
For him the simple words
Acts
So little talk, none needed
The drug
The sweet, natural drug
I have lost my sickness, I have lost my anxiety, I feel calm...

SUNDAY, NOVEMBER 24, 1946

I work at being at peace. At the moment, I have no anxiety...in between anxiety is
the inferno and the sickness. Albert is there, but I fear a blow. Instead of anxiety, there is
an inner resignation—something has broken my exaltation. To not fall as dangerously,
I do not soar as high...

NOVEMBER 29, 1946

An evening at Albert's hotel...such sensuality, yet I am still frigid. I have *always*
been with Albert, and I cannot understand it. I am not so with Chinchilito, yet I like
Albert better and have more desire and tenderness for him.

"Why? Why?" I ask Staff. He cannot answer yet, but he thinks any relationship
I have now would be incomplete because the eroticism caused by my illusions has
disappeared. I know this is not a complete relationship, and I don't want it. It is once
again stolen moments filled with obstacles. He lives outside of the city, and he comes
here rarely. We are not spiritually or mentally attached. It is too partial, too...I don't
know...based in reality, and the reality is that he is too calm, too passive for me, like a
plant. There is no real contact.

DECEMBER 11, 1946

I left Tuesday, the 3rd, for my tour of the colleges.

At Harvard, I stayed at Carlton Lake's house. Carlton is a cultured, intelligent,
sincere man, interested for many years in my work, starting a publishing house.

A real friendship.

But I want to understand this: I give myself to the situation. The present becomes
the center. I take an interest in Carlton, in his way of life. I enter his and his wife's
lives, secrets, hungers. I felt for his wife, who is intellectually inadequate but childlike
and real, and helped her to have confidence, took her fears away. The entire scene
becomes vivid, near, glowing...I experience their lives with them...I feel warm and
close to them. It all *glows* with humanity, with understanding. But why does my parting
dissolve them? As I leave, I could easily forget them, though we exchanged feelings, a
part of ourselves.

And that is why so many people claim a relationship with me, and while it is real
for me at the time, afterwards they dissolve and fade away. This frightened me: the

intense reality of my two days and two nights spent in Carlton's house, the confidences, and how it becomes so easily effaced for me.

On the 4th I spoke at the Poetry Room of Harvard's Widener Library. The lecture and reading were received with great absorption, not a rustle of inattention. I wore a black dress and a vivid fuchsia scarf. I spoke strongly and read well. I won many people, even some of the prejudiced ones.

The next day I left for Dartmouth, and the following morning I spoke at the auditorium to 400 students, and again I captured their full attention. Professor Herbert West said it moved him to see me so slight and small facing this hall full of men.

And all the time I was thinking that the height of my trip was going to be Bill Burford. I forgot about Albert, I forgot about my triumphs. Burford had sent me two telegrams, one eager, wanting to meet my train, the other an imaginative answer to my sending him a seahorse. And when I opened his telegram, I got a feeling of warmth and intimacy, but it is as if this feeling were transferable, no longer personal. As with Henry, it runs like a river, it is not fixed on one person, does attempt to fix itself, and when faced with an obstacle (in Burford's case, homosexuality) it is easily deviated.

I dare not risk another shattering.

At Dartmouth I saw so many desirable and beautiful men, but none in the sensitive way of Bill Pinckard or in the dark, fiery way of Burford.

After Dartmouth, I went to Goddard College. Every hour of the trip, every meal, was filled with questions from students, a constant "interview." I learned to talk freely, to parry attacks, to resist intellectualization, to answer irrelevant questions.

Exhaustion.

After a long, five-hour drive to Amherst, I stayed at James Merrill's place, and Bill Burford came. We had dinner with champagne, were happy, talking fabulously, freely.

Bill is nineteen, was born in Texas on February 20. He is tall, manly-looking, dark hair, and intense dark eyes. His face is rough-hewn, and his sensibility is only betrayed by his eyes and his hands. There is something feminine about his appearance. He is immature only in his anxiety and his stuttering. Being with Jimmy made everything more difficult, but at the same time Jimmy has a playfulness and humor which relieved the tension of Bill's tremendous anxiety.

All through the trip I felt I was traveling to reach him, all the little waves of vibrancy converged towards him, but this time poor Anaïs is afraid and pauses before the obstacle of his homosexuality.

When word got out that I was there, strangers began to appear. Bill was angry, and I was too.

DECEMBER 21, 1946

I work on Volume II of *Cities of the Interior*.

I throw myself into sensuality with Albert. It is not like my drugged hours with Pinckard, but something more animal, more real, more sexual and less erotic. Albert's body has less eroticism—it is more sexual, more concentrated. I love the way he moves his sex in my mouth, how he sighs and moans. Today I became roused by his hands while I kissed his penis and had an orgasm from his caress, a caress only Henry used to give me at times, the fingers in both my sex and my anus.

"*Comme tu caresse bien, comme tu fais ça bien, Anaïs.*"

Then, erotically roused, we took our clothes off and he said, "I want to take you in every way possible," as if he wanted to pierce me with his sex everywhere at once. I love how he lingers outside of the womb, sliding his wet penis all over, around it, the folds, between the legs, the anus, arousing all the regions between the legs, tantalizing me, and his vital, vital taking me afterwards. I gave myself this time, sank into it, enjoyed him. I was happy. Relaxed.

People are miserable and tense because they don't make love enough.

I felt as if I had been swimming or running, relaxed and content…

DECEMBER 1946

Letter from Hugo in Cuba:

Darling:

I still can't bear the thought of hurting you. Please forgive me. I love you more than ever, but with a self that is just beginning to find out who he is. That person is different from you, but he is in love with *you*.

Remember that always, because if you will be patient, this new love will be far stronger than the old.

Your Hugo

Bill Howell. He looks like a photograph of my father when my father was twenty years old. The same sensitive features, the small nose, the feminine smile, the boyish, slender body. But my nights with him put a painful end to my sensual frenzies. He was suffering from a break with his girlfriend and was fearful of loving me, fearful of a relationship, yet yielding, perverse, jealous.

Our last night together, he got drunk, flirted with a girl, and I felt he would not return with me since we are not lovers, we are not bound, and it is natural. But I couldn't bear it. I was so full of anguish I could not enjoy the party… We agreed I would go home alone with a friend and he would follow later. I felt deserted, betrayed, neurotic again. But he did come and was gentle, sweet, tender. "I would never hurt you or endanger what we have for the sake of a little whoring!" He lay beside me with his small, straight nose against my breast.

I was grateful for his not harming me. He was there. He was human and tender. I had expected callousness (oh the fear of cruelty!). I was at peace.

The fear of loss and betrayal had not materialized.

One night, he called me up to tell me that he met Hazel McKinley at a party, got drunk and slept with her. This, after having told me a while ago that "she is repulsive" and that he did not want to see her. He said: "It was gruesome. I hate myself. I hate her. I never want to see her again. Oh, honey, honey, honey, don't cry—oh, don't—I can't bear that. My feelings for you are growing and growing and growing. You must understand that I couldn't be casual with you, as you asked me to be. We would have to be involved. I respect you too much. You are too wonderful. I couldn't treat you as I treated Hazel."

Hugo came home from Cuba this evening.

JANUARY 1947

This hunger is unsatiated because it is no longer disguised as a hunger for the marvelous, but as a simple hunger of the body, one that is unsatisfied by Hugo for whom I have no desire, unsatisfied by the intermittent visits from Albert, unsatisfied by the smaller constellations of effusive relationships to Gore, Pablo, Bill Howell, all of which are insubstantial.

A day:

Gonzalo comes at eleven. When I say our love is dead, he denies it, but it is so clear that all we hold together is a wake for a dead relationship, a wistful wake, sometimes a violent one in which I, realizing fully all that he has destroyed, break into sudden frenzied sobbing and he looks blind, baffled.

Any "job" in New York is impossible because of his anarchism and his real handicap of being Helba's nursemaid. He will not go to Peru to claim his inheritance because he can't bear the thought of his mother seeing him in his humiliating poverty-stricken state. Although I would raise the money for him to go to France, he won't go without seeing his mother first. So he won't go to Peru, he won't go to France, and he can't find or keep a job. In three weeks the charity organization Hugo helped arrange will stop making him payments. He has not telephoned about two job prospects, he has not written to his mother, he has not written to France, and he lies on my couch inert, weak and fireless. I ask myself how I did I ever turn to this sick, sick, sick primitive for fire, a fire in the center of his being that I now can see is useless, raging, blind and destructive, a fire leading nowhere, a wasted fire.

At twelve Gore telephones. The day he came back from Guatemala we fused emotionally like two soft rivers. He said, "I made a house for *us*..." And then he said, "I have not been as happy for two months as I am right now." And, dipping in this happiness, with his childish and none-too-warm penis, he carries his limited supply of sensuality to an Irish boy, and a few days later he has lost the healthy glow of Guatemala, looks pale, has rings under his eyes.

At two o'clock I get a telegram from Bill Burford. Just as much as his writing is orderly, minute, perfect, his handwritten letters are chaotic and mad... He is unlike Gore: not nearly as human or simple, but complicated and perverse. But the friction and spark between our two imaginations generate writing, our only thread.

At three o'clock Staff and I are still unraveling my first humiliation at the hands of man (my father's violent spankings) and my slavery to it.

At four o'clock I receive a love letter from Bill Pinckard, which inundates me with pleasure and balances the pain he has inflicted.

At nine o'clock we are off to a New Year's party where I still pursue the echo of John Paanacker in Bill Howell…another mirage where all of us, drunk, indulged in effusions of caresses and wild words—love, love, love, love, love, love. I stayed away from the party where Gore was because there is no physical effusion there and my body is frustrated… So I deserted him as the most painful of all relationships (we are only happy alone because then we give each other the illusion of possessing each other, but in the world it is clear we do not, since any stranger can lay hold of our bodies).

Fell asleep sad that I am living in fragments in spite of a greater wholeness, greater stability, greater confidence, lessened anxiety, lessened fears.

RENUNCIATION

There was a stranger in my bed

Shock—

Gore had told me that he made a wonderful portrait of me in his third novel, *The City and the Pillar*, the ideal woman, and I discovered instead a caricature, a cheapened, superficial, distorted image, in his own terms.

I am being forced to face the mediocrity of his writing—he is almost a pulp writer. This is the reality of Gore and the loss of my dream. The other Gore is ruthless and cheap. This is the first inkling that I was *mad*, that I was inventing people! Such pain at the betrayal and, worse, his unawareness. He does not know what he killed. Why do I pity him?

Staff agrees it would not have been right to strike Gore down with the full strength of my anger:

1. He is only twenty years old
2. He has lived in the cheapest worlds: society, Hollywood
3. He is not conscious
4. He has been crippled by his mother

So I forgave him. He is a lost soul. Why does he cling to me or love me? Why doesn't he have a Hazel McKinley? He cannot distinguish between this sort of vulgarity and me, and yet he makes me his ideal. But I am the one who can destroy him.

The relationship is now a lie. I have to conceal my real opinion of his writing (I had hoped for a change). Nicholas Wredon, my editor at Dutton said, "It is a book on one-dimensional love, sex in a void," and he hated it. Gore is overwhelmed by the reactions. He calls on me for help, "Please tell me it is my greatest book, my biggest book." So I have to defend the motherless boy while hating the vulgarity of his work.

At the Gotham, he crystallizes his personae for the world: arrogance and egotism. A nice little monster I have taken to my breast, whose only human feelings are for me, but who is still capable of harming me in his writing. His mother said: "You are full of venom. You love no one. You are grey and cold." And this is what I take into my warm breast and love, reflecting on him my own glow.

Anaïs, *tu es folle. Bon.* That is finished. His telephone call every day has lost its magic. I see him as he is, a very sick boy. Staff saved me. I realized the incredible extent of my romanticism, my sentimentalism.

I write every day, all day. Something is seeking to break through, to flood me, to destroy my art form: my humanity. Something is seeking to live richly after being denied: my sensuality.

I try again to make a larger, more inclusive relationship with Hugo, whom I *trust.* In the eyes of the world I am happy.

When there is a party going on, someone is sure to name me, discuss me. There is always someone who knows me, whom the others envy and ask to be introduced to me. There is always "someone who wants to know you." They come, they are grateful, they are worshipful. It is a stream. I enjoy the friendships, but it is not enough.

Terrible depression. I lie like a dying animal, but then I flow. Staff helps. I write, I write, I hope, I revive, I try again.

This evening Bill Howell was going to come. We were going to make love. He called me up in the afternoon, elated, to make sure all was well. Then at seven, when I expected him here, he, upset and unhappy, called to tell me that his old girlfriend is back, pregnant. This has happened before—he married the first time in such an emergency and then divorced, never loving the woman. Now he once again feels trapped and miserable, and instead of a lover, I have an unhappy young man taking refuge in my understanding.

Hugo is my jailer and my lifesaver. My need of him is my own weakness. The child in me in need of kindness is more important than the woman in need of passion—*la fatalité intérieur...*

JANUARY 1947

Something marvelous has come of analysis, of the bitter struggle against neurosis: the loss of tension and a state of flower-like ease which I have only known intermittently. After we searched the bottom, Staff and I, raking all the murky walls of masochism, I reached relaxation. This *melting* which I only felt at moments—usually erotic moments in the presence of the relaxed men I did not fear, or the gentle ones, the feminine ones—I reached naturally.

I was relaxed about lecturing and reading, absolutely calm. I was relaxed when Carlton came for a visit and we went to the Vanguard to watch Josephine while Albert and his wife were there. Carlton brought me home, and at the door he had a *coup de passion*. After I answered him physically, we went to his hotel where I enjoyed his violent thrusts, his lack of caressing, his male sexual act. At one moment (as with Wilson) I felt that it was too rough, that it would bruise me. But I took my pleasure and he his, and I felt like a man, as I was a little irritated that he kept saying, "Oh, my darling," when I did not feel any tenderness. I want my older men hard, and I want to be hard with them (Carlton is only thirty-one, but behaves like a man of fifty).

Next day a party. Pablo questioned me about the bruises on my shoulder, and then all of them sought to surpass Carlton's bites, so they bit me hard. It was like an orgy without final climax. I danced deliriously with everyone, feeling a true gayety, wildness. I looked very beautiful that night, my hair with bangs, great animation, my violet Hindu sari, shoulders bare, waist very slender.

It was Hugo who spoke like a voice from the past, echoing my romantic dissatisfaction: "I watched you, and you did not belong there. You are so much more. You must find your level..."

No. I must first find ease and pleasure—anywhere—by surrendering my fantasies, exigencies, sorrows...

I expect nothing.

But this is the miracle: the loss of tension affects the others—they feel more at ease, they come nearer. A few weeks ago I felt no one desiring me. Suddenly, because of the ease, Carlton became passionate. And then today Bill Howell (whom I had given up on) was so simple, so warm, so direct, that he began to talk of why we couldn't have a relationship. He sat near. I lay back quietly, and when his hand touched my breast I experienced this rare moment, one so valued, so marvelous, of sudden blind impulse and passion—joy. So lovely. He is like a woman—he is tender afterwards, does not retract or feel anxiety.

"I am very happy," said Howell, and he talked about himself, his dancing and acting careers, his relationships.

Such mysteries! Mysteries, endless mysteries of the life of desire!

This act remained in me, penetrated me.

I went to dinner with Gore. Same place, same dinner as Gore likes it, but I am free of him. I feel compassion, but I am free.

Letter to Bill Burford:

My feelings became so strong and clear this time through a dream I had: I feel such a deep, devoted, total love of your writing (which is the essence of you), but more than that I feel a kind of communion or marriage between our writing, and the only incertitude which clouds my elation at this is one created by your silence or perhaps something like a non-participation in you in this elation, so I do not feel a confirmation of my feelings. Bill, this is a rare form of love, and if (because of my own incertitudes) you could only help me to believe in this magic unity.

I feel that it would give you and me all of love's power, for there are times when I want to cry out in desperation: if no one hears me, if no one answers this, I cannot go on. Oh Bill, this, if you would know it (and it is why I must say it to you!), would establish your faith forever. In this communion of the writing (because that is all we are permitted to have due to the obstacles) there is such richness. If you only knew that every word, every thought is echoed, echoed, echoed. If you could know this as I do, you could write against time, against circumstances, against every obstacle.

February 1, 1947

Bill Howell: an afternoon of passion and sweetness.

Dinner with Gore: compassion, but awareness of a difference of levels when he said, "Someone said you and I should write a book together, for you overwrite and I underwrite; you are too warm and I am too cold. I have all you lack..."

My first true unfaithfulness to Gore: I postponed the evening with him to be with Burford the day before Gore leaves for Guatemala for six weeks.

Last night a party.

I met Nancy Harman first at one of my book parties, took an interest in her writing, and promised to invite her over. Finally, they came one day, and I was struck by her husband Carter, who is a composer. He has an open, quiet friendliness, intelligence, a contagious simplicity. He is about twenty-six or twenty-seven, slender, blue-eyed, natural. Carter, through the experience of war, is without neurosis and is composing music for the Ballet Society. He is immensely likable because he so open, so unretracted. He was moved by my writing, which he understands and wants to set to music.

My immediate feeling for him was total. He is a person I could give everything to, but this is suspended by his marriage and its unity. They are close and so right together in their youth and physical appearance—it is a marriage of children. So I lay aside the curious feeling that I could live for him. But why would I *die* for him? It is because he is so complete, not inhumane and incomplete as Bill Burford and his homosexuality, or Bill Pinckard and his hollow shells.

Last night we danced together for the first time, and it gave me joy. Not the joy of eroticism, but the joy of a balanced completion in which fire, feeling and intelligence are in accord.

The rigidity and tension in Burford would make love so difficult and painful even if it were not impossible because of his homosexuality. His tension constricts me. I can no longer love constricted beings with the hope of melting them. They harm me and

I cannot change this constriction into flow. That was the harm Hugo did me, why the elation in me died in the marriage.

I understand better now my need of expansiveness, dilation, my pleasure with Pablo, my feeling for Carter, who is not exuberant but flows easily, naturally.

How one's taste changes, and with it one's fatalities.

SUNDAY, FEBRUARY 9, 1947

At ten o'clock last night I was reading at the Poetry Center from the *House of Incest*, with a power and dramatic intensity I have never reached before, a real actress's performance, where face and body and voice fused into a new art, reading with passion, fervor, and yet restraint.

At ten o'clock Pablo was listening to a concert of French Renaissance music with Nouche, a French-Spanish girl of his age who attracts him.

At ten o'clock Hugo sat listening to me and wept.

At ten o'clock Bill Howell sat waiting for us to pick him up after the lecture to go to the Haitian party together.

At eleven o'clock I touched Bill Howell's sensitive hand, looked at the modulations of his face and desired him as I desire the remote, the elusive, the adolescent, the unformed, the gentle, the passive, the beautiful woman with a phallus.

At eleven o'clock we came to the Haitian party and waved at Albert in a red shirt, and when he and I danced together, the current of desire welded us together. He has a purity and childlike passivity in him too. He sings and plays the drum, but he is married and rarely sees me, so I continue my relationship with Howell, courting him as he demands to be courted, yielding and faithless, easily won and easily lost, tender, beautiful, and not deep.

I will no longer seek a whole love, for I know now my match in creation and imagination is among the sick ones, such as Burford, and my body, unlike theirs, is not sick and can only find a match in Albert, the sensual ones. This is my renunciation of the immense dream of a match on earth. I accept everything new, but let me at least have the sensual life, pure and free, and then I can create.

How clear it was last night: Burford is homosexual, guilty, frustrated, and frustrating; Albert is a beautiful, virile plant; Howell is a pretty woman.

Carter, Nancy, Hugo and I tried to create a new opera. As we listened to Carter's records of songs written to e. e. cummings' words, which are very beautiful, poetic, lyrical and remote, I read from *House of Incest* and Hugo cast shadows on the walls.

Carter is intuitive. I could love him deeply. He moves me. He completes me in music, and he feels the same about my writing. There are those one feels close to without effort…naturally.

Hugo is leaving Friday for three weeks.

What I feel now is the loss of interest in the difficult, the courting of mollusks, chestnuts, snails. Courting Burford mystically and rejoicing over abstract victories, seeking the most remote ones and finding joy in winning them obliquely no longer lures me.

Oh, to be cured of the impossible, the unattainable, the myth. Staff says these pursuits are an evasion of *big* fulfillments, the fear of being swallowed, swamped, overwhelmed.

Unable to find in Burford a passionate friendship, I turn away. Unable to obtain from Albert a passionate continuity, I turn away. Or else I measure exactly what I *can* find, as in Howell, a small sweetness, narcissism. At thirty, he is like a boy of seventeen, with a frustrated violence, drinking, yielding, postponing. But I just like to caress him, to see his body like Pinckard's, his face like Paanacker's.

As Gonzalo is living out the consequences of his laziness, self-indulgence and lies (oh, the lies he has told me, his constant lying which I would not see, so many that Staff and Bogner have diagnosed him as "pathological"), at first I had guilt. If I ate in a good restaurant with Gore, I had difficulty in enjoying the dinner while thinking of Gonzalo sinking, his shoes torn, his suit worn out, etc.

Tonight for the first time, as I prepared the candles for Saturday's party, I felt free of guilt because now it is clear Gonzalo created his own destiny as I created mine. Even today he lies. His reactions are utterly selfish. But Staff says he would ruthlessly cling to me and suckle my breast until I *died* if I permitted it, that he does not care, that he idealizes what he calls his "bad luck."

But what a painful irony: Hugo will no longer give me $5 for Gonzalo's food every day, so *somehow* I must find it, by seeking orders to print writing paper, or by selling books, magazines, etc. So when Gonzalo went to the bookshop where I sent him to sell some books, the bookseller gave him a printing job to reprint my preface to *Tropic of Cancer*! That was a Dantesque punishment for his attempt at destroying my writing (he accused me of being a decadent reactionary writer, but his life is so decadent that his criticism cannot affect me).

Now, with all illusions lost, I see his selfishness starkly, the terrible weakness of his mouth, his sloth all revealed in the limp lines of his body, a body that has not held its firmness at fifty years old. His attempt at pride now seems infantile.

Hugo left Friday morning, and by sheer coincidence Chinchilito telephoned in the afternoon, "May I come?" So my holiday began with fireworks—violent lovemaking, the opening of a symphony of sensuality and frenzy.

A curious incident while Chinchilito (earthy, vulgar, violent, animal) was making love, came the hour for Carter's children's songs to be heard over the radio, and as I had mentioned this to Chinchilito, during a pause in the lovemaking he said (so sure his eroticism would continue), "Go and turn on your young friend's composition."

I leaped up, naked, and turned on the Carter songs, and to this delicate, innocent, playful music, we made love.

Strange, because in this new life of pleasure, this shallow life, I have moments when I wonder whether my capacity for feeling has been killed by too much suffering. But when I heard Carter's songs, lying beside Siegfried, the Tarzan who would give me the violent climax, my feelings were all in Carter's music, which has the same acute, nostalgic sadness, the same soulfulness that touches me when I listen to Debussy's *Sonata*. So my feelings are not dead.

Now I want to write about the party, not to achieve enjoyment or reality by way of the writing as I did before, but to *enjoy it twice*.

A group of thirty-five came, and many were vulgar, ugly, and uninteresting. But among them were three striking and unusual figures in contrast to this frustrating homosexual world, three Don Juans: Arthur, Anatole and Vincent. Arthur has negro or Jewish blood and is tall, handsome, dashing. Anatole is New Orleans French, handsome, sensual, ironic. And Vincent is tall and dark, like a Spaniard (he is of Italian origin). Three woman hungers.

Vincent, captivated by my writing and legend, had first met me at my book party. He told Anatole, "She has a beautiful body." Anatole asked permission to bring him to the party.

Being, as usual, dressed too early (I wore a clinging white dress without any underclothes, my heavy gold Arabian necklace, bangs and hair up—I was *en beauté*, soft, relaxed, luminous—I looked, as everybody said, like Cleopatra) and impatient, I decided to telephone Anatole, who has a book shop, to tell him to come before the crowd so I could speak to Vincent. Anatole was not there, and it was Vincent who answered, "But I am coming!"

Up the stairs came Vincent with his curly, jet black hair, dark eyes, slim body. We did not talk. He put on African-Cuban records, and we danced. He is a professional dancer, lascivious, smooth, undulatory. And instantaneously there was a strong sensual current established. Each dance exhausted us. He drummed on my back, he dug his nails into me, he lowered his hands over my hips, and we pressed against each other until it was unbearable.

The mood was set. All evening we either fled from the violence of the welding between us, or we yielded and made a striking couple, dancing deliriously, fused together. A delirious party, all in candlelight, sensual, full of incidents. Dick, who was rejected by Pablo in favor of Nouche, became utterly drunk and nearly fell off the terrace to his death, but Vincent, at the risk of his own life, held him back. Others were drunk, bestial and vulgar, demanding to be taken right then and there.

Fortunately Carter and Nancy did not stay late enough for the dregs to appear. I danced with Carter with such a piercing sweetness, gentle warmth, yearning to possess him rather than Vincent, but I was relieved when he left because then I could allow my body to hold sway.

Everyone stopped me to say I have never looked more beautiful! Two of the women said, "You make me wish I were a lesbian."

Candlelight, alcohol, violent music, dancing.

Vincent stayed until the end, but the lovemaking was not as violent or as good as the eroticism of the dancing. He was nervous. He kept saying: "I'm not used to your delicacy, your expertise, your style. I'm used to…roughness." Every word he said was foreign to me, and with the violent magnetism gone, there was a stranger in my bed. When I awakened at dawn, I had a moment of repulsion, of shame. When my feelings aren't touched, I feel shame, as man does with the whore.

We had breakfast. He dressed, stylishly, smoothly, and we parted. No echo left in the being.

I cannot have Pinckard, or Burford, or Carter—and here I am lost among strangers.

FEBRUARY 1947

The morning after the party, so different from the one described in *Ladders to Fire*, which was suspended in unfulfillment and romanticism. This one left stains of wine, candle wax on the floor, cigarette stubs, broken glasses, crumbs from sandwiches, empty bottles, ashes, dregs, devastation. The record of Debussy's *Sonata* for violin and piano, which I call the saddest piece of music ever written, was broken… I had to clean the apartment, take a bath, find my purity again before I could sleep. Yet, I found sensual fulfillment in this debauchery. This same taste, the bitter taste of desecration, must have struck Rimbaud, Beaudelaire.

When the dream dies…the romantic becomes unattainable… I thought I would die, too, die with it, be buried with it like the Inca aristocrats with their jewels. But I am *alive*. I am in reality. This was what I sought to attain? Reality.

Alone in my rarified house. Everything is in order. *Cities of the Interior* lies on my table. I have to write the *end*.

Vincent telephones, "Think of me a little!"

Bill Howell runs away from the conflict between his girlfriend and me, his unattainable job, home, broken relationships. "I have to make a decision. It can't be you and Patsy. I feel torn apart."

Bill Burford, who takes up the theme of my diary at twelve years old, "*Mon journal, un jour je pourrais dire: je suis arrivée au fond,*" writes me desperate letters from *au fond* of the abyss.

Aging is not a physical phenomenon. It comes when one wearies of repetitious motifs. I am beginning to know the next move, the next word, too well—to know the gesture that is coming, the themes, the motifs. Yet I find myself responding to Burford's despair with a deep letter. So I am not aging, but perhaps ready for a new experience, a new world, a new lover, a new passion…perhaps for the biggest one of all!

FEBRUARY 19, 1947

I rushed to borrow a Spanish dress from Tana, whom I recently met, for the Haitian carnival. We went to the cellar together. I kissed her childishly with delight at the beauty of the dress, and she responded with passion. As I walked in front of her she came up behind me and encircled me. I turned my head to face her and we then kissed as lovers, violently and wildly.

Up in her apartment we went to her bathroom to try on the dress. After I undressed, she dressed me herself in the Spanish costume and again we embraced wildly, mouth to mouth, body against body. She pulled my skirt away. She said, "*Eres una niña, como una niña*, like a child," and fell with frenzy upon me. Her husband was playing a record loudly in the next room…the music, loud, strong, and these kisses! Tana is beautiful, and like June—the same sun coloring her red-gold hair, tawny, burning eyes, softly curved, but so active, holding my body as a man would. Drunk on desire.

"I'm afraid," she said.

And I came away feeling I want to live like this. This is the way I am! Even if it means death and destruction.

So many desecrations.

Burford's answer to my letter is filled with devotional, fervent friendship, and a wonderful poem he wrote for me. I am happy as if he had made love to me. He has said I am a wonderful woman. To extract this acknowledgment from him I used most intricate, subtle, mystical courtship. I courted him with all the splendors of my brocaded words, of my true compassion for his suffering, with my clairvoyance and my eyes. I courted him and won him, spiritually.

So today I awakened feeling like a flower, suave, smooth and gentle, with the innocence, the confidence, the pure aloneness that is not loneliness. I looked at the clock. Nine. There is a page in the typewriter—page 45 of the polished version of *Cities*—work awaiting me. The party stirs up comparisons in my head.

Burford's poem on my lap, the day is opening, there are pages to write, coffee to make, and then the telephone:

"*Bonjour, Anaïs. C'est Albert.* Are you free today?"

"*Oui, Albert…*"

At six o'clock he arrives. We try to talk, but the nearness of his firm, rounded, full, compact, sun-browned body, his full, firm mouth, his face…and my nearness. When reaches for me, the blood rises instantly. Kneeling over me, he cries, "You have awakened in me a terrible sensuality!"

With Albert possession is all *enroulement*, undulation, rhythmic smoothness. It's the seeking of curve to curve, like snakes, a possession without air in between, without empty places, a welding of sinuosities, a tropical, voluptuous fusion. It is in the evenness of the rhythms, in their completeness, like two perfect negro dancers making one body. No need of violence.

It is as if we did not have enough ways of touching and taking each other, as if we wanted a thousand openings, a thousand thrusts. The tip of his penis around the tip of my breasts. His hands everywhere. My mouth everywhere. His flesh is so soft and firm, rich, dense. He is virile and voluptuous. He arouses me frenziedly. He arouses something close to love, a passionate feminine submission, a desire that he should take me and no one else, that he should keep me.

I lie here alone
content
Plant, flowers, mystic, creation, woman
all blooming
I want to live alone!
alone!
And not lonely!

FEBRUARY 20, 1947

I had lunch with Caresse, who confesses how, before his marriage, her son Bill acknowledged his love and possessed her physically twice, with happiness. Caresse said, "Now I have had everything!" I was moved and felt that this was so utterly right, so primitive, to return as a man to the womb from where he was born. How complete and human, how tremendous the feeling, as when Pinckard took me. Caresse is the mother of my erotic self, the one woman who truly made one impulse of the heart and womb and opened them simultaneously.

I hate to witness the death of my great passion for Gonzalo. I cannot be tender with him, because I feel *he* destroyed it. He wore out my courage, my faith, my love. I feel that if I soften he will crawl back to me. His clothes are wearing out. He looks old now, worn, sad and bitter.

Since Gonzalo savagely attacked my books, I have refrained from discussing them with him. One day I forgot myself and, bathed in the warmth of my work, began to talk about an idea I had. Suddenly, realizing the hopelessness of it, the wreckage caused by his violence, the blindness of my faith, the death of my faith and trust, I broke into a violent, agonizing sob, which Gonzalo did not understand.

FEBRUARY 22, 1947

Yesterday my birthday.

A snowstorm.

I went out at ten o'clock with my typewriter, which had started to skip frenziedly (the right metaphor for *my* typewriter) to get it repaired.

I went to Gonzalo's house to take him $5 to keep him from starving. His kiss on my cheek is a child's kiss. I cannot bear his expression of innocence, his expression that "It is not my fault. I do not understand the cruelty of the world." It is because I still believe he is blind and cannot see his own demon that makes me want to help him.

Came home to iron my Spanish dress, to read a cable from Hugo.

I had forgotten bobby pins for my flowers. Millicent was going home, but climbed five flights of stairs without my asking her, to bring me some. This pleased me more than any present, that after six years of serving me, Millicent, tired and not well, should want to do this for me, that she does not want to stop working even through her children are grown, that it is out of faithfulness to me that she keeps coming. The children say to her, "Not until Mrs. Hugo goes to Europe will you give her up."

Then I work on *Cities of the Interior*, now named *Children of the Albatross*. At eight-thirty Pablo came over in his Panama shirt and said, "You look ravishing, Anaïs! Oh, you look so utterly feminine!" And, "In your book you showed a startling insight into homosexuality." And: "Oh Anaïs, what you become when Hugo is not here. You are like an open flower! You are so free and relaxed."

Oh, my diary, may I be granted the wish to live alone like this. May it happen that Hugo may feel free without me, for I would not have the courage to desert him. May it happen simultaneously and painlessly, for then my life would match my writing and my writing my life, and it would all be integrated.

At the Haitian carnival, I danced deliriously with Pablo and once with Albert. A Haitian invited me to dance, and then a group of other young Haitians began to cut in, ravenously, one after the other, and each one immediately began a sexual dance, rubbing their hard sex against me. I could not completely submit for fear of losing Albert. At this moment I realized that what had blocked, harmed, enslaved, and tormented me in the past was not Hugo, or Henry, or Gonzalo, or my homosexual loves, but the fear of my own sensual nature. But I am no longer afraid. I have used even my dreams against this, and last night I used Albert as a defense against the others...

I came home at four o'clock in the morning and had this dream:

Bill Burford and I were talking on a divan. He had said something, and as so often happens in reality, I had already written his exact words. Such a twinship of thought, which I acknowledged. I lay back utterly passive, and suddenly he kissed me passionately. I was exultant, surprised, in ecstasy. We kissed, and he wanted to take me. I said, "Not here, we must find a room of our own." The apartment we were in had an empty wing. I said: "Come here, away from Hugo. We'll move in a bed and close the door."

Each time I brought something for our room—a bed, a curtain—I was met with an obstacle. People came in. I sent them away. I tried to lock the doors, but there were too many of them. Someone was cooking. I sent him away. I was angry at the invasion, the lack of privacy. I fought against it. Then I went into a bathroom and looked in the mirror. A dreadful growth had appeared on my chest almost between the breasts, a pale pink protuberance. I realize now it was like a rubber penis, growing right out of my chest. I pulled at it. I wanted to yank it off. I couldn't go to Bill this way. I had to tear it off. Then I saw a man was in the bathroom with me.

He said, "I am a doctor."

"Then take this off," I said.

He clipped it off but left a stub with roots. Then he said, "You must come with me."

I followed him out. "But where are we going?"

"To get an examination. A special test. Something you need badly."

"But what, what? I can't do it now anyway. Someone is waiting for me. He will leave. I'll come tomorrow. Any other time, but not now."

He agreed, but then he said: "I'm afraid I can't do anything for you for three weeks. I'm too busy."

So I left and returned to the apartment. From the view out the window, this wing seemed terrifically high up, too high, precarious. It made me uneasy, dizzy. I said, "I must get used to it." But it was like the top of the Empire State Building.

I awakened horrified by the realism of the penis on my chest.

LIFE!

Touch, oh, touch this man of fire

The evening of Hazel McKinley's party I met Rupert Pole, an actor who is Welsh and looks like Pinckard, but as soon as I saw his handsome face, I felt: Caution. Danger. He is probably homosexual. He spoke first, having heard I was Spanish. Ordinary remarks. We sat on the couch with a friend of his, discussing Schoenenberg, whom he had met in Hollywood. He intimated his belief of pacifism and mystical studies. Then people intervened.

I remember that as we talked we plunged deep, deep eyes into each other. The homosexual is passive, so I was surprised when I was getting ready to leave, Rupert came up and said, "I would like to see you again." Hazel told me afterward: "He asked about you. He was interested in you."

That night I came home with someone else, Bernard, and we made love, but during the entire time I maintained my image of Rupert as a more luminous, more spirited image.

The next day Chinchilito called and came.

Then I had enough. I realized this was a phase: a phase on the way towards reality. Man is there, sensual life is there, all obtainable, when you turn away from the masochistic traps. When Carlton Lake appeared, hoping for an orgiastic weekend, I had to tell him it would not be because Rupert had said he might come. He was hurt, and then it all seemed reverse, the way man leaves woman and woman becomes emotional. I am without feeling, possibly animated by revenge, resentment to have been possessed by them somehow: Bernard, Carlton, Chinchilito…

Rupert arrived in his working clothes, from printing. There was something marvelous in the contrast of his clothes, stained and dirty, and the finely chiseled face.

He is very tall, as tall as Hugo, but with an elongated boy's body. His face is long, sensitive, narrow, the eyes deep-set and brilliant, a blue, gold and green changefulness. His black hair, his long, heavy eyelashes, and something passionate about the face. He is all vitality, there is a fire in him. Voluptuousness again.

We talked. He is idealistic and romantic, wants to give up stage acting and the city, is proud, independent, wants to live out west, free, simply. He is full of poetry, has a young man's seriousness, intermittent depths, imagination.

We ate by candlelight. He talked and talked, confided in me. His face is so beautiful, so pure, and feminine, yet with a masculine assurance. As he sat on the couch, he made me feel feminine and passive. I let him be active. He continued talking. As I stood with him, looking over the table, he put his arm around me. He then kissed me as I love to be kissed—hungrily, for a long time, passionately. He carried me to the couch. He was strong, passionate. We undressed, lay in the dim light of the driftwood lamp, the same light which illumined my last night with Pinckard.

And, as with John Paanacker, I recaptured the sensation of making love with Pinckard. Is it the body? No, it's more than that. It's a kind of passion which matches mine. It is not bestial, it is voluptuous and welding, something I do not feel with the young.

Rupert was not only more penetrating than the older men, but he moved me as well. He is impetuous, and I feel both eroticism and tenderness. His long kiss prepared me, dissolved me. He said, "You have the body of a young girl." He was tireless. He took me twice, and once more before he fell asleep. No retractions. Emotionalism. We fell asleep clasped together as if we had always known each other. I didn't want to sleep all night with anyone but Paanacker and Pinckard, for Paanacker was a continuation of my interrupted love for Pinckard, and this is true of Rupert too.

His face was on my pillow, asleep, and the resemblance was startling. (Pinckard was Welsh too!) The full, well-balanced mouth, beautiful teeth, the passion. Rupert closes his eyes when we kiss. Such a beautiful night, like my nights with Pinckard and Paanacker. Such fantasy they have, capacity for dreaming.

Rupert awakened with sea-blue eyes and said, "Oh, this blue light—I thought I was at the bottom of the sea." (Pinckard's very words.) But Rupert has no fears. Until the last moment, he held me, kissed me, was both tender and passionate. Upon awakening, he clasped me again. I felt bathed in caresses. I was terribly, terribly happy. He said: "I would like to be on a beach with you. I would like to take you sailing." He was full of charm.

It's not only the actual beauty of their features, but the quality, the finesse of the three faces. It's their voices. Rupert sings and plays the guitar.

But I must not love him as I love Pinckard, for he has to go to New Mexico for a job. He is not here for long (oh my destiny!). Or is it that they unconsciously prepare all their lives for these flights from permanency? Not Rupert. He was married, is now divorced. His father is a writer and an actor, was a friend of Rupert Brooke, and that is where his name comes from. He won a scholarship for Harvard.

I could not work. I was exhausted, but so happy.

If Pinckard had no fears, he would be like this. But he has cold parents, whereas Rupert was loved.

Rupert said: "I surprised myself. I have been so asocial lately. I am surprised to be here, to have talked so much, to have made love to you. I had forgotten this wonderful thing woman gives."

Chinchilito, Bernard, Albert, Vincent, Carlton left no echoes, but Rupert did. I felt the need to recapture my purity for him, to be faithful to him. I deserted all of them. I refused to have Vincent over last night. I went back to my book.

Mysteries. Always the mystery of relationships.

Sunday, March 2, 1947

Finished *Children of the Albatross*—a slender volume, but so rich!

I lie alone and content.

Rupert took away the sedimentary taste left over from my other sensual encounters. I see him with his printer's stained hands, driving a small, dilapidated car, but with such a dashing spirit. I see his deep, deep, large, blue eyes looking at me intently when we parted. I thought: this will inspire my whole weekend.

No fears.

The last kiss was as passionate as the first, active, possessive, strong. He is too proud for stage life, too proud to beg for jobs and sell one's self. He dreams of open spaces. He is full of quotations and aphorisms, Lao Tze's sayings. "There was a woman out west who introduced me to mysticism. I met Khrishnamurti. But it was unbalanced. I am earthy. I want a better balance between body and spirit."

In his arms the pleasure was deeper. This young colt's body I love, skinny, the bones tender, the neck long and thin, like a bird without feathers. There is something breakable and vulnerable in him, as if the dream were still consuming the flesh and the flesh never consuming the dream.

In the morning, in the bathroom taking a shower, he sang in a rich voice, an Irish voice. I first saw him as the only one who could play the role of Pinckard on the stage.

I asked him, "How were you at seventeen?"

"Horribly shy and terrified of women."

Finished copying and polishing my book, which is to be delivered tomorrow.

I want to write an essay on the similarity between oriental philosophy and psychoanalysis. There is *orientalism* in my work.

MARCH 1947

Vincent came last night.

Suave, soft, smooth, darling of women, a dancing partner. The type of "gigolo" who lives by his dancing and lovemaking in Florida, protected by older women, his black hair curled, he handsomely dressed. Thin like a colt too, but made for the boudoir, with a trace of a common accent from a poor childhood. Crude in speech, unromantic, yet sensitive.

"Anaïs, you are not like other women. We will dance together again, smoke marijuana, make love while dancing."

Not tonight, Vincent. I have Rupert, proud and romantic, full of finesse and quality. This is beautiful, this is health.

I am learning *passivity*, which I once feared. I identified with my triumphant father and played the role of the *active* lover. I could not yield, I could not be taken. I gave either body or spirit, never both—there was always a part of me unpossessed.

MARCH 5, 1947

As soon as someone touches my feelings, as Rupert did, the great enemy, anxiety, sets in:

expectation of a telephone call

fear of his retraction

fear of failure

fear that it would be lost

I talked with Staff. He thinks I have made enormous progress. I was happy and well as long as I did not feel. As soon as feeling enters me (Rupert), then comes fear. Staff explained I became ill because Rupert did not call Monday.

I called Rupert up Tuesday after seeing Staff, in a casual way. He said that his finger was infected from a printing accident, that he couldn't sleep, and that there was a conflict between jobs. The lightness of his voice, even of the word "darling," sounded insincere to me (through the ear of my doubt, or justly?). He would come Thursday, he said.

But the fear is there.

Strange days.

Bill Howell comes, weak, not well, neurotic, takes refuge in me. It is now a chaste, affectionate relationship. His sleeps in Hugo's bed. We live like husband and wife, but without sensuality. He comes to say goodnight, lies beside me, naked, without desire, sleeps. Humble, sweet, perverse, lost, full of vacillations, fears too, and poor. He wishes to seek strength by logging in the mountains. I let him come…and go… We lie on the couch reading. He rummages through my photos, takes the ones he likes.

Bernard is sad that I would not let him take me again, longing, hungry, calling at midnight.

Everyone pursuing the one he cannot have.

A maze, a blind maze.

But I am coming out

Out of hell

Out of hell…

All this pity I can no longer give to Gonzalo because of his weakness now flows to Howell, who is tired, sick, with rings under his eyes, perverse, drunk. We visited Richard Wright together, but I took him away before he spoiled his relationship with Wright by obstinate argumentativeness. A child.

I half carried him to Hugo's bed (he is so light). In bed he awakened, smoked, and said: "You know so many interesting people. Why do you bother with me? Why?"

I left my bed and lay beside him, reassuring him, kissing him. He murmured in the dark: "You are wonderful. I love you. I adore you. If we could be together I would stay in New York. But your life is too complicated, too many men."

I said, "You're going through a difficult moment."

The tragic impasse is that a woman who feels like this, lost, childish, inadequate, is not ashamed to accept a man's protection. But these *jeunes filles* with phalluses are ashamed to be wives. Howell could not be content being my lover, be proud of my achievements, of who I am, be strengthened by me, or even supported.

This terrible bond with the adolescent—what happens is that at the moment of gentleness, a unbreakable fusion takes place. John Paanacker at East Hampton—if he had only taken me as a man, if he had only taken me and that was all…but at the beach, after possession, we returned to the bath house and we washed the sand off our feet. Then he took my feet and dried them so delicately, so tenderly. And after possession in the room, he would say, "I will tuck you in," and cover and arrange me in my bed as if I were a child. Such gestures take possession of the heart (to cause later the most cruel pains), and I cannot forget them.

It's funny, for a maturing woman trying to learn detachment:

Burford's stories can hurt me.

Howell can make me weep.

Rupert can kill my joyousness by calling up but not coming for ten days after our magnificent night.

Bill Howell leaves for the Cooneys' farm because he wants to earn money, to work until he gets a theatre job. He leaves without my help, but I am glad.

Howell was on the train at ten after six, exactly when Rupert rang the bell. He entered with vigor, with vitality, in an active role. We talked about going out to dinner.

We sat down and talked, drank. He sat near. His leg touched mine. I had almost forgotten his face, his black straight hair, his eyes changing from blue to gold, his clear but warm-toned skin, blood tones. No paleness. He is electric.

As I got up to go out with him, he embraced me. Once we began to kiss we could not separate. Desire, desire, desire, desire. His gestures are strong and romantic. Where did he learn to carry the woman to the couch? His long, long slender body. Lean. Lean and strong. His nervous, wiry, electric quality suits mine.

For ten days I thought my night with him would not be repeated.

He challenges my strength, my softness.

We never went out to dinner. We cooked here, together. He is active, capable, free. He travels on little money. He plays the guitar. He sings. He speaks Spanish. He prints to earn a living. He is healthy and beautiful and alive.

He loves another girl, who is mystical but confused, and, I gather, puritanical. She thwarts his lustiness. He cannot seriously think of her as a part of his life. She loves him, but not enough to lead his erratic, adventurous life with him.

The children entered my womb seeking refuge and peace, and while I felt desire immediately, another part of me, the strong part, lay dormant, aroused only occasionally. But Rupert challenges this part of me. He does not seek softness. He seeks strength. He says Debussy is too feminine. He likes rhythm. His impulsiveness is a delight, his vehemence, his beauty. I suppose when I did not believe in my own beauty, I did not dare love beauty. With Pinckard, beauty entered into my life. Rupert's leanness is vital. His spiritual face, intense, glowing.

Life heals you if you allow it to flow, if you do not allow it to trap you.

Have I achieved freedom? Freedom? Freedom?

That no one should be able to destroy you, enslave you, paralyze you.

Mon Journal,

How the illness makes the choices. How it caused the suffering—not Gore, not Burford, not Howell... The flow of desire went to Rupert Pole.

Thursday I went to help him with his printing job. Again a press, Rupert serious, wearing glasses, his guitar lying in the corner. Strange irony. We work together. He drives me in his little two-seater, old and dingy, but he drives electrically, impulsively. His vitality drives the car. We had dinner afterwards at the Spanish restaurant and went back to his place, a poor apartment, but his viola was there. We lie listening to music. He seems asleep, but suddenly—it is always sudden with him—he kisses me. His kiss is strong, appropriating, willful, full of assurance. The caresses—all of our caresses are strong, nervous—are the caresses of musicians, not tender and light, but strong and of the nerves. Our rhythm together is quick, tense, determined, but artful too, not only phallic, for he waits until we get into such a frenzy that we have to tear each other's clothes off. His hands on my backside have a nervous tapping, drumming, kneading frenzy, which awakens the nerves. Everything is electric, swift, strong. Once inside, his penis is slender, not large, and he moves so actively, so tantalizingly, as if my womb had to reach out for him, the little air between us a tease, as if he was not going to fill me, but he draws such excitement from me, such a long, long orgasm, reaching to the end of my nerves.

I feel fear. His body reaches too deeply into me. He is dangerous. He leaves drunkenness afterwards, ecstasy. I feel both his strength and his sensitivity.

At dinner, he had said: "Drive with me to California. I have to visit my parents. I have to get a job there."

I said, "Yes."

There is now passivity in me. I do not court. I have no anxiety. I do not seek certitudes.

He is full of delicacies, romanticisms, but vital, lusty, wiry, courageous...

I hold back

And I am happy

He plays the active role

I want this

Strange

I dream of the trip.

I have fears: will I have the physical endurance? He is twenty-eight. He is a lusty lover. That night, we lay together, his sex inside of me, waiting, and after a moment he took me again. He said, "I want to take you in the water, in the sea."

He can eat anything.

I can't.

He can go without sleep.

I can't.

Oh, Anaïs!

Look at his great beauty—he is too beautiful for me.

He is poor.

A fiery evening. He read from *The Prophet* (his Bible!).

While I lie down with Rupert, Gonzalo is working alone and discovering the enormity of the work I did for him, all the "chores," the realities of printing.

While I lie down with Rupert, Gore is at the Blue Angel with an Irish boy who "bores him." He looks worn, pale, has an infection of the throat, his eyes are bad, he can live months without sensuality, yet he still wants to marry me and lock me up in his house in Guatemala.

While I lie down with Rupert, making love violently, Josephine is singing at the Ruban Bleu, Bill Pinckard is lonely in Korea, Burford is with Merrill at Amherst, Pablo is in Panama with the girl he may marry.

The Anaïs who writes here tonight is the same child Anaïs who could not believe in happiness. I write tonight to reassure myself that it is true and palpable. With words, I must touch this.

With words, I touch the face of Rupert, caress his straight, dark, rich hair which smells of the aromatic tobacco of his pipe. With words, I touch the silky skin of his face, the ascetic temples, the leanness of the lines, long, pure, oval, the heavily lashed, deep-set blue eyes, the eyes of the dreamer and of the earth.

Touch, oh, touch this man of fire, who enters smiling, who throws off his coat, who is free and timeless, who comes with his guitar. We forget to make dinner, because he begins to kiss me, to kiss me, to kiss me, until we are in a frenzy. His mouth. It is *he* who kisses, takes, and every move is strong. I feel for the first time the reality of a phrase June used to say to Henry, "Up to the hilt, my love." I feel his sex against mine, the sexual act is so violent, each spurt of semen causing a tremor through his body, a somersault, and he puts me in such a frenzy that I feel as if I were not experiencing one orgasm or two, but hundreds of them. Frenzy! Frenzy! He comes twice without leaving me.

Rupert enjoys his food, enjoys his pipe, enjoys resting after dinner with his head on my breast, enjoys playing his guitar, enjoys singing. Oh, god, he is a man, a sensual man, a romantic.

Wildly beautiful. Intense. Healthy.

I cannot believe it…

As he sits there singing warmly with color and power, playing the guitar he taught himself to play, with his beautiful face, his long, slender neck, his ruddy hands which are not delicate, but strong, the rich, warm tones of his skin, his beautiful teeth, I cannot believe it.

Has my charm brought me this?

For the first time, I allowed my joy to explode. I had been subdued, passive. I received him with effervescence, but not love, no words of love, for this is passion. How good it is to be so thoroughly caressed, to be caressed and kissed while I cook, to be caressed and kissed every moment.

He looks at *Under a Glass Bell*, which I finally decided to give to him, and like me, he reads one phrase and divines the rest. One phrase of my preface, and taking me in his arms, he rocks me and says: "But we need the dreamer! We need dreamers!"

After making love to exhaustion, he says, "You destroy me, you destroy me only to give birth to me again, each time a new man!"

LIFE AGAIN! LIFE!

ALAN SWALLOW ✦ A TRIBUTE

By 1961, Anaïs Nin's efforts to find an American publisher for her work had been in vain for more than twenty years. Her agent, Gunther Stuhlmann, once said, "I couldn't sell Anaïs on 42nd Street." As a lark, Nin contacted Alan Swallow, the small publisher with a reputation for relentlessness and who worked out of his garage in Denver, Colorado. What follows is Swallow's letter to Nin agreeing to be her publisher, which marked the dawn of her eventual success.

March 6, 1961

Dear Anaïs,

I have now read the materials you sent me, including the manuscript of the new novel which came from Mr. Gunther Stuhlmann. (I am sending a copy of this letter to Mr. Stuhlmann as your agent.) I think it makes just about perfect sense that I become your U.S. publisher. The sales of your works have apparently demonstrated that they are not suitable or of interest to the large commercial publishers. Yet, there is a kind of victimization involved for an author to be handled by too many smallish "avant garde" publishers—who seem to be fly-by-night much of the time, who appeal to a certain clientele (an avid one but a limited and changeable one); or for you to be attempting self publication of the works. I fall in between. I don't manage the very large, large sales; but I am a determined and persistent devil, and I manage a very respectable sale for the materials in which I am interested. (Indeed, for many books I feel that my methods will get more sales over a period of time than can be achieved by others—for I have seemed to develop them for the kind of work in which I am interested, which I find will not support themselves well upon a publishing situation of high overhead, etc., but are quite satisfying to me and, in the end, to the author.) As I say, for the kind of sales which seems to me your destiny in this country, I feel that I am in a better situation than anyone else. I am loyal to my titles; I keep them in print if humanly possible (for example, such a book as Winters' *In Defense of Reason*, which bigwigs in NY publishing told me I could not sell in 2,000 quantity, is now in its third edition, has sold more than 5,000 copies and still sells as fast as it ever did; and 8 years ago I did his *Collected Poems*, stuck with them, sold them out, then in 1960 reissued a new, slightly augmented edition, placed it both in cloth and in Swallow Paperbooks, and it won the big Bollingen Prize for 1960 and was one of 13 finalists for the National Book Award in poetry.). This is the sort of thing I can do better, I feel, than other publishers and is the particular role I can play in the over-all field of publishing. Furthermore, I publish only what I admire, and everybody knows this; and I admire your work. So it should be a fairly good "wedding" of work and publisher, I think. I shall hope so, anyway! [...]

(By the way, also, if my idea about the stories is good—you may wish to let them go out of print after you lift the 2 novelettes from *Under a Glass Bell*—what would such a volume be called?)

All right, in summary: I am willing to embark on the long-range project for your work as it seems best. First steps would be preparation of a contract for *Seduction of the Minotaur*, your indication of exact stock you have of the material in print, and your cost figure for that stock, and its exact condition—cloth, paper, unbound sheets, etc.; signature of contracts covering rights and royalties upon such stock; signature of contracts for books "intended" as above. I am indicating my willingness, even my eagerness to do this. I would sign any contracts, of course, after seeing your willingness in the over-all plan and the particular contracts, etc., that is, that they be such that I can approve. I don't think we would have any problems there. The big problem now is the ultimate intent and then the development of the plans.

Cordially,
Alan Swallow[†]

Alan Swallow published all of Nin's fiction and was co-publisher of The Diary of Anaïs Nin, Volume One, *which was the book that propelled her to fame. Swallow died at the age of 50 at his typewriter only weeks after the diary's release. He remains an inspiration to small publishers far and wide.*

[†]*Excerpted from Volume 4 of* A Café in Space: The Anaïs Nin Literary Journal.

INDEX